2020 DAILY & SUNDAY MASS READINGS

CATHOLIC MISSAL (USA EDITION)

CATHOLIC LITURGICAL WORLD

DEDICATION

This book is dedicated to the Holy Trinity through the intercession of the Most Blessed Virgin Mary.

CONTENTS

ACKNOWLEDGMENTS

This is to acknowledge the unquantifiable contributions made by each member of the Catholic Liturgical World Team coordinated by headed by Rev Fr. Martins and Rev. Sr. Lucia. May the Most Holy Trinity meet all those who will use this book at the points of their needs and uplift them spiritually and materially, so that at the end of our earthly sojourn we all will be crowned with the supreme Crown of Heaven. We ask all these through the intercession of the Blessed Virgin Mary, through Christ our Lord, amen.

JANUARY

Sunday	Monday	Tuesday	Wednesday	Thursday	Friday	Saturday
			1 Solemnity of Mary, Mother of God SOLEMNITY **NEW YEAR'S DAY**	2 Basil the Great and Gregory Nazianzen, Bb & Dd Memorial	3 The Most Holy Name of Jesus Opt. Mem.	4 Elizabeth Ann Seton, Rel Memorial
5 Epiphany of the Lord SOLEMNITY	6 Andre Bessette, Rel Opt. Mem.	7 Raymond of Penyafort, P Opt. Mem.	8 Wednesday after Epiphany Weekday	9 Thursday after Epiphany Weekday	10 Friday after Epiphany Weekday	11 Saturday after Epiphany Weekday
12 Baptism of the Lord Feast	13 Hilary, B & D Opt. Mem.	14 Tuesday of the First Week of Ordinary Time Weekday	15 Wednesday of the First Week of Ordinary Time Weekday	16 Thursday of the First Week of Ordinary Time Weekday	17 Anthony, Ab Memorial	18 Saturday of the First Week of Ordinary Time Weekday
19 Second Sunday of Ordinary Time Sunday	20 Fabian, Po & M; Sebastian, M Opt. Mem. **MARTIN LUTHER KING'S DAY**	21 Agnes, V & M Memorial	22 Vincent, De & M Opt. Mem.	23 Marianne Cope, V Opt. Mem.	24 Francis de Sales, B & D Memorial	25 Conversion of St. Paul, Ap Feast
26 Third Sunday of Ordinary Time Sunday	27 Angela Merici, V Opt. Mem.	28 Thomas Aquinas, P & D Memorial	29 Wednesday of the Third Week of Ordinary Time Weekday	30 Thursday of the Third Week of Ordinary Time Weekday	31 John Bosco, P Memorial	

FEBRUARY

Sunday	Monday	Tuesday	Wednesday	Thursday	Friday	Saturday
						1 Saturday of the Third Week of Ordinary Time Weekday
2 Presentation of the Lord Feast	3 Blase, B & M; Ansgar, B Opt. Mem.	4 Tuesday of the Fourth Week of Ordinary Time Weekday	5 Agatha, V & M Memorial	6 Paul Miki and Companions, Mm Memorial	7 Friday of the Fourth Week of Ordinary Time Weekday	8 Jerome Emiliani; Josephine Bakhita, V Opt. Mem.
9 Fifth Sunday of Ordinary Time Sunday	10 Scholastica, V Memorial	11 Our Lady of Lourdes Opt. Mem.	12 Wednesday of the Fifth Week of Ordinary Time Weekday	13 Thursday of the Fifth Week of Ordinary Time Weekday	14 Cyril, monk, and Methodius, B Memorial	15 Saturday of the Fifth Week of Ordinary Time Weekday
16 Sixth Sunday of Ordinary Time Sunday	17 Seven Founders of the Order of Servites Opt. Mem. PRESIDENT'S DAY	18 Tuesday of the Sixth Week of Ordinary Time Weekday	19 Wednesday of the Sixth Week of Ordinary Time Weekday	20 Thursday of the Sixth Week of Ordinary Time Weekday	21 Peter Damian, B & D Opt. Mem.	22 Chair of Peter, Ap Feast
23 Seventh Sunday of Ordinary Time Sunday	24 Monday of the Seventh Week of Ordinary Time Weekday	25 Tuesday of the Seventh Week of Ordinary Time Weekday	26 Ash Wednesday Weekday	27 Thursday after Ash Wednesday Weekday	28 Friday after Ash Wednesday Weekday	29 Saturday after Ash Wednesday Weekday

MARCH

Sunday	Monday	Tuesday	Wednesday	Thursday	Friday	Saturday
1 First Sunday of Lent Sunday	2 Monday of the First Week of Lent Weekday	3 Katharine Drexel, V Commem.	4 Casimir Commem.	5 Thursday of the First Week of Lent Weekday	6 Friday of the First Week of Lent Weekday	7 Perpetua and Felicity, Mm Commem.
8 Second Sunday of Lent Sunday	9 Frances of Rome, Rel Commem.	10 Tuesday of the Second Week of Lent Weekday	11 Wednesday of the Second Week of Lent Weekday	12 Thursday of the Second Week of Lent Weekday	13 Friday of the Second Week of Lent Weekday	14 Saturday of the Second Week of Lent Weekday
15 Third Sunday of Lent Sunday	16 Monday of the Third Week of Lent Weekday	17 Patrick, B Commem.	18 Cyril of Jerusalem, B & D Commem.	19 Joseph, Husband of Mary SOLEMNITY	20 Friday of the Third Week of Lent Weekday	21 Saturday of the Third Week of Lent Weekday
22 Fourth Sunday of Lent Sunday	23 Turibius de Mogrovejo, B Commem.	24 Tuesday of the Fourth Week of Lent Weekday	25 Annunciation SOLEMNITY	26 Thursday of the Fourth Week of Lent Weekday	27 Friday of the Fourth Week of Lent Weekday	28 Saturday of the Fourth Week of Lent Weekday
29 Fifth Sunday of Lent Sunday	30 Monday of the Fifth Week of Lent Weekday	31 Tuesday of the Fifth Week of Lent Weekday				

APRIL

Sunday	Monday	Tuesday	Wednesday	Thursday	Friday	Saturday
			1 Wednesday of the Fifth Week of Lent Weekday	2 Francis of Paola, hermit Commem.	3 Friday of the Fifth Week of Lent Weekday	4 Isidore, B & D Commem.
5 Palm Sunday Sunday	6 Monday of Holy Week Holy Week	7 Tuesday of Holy Week Holy Week	8 Wednesday of Holy Week Holy Week	9 Holy Thursday Triduum	10 Good Friday Triduum	11 Easter Vigil Triduum
12 Easter Sunday SOLEMNITY	13 Monday in the Octave of Easter SOLEMNITY	14 Tuesday in the Octave of Easter SOLEMNITY	15 Wednesday in the Octave of Easter SOLEMNITY	16 Thursday in the Octave of Easter SOLEMNITY	17 Friday in the Octave of Easter SOLEMNITY	18 Saturday in the Octave of Easter SOLEMNITY
19 Sunday of Divine Mercy SOLEMNITY	20 Monday of the Second Week of Easter Weekday	21 Anselm, B & D Opt. Mem.	22 Wednesday of the Second Week of Easter Weekday	23 George, M; Adalbert, B & M Opt. Mem.	24 Fidelis of Sigmaringen, P & M Opt. Mem.	25 Mark, Evangelist Feast
26 Third Sunday of Easter Sunday	27 Monday of the Third Week of Easter Weekday	28 Peter Chanel, P & M; Louis Grignion de Montfort, P Opt. Mem.	29 Catherine of Siena, V & D Memorial	30 Pius V, Po Opt. Mem.		

MAY

Sunday	Monday	Tuesday	Wednesday	Thursday	Friday	Saturday
					1 Joseph the Worker Opt. Mem.	2 Athanasius, B & D Memorial
3 Fourth Sunday of Easter Sunday	4 Monday of the Fourth Week of Easter Weekday	5 Tuesday of the Fourth Week of Easter Weekday	6 Wednesday of the Fourth Week of Easter Weekday	7 Thursday of the Fourth Week of Easter Weekday	8 Friday of the Fourth Week of Easter Weekday	9 Saturday of the Fourth Week of Easter Weekday
10 Fifth Sunday of Easter Sunday	11 Monday of the Fifth Week of Easter Weekday	12 Nereus and Achilleus, Mm; Pancras, M Opt. Mem.	13 Our Lady of Fatima Opt. Mem.	14 Matthias, Ap Feast	15 Isidore, Farmer Opt. Mem.	16 Saturday of the Fifth Week of Easter Weekday
17 Sixth Sunday of Easter Sunday	18 John I, Po & M Opt. Mem.	19 Tuesday of the Sixth Week of Easter Weekday	20 Bernardine of Siena, P Opt. Mem.	21 Ascension of the Lord SOLEMNITY	22 Rita of Casica, Rel Opt. Mem.	23 Saturday of the Sixth Week of Easter Weekday
24 Seventh Sunday of Easter Sunday	25 Venerable Bede, P & D; Gregory VII, Po; Mary Magdalene de Pazzi, V Opt. Mem. MEMORIAL DAY	26 Philip Neri, P Memorial	27 Augustine of Canterbury, B Opt. Mem.	28 Thursday of the Seventh Week of Easter Weekday	29 Friday of the Seventh Week of Easter Weekday	30 Saturday of the Seventh Week of Easter Weekday
31 Pentecost Sunday SOLEMNITY						

JUNE

Sunday	Monday	Tuesday	Wednesday	Thursday	Friday	Saturday
	1 Mary, the Mother of the Church Memorial	2 Marcellinus and Peter, Mm Opt. Mem.	3 Charles Lwanga and Companions, Mm Memorial	4 Thursday of the Ninth Week of Ordinary Time Weekday	5 Boniface, B & M Memorial	6 Norbert, B Opt. Mem.
7 Trinity Sunday SOLEMNITY	8 Monday of the Tenth Week of Ordinary Time Weekday	9 Ephrem, De & D Opt. Mem.	10 Wednesday of the Tenth Week of Ordinary Time Weekday	11 Barnabas, Ap Memorial	12 Friday of the Tenth Week of Ordinary Time Weekday	13 Anthony of Padua, P & D Memorial
14 Corpus Christi SOLEMNITY	15 Monday of the Eleventh Week of Ordinary Time Weekday	16 Tuesday of the Eleventh Week of Ordinary Time Weekday	17 Wednesday of the Eleventh Week of Ordinary Time Weekday	18 Thursday of the Eleventh Week of Ordinary Time Weekday	19 Sacred Heart of Jesus SOLEMNITY	20 Immaculate Heart of Mary Memorial
21 Twelfth Sunday of Ordinary Time Sunday	22 Paulinus of Nola, B; John Fisher, B & M and Thomas More, M Opt. Mem.	23 Tuesday of the Twelfth Week of Ordinary Time Weekday	24 Birth of John the Baptist SOLEMNITY	25 Thursday of the Twelfth Week of Ordinary Time Weekday	26 Friday of the Twelfth Week of Ordinary Time Weekday	27 Cyril of Alexandria, B & D Opt. Mem.
28 Thirteenth Sunday of Ordinary Time Sunday	29 Peter and Paul, Ap SOLEMNITY	30 First Martyrs of the Church of Rome Opt. Mem.				

JULY

Sunday	Monday	Tuesday	Wednesday	Thursday	Friday	Saturday
			1 Junipero Serra, P Opt. Mem.	2 Thursday of the Thirteenth Week of Ordinary Time Weekday	3 Thomas, Ap Feast **INDEPENDENCE DAY (observed)**	4 Elizabeth of Portugal Opt. Mem. **INDEPENDENCE DAY**
5 Fourteenth Sunday of Ordinary Time Sunday	6 Maria Goretti, V & M Opt. Mem.	7 Tuesday of the Fourteenth Week of Ordinary Time Weekday	8 Wednesday of the Fourteenth Week of Ordinary Time Weekday	9 Augustine Zhao Rong, P & M, and Companions, Mm Opt. Mem.	10 Friday of the Fourteenth Week of Ordinary Time Weekday	11 Benedict, Ab Memorial
12 Fifteenth Sunday of Ordinary Time Sunday	13 Henry Opt. Mem.	14 Kateri Tekakwitha, V Memorial	15 Bonaventure, B & D Memorial	16 Our Lady of Mount Carmel Opt. Mem.	17 Friday of the Fifteenth Week of Ordinary Time Weekday	18 Camillus de Lellis, P Opt. Mem.
19 Sixteenth Sunday of Ordinary Time Sunday	20 Apollinarus, B & M Opt. Mem.	21 Lawrence of Brindisi, P & D Opt. Mem.	22 Mary Magdalene Memorial	23 Bridget, Rel Opt. Mem.	24 Sharbel Makhluf, P Opt. Mem.	25 James, Ap Feast
26 Seventeenth Sunday of Ordinary Time Sunday	27 Monday of the Seventeenth Week of Ordinary Time Weekday	28 Tuesday of the Seventeenth Week of Ordinary Time Weekday	29 Martha Memorial	30 Peter Chrysologus, B & D Opt. Mem.	31 Ignatius of Loyola, P Memorial	

AUGUST

Sunday	Monday	Tuesday	Wednesday	Thursday	Friday	Saturday
						1 Alphonsus Liguori, B & D Memorial
2 Eighteenth Sunday of Ordinary Time Sunday	3 Monday of the Eighteenth Week of Ordinary Time Weekday	4 John Vianney, P Memorial	5 Dedication of St. Mary Major Opt. Mem.	6 Transfiguration Feast	7 Sixtus II, Po & M, and Companions, Mm; Cajetan, P Opt. Mem.	8 Dominic, P Memorial
9 Nineteenth Sunday of Ordinary Time Sunday	10 Lawrence, De & M Feast	11 Clare, V Memorial	12 Jane Frances de Chantal, Rel Opt. Mem.	13 Pontian, Po & M and Hippolytus, P & M Opt. Mem.	14 Maximilian Kolbe, P & M Memorial	15 Assumption SOLEMNITY
16 Twentieth Sunday of Ordinary Time Sunday	17 Monday of the Twentieth Week of Ordinary Time Weekday	18 Tuesday of the Twentieth Week of Ordinary Time Weekday	19 John Eudes, P Opt. Mem.	20 Bernard, Ab & D Memorial	21 Pius X, Po Memorial	22 Queenship of Mary Memorial
23 Twenty-First Sunday of Ordinary Time Sunday	24 Bartholomew, Ap Feast	25 Louis of France; Joseph Calasanz, P Opt. Mem.	26 Wednesday of the Twenty-First Week of Ordinary Time Weekday	27 Monica Memorial	28 Augustine, B & D Memorial	29 Beheading of John the Baptist, M Memorial
30 Twenty-Second Sunday of Ordinary Time Sunday	31 Monday of the Twenty-Second Week of Ordinary Time Weekday					

SEPTEMBER

Sunday	Monday	Tuesday	Wednesday	Thursday	Friday	Saturday
		1 Tuesday of the Twenty-Second Week of Ordinary Time Weekday	2 Wednesday of the Twenty-Second Week of Ordinary Time Weekday	3 Gregory the Great, Po & D Memorial	4 Friday of the Twenty-Second Week of Ordinary Time Weekday	5 Saturday of the Twenty-Second Week of Ordinary Time Weekday
6 Twenty-Third Sunday of Ordinary Time Sunday	7 Monday of the Twenty-Third Week of Ordinary Time Weekday **LABOUR DAY**	8 Birth of Mary Feast	9 Peter Claver, P Memorial	10 Thursday of the Twenty-Third Week of Ordinary Time Weekday	11 Friday of the Twenty-Third Week of Ordinary Time Weekday	12 The Most Name of the Blessed Virgin Mary Opt. Mem.
13 Twenty-Fourth Sunday of Ordinary Time Sunday	14 Triumph of the Cross Feast	15 Our Lady of Sorrows Memorial	16 Cornelius, Po & M and Cyprian, B & M Memorial	17 Robert Bellarmine, B & D Opt. Mem.	18 Friday of the Twenty-Fourth Week of Ordinary Time Weekday	19 Janurius, B & M Opt. Mem.
20 Twenty-Fifth Sunday of Ordinary Time Sunday	21 Matthew, Ap & Evangelist Feast	22 Tuesday of the Twenty-Fifth Week of Ordinary Time Weekday	23 Pio of Pietreclina, P Opt. Mem.	24 Thursday of the Twenty-Fifth Week of Ordinary Time Weekday	25 Friday of the Twenty-Fifth Week of Ordinary Time Weekday	26 Cosmas and Damian, Mm Opt. Mem.
27 Twenty-Sixth Sunday of Ordinary Time Sunday	28 Wenceslaus, M; Lawrence Ruiz and Companions, Mm Opt. Mem.	29 Michael, Gabriel, and Raphael, Archangels Feast	30 Jerome, P & D Memorial			

OCTOBER

Sunday	Monday	Tuesday	Wednesday	Thursday	Friday	Saturday
				1 Therese of the Child Jesus, V & D Memorial	2 Guardian Angels Memorial	3 Saturday of the Twenty-Sixth Week of Ordinary Time Weekday
4 Twenty-Seventh Sunday of Ordinary Time Sunday	5 Bl. Francis Xavier Seelos, P Opt. Mem.	6 Bruno, P; Bl. Marie Rose Durocher, V Opt. Mem.	7 Our Lady of the Rosary Memorial	8 Thursday of the Twenty-Seventh Week of Ordinary Time Weekday	9 Denis, B & M, and Companions, Mm; John Leonardi, P Opt. Mem.	10 Saturday of the Twenty-Seventh Week of Ordinary Time Weekday
11 Twenty-Eighth Sunday of Ordinary Time Sunday	12 Monday of the Twenty-Eighth Week of Ordinary Time Weekday **COLOMBUS DAY**	13 Tuesday of the Twenty-Eighth Week of Ordinary Time Weekday	14 Callistus I, Po & M Opt. Mem.	15 Teresa of Avila, V & D Memorial	16 Hedwig, Rel; Margaret Mary Alacoque, V Opt. Mem.	17 Ignatius of Antioch, B & M Memorial
18 Twenty-Ninth Sunday of Ordinary Time Sunday	19 John de Brebeuf and Isaac Jogues, P & Mm, and Companions, Mm Memorial	20 Paul of the Cross, P Opt. Mem.	21 Wednesday of the Twenty-Ninth Week of Ordinary Time Weekday	22 John Paul II, Po Opt. Mem.	23 John of Capistrano, P Opt. Mem.	24 Anthony Claret, B Opt. Mem.
25 Thirtieth Sunday of Ordinary Time Sunday	26 Monday of the Thirtieth Week of Ordinary Time Weekday	27 Tuesday of the Thirtieth Week of Ordinary Time Weekday	28 Simon and Jude, Ap Feast	29 Thursday of the Thirtieth Week of Ordinary Time Weekday	30 Friday of the Thirtieth Week of Ordinary Time Weekday	31 Saturday of the Thirtieth Week of Ordinary Time Weekday

NOVEMBER

Sunday	Monday	Tuesday	Wednesday	Thursday	Friday	Saturday
1 All Saints SOLEMNITY	2 All Souls Feast	3 Martin de Porres, Rel Opt. Mem.	4 Charles Borromeo, B Memorial	5 Thursday of the Thirty-First Week of Ordinary Time Weekday	6 Friday of the Thirty- First Week of Ordinary Time Weekday	7 Saturday of the Thirty- First Week of Ordinary Time Weekday
8 Thirty-Second Sunday of Ordinary Time Sunday	9 Dedication of St. John Lateran Feast	10 Leo the Great, Po & D Memorial	11 Martin of Tours, B Memorial **VETERANS DAY**	12 Josaphat, B & M Memorial	13 Frances Xavier Cabrini, V Memorial	14 Saturday of the Thirty- Second Week of Ordinary Time Weekday
15 Thirty-Third Sunday of Ordinary Time Sunday	16 Margaret of Scotland; Gertrude, V Opt. Mem.	17 Elizabeth of Hungary, Rel Memorial	18 Dedication of Churches of Peter & Paul; Rose Philippine Duchesne, V Opt. Mem.	19 Thursday of the Thirty-Third Week of Ordinary Time Weekday	20 Friday of the Thirty- Third Week of Ordinary Time Weekday	21 Presentation of Mary Memorial
22 Christ the King SOLEMNITY	23 Clement I, Po & M; Columban, Ab; Bl. Miguel Pro, P & M Opt. Mem.	24 Andrew Dung-Lac, P & M, and Companions, Mm Memorial	25 Catherine of Alexandria, V & M Opt. Mem.	26 Thursday of the Thirty-Fourth Week of Ordinary Time Weekday **THANKSGIVING DAY**	27 Friday of the Thirty- Fourth Week of Ordinary Time Weekday	28 Saturday of the Thirty- Fourth Week of Ordinary Time Weekday
29 First Sunday of Advent Sunday	30 Andrew, Ap Feast					

DECEMBER

Sunday	Monday	Tuesday	Wednesday	Thursday	Friday	Saturday
		1 Tuesday of the First Week of Advent Weekday	2 Wednesday of the First Week of Advent Weekday	3 Frances Xavier, P Memorial	4 John Damascene, P & D Opt. Mem.	5 Saturday of the First Week of Advent Weekday
6 Second Sunday of Advent Sunday	7 Ambrose, B & D Memorial	8 Immaculate Conception SOLEMNITY	9 Juan Diego Opt. Mem.	10 Thursday of the Second Week of Advent Weekday	11 Damasus I, Po Opt. Mem.	12 Our Lady of Guadalupe Feast
13 Third Sunday of Advent Sunday	14 John of the Cross, P & D Memorial	15 Tuesday of the Third Week of Advent Weekday	16 Wednesday of the Third Week of Advent Weekday	17 Thursday of the Third Week of Advent Weekday	18 Friday of the Third Week of Advent Weekday	19 Saturday of the Third Week of Advent Weekday
20 Fourth Sunday of Advent Sunday	21 Peter Canisius, P & D Opt. Mem.	22 Tuesday of the Fourth Week of Advent Weekday	23 John of Kanty, P Opt. Mem.	24 Thursday of the Fourth Week of Advent Weekday	25 Christmas SOLEMNITY **CHRISTMAS DAY**	26 Stephen, M Feast
27 Holy Family Feast	28 Holy Innocents, Mm Feast	29 Thomas Becket, B & M Opt. Mem.	30 Sixth day in the Octave of Christmas Weekday	31 Sylvester I, Po Opt. Mem.		

Introductory Rites

Greeting

P. In the name of the Father, and of the Son, and of the Holy Spirit.
C. Amen.

P. In nómine Patris, et Fílii, et Spíritus Sancti.
C. Amen.

(FORM A)

P: The grace of our Lord Jesus Christ and the love of God and the fellowship of the Holy Spirit be with you all.
C: And with your spirit.

(FORM A)

P: Grátia Dòmini nostri Jesu Christi, et càritas Dei, et communicàtio Sancti Spìritus sit cum òmnibus vobis.
C: Et cum spiritu tuo.

(FORM B)

P: The grace and peace of God our Father and the Lord Jesus Christ be with you.
C: And with your spirit.
(or)
C: Blessed be God, the Father of our Lord Jesus Chirst.

(FORM B)

P: Gratia vobis et pax a Deo Patre   nostro et Dominio Jesu Christo.
C: Et cum spiritu tuo.
(or)
C: Benedictus Deus et Pater Domini nostri Jesu Christi.

(FORMC)

P: The Lord be with you. (or a bishop says "Peace be with you")
C: and with your spirit.

(FORMC)

P: Dòminus vobìscum. (B: Pax vobis)

C: Et cum spiritu tuo.

PENITENTIAL RITE
(FORM A)

P: Brethren (brothers and sisters), to prepare ourselves to celebrate the sacred mysteries, let us call to mind our sins.

ACTUS PAENITENTIALIS
(FORM A)

P: Fratres, agnoscàmus peccàta nostra, ut apti simus ad sacra mystèria celebrànda.

A: I confess to almighty God and to you, my brothers and sisters, that I have greatly sinned, in my thoughts and in my words, in

A: Confíteor Deo omnipoténti et vobis, fratres, quia peccavi nimis cogitatione, verbo, opere et omissione: mea culpa, mea culpa, mea maxima what I have done and in what I have failed to do, through my fault, through my fault, through my most grievous fault; therefore I ask blessed Mary ever-Virgin, all the Angels and Saints, and you, my brothers and sisters, to pray for me to the Lord our God.

culpa. Ideo precor beatam Mariam semper Virginem, omnes Angelos et Sanctos, et vos, fratres, orare pro me ad Dominum Deum nostrum.

P: Lord have mercy.
C: Lord have mercy.
P: Christ have mercy.
C: Christ have mercy
P: Lord have mercy.
C: Lord have mercy

P: Kyrie elèison.
C: Kyrie elèison.
P: Christe elèison.
C: Christe elèison.
P: Kyrie elèison.
C: Kyrie elèison.

P: May almighty God have mercy on us, forgive us our sins, and bring us to everlasting life
C: Amen.

P: Misereàtur nostri omnìpotens Deus et, dimìssis peccàtis nostris, perdùcat nos ad vitam aetèrnam.
C: Amen.

(FORM B)
P: Lord, we have sinned against you.
C: Lord, have mercy.
P: Lord, show us your mercy and love.

C: And grant us your salvation.
P: May almighty God have mercy on us, forgive us our sins, and bring us to everlasting life.
C: Amen.

(FORM B)
P: Miserere nostri, Domine.
C: Quia peccavimus tibi.
P: Ostende nobis, Domine, misericordiam tuam.

C: Et salutare tuum da nobis.
P: Misereàtur nostri omnìpotens Deus et, dimìssis peccàtis nostris, perdùcat nos ad vitam aetèrnam.
C: Amen.

(FORM C)
P: You were sent to heal the contrite: Lord have mercy.
C: Lord have mercy.
P: You came to call sinners: Christ have mercy.
C: Christ have mercy.

(FORM C)
P: Qui missus es sanare contritos corde: Kyrie elèison.
C: Kyrie elèison.
P: Qui peccatores vocare venisti: Christe, elèison.
C: Christe, elèison.

P: You plead for us at the right hand of the Father: Lord have mercy.

C: Lord have mercy.

P: May almighty God have mercy on us, forgive us our sins, and bring us to everlasting life.

C: Amen

(please omit the Gloria during Advent and Lent)

GLORY TO GOD IN THE HIGHEST

Glory to God in the Highest. And on earth peace to people of good will. We praise You. We bless You. We adore You. We glorify You. We give You thanks for Your great glory, Lord God, heavenly King, O God Almighty Father. Lord Jesus Christ, Only-begotten Son. Lord God, Lamb of God, Son of the Father, You take away the sins of the world, have mercy on us. You take away the sins of the world, receive our prayer. You are seated at the right hand of the Father, have mercy on us. For You alone are the Holy; You alone are Lord; You alone are the Most High, Jesus Christ, with the Holy Spirit, in the Glory of God the Father. *Amen.*

OPENING PRAYER

P: Let us pray.

(prayer)

C: Amen.

LITURGY OF THE WORD

(after the reading)

L: The word of the Lord.

C. Thanks be to God.

P: Qui ad dexteram Patris sedes, ad interpellandum pro nobis: Kyrie elèison.

C: Kyrie elèison.

P: Misereàtur nostri omnìpotens Deus et, dimìssis peccàtis nostris, perdùcat nos ad vitam aetèrnam.

C: Amen.

(please omit the Gloria during Advent and Lent)

GLORIA IN EXCELSIS DEO

Gloria in excelsis deo. Et in terra pax hominibus bonae voluntatis. Laudamus te. Benedicimus te. Adoramus te. Glorificamus te. Gratiam agimus tibi propter magnam gloriam tuam. Domine deus, rex coelestis, deus pater omnipotens. Domine fili unigenite, Jesu Christe. Domine deus, agnus dei, filius patris. Qui tollis peccata mundi, miserere nobis. Qui tollis peccata mundi, suscipe deprecationem nostram. Qui sedes ad dexteram patris, miserere nobis. Quoniam tu solus sanctus. Tu solus dominus. Tu solus altissimus, jesu christe. Cum sancto spiritu in gloria dei patris. *Amen.*

COLLECTA

P: Oremus.

(prayer)

C: Amen.

LECTIO PRIMA

(after the reading)

L: Verbum Dòmini.

C: Deo gratias.

RESPONSORIAL PSALM

Second Reading

(after the reading)

L: The word of the Lord.

C. Thanks be to God.

Alleluia

Gospel

P: the Lord be with you

C: and with your spirit

P: A reading from the holy gospel according to N.

C: glory to you O, Lord.

(after the reading)

P: the gospel of the Lord.

C: praise to you Lord Jesus Christ.

HOMILY

Profession of Faith

The Creed

I believe in one God, the Father Almighty, maker of heaven and earth, of all things visible and invisible. I believe in one Lord Jesus Christ, the Only Begotten Son of God, born of the Father before all ages.

God from God, Light from Light, true God from true God, begotten, not made, consubstantial with the Father; through him all things were made. For us men and for our salvation. He came down from heaven, and by the Holy Spirit was incarnate of the Virgin

PSALMUS

Lectio Secunda

(after the reading)

L: Verbum Dòmini.

C: Deo gratias.

Alleluia

Evangelium

P: Dòminus vobìscum.

C: Et cum spiritu tuo.

P: Lèctio sancti Evangèlii secùndum N.

C: Glòria tibi, Domine.

(after the reading)

P: Verbum Dòmini.

C: Laus tibi, Christe.

HOMILIA

Credo

Credo in unum Deum, Patrem omnipotentem, factorem caeli et terrae, visibilium omnium et invisibilium, Et in unum Dominum Iesum Christum, Filium Dei unigenitum, et ex Patre natum, ante omnia saecula,

Deum de Deo, lumen de Lumine, Deum verum de Deo vero, genitum, non factum, consubstantialem Patri: per quem omnia facta sunt. Qui propter nos homines et propter nostram salutem descendit de caelis. Et incarnatus est de Spiritu Sancto ex Maria

Mary, and became man.

For our sake he was crucified under Pontius Pilate, he suffered death and was buried, and rose again on the third day in accordance with the Scriptures. He ascended into heaven and is seated at the right hand of the Father.

He will come again in glory to judge the living and the dead and his kingdom will have no end.

I believe in the Holy Spirit, the Lord, the giver of life, who proceeds from the Father and the Son.

Who with the Father and the Son is adored and glorified, who has spoken through the prophets.

I believe in one, holy, catholic and apostolic Church.
I confess one Baptism for the forgiveness of sinsand I look forward to the resurrection of the dead and the life of the world to come. Amen.

Virgine, et homo factus est.

Crucifixus etiam pro nobis sub Pontio Pilato; passus et sepultus est, et resurrexit tertia die, secundem Scripturas, et ascendit in caelum, sedet ad dexteram Patris.

Et iterum venturus est cum gloria, iudicare vivos et mortuos, cuius regni non erit finis.

Et in Spiritum Sanctum, Dominum et vivificantem: qui ex Patre Filioque procedit.

Qui cum Patre et Filio simul adoratur et conglorificatur: qui locutus est per prophetas.

Et nuam, sanctam, catholicam et apostolicam Ecclesiam.
Confiteor unum baptisma in remissionem peccatorum. Et exspecto resurrectionem mortuorum, et vitam venturi saeculi. Amen.

PREPARATION OF THE ALTAR AND THE GIFTS

P. Blessed are you, Lord God of all creation, for through your goodness we have received the bread we offer you: fruit of the earth and work of human hands, it will become for us the bread of life.

C: Blessed be God forever.

P. Pray, brethren (brothers and sisters), that my sacrifice and yours may be acceptable to

P. Benedictus es, Dómine, Deus univérsi, quia de tua largitáte accépimus panem, quem tibi of férimus, fructum terræ et óperis mánuum hóminum: ex quo nobis fiet panis vitæ.

C: Benedìctus Deus in Sàecula.

P. Oráte, fratres: ut meum acvestrum sacrifícium acceptàbile fiat apud Deum

God, the almighty Father.

C. May the Lord accept the sacrifice at your hands for the praise and glory of his name, for our good and the good of all his holy Church.

PRAYER OVER THE GIFTS
P: (prayer)
C: Amen.

EUCHARISTIC PRAYER II
P. The Lord be with you.
C. And with your spirit.
P. Lift up your hearts.
C. We lift them up to the Lord.
P. Let us give thanks to the Lord our God.
C. It is right and just.
P: It is truly right and just, our duty and our salvation, always and everywhere to give you thanks Father most holy through your beloved Son, Jesus Christ, your word through whom you made all things, whom you sent as our Savior and Redeemer, incarnate by the Holy Spirit and born of the Virgin.

Fulfilling your will and gaining for you a holy people, He stretched out His hands and as He endured His Passion, so as to break the bonds of death and manifest the resurrection.

And so with all the angels and the saints we declare your glory, as with one voice we acclaim:

Holy, Holy, Holy Lord God of hosts. Heaven and earth are full of your glory. Hosanna in the highest. Blessed is He who comes in the

---

Patrem omnipoténtem.

C. Suscípiat Dóminus sacrifícium de mánibus tuis praiad laudem et glóriam nóminis sui, ad utilitátem quoque nostram totiúsque Ecclésiæ suæ sanctæ.

ORATIO SUPER OBLATA
P: (prayer)
C: Amen.

PREX EUCHARISTICA II
P: Dòminus vobìscum
C: Et cum spiritu tuo.
C: Sursum Corda.
C: Habèmus ad Dòminum.
P: Gràtias agàmus Dòmino Deo nostro
C: Dignum et iustum est.
P: Vere dignum et iustum est aequum et salutàre, nos tibi sancte Pater, semper et ubìque gràtias àgere per Filium dilectiònis tuae Jesum Christum.

Verbum tuum, per quod cuncta fecìsti: quem misìsti nobis Salvatòrem et Redemptòrem, incarnàtum de Spìritu Sancto et ex Virgine natum.

Qui voluntàtem tuam adìmplens et pòpulum tibi sanctum acquirens extèndit manus cum paterètur, ut mortem sòlveret et resurrectiònem manifestàret.

Et ìdeo cum Angelis et òmnibus Sanctis glòriam tuam una voce dicèntes:

Sanctus, Sanctus, Sanctus, Dóminus Deus Sábaoth. Pleni sunt caeli et terra glória tua. Hosánna in excélsis. Benedíctus qui venit in name of the Lord. Hosanna in the highest.

P. You are indead Holy, O Lord, the fount of all holiness. Make holy, therefore, these gifts, we pray, by sending down Your Spirit upon them like the dewfall, so that they may become for us the Body ✝ and Blood of our Lord, Jesus Christ.

At the time He was betrayed and entered willingly into His Passion, He took bread and, giving thanks, broke it and gave it to His disciples, saying:

TAKE THIS, ALL OF YOU, AND EAT OF IT: FOR THIS IS MY BODY WHICH WILL BE GIVEN UP FOR YOU.

In a similar way when supper was ended, he took the chalice and, once more giving thanks He gave it to His disciples, saying:

TAKE THIS ALL OF YOU AND DRINK FROM IT: FOR THIS IS THE CHALICE OF MY BLOOD, THE BLOOD OF THE NEW AND EVERLASTING COVENANT, WHICH WILL BE POURED OUT FOR YOU AND FOR MANY FOR THE FORGIVENESS OF SINS. DO THIS IN MEMORY OF ME.

P: LET US PROCLAIM THE MYSTERY OF FAITH

A. we proclaim your Death, O Lord, and profess your resurrection until you come

---

nómine Domini. Hosánna in excélsis.

P. **V**ere Sanctus es, Domine, fons omnis sanctitatis. Haec ergo dona, quaesumus, Spiritus tui rore sanctifica, ut nobis Corpus et ✝ Sanguis fiant Domini nostri Iesu Christi.

Qui, pridie quam pateretur, accepit panem in sanctas ac venerabiles manus suas, et elevatis oculis in caelum ad te Deum Patrem suum omnipotentem, tibi gratias agens benedixit, fregit, deditque discipulis suis, dicens:

ACCIPITE ET MANDUCATE EX HOC OMNES: HOC EST ENIM CORPUS MEUM, QUOD PRO VOBIS TRADETUR.

Simili modo, postquam cenatum est, accipiens et hunc praeclarum calicem in sanctas ac venerabiles manus suas, item tibi grtias agens benedixit, deditque discipulis suis, dicens:

ACCIPITE ET BIBITE EX EO OMNES: HIC EST ENIM CALIX SANGUINIS MEI NOVI ET AETERNI TESTAMENTI, QUI PRO VOBIS ET PRO MULTIS EFFUNDETUR IN REMISSIONEM PECCATORUM.
HOC FACITE IN MEAM COMMEMORATIONEM.

P: MYSTERIUM FÌDEI.

A. Mortem tuam annuntiamus, Domine, et tuam resurrectionem confitemur, donec again

B. When we eat this bread and drink this cup, we proclaim your death, Lord Jesus, until you come in glory.

C. Save us Saviour of the world, for by Your by your cross and resurrection you have set us free.

P. Therefore, as we celebrate the memorial of His Death and Resurrection, we offer You, Lord the Bread of Life and the Chalice of salvation, giving thanks that you have held us worthy to be in Your presence and minister to You. Humbly we pray that, partaking of the Body and Blood of Christ, we may be gathered into one by the Holy Spirit.

Remember, Lord, Your Church spread throughout the world; and bring her to the fullness of charity, together with N. our Pope, N. our bishop, and all the clergy.

Remember also our brothers and sisters who have fallen asleep in the hope of the resurrection, and all who have died in Your mercy: welcome them into the light of Your face. Have mercy on us all, we pray, that with the Virgin Mary, Blessed Joseph, her Spouse, with the Blessed Apostles, and all the Saints who have pleased You throughout the ages, we may merit to be coheirs to eternal life, and may praise and glorify You through Your Son Jesus Christ.

venias.

B. Quotiescumque manducamus panem hunc et calicem bibimus, mortem tuam annuntiamus, Domine, donec venias.

C. Salvator mundi, salva nos, qui per crucem et resurrectionem tuam liberasti nos.

P. Memores igitur mortis et resurrectionis eius, tibi, Domine, panem vitae et calicem salutis afferimus, gratias agentes quia nos dignos habuisti astare coram te et tibi ministrare. Et supplices deprecamur ut Corporis et Sanguinis Christi participes a Spiritu Sancto congregemur in unum.

Recordare, Domine, Ecclesiae tuae toto orbe diffusae, ut eam in caritate perficias una cum Papa nostro N. et Episcopo nostro N. et universo clero.

Memento etiam fratrum nostrorum, qui in spe resurrectionis dormierunt, omniumque in tua miseratione defunctorum, et eos in lumen vultus tui admitte. Omnium nostrum, quaesumus, miserere, ut cum beata Dei Genetrice Virgine Maria, beatis Apostolis et omnibus Sanctis, qui tibi a saeculo placuerunt, aeternae vitae mereamur esse consortes, et te laudemus et glorificemus.

CONCLUDING DOXOLGY

P. Through him, and with him, and in him, O God, Almighty Father, in the unity of the Holy Spirit, all glory and honor is yours, for ever and ever.

C. Amen

COMMUNION RITE

Lord's Prayer

P: At the Saviour's command and formed by divine teaching, we dare to say:

Our Father, who art in heaven, hallowed be Thy name. Thy kingdom come. Thy will be done on earth as it is in heaven. Give us this day our daily bread and forgive us our trespasses as we forgive those who trespass against us. And lead us not into temptation, but deliver us from evil. Amen.

DOXOLOGY

P. Deliver us, Lord, we pray, from every evil, graciously grant peace in our days, that, by the help of your mercy, we may be always free from sin and safe from all distress, as we await the blessed hope and the coming of our Savior, Jesus Christ. Christi.

C. For the kingdom, the power and the glory are yours now and forever.

SIGN OF PEACE

P. Lord Jesus Christ, who said to your Apostles: Peace I leave you, my peace I give you, look not on our sins, but on the faith of your Church, and graciously grant her peace

RITUS COMMUNINIS

Pater Noster

P: Praecèptis salutàribus mòniti et divìna institutiòne formàti, audèmus dicere:

Páter nóster, qui es in cáelis, sanctificétur nómen túum. Advéniat régnum túum. Fíat volúntas túa, sícut in cáelo et in térra. Pánem nóstrum quotidiánum da nóbis hódie, et dimítte nóbis débita nóstra, sícut et nos dimíttimus debitóribus nóstris. Et ne nos indúcas in tentatiónem: sed líbera nos a málo. Amen.

P: Líbera nos, quǽsumus, Dómine, ab ómnibus malis, da pro pítius pacem in diébus nostris, ut, ope misericórdiæ tuæ adiúti, et a peccáto simus semper líberi et ab omni perturbatióne secúri: exspectántes beátam spem et advéntum Salvatóris nostri Iesu

C. Quia tuum est regnum, et potéstas, et glória in sǽcula.

P. Dómine Iesu Christe, qui dixí- sti Apóstolis tuis: Pacem relínquo vobis, pacem meam do vobis: ne respícias peccáta nostra, sed fidem Ecclésiæ tuæ; eám que secúndum voluntátem

CONCLUDING DOXOLGY

P. Per ipsum, et cum ipso, et in ipso, est tibi Deo Patris omnipotenti, in unitate Spiritus Sancti, omnis honor et gloria per omnia saecula saeculorum.

C. Amen

and unity in accordance with your will. Who live and reign for ever and ever.

C. Amen

P. The peace of the Lord be with you always,

C. and with your spirit.

P: Let us offer each other the sign of peace.

tuam pacificáre et coadunáre digne ris. Qui vivis et regnas in sǽcula sǽculorum.

C. Amen

P. Pax Dòmini sit semper;

C. Et cum spiritu tuo.

P: Offèrte vobis pacem.

BREAKING OF THE BREAD

A: Lamb of God, you take away the sins of the world, have mercy on us.

A: Lamb of God, you take away the sins of the world, have mercy on us.

A: Lamb of God, you take away the sins of the world, grant us peace.

P. Behold the Lamb of God, behold Him who takes away the sins of the world. Blessed are those called to the supper of the Lamb.

C. Lord, I am not worthy that you should enter under my roof, but only say the word and my soul shall be healed.

P. May the Body and Blood of Christ keep me safe for eternal life.

C. Amen

A: Agnus Dei, qui tollis peccàta mundi; miserère nobis.

A: Agnus Dei, qui tollis peccàta mundi; miserère nobis.

A: Agnus Dei, qui tollis peccàta mundi; dona nobis pacem.

P. Ecce Agnus Dei, ecce qui tollis peccáta mundi. Beáti qui ad cenam Agni vocáti sunt.

C. Dómine, non sum dignus, ut intres sub tectum meum, sed tantum dic verbo et sanábitur ánima mea.

P. Corpus et SanguisChristi custódiat me in vitam ætérnam.

C. Amen

COMMUNION

P. The Body of Christ.

C. Amen

P. The Blood of Christ.

C. Amen

P. Corpus Christi.

C. Amen

P. Sanguis Christi.

C. Amen

Prayer After Communion

P. Let us pray.

(Prayer)

C: Amen.

Postcommunio

P. Oremus

(Prayer)

C: Amen.

Concluding Rite

P: The Lord be with you.

Ritus Conclusionis

P: Dòminus vobìscum.

C: And with your spirit.

C: Et cum spìritu tuo.

BLESSING

(form A)

P: May almighty God bless you: the Father, and the Son, ✠ and the Holy Spirit.

C: Amen

(form A)

P: Benedícat vos omnípotens De us, Pater, et Filius, ✠ et Spíritus Sanctus.

C: Amen

DISMISSAL

P: Go forth, the Mass is ended.

C: Thanks be to God.

P: Ite, missa est.

C: Deo gratias.

3   JANUARY

WEDNESDAY 1 JANUARY; THE OCTAVE DAY OF CHRISTMAS SOLEMNITY OF MARY, MOTHER OF GOD

FIRST READING   Numbers 6:22—27

The LORD said to Moses: "Speak to Aaron and his sons and tell them: This is how you shall bless the Israelites. Say to them: The LORD bless you and keep you! The LORD let his face shine upon you, and be gracious to you! The LORD look upon you kindly and give you peace! So shall they invoke my name
 upon the Israelites, and I will bless them."

RESPONSORIAL PSALM   *Psalm 67:2—3, 5, 6, 8 (2a)*

R. May God bless us in his mercy.

May God have pity on us and bless us; **/** may he let his face shine upon us. **/**
So may your way be known upon earth; **/** among all nations, your salvation. **R.**
May the nations be glad and exult **/** because you rule the peoples in equity; **/** the nations on the earth you guide. **R.**
May the peoples praise you, O God; **/** may all the peoples praise you! **/** May God bless us, **/** and may all the ends of the earth fear him! **R.**

SECOND READING   *Galatians 4: 4 — 7*

Brothers and sisters: When the fullness of time had come, God sent his Son, born of a woman, born under the law, to ransom those under the law, so that we might receive adoption as sons. As proof that you are sons, God sent the Spirit of his Son into our hearts, crying out, "Abba, Father!" So you are no longer a slave but a son, and if a son then also an heir, through God.

ALLELUIA *Hebrews 1:1—2*

R. Alleluia, alleluia. In the past God spoke to our ancestors through the prophets; in these last days, he has spoken to us through the Son. **R.**

GOSPEL *Luke 2:16—21*

The shepherds went in haste to Bethlehem and found Mary and Joseph, and the infant lying in the manger. When they saw this, they made known the message that had been told them about this child. All who heard it were amazed by what had been told them by the shepherds. And Mary kept all these things, reflecting on them in her heart. Then the shepherds returned, glorifying and praising God for all they had heard and seen, just as it had been told to them.

When eight days were completed for his circumcision, he was named Jesus, the name given him by the angel before he was conceived in the womb.

THURSDAY JANUARY 2;
ST. BASIL THE GREAT AND ST. GREGORY NAZIANZEN

FIRST READING *1John 2:22–28*

Beloved: Who is the liar? Whoever denies that Jesus is the Christ. Whoever denies the Father and the Son, this is the antichrist. Anyone who denies the Son does not have the Father, but whoever confesses the Son has the Father as well.

Let what you heard from the beginning remain in you. If what you heard from the beginning remains in you, then you will remain in the Son and in the Father. And this is the promise that he made us: eternal life. I write you these things about those who would deceive you. As for you, the anointing that you received from him remains in you, so that you do not need anyone to teach you. But his anointing teaches you about everything and is true and not false; just as it taught you, remain in him.

And now, children, remain in him, so that when he appears we may have confidence and not be put to shame by him at his coming.

RESPONSORIAL PSALM *Psalm 98:1, 2–3ab, 3cd–4*

R. (3cd) All the ends of the earth have seen the saving power of God.

Sing to the LORD a new song, / for he has done wondrous deeds; / His right hand has won victory for him, his holy arm. **R.**

The LORD has made his salvation known: / in the sight of the nations he has revealed his justice. / He has remembered his kindness / and his faithfulness toward the house of Israel. **R.**

All the ends of the earth have seen / the salvation by our God. / Sing joyfully to the LORD, all you lands; / break into song; sing praise. **R.**

ALLELUIA *Hebrews 1:1–2*

R. Alleluia, alleluia. In times past, God spoke to our ancestors through the prophets: in these last days, he has spoken to us through his Son. **R.**

GOSPEL *John 1:19–28*

This is the testimony of John. When the Jews from Jerusalem sent priests and Levites to him to ask him, "Who are you?" He admitted and did not deny it, but admitted, "I am not the Christ." So they asked him, "What are you then? Are you Elijah?" And he said, "I am not." "Are you the Prophet?" He answered, "No." So they said to him, "Who are you, so we can give an answer to those who sent us? What do you have to say for yourself?" He said: *"I am the voice of one crying out in the desert, 'Make straight the way of the Lord,'* as Isaiah the prophet said." Some Pharisees were also sent. They asked him, "Why then do you baptize if you are not the Christ or Elijah or the Prophet?" John answered them, "I baptize with water; but there is one among you whom you do not recognize, the one who is coming after me, whose sandal strap I am not worthy to untie." This happened in Bethany across the Jordan, where John was baptizing.

FRIDAY 3 JANUARY; THE MOST HOLY NAME OF JESUS
FIRST READING *1John 2:29–3 :6*

If you consider that God is righteous, you also know that everyone who acts in righteousness is begotten by him.

See what love the Father has bestowed on us that we may be called the children of God. Yet so we are. The reason the world does not know us is that it did not know him. Beloved, we are God's children now; what we shall be has not yet been revealed. We do know that when it is revealed we shall be like him, for we shall see him as he is. Everyone who has this hope based on him makes himself pure, as he is pure.

Everyone who commits sin commits lawlessness, for sin is lawlessness. You know that he was revealed to take away sins, and in him there is no sin. No one who remains in him sins; no one who sins has seen him or known him.

PSALM *Psalm 98:1, 3cd–4, 5–6*
R. (3cd) All the ends of the earth have seen the saving power of God.
Sing to the LORD a new song, **/** for he has done wondrous deeds; **/** His right hand has won victory for him, **/** his holy arm. **R.**
All the ends of the earth have seen **/** the salvation by our God. **/** Sing joyfully to the LORD, **/** all you lands; break into song; sing praise. **R.**
Sing praise to the LORD with the harp, **/** with the harp and melodious song. **/** With trumpets and the sound of the horn**/** sing joyfully before the King, the LORD. **R.**
ALLELUIA *John 1:14a, 12a*
R. Alleluia, alleluia. The Word of God became flesh and dwelt among us. To those who accepted him, he gave power to become children of God. **R.**

GOSPEL *John 1:29–34*

John the Baptist saw Jesus coming toward him and said, "Behold, the Lamb of God, who takes away the sin of the world. He is the one of whom I said, 'A man is coming after me who ranks ahead of me because he existed before me.' I did not know him, but the reason why I came baptizing with water was that he might be made known to Israel." John testified further, saying, "I saw the Spirit come down like a dove from the sky and remain upon him. I did not know him, but the one who sent me to baptize with water told me, 'On whomever you see the Spirit come down and remain, he is the one who will baptize with the Holy Spirit.' Now I have seen and testified that he is the Son of God."

SATURDAY 4 JANUARY; ST. ELIZABETH ANN SETON

FIRST READING *1John 3:7–10*

Children, let no one deceive you. The person who acts in righteousness is righteous, just as he is righteous. Whoever sins belongs to the Devil, because the Devil has sinned from the beginning. Indeed, the Son of God was revealed to destroy the works of the Devil. No one who is begotten by God commits sin, because God's seed remains in him; he cannot sin because he is begotten by God. In this way, the children of God and the children of the Devil are made plain; no one who fails to act in righteousness belongs to God, nor anyone who does not love his brother.

RESPONSORIAL PSALM *Psalm 98:1, 7–8, 9*

R. (3cd) All the ends of the earth have seen the saving power of God.

Sing to the LORD a new song, **/** for he has done wondrous deeds; **/** His right hand has won victory for him, his holy arm. **R.**

Let the sea and what fills it resound, **/** the world and those who dwell in it; **/** Let the rivers clap their hands, **/** the mountains shout with them for joy before the LORD. **R.**

The LORD comes; he comes to rule the earth; **/** He will rule the world with justice **/** and the peoples with equity. **R.**

ALLELUIA *Hebrews 1:1–2*

R. Alleluia, alleluia. In the past God spoke to our ancestors through the prophets: in these last days, he has spoken to us through the Son. **R.**

GOSPEL *John 1:35–42*

John was standing with two of his disciples, and as he watched Jesus walk by, he said, "Behold, the Lamb of God." The two disciples heard what he said and followed Jesus. Jesus turned and saw them following him and said to them, "What are you looking for?" They said to him, "Rabbi" (which translated means Teacher), "where are you staying?" He said to them, "Come, and you will see." So they went and saw where he was staying, and they stayed with him that day. It was about four in the afternoon. Andrew, the brother of Simon Peter, was one of the two who heard John and followed Jesus. He first found his own brother Simon and told him, "We have found the Messiah," which is translated Christ. Then he brought him to Jesus. Jesus looked at him and said, "You are Simon the son of John; you will be called Cephas," which is translated Peter.

SUNDAY 5 JANUARY; SOLEMNITY OF THE EPIPHANY OF THE LORD; ST. JOHN NEUMANN

FIRST READING   *Isaiah 60:1—6*

Rise up in splendor, Jerusalem! Your light has come, the glory of the Lord shines upon you. See, darkness covers the earth, and thick clouds cover the peoples; but upon you the LORD shines, and over you appears his glory. Nations shall walk by your light, and kings by your shining radiance. Raise your eyes and look about; they all gather and come to you: your sons come from afar, and your daughters in the arms of their nurses.

Then you shall be radiant at what you see, your heart shall throb and overflow, for the riches of the sea shall be emptied out before you, the wealth of nations shall be brought to you. Caravans of camels shall fill you, dromedaries from Midian and Ephah; all from Sheba shall come bearing gold and frankincense, and proclaiming the praises of the LORD.

RESPONSORIAL PSALM: *Psalm 72:1—2, 7—8, 10—11, 12—13 (see 11)*

R. Lord, every nation on earth will adore you.

O God, with your judgment endow the king, **/** and with your justice, the king's son; **/**
He shall govern your people with justice **/** and your afflicted ones with judgment. **R.**
Justice shall flower in his days, **/** and profound peace, till the moon be no more. **/**
May he rule from sea to sea, **/** and from the River to the ends of the earth. **R.**
The kings of Tarshish and the Isles shall offer gifts; **/** the kings of Arabia and Seba shall bring tribute. **/** All kings shall pay him homage, **/** all nations shall serve him. **R.**
For he shall rescue the poor when he cries out, **/** and the afflicted when he has no one to help him. **/** He shall have pity for the lowly and the poor; **/**
the lives of the poor he shall save. **R.**

SECOND READING   *Ephesians 3:2—3a, 5—6*

Brothers and sisters: You have heard of the stewardship of God's grace that was given to me for your benefit, namely, that the mystery was made known to me by revelation. It was not made known to people in other generations as it has now been revealed to his holy apostles and prophets by the Spirit: that the Gentiles are coheirs, members of the same body, and copartners in the promise in Christ Jesus through the gospel.

ALLELUIA   *Matthew 2:2*

R. Alleluia, alleluia. We saw his star at its rising and have come to do him homage. **R.**

GOSPEL   *Matthew 2:1—12*

When Jesus was born in Bethlehem of Judea, in the days of King Herod, behold, magi from the east arrived in Jerusalem, saying, "Where is the newborn king of the Jews? We saw his star at its rising and have come to do him homage." When King Herod heard this, he was greatly troubled, and all Jerusalem with him. Assembling all the chief priests and the scribes of the people, he inquired of them where the Christ was to be born. They said to him, "In Bethlehem of Judea, for thus it has been written through the prophet:

And you, Bethlehem, land of Judah, are by no means least among the rulers of Judah; since from you shall come a ruler, who is to shepherd my people Israel."

Then Herod called the magi secretly and ascertained from them the time of the star's appearance. He sent them to Bethlehem and said, "Go and search diligently for the child. When you have found him, bring me word, that I too may go and do him homage." After their audience with the king they set out. And behold, the star that they had seen at its rising preceded them, until it came and stopped over the place where the child was. They were overjoyed at seeing the star, and on entering the house they saw the child with Mary his mother. They prostrated themselves and did him homage. Then they opened their treasures and offered him gifts of gold, frankincense, and myrrh. And having been warned in a dream not to return to Herod, they departed for their country by another way.

JANUARY 6, MONDAY AFTER EPIPHANY; ST. ANDRÉ BESSETTE
FIRST READING   *1John 3:22 – 4 :6*

Beloved: we receive from him whatever we ask, because we keep his commandments and do what pleases him. And his commandment is this: we should believe in the name of his Son, Jesus Christ, and love one another just as he commanded us. Those who keep his commandments remain in him, and he in them, and the way we know that he remains in us is from the Spirit whom he gave us.

Beloved, do not trust every spirit but test the spirits to see whether they belong to God, because many false prophets have gone out into the world. This is how you can know the Spirit of God: every spirit that acknowledges Jesus Christ come in the flesh belongs to God, and every spirit that does not acknowledge Jesus does not belong to God. This is the spirit of the antichrist who, as you heard, is to come, but in fact is already in the world. You belong to God, children, and you have conquered them, for the one who is in you is greater than the one who is in the world. They belong to the world; accordingly, their teaching belongs to the world, and the world listens to them. We belong to God, and anyone who knows God listens to us, while anyone who does not belong to God refuses to hear us. This is how we know the spirit of truth and the spirit of deceit.

RESPONSORIAL PSALM   *Psalm 2:7bc–8, 10–12a*

R. (8ab) **I will give you all the nations for an inheritance.**

The LORD said to me, / "You are my Son; / this day I have begotten you. / Ask of me and I will give you the nations for an inheritance / and the ends of the earth for your possession." **R.**

And now, O kings, give heed; / take warning, you rulers of the earth. / Serve the LORD with fear, / and rejoice before him; with trembling rejoice. **R.**

ALLELUIA   *See Matthew 4:23*

R. Alleluia, alleluia. Jesus proclaimed the Gospel of the Kingdom and cured every disease among the people. **R.**

GOSPEL   *Matthew 4:12–17, 23–25*

When Jesus heard that John had been arrested, he withdrew to Galilee. He left Nazareth and went to live in Capernaum by the sea, in the region of Zebulun and Naphtali, that what had been said through Isaiah the prophet might be fulfilled:

Land of Zebulun and land of Naphtali, the way to the sea, beyond the Jordan, Galilee of the Gentiles, the people who sit in darkness have seen a great light, on those dwelling in a land overshadowed by death light has arisen.

From that time on, Jesus began to preach and say, "Repent, for the Kingdom of heaven is at hand."

He went around all of Galilee, teaching in their synagogues, proclaiming the Gospel of the Kingdom, and curing every disease and illness among the people. His fame spread to all of Syria, and they brought to him all who were sick with various diseases and racked with pain, those who were possessed, lunatics, and paralytics, and he cured them. And great crowds from Galilee, the Decapolis, Jerusalem, and Judea, and from beyond the Jordan followed him.

JANUARY 7, TUESDAY AFTER EPIPHANY; ST. RAYMOND OF PEÑAFORT

FIRST READING   *1John 4:7–10*

Beloved, let us love one another, because love is of God; everyone who loves is begotten by God and knows God. Whoever is without love does not know God, for God is love. In this way the love of God was revealed to us: God sent his only–begotten Son into the world so that we might have life through him. In this is love: not that we have loved God, but that he loved us and sent his Son as expiation for our sins.

RESPONSORIAL PSALM   *Psalm 72:1–2, 3–4, 7–8*

R. (see 11) Lord, every nation on earth will adore you.

O God, with your judgment endow the king, / and with your justice, the king's son; / He shall govern your people with justice/ and your afflicted ones with judgment. **R.**

The mountains shall yield peace for the people, / and the hills justice. / He shall defend the afflicted among the people, / save the children of the poor. **R.**

Justice shall flower in his days, / and profound peace, till the moon be no more. / May he rule from sea to sea, / and from the River to the ends of the earth. **R.**

ALLELUIA   *Luke 4:18*

R. Alleluia, alleluia. The Lord has sent me to bring glad tidings to the poor and to proclaim liberty to captives. **R.**

GOSPEL   *Mark 6:34–44*

When Jesus saw the vast crowd, his heart was moved with pity for them, for they were like sheep without a shepherd; and he began to teach them many things. By now it was already late and his disciples approached him and said, "This is a deserted place and it is already very late. Dismiss them so that they can go to the surrounding farms and villages and buy themselves something to eat." He said to them in reply, "Give them some food yourselves." But they said to him, "Are we to buy two hundred days' wages worth of food and give it to them to eat?" He asked them, "How many loaves do you have? Go and see." And when they had found out they said, "Five loaves and two fish." So he gave orders to have them sit down in groups on the green grass. The people took their places in rows by hundreds and by fifties. Then, taking the five loaves and the two fish and looking up to heaven, he said the blessing, broke the loaves, and gave them to his disciples to set before the people; he also divided the two fish among them all. They all ate and were satisfied. And they picked up twelve wicker baskets full of fragments and what was left of the fish. Those who ate of the loaves were five thousand men.

JANUARY 8, WEDNESDAY AFTER EPIPHANY; ST. ANDREW CORSINI

FIRST READING
1John 4:11–18

Beloved, if God so loved us, we also must love one another. No one has ever seen God. Yet, if we love one another, God remains in us, and his love is brought to perfection in us.

This is how we know that we remain in him and he in us, that he has given us of his Spirit. Moreover, we have seen and testify that the Father sent his Son as savior of the world. Whoever acknowledges that Jesus is the Son of God, God remains in him and he in God. We have come to know and to believe in the love God has for us.

God is love, and whoever remains in love remains in God and God in him. In this is love brought to perfection among us, that we have confidence on the day of judgment because as he is, so are we in this world. There is no fear in love, but perfect love drives out fear because fear has to do with punishment, and so one who fears is not yet perfect in love.

RESPONSORIAL PSALM
Psalm 72:1–2, 10, 12–13

R. (see 11) **Lord, every nation on earth will adore you.**

O God, with your judgment endow the king, / and with your justice, the king's son; / He shall govern your people with justice / and your afflicted ones with judgment. **R.**

The kings of Tarshish and the Isles shall offer gifts; / the kings of Arabia and Seba shall bring tribute. **R.**

For he shall rescue the poor when he cries out, / and the afflicted when he has no one to help him. / He shall have pity for the lowly and the poor; the lives of the poor he shall save. **R.**

ALLELUIA
See 1 Timothy 3:16

R. **Alleluia, alleluia.** Glory to you, O Christ, proclaimed to the Gentiles. Glory to you, O Christ, believed in throughout the world. **R.**

GOSPEL
Mark 6:45–52

After the five thousand had eaten and were satisfied, Jesus made his disciples get into the boat and precede him to the other side toward Bethsaida, while he dismissed the crowd.

And when he had taken leave of them, he went off to the mountain to pray. When it was evening, the boat was far out on the sea and he was alone on shore. Then he saw that they were tossed about while rowing, for the wind was against them. About the fourth watch of the night, he came toward them walking on the sea. He meant to pass by them. But when they saw him walking on the sea, they thought it was a ghost and cried out. They had all seen him and were terrified. But at once he spoke with them, "Take courage, it is I, do not be afraid!" He got into the boat with them and the wind died down. They were completely astounded. They had not understood the incident of the loaves. On the contrary, their hearts were hardened.

JANUARY 9 THURSDAY AFTER EPIPHANY; ST. ADRIAN OF CANTERBURY
FIRST READING *1John 4:19 – 5:4*

Beloved, we love God because he first loved us. If anyone says, "I love God," but hates his brother, he is a liar; for whoever does not love a brother whom he has seen cannot love God whom he has not seen. This is the commandment we have from him: Whoever loves God must also love his brother.

Everyone who believes that Jesus is the Christ is begotten by God, and everyone who loves the Father loves also the one begotten by him. In this way we know that we love the children of God when we love God and obey his commandments. For the love of God is this, that we keep his commandments. And his commandments are not burdensome, for whoever is begotten by God conquers the world. And the victory that conquers the world is our faith.

RESPONSORIAL PSALM: *Psalm 72:1–2, 14 and 15bc, 17*

R. (see 11) **Lord, every nation on earth will adore you.**

O God, with your judgment endow the king, / and with your justice, the king's son; / He shall govern your people with justice / and your afflicted ones with judgment. **R.**

From fraud and violence he shall redeem them, / and precious shall their blood be in his sight. / May they be prayed for continually; / day by day shall they bless him. **R.**

May his name be blessed forever; / as long as the sun his name shall remain. / In him shall all the tribes of the earth be blessed; / all the nations shall proclaim his happiness. **R.**

ALLELUIA *Luke 4:18*

R. **Alleluia, alleluia.** The Lord has sent me to bring glad tidings to the poor and to proclaim liberty to captives. **R.**

GOSPEL *Luke 4:14–22*

Jesus returned to Galilee in the power of the Spirit, and news of him spread throughout the whole region. He taught in their synagogues and was praised by all.

He came to Nazareth, where he had grown up, and went according to his custom into the synagogue on the sabbath day. He stood up to read and was handed a scroll of the prophet Isaiah. He unrolled the scroll and found the passage where it was written:

The Spirit of the Lord is upon me, because he has anointed me to bring glad tidings to the poor. He has sent me to proclaim liberty to captives and recovery of sight to the blind, to let the oppressed go free, and to proclaim a year acceptable to the Lord.

Rolling up the scroll, he handed it back to the attendant and sat down, and the eyes of all in the synagogue looked intently at him. He said to them, "Today this Scripture passage is fulfilled in your hearing." And all spoke highly of him and were amazed at the gracious words that came from his mouth.

JANUARY 10, FRIDAY AFTER EPIPHANY; ST. JOHN THE ALMSGIVER

FIRST READING   *1John 5:5–13*

Beloved: Who indeed is the victor over the world but the one who believes that Jesus is the Son of God?

This is the one who came through water and Blood, Jesus Christ, not by water alone, but by water and Blood. The Spirit is the one who testifies, and the Spirit is truth. So there are three who testify, the Spirit, the water, and the Blood, and the three are of one accord. If we accept human testimony, the testimony of God is surely greater. Now the testimony of God is this, that he has testified on behalf of his Son. Whoever believes in the Son of God has this testimony within himself. Whoever does not believe God has made him a liar by not believing the testimony God has given about his Son. And this is the testimony: God gave us eternal life, and this life is in his Son. Whoever possesses the Son has life; whoever does not possess the Son of God does not have life.

I write these things to you so that you may know that you have eternal life, you who believe in the name of the Son of God.

PSALM: *Psalm 147:12–13, 14–15, 19–20*

R. Praise the Lord, Jerusalem. or: R. Alleluia.

Glorify the LORD, O Jerusalem; / praise your God, O Zion. / For he has strengthened the bars of your gates; / he has blessed your children within you.**R.**

He has granted peace in your borders; / with the best of wheat he fills you. / He sends forth his command to the earth; / swiftly runs his word! **R.**

He has proclaimed his word to Jacob, / his statutes and his ordinances to Israel. / He has not done thus for any other nation; / his ordinances he has not made known to them. **R.**

ALLELUIA: *See Matthew 4:23*

R. Alleluia, alleluia.

Jesus proclaimed the Gospel of the Kingdom / and cured every disease among the people. **R.**

GOSPEL   *Luke 5:12–16*

It happened that there was a man full of leprosy in one of the towns where Jesus was; and when he saw Jesus, he fell prostrate, pleaded with him, and said, "Lord, if you wish, you can make me clean." Jesus stretched out his hand, touched him, and said, "I do will it. Be made clean." And the leprosy left him immediately. Then he ordered him not to tell anyone, but

"Go, show yourself to the priest and offer for your cleansing what Moses prescribed; that will be proof for them." The report about him spread all the more, and great crowds assembled to listen to him and to be cured of their ailments, but he would withdraw to deserted places to pray.

JANUARY 11, SATURDAY AFTER EPIPHANY; BLESSED BERNARD OF CORLEONE

First Reading   *1John 5:14–21*

Beloved: We have this confidence in him that if we ask anything according to his will, he hears us. And if we know that he hears us in regard to whatever we ask, we know that what we have asked him for is ours. If anyone sees his brother sinning, if the sin is not deadly, he should pray to God and he will give him life. This is only for those whose sin is not deadly. There is such a thing as deadly sin, about which I do not say that you should pray. All wrongdoing is sin, but there is sin that is not deadly.

We know that anyone begotten by God does not sin; but the one begotten by God he protects, and the Evil One cannot touch him. We know that we belong to God, and the whole world is under the power of the Evil One. We also know that the Son of God has come and has given us discernment to know the one who is true. And we are in the one who is true, in his Son Jesus Christ. He is the true God and eternal life. Children, be on your guard against idols.

PSALM: *Psalm 149:1–2, 3–4, 5–6a and 9b*

R. The Lord takes delight in his people. or: R. Alleluia.

Sing to the LORD a new song of praise/ in the assembly of the faithful. / Let Israel be glad in their maker, / let the children of Zion rejoice in their king. **R.**

Let them praise his name in the festive dance, / let them sing praise to him with timbrel and harp. / For the LORD loves his people, / and he adorns the lowly with victory. **R.**

Let the faithful exult in glory; / let them sing for joy upon their couches; / Let the high praises of God be in their throats. / This is the glory of all his faithful. Alleluia. **R.**

ALLELUIA   *Matthew 4:16*

R. Alleluia, alleluia. The people who sit in darkness have seen a great light, on those dwelling in a land overshadowed by death light has arisen. **R.**

GOSPEL   *John 3:22–30*

Jesus and his disciples went into the region of Judea, where he spent some time with them baptizing. John was also baptizing in Aenon near Salim, because there was an abundance of water there, and people came to be baptized, for John had not yet been imprisoned. Now a dispute arose between the disciples of John and a Jew about ceremonial washings. So they came to John and said to him, "Rabbi, the one who was with you across the Jordan, to whom you testified, here he is baptizing and everyone is coming to him." John answered and said, "No one can receive anything except what has been given from heaven. You yourselves can testify that I said that I am not the Christ, but that I was sent before him. The one who has the bride is the bridegroom; the best man, who stands and listens for him, rejoices greatly at the bridegroom's voice. So this joy of mine has been made complete. He must increase; I must decrease."

SUNDAY 12, JANUARY; FEAST OF THE BAPTISM OF THE LORD

First Reading   *Isaiah 42:1—4, 6—7*

Thus says the LORD: Here is my servant whom I uphold, my chosen one with whom I am pleased, upon whom I have put my spirit; he shall bring forth justice to the nations, not crying out, not shouting, not making his voice heard in the street. A bruised reed he shall not break, and a smoldering wick he shall not quench, until he establishes justice on the earth; the coastlands will wait for his teaching.

I, the LORD, have called you for the victory of justice, I have grasped you by the hand; I formed you, and set you as a covenant of the people, a light for the

nations, to open the eyes of the blind, to bring out prisoners from confinement, and from the dungeon, those who live in

darkness.

PSALM   *Psalm 29:1—2, 3—4, 3, 9—10 (11b)*

R. The Lord will bless his people with peace.

Give to the LORD, you sons of God, **/** give to the LORD glory and praise, **/** Give to the LORD the glory due his name; **/** adore the LORD in holy attire. **R.**

The voice of the LORD is over the waters, **/** the LORD, over vast waters. **/** The voice of the LORD is mighty; **/** the voice of the LORD is majestic. **R.**

The God of glory thunders, **/** and in his temple all say, "Glory!" **/** The LORD is enthroned above the flood; **/** the LORD is enthroned as king forever. **R.**

SECOND READING   *Acts 10:34—38*

Peter proceeded to speak to those gathered in the house of Cornelius, saying: "In truth, I see that God shows no partiality. Rather, in every nation whoever fears him and acts uprightly is acceptable to him. You know the word that he sent to the Israelites as he proclaimed peace through Jesus Christ, who is Lord of all, what has happened all over Judea, beginning in Galilee after the baptism that John preached, how God anointed Jesus of Nazareth with the Holy Spirit and power. He went about doing good and healing all those oppressed by the devil, for God was with him."

ALLELUIA   *see Mark 9:7*

R. Alleluia, alleluia. The heavens were opened and the voice of the Father thundered: this is my beloved Son, listen to him. **R.**

GOSPEL   *Matthew 3:13—17*

Jesus came from Galilee to John at the Jordan to be baptized by him. John tried to prevent him, saying, "I need to be baptized by you, and yet you are coming to me?" Jesus said to him in reply, "Allow it now, for thus it is fitting for us to fulfill all righteousness." Then he allowed him. After Jesus was baptized, he came up from the water and behold, the heavens were opened for him, and he saw the Spirit of God descending like a dove and coming upon him. And a voice came from the heavens, saying, "This is my beloved Son, with whom I am well pleased."

MONDAY 13 JANUARY, ST. HILARY OF POITIERS

FIRST READING   *1 Samuel 1:1–8*

There was a certain man from Ramathaim, Elkanah by name, a Zuphite from the hill country of Ephraim. He was the son of Jeroham, son of Elihu, son of Tohu, son of Zuph, an Ephraimite. He had two wives, one named Hannah, the other Peninnah; Peninnah had children, but Hannah was childless. This man regularly went on pilgrimage from his city to worship the LORD of hosts and to sacrifice to him at Shiloh, where the two sons of Eli, Hophni and Phinehas, were ministering as priests of the LORD. When the day came for Elkanah to offer sacrifice, he used to give a portion each to his wife Peninnah and to all her sons and daughters, but a double portion to Hannah because he loved her, though the LORD had made her barren. Her rival, to upset her, turned it into a constant reproach to her that the LORD had left her barren. This went on year after year; each time they made their pilgrimage to the sanctuary of the LORD, Peninnah would approach her, and Hannah would weep and refuse to eat. Her husband Elkanah used to ask her: "Hannah, why do you weep, and why do you refuse to eat? Why do you grieve? Am I not more to you than ten sons?"

RESPONSORIAL PSALM   *Psalm 116:12–13, 14–17, 18–19*

R. To you, Lord, I will offer a sacrifice of praise. or: Alleluia

How shall I make a return to the LORD / for all the good he has done for me? / The cup of salvation I will take up, / and I will call upon the name of the LORD. **R.**

My vows to the LORD I will pay / in the presence of all his people. / Precious in the eyes of the LORD / is the death of his faithful ones. / O LORD, I am your servant; / I am your servant, the son of your handmaid; / you have loosed my bonds. **R.**

My vows to the LORD I will pay / in the presence of all his people, / In the courts of the house of the LORD, / in your midst, O Jerusalem. **R.**

ALLELUIA   *Mark 1:15*

R. Alleluia, alleluia. The Kingdom of God is at hand; repent and believe in the Gospel. **R.**

GOSPEL   *Mark 1:14–20*

After John had been arrested, Jesus came to Galilee proclaiming the Gospel of God: "This is the time of fulfillment. The Kingdom of God is at hand. Repent, and believe in the Gospel."

As he passed by the Sea of Galilee, he saw Simon and his brother Andrew casting their nets into the sea; they were fishermen. Jesus said to them, "Come after me, and I will make you fishers of men." Then they left their nets and followed him. He walked along a little farther and saw James, the son of Zebedee, and his brother John. They too were in a boat mending their nets. Then he called them. So they left their father Zebedee in the boat along with the hired men and followed him.

TUESDAY 14 JANUARY, ST. MACRINA THE ELDER

FIRST READING *1 Samuel 1:9–20*

Hannah rose after a meal at Shiloh, and presented herself before the LORD; at the time, Eli the priest was sitting on a chair near the doorpost of the LORD's temple. In her bitterness she prayed to the LORD, weeping copiously, and she made a vow, promising: "O LORD of hosts, if you look with pity on the misery of your handmaid, if you remember me and do not forget me, if you give your handmaid a male child, I will give him to the LORD for as long as he lives; neither wine nor liquor shall he drink, and no razor shall ever touch his head." As she remained long at prayer before the LORD, Eli watched her mouth, for Hannah was praying silently; though her lips were moving, her voice could not be heard. Eli, thinking her drunk, said to her, "How long will you make a drunken show of yourself? Sober up from your wine!" "It isn't that, my lord," Hannah answered. "I am an unhappy woman. I have had neither wine nor liquor; I was only pouring out my troubles to the LORD. Do not think your handmaid a ne'er–do–well; my prayer has been prompted by my deep sorrow and misery." Eli said, "Go in peace, and may the God of Israel grant you what you have asked of him." She replied, "Think kindly of your maidservant," and left. She went to her quarters, ate and drank with her husband, and no longer appeared downcast. Early the next morning they worshiped before the LORD, and then returned to their home in Ramah.

When Elkanah had relations with his wife Hannah, the LORD remembered her. She conceived, and at the end of her term bore a son whom she called Samuel, since she had asked the LORD for him.

RESPONSORIALPSALM *1 Samuel 2:1, 4–5, 6–7, 8abcd*

R. (see 1) My heart exults in the Lord, my Savior.

"My heart exults in the LORD, / my horn is exalted in my God. / I have swallowed up my enemies; / I rejoice in my victory." **R.**

"The bows of the mighty are broken, / while the tottering gird on strength. / The well–fed hire themselves out for bread, / while the hungry batten on spoil. / The barren wife bears seven sons, / while the mother of many languishes." **R.**

"The LORD puts to death and gives life; / he casts down to the nether world; he raises up again. / The LORD makes poor and makes rich; / he humbles, he also exalts." **R.**

"He raises the needy from the dust; / from the dung heap he lifts up the poor, / to seat them with nobles / and make a glorious throne their heritage." **R.**

ALLELUIA *See 1 Thessalonians 2:13*

R. Alleluia, alleluia. Receive the word of God, not as the word of men, but as it truly is, the word of God. **R.**

GOSPEL *Mark 1:21–28*

Jesus came to Capernaum with his followers, and on the Sabbath he entered the synagogue and taught. The people were astonished at his teaching, for he taught them as one having authority and not as the scribes. In their synagogue was a man with an unclean spirit; he cried out, "What have you to do with us, Jesus of Nazareth? Have you come to destroy us? I know who you are—the Holy One of God!" Jesus rebuked him and said, "Quiet! Come out of him!" The unclean spirit convulsed him and with a loud cry came out of him. All were amazed and asked one another, "What is this? A new teaching with authority. He commands even the unclean spirits and they obey him." His fame spread everywhere throughout the whole region of Galilee.

WEDNESDAY 15 JANUARY, ST. PAUL THE HERMIT

FIRST READING *1 Samuel 3:1–10, 19–20*

During the time young Samuel was minister to the LORD under Eli, a revelation of the LORD was uncommon and vision infrequent. One day Eli was asleep in his usual place. His eyes had lately grown so weak that he could not see. The lamp of God was not yet extinguished, and Samuel was sleeping in the temple of the LORD where the ark of God was. The LORD called to Samuel, who answered, "Here I am." Samuel ran to Eli and said, "Here I am. You called me." "I did not call you," Eli said. "Go back to sleep." So he went back to sleep. Again the LORD called Samuel, who rose and went to Eli. "Here I am," he said. "You called me." But Eli answered, "I did not call you, my son. Go back to sleep." At that time Samuel was not familiar with the LORD, because the LORD had not revealed anything to him as yet. The LORD called Samuel again, for the third time. Getting up and going to Eli, he said, "Here I am. You called me." Then Eli understood that the LORD was calling the youth. So Eli said to Samuel, "Go to sleep, and if you are called, reply, 'Speak, LORD, for your servant is listening.'" When Samuel went to sleep in his place, the LORD came and revealed his presence, calling out as before, "Samuel, Samuel!" Samuel answered, "Speak, for your servant is listening."

Samuel grew up, and the LORD was with him, not permitting any word of his to be without effect. Thus all Israel from Dan to Beersheba came to know that Samuel was an accredited prophet of the LORD.

RESPONSORIAL PSALM *Psalm 40:2 and 5, 7–8a, 8b–9, 10*

R. (8a and 9a) Here am I, Lord; I come to do your will.

I have waited, waited for the LORD, / and he stooped toward me and heard my cry. / Blessed the man who makes the LORD his trust; / who turns not to idolatry or to those who stray after falsehood. **R.**

Sacrifice or oblation you wished not, / but ears open to obedience you gave me. / Burnt offerings or sin–offerings you sought not; / then said I, "Behold I come." **R.**

"In the written scroll it is prescribed for me. / To do your will, O my God, is my delight, / and your law is within my heart!" **R.**

I announced your justice in the vast assembly; / I did not restrain my lips, as you, O LORD, know.**R.**

ALLELUIA *John 10:27*

R. Alleluia, alleluia.

My sheep hear my voice, says the Lord. I know them, and they follow me. **R.**

GOSPEL

Mark 1:29–39

On leaving the synagogue Jesus entered the house of Simon and Andrew with James and John. Simon's mother–in–law lay sick with a fever. They immediately told him about her. He approached, grasped her hand, and helped her up. Then the fever left her and she waited on them.

When it was evening, after sunset, they brought to him all who were ill or possessed by demons. The whole town was gathered at the door. He cured many who were sick with various diseases, and he drove out many demons, not permitting them to speak because they knew him.

Rising very early before dawn, he left and went off to a deserted place, where he prayed. Simon and those who were with him pursued him and on finding him said, "Everyone is looking for you." He told them, "Let us go on to the nearby villages that I may preach there also. For this purpose have I come." So he went into their synagogues, preaching and driving out demons throughout the whole of Galilee.

THURSDAY 16 JANUARY; ST. BERARD AND COMPANIONS

FIRST READING

1 Samuel 4:1–11

The Philistines gathered for an attack on Israel. Israel went out to engage them in battle and camped at Ebenezer, while the Philistines camped at Aphek. The Philistines then drew up in battle formation against Israel. After a fierce struggle Israel was defeated by the Philistines, who slew about four thousand men on the battlefield. When the troops retired to the camp, the elders of Israel said, "why has the LORD permitted us to be defeated today by the Philistines? Let us fetch the ark of the LORD from Shiloh that it may go into battle among us and save us from the grasp of our enemies."

So the people sent to Shiloh and brought from there the ark of the LORD of hosts, who is enthroned upon the cherubim. The two sons of Eli, Hophni and Phinehas, were with the ark of God. When the ark of the LORD arrived in the camp, all Israel shouted so loudly that the earth resounded. The Philistines, hearing the noise of shouting, asked, "What can this loud shouting in the camp of the Hebrews mean?" On learning that the ark of the LORD had come into the camp, the Philistines were frightened. They said, "Gods have come to their camp." They said also, "Woe to us! This has never happened before. Woe to us! Who can deliver us from the power of these mighty gods? These are the gods that struck the Egyptians with various plagues and with pestilence. Take courage and be manly, Philistines; otherwise you will become slaves to the Hebrews, as they were your slaves. So fight manfully!" The Philistines fought and Israel was defeated; every man fled to his own tent. It was a disastrous defeat, in which Israel lost thirty thousand foot soldiers. The ark of God was captured, and Eli's two sons, Hophni and Phinehas, were among the dead.

RESPONSORIAL PSALM

Psalm 44:10–11, 14–15, 24–25

R. (27b) Redeem us, Lord, because of your mercy.

Yet now you have cast us off and put us in disgrace, / and you go not forth with our armies. / You have let us be driven back by our foes; / those who hated us plundered us at will. **R.**

You made us the reproach of our neighbors, / the mockery and the scorn of those around us. / You made us a byword among the nations, / a laughingstock among the peoples. **R.**
Why do you hide your face, / forgetting our woe and our oppression? / For our souls are bowed down to the dust, / our bodies are pressed to the earth. **R.**

ALLELUIA   *See Matthew 4:23*

R. Alleluia, alleluia.
Jesus preached the Gospel of the Kingdom and cured every disease among the people. **R.**

GOSPEL   *Mark 1:40–45*
A leper came to him and kneeling down begged him and said, "If you wish, you can make me clean." Moved with pity, he stretched out his hand, touched the leper, and said to him, "I do will it. Be made clean." The leprosy left him immediately, and he was made clean. Then, warning him sternly, he dismissed him at once. Then he said to him, "See that you tell no one anything, but go, show yourself to the priest and offer for your cleansing what Moses prescribed; that will be proof for them." The man went away and began to publicize the whole matter. He spread the report abroad so that it was impossible for Jesus to enter a town openly. He remained outside in deserted places, and people kept coming to him from everywhere.

FRIDAY 17, JANUARY; ST. ANTHONY OF EGYPT

FIRST READING   *1 Samuel 8:4–7, 10–22a*
All the elders of Israel came in a body to Samuel at Ramah and said to him, "Now that you are old, and your sons do not follow your example, appoint a king over us, as other nations have, to judge us."

Samuel was displeased when they asked for a king to judge them. He prayed to the LORD, however, who said in answer: "Grant the people's every request. It is not you they reject, they are rejecting me as their king."

Samuel delivered the message of the LORD in full to those who were asking him for a king. He told them: "The rights of the king who will rule you will be as follows: He will take your sons and assign them to his chariots and horses, and they will run before his chariot. He will also appoint from among them his commanders of groups of a thousand and of a hundred soldiers. He will set them to do his plowing and his harvesting, and to make his implements of war and the equipment of his chariots. He will use your daughters as ointment makers, as cooks, and as bakers. He will take the best of your fields, vineyards, and olive groves, and give them to his officials. He will tithe your crops and your vineyards, and give the revenue to his eunuchs and his slaves. He will take your male and female servants, as well as your best oxen and your asses, and use them to do his work. He will tithe your flocks and you yourselves will become his slaves. When this takes place, you will complain against the king whom you have chosen, but on that day the LORD will not answer you."

The people, however, refused to listen to Samuel's warning and said, "Not so! There must be a king over us. We too must be like other nations, with a king to rule us and to lead us in warfare and fight our battles." When Samuel had listened to all the people had to say, he repeated it to the LORD, who then said to him, "Grant their request and appoint a king to rule them."

RESPONSORIAL PSALM   *Psalm 89:16–17, 18–19*
R. (2) For ever I will sing the goodness of the Lord.
Blessed the people who know the joyful shout; / in the light of your countenance, O LORD, they walk. / At your name they rejoice all the day, / and through your justice they are exalted. **R.**
For you are the splendor of their strength, / and by your favor our horn is exalted. / For to the LORD belongs our shield, / and to the Holy One of Israel, our King. **R.**
ALLELUIA   *Luke 7:16*
R. Alleluia, alleluia. A great prophet has arisen in our midst and God has visited his people. **R.**

GOSPEL   *Mark 2:1–12*
When Jesus returned to Capernaum after some days, it became known that he was at home. Many gathered together so that there was no longer room for them, not even around the door, and he preached the word to them. They came bringing to him a paralytic carried by four men. Unable to get near Jesus because of the crowd, they opened up the roof above him. After they had broken through, they let down the mat on which the paralytic was lying. When Jesus saw their faith, he said to him, "Child, your sins are forgiven." Now some of the scribes were sitting there asking themselves, "Why does this man speak that way? He is blaspheming. Who but God alone can forgive sins?" Jesus immediately knew in his mind what they were thinking to themselves, so he said, "Why are you thinking such things in your hearts? Which is easier, to say to the paralytic, 'Your sins are forgiven,' or to say, 'Rise, pick up your mat and walk'? But that you may know that the Son of Man has authority to forgive sins on earth" —he said to the paralytic, "I say to you, rise, pick up your mat, and go home." He rose, picked up his mat at once, and went away in the sight of everyone. They were all astounded and glorified God, saying, "We have never seen anything like this."

SATURDAY 18, JANUARY; BLESSED CHRISTINA CICCARELLI
FIRST READING   *1 Samuel 9:1–4, 17–19; 10:1*
There was a stalwart man from Benjamin named Kish, who was the son of Abiel, son of Zeror, son of Becorath, son of Aphiah, a Benjaminite. He had a son named Saul, who was a handsome young man. There was no other child of Israel more handsome than Saul; he stood head and shoulders above the people.

Now the asses of Saul's father, Kish, had wandered off. Kish said to his son Saul, "Take one of the servants with you and go out and hunt for the asses." Accordingly they went through the hill country of Ephraim, and through the land of Shalishah. Not finding them there, they continued through the land of Shaalim without success. They also went through the land of Benjamin, but they failed to find the animals.

When Samuel caught sight of Saul, the LORD assured him, "This is the man of whom I told you; he is to govern my people."

Saul met Samuel in the gateway and said, "Please tell me where the seer lives." Samuel answered Saul: "I am the seer. Go up ahead of me to the high place and eat with me today. In the morning, before dismissing you, I will tell you whatever you wish."

Then, from a flask he had with him, Samuel poured oil on Saul's head; he also kissed him, saying: "The LORD anoints you commander over his heritage. You are to govern the LORD's people Israel, and to save them from the grasp of their enemies roundabout.

"This will be the sign for you that the LORD has anointed you commander over his heritage."

RESPONSORIAL PSALM

Psalm 21:2–3, 4–5, 6–7

R. (2a) Lord, in your strength the king is glad.
O LORD, in your strength the king is glad; / in your victory how greatly he rejoices! / You have granted him his heart's desire; / you refused not the wish of his lips. **R.**
For you welcomed him with goodly blessings, / you placed on his head a crown of pure gold. / He asked life of you: / you gave him length of days forever and ever. **R.**
Great is his glory in your victory; / majesty and splendor you conferred upon him. / For you made him a blessing forever; / you gladdened him with the joy of your face.
R. ALLELUIA

Luke 4:18

R. Alleluia, alleluia. The Lord sent me to bring glad tidings to the poor and to proclaim liberty to captives. **R.**

GOSPEL

Mark 2:13–17

Jesus went out along the sea. All the crowd came to him and he taught them. As he passed by, he saw Levi, son of Alphaeus, sitting at the customs post. Jesus said to him, "Follow me." And he got up and followed Jesus. While he was at table in his house, many tax collectors and sinners sat with Jesus and his disciples; for there were many who followed him. Some scribes who were Pharisees saw that Jesus was eating with sinners and tax collectors and said to his disciples, "Why does he eat with tax collectors and sinners?" Jesus heard this and said to them, "Those who are well do not need a physician, but the sick do. I did not come to call the righteous but sinners."

SUNDAY 19, JANUARY; ST. PAULA

FIRST READING

Isaiah 49:3, 5—6

The LORD said to me: You are my servant, Israel, through whom I show my glory. Now the LORD has spoken who formed me as his servant from the womb, that Jacob may be brought back to him and Israel gathered to him; and I am made glorious in the sight of the LORD, and my God is now my strength! It is too little, the LORD says, for you to be my servant, to raise up the tribes of Jacob, and restore the survivors of Israel; I will make you a light to the nations, that my salvation may reach to the ends of the earth.

RESPONSORIAL PSALM *Psalm 40:2, 4, 7—8, 8—9, 10 (8a, 9a)*
R. Here am I, Lord; I come to do your will.
I have waited, waited for the LORD, **/** and he stooped toward me and heard my cry. **/** And he put a new song into my mouth, **/** a hymn to our God. **R.**
Sacrifice or offering you wished not, **/** but ears open to obedience you gave me. **/** Holocausts or sin—offerings you sought not; **/** then said I, "Behold I come." **R.**
"In the written scroll it is prescribed for me, **/** to do your will, O my God, is my delight, **/** and your law is within my heart!" **R.**
I announced your justice in the vast assembly; **/** I did not restrain my lips, **/** as you, O LORD, know. **R.**

SECOND READING *1 Corinthians 1:1—3*
Paul, called to be an apostle of Christ Jesus by the will of God, and Sosthenes our brother, to the church of God that is in Corinth, to you who have been sanctified in Christ Jesus, called to be holy, with all those everywhere who call upon the name of our Lord Jesus Christ, their Lord and ours. Grace to you and peace from God our Father and the Lord Jesus Christ.

ALLELUIA *John 1:14a, 12a*
R. Alleluia, alleluia. The Word of God became flesh and dwelt among us. **/** To those who accepted him, **/** he gave power to become children of God. **R.**

GOSPEL *John 1:29—34*
John the Baptist saw Jesus coming toward him and said, "Behold, the Lamb of God, who takes away the sin of the world. He is the one of whom I said, 'A man is coming after me who ranks ahead of me because he existed before me.' I did not know him, but the reason why I came baptizing with water was that he might be made known to Israel." John testified further, saying, "I saw the Spirit come down like a dove from heaven and remain upon him. I did not know him, but the one who sent me to baptize with water told me, 'On whomever you see the Spirit come down and remain, he is the one who will baptize with the Holy Spirit.' Now I have seen and testified that he is the Son of God."

MONDAY 20, JANUARY; ST. FABIAN & ST. SEBASTIAN
FIRST READING *1 Samuel 15:16—23*
Samuel said to Saul: "Stop! Let me tell you what the LORD said to me last night." Saul replied, "Speak!" Samuel then said: "Though little in your own esteem, are you not leader of the tribes of Israel? The LORD anointed you king of Israel and sent you on a mission, saying, 'Go and put the sinful Amalekites under a ban of destruction. Fight against them until you have exterminated them.' Why then have you disobeyed the LORD? You have pounced on the spoil, thus displeasing the LORD." Saul answered Samuel: "I did indeed

obey the LORD and fulfill the mission on which the LORD sent me. I have brought back Agag, and I have destroyed Amalek under the ban. But from the spoil the men took sheep and oxen, the best of what had been banned, to sacrifice to the LORD their God in Gilgal." But Samuel said: "Does the LORD so delight in burnt offerings and sacrifices as in obedience to the command of the LORD? Obedience is better than sacrifice, and submission than the fat of rams. For a sin like divination is rebellion, and presumption is the crime of idolatry. Because you have rejected the command of the LORD, he, too, has rejected you as ruler."

RESPONSORIAL PSALM *Psalm 50:8–9, 16bc–17, 21 and 23*
R. (23b) To the upright I will show the saving power of God.
"Not for your sacrifices do I rebuke you, / for your burnt offerings are before me always. / I take from your house no bullock, / no goats out of your fold." **R.**
"Why do you recite my statutes, / and profess my covenant with your mouth, / though you hate discipline / and cast my words behind you?" **R.**
"When you do these things, shall I be deaf to it? / Or do you think that I am like yourself? / I will correct you by drawing them up before your eyes. / He that offers praise as a sacrifice glorifies me; / and to him that goes the right way / I will show the salvation of God." **R.**

ALLELUIA *Hebrews 4:12*
R. Alleluia, alleluia. The word of God is living and effective, able to discern reflections and thoughts of the heart. **R.**

GOSPEL *Mark 2:18–22*
The disciples of John and of the Pharisees were accustomed to fast. People came to Jesus and objected, "Why do the disciples of John and the disciples of the Pharisees fast, but your disciples do not fast?" Jesus answered them, "Can the wedding guests fast while the bridegroom is with them? As long as they have the bridegroom with them they cannot fast. But the days will come when the bridegroom is taken away from them, and then they will fast on that day. No one sews a piece of unshrunken cloth on an old cloak. If he does, its fullness pulls away, the new from the old, and the tear gets worse. Likewise, no one pours new wine into old wineskins. Otherwise, the wine will burst the skins, and both the wine and the skins are ruined. Rather, new wine is poured into fresh wineskins."

TUESDAY 21, JANUARY; ST. AGNES

FIRST READING *1 Samuel 16:1–13*
The LORD said to Samuel: "How long will you grieve for Saul, whom I have rejected as king of Israel? Fill your horn with oil, and be on your way. I am sending you to Jesse of Bethlehem, for I have chosen my king from among his sons." But Samuel replied: "How can I go? Saul will hear of it and kill me." To this the LORD answered: "Take a heifer along and say, 'I have come to sacrifice to the LORD.' Invite Jesse to the sacrifice, and I myself will tell you what to do; you are to anoint for me the one I point out to you."

Samuel did as the LORD had commanded him. When he entered Bethlehem, the elders of the city came trembling to meet him and inquired, "Is your visit peaceful, O seer?"

He replied: "Yes! I have come to sacrifice to the LORD. So cleanse yourselves and join me today for the banquet." He also had Jesse and his sons cleanse themselves and invited them to the sacrifice. As they came, he looked at Eliab and thought, "Surely the LORD's anointed is here before him." But the LORD said to Samuel: "Do not judge from his appearance or from his lofty stature, because I have rejected him. Not as man sees does God see, because he sees the appearance but the LORD looks into the heart." Then Jesse called Abinadab and presented him before Samuel, who said, "The LORD has not chosen him." Next Jesse presented Shammah, but Samuel said, "The LORD has not chosen this one either." In the same way Jesse presented seven sons before Samuel, but Samuel said to Jesse, "The LORD has not chosen any one of these." Then Samuel asked Jesse, "Are these all the sons you have?" Jesse replied, "There is still the youngest, who is tending the sheep." Samuel said to Jesse, "Send for him; we will not begin the sacrificial banquet until he arrives here." Jesse sent and had the young man brought to them. He was ruddy, a youth handsome to behold and making a splendid appearance. The LORD said, "There—anoint him, for this is he!" Then Samuel, with the horn of oil in hand, anointed him in the midst of his brothers; and from that day on, the Spirit of the LORD rushed upon David. When Samuel took his leave, he went to Ramah.

RESPONSORIAL PSALM   *Psalm 89:20, 21–22, 27–28*
R. (21a) I have found David, my servant.
Once you spoke in a vision, **/** and to your faithful ones you said: **/** "On a champion I have placed a crown; **/** over the people I have set a youth." **R.**
"I have found David, my servant; **/** with my holy oil I have anointed him, **/** that my hand may be always with him, **/** and that my arm may make him strong." **R.**
"He shall say of me, **/** 'You are my father, my God, the Rock, my savior.' **/** And I will make him the first–born, **/** highest of the kings of the earth." **R.**
ALLELUIA   *See Ephesians 1:17–18*
R. Alleluia, alleluia. May the Father of our Lord Jesus Christ enlighten the eyes of our hearts, **/** that we may know what is the hope that belongs to our call. **R.**

GOSPEL   *Mark 2:23–28*
As Jesus was passing through a field of grain on the Sabbath, his disciples began to make a path while picking the heads of grain. At this the Pharisees said to him, "Look, why are they doing what is unlawful on the Sabbath?" He said to them, "Have you never read what David did when he was in need and he and his companions were hungry? How he went into the house of God when Abiathar was high priest and ate the bread of offering that only the priests could lawfully eat, and shared it with his companions?" Then he said to them, "The Sabbath was made for man, not man for the Sabbath. That is why the Son of Man is lord even of the Sabbath."

WEDNESDAY 22 JANUARY; ST. VINCENT OF SARAGOSSA

FIRST READING   *1 Samuel 17:32–33, 37, 40–51*

David spoke to Saul: "Let your majesty not lose courage. I am at your service to go and fight this Philistine." But Saul answered David, "You cannot go up against this Philistine and fight with him, for you are only a youth, while he has been a warrior from his youth."

David continued: "The LORD, who delivered me from the claws of the lion and the bear, will also keep me safe from the clutches of this Philistine." Saul answered David, "Go! the LORD will be with you."

Then, staff in hand, David selected five smooth stones from the wadi and put them in the pocket of his shepherd's bag. With his sling also ready to hand, he approached the Philistine.

With his shield bearer marching before him, the Philistine also advanced closer and closer to David. When he had sized David up, and seen that he was youthful, and ruddy, and handsome in appearance, the Philistine held David in contempt. The Philistine said to David, "Am I a dog that you come against me with a staff?" Then the Philistine cursed David by his gods and said to him, "Come here to me, and I will leave your flesh for the birds of the air and the beasts of the field." David answered him: "You come against me with sword and spear and scimitar, but I come against you in the name of the LORD of hosts, the God of the armies of Israel that you have insulted. Today the LORD shall deliver you into my hand; I will strike you down and cut off your head. This very day I will leave your corpse and the corpses of the Philistine army for the birds of the air and the beasts of the field; thus the whole land shall learn that Israel has a God. All this multitude, too, shall learn that it is not by sword or spear that the LORD saves. For the battle is the LORD's and he shall deliver you into our hands."

The Philistine then moved to meet David at close quarters, while David ran quickly toward the battle line in the direction of the Philistine. David put his hand into the bag and took out a stone, hurled it with the sling, and struck the Philistine on the forehead. The stone embedded itself in his brow, and he fell prostrate on the ground. Thus David overcame the Philistine with sling and stone; he struck the Philistine mortally, and did it without a sword. Then David ran and stood over him; with the Philistine's own sword which he drew from its sheath he dispatched him and cut off his head.

RESPONSORIAL PSALM   *Psalm 144:1b, 2, 9–10*

R. (1) Blessed be the Lord, my Rock!

Blessed be the LORD, my rock, / who trains my hands for battle, / my fingers for war. **R.** My refuge and my fortress, / my stronghold, my deliverer, / My shield, in whom I trust, / who subdues my people under me. **R.**

O God, I will sing a new song to you; / with a ten–stringed lyre I will chant your praise, / You who give victory to kings, / and deliver David, your servant from the evil sword. **R.**

ALLELUIA   *See Matthew 4:23*

R. Alleluia, alleluia. Jesus preached the Gospel of the Kingdom and cured every disease among the people. **R.**

GOSPEL

Mark 3:1–6

Jesus entered the synagogue. There was a man there who had a withered hand. They watched Jesus closely to see if he would cure him on the sabbath so that they might accuse him. He said to the man with the withered hand, "Come up here before us." Then he said to the Pharisees, "Is it lawful to do good on the sabbath rather than to do evil, to save life rather than to destroy it?" But they remained silent. Looking around at them with anger and grieved at their hardness of heart, Jesus said to the man, "Stretch out your hand." He stretched it out and his hand was restored. The Pharisees went out and immediately took counsel with the Herodians against him to put him to death.

THURSDAY 23, JANUARY; ST. WILLIAM OF BOURGES

FIRST READING

1 Samuel 18:6–9; 19:1–7

When David and Saul approached (on David's return after slaying the Philistine), women came out from each of the cities of Israel to meet King Saul, singing and dancing, with tambourines, joyful songs, and sistrums. The women played and sang:

"Saul has slain his thousands, and David his ten thousands."

Saul was very angry and resentful of the song, for he thought: "they give David ten thousands, but only thousands to me. All that remains for him is the kingship." And from that day on, Saul was jealous of David.

Saul discussed his intention of killing David with his son Jonathan and with all his servants. But Saul's son Jonathan, who was very fond of David, told him: "My father Saul is trying to kill you. Therefore, please be on your guard tomorrow morning; get out of sight and remain in hiding. I, however, will go out and stand beside my father in the countryside where you are, and will speak to him about you. If I learn anything, I will let you know."

Jonathan then spoke well of David to his father Saul, saying to him: "Let not your majesty sin against his servant David, for he has committed no offense against you, but has helped you very much by his deeds. When he took his life in his hands and slew the Philistine, and the LORD brought about a great victory for all Israel through him, you were glad to see it. Why, then, should you become guilty of shedding innocent blood by killing David without cause?" Saul heeded Jonathan's plea and swore, "As the LORD lives, he shall not be killed." So Jonathan summoned David and repeated the whole conversation to him. Jonathan then brought David to Saul, and David served him as before.

RESPONSORIAL PSALM

Psalm 56:2–3, 9–10a, 10b–11, 12–13

R. (5b) In God I trust; I shall not fear.

Have mercy on me, O God, / for men trample upon me; / all the day they press their attack against me. / My adversaries trample upon me all the day; / yes, many fight against me. **R.**

My wanderings you have counted; / my tears are stored in your flask; / are they not recorded in your book? / Then do my enemies turn back, / when I call upon you. **R.**

Now I know that God is with me. / In God, in whose promise I glory, / in God I trust without fear; / what can flesh do against me? **R.**

I am bound, O God, by vows to you; / your thank offerings I will fulfill. / For you have rescued me from death, / my feet, too, from stumbling; / that I may walk before God in / the light of the living. **R.**

ALLELUIA   *See 2 Timothy 1:10*

R. Alleluia, alleluia. Our Savior Jesus Christ has destroyed death and brought life to light through the Gospel. **R.**

GOSPEL   *Mark 3:7–12*

Jesus withdrew toward the sea with his disciples. A large number of people followed from Galilee and from Judea. Hearing what he was doing, a large number of people came to him also from Jerusalem, from Idumea, from beyond the Jordan, and from the neighborhood of Tyre and Sidon. He told his disciples to have a boat ready for him because of the crowd, so that they would not crush him. He had cured many and, as a result, those who had diseases were pressing upon him to touch him. And whenever unclean spirits saw him they would fall down before him and shout, "You are the Son of God." He warned them sternly not to make him known.

FRIDAY 24, JANUARY; ST. FRANCIS DE SALES

FIRST READING   *1 Samuel 24:3–21*

Saul took three thousand picked men from all Israel and went in search of David and his men in the direction of the wild goat crags. When he came to the sheepfolds along the way, he found a cave, which he entered to relieve himself. David and his men were occupying the inmost recesses of the cave.

David's servants said to him, "This is the day of which the LORD said to you, 'I will deliver your enemy into your grasp; do with him as you see fit.'" So David moved up and stealthily cut off an end of Saul's mantle. Afterward, however, David regretted that he had cut off an end of Saul's mantle. He said to his men, "The LORD forbid that I should do such a thing to my master, the LORD's anointed, as to lay a hand on him, for he is the LORD's anointed." With these words David restrained his men and would not permit them to attack Saul. Saul then left the cave and went on his way. David also stepped out of the cave, calling to Saul, "My lord the king!" When Saul looked back, David bowed to the ground in homage and asked Saul: "Why do you listen to those who say, 'David is trying to harm you'? You see for yourself today that the LORD just now delivered you into my grasp in the cave. I had some thought of killing you, but I took pity on you instead. I decided, 'I will not raise a hand against my lord, for he is the LORD's anointed and a father to me.' Look here at this end of your mantle which I hold. Since I cut off an end of your mantle and did not kill you, see and be convinced that I plan no harm and no rebellion. I have done you no wrong, though you are hunting me down to take my life. The Lord will judge between me and you, and the LORD will exact justice from you in my case. I shall not touch you. The old proverb says, 'From the wicked comes forth wickedness.' So I will take no action against you. Against whom are you on campaign, O king of Israel? Whom are you pursuing? A dead dog, or a single flea! The Lord will be the judge; he will decide between me and you. May he see this, and take my part, and grant me justice beyond your reach!" When David finished saying these things to Saul, Saul answered, "Is that your voice, my son David?" And Saul wept aloud. Saul then said to David: "You are in the right rather than I; you have treated me generously, while I have done you harm. Great is the generosity you showed me today, when the LORD delivered me into your grasp and you did not kill me. For if a man meets his enemy, does he send him away unharmed? May the LORD reward you generously for what you have done this day. And now, I know that you shall surely be king and that sovereignty over Israel shall come into your possession."

RESPONSORIAL PSALM *Psalm 57:2, 3–4, 6 and 11*
R. (2a) Have mercy on me, God, have mercy.
Have mercy on me, O God; / have mercy on me, for in you I take refuge. / In the shadow of your wings I take refuge, / till harm pass by. **R.**
I call to God the Most High, to God, my benefactor. / May He send from heaven and save me; / may He make those a reproach who trample upon me; / may God send his mercy and his faithfulness. **R.**
Be exalted above the heavens, O God; / above all the earth be your glory! / For your mercy towers to the heavens, / and your faithfulness to the skies. **R.**

ALLELUIA *2 Corinthians 5:19*
R. Alleluia, alleluia. God was reconciling the world to himself in Christ, and entrusting to us the message of reconciliation. **R.**

GOSPEL *Mark 3:13–19*
Jesus went up the mountain and summoned those whom he wanted and they came to him. He appointed Twelve, whom he also named Apostles, that they might be with him and he might send them forth to preach and to have authority to drive out demons: He appointed the Twelve: Simon, whom he named Peter; James, son of Zebedee, and John the brother of James, whom he named Boanerges, that is, sons of thunder; Andrew, Philip, Bartholomew, Matthew, Thomas, James the son of Alphaeus; Thaddeus, Simon the Cananean, and Judas Iscariot who betrayed him.

SATURDAY 25, JANUARY THE CONVERSION OF SAINT PAUL, APOSTLE - FEAST
FIRST READING *Acts 22:3–16*
Paul addressed the people in these words: "I am a Jew, born in Tarsus in Cilicia, but brought up in this city. At the feet of Gamaliel I was educated strictly in our ancestral law and was zealous for God, just as all of you are today. I persecuted this Way to death, binding both men and women and delivering them to prison. Even the high priest and the whole council of elders can testify on my behalf. For from them I even received letters to the brothers and set out for Damascus to bring back to Jerusalem in chains for punishment those there as well.

"On that journey as I drew near to Damascus, about noon a great light from the sky suddenly shone around me. I fell to the ground and heard a voice saying to me, 'Saul, Saul, why are you persecuting me?' I replied, 'Who are you, sir?' And he said to me, 'I am Jesus the Nazorean whom you are persecuting.' My companions saw the light but did not hear the voice of the one who spoke to me. I asked, 'What shall I do, sir?' The Lord answered me, 'Get up and go into Damascus, and there you will be told about everything appointed for you to do.' Since I could see nothing because of the brightness of that light, I was led by hand by my companions and entered Damascus.

"A certain Ananias, a devout observer of the law, and highly spoken of by all the Jews who lived there, came to me and stood there and said, 'Saul, my brother, regain your sight.' And at that very moment I regained my sight and saw him. Then he said, 'The God of our ancestors designated you to know his will, to see the Righteous One, and to hear the sound of his voice; for you will be his witness before all to what you have seen and heard. Now, why delay? Get up and have yourself baptized and your sins washed away, calling upon his name.'"

ALTERNATIVE READING: Acts 9:1–22

Saul, still breathing murderous threats against the disciples of the Lord, went to the high priest and asked him for letters to the synagogues in Damascus, that, if he should find any men or women who belonged to the Way, he might bring them back to Jerusalem in chains. On his journey, as he was nearing Damascus, a light from the sky suddenly flashed around him. He fell to the ground and heard a voice saying to him, "Saul, Saul, why are you persecuting me?" He said, "Who are you, sir?" The reply came, "I am Jesus, whom you are persecuting. Now get up and go into the city and you will be told what you must do." The men who were traveling with him stood speechless, for they heard the voice but could see no one. Saul got up from the ground, but when he opened his eyes he could see nothing; so they led him by the hand and brought him to Damascus. For three days he was unable to see, and he neither ate nor drank.

There was a disciple in Damascus named Ananias, and the Lord said to him in a vision, Ananias." He answered, "Here I am, Lord." The Lord said to him, "Get up and go to the street called Straight and ask at the house of Judas for a man from Tarsus named Saul. He is there praying, and in a vision he has seen a man named Ananias come in and lay his hands on him, that he may regain his sight." But Ananias replied, "Lord, I have heard from many sources about this man, what evil things he has done to your holy ones in Jerusalem. And here he has authority from the chief priests to imprison all who call upon your name." But the Lord said to him, "Go, for this man is a chosen instrument of mine to carry my name before Gentiles, kings, and children of Israel, and I will show him what he will have to suffer for my name." So Ananias went and entered the house; laying his hands on him, he said, "Saul, my brother, the Lord has sent me, Jesus who appeared to you on the way by which you came, that you may regain your sight and be filled with the Holy Spirit." Immediately things like scales fell from his eyes and he regained his sight. He got up and was baptized, and when he had eaten, he recovered his strength.

He stayed some days with the disciples in Damascus, and he began at once to proclaim Jesus in the synagogues, that he is the Son of God. All who heard him were astounded and said, "Is not this the man who in Jerusalem ravaged those who call upon this name, and came here expressly to take them back in chains to the chief priests?" But Saul grew all the stronger and confounded the Jews who lived in Damascus, proving that this is the Christ.

RESPONSORIALPSALM   *Psalm 117:1bc, 2*
R. Go out to all the world and tell the Good News.   or: R. Alleluia, alleluia.
Praise the Lord, all you nations; glorify him, all you peoples! **R.**
For steadfast is his kindness toward us, and the fidelity of the LORD endures forever. **R.**
ALLELUIA   *See John 15:16*
R. Alleluia, alleluia. I chose you from the world, to go and bear fruit that will last, says the Lord. **R.**

GOSPEL   *Mark 16:15–18*
Jesus appeared to the Eleven and said to them: "Go into the whole world and proclaim the Gospel to every creature. Whoever believes and is baptized will be saved; whoever does not believe will be condemned. These signs will accompany those who believe: in my name they will drive out demons, they will speak new languages. They will pick up serpents with their hands, and if they drink any deadly thing, it will not harm them. They will lay hands on the sick, and they will recover."

JANUARY 26, 3RD SUNDAY IN ORDINARY TIME; ST. TIMOTHY AND ST. TITUS
FIRST READING   *Isaiah 8:23—9:3*
First the Lord degraded the land of Zebulun and the land of Naphtali; but in the end he has glorified the seaward road, the land west of the Jordan, the District of the Gentiles.

Anguish has taken wing, dispelled its darkness: for there is no gloom where but now there was distress.
The people who walked in darkness have seen a great light; upon those who dwelt in the land of gloom a light has shone. You have brought them abundant joy and great rejoicing, as they rejoice before you as at the harvest, as people make merry when dividing spoils. For the yoke that burdened them, the pole on their shoulder, and the rod of their taskmaster you have smashed, as on the day of Midian.

RESPONSORIAL PSALM   *Psalm 27:1, 4, 13—14 (1a)*
R. The Lord is my light and my salvation.
The Lord is my light and my salvation; / whom should I fear? The Lord is my life's refuge; / of whom should I be afraid? **R.**
One thing I ask of the Lord; this I seek: / to dwell in the house of the Lord all the days of my life, / that I may gaze on the loveliness of the Lord / and contemplate his temple. **R.**
I believe that I shall see the bounty of the Lord / in the land of the living. / Wait for the LORD with courage; / be stouthearted, and wait for the Lord. **R.**

SECOND READING
1 Corinthians 1:10—13, 17

I urge you, brothers and sisters, in the name of our Lord Jesus Christ, that all of you agree in what you say, and that there be no divisions among you, but that you be united in the same mind and in the same purpose. For it has been reported to me about you, my brothers and sisters, by Chloe's people, that there are rivalries among you. I mean that each of you is saying, "I belong to Paul," or "I belong to Apollos," or "I belong to Cephas," or "I belong to Christ." Is Christ divided? Was Paul crucified for you? Or were you baptized in the name of Paul? For Christ did not send me to baptize but to preach the gospel, and not with the wisdom of human eloquence, so that the cross of Christ might not be emptied of its meaning.

ALLELUIA
see Matthew 4:23

R. **Alleluia, alleluia.** Jesus proclaimed the Gospel of the kingdom and cured every disease among the people. **R.**

GOSPEL
Longer Form Matthew 4:12—23

When Jesus heard that John had been arrested, he withdrew to Galilee. He left Nazareth and went to live in Capernaum by the sea, in the region of Zebulun and Naphtali, that what had been said through Isaiah the prophet might be fulfilled: *Land of Zebulun and land of Naphtali, the way to the sea, beyond the Jordan, Galilee of the Gentiles, the people who sit in darkness have seen a great light, on those dwelling in a land overshadowed by death light has arisen.* From that time on, Jesus began to preach and say, "Repent, for the kingdom of heaven is at hand."

As he was walking by the Sea of Galilee, he saw two brothers, Simon who is called Peter, and his brother Andrew, casting a net into the sea; they were fishermen. He said to them, "Come after me, and I will make you fishers of men." At once they left their nets and followed him. He walked along from there and saw two other brothers, James, the son of Zebedee, and his brother John. They were in a boat, with their father Zebedee, mending their nets. He called them, and immediately they left their boat and their father and followed him. He went around all of Galilee, teaching in their synagogues, proclaiming the gospel of the kingdom, and curing every disease and illness among the people.

ALTERNATIVE GOSPEL READING
Matthew 4:12—17

When Jesus heard that John had been arrested, he withdrew to Galilee. He left Nazareth and went to live in Capernaum by the sea, in the region of Zebulun and Naphtali, that what had been said through Isaiah the prophet might be fulfilled: *Land of Zebulun and land of Naphtali, the way to the sea, beyond the Jordan, Galilee of the Gentiles, the people who sit in darkness have seen a great light, on those dwelling in a land overshadowed by death light has arisen.* From that time on, Jesus began to preach and say, "Repent, for the kingdom of heaven is at hand."

JANUARY 27, MONDAY OF WEEK 3; ST. ANGELA MERICI

FIRST READING *2 Samuel 5:1–7, 10*

All the tribes of Israel came to David in Hebron and said: "Here we are, your bone and your flesh. In days past, when Saul was our king, it was you who led the children of Israel out and brought them back. And the LORD said to you, 'You shall shepherd my people Israel and shall be commander of Israel.'" When all the elders of Israel came to David in Hebron, King David made an agreement with them there before the LORD, and they anointed him king of Israel. David was thirty years old when he became king, and he reigned for forty years: seven years and six months in Hebron over Judah, and thirty–three years in Jerusalem over all Israel and Judah.

Then the king and his men set out for Jerusalem against the Jebusites who inhabited the region. David was told, "You cannot enter here: the blind and the lame will drive you away!" which was their way of saying, "David cannot enter here." But David did take the stronghold of Zion, which is the City of David.

David grew steadily more powerful, for the LORD of hosts was with him.

RESPONSORIAL PSALM *Psalm 89:20, 21–22, 25–26*

R. (25a) My faithfulness and my mercy shall be with him.

Once you spoke in a vision, / and to your faithful ones you said: / "On a champion I have placed a crown; / over the people I have set a youth." **R.**

"I have found David, my servant; / with my holy oil I have anointed him, / That my hand may be always with him, / and that my arm may make him strong." **R.**

"My faithfulness and my mercy shall be with him, / and through my name shall his horn be exalted. / I will set his hand upon the sea, / his right hand upon the rivers." **R.**

ALLELUIA *See 2 Timothy 1:10*

R. Alleluia, alleluia. Our Savior Jesus Christ has destroyed death and brought life to light through the Gospel. **R.**

GOSPEL *Mark 3:22–30*

The scribes who had come from Jerusalem said of Jesus, "He is possessed by Beelzebul," and "By the prince of demons he drives out demons."

Summoning them, he began to speak to them in parables, "How can Satan drive out Satan? If a kingdom is divided against itself, that kingdom cannot stand. And if a house is divided against itself, that house will not be able to stand. And if Satan has risen up against himself and is divided, he cannot stand; that is the end of him. But no one can enter a strong man's house to plunder his property unless he first ties up the strong man. Then he can plunder his house. Amen, I say to you, all sins and all blasphemies that people utter will be forgiven them. But whoever blasphemes against the Holy Spirit will never have forgiveness, but is guilty of an everlasting sin." For they had said, "He has an unclean spirit."

JANUARY 28, TUESDAY OF WEEK 3; ST. THOMAS AQUINAS

FIRST READING *2 Samuel 6:12b–15, 17–19*

David went to bring up the ark of God from the house of Obed–edom into the City of David amid festivities. As soon as the bearers of the ark of the LORD had advanced six steps, he sacrificed an ox and a fatling. Then David, girt with a linen apron, came dancing before the LORD with abandon, as he and all the house of Israel were bringing up the ark of the LORD with shouts of joy and to the sound of the horn. The ark of the LORD was brought in and set in its place within the tent David had pitched for it. Then David offered burnt offerings and peace offerings before the LORD. When he finished making these offerings, he blessed the people in the name of the LORD of hosts. He then distributed among all the people, to each man and each woman in the entire multitude of Israel, a loaf of bread, a cut of roast meat, and a raisin cake. With this, all the people left for their homes.

RESPONSORIAL PSALM *Psalm 24:7, 8, 9, 10*

R. (8) Who is this king of glory? It is the Lord!

Lift up, O gates, your lintels; / reach up, you ancient portals, / that the king of glory may come in! **R.**

Who is this king of glory? / The Lord, strong and mighty, / the Lord, mighty in battle. **R.** Lift up, O gates, your lintels; / reach up, you ancient portals, / that the king of glory may come in! **R.**

Who is this king of glory? / The Lord of hosts; he is the king of glory. **R.**

ALLELUIA *See Matthew 11:25*

R. Alleluia, alleluia. Blessed are you, Father, Lord of heaven and earth; you have revealed to little ones the mysteries of the Kingdom. **R.**

GOSPEL *Mark 3:31–35*

The mother of Jesus and his brothers arrived at the house. Standing outside, they sent word to Jesus and called him. A crowd seated around him told him, "Your mother and your brothers and your sisters are outside asking for you." But he said to them in reply, "Who are my mother and my brothers?" And looking around at those seated in the circle he said, "Here are my mother and my brothers. For whoever does the will of God is my brother and sister and mother."

JANUARY 29, WEDNESDAY OF WEEK 3; ST. GENEVIEVE

FIRST READING *2 Samuel 7:4–17*

That night the LORD spoke to Nathan and said: "Go, tell my servant David, 'Thus says the LORD: Should you build me a house to dwell in? I have not dwelt in a house from the day on which I led the children of Israel out of Egypt to the present, but I have been going about in a tent under cloth. In all my wanderings everywhere among the children of Israel, did I ever utter a word to any one of the judges whom I charged to tend my people Israel, to ask: Why have you not built me a house of cedar?'

"Now then, speak thus to my servant David, 'The LORD of hosts has this to say: It was I who took you from the pasture and from the care of the flock to be commander of my people Israel. I have been with you wherever you went, and I have destroyed all your enemies before you. And I will make you famous like the great ones of the earth. I will fix a place for my people Israel; I will plant them so that they may dwell in their place without further disturbance. Neither shall the wicked continue to afflict them as they did of old, since the time I first appointed judges over my people Israel. I will give you rest from all your enemies. The LORD also reveals to you that he will establish a house for you. And when your time comes and you rest with your ancestors, I will raise up your heir after you, sprung from your loins, and I will make his Kingdom firm. It is he who shall build a house for my name. And I will make his royal throne firm forever. I will be a father to him, and he shall be a son to me. And if he does wrong, I will correct him with the rod of men and with human chastisements; but I will not withdraw my favor from him as I withdrew it from your predecessor Saul, whom I removed from my presence. Your house and your kingdom shall endure forever before me; your throne shall stand firm forever.'"

Nathan reported all these words and this entire vision to David.

RESPONSORIAL PSALM *Psalm 89:4–5, 27–28, 29–30*

R. (29a) For ever I will maintain my love for my servant.

"I have made a covenant with my chosen one; I have sworn to David my servant: I will make your dynasty stand forever and establish your throne through all ages." **R.**

"He shall cry to me, 'You are my father, my God, the Rock that brings me victory!' I myself make him firstborn, Most High over the kings of the earth." **R.**

"Forever I will maintain my love for him; my covenant with him stands firm. I will establish his dynasty forever, his throne as the days of the heavens." **R.**

R. Alleluia, alleluia. The seed is the word of God, Christ is the sower; all who come to him will live for ever. **R.**

GOSPEL *Mark 4:1–20*

On another occasion, Jesus began to teach by the sea. A very large crowd gathered around him so that he got into a boat on the sea and sat down. And the whole crowd was beside the sea on land. And he taught them at length in parables, and in the course of his instruction he said to them, "Hear this! A sower went out to sow. And as he sowed, some seed fell on the path, and the birds came and ate it up. Other seed fell on rocky ground where it had little soil. It sprang up at once because the soil was not deep. And when the sun rose, it was scorched and it withered for lack of roots. Some seed fell among thorns, and the thorns grew up and choked it and it produced no grain. And some seed fell on rich soil and produced fruit. It came up and grew and yielded thirty, sixty, and a hundredfold." He added, "Whoever has ears to hear ought to hear."

And when he was alone, those present along with the Twelve questioned him about the parables. He answered them, "The mystery of the Kingdom of God has been granted to you. But to those outside everything comes in parables, so that *they may look and see but not perceive, and hear and listen but not understand, in order that they may not be converted and be forgiven."*

Jesus said to them, "Do you not understand this parable? Then how will you understand any of the parables? The sower sows the word. These are the ones on the path where the word is sown. As soon as they hear, Satan comes at once and takes away the word sown in them. And these are the ones sown on rocky ground who, when they hear the word, receive it at once with joy. But they have no roots; they last only for a time. Then when tribulation or persecution comes because of the word, they quickly fall away. Those sown among thorns are another sort. They are the people who hear the word, but worldly anxiety, the lure of riches, and the craving for other things intrude and choke the word, and it bears no fruit. But those sown on rich soil are the ones who hear the word and accept it and bear fruit thirty and sixty and a hundredfold."

JANUARY 30, THURSDAY OF WEEK 3; ST. MARIA SOLEDAD TORRES-ACOSTA

FIRST READING *2 Samuel 7:18–19, 24–29*

After Nathan had spoken to King David, the king went in and sat before the LORD and said, "Who am I, Lord GOD, and who are the members of my house, that you have brought me to this point? Yet even this you see as too little, Lord GOD; you have also spoken of the house of your servant for a long time to come: this too you have shown to man, Lord GOD!

"You have established for yourself your people Israel as yours forever, and you, LORD, have become their God. And now, LORD God, confirm for all time the prophecy you have made concerning your servant and his house, and do as you have promised. Your name will be forever great, when men say, 'The LORD of hosts is God of Israel,' and the house of your servant David stands firm before you. It is you, LORD of hosts, God of Israel, who said in a revelation to your servant, 'I will build a house for you.' Therefore your servant now finds the courage to make this prayer to you. And now, Lord GOD, you are God and your words are truth; you have made this generous promise to your servant. Do, then, bless the house of your servant that it may be before you forever; for you, Lord GOD, have promised, and by your blessing the house of your servant shall be blessed forever."

RESPONSORIAL PSALM *Psalm 132:1–2, 3–5, 11, 12, 13–14*

R. (Lk 1:32b) **The Lord God will give him the throne of David, his father.**

LORD, remember David and all his anxious care; / How he swore an oath to the LORD, / vowed to the Mighty One of Jacob. **R.**

"I will not enter the house where I live, / nor lie on the couch where I sleep; / I will give my eyes no sleep, my eyelids no rest, / Till I find a home for the LORD, / a dwelling for the Mighty One of Jacob." **R.**

The LORD swore an oath to David / a firm promise from which he will not withdraw: / "Your own offspring I will set upon your throne." **R.**

"If your sons keep my covenant, / and the decrees which I shall teach them, / Their sons, too, forever shall sit upon your throne." **R.**

For the LORD has chosen Zion, / he prefers her for his dwelling: / "Zion is my resting place forever; in her I will dwell, for I prefer her." **R.**

ALLELUIA *Psalm 119:105*

R. Alleluia, alleluia. A lamp to my feet is your word, a light to my path. **R.**

GOSPEL *Mark 4:21–25*

Jesus said to his disciples, "Is a lamp brought in to be placed under a bushel basket or under a bed, and not to be placed on a lampstand? For there is nothing hidden except to be made visible; nothing is secret except to come to light. Anyone who has ears to hear ought to hear." He also told them, "Take care what you hear. The measure with which you measure will be measured out to you, and still more will be given to you. To the one who has, more will be given; from the one who has not, even what he has will be taken away."

JANUARY 31, FRIDAY OF WEEK 3; ST. JOHN BOSCO

FIRST READING *2 Samuel 11:1–4a, 5–10a, 13–17*

At the turn of the year, when kings go out on campaign, David sent out Joab along with his officers and the army of Israel, and they ravaged the Ammonites and besieged Rabbah.

David, however, remained in Jerusalem. One evening David rose from his siesta and strolled about on the roof of the palace. From the roof he saw a woman bathing, who was very beautiful. David had inquiries made about the woman and was told, "She is Bathsheba, daughter of Eliam, and wife of Joab's armor bearer Uriah the Hittite." Then David sent messengers and took her. When she came to him, he had relations with her. She then returned to her house. But the woman had conceived, and sent the information to David, "I am with child."

David therefore sent a message to Joab, "Send me Uriah the Hittite." So Joab sent Uriah to David. When he came, David questioned him about Joab, the soldiers, and how the war was going, and Uriah answered that all was well. David then said to Uriah, "Go down to your house and bathe your feet." Uriah left the palace, and a portion was sent out after him from the king's table. But Uriah slept at the entrance of the royal palace with the other officers of his lord, and did not go down to his own house.

David was told that Uriah had not gone home. On the day following, David summoned him, and he ate and drank with David, who made him drunk. But in the evening Uriah went out to sleep on his bed among his lord's servants, and did not go down to his home.

The next morning David wrote a letter to Joab which he sent by Uriah. In it he directed: "Place Uriah up front, where the fighting is fierce. Then pull back and leave him to be struck down dead." So while Joab was besieging the city, he assigned Uriah to a place where he knew the defenders were strong. When the men of the city made a sortie against Joab, some officers of David's army fell, and among them Uriah the Hittite died.

RESPONSORIAL PSALM *Psalm 51:3–4, 5–6a, 6bcd–7, 10–11*

R. (see 3a) Be merciful, O Lord, for we have sinned.

Have mercy on me, O God, in your goodness; / in the greatness of your compassion wipe out my offense. / Thoroughly wash me from my guilt and of my sin cleanse me. **R.**

For I acknowledge my offense, and my sin is before me always: / "Against you only have I sinned, / and done what is evil in your sight." **R.**

I have done such evil in your sight / that you are just in your sentence, / blameless when you condemn. True, I was born guilty, / a sinner, even as my mother conceived me. **R.**

Let me hear the sounds of joy and gladness; / the bones you have crushed shall rejoice. / Turn away your face from my sins, / and blot out all my guilt. **R.**

ALLELUIA   *See Matthew 11:25*

R. Alleluia, alleluia. Blessed are you, Father, Lord of heaven and earth; you have revealed to little ones the mysteries of the Kingdom. **R.**

GOSPEL   *Mark 4:26–34*

Jesus said to the crowds: "This is how it is with the Kingdom of God; it is as if a man were to scatter seed on the land and would sleep and rise night and day and the seed would sprout and grow, he knows not how. Of its own accord the land yields fruit, first the blade, then the ear, then the full grain in the ear. And when the grain is ripe, he wields the sickle at once, for the harvest has come."

He said, "To what shall we compare the Kingdom of God, or what parable can we use for it? It is like a mustard seed that, when it is sown in the ground, is the smallest of all the seeds on the earth. But once it is sown, it springs up and becomes the largest of plants and puts forth large branches, so that the birds of the sky can dwell in its shade." With many such parables he spoke the word to them as they were able to understand it. Without parables he did not speak to them, but to his own disciples he explained everything in private.

4   FEBRUARY

FEBRUARY 1, SATURDAY OF WEEK 3; ST. BRIGID OF IRELAND

FIRST READING   *2 Samuel 12:1–7a, 10–17*

The LORD sent Nathan to David, and when he came to him, Nathan said: "Judge this case for me! In a certain town there were two men, one rich, the other poor. The rich man had flocks and herds in great numbers. But the poor man had nothing at all except one little ewe lamb that he had bought. He nourished her, and she grew up with him and his children. She shared the little food he had and drank from his cup and slept in his bosom. She was like a daughter to him. Now, the rich man received a visitor, but he would not take from his own flocks and herds to prepare a meal for the wayfarer who had come to him. Instead he took the poor man's ewe lamb and made a meal of it for his visitor." David grew very angry with that man and said to him: "As the LORD lives, the man who has done this merits death! He shall restore the ewe lamb fourfold because he has done this and has had no pity."

Then Nathan said to David: "You are the man! Thus says the LORD God of Israel: 'The sword shall never depart from your house, because you have despised me and have taken the wife of Uriah to be your wife.' Thus says the LORD: 'I will bring evil upon you out of your own house. I will take your wives while you live to see it, and will give them to your neighbor. He shall lie with your wives in broad daylight. You have done this deed in secret, but I will bring it about in the presence of all Israel, and with the sun looking down.'"

Then David said to Nathan, "I have sinned against the LORD." Nathan answered David: "The LORD on his part has forgiven your sin: you shall not die. But since you have utterly spurned the LORD by this deed, the child born to you must surely die." Then Nathan returned to his house.

The LORD struck the child that the wife of Uriah had borne to David, and it became desperately ill. David besought God for the child. He kept a fast, retiring for the night to lie on the ground clothed in sackcloth. The elders of his house stood beside him urging him to rise from the ground; but he would not, nor would he take food with them.

RESPONSORIAL PSALM   *Psalm 51:12–13, 14–15, 16–17*
R. (12a) Create a clean heart in me, O God.
A clean heart create for me, O God, / and a steadfast spirit renew within me. / Cast me not out from your presence, / and your Holy Spirit take not from me. **R.**
Give me back the joy of your salvation, /and a willing spirit sustain in me. / I will teach transgressors your ways, / and sinners shall return to you. **R.**
Free me from blood guilt, O God, my saving God; /then my tongue shall revel in your justice. / O Lord, open my lips, / and my mouth shall proclaim your praise. **R.**

ALLELUIA   *John 3:16*
R. Alleluia, alleluia. God so loved the world that he gave his only–begotten Son, so that everyone who believes in him might have eternal life. **R.**

GOSPEL   *Mark 4:35–41*
On that day, as evening drew on, Jesus said to his disciples: "Let us cross to the other side." Leaving the crowd, they took Jesus with them in the boat just as he was. And other boats were with him. A violent squall came up and waves were breaking over the boat, so that it was already filling up. Jesus was in the stern, asleep on a cushion. They woke him and said to him, "Teacher, do you not care that we are perishing?" He woke up, rebuked the wind, and said to the sea, "Quiet! Be still!" The wind ceased and there was great calm. Then he asked them, "Why are you terrified? Do you not yet have faith?" They were filled with great awe and said to one another, "Who then is this whom even wind and sea obey?"

FEBRUARY 2, THE PRESENTATION OF THE LORD

FIRST READING *Malachi 3:1—4*

Thus says the Lord God: Lo, I am sending my messenger to prepare the way before me; And suddenly there will come to the temple the LORD whom you seek, And the messenger of the covenant whom you desire. Yes, he is coming, says the LORD of hosts. But who will endure the day of his coming? And who can stand when he appears? For he is like the refiner's fire, or like the fuller's lye. He will sit refining and purifying silver, and he will purify the sons of Levi, Refining them like gold or like silver that they may offer due sacrifice to the LORD. Then the sacrifice of Judah and Jerusalem will please the LORD, as in the days of old, as in years gone by.

RESPONSORIAL PSALM *Psalm 24:7, 8, 9, 10 (8)*

R. Who is this king of glory? It is the Lord!

Lift up, O gates, your lintels; / reach up, you ancient portals, / that the king of glory may come in! **R.**

Who is this king of glory? / The LORD, strong and mighty, / the LORD, mighty in battle. **R.**

Lift up, O gates, your lintels; / reach up, you ancient portals, / that the king of glory may come in! **R.**

Who is this king of glory? / The LORD of hosts; / He is the king of glory. **R.**

SECOND READING *Hebrews 2:14—18*

Since the children share in blood and flesh, Jesus likewise shared in them, that through death he might destroy the one who has the power of death, that is, the devil, and free those who through fear of death had been subject to slavery all their life. Surely he did not help angels but rather the descendants of Abraham; therefore, he had to become like his brothers and sisters in every way, that he might be a merciful and faithful high priest before God to expiate the sins of the people. Because he himself was tested through what he suffered, he is able to help those who are being tested.

ALLELUIA *Luke 2:32*

R. Alleluia, alleluia. A light of revelation to the Gentiles, and glory for your people Israel. **R.**

GOSPEL *Longer Form Luke 2:22—40*

When the days were completed for their purification according to the law of Moses, Mary and Joseph took Jesus up to Jerusalem to present him to the Lord, just as it is written in the law of the Lord, *Every male that opens the womb shall be consecrated to the Lord,* and to offer the sacrifice of *a pair of turtledoves or two young pigeons,* in accordance with the dictate in the law of the Lord.

Now there was a man in Jerusalem whose name was Simeon. This man was righteous and devout, awaiting the consolation of Israel, and the Holy Spirit was upon him. It had been revealed to him by the Holy Spirit that he should not see death before he had seen the Christ of the Lord. He came in the Spirit into the temple; and when the parents brought in the child Jesus to perform the custom of the law in regard to him, he took him into his arms and blessed God, saying:

"Now, Master, you may let your servant go in peace, according to your word, for my eyes have seen your salvation, which you prepared in sight of all the peoples: a light for revelation to the Gentiles, and glory for your people Israel."

The child's father and mother were amazed at what was said about him; and Simeon blessed them and said to Mary his mother, "Behold, this child is destined for the fall and rise of many in Israel, and to be a sign that will be contradicted —and you yourself a sword will pierce— so that the thoughts of many hearts may be revealed." There was also a prophetess, Anna, the daughter of Phanuel, of the tribe of Asher. She was advanced in years, having lived seven years with her husband after her marriage, and then as a widow until she was eighty–four. She never left the temple, but worshiped night and day with fasting and prayer. And coming forward at that very time, she gave thanks to God and spoke about the child to all who were awaiting the redemption of Jerusalem.

When they had fulfilled all the prescriptions of the law of the Lord, they returned to Galilee, to their own town of Nazareth. The child grew and became strong, filled with wisdom; and the favor of God was upon him.

ALTERNATIVE GOSPEL   *horter Form Luke 2:22—32*

When the days were completed for their purification according to the law of Moses, Mary and Joseph took Jesus up to Jerusalem to present him to the Lord, just as it is written in the law of the Lord, *Every male that opens the womb shall be consecrated to the Lord,* and to offer the sacrifice of *a pair of turtledoves or two young pigeons,* in accordance with the dictate in the law of the Lord.

Now there was a man in Jerusalem whose name was Simeon. This man was righteous and devout, awaiting the consolation of Israel, and the Holy Spirit was upon him. It had been revealed to him by the Holy Spirit that he should not see death before he had seen the Christ of the Lord. He came in the Spirit into the temple; and when the parents brought in the child Jesus to perform the custom of the law in regard to him, he took him into his arms and blessed God, saying:

"Now, Master, you may let your servant go in peace, according to your word, for my eyes have seen your salvation, which you prepared in sight of all the peoples: a light for revelation to the Gentiles, and glory for your people Israel."

FEBRUARY 3, MONDAY OF WEEK 4; ST. BLASE

FIRST READING   *2 Samuel 15:13–14, 30; 16:5–13*

An informant came to David with the report, "The children of Israel have transferred their loyalty to Absalom." At this, David said to all his servants who were with him in Jerusalem: "Up! Let us take flight, or none of us will escape from Absalom. Leave quickly, lest he hurry and overtake us, then visit disaster upon us and put the city to the sword."

As David went up the Mount of Olives, he wept without ceasing. His head was covered, and he was walking barefoot. All those who were with him also had their heads covered and were weeping as they went.

As David was approaching Bahurim, a man named Shimei, the son of Gera of the same clan as Saul's family, was coming out of the place, cursing as he came. He threw stones at David and at all the king's officers, even though all the soldiers, including the royal guard, were on David's right and on his left. Shimei was saying as he cursed: "Away, away, you murderous and wicked man! The LORD has requited you for all the bloodshed in the family of Saul, in whose stead you became king, and the LORD has given over the kingdom to your son Absalom. And now you suffer ruin because you are a murderer." Abishai, son of Zeruiah, said to the king: "Why should this dead dog curse my lord the king? Let me go over, please, and lop off his head." But the king replied: "What business is it of mine or of yours, sons of Zeruiah, that he curses? Suppose the LORD has told him to curse David; who then will dare to say, 'Why are you doing this?'" Then the king said to Abishai and to all his servants: "If my own son, who came forth from my loins, is seeking my life, how much more might this Benjaminite do so? Let him alone and let him curse, for the LORD has told him to. Perhaps the LORD will look upon my affliction and make it up to me with benefits for the curses he is uttering this day." David and his men continued on the road, while Shimei kept abreast of them on the hillside, all the while cursing and throwing stones and dirt as he went.

RESPONSORIAL PSALM   *Psalm 3:2–3, 4–5, 6–7*

R. (8a) Lord, rise up and save me.

O LORD, how many are my adversaries! / Many rise up against me! / Many are saying of me, / "There is no salvation for him in God." **R.**

But you, O LORD, are my shield; / my glory, you lift up my head! / When I call out to the LORD, / he answers me from his holy mountain. **R.**

When I lie down in sleep, I wake again, / for the LORD sustains me. / I fear not the myriads of people arrayed against me on every side. **R.**

ALLELUIA   *Luke 7:16*

R. Alleluia, alleluia. A great prophet has arisen in our midst and God has visited his people. **R.**

GOSPEL   *Mark 5:1–20*

Jesus and his disciples came to the other side of the sea, to the territory of the Gerasenes. When he got out of the boat, at once a man from the tombs who had an unclean spirit met him. The man had been dwelling among the tombs, and no one could restrain him any longer, even with a chain. In fact, he had frequently been bound with shackles and chains, but the chains had been pulled apart by him and the shackles smashed, and no one was strong enough to subdue him. Night and day among the tombs and on the hillsides he was always crying out and bruising himself with stones. Catching sight of Jesus from a distance, he ran up and prostrated himself before him, crying out in a loud voice, "What have you to do with me, Jesus, Son of the Most High God? I adjure you by God, do not torment me!"

(He had been saying to him, "Unclean spirit, come out of the man!") He asked him, "What is your name?" He replied, "Legion is my name. There are many of us." And he pleaded earnestly with him not to drive them away from that territory.

Now a large herd of swine was feeding there on the hillside. And they pleaded with him, "Send us into the swine. Let us enter them." And he let them, and the unclean spirits came out and entered the swine. The herd of about two thousand rushed down a steep bank into the sea, where they were drowned. The swineherds ran away and reported the incident in the town and throughout the countryside. And people came out to see what had happened. As they approached Jesus, they caught sight of the man who had been possessed by Legion, sitting there clothed and in his right mind. And they were seized with fear. Those who witnessed the incident explained to them what had happened to the possessed man and to the swine. Then they began to beg him to leave their district. As he was getting into the boat, the man who had been possessed pleaded to remain with him. But Jesus would not permit him but told him instead, "Go home to your family and announce to them all that the Lord in his pity has done for you." Then the man went off and began to proclaim in the Decapolis what Jesus had done for him; and all were amazed.

FEBRUARY 4, TUESDAY OF WEEK 4; ST. JANE VALOIS

FIRST READING   *2 Samuel 18:9–10, 14b, 24–25a, 30—19:3*

Absalom unexpectedly came up against David's servants. He was mounted on a mule, and, as the mule passed under the branches of a large terebinth, his hair caught fast in the tree. He hung between heaven and earth while the mule he had been riding ran off. Someone saw this and reported to Joab that he had seen Absalom hanging from a terebinth. And taking three pikes in hand, he thrust for the heart of Absalom, still hanging from the tree alive.

Now David was sitting between the two gates, and a lookout went up to the roof of the gate above the city wall, where he looked about and saw a man running all alone. The lookout shouted to inform the king, who said, "If he is alone, he has good news to report." The king said, "Step aside and remain in attendance here." So he stepped aside and remained there. When the Cushite messenger came in, he said, "Let my lord the king receive the good news that this day the LORD has taken your part, freeing you from the grasp of all who rebelled against you." But the king asked the Cushite, "Is young Absalom safe?" The Cushite replied, "May the enemies of my lord the king and all who rebel against you with evil intent be as that young man!"

The king was shaken, and went up to the room over the city gate to weep. He said as he wept, "My son Absalom! My son, my son Absalom! If only I had died instead of you, Absalom, my son, my son!"

Joab was told that the king was weeping and mourning for Absalom; and that day's victory was turned into mourning for the whole army when they heard that the king was grieving for his son.

RESPONSORIAL PSALM   *Psalm 86:1–2, 3–4, 5–6*

R. (1a) Listen, Lord, and answer me.

Incline your ear, O LORD; answer me, **/** for I am afflicted and poor. **/** Keep my life, for I am devoted to you; **/** save your servant who trusts in you. **/** You are my God. **R.**

Have mercy on me, O Lord, for to you I call all the day. **/** Gladden the soul of your servant, **/** for to you, O Lord, I lift up my soul. **R.**

For you, O Lord, are good and forgiving, **/** abounding in kindness to all who call upon you. **/** Hearken, O LORD, to my prayer and **/** attend to the sound of my pleading. **R.**

ALLELUIA   *Matthew 8:17*

R. Alleluia, alleluia. Christ took away our infirmities and bore our diseases. **R.**

GOSPEL   *Mark 5:21–43*

When Jesus had crossed again in the boat to the other side, a large crowd gathered around him, and he stayed close to the sea. One of the synagogue officials, named Jairus, came forward. Seeing him he fell at his feet and pleaded earnestly with him, saying, "My daughter is at the point of death. Please, come lay your hands on her that she may get well and live." He went off with him and a large crowd followed him.

There was a woman afflicted with hemorrhages for twelve years. She had suffered greatly at the hands of many doctors and had spent all that she had. Yet she was not helped but only grew worse. She had heard about Jesus and came up behind him in the crowd and touched his cloak. She said, "If I but touch his clothes, I shall be cured." Immediately her flow of blood dried up. She felt in her body that she was healed of her affliction. Jesus, aware at once that power had gone out from him, turned around in the crowd and asked, "Who has touched my clothes?" But his disciples said to him, "You see how the crowd is pressing upon you, and yet you ask, Who touched me?" And he looked around to see who had done it. The woman, realizing what had happened to her, approached in fear and trembling. She fell down before Jesus and told him the whole truth. He said to her, "Daughter, your faith has saved you. Go in peace and be cured of your affliction."

While he was still speaking, people from the synagogue official's house arrived and said, "Your daughter has died; why trouble the teacher any longer?" Disregarding the message that was reported, Jesus said to the synagogue official, "Do not be afraid; just have faith." He did not allow anyone to accompany him inside except Peter, James, and John, the brother of James. When they arrived at the house of the synagogue official, he caught sight of a commotion, people weeping and wailing loudly. So he went in and said to them, "Why this commotion and weeping? The child is not dead but asleep." And they ridiculed him. Then he put them all out. He took along the child's father and mother and those who were with him and entered the room where the child was. He took the child by the hand and said to her, "Talitha koum," which means, "Little girl, I say to you, arise!" The girl, a child of twelve, arose immediately and walked around. At that they were utterly astounded. He gave strict orders that no one should know this and said that she should be given something to eat.

FEBRUARY 5, WEDNESDAY OF WEEK 4; ST. AGATHA

FIRST READING *2 Samuel 24:2, 9–17*

King David said to Joab and the leaders of the army who were with him, "Tour all the tribes in Israel from Dan to Beer–sheba and register the people, that I may know their number." Joab then reported to the king the number of people registered: in Israel, eight hundred thousand men fit for military service; in Judah, five hundred thousand.

Afterward, however, David regretted having numbered the people, and said to the LORD: "I have sinned grievously in what I have done. But now, LORD, forgive the guilt of your servant, for I have been very foolish." When David rose in the morning, the LORD had spoken to the prophet Gad, David's seer, saying: "Go and say to David, 'This is what the LORD says: I offer you three alternatives; choose one of them, and I will inflict it on you.'" Gad then went to David to inform him. He asked: "Do you want a three years' famine to come upon your land, or to flee from your enemy three months while he pursues you, or to have a three days' pestilence in your land? Now consider and decide what I must reply to him who sent me." David answered Gad: "I am in very serious difficulty. Let us fall by the hand of God, for he is most merciful; but let me not fall by the hand of man." Thus David chose the pestilence. Now it was the time of the wheat harvest when the plague broke out among the people. The LORD then sent a pestilence over Israel from morning until the time appointed, and seventy thousand of the people from Dan to Beer–sheba died. But when the angel stretched forth his hand toward Jerusalem to destroy it, the LORD regretted the calamity and said to the angel causing the destruction among the people, "Enough now! Stay your hand." The angel of the LORD was then standing at the threshing floor of Araunah the Jebusite. When David saw the angel who was striking the people, he said to the LORD: "It is I who have sinned; it is I, the shepherd, who have done wrong. But these are sheep; what have they done? Punish me and my kindred."

RESPONSORIAL PSALM *Psalm 32:1–2, 5, 6, 7*

R. (see 5c) Lord, forgive the wrong I have done.

Blessed is he whose fault is taken away, / whose sin is covered. / Blessed the man to whom the LORD imputes not guilt, / in whose spirit there is no guile. **R.**

Then I acknowledged my sin to you, / my guilt I covered not. I said, "I confess my faults to the LORD," / and you took away the guilt of my sin. **R.**

For this shall every faithful man pray to you in time of stress. / Though deep waters overflow, they shall not reach him. **R.**

You are my shelter; / from distress you will preserve me; / with glad cries of freedom you will ring me round. **R.**

ALLELUIA *John 10:27*

R. Alleluia, alleluia. My sheep hear my voice, says the Lord; I know them, and they follow me. **R.**

GOSPEL   *Mark 6:1–6*

Jesus departed from there and came to his native place, accompanied by his disciples. When the Sabbath came he began to teach in the synagogue, and many who heard him were astonished. They said, "Where did this man get all this? What kind of wisdom has been given him? What mighty deeds are wrought by his hands! Is he not the carpenter, the son of Mary, and the brother of James and Joseph and Judas and Simon? And are not his sisters here with us?" And they took offense at him. Jesus said to them, "A prophet is not without honor except in his native place and among his own kin and in his own house." So he was not able to perform any mighty deed there, apart from curing a few sick people by laying his hands on them. He was amazed at their lack of faith.

FEBRUARY 6, THURSDAY OF WEEK 4; ST. PAUL MIKI AND COMPANIONS

FIRST READING   *1 Kings 2:1–4, 10–12*

When the time of David's death drew near, he gave these instructions to his son Solomon: "I am going the way of all flesh. Take courage and be a man. Keep the mandate of the LORD, your God, following his ways and observing his statutes, commands, ordinances, and decrees as they are written in the law of Moses, that you may succeed in whatever you do, wherever you turn, and the LORD may fulfill the promise he made on my behalf when he said, 'If your sons so conduct themselves that they remain faithful to me with their whole heart and with their whole soul, you shall always have someone of your line on the throne of Israel.'"

David rested with his ancestors and was buried in the City of David. The length of David's reign over Israel was forty years: he reigned seven years in Hebron and thirty–three years in Jerusalem.

Solomon was seated on the throne of his father David, with his sovereignty firmly established.

RESPONSORIAL PSALM: *1 Chronicles 29:10, 11ab, 11d–12a, 12bcd*
R. (12b) Lord, you are exalted over all.
"Blessed may you be, O LORD, God of Israel our father, / from eternity to eternity." **R.**
"Yours, O LORD, are grandeur and power, / majesty, splendor, and glory." **R.**
"LORD, you are exalted over all. / Yours, O LORD, is the sovereignty; /you are exalted as head over all. / Riches and honor are from you." **R.**
"In your hand are power and might; / it is yours to give grandeur and strength to all." **R.**

ALLELUIA   *Mark 1:15*

R. Alleluia, alleluia. The Kingdom of God is at hand; repent and believe in the Gospel. **R.**

GOSPEL   *Mark 6:7–13*

Jesus summoned the Twelve and began to send them out two by two and gave them authority over unclean spirits. He instructed them to take nothing for the journey but a walking stick —no food, no sack, no money in their belts. They were, however, to wear sandals but not a second tunic. He said to them, "Wherever you enter a house, stay there until you leave from there. Whatever place does not welcome you or listen to you, leave there and shake the dust off your feet in testimony against them." So they went off and preached repentance. The Twelve drove out many demons, and they anointed with oil many who were sick and cured them.

FEBRUARY 7, FRIDAY OF WEEK 4; BLESSED GILES MARY

FIRST READING *Sirach 47:2–11*

Like the choice fat of the sacred offerings, so was David in Israel. He made sport of lions as though they were kids, and of bears, like lambs of the flock. As a youth he slew the giant and wiped out the people's disgrace, when his hand let fly the slingstone that crushed the pride of Goliath. Since he called upon the Most High God, who gave strength to his right arm to defeat the skilled warrior and raise up the might of his people, Therefore the women sang his praises, and ascribed to him tens of thousands and praised him when they blessed the Lord. When he assumed the royal crown, he battled and subdued the enemy on every side. He destroyed the hostile Philistines and shattered their power till our own day. With his every deed he offered thanks to God Most High, in words of praise. With his whole being he loved his Maker and daily had his praises sung; he set singers before the altar and by their voices he made sweet melodies, he added beauty to the feasts and solemnized the seasons of each year So that when the Holy Name was praised, before daybreak the sanctuary would resound. The LORD forgave him his sins and exalted his strength forever; He conferred on him the rights of royalty and established his throne in Israel.

RESPONSORIAL PSALM *Psalm 18:31, 47 and 50, 51*

R. (see 47b) Blessed be God my salvation!

God's way is unerring, **/** the promise of the LORD is fire–tried; **/** He is a shield to all who take refuge in him. **R.**

The LORD live! And blessed be my Rock! **/** Extolled be God my savior. **/** Therefore will I proclaim you, O LORD, among the nations, **/** and I will sing praise to your name. **R.**

You who gave great victories to your king **/** and showed kindness to your anointed, **/** to David and his posterity forever. **R.**

ALLELUIA *See Luke 8:15*

R. Alleluia, alleluia. Blessed are they who have kept the word with a generous heart, and yield a harvest through perseverance. **R.**

GOSPEL *Mark 6:14–29*

King Herod heard about Jesus, for his fame had become widespread, and people were saying, "John the Baptist has been raised from the dead; That is why mighty powers are at work in him." Others were saying, "He is Elijah"; still others, "He is a prophet like any of the prophets." But when Herod learned of it, he said, "It is John whom I beheaded. He has been raised up." Herod was the one who had John arrested and bound in prison on account of Herodias, the wife of his brother Philip, whom he had married. John had said to Herod, "It is not lawful for you to have your brother's wife." Herodias harbored a grudge against him and wanted to kill him but was unable to do so. Herod feared John, knowing him to be a righteous and holy man, and kept him in custody. When he heard him speak he was very much perplexed, yet he liked to listen to him. Herodias had an opportunity one day when Herod, on his birthday, gave a banquet for his courtiers, his military officers, and the leading men of Galilee. His own daughter came in and performed a dance that delighted Herod and his guests. The king said to the girl, "Ask of me whatever you wish and I will grant it to you." He even swore many things to her, "I will grant you whatever you ask of me, even to half of my kingdom."

She went out and said to her mother, "What shall I ask for?" Her mother replied, "The head of John the Baptist." The girl hurried back to the king's presence and made her request, "I want you to give me at once on a platter the head of John the Baptist." The king was deeply distressed, but because of his oaths and the guests he did not wish to break his word to her. So he promptly dispatched an executioner with orders to bring back his head. He went off and beheaded him in the prison. He brought in the head on a platter and gave it to the girl. The girl in turn gave it to her mother. When his disciples heard about it, they came and took his body and laid it in a tomb.

FEBRUARY 8, SATURDAY OF WEEK 4; ST. JOSEPHINE BAKHITA

FIRST READING   *1 Kings 3:4–13*

Solomon went to Gibeon to sacrifice there, because that was the most renowned high place. Upon its altar Solomon offered a thousand burnt offerings. In Gibeon the LORD appeared to Solomon in a dream at night. God said, "Ask something of me and I will give it to you." Solomon answered: "You have shown great favor to your servant, my father David, because he behaved faithfully toward you, with justice and an upright heart; and you have continued this great favor toward him, even today, seating a son of his on his throne. O LORD, my God, you have made me, your servant, king to succeed my father David; but I am a mere youth, not knowing at all how to act. I serve you in the midst of the people whom you have chosen, a people so vast that it cannot be numbered or counted. Give your servant, therefore, an understanding heart to judge your people and to distinguish right from wrong. For who is able to govern this vast people of yours?"

The LORD was pleased that Solomon made this request. So God said to him: "Because you have asked for this— not for a long life for yourself, nor for riches, nor for the life of your enemies, but for understanding so that you may know what is right— I do as you requested. I give you a heart so wise and understanding that there has never been anyone like you up to now, and after you there will come no one to equal you. In addition, I give you what you have not asked for, such riches and glory that among kings there is not your like."

RESPONSORIAL PSALM   *Psalm 119:9, 10, 11, 12, 13, 14*
R. (12b) Lord, teach me your statutes.
How shall a young man be faultless in his way? By keeping to your words. **R.**
With all my heart I seek you; let me not stray from your commands. **R.**

Within my heart I treasure your promise, that I may not sin against you. **R.**

Blessed are you, O LORD; teach me your statutes. **R.**

With my lips I declare all the ordinances of your mouth. **R.**

In the way of your decrees I rejoice, as much as in all riches. **R.**

ALLELUIA   *John 10:27*

R. Alleluia, alleluia. My sheep hear my voice, says the Lord; I know them, and they follow me. **R.**

GOSPEL   Mark *6:30–34*

The Apostles gathered together with Jesus and reported all they had done and taught. He said to them, "Come away by yourselves to a deserted place and rest a while." People were coming and going in great numbers, and they had no opportunity even to eat. So they went off in the boat by themselves to a deserted place. People saw them leaving and many came to know about it. They hastened there on foot from all the towns and arrived at the place before them.

When Jesus disembarked and saw the vast crowd, his heart was moved with pity for them, for they were like sheep without a shepherd; and he began to teach them many things.

FEBRUARY9, 5TH SUNDAY IN ORDINARY TIME;
ST. APOLLONIA AND THE MARTYRS OF ALEXANDRIA

FIRST READING   *Isaiah 58:7—10*

Thus says the LORD: Share your bread with the hungry, shelter the oppressed and the homeless; clothe the naked when you see them, and do not turn your back on your own. Then your light shall break forth like the dawn, and your wound shall quickly be healed; your vindication shall go before you, and the glory of the LORD shall be your rear guard. Then you shall call, and the LORD will answer; you shall cry for help, and he will say: Here I am! If you remove from your midst oppression, false accusation and malicious speech; if you bestow your bread on the hungry and satisfy the afflicted; then light shall rise for you in the darkness, and the gloom shall become for you like midday.

RESPONSORIAL PSALM   *Psalm 112:4—5, 6—7, 8—9 (4a)*

R. The just man is a light in darkness to the upright. or R. Alleluia.

Light shines through the darkness for the upright; / He is gracious and merciful and just. / Well for the man who is gracious and lends, / who conducts his affairs with justice. **R.**

He shall never be moved; / the just one shall be in everlasting remembrance. / An evil report he shall not fear; / his heart is firm, trusting in the LORD. **R.**

His heart is steadfast; he shall not fear. / Lavishly he gives to the poor; his justice shall endure forever; / his horn shall be exalted in glory. **R.**

SECOND READING   *1 Corinthians 2:1—5*

When I came to you, brothers and sisters, proclaiming the mystery of God, I did not come with sublimity of words or of wisdom. For I resolved to know nothing while I was with you except Jesus Christ, and him crucified. I came to you in weakness and fear and much trembling, and my message and my proclamation were not with persuasive words of wisdom, but with a demonstration of Spirit and power, so that your faith might rest not on human wisdom but on the power of God.

ALLELUIA   *John 8:12*

R. Alleluia, alleluia. I am the light of the world, says the Lord; whoever follows me will have the light of life. **R.**

GOSPEL   *Matthew 5:13—16*

Jesus said to his disciples: "You are the salt of the earth. But if salt loses its taste, with what can it be seasoned? It is no longer good for anything but to be thrown out and trampled underfoot. You are the light of the world. A city set on a mountain cannot be hidden. Nor do they light a lamp and then put it under a bushel basket; it is set on a lampstand, where it gives light to all in the house. Just so, your light must shine before others, that they may see your good deeds and glorify your heavenly Father."

FEBRUARY 10, MONDAY OF WEEK 5; ST. SCHOOLASTICA

FIRST READING   *1 Kings 8:1–7, 9–13*

The elders of Israel and all the leaders of the tribes, the princes in the ancestral houses of the children of Israel, came to King Solomon in Jerusalem, to bring up the ark of the LORD's covenant from the City of David, which is Zion. All the people of Israel assembled before King Solomon during the festival in the month of Ethanim (the seventh month). When all the elders of Israel had arrived, the priests took up the ark; they carried the ark of the LORD and the meeting tent with all the sacred vessels that were in the tent. (The priests and Levites carried them.)

King Solomon and the entire community of Israel present for the occasion sacrificed before the ark sheep and oxen too many to number or count. The priests brought the ark of the covenant of the LORD to its place beneath the wings of the cherubim in the sanctuary, the holy of holies of the temple. The cherubim had their wings spread out over the place of the ark, sheltering the ark and its poles from above. There was nothing in the ark but the two stone tablets which Moses had put there at Horeb, when the LORD made a covenant with the children of Israel at their departure from the land of Egypt.

When the priests left the holy place, the cloud filled the temple of the LORD so that the priests could no longer minister because of the cloud, since the LORD's glory had filled the temple of the LORD. Then Solomon said, "The LORD intends to dwell in the dark cloud; I have truly built you a princely house, a dwelling where you may abide forever."

RESPONSORIAL PSALM   *Psalm 132:6–7, 8–10*

R. (8a) Lord, go up to the place of your rest!

Behold, we heard of it in Ephrathah; / we found it in the fields of Jaar. / Let us enter into his dwelling, / let us worship at his footstool. **R.**

Advance, O LORD, to your resting place, / you and the ark of your majesty. / May your priests be clothed with justice; / let your faithful ones shout merrily for joy. / For the sake of David your servant, / reject not the plea of your anointed. **R.**

ALLELUIA *See Matthew 4:23*

R. Alleluia, alleluia. Jesus preached the Gospel of the Kingdom and cured every disease among the people. **R.**

GOSPEL *Mark 6:53–56*

After making the crossing to the other side of the sea, Jesus and his disciples came to land at Gennesaret and tied up there. As they were leaving the boat, people immediately recognized him. They scurried about the surrounding country and began to bring in the sick on mats to wherever they heard he was. Whatever villages or towns or countryside he entered, they laid the sick in the marketplaces and begged him that they might touch only the tassel on his cloak; and as many as touched it were healed.

FEBRUARY 11, TUESDAY OF WEEK 5; OUR LADY OF LOURDES

FIRST READING *1 Kings 8:22–23, 27–30*

Solomon stood before the altar of the LORD in the presence of the whole community of Israel, and stretching forth his hands toward heaven, he said, "LORD, God of Israel, there is no God like you in heaven above or on earth below; you keep your covenant of mercy with your servants who are faithful to you with their whole heart.

"Can it indeed be that God dwells on earth? If the heavens and the highest heavens cannot contain you, how much less this temple which I have built! Look kindly on the prayer and petition of your servant, O LORD, my God, and listen to the cry of supplication which I, your servant, utter before you this day. May your eyes watch night and day over this temple, the place where you have decreed you shall be honored; may you heed the prayer which I, your servant, offer in this place. Listen to the petitions of your servant and of your people Israel which they offer in this place. Listen from your heavenly dwelling and grant pardon."

RESPONSORIAL PSALM *Psalm 84:3, 4, 5 and 10, 11*

R. (2) How lovely is your dwelling place, Lord, mighty God!

My soul yearns and pines for the courts of the LORD. / My heart and my flesh cry out for the living God. **R.**

Even the sparrow finds a home, / and the swallow a nest in which she puts her young— Your altars, / O LORD of hosts, my king and my God! **R.**

Blessed they who dwell in your house! / continually they praise you. O God, behold our shield, / and look upon the face of your anointed. **R.**

I had rather one day in your courts / than a thousand elsewhere; / I had rather lie at the threshold of the house of my God / than dwell in the tents of the wicked. **R.**

ALLELUIA   *Psalm 119:36, 29b*

R. Alleluia, alleluia. Incline my heart, O God, to your decrees; and favor me with your law. **R.**

GOSPEL   *Mark 7:1–13*

When the Pharisees with some scribes who had come from Jerusalem gathered around Jesus, they observed that some of his disciples ate their meals with unclean, that is, unwashed, hands. (For the Pharisees and, in fact, all Jews, do not eat without carefully washing their hands, keeping the tradition of the elders. And on coming from the marketplace they do not eat without purifying themselves. And there are many other things that they have traditionally observed, the purification of cups and jugs and kettles and beds.) So the Pharisees and scribes questioned him, "Why do your disciples not follow the tradition of the elders but instead eat a meal with unclean hands?" He responded, "Well did Isaiah prophesy about you hypocrites, as it is written:

This people honors me with their lips, but their hearts are far from me; in vain do they worship me, teaching as doctrines human precepts.

You disregard God's commandment but cling to human tradition." He went on to say, "How well you have set aside the commandment of God in order to uphold your tradition! For Moses said, *Honor your father and your mother, and whoever curses father or mother shall die.* Yet you say, 'If someone says to father or mother, "Any support you might have had from me is qorban"' (meaning, dedicated to God), you allow him to do nothing more for his father or mother. You nullify the word of God in favor of your tradition that you have handed on. And you do many such things."

FEBRUARY 12, WEDNESDAY OF WEEK 5; ST. MELETIUS

FIRST READING   *1 Kings 10:1–10*

The queen of Sheba, having heard of Solomon's fame, came to test him with subtle questions. She arrived in Jerusalem with a very numerous retinue, and with camels bearing spices, a large amount of gold, and precious stones. She came to Solomon and questioned him on every subject in which she was interested. King Solomon explained everything she asked about, and there remained nothing hidden from him that he could not explain to her.

When the queen of Sheba witnessed Solomon's great wisdom, the palace he had built, the food at his table, the seating of his ministers, the attendance and garb of his waiters, his banquet service, and the burnt offerings he offered in the temple of the LORD, she was breathless. "The report I heard in my country about your deeds and your wisdom is true," she told the king. "Though I did not believe the report until I came and saw with my own eyes, I have discovered that they were not telling me the half. Your wisdom and prosperity surpass the report I heard. Blessed are your men, blessed these servants of yours, who stand before you always and listen to your wisdom. Blessed be the LORD, your God, whom it has pleased to place you on the throne of Israel. In his enduring love for Israel, the LORD has made you king to carry out judgment and justice." Then she gave the king one hundred and twenty gold talents, a very large quantity of spices, and precious stones. Never again did anyone bring such an abundance of spices as the queen of Sheba gave to King Solomon.

RESPONSORIAL PSALM   *Psalm 37:5–6, 30–31, 39–40*
R. (30a) The mouth of the just murmurs wisdom.
Commit to the LORD your way; / trust in him, and he will act. / He will make justice dawn for you like the light; / bright as the noonday shall be your vindication. **R.**
The mouth of the just man tells of wisdom / and his tongue utters what is right. / The law of his God is in his heart, / and his steps do not falter. **R.**
The salvation of the just is from the LORD; / He is their refuge in time of distress. / And the LORD helps them and delivers them; / He delivers them from the wicked and saves them, / because they take refuge in him. **R.**

ALLELUIA   *See John 17:17b, 17a*
R. Alleluia, alleluia. Your word, O Lord, is truth: consecrate us in the truth. **R.**

GOSPEL   *Mark 7:14–23*
Jesus summoned the crowd again and said to them, "Hear me, all of you, and understand. Nothing that enters one from outside can defile that person; but the things that come out from within are what defile."

When he got home away from the crowd his disciples questioned him about the parable. He said to them, "Are even you likewise without understanding? Do you not realize that everything that goes into a person from outside cannot defile, since it enters not the heart but the stomach and passes out into the latrine?" (Thus he declared all foods clean.) "But what comes out of the man, that is what defiles him. From within the man, from his heart, come evil thoughts, unchastity, theft, murder, adultery, greed, malice, deceit, licentiousness, envy, blasphemy, arrogance, folly. All these evils come from within and they defile."

FEBRUARY 13, THURSDAY OF WEEK 5; ST. CATHERINE OF RICCI
FIRST READING   *1 Kings 11:4–13*
When Solomon was old his wives had turned his heart to strange gods, and his heart was not entirely with the LORD, his God, as the heart of his father David had been. By adoring Astarte, the goddess of the Sidonians, and Milcom, the idol of the Ammonites, Solomon did evil in the sight of the LORD; he did not follow him unreservedly as his father David had done. Solomon then built a high place to Chemosh, the idol of Moab, and to Molech, the idol of the Ammonites, on the hill opposite Jerusalem. He did the same for all his foreign wives who burned incense and sacrificed to their gods. The LORD, therefore, became angry with Solomon, because his heart was turned away from the LORD, the God of Israel, who had appeared to him twice (for though the LORD had forbidden him this very act of following strange gods, Solomon had not obeyed him).

So the LORD said to Solomon: "Since this is what you want, and you have not kept my covenant and my statutes which I enjoined on you, I will deprive you of the kingdom and give it to your servant. I will not do this during your lifetime, however, for the sake of your father David; it is your son whom I will deprive. Nor will I take away the whole kingdom. I will leave your son one tribe for the sake of my servant David and of Jerusalem, which I have chosen."

RESPONSORIAL PSALM   *Psalm 106:3–4, 35–36, 37 and 40*
R. (4a) **Remember us, O Lord, as you favor your people.**
Blessed are they who observe what is right, / who do always what is just. / Remember us, O LORD, as you favor your people; / visit us with your saving help. **R.**
But they mingled with the nations and learned their works. / They served their idols, which became a snare for them. **R.**
They sacrificed their sons and their daughters to demons. / And the LORD grew angry with his people, and abhorred his inheritance. **R.**

ALLELUIA   *James 1:21bc*
R. **Alleluia, alleluia.** Humbly welcome the word that has been planted in you and is able to save your souls. **R.**

GOSPEL   *Mark 7:24–30*
Jesus went to the district of Tyre. He entered a house and wanted no one to know about it, but he could not escape notice. Soon a woman whose daughter had an unclean spirit heard about him. She came and fell at his feet. The woman was a Greek, a Syrophoenician by birth, and she begged him to drive the demon out of her daughter. He said to her, "Let the children be fed first. For it is not right to take the food of the children and throw it to the dogs." She replied and said to him, "Lord, even the dogs under the table eat the children's scraps." Then he said to her, "For saying this, you may go. The demon has gone out of your daughter." When the woman went home, she found the child lying in bed and the demon gone.

FEBRUARY 14 FRIDAY OF WEEK 5; ST. CYRIL AND ST. METHODIUS & ST. VALENTINE
FIRST READING   *1 Kings 11:29–32; 12:19*
Jeroboam left Jerusalem, and the prophet Ahijah the Shilonite met him on the road. The two were alone in the area, and the prophet was wearing a new cloak. Ahijah took off his new cloak, tore it into twelve pieces, and said to Jeroboam:

"Take ten pieces for yourself; the LORD, the God of Israel, says: 'I will tear away the kingdom from Solomon's grasp and will give you ten of the tribes. One tribe shall remain to him for the sake of David my servant, and of Jerusalem, the city I have chosen out of all the tribes of Israel.'"

Israel went into rebellion against David's house to this day.

RESPONSORIAL PSALM   *Psalm 81:10–11ab, 12–13, 14–15*
R. (11a and 9a) **I am the Lord, your God: hear my voice.**

"There shall be no strange god among you / nor shall you worship any alien god. / I, the LORD, am your God / who led you forth from the land of Egypt." **R.**

"My people heard not my voice, / and Israel obeyed me not; / So I gave them up to the hardness of their hearts; / they walked according to their own counsels." **R.**

"If only my people would hear me, / and Israel walk in my ways, / Quickly would I humble their enemies; / against their foes I would turn my hand." **R.**

ALLELUIA   *See Acts 16:14b*

R. Alleluia, alleluia. Open our hearts, O Lord, to listen to the words of your Son. **R.**

GOSPEL   *Mark 7:31–37*

Jesus left the district of Tyre and went by way of Sidon to the Sea of Galilee, into the district of the Decapolis. And people brought to him a deaf man who had a speech impediment and begged him to lay his hand on him. He took him off by himself away from the crowd. He put his finger into the man's ears and, spitting, touched his tongue; then he looked up to heaven and groaned, and said to him, "Ephphatha!" (that is, "Be opened!") And immediately the man's ears were opened, his speech impediment was removed, and he spoke plainly. He ordered them not to tell anyone. But the more he ordered them not to, the more they proclaimed it. They were exceedingly astonished and they said, "He has done all things well. He makes the deaf hear and the mute speak."

FEBRUARY 15, SATURDAY OF WEEK 5; ST. FAUSTINUS AND ST. JOVITA

FIRST READING   *Kings 12:26–32; 13:33–34*

Jeroboam thought to himself: "The kingdom will return to David's house. If now this people go up to offer sacrifices in the temple of the LORD in Jerusalem, the hearts of this people will return to their master, Rehoboam, king of Judah, and they will kill me." After taking counsel, the king made two calves of gold and said to the people: "You have been going up to Jerusalem long enough. Here is your God, O Israel, who brought you up from the land of Egypt." And he put one in Bethel, the other in Dan. This led to sin, because the people frequented those calves in Bethel and in Dan. He also built temples on the high places and made priests from among the people who were not Levites. Jeroboam established a feast in the eighth month on the fifteenth day of the month to duplicate in Bethel the pilgrimage feast of Judah, with sacrifices to the calves he had made; and he stationed in Bethel priests of the high places he had built.

Jeroboam did not give up his evil ways after this, but again made priests for the high places from among the common people. Whoever desired it was consecrated and became a priest of the high places. This was a sin on the part of the house of Jeroboam for which it was to be cut off and destroyed from the earth.

RESPONSORIAL PSALM   *Psalm 106:6–7ab, 19–20, 21–22*

R. (4a) Remember us, O Lord, as you favor your people.

We have sinned, we and our fathers; / we have committed crimes; we have done wrong. / Our fathers in Egypt considered not your wonders. **R.**

They made a calf in Horeb and adored a molten image; / They exchanged their glory for the image of a grass–eating bullock. **R.**

They forgot the God who had saved them, / who had done great deeds in Egypt, / Wondrous deeds in the land of Ham, / terrible things at the Red Sea. **R.**

ALLELUIA   *Matthew 4:4b*

R. Alleluia, alleluia. One does not live on bread alone, but on every word that comes forth from the mouth of God. **R.**

GOSPEL   *Mark 8:1–10*

In those days when there again was a great crowd without anything to eat, Jesus summoned the disciples and said, "My heart is moved with pity for the crowd, because they have been with me now for three days and have nothing to eat. If I send them away hungry to their homes, they will collapse on the way, and some of them have come a great distance." His disciples answered him, "Where can anyone get enough bread to satisfy them here in this deserted place?" Still he asked them, "How many loaves do you have?" They replied, "Seven." He ordered the crowd to sit down on the ground. Then, taking the seven loaves he gave thanks, broke them, and gave them to his disciples to distribute, and they distributed them to the crowd. They also had a few fish. He said the blessing over them and ordered them distributed also. They ate and were satisfied. They picked up the fragments left over—seven baskets. There were about four thousand people.

He dismissed the crowd and got into the boat with his disciples and came to the region of Dalmanutha.

FEBRUARY 16, 6TH SUNDAY IN ORDINARY TIME; ST. ONESIMUS

FIRST READING   *Sirach 15:15—20*

If you choose you can keep the commandments, they will save you; if you trust in God, you too shall live; he has set before you fire and water; to whichever you choose, stretch forth your hand. Before man are life and death, good and evil, whichever he chooses shall be given him. Immense is the wisdom of the LORD; he is mighty in power, and all–seeing. The eyes of God are on those who fear him; he understands man's every deed. No one does he command to act unjustly, to none does he give license to sin.

RESPONSORIAL PSALM: *Psalm 119:1—2, 4—5, 17—18, 33—34 (1b)*

R. Blessed are they who follow the law of the Lord!

Blessed are they whose way is blameless, / who walk in the law of the LORD. / Blessed are they who observe his decrees, / who seek him with all their heart. **R.**

You have commanded that your precepts be diligently kept. / Oh, that I might be firm in the ways of keeping your statutes! **R.**

Be good to your servant, that I may live and keep your words. / Open my eyes, that I may consider the wonders of your law. **R.**

Instruct me, O LORD, in the way of your statutes, / that I may exactly observe them. / Give me discernment, that I may observe your law / and keep it with all my heart. **R.**

SECOND READING
1 Corinthians 2:6—10

Brothers and sisters: We speak a wisdom to those who are mature, not a wisdom of this age, nor of the rulers of this age who are passing away. Rather, we speak God's wisdom, mysterious, hidden, which God predetermined before the ages for our glory, and which none of the rulers of this age knew; or, if they had known it, they would not have crucified the Lord of glory. But as it is written: *What eye has not seen, and ear has not heard, and what has not entered the human heart, what God has prepared for those who love him, this God has revealed to us through the Spirit.*

For the Spirit scrutinizes everything, even the depths of God.

ALLELUIA
see Matthew 11:25

R. Alleluia, alleluia. Blessed are you, Father, Lord of heaven and earth; you have revealed to little ones the mysteries of the kingdom. R.

GOSPEL
Longer Form Matthew 5:17—37

Jesus said to his disciples: "Do not think that I have come to abolish the law or the prophets. I have come not to abolish but to fulfill. Amen, I say to you, until heaven and earth pass away, not the smallest letter or the smallest part of a letter will pass from the law, until all things have taken place. Therefore, whoever breaks one of the least of these commandments and teaches others to do so will be called least in the kingdom of heaven. But whoever obeys and teaches these commandments will be called greatest in the kingdom of heaven. I tell you, unless your righteousness surpasses that of the scribes and Pharisees, you will not enter the kingdom of heaven. You have heard that it was said to your ancestors, *You shall not kill; and whoever kills will be liable to judgment.* But I say to you, whoever is angry with his brother will be liable to judgment; and whoever says to his brother, 'Raqa,' will be answerable to the Sanhedrin; and whoever says, 'You fool,' will be liable to fiery Gehenna. Therefore, if you bring your gift to the altar, and there recall that your brother has anything against you, leave your gift there at the altar, go first and be reconciled with your brother, and then come and offer your gift. Settle with your opponent quickly while on the way to court. Otherwise your opponent will hand you over to the judge, and the judge will hand you over to the guard, and you will be thrown into prison. Amen, I say to you, you will not be released until you have paid the last penny.

"You have heard that it was said, *You shall not commit adultery.* But I say to you, everyone who looks at a woman with lust has already committed adultery with her in his heart. If your right eye causes you to sin, tear it out and throw it away. It is better for you to lose one of your members than to have your whole body thrown into Gehenna. And if your right hand causes you to sin, cut it off and throw it away. It is better for you to lose one of your members than to have your whole body go into Gehenna.

"It was also said, *Whoever divorces his wife must give her a bill of divorce.* But I say to you, whoever divorces his wife—unless the marriage is unlawful— causes her to commit adultery, and whoever marries a divorced woman commits adultery.

"Again you have heard that it was said to your ancestors, *Do not take a false oath, but make good to the Lord all that you vow.* But I say to you, do not swear at all; not by heaven, for it is God's throne; nor by the earth, for it is his footstool; nor by Jerusalem, for it is the city of the great King. Do not swear by your head, for you cannot make a single hair white or black. Let your 'Yes' mean 'Yes,' and your 'No' mean 'No.' Anything more is from the evil one."

SHORTER FORM   *Matthew 5:20—22a, 27—28, 33—34a, 37*

Jesus said to his disciples: "I tell you, unless your righteousness surpasses that of the scribes and Pharisees, you will not enter the kingdom of heaven.

"You have heard that it was said to your ancestors, *You shall not kill; and whoever kills will be liable to judgment.* But I say to you, whoever is angry with his brother will be liable to judgment.

"You have heard that it was said, *You shall not commit adultery.* But I say to you, everyone who looks at a woman with lust has already committed adultery with her in his heart.

"Again you have heard that it was said to your ancestors, *Do not take a false oath, but make good to the Lord all that you vow.* But I say to you, do not swear at all. Let your 'Yes' mean 'Yes,' and your 'No' mean 'No.' Anything more is from the evil one."

FEBRUARY 17 MONDAY OF WEEK 6; SEVEN FOUNDERS OF THE ORDER OF SERVITES
FIRST READING   *James 1:1—11*

James, a servant of God and of the Lord Jesus Christ, to the twelve tribes in the dispersion, greetings.

Consider it all joy, my brothers and sisters, when you encounter various trials, for you know that the testing of your faith produces perseverance. And let perseverance be perfect, so that you may be perfect and complete, lacking in nothing. But if any of you lacks wisdom, he should ask God who gives to all generously and ungrudgingly, and he will be given it. But he should ask in faith, not doubting, for the one who doubts is like a wave of the sea that is driven and tossed about by the wind. For that person must not suppose that he will receive anything from the Lord, since he is a man of two minds, unstable in all his ways.

The brother in lowly circumstances should take pride in high standing, and the rich one in his lowliness, for he will pass away "like the flower of the field." For the sun comes up with its scorching heat and dries up the grass, its flower droops, and the beauty of its appearance vanishes. So will the rich person fade away in the midst of his pursuits.

RESPONSORIAL PSALM   *Psalm 119:67, 68, 71, 72, 75, 76*

R. (77a) Be kind to me, Lord, and I shall live.
Before I was afflicted I went astray, **/** but now I hold to your promise. **R.**
You are good and bountiful; **/** teach me your statutes. **R.**
It is good for me that I have been afflicted, **/** that I may learn your statutes. **R.**
The law of your mouth is to me **/** more precious than thousands of gold and silver pieces. **R.**

I know, O LORD, that your ordinances are just, / and in your faithfulness you have afflicted me. **R.**

Let your kindness comfort me / according to your promise to your servants. **R.**

ALLELUIA *John 14:6*

R. Alleluia, alleluia. I am the way and the truth and the life, says the Lord; no one comes to the Father except through me. **R.**

GOSPEL *Mark 8:11–13*

The Pharisees came forward and began to argue with Jesus, seeking from him a sign from heaven to test him. He sighed from the depth of his spirit and said, "Why does this generation seek a sign? Amen, I say to you, no sign will be given to this generation." Then he left them, got into the boat again, and went off to the other shore.

FEBRUARY 18, TUESDAY OF WEEK 6; BLESSED ELISABETTA CANORI-MORA

FIRST READING *James 1:12–18*

Blessed is he who perseveres in temptation, for when he has been proven he will receive the crown of life that he promised to those who love him. No one experiencing temptation should say, "I am being tempted by God"; for God is not subject to temptation to evil, and he himself tempts no one. Rather, each person is tempted when lured and enticed by his desire. Then desire conceives and brings forth sin, and when sin reaches maturity it gives birth to death.

Do not be deceived, my beloved brothers and sisters: all good giving and every perfect gift is from above, coming down from the Father of lights, with whom there is no alteration or shadow caused by change. He willed to give us birth by the word of truth that we may be a kind of firstfruits of his creatures.

RESPONSORIAL PSALM *Psalm 94:12–13a, 14–15, 18–19*

R. (12a) Blessed the man you instruct, O Lord.

Blessed the man whom you instruct, O LORD, / whom by your law you teach, / Giving him rest from evil days. **R.**

For the LORD will not cast off his people, / nor abandon his inheritance; / But judgment shall again be with justice, / and all the upright of heart shall follow it. **R.**

When I say, "My foot is slipping," / your mercy, O LORD, sustains me; / When cares abound within me, / your comfort gladdens my soul. **R.**

ALLELUIA *John 14:23*

R. Alleluia, alleluia. Whoever loves me will keep my word, says the Lord; and my Father will love him and we will come to him. **R.**

GOSPEL *Mark 8:14–21*

The disciples had forgotten to bring bread, and they had only one loaf with them in the boat. Jesus enjoined them, "Watch out, guard against the leaven of the Pharisees and the leaven of Herod." They concluded among themselves that it was because they had no bread. When he became aware of this he said to them, "Why do you conclude that it is because you have no bread? Do you not yet understand or comprehend? Are your hearts hardened? Do you have eyes and not see, ears and not hear? And do you not remember, when I broke the five loaves for the five thousand, how many wicker baskets full of fragments you picked up?" They answered him, "Twelve." "When I broke the seven loaves for the four thousand, how many full baskets of fragments did you pick up?" They answered him, "Seven." He said to them, "Do you still not understand?"

FEBRUARY 19, WEDNESDAY OF WEEK 6; ST. BARBATUS

FIRST READING *James 1:19–27*

Know this, my dear brothers and sisters: everyone should be quick to hear, slow to speak, slow to anger for anger does not accomplish the righteousness of God. Therefore, put away all filth and evil excess and humbly welcome the word that has been planted in you and is able to save your souls.

Be doers of the word and not hearers only, deluding yourselves. For if anyone is a hearer of the word and not a doer, he is like a man who looks at his own face in a mirror. He sees himself, then goes off and promptly forgets what he looked like. But the one who peers into the perfect law of freedom and perseveres, and is not a hearer who forgets but a doer who acts; such a one shall be blessed in what he does.

If anyone thinks he is religious and does not bridle his tongue but deceives his heart, his religion is vain. Religion that is pure and undefiled before God and the Father is this: to care for orphans and widows in their affliction and to keep oneself unstained by the world.

RESPONSORIAL PSALM *Psalm 15:2–3a, 3bc–4ab, 5*

R. (1b) Who shall live on your holy mountain, O Lord?

He who walks blamelessly and does justice; / who thinks the truth in his heart and slanders not with his tongue. **R.**

Who harms not his fellow man, / nor takes up a reproach against his neighbor; / By whom the reprobate is despised, / while he honors those who fear the LORD. **R.**

Who lends not his money at usury / and accepts no bribe against the innocent. / He who does these things shall never be disturbed. **R.**

ALLELUIA *See Ephesians 1:17–18*

R. Alleluia, alleluia. May the Father of our Lord Jesus Christ enlighten the eyes of our hearts, that we may know what is the hope that belongs to his call. **R.**

GOSPEL *Mark 8:22–26*

When Jesus and his disciples arrived at Bethsaida, people brought to him a blind man and begged Jesus to touch him. He took the blind man by the hand and led him outside the village. Putting spittle on his eyes he laid his hands on the man and asked, "Do you see anything?" Looking up the man replied, "I see people looking like trees and walking." Then he laid hands on the man's eyes a second time and he saw clearly; his sight was restored and he could see everything distinctly. Then he sent him home and said, "Do not even go into the village."

FEBRUARY 20, THURSDAY OF WEEK 6; ST. MARGARET OF CORTONA

FIRST READING   *James 2:1–9*

My brothers and sisters, show no partiality as you adhere to the faith in our glorious Lord Jesus Christ. For if a man with gold rings and fine clothes comes into your assembly, and a poor person with shabby clothes also comes in, and you pay attention to the one wearing the fine clothes and say, "Sit here, please," while you say to the poor one, "Stand there," or "Sit at my feet," have you not made distinctions among yourselves and become judges with evil designs?

Listen, my beloved brothers and sisters. Did not God choose those who are poor in the world to be rich in faith and heirs of the Kingdom that he promised to those who love him? But you dishonored the poor. Are not the rich oppressing you? And do they themselves not haul you off to court? Is it not they who blaspheme the noble name that was invoked over you? However, if you fulfill the royal law according to the Scripture, *You shall love your neighbor as yourself*, you are doing well. But if you show partiality, you commit sin, and are convicted by the law as transgressors.

RESPONSORIAL PSALM   *Psalm 34:2–3, 4–5, 6–7*

R. (7a) The Lord hears the cry of the poor.

I will bless the LORD at all times; / His praise shall be ever in my mouth. / Let my soul glory in the LORD; / the lowly will hear me and be glad. **R.**

Glorify the LORD with me, / let us together extol his name. / I sought the LORD, and He answered me / and delivered me from all my fears. **R.**

Look to him that you may be radiant with joy, / and your faces may not blush with shame. / When the poor one called out, the LORD heard, / and from all his distress He saved him. **R.**

ALLELUIA   *See John 6:63c, 68c*

R. Alleluia, alleluia. Your words, Lord, are Spirit and life; you have the words of everlasting life. **R.**

GOSPEL   *Mark 8:27–33*

Jesus and his disciples set out for the villages of Caesarea Philippi. Along the way he asked his disciples, "Who do people say that I am?" They said in reply, "John the Baptist, others Elijah, still others one of the prophets." And he asked them, "But who do you say that I am?" Peter said to him in reply, "You are the Christ." Then he warned them not to tell anyone about him.

He began to teach them that the Son of Man must suffer greatly and be rejected by the elders, the chief priests, and the scribes, and be killed, and rise after three days. He spoke this openly. Then Peter took him aside and began to rebuke him. At this he turned around and, looking at his disciples, rebuked Peter and said, "Get behind me, Satan. You are thinking not as God does, but as human beings do."

FEBRUARY 21, FRIDAY OF WEEK 6; ST. PETER DAMIAN

FIRST READING *James 2:14–24, 26*

What good is it, my brothers and sisters, if someone says he has faith but does not have works? Can that faith save him? If a brother or sister has nothing to wear and has no food for the day, and one of you says to them, "Go in peace, keep warm, and eat well," but you do not give them the necessities of the body, what good is it? So also faith of itself, if it does not have works, is dead.

Indeed someone might say, "You have faith and I have works." Demonstrate your faith to me without works, and I will demonstrate my faith to you from my works. You believe that God is one. You do well. Even the demons believe that and tremble. Do you want proof, you ignoramus, that faith without works is useless? Was not Abraham our father justified by works when he offered his son Isaac upon the altar? You see that faith was active along with his works, and faith was completed by the works. Thus the Scripture was fulfilled that says, *Abraham believed God, and it was credited to him as righteousness, and he was called the friend of God.* See how a person is justified by works and not by faith alone. For just as a body without a spirit is dead, so also faith without works is dead.

RESPONSORIAL PSALM *Psalm 112:1–2, 3–4, 5–6*

R. (see 1b) Blessed the man who greatly delights in the Lord's commands.

Blessed the man who fears the LORD, / who greatly delights in his commands. / His posterity shall be mighty upon the earth; / the upright generation shall be blessed. **R.**
Wealth and riches shall be in his house; / his generosity shall endure forever. / Light shines through the darkness for the upright; / he is gracious and merciful and just. **R.**
Well for the man who is gracious and lends, / who conducts his affairs with justice; / He shall never be moved; / the just man shall be in everlasting remembrance. **R.**

ALLELUIA *John 15:15b*

R. Alleluia, alleluia. I call you my friends, says the Lord, for I have made known to you all that the Father has told me. **R.**

GOSPEL *Mark 8:34—9:1*

Jesus summoned the crowd with his disciples and said to them, "Whoever wishes to come after me must deny himself, take up his cross, and follow me. For whoever wishes to save his life will lose it, but whoever loses his life for my sake and that of the Gospel will save it. What profit is there for one to gain the whole world and forfeit his life? What could one give in exchange for his life? Whoever is ashamed of me and of my words in this faithless and sinful generation, the Son of Man will be ashamed of when he comes in his Father's glory with the holy angels."

He also said to them, "Amen, I say to you, there are some standing here who will not taste death until they see that the Kingdom of God has come in power."

FEBRUARY 22, SATURDAY OF WEEK 6; CHAIR OF SAINT PETER

First Reading   1 Pt 5:1-4

Beloved: I exhort the presbyters among you, as a fellow presbyter and witness to the sufferings of Christ and one who has a share in the glory to be revealed. Tend the flock of God in your midst, overseeing not by constraint but willingly, as God would have it, not for shameful profit but eagerly. Do not lord it over those assigned to you, but be examples to the flock. And when the chief Shepherd is revealed, you will receive the unfading crown of glory.

RESPONSORIAL PSALM   *Psalm 23:1—3a, 3b—4, 5, 6 (1) (4ab)*
R. The Lord is my shepherd; there is nothing I shall want.
The LORD is my shepherd; I shall not want. **/** In verdant pastures he gives me repose; **/** beside restful waters he leads me; **/** he refreshes my soul. **R.**
He guides me in right paths **/** for his name's sake. **/** Even though I walk in the dark valley **/** I fear no evil; for you are at my side **/** with your rod and your staff **/** that give me courage. **R.**
You spread the table before me **/** in the sight of my foes; **/** You anoint my head with oil; **/** my cup overflows. **R.**
Only goodness and kindness follow me **/** all the days of my life; **/** and I shall dwell in the house of the LORD **/** for years to come. **R.**

ALLELUIA   **Mt 16:18**
R. Alleluia, alleluia. You are Peter, and upon this rock I will build my Church; the gates of the netherworld shall not prevail against it. **R.**

Gospel   Mt 16:13-19
When Jesus went into the region of Caesarea Philippi he asked his disciples, "Who do people say that the Son of Man is?" They replied, "Some say John the Baptist, others Elijah, still others Jeremiah or one of the prophets." He said to them, "But who do you say that I am?" Simon Peter said in reply, "You are the Christ, the Son of the living God." Jesus said to him in reply, "Blessed are you, Simon son of Jonah. For flesh and blood has not revealed this to you, but my heavenly Father. And so I say to you, you are Peter, and upon this rock I will build my Church, and the gates of the netherworld shall not prevail against it. I will give you the keys to the Kingdom of heaven. Whatever you bind on earth shall be bound in heaven; and whatever you loose on earth shall be loosed in heaven."

FEBRUARY 23 7TH SUNDAY IN ORDINARY TIME; ST. POLYCARP
FIRST READING   *Leviticus 19:1—2, 17—18*
The LORD said to Moses, "Speak to the whole Israelite community and tell them: Be holy, for I, the LORD, your God, am holy.

"You shall not bear hatred for your brother or sister in your heart. Though you may have to reprove your fellow citizen, do not incur sin because of him. Take no revenge and cherish no grudge against any of your people. You shall love your neighbor as yourself. I am the LORD."

RESPONSORIAL PSALM *Psalm 103:1—2, 3—4, 8, 10, 12—13 (8a)*
R. The Lord is kind and merciful.
Bless the LORD, O my soul; **/** and all my being, bless His holy name. **/** Bless the LORD, O my soul, **/** and forget not all his benefits. **R.**
He pardons all your iniquities, heals all your ills. **/** He redeems your life from destruction, **/** crowns you with kindness and compassion. **R.**
Merciful and gracious is the LORD, **/** slow to anger and abounding in kindness. **/** Not according to our sins does He deal with us, **/** nor does He requite us according to our crimes. **R.**
As far as the east is from the west, **/** so far has he put our transgressions from us. **/** As a father has compassion on his children, **/** so the LORD has compassion on those who fear him. **R.**

SECOND READING *1 Corinthians 3:16—23*
Brothers and sisters: Do you not know that you are the temple of God, and that the Spirit of God dwells in you? If anyone destroys God's temple, God will destroy that person; for the temple of God, which you are, is holy.

Let no one deceive himself. If any one among you considers himself wise in this age, let him become a fool, so as to become wise. For the wisdom of this world is foolishness in the eyes of God, for it is written: *God catches the wise in their own ruses,* and again: *The Lord knows the thoughts of the wise, that they are vain.*

So let no one boast about human beings, for everything belongs to you, Paul or Apollos or Cephas, or the world or life or death, or the present or the future: all belong to you, and you to Christ, and Christ to God.

ALLELUIA *1 John 2:5*
R. Alleluia, alleluia. Whoever keeps the word of Christ, the love of God is truly perfected in him. **R.**

GOSPEL *Matthew 5:38—48*
Jesus said to his disciples: *"You have heard that it was said, An eye for an eye and a tooth for a tooth.* But I say to you, offer no resistance to one who is evil. When someone strikes you on your right cheek, turn the other one as well. If anyone wants to go to law with you over your tunic, hand over your cloak as well. Should anyone press you into service for one mile, go for two miles. Give to the one who asks of you, and do not turn your back on one who wants to borrow.

"You have heard that it was said, *You shall love your neighbor and hate your enemy.* But I say to you, love your enemies and pray for those who persecute you, that you may be children of your heavenly Father, for he makes his sun rise on the bad and the good, and causes rain to fall on the just and the unjust. For if you love those who love you, what recompense will you have? Do not the tax collectors do the same? And if you greet your brothers only, what is unusual about that? Do not the pagans do the same? So be perfect, just as your heavenly Father is perfect."

FEBRUARY 24, MONDAY OF WEEK 7; BLESSED JOSEFA NAVAL GIRBES

FIRST READING *James 3:13–18*

Beloved: Who among you is wise and understanding? Let him show his works by a good life in the humility that comes from wisdom. But if you have bitter jealousy and selfish ambition in your hearts, do not boast and be false to the truth. Wisdom of this kind does not come down from above but is earthly, unspiritual, demonic. For where jealousy and selfish ambition exist, there is disorder and every foul practice. But the wisdom from above is first of all pure, then peaceable, gentle, compliant, full of mercy and good fruits, without inconstancy or insincerity. And the fruit of righteousness is sown in peace for those who cultivate peace.

RESPONSORIAL PSALM *Psalm 19:8, 9, 10, 15*

R. (9a) The precepts of the Lord give joy to the heart.

The law of the LORD is perfect, / refreshing the soul; The decree of the LORD is trustworthy, / giving wisdom to the simple. **R.**

The precepts of the LORD are right, / rejoicing the heart; / The command of the LORD is clear, / enlightening the eye. **R.**

The fear of the LORD is pure, / enduring forever; / The ordinances of the LORD are true, / all of them just. **R.**

Let the words of my mouth and the thought of my heart / find favor before you, O LORD, / my rock and my redeemer. **R.**

ALLELUIA *See 2 Timothy 1:10*

R. Alleluia, alleluia. Our Savior Jesus Christ has destroyed death and brought life to light through the Gospel. **R.**

GOSPEL *Mark 9:14–29*

As Jesus came down from the mountain with Peter, James, John and approached the other disciples, they saw a large crowd around them and scribes arguing with them. Immediately on seeing him, the whole crowd was utterly amazed. They ran up to him and greeted him. He asked them, "What are you arguing about with them?" Someone from the crowd answered him, "Teacher, I have brought to you my son possessed by a mute spirit. Wherever it seizes him, it throws him down; he foams at the mouth, grinds his teeth, and becomes rigid. I asked your disciples to drive it out, but they were unable to do so." He said to them in reply, "O faithless generation, how long will I be with you? How long will I endure you? Bring him to me." They brought the boy to him. And when he saw him, the spirit immediately threw the boy into convulsions. As he fell to the ground, he began to roll around and foam at the mouth. Then he questioned his father, "How long has this been happening to him?" He replied, "Since childhood. It has often thrown him into fire and into water to kill him. But if you can do anything, have compassion on us and help us." Jesus said to him, "'If you can!' Everything is possible to one who has faith." Then the boy's father cried out, "I do believe, help my unbelief!" Jesus, on seeing a crowd rapidly gathering, rebuked the unclean spirit and said to it, "Mute and deaf spirit, I command you: come out of him and never enter him again!" Shouting and throwing the boy into convulsions, it came out. He became like a corpse, which caused many to say, "He is dead!" But Jesus took him by the hand, raised him, and he stood up. When he entered the house, his disciples asked him in private, "Why could we not drive the spirit out?" He said to them, "This kind can only come out through prayer."

FEBRUARY 25 TUESDAY OF WEEK 7; ST. CAESARIUS OF NAZIANZEN

FIRST READING   *James 4:1–10*

Beloved: Where do the wars and where do the conflicts among you come from? Is it not from your passions that make war within your members? You covet but do not possess. You kill and envy but you cannot obtain; you fight and wage war. You do not possess because you do not ask. You ask but do not receive, because you ask wrongly, to spend it on your passions. Adulterers! Do you not know that to be a lover of the world means enmity with God? Therefore, whoever wants to be a lover of the world makes himself an enemy of God. Or do you suppose that the Scripture speaks without meaning when it says, *The spirit that he has made to dwell in us tends toward jealousy?* But he bestows a greater grace; therefore, it says: *God resists the proud, but gives grace to the humble.*

So submit yourselves to God. Resist the Devil, and he will flee from you. Draw near to God, and he will draw near to you. Cleanse your hands, you sinners, and purify your hearts, you of two minds. Begin to lament, to mourn, to weep. Let your laughter be turned into mourning and your joy into dejection. Humble yourselves before the Lord and he will exalt you.

RESPONSORIAL PSALM   *Psalm 55:7–8, 9–10a, 10b–11a, 23*

R. (23a) Throw your cares on the Lord, and he will support you.
And I say, "Had I but wings like a dove, / I would fly away and be at rest. / Far away I would flee; / I would lodge in the wilderness." **R.**
"I would wait for him who saves me / from the violent storm and the tempest." / Engulf them, O Lord; divide their counsels. **R.**
In the city I see violence and strife, / day and night they prowl about upon its walls. **R.** Cast your care upon the LORD, / and He will support you; / never will He permit the just man to be disturbed. **R.**

ALLELUIA   *Galatians 6:14*

R. Alleluia, alleluia. May I never boast except in the Cross of our Lord Jesus Christ, through which the world has been crucified to me and I to the world. **R.**

GOSPEL   *Mark 9:30–37*

Jesus and his disciples left from there and began a journey through Galilee, but he did not wish anyone to know about it. He was teaching his disciples and telling them, "The Son of

Man is to be handed over to men and they will kill him, and three days after his death the Son of Man will rise." But they did not understand the saying, and they were afraid to question him.

They came to Capernaum and, once inside the house, he began to ask them, "What were you arguing about on the way?" But they remained silent. For they had been discussing among themselves on the way who was the greatest. Then he sat down, called the Twelve, and said to them, "If anyone wishes to be first, he shall be the last of all and the servant of all." Taking a child, he placed it in their midst, and putting his arms around it, he said to them, "Whoever receives one child such as this in my name, receives me; and whoever receives me, receives not me but the One who sent me."

FEBRUARY 26, ASH WEDNESDAY; ST. PORPHYRY

FIRST READING   *Joel 2:12–18*

Even now, says the LORD, return to me with your whole heart, with fasting, and weeping, and mourning; Rend your hearts, not your garments, and return to the LORD, your God. For gracious and merciful is he, slow to anger, rich in kindness, and relenting in punishment. Perhaps he will again relent and leave behind him a blessing, Offerings and libations for the LORD, your God.

Blow the trumpet in Zion! proclaim a fast, call an assembly; Gather the people, notify the congregation; Assemble the elders, gather the children and the infants at the breast; Let the bridegroom quit his room and the bride her chamber. Between the porch and the altar let the priests, the ministers of the LORD, weep, And say, "Spare, O LORD, your people, and make not your heritage a reproach, with the nations ruling over them! Why should they say among the peoples, 'Where is their God?'"

Then the LORD was stirred to concern for his land and took pity on his people.

RESPONSORIAL PSALM   *Psalm 51:3–4, 5–6ab, 12–13, 14 and 17*
R. (see 3a) Be merciful, O Lord, for we have sinned.
Have mercy on me, O God, in your goodness; / in the greatness of your compassion / wipe out my offense. / Thoroughly wash me from my guilt and of my sin cleanse me. **R.**
For I acknowledge my offense, / and my sin is before me always: / "Against you only have I sinned, / and done what is evil in your sight." **R.**
A clean heart create for me, O God, / and a steadfast spirit renew within me. / Cast me not out from your presence, / and your Holy Spirit take not from me. **R.**
Give me back the joy of your salvation, / and a willing spirit sustain in me. / O Lord, open my lips, / and my mouth shall proclaim your praise. **R.**

SECOND READING   *2 Corinthians 5:20–6:2*

Brothers and sisters: We are ambassadors for Christ, as if God were appealing through us. We implore you on behalf of Christ, be reconciled to God. For our sake he made him to be sin who did not know sin, so that we might become the righteousness of God in him.

Working together, then, we appeal to you not to receive the grace of God in vain. For he says:

In an acceptable time I heard you, and on the day of salvation I helped you. Behold, now is a very acceptable time; behold, now is the day of salvation.

VERSE BEFORE THE GOSPEL
See Psalm 95:8

R. Praise to you, O Christ, King of Eternal Glory! If today you hear his voice, harden not your hearts. **R.**

GOSPEL
Matthew 6:1–6, 16–18

Jesus said to his disciples: "Take care not to perform righteous deeds in order that people may see them; otherwise, you will have no recompense from your heavenly Father. When you give alms, do not blow a trumpet before you, as the hypocrites do in the synagogues and in the streets to win the praise of others. Amen, I say to you, they have received their reward. But when you give alms, do not let your left hand know what your right is doing, so that your almsgiving may be secret. And your Father who sees in secret will repay you.

"When you pray, do not be like the hypocrites, who love to stand and pray in the synagogues and on street corners so that others may see them. Amen, I say to you, they have received their reward. But when you pray, go to your inner room, close the door, and pray to your Father in secret. And your Father who sees in secret will repay you.

"When you fast, do not look gloomy like the hypocrites. They neglect their appearance, so that they may appear to others to be fasting. Amen, I say to you, they have received their reward. But when you fast, anoint your head and wash your face, so that you may not appear to be fasting, except to your Father who is hidden. And your Father who sees what is hidden will repay you."

FEBRUARY 27, THURSDAY AFTER ASH WEDNESDAY; ST. GABRIEL POSSENTI
FIRST READING
Deuteronomy 30:15–20

Moses said to the people: "Today I have set before you life and prosperity, death and doom. If you obey the commandments of the LORD, your God, which I enjoin on you today, loving him, and walking in his ways, and keeping his commandments, statutes and decrees, you will live and grow numerous, and the LORD, your God, will bless you in the land you are entering to occupy. If, however, you turn away your hearts and will not listen, but are led astray and adore and serve other gods, I tell you now that you will certainly perish; you will not have a long life on the land that you are crossing the Jordan to enter and occupy. I call heaven and earth today to witness against you: I have set before you life and death, the blessing and the curse. Choose life, then, that you and your descendants may live, by loving the LORD, your God, heeding his voice, and holding fast to him. For that will mean life for you, a long life for you to live on the land that the LORD swore he would give to your fathers Abraham, Isaac and Jacob.

RESPONSORIAL PSALM   *Psalm 1:1–2, 3, 4 and 6*

R. (40:5a) Blessed are they who hope in the Lord.

Blessed the man who follows not the counsel of the wicked / Nor walks in the way of sinners, / nor sits in the company of the insolent, / But delights in the law of the LORD / and meditates on his law day and night. **R.**

He is like a tree planted near running water, / That yields its fruit in due season, / and whose leaves never fade. / Whatever he does, prospers. **R.**

Not so the wicked, not so; / they are like chaff which the wind drives away. / For the LORD watches over the way of the just, / but the way of the wicked vanishes. **R.**

VERSE BEFORE THE GOSPEL   *Matthew 4:17*

R. Praise to you, O Christ, King of Eternal Glory! Repent, says the Lord; the Kingdom of heaven is at hand. **R.**

GOSPEL   *Luke 9:22–25*

Jesus said to his disciples: "The Son of Man must suffer greatly and be rejected by the elders, the chief priests, and the scribes, and be killed and on the third day be raised."

Then he said to all, "If anyone wishes to come after me, he must deny himself and take up his cross daily and follow me. For whoever wishes to save his life will lose it, but whoever loses his life for my sake will save it. What profit is there for one to gain the whole world yet lose or forfeit himself?"

FEBRUARY 28, FRIDAY AFTER ASH WEDNESDAY; ST. ROMANUS AND ST. LUPICINUS

FIRST READING   *Isaiah 58:1–9a*

Thus says the Lord GOD: Cry out full–throated and unsparingly, lift up your voice like a trumpet blast; Tell my people their wickedness, and the house of Jacob their sins. They seek me day after day, and desire to know my ways, Like a nation that has done what is just and not abandoned the law of their God; They ask me to declare what is due them, pleased to gain access to God. "Why do we fast, and you do not see it? afflict ourselves, and you take no note of it?"

Lo, on your fast day you carry out your own pursuits, and drive all your laborers. Yes, your fast ends in quarreling and fighting, striking with wicked claw. Would that today you might fast so as to make your voice heard on high! Is this the manner of fasting I wish, of keeping a day of penance: That a man bow his head like a reed and lie in sackcloth and ashes? Do you call this a fast, a day acceptable to the LORD? This, rather, is the fasting that I wish: releasing those bound unjustly, untying the thongs of the yoke; Setting free the oppressed, breaking every yoke; Sharing your bread with the hungry, sheltering the oppressed and the homeless; Clothing the naked when you see them, and not turning your back on your own. Then your light shall break forth like the dawn, and your wound shall quickly be healed; Your vindication shall go before you, and the glory of the LORD shall be your rear guard. Then you shall call, and the LORD will answer, you shall cry for help, and he will say: Here I am!

RESPONSORIAL PSALM   *Psalm 51:3–4, 5–6ab, 18–19*

R. (19b) A heart contrite and humbled, O God, you will not spurn.

Have mercy on me, O God, in your goodness; / in the greatness of your compassion wipe out my offense. / Thoroughly wash me from my guilt / and of my sin cleanse me. **R.**

For I acknowledge my offense, and my sin is before me always: / "Against you only have I sinned, / and done what is evil in your sight." **R.**

For you are not pleased with sacrifices; / should I offer a burnt offering, you would not accept it. / My sacrifice, O God, is a contrite spirit; / a heart contrite and humbled, O God, you will not spurn. **R.**

VERSE BEFORE THE GOSPEL   *See Amos 5:14*

R. Praise to you, O Christ, King of Eternal Glory! Seek good and not evil so that you may live, and the LORD will be with you. **R.**

GOSPEL   *Matthew 9:14–15*

The disciples of John approached Jesus and said, "Why do we and the Pharisees fast much, but your disciples do not fast?" Jesus answered them, "Can the wedding guests mourn as long as the bridegroom is with them? The days will come when the bridegroom is taken away from them, and then they will fast."

FEBRUARY 29, SATURDAY AFTER ASH WEDNESDAY MARY QUEEN OF APOSTLES

FIRST READING   *Isaiah 58:9b–14*

Thus says the LORD: If you remove from your midst oppression, false accusation and malicious speech; If you bestow your bread on the hungry and satisfy the afflicted; Then light shall rise for you in the darkness, and the gloom shall become for you like midday; Then the LORD will guide you always and give you plenty even on the parched land. He will renew your strength, and you shall be like a watered garden, like a spring whose water never fails. The ancient ruins shall be rebuilt for your sake, and the foundations from ages past you shall raise up; "Repairer of the breach," they shall call you, "Restorer of ruined homesteads."

If you hold back your foot on the sabbath from following your own pursuits on my holy day; If you call the sabbath a delight, and the LORD's holy day honorable; If you honor it by not following your ways, seeking your own interests, or speaking with malice Then you shall delight in the LORD, and I will make you ride on the heights of the earth; I will nourish you with the heritage of Jacob, your father, for the mouth of the LORD has spoken.

RESPONSORIAL PSALM   *Psalm 86:1–2, 3–4, 5–6*

R. (11ab) Teach me your way, O Lord, that I may walk in your truth.

Incline your ear, O LORD; / answer me, for I am afflicted and poor. / Keep my life, for I am devoted to you; / save your servant who trusts in you. / You are my God. **R.**

Have mercy on me, O Lord, / for to you I call all the day. / Gladden the soul of your servant, / for to you, O Lord, I lift up my soul. **R.**

For you, O Lord, are good and forgiving, / abounding in kindness to all who call upon you. / Hearken, O LORD, to my prayer / and attend to the sound of my pleading. **R.**

VERSE BEFORE THE GOSPEL   *Ezekiel 33:11*

R. Praise to you, O Christ, King of Eternal Glory! I take no pleasure in the death of the wicked man, says the Lord, but rather in his conversion, that he may live. **R.**

GOSPEL   *Luke 5:27–32*

Jesus saw a tax collector named Levi sitting at the customs post. He said to him, "Follow me." And leaving everything behind, he got up and followed him. Then Levi gave a great banquet for him in his house, and a large crowd of tax collectors and others were at table with them. The Pharisees and their scribes complained to his disciples, saying, "Why do you eat and drink with tax collectors and sinners?" Jesus said to them in reply, "Those who are healthy do not need a physician, but the sick do. I have not come to call the righteous to repentance but sinners."

5   MARCH

MARCH 1, 1ST SUNDAY OF LENT; ST. DAVID OF WALES

FIRST READING   *Genesis 2:7—9; 3:1—7*

The LORD God formed man out of the clay of the ground and blew into his nostrils the breath of life, and so man became a living being.

Then the LORD God planted a garden in Eden, in the east, and placed there the man whom he had formed. Out of the ground the LORD God made various trees grow that were delightful to look at and good for food, with the tree of life in the middle of the garden and the tree of the knowledge of good and evil.

Now the serpent was the most cunning of all the animals that the LORD God had made. The serpent asked the woman, "Did God really tell you not to eat from any of the trees in the garden?" The woman answered the serpent: "We may eat of the fruit of the trees in the garden; it is only about the fruit of the tree in the middle of the garden that God said, 'You shall not eat it or even touch it, lest you die.'" But the serpent said to the woman: "You certainly will not die! No, God knows well that the moment you eat of it your eyes will be opened and you will be like gods who know what is good and what is evil." The woman saw that the tree was good for food, pleasing to the eyes, and desirable for gaining wisdom. So she took some of its fruit and ate it; and she also gave some to her husband, who was with her, and he ate it. Then the eyes of both of them were opened, and they realized that they were naked; so they sewed fig leaves together and made loincloths for themselves.

RESPONSORIAL PSALM: *Psalm 51:3—4, 5—6, 12—13, 17 (see 3a)*

R. Be merciful, O Lord, for we have sinned.

Have mercy on me, O God, in your goodness; / in the greatness of your compassion wipe out my offense. / Thoroughly wash me from my guilt / and of my sin cleanse me. **R.**

For I acknowledge my offense, / and my sin is before me always: / "Against you only have I sinned, / and done what is evil in your sight." **R.**

A clean heart create for me, O God, / and a steadfast spirit renew within me. / Cast me not out from your presence, / and your Holy Spirit take not from me. **R.**

Give me back the joy of your salvation, / and a willing spirit sustain in me. / O Lord, open my lips, / and my mouth shall proclaim your praise. **R.**

SECOND READING   *Longer Form Romans 5:12—19*

Brothers and sisters: Through one man sin entered the world, and through sin, death, and thus death came to all men, inasmuch as all sinned— for up to the time of the law, sin was in the world, though sin is not accounted when there is no law. But death reigned from Adam to Moses, even over those who did not sin after the pattern of the trespass of Adam, who is the type of the one who was to come.

But the gift is not like the transgression. For if by the transgression of the one, the many died, how much more did the grace of God and the gracious gift of the one man Jesus Christ overflow for the many. And the gift is not like the result of the one who sinned. For after one sin there was the judgment that brought condemnation; but the gift, after many transgressions, brought acquittal. For if, by the transgression of the one, death came to reign through that one, how much more will those who receive the abundance of grace and of the gift of justification come to reign in life through the one Jesus Christ. In conclusion, just as through one transgression condemnation came upon all, so, through one righteous act, acquittal and life came to all. For just as through the disobedience of the one man the many were made sinners, so, through the obedience of the one, the many will be made righteous.

SHORTER FORM   *Romans 5:12, 17—19*

Brothers and sisters: Through one man sin entered the world, and through sin, death, and thus death came to all men, inasmuch as all sinned.

For if, by the transgression of the one, death came to reign through that one, how much more will those who receive the abundance of grace and of the gift of justification come to reign in life through the one Jesus Christ. In conclusion, just as through one transgression condemnation came upon all, so, through one righteous act, acquittal and life came to all. For just as through the disobedience of the one man the many were made sinners, so, through the obedience of the one, the many will be made righteous.

VERSE BEFORE THE GOSPEL   *Matthew 4:4b*

R. Praise to you, O Christ, King of Eternal Glory! One does not live on bread alone, but on every word that comes forth from the mouth of God. **R.**

GOSPEL   *Matthew 4:1—11*

At that time Jesus was led by the Spirit into the desert to be tempted by the devil. He fasted for forty days and forty nights, and afterwards he was hungry. The tempter approached and said to him, "If you are the Son of God, command that these stones become loaves of bread." He said in reply, "It is written: *One does not live on bread alone, but on every word that comes forth from the mouth of God."*

Then the devil took him to the holy city, and made him stand on the parapet of the temple, and said to him, "If you are the Son of God, throw yourself down. For it is written: *He will command his angels concerning you and with their hands they will support you, lest you dash your foot against a stone."* Jesus answered him, "Again it is written, *You shall not put the Lord, your God, to the test."* Then the devil took him up to a very high mountain, and showed him all the kingdoms of the world in their magnificence, and he said to him, "All these I shall give to you, if you will prostrate yourself and worship me." At this, Jesus said to him, "Get away, Satan! It is written: *The Lord, your God, shall you worship and him alone shall you serve."*

Then the devil left him and, behold, angels came and ministered to him.

MARCH 2, 1ST WEEK OF LENT – MONDAY; BLESSED AGNES OF BOHEMIA
FIRST READING *Leviticus 19:1–2, 11–18*

The LORD said to Moses, "Speak to the whole assembly of the children of Israel and tell them: Be holy, for I, the LORD, your God, am holy.

"You shall not steal. You shall not lie or speak falsely to one another. You shall not swear falsely by my name, thus profaning the name of your God. I am the LORD.

"You shall not defraud or rob your neighbor. You shall not withhold overnight the wages of your day laborer. You shall not curse the deaf, or put a stumbling block in front of the blind, but you shall fear your God. I am the LORD.

"You shall not act dishonestly in rendering judgment. Show neither partiality to the weak nor deference to the mighty, but judge your fellow men justly. You shall not go about spreading slander among your kin; nor shall you stand by idly when your neighbor's life is at stake. I am the LORD.

"You shall not bear hatred for your brother in your heart. Though you may have to reprove him, do not incur sin because of him. Take no revenge and cherish no grudge against your fellow countrymen. You shall love your neighbor as yourself. I am the LORD."

RESPONSORIAL PSALM *Psalm 19:8, 9, 10, 15*
R. (John 6:63b) Your words, Lord, are Spirit and life.
The law of the LORD is perfect, / refreshing the soul. / The decree of the LORD is trustworthy, / giving wisdom to the simple. **R.**
The precepts of the LORD are right, rejoicing the heart. / The command of the LORD is clear, / enlightening the eye. **R.**
The fear of the LORD is pure, / enduring forever; / the ordinances of the LORD are true, / all of them just. R.
Let the words of my mouth and the thought of my heart / find favor before you, O LORD, / my rock and my redeemer. **R.**
VERSE BEFORE THE GOSPEL *2 Corinthians 6:2b*

R. Praise to you, O Christ, King of Eternal Glory! Behold, now is a very acceptable time; behold, now is the day of salvation. **R.**

GOSPEL   *Matthew 25:31–46*

Jesus said to his disciples: "When the Son of Man comes in his glory, and all the angels with him, he will sit upon his glorious throne, and all the nations will be assembled before him. And he will separate them one from another, as a shepherd separates the sheep from the goats. He will place the sheep on his right and the goats on his left. Then the king will say to those on his right, 'Come, you who are blessed by my Father. Inherit the kingdom prepared for you from the foundation of the world. For I was hungry and you gave me food, I was thirsty and you gave me drink, a stranger and you welcomed me, naked and you clothed me, ill and you cared for me, in prison and you visited me.' Then the righteous will answer him and say, 'Lord, when did we see you hungry and feed you, or thirsty and give you drink? When did we see you a stranger and welcome you, or naked and clothe you? When did we see you ill or in prison, and visit you?' And the king will say to them in reply, 'Amen, I say to you, whatever you did for one of these least brothers of mine, you did for me.' Then he will say to those on his left, 'Depart from me, you accursed, into the eternal fire prepared for the Devil and his angels. For I was hungry and you gave me no food, I was thirsty and you gave me no drink, a stranger and you gave me no welcome, naked and you gave me no clothing, ill and in prison, and you did not care for me.' Then they will answer and say, 'Lord, when did we see you hungry or thirsty or a stranger or naked or ill or in prison, and not minister to your needs?' He will answer them, 'Amen, I say to you, what you did not do for one of these least ones, you did not do for me.' And these will go off to eternal punishment, but the righteous to eternal life."

MARCH 3, 1ST WEEK OF LENT TUESDAY; ST. KATHARINE DREXEL

FIRST READING   *Isaiah 55:10–11*

Thus says the LORD: Just as from the heavens the rain and snow come down And do not return there till they have watered the earth, making it fertile and fruitful, Giving seed to the one who sows and bread to the one who eats, So shall my word be that goes forth from my mouth; It shall not return to me void, but shall do my will, achieving the end for which I sent it.

RESPONSORIAL PSALM   *Psalm 34:4–5, 6–7, 16–17, 18–19*

R. (18b) From all their distress God rescues the just.
Glorify the LORD with me, / let us together extol his name. / I sought the LORD, and He answered me / and delivered me from all my fears. **R.**
Look to him that you may be radiant with joy, and your faces may not blush with shame. When the poor one called out, the LORD heard, / and from all his distress. / He saved him. **R.**
The LORD has eyes for the just, / and ears for their cry. / The LORD confronts the evildoers, / to destroy remembrance of them from the earth. **R.**

When the just cry out, **/** the LORD hears them, **/** and from all their distress He rescues them. **/** The LORD is close to the brokenhearted; **/** and those who are crushed in spirit he saves. **R.**

VERSE BEFORE THE GOSPEL   *Matthew 4:4b*
R. Praise to you, O Christ, King of Eternal Glory! One does not live on bread alone, but on every word that comes forth from the mouth of God. **R.**

GOSPEL   *Matthew 6:7–15*
Jesus said to his disciples: "In praying, do not babble like the pagans, who think that they will be heard because of their many words. Do not be like them. Your Father knows what you need before you ask him.

"This is how you are to pray: Our Father who art in heaven, hallowed be thy name, thy Kingdom come, thy will be done, on earth as it is in heaven. Give us this day our daily bread; and forgive us our trespasses, as we forgive those who trespass against us; and lead us not into temptation, but deliver us from evil.

"If you forgive men their transgressions, your heavenly Father will forgive you. But if you do not forgive men, neither will your Father forgive your transgressions."

MARCH 4, 1ST WEEK OF LENT – WEDNESDAY; ST. CASIMIR
FIRST READING   *Jonah 3:1–10*
The word of the LORD came to Jonah a second time: "Set out for the great city of Nineveh, and announce to it the message that I will tell you." So Jonah made ready and went to Nineveh, according to the LORD's bidding. Now Nineveh was an enormously large city; it took three days to go through it. Jonah began his journey through the city, and had gone but a single day's walk announcing, "Forty days more and Nineveh shall be destroyed," when the people of Nineveh believed God; they proclaimed a fast and all of them, great and small, put on sackcloth.

When the news reached the king of Nineveh, he rose from his throne, laid aside his robe, covered himself with sackcloth, and sat in the ashes. Then he had this proclaimed throughout Nineveh, by decree of the king and his nobles: "Neither man nor beast, neither cattle nor sheep, shall taste anything; they shall not eat, nor shall they drink water. Man and beast shall be covered with sackcloth and call loudly to God; every man shall turn from his evil way and from the violence he has in hand. Who knows, God may relent and forgive, and withhold his blazing wrath, so that we shall not perish." When God saw by their actions how they turned from their evil way, he repented of the evil that he had threatened to do to them; he did not carry it out.

RESPONSORIAL PSALM   *Psalm 51:3–4, 12–13, 18–19*
R. (19b) A heart contrite and humbled, O God, you will not spurn.
Have mercy on me, O God, in your goodness; **/** in the greatness of your compassion wipe out my offense. **/** Thoroughly wash me from my guilt **/** and of my sin cleanse me. **R.**

A clean heart create for me, O God, / and a steadfast spirit renew within me. / Cast me not out from your presence, / and your Holy Spirit take not from me. **R.**

For you are not pleased with sacrifices; / should I offer a burnt offering, you would not accept it. / My sacrifice, O God, is a contrite spirit; / a heart contrite and humbled, / O God, you will not spurn. **R.**

VERSE BEFORE THE GOSPEL *Joel 2:12–13*

R. Praise to you, O Christ, King of Eternal Glory! Even now, says the LORD, return to me with your whole heart for I am gracious and merciful. **R.**

GOSPEL *Luke 11:29–32*

While still more people gathered in the crowd, Jesus said to them, "This generation is an evil generation; it seeks a sign, but no sign will be given it, except the sign of Jonah. Just as Jonah became a sign to the Ninevites, so will the Son of Man be to this generation. At the judgment the queen of the south will rise with the men of this generation and she will condemn them, because she came from the ends of the earth to hear the wisdom of Solomon, and there is something greater than Solomon here. At the judgment the men of Nineveh will arise with this generation and condemn it, because at the preaching of Jonah they repented, and there is something greater than Jonah here."

MARCH 5, 1ST WEEK OF LENT – THURSDAY; ST. JOHN JOSEPH OF THE CROSS

FIRST READING *Esther C:12, 14–16, 23–25*

Queen Esther, seized with mortal anguish, had recourse to the LORD. She lay prostrate upon the ground, together with her handmaids, from morning until evening, and said: "God of Abraham, God of Isaac, and God of Jacob, blessed are you. Help me, who am alone and have no help but you, for I am taking my life in my hand. As a child I used to hear from the books of my forefathers that you, O LORD, always free those who are pleasing to you. Now help me, who am alone and have no one but you, O LORD, my God.

"And now, come to help me, an orphan. Put in my mouth persuasive words in the presence of the lion and turn his heart to hatred for our enemy, so that he and those who are in league with him may perish. Save us from the hand of our enemies; turn our mourning into gladness and our sorrows into wholeness."

RESPONSORIAL PSALM *Psalm 138:1–2ab, 2cde–3, 7c–8*

R. (3a) Lord, on the day I called for help, you answered me.

I will give thanks to you, O LORD, with all my heart, / for you have heard the words of my mouth; / in the presence of the angels I will sing your praise; / I will worship at your holy temple / and give thanks to your name. **R.**

Because of your kindness and your truth; / for you have made great above all things your name and your promise. / When I called, you answered me; / you built up strength within me. **R.**

Your right hand saves me. / The LORD will complete what He has done for me; / your kindness, O LORD, endures forever; / forsake not the work of your hands. **R.**

VERSE BEFORE THE GOSPEL   *Psalm 51:12a, 14a*

R. Praise to you, O Christ, King of Eternal Glory! A clean heart create for me, God; give me back the joy of your salvation. **R.**

GOSPEL   *Matthew 7:7–12*

Jesus said to his disciples: "Ask and it will be given to you; seek and you will find; knock and the door will be opened to you. For everyone who asks, receives; and the one who seeks, finds; and to the one who knocks, the door will be opened. Which one of you would hand his son a stone when he asked for a loaf of bread, or a snake when he asked for a fish? If you then, who are wicked, know how to give good gifts to your children, how much more will your heavenly Father give good things to those who ask him.

"Do to others whatever you would have them do to you. This is the law and the prophets."

MARCH 6, 1ST WEEK OF LENT - FRIDAY; ST. COLETTE

FIRST READING   *Ezekiel 18:21–28*

Thus says the Lord GOD: If the wicked man turns away from all the sins he committed, if he keeps all my statutes and does what is right and just, he shall surely live, he shall not die. None of the crimes he committed shall be remembered against him; he shall live because of the virtue he has practiced. Do I indeed derive any pleasure from the death of the wicked? says the Lord GOD. Do I not rather rejoice when he turns from his evil way that he may live?

And if the virtuous man turns from the path of virtue to do evil, the same kind of abominable things that the wicked man does, can he do this and still live? None of his virtuous deeds shall be remembered, because he has broken faith and committed sin; because of this, he shall die. You say, "The LORD's way is not fair!" Hear now, house of Israel: Is it my way that is unfair, or rather, are not your ways unfair? When someone virtuous turns away from virtue to commit iniquity, and dies, it is because of the iniquity he committed that he must die. But if the wicked, turning from the wickedness he has committed, does what is right and just, he shall preserve his life; since he has turned away from all the sins that he committed, he shall surely live, he shall not die.

RESPONSORIAL PSALM   *Psalm 130:1–2, 3–4, 5–7a, 7bc–8*

R. (3) If you, O Lord, mark iniquities, who can stand?

Out of the depths I cry to you, O LORD; / LORD, hear my voice! / Let your ears be attentive to my voice in supplication. **R.**

If you, O LORD, mark iniquities, / LORD, who can stand? / But with you is forgiveness, / that you may be revered. **R.**

I trust in the LORD; my soul trusts in his word. / My soul waits for the LORD more than sentinels wait for the dawn. / Let Israel wait for the LORD. **R.**

For with the LORD is kindness / and with him is plenteous redemption; / And He will redeem Israel from all their iniquities. **R.**

VERSE BEFORE THE GOSPEL   *Ezekiel 18:31*

R. Praise to you, O Christ, King of Eternal Glory! Cast away from you all the crimes you have committed, says the Lord, and make for yourselves a new heart and a new spirit. **R.**

GOSPEL
Matthew 5:20–26

Jesus said to his disciples: "I tell you, unless your righteousness surpasses that of the scribes and Pharisees, you will not enter into the Kingdom of heaven.

"You have heard that it was said to your ancestors, *You shall not kill; and whoever kills will be liable to judgment.* But I say to you, whoever is angry with his brother will be liable to judgment, and whoever says to his brother, Raqa, will be answerable to the Sanhedrin, and whoever says, 'You fool,' will be liable to fiery Gehenna. Therefore, if you bring your gift to the altar, and there recall that your brother has anything against you, leave your gift there at the altar, go first and be reconciled with your brother, and then come and offer your gift. Settle with your opponent quickly while on the way to court. Otherwise your opponent will hand you over to the judge, and the judge will hand you over to the guard, and you will be thrown into prison. Amen, I say to you, you will not be released until you have paid the last penny."

MARCH 7, 1ST WEEK OF LENT – SATURDAY; ST. PERPETUA AND ST. FELICITY

FIRST READING *Deuteronomy 26:16–19*

Moses spoke to the people, saying: "This day the LORD, your God, commands you to observe these statutes and decrees. Be careful, then, to observe them with all your heart and with all your soul. Today you are making this agreement with the LORD: he is to be your God and you are to walk in his ways and observe his statutes, commandments and decrees, and to hearken to his voice. And today the LORD is making this agreement with you: you are to be a people peculiarly his own, as he promised you; and provided you keep all his commandments, he will then raise you high in praise and renown and glory above all other nations he has made, and you will be a people sacred to the LORD, your God, as he promised."

RESPONSORIAL PSALM *Psalm 119:1–2, 4–5, 7–8*

R. (1b) Blessed are they who follow the law of the Lord!

Blessed are they whose way is blameless, / who walk in the law of the LORD. / Blessed are they who observe His decrees, / who seek him with all their heart. **R.**

You have commanded that your precepts be diligently kept. / Oh, that I might be firm in the ways of keeping your statutes! **R.**

I will give you thanks with an upright heart, / when I have learned your just ordinances. / I will keep your statutes; / do not utterly forsake me. **R.**

VERSE BEFORE THE GOSPEL *2 Corinthians 6:2b*

R. Praise to you, O Christ, King of Eternal Glory! Behold, now is a very acceptable time; behold, now is the day of salvation. **R.**

GOSPEL   *Matthew 5:43–48*

Jesus said to his disciples: "You have heard that it was said, *You shall love your neighbor and hate your enemy.* But I say to you, love your enemies, and pray for those who persecute you, that you may be children of your heavenly Father, for he makes his sun rise on the bad and the good, and causes rain to fall on the just and the unjust. For if you love those who love you, what recompense will you have? Do not the tax collectors do the same? And if you greet your brothers and sisters only, what is unusual about that? Do not the pagans do the same? So be perfect, just as your heavenly Father is perfect."

MARCH 8, 2ND SUNDAY OF LENT; ST. JOHN OF GOD

FIRST READING   *Genesis 12:1—4a*

The LORD said to Abram: "Go forth from the land of your kinsfolk and from your father's house to a land that I will show you.

"I will make of you a great nation, and I will bless you; I will make your name great, so that you will be a blessing. I will bless those who bless you and curse those who curse you. All the communities of the earth shall find blessing in you." Abram went as the LORD directed him.

RESPONSORIAL PSALM   *Psalm 33:4—5, 18—19, 20, 22 (22)*

R. Lord, let your mercy be on us, as we place our trust in you.

Upright is the word of the LORD, / and all his works are trustworthy. / He loves justice and right; / of the kindness of the LORD the earth is full. **R.**

See, the eyes of the LORD are upon those who fear him, / upon those who hope for his kindness, / to deliver them from death / and preserve them in spite of famine. **R.**

Our soul waits for the LORD, / who is our help and our shield. / May your kindness, O LORD, be upon us / who have put our hope in you. **R.**

SECOND READING   *2 Timothy 1:8b—10*

Beloved: Bear your share of hardship for the gospel with the strength that comes from God.

He saved us and called us to a holy life, not according to our works but according to his own design and the grace bestowed on us in Christ Jesus before time began, but now made manifest through the appearance of our savior Christ Jesus, who destroyed death and brought life and immortality to light through the gospel.

VERSE BEFORE THE GOSPEL   *see Matthew 17:5*

R. Praise to you, O Christ, King of Eternal Glory! From the shining cloud the Father's voice is heard: This is my beloved Son, hear him. **R.**

GOSPEL   *Matthew 17:1—9*

Jesus took Peter, James, and John his brother, and led them up a high mountain by themselves. And he was transfigured before them; his face shone like the sun and his clothes became white as light. And behold, Moses and Elijah appeared to them, conversing with him. Then Peter said to Jesus in reply, "Lord, it is good that we are here. If you wish, I will make three tents here, one for you, one for Moses, and one for Elijah." While he was still speaking, behold, a bright cloud cast a shadow over them, then from the cloud came a voice that said, "This is my beloved Son, with whom I am well pleased; listen to him." When the disciples heard this, they fell prostrate and were very much afraid. But Jesus came and touched them, saying, "Rise, and do not be afraid." And when the disciples raised their eyes, they saw no one else but Jesus alone.

As they were coming down from the mountain, Jesus charged them, "Do not tell the vision to anyone until the Son of Man has been raised from the dead."

MARCH 9, 2ND WEEK OF LENT – MONDAY; ST. FRANCES OF ROME
FIRST READING   *Daniel 9:4b–10*

"Lord, great and awesome God, you who keep your merciful covenant toward those who love you and observe your commandments! We have sinned, been wicked and done evil; we have rebelled and departed from your commandments and your laws. We have not obeyed your servants the prophets, who spoke in your name to our kings, our princes, our fathers, and all the people of the land. Justice, O Lord, is on your side; we are shamefaced even to this day: we, the men of Judah, the residents of Jerusalem, and all Israel, near and far, in all the countries to which you have scattered them because of their treachery toward you. O LORD, we are shamefaced, like our kings, our princes, and our fathers, for having sinned against you. But yours, O Lord, our God, are compassion and forgiveness! Yet we rebelled against you and paid no heed to your command, O LORD, our God, to live by the law you gave us through your servants the prophets."

RESPONSORIAL PSALM   *Psalm 79:8, 9, 11 and 13*
R. (see 103:10a) Lord, do not deal with us according to our sins.
Remember not against us the iniquities of the past; / may your compassion quickly come to us, / for we are brought very low. **R.**
Help us, O God our savior, / because of the glory of your name; / Deliver us and pardon our sins for your name's sake. **R.**
Let the prisoners' sighing come before you; / with your great power free those doomed to death. / Then we, your people and the sheep of your pasture, / will give thanks to you forever; / through all generations we will declare your praise. **R.**

VERSE BEFORE THE GOSPEL   *See John 6:63c, 68c*
R. Praise to you, O Christ, King of Eternal Glory! Your words, Lord, are Spirit and life; you have the words of everlasting life. **R.**

GOSPEL   *Luke 6:36–38*
Jesus said to his disciples: "Be merciful, just as your Father is merciful.

"Stop judging and you will not be judged. Stop condemning and you will not be condemned. Forgive and you will be forgiven. Give and gifts will be given to you; a good measure, packed together, shaken down, and overflowing, will be poured into your lap. For the measure with which you measure will in return be measured out to you."

MARCH 10, 2ND WEEK OF LENT - TUESDAY; ST. DOMINIC SAVIO

FIRST READING *Isaiah 1:10, 16–20*

Hear the word of the LORD, princes of Sodom! Listen to the instruction of our God, people of Gomorrah!

Wash yourselves clean! Put away your misdeeds from before my eyes; cease doing evil; learn to do good. Make justice your aim: redress the wronged, hear the orphan's plea, defend the widow.

Come now, let us set things right, says the LORD: Though your sins be like scarlet, they may become white as snow; though they be crimson red, they may become white as wool. If you are willing, and obey, you shall eat the good things of the land; but if you refuse and resist, the sword shall consume you: for the mouth of the LORD has spoken!

RESPONSORIAL PSALM *Psalm 50:8–9, 16bc–17, 21 and 23*

R. (23b) To the upright I will show the saving power of God.

"Not for your sacrifices do I rebuke you, / for your burnt offerings are before me always. / I take from your house no bullock, / no goats out of your fold." **R.**

"Why do you recite my statutes, / and profess my covenant with your mouth, / Though you hate discipline / and cast my words behind you?" **R.**

"When you do these things, shall I be deaf to it? / Or do you think that I am like yourself? / I will correct you by drawing them up before your eyes. / He that offers praise as a sacrifice glorifies me; / and to him that goes the right way / I will show the salvation of God." **R.**

VERSE BEFORE THE GOSPEL *Ezekiel 18:31*

R. Praise to you, O Christ, King of Eternal Glory! Cast away from you all the crimes you have committed, says the Lord, and make for yourselves a new heart and a new spirit. **R.**

GOSPEL *Matthew 23:1–12*

Jesus spoke to the crowds and to his disciples, saying, "The scribes and the Pharisees have taken their seat on the chair of Moses. Therefore, do and observe all things whatsoever they tell you, but do not follow their example. For they preach but they do not practice. They tie up heavy burdens hard to carry and lay them on people's shoulders, but they will not lift a finger to move them. All their works are performed to be seen. They widen their phylacteries and lengthen their tassels. They love places of honor at banquets, seats of honor in synagogues, greetings in marketplaces, and the salutation 'Rabbi.' As for you, do not be called 'Rabbi.' You have but one teacher, and you are all brothers. Call no one on earth your father; you have but one Father in heaven. Do not be called 'Master'; you have but one master, the Christ. The greatest among you must be your servant. Whoever exalts himself will be humbled; but whoever humbles himself will be exalted."

MARCH 11, 2ND WEEK OF LENT – WEDNESDAY; ST. GEMMA GALGANI

FIRST READING *Jeremiah 18:18–20*

The people of Judah and the citizens of Jerusalem said, "Come, let us contrive a plot against Jeremiah. It will not mean the loss of instruction from the priests, nor of counsel from the wise, nor of messages from the prophets. And so, let us destroy him by his own tongue; let us carefully note his every word."

Heed me, O LORD, and listen to what my adversaries say. Must good be repaid with evil that they should dig a pit to take my life? Remember that I stood before you to speak in their behalf, to turn away your wrath from them.

RESPONSORIAL PSALM *Psalm 31:5–6, 14, 15–16*

R. (17b) Save me, O Lord, in your kindness.

You will free me from the snare they set for me, / for you are my refuge. / Into your hands I commend my spirit; / you will redeem me, O LORD, O faithful God. **R.**

I hear the whispers of the crowd, / that frighten me from every side, / as they consult together against me, / plotting to take my life. **R.**

But my trust is in you, O LORD; / I say, "You are my God." / In your hands is my destiny; / rescue me from the clutches of my enemies and my persecutors. **R.**

VERSE BEFORE THE GOSPEL *John 8:12*

R. Praise to you, O Christ, King of Eternal Glory! I am the light of the world, says the Lord; whoever follows me will have the light of life. **R.**

GOSPEL *Matthew 20:17–28*

As Jesus was going up to Jerusalem, he took the Twelve disciples aside by themselves, and said to them on the way, "Behold, we are going up to Jerusalem, and the Son of Man will be handed over to the chief priests and the scribes, and they will condemn him to death, and hand him over to the Gentiles to be mocked and scourged and crucified, and he will be raised on the third day."

Then the mother of the sons of Zebedee approached Jesus with her sons and did him homage, wishing to ask him for something. He said to her, "What do you wish?" She answered him, "Command that these two sons of mine sit, one at your right and the other at your left, in your kingdom." Jesus said in reply, "You do not know what you are asking. Can you drink the chalice that I am going to drink?" They said to him, "We can." He replied, "My chalice you will indeed drink, but to sit at my right and at my left, this is not mine to give but is for those for whom it has been prepared by my Father." When the ten heard this, they became indignant at the two brothers. But Jesus summoned them and said, "You know that the rulers of the Gentiles lord it over them, and the great ones make their authority over them felt. But it shall not be so among you. Rather, whoever wishes to be great among you shall be your servant; whoever wishes to be first among you shall be your slave. Just so, the Son of Man did not come to be served but to serve and to give his life as a ransom for many."

MARCH 12, 2ND WEEK OF LENT – THURSDAY; BLESSED ANIELA SALAWA

FIRST READING *Jeremiah 17:5–10*

Thus says the LORD: Cursed is the man who trusts in human beings, who seeks his strength in flesh, whose heart turns away from the LORD. He is like a barren bush in the desert that enjoys no change of season, but stands in a lava waste, a salt and empty earth. Blessed is the man who trusts in the LORD, whose hope is the LORD. He is like a tree planted beside the waters that stretches out its roots to the stream: It fears not the heat when it comes, its leaves stay green; In the year of drought it shows no distress, but still bears fruit. More tortuous than all else is the human heart, beyond remedy; who can understand it? I, the LORD, alone probe the mind and test the heart, to reward everyone according to his ways, according to the merit of his deeds.

RESPONSORIAL PSALM *Psalm 1:1–2, 3, 4 and 6*

R. (40:5a) Blessed are they who hope in the Lord.

Blessed the man who follows not the counsel of the wicked / Nor walks in the way of sinners, / nor sits in the company of the insolent, / But delights in the law of the LORD / and meditates on his law day and night. **R.**

He is like a tree planted near running water, / That yields its fruit in due season, / and whose leaves never fade. / Whatever he does, prospers. **R.**

Not so, the wicked, not so; / they are like chaff which the wind drives away. / For the LORD watches over the way of the just, / but the way of the wicked vanishes. **R.**

VERSE BEFORE THE GOSPEL *See Luke 8:15*

R. Praise to you, O Christ, King of Eternal Glory! Blessed are they who have kept the word with a generous heart and yield a harvest through perseverance. **R.**

GOSPEL *Luke 16:19–31*

Jesus said to the Pharisees: "There was a rich man who dressed in purple garments and fine linen and dined sumptuously each day. And lying at his door was a poor man named Lazarus, covered with sores, who would gladly have eaten his fill of the scraps that fell from the rich man's table. Dogs even used to come and lick his sores. When the poor man died, he was carried away by angels to the bosom of Abraham. The rich man also died and was buried, and from the netherworld, where he was in torment, he raised his eyes and saw Abraham far off and Lazarus at his side. And he cried out, 'Father Abraham, have pity on me. Send Lazarus to dip the tip of his finger in water and cool my tongue, for I am suffering torment in these flames.' Abraham replied, 'My child, remember that you received what was good during your lifetime while Lazarus likewise received what was bad; but now he is comforted here, whereas you are tormented. Moreover, between us and you a great chasm is established to prevent anyone from crossing who might wish to go from our side to yours or from your side to ours.' He said, 'Then I beg you, father, send him to my father's house, for I have five brothers, so that he may warn them, lest they too come to this place of torment.' But Abraham replied, 'They have Moses and the prophets. Let them listen to them.' He said, 'Oh no, father Abraham, but if someone from the dead goes to them, they will repent.' Then Abraham said, 'If they will not listen to Moses and the prophets, neither will they be persuaded if someone should rise from the dead.'"

MARCH 13, 2ND WEEK OF LENT - FRIDAY; ST. SERAPHINA (FINA)

FIRST READING   *Genesis 37:3–4, 12–13a, 17b–28a*

Israel loved Joseph best of all his sons, for he was the child of his old age; and he had made him a long tunic. When his brothers saw that their father loved him best of all his sons, they hated him so much that they would not even greet him.

One day, when his brothers had gone to pasture their father's flocks at Shechem, Israel said to Joseph, "Your brothers, you know, are tending our flocks at Shechem. Get ready; I will send you to them."

So Joseph went after his brothers and caught up with them in Dothan. They noticed him from a distance, and before he came up to them, they plotted to kill him. They said to one another: here comes that master dreamer! Come on, let us kill him and throw him into one of the cisterns here; we could say that a wild beast devoured him. We shall then see what comes of his dreams."

When Reuben heard this, he tried to save him from their hands, saying, "We must not take his life. Instead of shedding blood," he continued, "just throw him into that cistern there in the desert; but do not kill him outright." His purpose was to rescue him from their hands and return him to his father. So when Joseph came up to them, they stripped him of the long tunic he had on; then they took him and threw him into the cistern, which was empty and dry.

They then sat down to their meal. Looking up, they saw a caravan of Ishmaelites coming from Gilead, their camels laden with gum, balm and resin to be taken down to Egypt. Judah said to his brothers: "What is to be gained by killing our brother and concealing his blood? Rather, let us sell him to these Ishmaelites, instead of doing away with him ourselves. After all, he is our brother, our own flesh." His brothers agreed. They sold Joseph to the Ishmaelites for twenty pieces of silver.

RESPONSORIAL PSALM   *Psalm 105:16–17, 18–19, 20–21*

R. (5a) Remember the marvels the Lord has done.

When the LORD called down a famine on the land / and ruined the crop that sustained them, / He sent a man before them, / Joseph, sold as a slave. **R.**

They had weighed him down with fetters, / and he was bound with chains, / Till his prediction came to pass / and the word of the LORD proved him true. **R.**

The king sent and released him, / the ruler of the peoples set him free. / He made him lord of his house / and ruler of all his possessions. **R.**

VERSE BEFORE THE GOSPEL   *John 3:16*

R. Praise to you, O Christ, King of Eternal Glory! God so loved the world that he gave his only–begotten Son; so that everyone who believes in him might have eternal life. **R.**

GOSPEL
Matthew 21:33–43, 45–46

Jesus said to the chief priests and the elders of the people: "Hear another parable. There was a landowner who planted a vineyard, put a hedge around it, dug a wine press in it, and built a tower. Then he leased it to tenants and went on a journey. When vintage time drew near, he sent his servants to the tenants to obtain his produce. But the tenants seized the servants and one they beat, another they killed, and a third they stoned. Again he sent other servants, more numerous than the first ones, but they treated them in the same way. Finally, he sent his son to them, thinking, 'They will respect my son.' But when the tenants saw the son, they said to one another, 'This is the heir. Come, let us kill him and acquire his inheritance.' They seized him, threw him out of the vineyard, and killed him. What will the owner of the vineyard do to those tenants when he comes?" They answered him, He will put those wretched men to a wretched death and lease his vineyard to other tenants who will give him the produce at the proper times." Jesus said to them, did you never read in the Scriptures:

The stone that the builders rejected has become the cornerstone; by the Lord has this been done, and it is wonderful in our eyes?

Therefore, I say to you, the Kingdom of God will be taken away from you and given to a people that will produce its fruit." When the chief priests and the Pharisees heard his parables, they knew that he was speaking about them. And although they were attempting to arrest him, they feared the crowds, for they regarded him as a prophet.

MARCH 14, 2ND WEEK OF LENT – SATURDAY; ST. MATILDA
FIRST READING
Micah 7:14–15, 18–20

Shepherd your people with your staff, the flock of your inheritance, that dwells apart in a woodland, in the midst of Carmel. Let them feed in Bashan and Gilead, as in the days of old; As in the days when you came from the land of Egypt, show us wonderful signs.

Who is there like you, the God who removes guilt and pardons sin for the remnant of his inheritance; Who does not persist in anger forever, but delights rather in clemency, and will again have compassion on us, treading underfoot our guilt? You will cast into the depths of the sea all our sins; You will show faithfulness to Jacob, and grace to Abraham, As you have sworn to our fathers from days of old.

RESPONSORIAL PSALM
Psalm 103:1–2, 3–4, 9–10, 11–12

R. (8a) The Lord is kind and merciful.

Bless the LORD, O my soul; / and all my being, bless his holy name. / Bless the LORD, O my soul, / and forget not all his benefits. **R.**

He pardons all your iniquities, / He heals all your ills. / He redeems your life from destruction, / He crowns you with kindness and compassion. **R.**

He will not always chide, / nor does He keep His wrath forever. / Not according to our sins does he deal with us, / nor does he requite us according to our crimes. **R.**

For as the heavens are high above the earth, / so surpassing is His kindness toward those who fear him. / As far as the east is from the west, / so far has He put our transgressions from us. **R.**

VERSE BEFORE THE GOSPEL   *Luke 15:18*
R. Praise to you, O Christ, King of Eternal Glory! I will get up and go to my father and shall say to him, Father; I have sinned against heaven and against you. **R.**

GOSPEL   *Luke 15:1–3, 11–32*
Tax collectors and sinners were all drawing near to listen to Jesus, but the Pharisees and scribes began to complain, saying, "This man welcomes sinners and eats with them." So to them Jesus addressed this parable. "A man had two sons, and the younger son said to his father, 'Father, give me the share of your estate that should come to me.' So the father divided the property between them. After a few days, the younger son collected all his belongings and set off to a distant country where he squandered his inheritance on a life of dissipation. When he had freely spent everything, a severe famine struck that country, and he found himself in dire need. So he hired himself out to one of the local citizens who sent him to his farm to tend the swine. And he longed to eat his fill of the pods on which the swine fed, but nobody gave him any. Coming to his senses he thought, 'How many of my father's hired workers have more than enough food to eat, but here am I, dying from hunger. I shall get up and go to my father and I shall say to him, "Father, I have sinned against heaven and against you. I no longer deserve to be called your son; treat me as you would treat one of your hired workers."' So he got up and went back to his father. While he was still a long way off, his father caught sight of him, and was filled with compassion. He ran to his son, embraced him and kissed him. His son said to him, 'Father, I have sinned against heaven and against you; I no longer deserve to be called your son.' But his father ordered his servants, 'Quickly, bring the finest robe and put it on him; put a ring on his finger and sandals on his feet. Take the fattened calf and slaughter it. Then let us celebrate with a feast, because this son of mine was dead, and has come to life again; he was lost, and has been found.' Then the celebration began. Now the older son had been out in the field and, on his way back, as he neared the house, he heard the sound of music and dancing. He called one of the servants and asked what this might mean. The servant said to him, 'Your brother has returned and your father has slaughtered the fattened calf because he has him back safe and sound.' He became angry, and when he refused to enter the house, his father came out and pleaded with him. He said to his father in reply, 'Look, all these years I served you and not once did I disobey your orders; yet you never gave me even a young goat to feast on with my friends. But when your son returns who swallowed up your property with prostitutes, for him you slaughter the fattened calf.' He said to him, 'My son, you are here with me always; everything I have is yours. But now we must celebrate and rejoice, because your brother was dead and has come to life again; he was lost and has been found.'"

MARCH 15, 3RD SUNDAY OF LENT; ST. ZACHARY

FIRST READING   *Exodus 17:3—7*

In those days, in their thirst for water, the people grumbled against Moses, saying, "Why did you ever make us leave Egypt? Was it just to have us die here of thirst with our children and our livestock?" So Moses cried out to the LORD, "What shall I do with this people? A little more and they will stone me!" The LORD answered Moses, "Go over there in front of the people, along with some of the elders of Israel, holding in your hand, as you go, the staff with which you struck the river. I will be standing there in front of you on the rock in Horeb. Strike the rock, and the water will flow from it for the people to drink." This Moses did, in the presence of the elders of Israel. The place was called Massah and Meribah, because the Israelites quarreled there and tested the LORD, saying, "Is the LORD in our midst or not?"

RESPONSORIAL PSALM   *Psalm 95:1—2, 6—7, 8—9 (8)*

R. If today you hear his voice, harden not your hearts.

Come, let us sing joyfully to the LORD; / let us acclaim the Rock of our salvation. / Let us come into his presence with thanksgiving; / let us joyfully sing psalms to him. **R.**

Come, let us bow down in worship; / let us kneel before the LORD who made us. / For He is our God, / and we are the people he shepherds, / the flock he guides. **R.**

Oh, that today you would hear his voice: / "Harden not your hearts as at Meribah, / as in the day of Massah in the desert. / Where your fathers tempted me; / they tested me though they had seen my works." **R.**

SECOND READING   *Romans 5:1—2, 5—8*

Brothers and sisters: Since we have been justified by faith, we have peace with God through our Lord Jesus Christ, through whom we have gained access by faith to this grace in which we stand, and we boast in hope of the glory of God.

And hope does not disappoint, because the love of God has been poured out into our hearts through the Holy Spirit who has been given to us. For Christ, while we were still helpless, died at the appointed time for the ungodly. Indeed, only with difficulty does one die for a just person, though perhaps for a good person one might even find courage to die. But God proves his love for us in that while we were still sinners Christ died for us.

VERSE BEFORE THE GOSPEL   *see John 4:42, 15*

R. Praise to you, O Christ, King of Eternal Glory! Lord, you are truly the Savior of the world; give me living water, that I may never thirst again. **R.**

GOSPEL   *Longer Form John 4:5—42*

Jesus came to a town of Samaria called Sychar, near the plot of land that Jacob had given to his son Joseph. Jacob's well was there. Jesus, tired from his journey, sat down there at the well. It was about noon.

A woman of Samaria came to draw water. Jesus said to her, "Give me a drink." His disciples had gone into the town to buy food. The Samaritan woman said to him, "How can you, a Jew, ask me, a Samaritan woman, for a drink?" —For Jews use nothing in common with Samaritans.— Jesus answered and said to her, "If you knew the gift of God and who is saying to you, 'Give me a drink,' you would have asked him and he would have given you living water." The woman said to him, "Sir, you do not even have a bucket and the cistern is deep; where then can you get this living water? Are you greater than our father Jacob, who gave us this cistern and drank from it himself with his children and his flocks?" Jesus answered and said to her, "Everyone who drinks this water will be thirsty again; but whoever drinks the water I shall give will never thirst; the water I shall give will become in him a spring of water welling up to eternal life." The woman said to him, "Sir, give me this water, so that I may not be thirsty or have to keep coming here to draw water."

Jesus said to her, "Go call your husband and come back." The woman answered and said to him, "I do not have a husband." Jesus answered her, "You are right in saying, 'I do not have a husband.' For you have had five husbands, and the one you have now is not your husband. What you have said is true." The woman said to him, "Sir, I can see that you are a prophet. Our ancestors worshiped on this mountain; but you people say that the place to worship is in Jerusalem." Jesus said to her, "Believe me, woman, the hour is coming when you will worship the Father neither on this mountain nor in Jerusalem. You people worship what you do not understand; we worship what we understand, because salvation is from the Jews. But the hour is coming, and is now here, when true worshipers will worship the Father in Spirit and truth; and indeed the Father seeks such people to worship him. God is Spirit, and those who worship him must worship in Spirit and truth." The woman said to him, "I know that the Messiah is coming, the one called the Christ; when he comes, he will tell us everything." Jesus said to her, "I am he, the one speaking with you."

At that moment his disciples returned, and were amazed that he was talking with a woman, but still no one said, "What are you looking for?" or "Why are you talking with her?" The woman left her water jar and went into the town and said to the people, "Come see a man who told me everything I have done. Could he possibly be the Christ?" They went out of the town and came to him. Meanwhile, the disciples urged him, "Rabbi, eat." But he said to them, "I have food to eat of which you do not know." So the disciples said to one another, "Could someone have brought him something to eat?" Jesus said to them, "My food is to do the will of the one who sent me and to finish his work. Do you not say, 'In four months the harvest will be here'? I tell you, look up and see the fields ripe for the harvest. The reaper is already receiving payment and gathering crops for eternal life, so that the sower and reaper can rejoice together. For here the saying is verified that 'One sows and another reaps.' I sent you to reap what you have not worked for; others have done the work, and you are sharing the fruits of their work."

Many of the Samaritans of that town began to believe in him because of the word of the woman who testified, "He told me everything I have done." When the Samaritans came to him, they invited him to stay with them; and he stayed there two days. Many more began to believe in him because of his word, and they said to the woman, "We no longer believe because of your word; for we have heard for ourselves, and we know that this is truly the savior of the world."

SHORTER FORM   *John 4:5—15, 19b—26, 39a, 40—42*

Jesus came to a town of Samaria called Sychar, near the plot of land that Jacob had given to his son Joseph. Jacob's well was there. Jesus, tired from his journey, sat down there at the well. It was about noon.

A woman of Samaria came to draw water. Jesus said to her, "Give me a drink." His disciples had gone into the town to buy food. The Samaritan woman said to him, "How can you, a Jew, ask me, a Samaritan woman, for a drink?" —For Jews use nothing in common with Samaritans.— Jesus answered and said to her, "If you knew the gift of God and who is saying to you, 'Give me a drink,' you would have asked him and he would have given you living water." The woman said to him, "Sir, you do not even have a bucket and the cistern is deep; where then can you get this living water? Are you greater than our father Jacob, who gave us this cistern and drank from it himself with his children and his flocks?" Jesus answered and said to her, "Everyone who drinks this water will be thirsty again; but whoever drinks the water I shall give will never thirst; the water I shall give will become in him a spring of water welling up to eternal life." The woman said to him, "Sir, give me this water, so that I may not be thirsty or have to keep coming here to draw water.

"I can see that you are a prophet. Our ancestors worshiped on this mountain; but you people say that the place to worship is in Jerusalem." Jesus said to her, "Believe me, woman, the hour is coming when you will worship the Father neither on this mountain nor in Jerusalem. You people worship what you do not understand; we worship what we understand, because salvation is from the Jews. But the hour is coming, and is now here, when true worshipers will worship the Father in Spirit and truth; and indeed the Father seeks such people to worship him. God is Spirit, and those who worship him must worship in Spirit and truth." The woman said to him, "I know that the Messiah is coming, the one called the Christ; when he comes, he will tell us everything." Jesus said to her, "I am he, the one who is speaking with you."

Many of the Samaritans of that town began to believe in him. When the Samaritans came to him, they invited him to stay with them; and he stayed there two days. Many more began to believe in him because of his word, and they said to the woman, "We no longer believe because of your word; for we have heard for ourselves, and we know that this is truly the savior of the world."

MARCH 16, 3RD WEEK OF LENT – MONDAY; BLESSED TORELLO
FIRST READING   *2 Kings 5:1–15ab*

Naaman, the army commander of the king of Aram, was highly esteemed and respected by his master, for through him the LORD had brought victory to Aram. But valiant as he was, the man was a leper. Now the Arameans had captured in a raid on the land of Israel a little girl, who became the servant of Naaman's wife. "If only my master would present himself to the prophet in Samaria," she said to her mistress, "he would cure him of his leprosy." Naaman went and told his lord just what the slave girl from the land of Israel had said. "Go," said the king of Aram. "I will send along a letter to the king of Israel." So Naaman set out, taking along ten silver talents, six thousand gold pieces, and ten festal garments. To the king of Israel he brought the letter, which read: "With this letter I am sending my servant Naaman to you, that you may cure him of his leprosy."

When he read the letter, the king of Israel tore his garments and exclaimed: "Am I a god with power over life and death, that this man should send someone to me to be cured of leprosy? Take note! You can see he is only looking for a quarrel with me!" When Elisha, the man of God, heard that the king of Israel had torn his garments, he sent word to the king: "Why have you torn your garments? Let him come to me and find out that there is a prophet in Israel."

Naaman came with his horses and chariots and stopped at the door of Elisha's house. The prophet sent him the message: "Go and wash seven times in the Jordan, and your flesh will heal, and you will be clean." But Naaman went away angry, saying, "I thought that he would surely come out and stand there to invoke the LORD his God, and would move his hand over the spot, and thus cure the leprosy. Are not the rivers of Damascus, the Abana and the Pharpar, better than all the waters of Israel? Could I not wash in them and be cleansed?" With this, he turned about in anger and left.

But his servants came up and reasoned with him. "My father," they said, "if the prophet had told you to do something extraordinary, would you not have done it? All the more now, since he said to you, 'Wash and be clean,' should you do as he said." So Naaman went down and plunged into the Jordan seven times at the word of the man of God. His flesh became again like the flesh of a little child, and he was clean.

He returned with his whole retinue to the man of God. On his arrival he stood before him and said, "Now I know that there is no God in all the earth, except in Israel."

RESPONSORIAL PSALM   *Psalm 42:2, 3; 43:3, 4*
R. (see 42:3) Athirst is my soul for the living God. When shall I go and behold the face of God?
As the hind longs for the running waters, / so my soul longs for you, O God. **R.**
Athirst is my soul for God, the living God. / When shall I go and behold the face of God? **R.**
Send forth your light and your fidelity; / they shall lead me on and bring me to your holy mountain, / to your dwelling–place. **R.**
Then will I go in to the altar of God, / the God of my gladness and joy; / Then will I give you thanks upon the harp, / O God, my God! **R.**

VERSE BEFORE THE GOSPEL   *See Psalm 130:5, 7*
R. Praise to you, O Christ, King of Eternal Glory! I hope in the LORD, I trust in his word; with him there is kindness and plenteous redemption. **R.**

GOSPEL   *Luke 4:24–30*
Jesus said to the people in the synagogue at Nazareth: "Amen, I say to you, no prophet is accepted in his own native place. Indeed, I tell you, there were many widows in Israel in the days of Elijah when the sky was closed for three and a half years and a severe famine spread over the entire land. It was to none of these that Elijah was sent, but only to a widow in Zarephath in the land of Sidon. Again, there were many lepers in Israel during the time of Elisha the prophet; yet not one of them was cleansed, but only Naaman the Syrian."

When the people in the synagogue heard this, they were all filled with fury. They rose up, drove him out of the town, and led him to the brow of the hill on which their town had been built, to hurl him down headlong. But he passed through the midst of them and went away.

MARCH 17, 3RD WEEK OF LENT - TUESDAY; ST. PATRICK

FIRST READING   *Daniel 3:25, 34–43*

"For your name's sake, O Lord, do not deliver us up forever, or make void your covenant. Do not take away your mercy from us, for the sake of Abraham, your beloved, Isaac your servant, and Israel your holy one, To whom you promised to multiply their offspring like the stars of heaven, or the sand on the shore of the sea. For we are reduced, O Lord, beyond any other nation, brought low everywhere in the world this day because of our sins. We have in our day no prince, prophet, or leader, no burnt offering, sacrifice, oblation, or incense, no place to offer first fruits, to find favor with you. But with contrite heart and humble spirit let us be received; As though it were burnt offerings of rams and bullocks, or thousands of fat lambs, So let our sacrifice be in your presence today as we follow you unreservedly; for those who trust in you cannot be put to shame. And now we follow you with our whole heart, we fear you and we pray to you. Do not let us be put to shame, but deal with us in your kindness and great mercy. Deliver us by your wonders, and bring glory to your name, O Lord."

RESPONSORIAL PSALM   *Psalm 25:4–5ab, 6 and 7bc, 8–9*

R. (6a) Remember your mercies, O Lord.

Your ways, O LORD, make known to me; / teach me your paths, / Guide me in your truth and teach me, / for you are God my savior. **R.**

Remember that your compassion, O LORD, / and your kindness are from of old. / In your kindness remember me, / because of your goodness, O LORD. **R.**

Good and upright is the LORD; / thus he shows sinners the way. / He guides the humble to justice, / He teaches the humble his way. **R.**

VERSE BEFORE THE GOSPEL   *Joel 2:12–13*

R. Praise to you, O Christ, King of Eternal Glory! Even now, says the LORD, return to me with your whole heart; for I am gracious and merciful. **R.**

GOSPEL   *Matthew 18:21–35*

Peter approached Jesus and asked him, "Lord, if my brother sins against me, how often must I forgive him? As many as seven times?" Jesus answered, "I say to you, not seven times but seventy–seven times. That is why the Kingdom of heaven may be likened to a king who decided to settle accounts with his servants. When he began the accounting, a debtor was brought before him who owed him a huge amount. Since he had no way of paying it back, his master ordered him to be sold, along with his wife, his children, and all his property, in payment of the debt. At that, the servant fell down, did him homage, and said, 'Be patient with me, and I will pay you back in full.' Moved with compassion the master of that servant let him go and forgave him the loan. When that servant had left, he found one of his fellow servants who owed him a much smaller amount. He seized him and started to choke him, demanding, 'Pay back what you owe.' Falling to his knees, his fellow servant begged him, 'Be patient with me, and I will pay you back.' But he refused. Instead, he had him put in prison until he paid back the debt. Now when his fellow servants saw what had happened, they were deeply disturbed, and went to their master and reported the whole affair. His master summoned him and said to him, 'You wicked servant! I forgave you your entire debt because you begged me to. Should you not have had pity on your fellow servant, as I had pity on you?' Then in anger his master handed him over to the torturers until he should pay back the whole debt. So will my heavenly Father do to you, unless each of you forgives your brother from your heart."

MARCH 18, 3RD WEEK OF LENT – WEDNESDAY; ST. CYRIL OF JERUSALEM

FIRST READING   *Deuteronomy 4:1, 5–9*

Moses spoke to the people and said: "Now, Israel, hear the statutes and decrees which I am teaching you to observe, that you may live, and may enter in and take possession of the land which the LORD, the God of your fathers, is giving you. Therefore, I teach you the statutes and decrees as the LORD, my God, has commanded me, that you may observe them in the land you are entering to occupy. Observe them carefully, for thus will you give evidence of your wisdom and intelligence to the nations, who will hear of all these statutes and say, 'This great nation is truly a wise and intelligent people.' For what great nation is there that has gods so close to it as the LORD, our God, is to us whenever we call upon him? Or what great nation has statutes and decrees that are as just as this whole law which I am setting before you today?

"However, take care and be earnestly on your guard not to forget the things which your own eyes have seen, nor let them slip from your memory as long as you live, but teach them to your children and to your children's children."

RESPONSORIAL PSALM   *Psalm 147:12–13, 15–16, 19–20*

R. (12a) Praise the Lord, Jerusalem.
Glorify the LORD, O Jerusalem; / praise your God, O Zion. / For He has strengthened the bars of your gates; / He has blessed your children within you. **R.**
He sends forth His command to the earth; / swiftly runs His word! He spreads snow like wool; / frost He strews like ashes. **R.**
He has proclaimed His word to Jacob, / His statutes and his ordinances to Israel. / He has not done thus for any other nation; / His ordinances he has not made known to them. **R.**

VERSE BEFORE THE GOSPEL   *See John 6:63c, 68c*

R. Praise to you, O Christ, King of Eternal Glory! Your words, Lord, are Spirit and life; you have the words of everlasting life. **R.**

GOSPEL   *Matthew 5:17–19*

Jesus said to his disciples: "Do not think that I have come to abolish the law or the prophets. I have come not to abolish but to fulfill. Amen, I say to you, until heaven and earth pass away, not the smallest letter or the smallest part of a letter will pass from the law, until all things have taken place. Therefore, whoever breaks one of the least of these commandments and teaches others to do so will be called least in the Kingdom of heaven. But whoever obeys and teaches these commandments will be called greatest in the Kingdom of heaven."

MARCH 19, SOLEMNITY OF SAINT JOSEPH, HUSBAND OF THE BLESSED VIRGIN MARY

FIRST READING   *2 Samuel 7:4—5a, 12—14a, 16*

The LORD spoke to Nathan and said: "Go, tell my servant David, 'When your time comes and you rest with your ancestors, I will raise up your heir after you, sprung from your loins, and I will make his kingdom firm. It is he who shall build a house for my name. And I will make his royal throne firm forever. I will be a father to him, and he shall be a son to me. Your house and your kingdom shall endure forever before me; your throne shall stand firm forever.'"

RESPONSORIAL PSALM   *Psalm 89:2—3, 4—5, 27, 29 (37)*

R. The son of David will live for ever.

The promises of the LORD I will sing for ever, / through all generations my mouth will proclaim your faithfulness, / For you have said, "My kindness is established forever"; / in heaven you have confirmed your faithfulness. **R.**

"I have made a covenant with my chosen one, / I have sworn to David my servant: / Forever will I confirm your posterity / and establish your throne for all generations." **R.** "He shall say of me, / 'You are my father, my God, the Rock, my savior.'/ Forever I will maintain my kindness toward him, / And my covenant with him stands firm." **R.**

SECOND READING   *Romans 4:13, 16—18, 22*

Brothers and sisters: It was not through the law that the promise was made to Abraham and his descendants that he would inherit the world, but through the righteousness that comes from faith. For this reason, it depends on faith, so that it may be a gift, and the promise may be guaranteed to all his descendants, not to those who only adhere to the law but to those who follow the faith of Abraham, who is the father of all of us, as it is written, I have made you father of many nations. He is our father in the sight of God, in whom he believed, who gives life to the dead and calls into being what does not exist. He believed, hoping against hope, that he would become the father of many nations, according to what was said, thus shall your descendants be. That is why it was credited to him as righteousness.

ALLELUIA   *Psalm 84:5*

R. Alleluia, alleluia. Blessed are those who dwell in your house, O Lord; they never cease to praise you. **R.**

GOSPEL   *Matthew 1:16, 18—21, 24a*

Jacob was the father of Joseph, the husband of Mary. Of her was born Jesus who is called the Christ.

Now this is how the birth of Jesus Christ came about. When his mother Mary was betrothed to Joseph, but before they lived together, she was found with child through the Holy Spirit. Joseph her husband, since he was a righteous man, yet unwilling to expose her to shame, decided to divorce her quietly. Such was his intention when, behold, the angel of the Lord appeared to him in a dream and said, "Joseph, son of David, do not be afraid to take Mary your wife into your home. For it is through the Holy Spirit that this child has been conceived in her. She will bear a son and you are to name him Jesus, because he will save his people from their sins." When Joseph awoke, he did as the angel of the Lord had commanded him and took his wife into his home.

ALTERNATIVE GOSPEL   *Luke 2:41—51a*

Each year Jesus' parents went to Jerusalem for the feast of Passover, and when he was twelve years old, they went up according to festival custom. After they had completed its days, as they were returning, the boy Jesus remained behind in Jerusalem, but his parents did not know it. Thinking that he was in the caravan, they journeyed for a day and looked for him among their relatives and acquaintances, but not finding him, they returned to Jerusalem to look for him. After three days they found him in the temple, sitting in the midst of the teachers, listening to them and asking them questions, and all who heard him were astounded at his understanding and his answers. When his parents saw him, they were astonished, and his mother said to him, "Son, why have you done this to us? Your father and I have been looking for you with great anxiety." And he said to them, "Why were you looking for me? Did you not know that I must be in my Father's house?" But they did not understand what he said to them. He went down with them and came to Nazareth, and was obedient to them.

MARCH 20, 3RD WEEK OF LENT - FRIDAY; ST. CUTHBERT

FIRST READING   *Hosea 14:2–10*

Thus says the LORD: Return, O Israel, to the LORD, your God; you have collapsed through your guilt. Take with you words, and return to the LORD; Say to him, "Forgive all iniquity, and receive what is good, that we may render as offerings the bullocks from our stalls. Assyria will not save us, nor shall we have horses to mount; We shall say no more, 'Our god,' to the work of our hands; for in you the orphan finds compassion."

I will heal their defection, says the LORD, I will love them freely; for my wrath is turned away from them. I will be like the dew for Israel: he shall blossom like the lily; He shall strike root like the Lebanon cedar, and put forth his shoots. His splendor shall be like the olive tree and his fragrance like the Lebanon cedar. Again they shall dwell in his shade and raise grain; They shall blossom like the vine, and his fame shall be like the wine of Lebanon.

Ephraim! What more has he to do with idols? I have humbled him, but I will prosper him. "I am like a verdant cypress tree"— Because of me you bear fruit!

Let him who is wise understand these things; let him who is prudent know them. Straight are the paths of the LORD, in them the just walk, but sinners stumble in them.

RESPONSORIAL PSALM *Psalm 81:6c–8a, 8bc–9, 10–11ab, 14 and 17*
R. (see 11 and 9a) I am the Lord your God: hear my voice.
An unfamiliar speech I hear: / "I relieved his shoulder of the burden; / his hands were freed from the basket. / In distress you called, and I rescued you." **R.**
"Unseen, I answered you in thunder; / I tested you at the waters of Meribah. / Hear, my people, and I will admonish you; / O Israel, will you not hear me?" **R.**
"There shall be no strange god among you / nor shall you worship any alien god. / I, the LORD, am your God / who led you forth from the land of Egypt." **R.**
"If only my people would hear me, / and Israel walk in my ways, / I would feed them with the best of wheat, / and with honey from the rock I would fill them." **R.**
VERSE BEFORE THE GOSPEL *Matthew 4:17*
R. Praise to you, O Christ, King of Eternal Glory! Repent, says the Lord; the Kingdom of heaven is at hand. **R.**

GOSPEL *Mark 12:28–34*
One of the scribes came to Jesus and asked him, "Which is the first of all the commandments?" Jesus replied, "The first is this: *Hear, O Israel! The Lord our God is Lord alone! You shall love the Lord your God with all your heart, with all your soul, with all your mind, and with all your strength.* The second is this: *You shall love your neighbor as yourself.* There is no other commandment greater than these." The scribe said to him, "Well said, teacher. You are right in saying, *He is One and there is no other than he.* And *to love him with all your heart, with all your understanding, with all your strength, and to love your neighbor as yourself* is worth more than all burnt offerings and sacrifices." And when Jesus saw that he answered with understanding, he said to him, "You are not far from the Kingdom of God." And no one dared to ask him any more questions.

MARCH 21, 3RD WEEK OF LENT – SATURDAY; ST. SERAPION
FIRST READING *Hosea 6:1–6*
"Come, let us return to the LORD, it is he who has rent, but he will heal us; he has struck us, but he will bind our wounds. He will revive us after two days; on the third day he will raise us up, to live in his presence. Let us know, let us strive to know the LORD; as certain as the dawn is his coming, and his judgment shines forth like the light of day! He will come to us like the rain, like spring rain that waters the earth."

What can I do with you, Ephraim? What can I do with you, Judah? Your piety is like a morning cloud, like the dew that early passes away. For this reason I smote them through the prophets, I slew them by the words of my mouth; For it is love that I desire, not sacrifice, and knowledge of God rather than burnt offerings.

RESPONSORIAL PSALM *Psalm 51:3–4, 18–19, 20–21ab*

R. (see Hosea 6:6) It is mercy I desire, and not sacrifice.

Have mercy on me, O God, in your goodness; / in the greatness of your compassion wipe out my offense. / Thoroughly wash me from my guilt / and of my sin cleanse me. **R.**

For you are not pleased with sacrifices; / should I offer a burnt offering, you would not accept it. / My sacrifice, O God, is a contrite spirit; / a heart contrite and humbled, / O God, you will not spurn. **R.**

Be bountiful, O LORD, to Zion in your kindness / by rebuilding the walls of Jerusalem; / Then shall you be pleased with due sacrifices, / burnt offerings and holocausts. **R.**

VERSE BEFORE THE GOSPEL *Psalm 95:8*

R. Praise to you, O Christ, King of Eternal Glory! If today you hear his voice, harden not your hearts.

GOSPEL *Luke 18:9–14*

Jesus addressed this parable to those who were convinced of their own righteousness and despised everyone else. "Two people went up to the temple area to pray; one was a Pharisee and the other was a tax collector. The Pharisee took up his position and spoke this prayer to himself, 'O God, I thank you that I am not like the rest of humanity – greedy, dishonest, adulterous – or even like this tax collector. I fast twice a week, and I pay tithes on my whole income.' But the tax collector stood off at a distance and would not even raise his eyes to heaven but beat his breast and prayed, 'O God, be merciful to me a sinner.' I tell you, the latter went home justified, not the former; for everyone who exalts himself will be humbled, and the one who humbles himself will be exalted."

MARCH 22, 4TH SUNDAY OF LENT; ST. DEOGRATIAS

FIRST READING *1 Samuel 16:1b, 6—7, 10—13a*

The LORD said to Samuel: "Fill your horn with oil, and be on your way. I am sending you to Jesse of Bethlehem, for I have chosen my king from among his sons."

As Jesse and his sons came to the sacrifice, Samuel looked at Eliab and thought, "Surely the LORD's anointed is here before him." But the LORD said to Samuel: "Do not judge from his appearance or from his lofty stature, because I have rejected him. Not as man sees does God see, because man sees the appearance but the LORD looks into the heart." In the same way Jesse presented seven sons before Samuel, but Samuel said to Jesse, "The LORD has not chosen any one of these." Then Samuel asked Jesse, "Are these all the sons you have?" Jesse replied, "There is still the youngest, who is tending the sheep." Samuel said to Jesse, "Send for him; we will not begin the sacrificial banquet until he arrives here." Jesse sent and had the young man brought to them. He was ruddy, a youth handsome to behold and making a splendid appearance. The LORD said, "There—anoint him, for this is the one!" Then Samuel, with the horn of oil in hand, anointed David in the presence of his brothers; and from that day on, the spirit of the LORD rushed upon David.

RESPONSORIAL PSALM
Psalm 23:1—3a, 3b—4, 5, 6 (1)

R. The Lord is my shepherd; there is nothing I shall want.

The LORD is my shepherd; / I shall not want. / In verdant pastures he gives me repose; / beside restful waters he leads me; / he refreshes my soul. **R.**

He guides me in right paths for his name's sake. / Even though I walk in the dark valley I fear no evil; / for you are at my side / with your rod and your staff that give me courage. **R.**

You spread the table before me in the sight of my foes; / you anoint my head with oil; / my cup overflows. **R.**

Only goodness and kindness follow me / all the days of my life; / and I shall dwell in the house of the LORD for years to come. **R.**

SECOND READING
Ephesians 5:8—14

Brothers and sisters: You were once darkness, but now you are light in the Lord. Live as children of light, for light produces every kind of goodness and righteousness and truth. Try to learn what is pleasing to the Lord. Take no part in the fruitless works of darkness; rather expose them, for it is shameful even to mention the things done by them in secret; but everything exposed by the light becomes visible, for everything that becomes visible is light. Therefore, it says: "Awake, O sleeper, and arise from the dead, and Christ will give you light."

VERSE BEFORE THE GOSPEL
John 8:12

R. Praise to you, O Christ, King of Eternal Glory! I am the light of the world, says the Lord; whoever follows me will have the light of life. **R.**

GOSPEL
Longer Form John 9:1—41

As Jesus passed by he saw a man blind from birth. His disciples asked him, "Rabbi, who sinned, this man or his parents, that he was born blind?" Jesus answered, "Neither he nor his parents sinned; it is so that the works of God might be made visible through him. We have to do the works of the one who sent me while it is day. Night is coming when no one can work. While I am in the world, I am the light of the world." When he had said this, he spat on the ground and made clay with the saliva, and smeared the clay on his eyes, and said to him, "Go wash in the Pool of Siloam"—which means Sent—. So he went and washed, and came back able to see.

His neighbors and those who had seen him earlier as a beggar said, "Isn't this the one who used to sit and beg?" Some said, "It is," but others said, "No, he just looks like him." He said, "I am." So they said to him, "How were your eyes opened?" He replied, "The man called Jesus made clay and anointed my eyes and told me, 'Go to Siloam and wash.' So I went there and washed and was able to see." And they said to him, "Where is he?" He said, "I don't know."

They brought the one who was once blind to the Pharisees. Now Jesus had made clay and opened his eyes on a sabbath. So then the Pharisees also asked him how he was able to see. He said to them, "He put clay on my eyes, and I washed, and now I can see." So some of the Pharisees said, "This man is not from God, because he does not keep the sabbath." But others said, "How can a sinful man do such signs?" And there was a division among them. So they said to the blind man again, "What do you have to say about him, since he opened your eyes?" He said, "He is a prophet."

Now the Jews did not believe that he had been blind and gained his sight until they summoned the parents of the one who had gained his sight. They asked them, "Is this your son, who you say was born blind? How does he now see?" His parents answered and said, "We know that this is our son and that he was born blind. We do not know how he sees now, nor do we know who opened his eyes. Ask him, he is of age; he can speak for himself." His parents said this because they were afraid of the Jews, for the Jews had already agreed that if anyone acknowledged him as the Christ, he would be expelled from the synagogue. For this reason his parents said, "He is of age; question him."

So a second time they called the man who had been blind and said to him, "Give God the praise! We know that this man is a sinner." He replied, "If he is a sinner, I do not know. One thing I do know is that I was blind and now I see." So they said to him, "What did he do to you? How did he open your eyes?" He answered them, "I told you already and you did not listen. Why do you want to hear it again? Do you want to become his disciples, too?" They ridiculed him and said, "You are that man's disciple; we are disciples of Moses! We know that God spoke to Moses, but we do not know where this one is from." The man answered and said to them, "This is what is so amazing, that you do not know where he is from, yet he opened my eyes. We know that God does not listen to sinners, but if one is devout and does his will, he listens to him. It is unheard of that anyone ever opened the eyes of a person born blind. If this man were not from God, he would not be able to do anything." They answered and said to him, "You were born totally in sin, and are you trying to teach us?" Then they threw him out.

When Jesus heard that they had thrown him out, he found him and said, "Do you believe in the Son of Man?" He answered and said, "Who is he, sir, that I may believe in him?" Jesus said to him, "You have seen him, and the one speaking with you is he." He said, "I do believe, Lord," and he worshiped him. Then Jesus said, "I came into this world for judgment, so that those who do not see might see, and those who do see might become blind."

Some of the Pharisees who were with him heard this and said to him, "Surely we are not also blind, are we?" Jesus said to them, "If you were blind, you would have no sin; but now you are saying, 'We see,' so your sin remains."

SHORTER FORM   *John 9:1, 6—9, 13—17, 34—38*

As Jesus passed by he saw a man blind from birth. He spat on the ground and made clay with the saliva, and smeared the clay on his eyes, and said to him, "Go wash in the Pool of Siloam"—which means Sent—. So he went and washed, and came back able to see.

His neighbors and those who had seen him earlier as a beggar said, "Isn't this the one who used to sit and beg?" Some said, "It is," but others said, "No, he just looks like him." He said, "I am."

They brought the one who was once blind to the Pharisees. Now Jesus had made clay and opened his eyes on a sabbath. So then the Pharisees also asked him how he was able to see. He said to them, "He put clay on my eyes, and I washed, and now I can see." So some of the Pharisees said, "This man is not from God, because he does not keep the sabbath." But others said, "How can a sinful man do such signs?" And there was a division among them. So they said to the blind man again, "What do you have to say about him, since he opened your eyes?" He said, "He is a prophet."

They answered and said to him, "You were born totally in sin, and are you trying to teach us?" Then they threw him out.

When Jesus heard that they had thrown him out, he found him and said, "Do you believe in the Son of Man?" He answered and said, "Who is he, sir, that I may believe in him?" Jesus said to him, "You have seen him, and the one speaking with you is he." He said, "I do believe, Lord," and he worshiped him.

MARCH 23, 4TH WEEK OF LENT – MONDAY; ST. TORIBIO DE MOGROVEJO

FIRST READING   *Isaiah 65:17–21*

Thus says the LORD: Lo, I am about to create new heavens and a new earth; the things of the past shall not be remembered or come to mind. Instead, there shall always be rejoicing and happiness in what I create; for I create Jerusalem to be a joy and its people to be a delight; I will rejoice in Jerusalem and exult in my people. No longer shall the sound of weeping be heard there, or the sound of crying; No longer shall there be in it an infant who lives but a few days, or an old man who does not round out his full lifetime; He dies a mere youth who reaches but a hundred years, and he who fails of a hundred shall be thought accursed. They shall live in the houses they build, and eat the fruit of the vineyards they plant.

RESPONSORIAL PSALM   *Psalm 30:2 and 4, 5–6, 11–12a and 13b*

R. (2a) I will praise you, Lord, for you have rescued me.

I will extol you, O LORD, / for you drew me clear and did not let my enemies rejoice over me. / O LORD, you brought me up from the nether world; / you preserved me from among those going down into the pit. **R.**

Sing praise to the LORD, / you his faithful ones, / and give thanks to his holy name. For his anger lasts but a moment; / a lifetime, his good will. / At nightfall, weeping enters in, / but with the dawn, rejoicing. **R.**

"Hear, O LORD, and have pity on me; / O LORD, be my helper." / You changed my mourning into dancing; / O LORD, my God, / forever will I give you thanks. **R.**

VERSE BEFORE THE GOSPEL   *Amos 5:14*

R. Praise to you, O Christ, King of Eternal Glory! Seek good and not evil so that you may live, and the LORD will be with you. **R.**

GOSPEL   *John 4:43–54*

At that time Jesus left [Samaria] for Galilee. For Jesus himself testified that a prophet has no honor in his native place. When he came into Galilee, the Galileans welcomed him, since they had seen all he had done in Jerusalem at the feast; for they themselves had gone to the feast. Then he returned to Cana in Galilee, where he had made the water wine. Now there was a royal official whose son was ill in Capernaum. When he heard that Jesus had arrived in Galilee from Judea, he went to him and asked him to come down and heal his son, who was near death. Jesus said to him, "Unless you people see signs and wonders, you will not believe." The royal official said to him, "Sir, come down before my child dies." Jesus said to him, "You may go; your son will live." The man believed what Jesus said to him and left. While the man was on his way back, his slaves met him and told him that his boy would live. He asked them when he began to recover. They told him, "The fever left him yesterday, about one in the afternoon." The father realized that just at that time Jesus had said to him, "Your son will live," and he and his whole household came to believe. Now this was the second sign Jesus did when he came to Galilee from Judea.

MARCH 24, 4TH WEEK OF LENT – TUESDAY; BLESSED DIEGO

FIRST READING   *Ezekiel 47:1–9, 12*

The angel brought me, Ezekiel, back to the entrance of the temple of the LORD, and I saw water flowing out from beneath the threshold of the temple toward the east, for the façade of the temple was toward the east; the water flowed down from the right side of the temple, south of the altar. He led me outside by the north gate, and around to the outer gate facing the east, where I saw water trickling from the right side. Then when he had walked off to the east with a measuring cord in his hand, he measured off a thousand cubits and had me wade through the water, which was ankle–deep. He measured off another thousand and once more had me wade through the water, which was now knee–deep. Again he measured off a thousand and had me wade; the water was up to my waist. Once more he measured off a thousand, but there was now a river through which I could not wade; for the water had risen so high it had become a river that could not be crossed except by swimming. He asked me, "Have you seen this, son of man?" Then he brought me to the bank of the river, where he had me sit. Along the bank of the river I saw very many trees on both sides. He said to me, "This water flows into the eastern district down upon the Arabah, and empties into the sea, the salt waters, which it makes fresh. Wherever the river flows, every sort of living creature that can multiply shall live, and there shall be abundant fish, for wherever this water comes the sea shall be made fresh. Along both banks of the river, fruit trees of every kind shall grow; their leaves shall not fade, nor their fruit fail. Every month they shall bear fresh fruit, for they shall be watered by the flow from the sanctuary. Their fruit shall serve for food, and their leaves for medicine."

RESPONSORIAL PSALM   *Psalm 46:2–3, 5–6, 8–9*

R. (8) The Lord of hosts is with us; our stronghold is the God of Jacob.

God is our refuge and our strength, / an ever–present help in distress. / Therefore we fear not, though the earth be shaken / and mountains plunge into the depths of the sea. **R.**

There is a stream whose runlets gladden the city of God, / the holy dwelling of the Most High. / God is in its midst; it shall not be disturbed; / God will help it at the break of dawn. **R.**

The LORD of hosts is with us; **/** our stronghold is the God of Jacob. **/** Come! behold the deeds of the LORD, **/** the astounding things he has wrought on earth. **R.**

VERSE BEFORE THE GOSPEL   *Psalm 51:12a, 14a*
R. Praise to you, O Christ, King of Eternal Glory! A clean heart create for me, O God; give me back the joy of your salvation. **R.**

GOSPEL   *John 5:1–16*
There was a feast of the Jews, and Jesus went up to Jerusalem. Now there is in Jerusalem at the Sheep Gate a pool called in Hebrew Bethesda, with five porticoes. In these lay a large number of ill, blind, lame, and crippled. One man was there who had been ill for thirty-eight years. When Jesus saw him lying there and knew that he had been ill for a long time, he said to him, "Do you want to be well?" The sick man answered him, "Sir, I have no one to put me into the pool when the water is stirred up; while I am on my way, someone else gets down there before me." Jesus said to him, "Rise, take up your mat, and walk." Immediately the man became well, took up his mat, and walked.

Now that day was a sabbath. So the Jews said to the man who was cured, "It is the sabbath, and it is not lawful for you to carry your mat." He answered them, "The man who made me well told me, 'Take up your mat and walk.'" They asked him, "Who is the man who told you, 'Take it up and walk'?" The man who was healed did not know who it was, for Jesus had slipped away, since there was a crowd there. After this Jesus found him in the temple area and said to him, "Look, you are well; do not sin any more, so that nothing worse may happen to you." The man went and told the Jews that Jesus was the one who had made him well. Therefore, the Jews began to persecute Jesus because he did this on a sabbath.

MARCH 25, SOLEMNITY OF THE ANNUNCIATION OF THE LORD

FIRST READING   *Isaiah 7:10—14; 8:10*
The LORD spoke to Ahaz, saying: Ask for a sign from the LORD, your God; let it be deep as the nether world, or high as the sky! But Ahaz answered, "I will not ask! I will not tempt the LORD!" Then Isaiah said: Listen, O house of David! Is it not enough for you to weary people, must you also weary my God? Therefore the Lord himself will give you this sign: the virgin shall be with child, and bear a son, and shall name him Emmanuel, which means "God is with us!"

RESPONSORIAL PSALM: *Psalm 40:7—8a, 8b—9, 10, 11 (8a, 9a)*
R. Here I am, Lord; I come to do your will.
Sacrifice or oblation you wished not, **/** but ears open to obedience you gave me. **/** Holocausts or sin–offerings you sought not; **/** then said I, "Behold I come." **R.**
"In the written scroll it is prescribed for me, **/** To do your will, O God, is my delight, **/** and your law is within my heart!" **R.**
I announced your justice in the vast assembly; **/**
I did not restrain my lips, as you, O LORD, know. **R.**

Your justice I kept not hid within my heart; **/** your faithfulness and your salvation I have spoken of; **/** I have made no secret of your kindness **/** and your truth in the vast assembly. **R.**

SECOND READING   *Hebrews 10:4—10*

Brothers and sisters: It is impossible that the blood of bulls and goats takes away sins. For this reason, when Christ came into the world, he said:

"Sacrifice and offering you did not desire, but a body you prepared for me; in holocausts and sin offerings you took no delight. Then I said, 'As is written of me in the scroll, behold, I come to do your will, O God.'"

First Christ says, "Sacrifices and offerings, holocausts and sin offerings, you neither desired nor delighted in." These are offered according to the law. Then he says, "Behold, I come to do your will." He takes away the first to establish the second. By this "will," we have been consecrated through the offering of the Body of Jesus Christ once for all.

ALLELUIA   *John 1:14ab*

R. Alleluia, alleluia. The Word became flesh and made his dwelling among us; and we saw his glory. **R.**

GOSPEL   *Luke 1:26—38*

The angel Gabriel was sent from God to a town of Galilee called Nazareth, to a virgin betrothed to a man named Joseph, of the house of David, and the virgin's name was Mary. And coming to her, he said, "Hail, full of grace! The Lord is with you." But she was greatly troubled at what was said and pondered what sort of greeting this might be. Then the angel said to her, "Do not be afraid, Mary, for you have found favor with God. Behold, you will conceive in your womb and bear a son, and you shall name him Jesus. He will be great and will be called Son of the Most High, and the Lord God will give him the throne of David his father, and he will rule over the house of Jacob forever, and of his Kingdom there will be no end." But Mary said to the angel, "How can this be, since I have no relations with a man?" And the angel said to her in reply, "The Holy Spirit will come upon you, and the power of the Most High will overshadow you. Therefore the child to be born will be called holy, the Son of God. And behold, Elizabeth, your relative, has also conceived a son in her old age, and this is the sixth month for her who was called barren; for nothing will be impossible for God." Mary said, "Behold, I am the handmaid of the Lord. May it be done to me according to your word." Then the angel departed from her.

MARCH 26, 4TH WEEK OF LENT - THURSDAY; ST. MARGARET CLITHEROW
FIRST READING   *Exodus 32:7—14*

The LORD said to Moses, "Go down at once to your people whom you brought out of the land of Egypt, for they have become depraved. They have soon turned aside from the way I pointed out to them, making for themselves a molten calf and worshiping it, sacrificing to it and crying out, 'This is your God, O Israel, who brought you out of the land of Egypt!' The

LORD said to Moses, "I see how stiff-necked this people is. Let me alone, then, that my wrath may blaze up against them to consume them. Then I will make of you a great nation."

But Moses implored the LORD, his God, saying, "Why, O LORD, should your wrath blaze up against your own people, whom you brought out of the land of Egypt with such great power and with so strong a hand? Why should the Egyptians say, 'With evil intent he brought them out, that he might kill them in the mountains and exterminate them from the face of the earth'? Let your blazing wrath die down; relent in punishing your people. Remember your servants Abraham, Isaac and Israel, and how you swore to them by your own self, saying, 'I will make your descendants as numerous as the stars in the sky; and all this land that I promised, I will give your descendants as their perpetual heritage.'" So the LORD relented in the punishment he had threatened to inflict on his people.

RESPONSORIAL PSALM

`Psalm 106:19–20, 21–22, 23`

R. (4a) Remember us, O Lord, as you favor your people.

Our fathers made a calf in Horeb and adored a molten image; / They exchanged their glory for the image of a grass-eating bullock. **R.**

They forgot the God who had saved them, / who had done great deeds in Egypt, / Wondrous deeds in the land of Ham, / terrible things at the Red Sea. **R.**

Then he spoke of exterminating them, / but Moses, his chosen one, / Withstood him in the breach to turn back his destructive wrath. **R.**

VERSE BEFORE THE GOSPEL

John 3:16

R. Praise to you, O Christ, King of Eternal Glory! God so loved the world that he gave his only-begotten Son, so that everyone who believes in him might have eternal life. **R.**

GOSPEL

John 5:31–47

Jesus said to the Jews: "If I testify on my own behalf, my testimony is not true. But there is another who testifies on my behalf, and I know that the testimony he gives on my behalf is true. You sent emissaries to John, and he testified to the truth. I do not accept human testimony, but I say this so that you may be saved. He was a burning and shining lamp, and for a while you were content to rejoice in his light. But I have testimony greater than John's. The works that the Father gave me to accomplish, these works that I perform testify on my behalf that the Father has sent me. Moreover, the Father who sent me has testified on my behalf. But you have never heard his voice nor seen his form, and you do not have his word remaining in you, because you do not believe in the one whom he has sent. You search the Scriptures, because you think you have eternal life through them; even they testify on my behalf. But you do not want to come to me to have life.

"I do not accept human praise; moreover, I know that you do not have the love of God in you. I came in the name of my Father, but you do not accept me; yet if another comes in his own name, you will accept him. How can you believe, when you accept praise from one another and do not seek the praise that comes from the only God? Do not think that I will accuse you before the Father: the one who will accuse you is Moses, in whom you have placed your hope. For if you had believed Moses, you would have believed me, because he wrote about me. But if you do not believe his writings, how will you believe my words?"

MARCH 27, 4TH WEEK OF LENT – FRIDAY; ST. JOHN OF EGYPT

FIRST READING   *Wisdom 2:1a, 12–22*

The wicked said among themselves, thinking not aright: "Let us beset the just one, because he is obnoxious to us; he sets himself against our doings, Reproaches us for transgressions of the law and charges us with violations of our training. He professes to have knowledge of God and styles himself a child of the LORD. To us he is the censure of our thoughts; merely to see him is a hardship for us, Because his life is not like that of others, and different are his ways. He judges us debased; he holds aloof from our paths as from things impure. He calls blest the destiny of the just and boasts that God is his Father. Let us see whether his words be true; let us find out what will happen to him. For if the just one be the son of God, he will defend him and deliver him from the hand of his foes. With revilement and torture let us put him to the test that we may have proof of his gentleness and try his patience. Let us condemn him to a shameful death; for according to his own words, God will take care of him." These were their thoughts, but they erred; for their wickedness blinded them, and they knew not the hidden counsels of God; neither did they count on a recompense of holiness nor discern the innocent souls' reward.

RESPONSORIAL PSALM   *Psalm 34:17–18, 19–20, 21 and 23*
R. (19a) The Lord is close to the brokenhearted.
The LORD confronts the evildoers, / to destroy remembrance of them from the earth. / When the just cry out, / the LORD hears them, / and from all their distress he rescues them. **R.**
The LORD is close to the brokenhearted; / and those who are crushed in spirit he saves. / Many are the troubles of the just man, / but out of them all the LORD delivers him. **R.**
He watches over all his bones; / not one of them shall be broken. / The LORD redeems the lives of his servants; / no one incurs guilt who takes refuge in him. **R.**

VERSE BEFORE THE GOSPEL   *Matthew 4:4b*
R. Praise to you, O Christ, King of Eternal Glory! One does not live on bread alone, but on every word that comes forth from the mouth of God. **R.**

GOSPEL   *John 7:1–2, 10, 25–30*

Jesus moved about within Galilee; he did not wish to travel in Judea, because the Jews were trying to kill him. But the Jewish feast of Tabernacles was near.

But when his brothers had gone up to the feast, he himself also went up, not openly but as it were in secret.

Some of the inhabitants of Jerusalem said, "Is he not the one they are trying to kill? And look, he is speaking openly and they say nothing to him. Could the authorities have realized that he is the Christ? But we know where he is from. When the Christ comes, no one will know where he is from." So Jesus cried out in the temple area as he was teaching and said, "You know me and also know where I am from. Yet I did not come on my own, but the one who sent me, whom you do not know, is true. I know him, because I am from him, and he sent me." So they tried to arrest him, but no one laid a hand upon him, because his hour had not yet come.

MARCH 28, 4TH WEEK OF LENT - SATURDAY; ST. TUTILO

FIRST READING *Jeremiah 11:18–20*

I knew their plot because the LORD informed me; at that time you, O LORD, showed me their doings.

Yet I, like a trusting lamb led to slaughter, had not realized that they were hatching plots against me: "Let us destroy the tree in its vigor; let us cut him off from the land of the living, so that his name will be spoken no more."

But, you, O LORD of hosts, O just Judge, searcher of mind and heart, Let me witness the vengeance you take on them, for to you I have entrusted my cause!

RESPONSORIAL PSALM *Psalm 7:2–3, 9bc–10, 11–12*

R. (2a) O Lord, my God, in you I take refuge.

O LORD, my God, in you I take refuge; / save me from all my pursuers and rescue me, / Lest I become like the lion's prey, / to be torn to pieces, with no one to rescue me. **R.**

Do me justice, O LORD, / because I am just, / and because of the innocence that is mine. / Let the malice of the wicked come to an end, / but sustain the just, / O searcher of heart and soul, / O just God. **R.**

A shield before me is God, / who saves the upright of heart; / A just judge is God, / a God who punishes day by day. **R.**

VERSE BEFORE THE GOSPEL *See Luke 8:15*

R. Praise to you, O Christ, King of Eternal Glory! Blessed are they who have kept the word with a generous heart and yield a harvest through perseverance. **R.**

GOSPEL *John 7:40–53*

Some in the crowd who heard these words of Jesus said, "This is truly the Prophet." Others said, "This is the Christ." But others said, "The Christ will not come from Galilee, will he? Does not Scripture say that the Christ will be of David's family and come from Bethlehem, the village where David lived?" So a division occurred in the crowd because of him. Some of them even wanted to arrest him, but no one laid hands on him.

So the guards went to the chief priests and Pharisees, who asked them, "Why did you not bring him?" The guards answered, "Never before has anyone spoken like this man." So the Pharisees answered them, "Have you also been deceived? Have any of the authorities or the Pharisees believed in him? But this crowd, which does not know the law, is accursed." Nicodemus, one of their members who had come to him earlier, said to them, "Does our law condemn a man before it first hears him and finds out what he is doing?" They answered and said to him, "You are not from Galilee also, are you? Look and see that no prophet arises from Galilee." Then each went to his own house.

MARCH 29, 5TH SUNDAY OF LENT; ST. JONAS AND ST. BARACHISIUS

FIRST READING   *Ezekiel 37:12—14*

Thus says the LORD God: O my people, I will open your graves and have you rise from them, and bring you back to the land of Israel. Then you shall know that I am the LORD, when I open your graves and have you rise from them, O my people! I will put my spirit in you that you may live, and I will settle you upon your land; thus you shall know that I am the LORD. I have promised, and I will do it, says the LORD.

RESPONSORIAL PSALM   *Psalm 130:1—2, 3—4, 5—6, 7—8 (7)*

R. With the Lord there is mercy and fullness of redemption.

Out of the depths I cry to you, O LORD; / LORD, hear my voice! / Let your ears be attentive to my voice in supplication. **R.**

If you, O LORD, mark iniquities, / LORD, who can stand? / But with you is forgiveness, / that you may be revered. **R.**

I trust in the LORD; my soul trusts in his word. / More than sentinels wait for the dawn, / let Israel wait for the LORD. **R.**

For with the LORD is kindness and with him is plenteous redemption; / and he will redeem Israel from all their iniquities. **R.**

SECOND READING   *Romans 8:8—11*

Brothers and sisters: Those who are in the flesh cannot please God. But you are not in the flesh; on the contrary, you are in the spirit, if only the Spirit of God dwells in you. Whoever does not have the Spirit of Christ does not belong to him. But if Christ is in you, although the body is dead because of sin, the spirit is alive because of righteousness. If the Spirit of the one who raised Jesus from the dead dwells in you, the One who raised Christ from the dead will give life to your mortal bodies also, through his Spirit dwelling in you.

VERSE BEFORE THE GOSPEL   *John 11:25a, 26*

R. Praise to you, O Christ, King of Eternal Glory! I am the resurrection and the life, says the Lord; whoever believes in me will never die. **R.**

GOSPEL   *Longer Form John 11:1—45*

Now a man was ill, Lazarus from Bethany, the village of Mary and her sister Martha. Mary was the one who had anointed the Lord with perfumed oil and dried his feet with her hair; it was her brother Lazarus who was ill. So the sisters sent word to Jesus saying, "Master, the one you love is ill." When Jesus heard this he said, "This illness is not to end in death, but is for the glory of God, that the Son of God may be glorified through it." Now Jesus loved Martha and her sister and Lazarus. So when he heard that he was ill, he remained for two days in the place where he was. Then after this he said to his disciples, "Let us go back to Judea." The disciples said to him, "Rabbi, the Jews were just trying to stone you, and you want to go back there?" Jesus answered, "Are there not twelve hours in a day? If one walks during the day, he does not stumble, because he sees the light of this world. But if one walks at night, he stumbles, because the light is not in him." He said this, and then told them, "Our friend Lazarus is asleep, but I am going to awaken him." So the disciples said to him, "Master, if he is asleep, he will be saved." But Jesus was talking about his death, while they thought that he meant ordinary sleep. So then Jesus said to them clearly, "Lazarus has died. And I am glad for you that I was not there, that you may believe. Let us go to him." So Thomas, called Didymus, said to his fellow disciples, "Let us also go to die with him."

When Jesus arrived, he found that Lazarus had already been in the tomb for four days. Now Bethany was near Jerusalem, only about two miles away. And many of the Jews had come to Martha and Mary to comfort them about their brother. When Martha heard that Jesus was coming, she went to meet him; but Mary sat at home. Martha said to Jesus, "Lord, if you had been here, my brother would not have died. But even now I know that whatever you ask of God, God will give you." Jesus said to her, "Your brother will rise." Martha said to him, "I know he will rise, in the resurrection on the last day." Jesus told her, "I am the resurrection and the life; whoever believes in me, even if he dies, will live, and everyone who lives and believes in me will never die. Do you believe this?" She said to him, "Yes, Lord. I have come to believe that you are the Christ, the Son of God, the one who is coming into the world."

When she had said this, she went and called her sister Mary secretly, saying, "The teacher is here and is asking for you." As soon as she heard this, she rose quickly and went to him. For Jesus had not yet come into the village, but was still where Martha had met him. So when the Jews who were with her in the house comforting her saw Mary get up quickly and go out, they followed her, presuming that she was going to the tomb to weep there. When Mary came to where Jesus was and saw him, she fell at his feet and said to him, "Lord, if you had been here, my brother would not have died." When Jesus saw her weeping and the Jews who had come with her weeping, he became perturbed and deeply troubled, and said, "Where have you laid him?" They said to him, "Sir, come and see." And Jesus wept. So the Jews said, "See how he loved him." But some of them said, "Could not the one who opened the eyes of the blind man have done something so that this man would not have died?"

So Jesus, perturbed again, came to the tomb. It was a cave, and a stone lay across it. Jesus said, "Take away the stone." Martha, the dead man's sister, said to him, "Lord, by now there will be a stench; he has been dead for four days." Jesus said to her, "Did I not tell you that if you believe you will see the glory of God?" So they took away the stone. And Jesus raised his eyes and said, "Father, I thank you for hearing me. I know that you always hear me; but because of the crowd here I have said this, that they may believe that you sent me." And when he had said this, he cried out in a loud voice, "Lazarus, come out!" The dead man came out, tied hand and foot with burial bands, and his face was wrapped in a cloth. So Jesus said to them, "Untie him and let him go."

Now many of the Jews who had come to Mary and seen what he had done began to believe in him.

SHORTER FORM   *John 11:3—7, 17, 20—27, 33b—45*

The sisters of Lazarus sent word to Jesus, saying, "Master, the one you love is ill." When Jesus heard this he said, "This illness is not to end in death, but is for the glory of God, that the Son of God may be glorified through it." Now Jesus loved Martha and her sister and Lazarus. So when he heard that he was ill, he remained for two days in the place where he was. Then after this he said to his disciples, "Let us go back to Judea."

When Jesus arrived, he found that Lazarus had already been in the tomb for four days. When Martha heard that Jesus was coming, she went to meet him; but Mary sat at home. Martha said to Jesus, "Lord, if you had been here, my brother would not have died. But even now I know that whatever you ask of God, God will give you." Jesus said to her, "Your brother will rise." Martha said, "I know he will rise, in the resurrection on the last day." Jesus told her, "I am the resurrection and the life; whoever believes in me, even if he dies, will live, and everyone who lives and believes in me will never die. Do you believe this?" She said to him, "Yes, Lord. I have come to believe that you are the Christ, the Son of God, the one who is coming into the world."

He became perturbed and deeply troubled, and said, "Where have you laid him?" They said to him, "Sir, come and see." And Jesus wept. So the Jews said, "See how he loved him." But some of them said, "Could not the one who opened the eyes of the blind man have done something so that this man would not have died?"

So Jesus, perturbed again, came to the tomb. It was a cave, and a stone lay across it. Jesus said, "Take away the stone." Martha, the dead man's sister, said to him, "Lord, by now there will be a stench; he has been dead for four days." Jesus said to her, "Did I not tell you that if you believe you will see the glory of God?" So they took away the stone. And Jesus raised his eyes and said, "Father, I thank you for hearing me. I know that you always hear me; but because of the crowd here I have said this, that they may believe that you sent me." And when he had said this, He cried out in a loud voice, "Lazarus, come out!" The dead man came out, tied hand and foot with burial bands, and his face was wrapped in a cloth. So Jesus said to them, "Untie him and let him go."

Now many of the Jews who had come to Mary and seen what he had done began to believe in him.

MARCH 30, 5TH WEEK OF LENT – MONDAY; ST. JOHN CLIMACUS

FIRST READING   *Daniel 13:1–9, 15–17, 19–30, 33–62*

In Babylon there lived a man named Joakim, who married a very beautiful and God–fearing woman, Susanna, the daughter of Hilkiah; her pious parents had trained their daughter according to the law of Moses. Joakim was very rich; he had a garden near his house, and the Jews had recourse to him often because he was the most respected of them all.

That year, two elders of the people were appointed judges, of whom the Lord said, "Wickedness has come out of Babylon: from the elders who were to govern the people as judges." These men, to whom all brought their cases, frequented the house of Joakim. When the people left at noon, Susanna used to enter her husband's garden for a walk. When the old men saw her enter every day for her walk, they began to lust for her. They suppressed their consciences; they would not allow their eyes to look to heaven, and did not keep in mind just judgments.

One day, while they were waiting for the right moment, she entered the garden as usual, with two maids only. She decided to bathe, for the weather was warm. Nobody else was there except the two elders, who had hidden themselves and were watching her. "Bring me oil and soap," she said to the maids, "and shut the garden doors while I bathe."

As soon as the maids had left, the two old men got up and hurried to her. "Look," they said, "the garden doors are shut, and no one can see us; give in to our desire, and lie with us. If you refuse, we will testify against you that you dismissed your maids because a young man was here with you."

"I am completely trapped," Susanna groaned. "If I yield, it will be my death; if I refuse, I cannot escape your power. Yet it is better for me to fall into your power without guilt than to sin before the Lord." Then Susanna shrieked, and the old men also shouted at her, as one of them ran to open the garden doors. When the people in the house heard the cries from the garden, they rushed in by the side gate to see what had happened to her. At the accusations by the old men, the servants felt very much ashamed, for never had any such thing been said about Susanna.

When the people came to her husband Joakim the next day, the two wicked elders also came, fully determined to put Susanna to death. Before all the people they ordered: "Send for Susanna, the daughter of Hilkiah, the wife of Joakim." When she was sent for, she came with her parents, children and all her relatives. All her relatives and the onlookers were weeping.

In the midst of the people the two elders rose up and laid their hands on her head. Through tears she looked up to heaven, for she trusted in the Lord wholeheartedly. The elders made this accusation: "As we were walking in the garden alone, this woman entered with two girls and shut the doors of the garden, dismissing the girls. A young man, who was hidden there, came and lay with her. When we, in a corner of the garden, saw this crime, we ran toward them. We saw them lying together, but the man we could not hold, because he was stronger than we; he opened the doors and ran off. Then we seized her and asked who the young man was, but she refused to tell us. We testify to this." The assembly believed them, since they were elders and judges of the people, and they condemned her to death.

But Susanna cried aloud: "O eternal God, you know what is hidden and are aware of all things before they come to be: you know that they have testified falsely against me. Here I am about to die, though I have done none of the things with which these wicked men have charged me."

The Lord heard her prayer. As she was being led to execution, God stirred up the holy spirit of a young boy named Daniel, and he cried aloud: "I will have no part in the death of this woman." All the people turned and asked him, "What is this you are saying?" He stood in their midst and continued, "Are you such fools, O children of Israel! To condemn a woman of Israel without examination and without clear evidence? Return to court, for they have testified falsely against her."

Then all the people returned in haste. To Daniel the elders said, ACome, sit with us and inform us, since God has given you the prestige of old age." But he replied, "Separate these two far from each other that I may examine them."

After they were separated one from the other, he called one of them and said: "How you have grown evil with age! Now have your past sins come to term: passing unjust sentences, condemning the innocent, and freeing the guilty, although the Lord says, 'The innocent and the just you shall not put to death.' Now, then, if you were a witness, tell me under what tree you saw them together." "Under a mastic tree," he answered. Daniel replied, "Your fine lie has cost you your head, for the angel of God shall receive the sentence from him and split you in two." Putting him to one side, he ordered the other one to be brought. Daniel said to him, "Offspring of Canaan, not of Judah, beauty has seduced you, lust has subverted your conscience. This is how you acted with the daughters of Israel, and in their fear they yielded to you; but a daughter of Judah did not tolerate your wickedness. Now, then, tell me under what tree you surprised them together." "Under an oak," he said. Daniel replied, "Your fine lie has cost you also your head, for the angel of God waits with a sword to cut you in two so as to make an end of you both."

The whole assembly cried aloud, blessing God who saves those who hope in him. They rose up against the two elders, for by their own words Daniel had convicted them of perjury. According to the law of Moses, they inflicted on them the penalty they had plotted to impose on their neighbor: they put them to death. Thus was innocent blood spared that day.

ALTERNATIVE READING   Daniel 13:41c–62

The assembly condemned Susanna to death.

But Susanna cried aloud: "O eternal God, you know what is hidden and are aware of all things before they come to be: you know that they have testified falsely against me. Here I am about to die, though I have done none of the things with which these wicked men have charged me."

The Lord heard her prayer. As she was being led to execution, God stirred up the holy spirit of a young boy named Daniel, and he cried aloud: "I will have no part in the death of this woman." All the people turned and asked him, "What is this you are saying?" He stood in their midst and continued, "Are you such fools, O children of Israel! To condemn a woman of Israel without examination and without clear evidence? Return to court, for they have testified falsely against her."

Then all the people returned in haste. To Daniel the elders said, "Come, sit with us and inform us, since God has given you the prestige of old age." But he replied, "Separate these two far from each other that I may examine them."

After they were separated one from the other, he called one of them and said: "How you have grown evil with age! Now have your past sins come to term: passing unjust sentences, condemning the innocent, and freeing the guilty, although the Lord says, 'The innocent and the just you shall not put to death.' Now, then, if you were a witness, tell me under what tree you saw them together." "Under a mastic tree," he answered. Daniel replied, "Your fine lie has cost you your head, for the angel of God shall receive the sentence from him and split you in two." Putting him to one side, he ordered the other one to be brought. Daniel said to him, "Offspring of Canaan, not of Judah, beauty has seduced you, lust has subverted your conscience. This is how you acted with the daughters of Israel, and in their fear they yielded to you; but a daughter of Judah did not tolerate your wickedness. Now, then, tell me under what tree you surprised them together." "Under an oak," he said. Daniel replied, "Your fine lie has cost you also your head," for the angel of God waits with a sword to cut you in two so as to make an end of you both."

The whole assembly cried aloud, blessing God who saves those who hope in him. They rose up against the two elders, for by their own words Daniel had convicted them of perjury. According to the law of Moses, they inflicted on them the penalty they had plotted to impose on their neighbor: they put them to death. Thus was innocent blood spared that day.

RESPONSORIAL PSALM   *Psalm 23:1–3a, 3b–4, 5, 6*
R. (4ab) Even though I walk in the dark valley I fear no evil; for you are at my side.
The LORD is my shepherd; / I shall not want. / In verdant pastures he gives me repose; / Beside restful waters he leads me; / he refreshes my soul. **R.**
He guides me in right paths for his name's sake. / Even though I walk in the dark valley I fear no evil; / for you are at my side / with your rod and your staff that give me courage. **R.**
You spread the table before me in the sight of my foes; / You anoint my head with oil; / my cup overflows. **R.**
Only goodness and kindness follow me / all the days of my life; / And I shall dwell in the house of the LORD for years to come. **R.**

VERSE BEFORE THE GOSPEL   *Ezekiel 33:11*
R. Praise to you, O Christ, King of Eternal Glory! I take no pleasure in the death of the wicked man, says the Lord, but rather in his conversion, that he may live. **R.**

GOSPEL   *John 8:1–11*
Jesus went to the Mount of Olives. But early in the morning he arrived again in the temple area, and all the people started coming to him, and he sat down and taught them. Then the scribes and the Pharisees brought a woman who had been caught in adultery and made her stand in the middle. They said to him, "Teacher, this woman was caught in the very act of committing adultery. Now in the law, Moses commanded us to stone such women. So what do you say?" They said this to test him, so that they could have some charge to bring against him. Jesus bent down and began to write on the ground with his finger. But when they continued asking him, he straightened up and said to them, "Let the one among you who is without sin be the first to throw a stone at her." Again he bent down and wrote on the ground. And in response, they went away one by one, beginning with the elders. So he was left alone with the woman before him. Then Jesus straightened up and said to her, "Woman, where are they? Has no one condemned you?" She replied, "No one, sir." Then Jesus said, "Neither do I condemn you. Go, and from now on do not sin any more."

MARCH 31, 5TH WEEK OF LENT – TUESDAY; ST. GUY OF POMPOSA

FIRST READING *Numbers 21:4–9*

From Mount Hor the children of Israel set out on the Red Sea road, to bypass the land of Edom. But with their patience worn out by the journey, the people complained against God and Moses, "Why have you brought us up from Egypt to die in this desert, where there is no food or water? We are disgusted with this wretched food!"

In punishment the LORD sent among the people saraph serpents, which bit the people so that many of them died. Then the people came to Moses and said, "We have sinned in complaining against the LORD and you. Pray the LORD to take the serpents away from us." So Moses prayed for the people, and the LORD said to Moses, "Make a saraph and mount it on a pole, and whoever looks at it after being bitten will live." Moses accordingly made a bronze serpent and mounted it on a pole, and whenever anyone who had been bitten by a serpent looked at the bronze serpent, he lived.

RESPONSORIAL PSALM *Psalm 102:2–3, 16–18, 19–21*

R. (2) O Lord, hear my prayer, and let my cry come to you.

O LORD, hear my prayer, and let my cry come to you. / Hide not your face from me in the day of my distress. / Incline your ear to me; / in the day when I call, answer me speedily. **R.**
The nations shall revere your name, O LORD, / and all the kings of the earth your glory, / When the LORD has rebuilt Zion and appeared in his glory; / when he has regarded the prayer of the destitute, / and not despised their prayer. **R.**
Let this be written for the generation to come, / and let his future creatures praise the LORD: / "The LORD looked down from his holy height, / from heaven he beheld the earth, / to hear the groaning of the prisoners, / to release those doomed to die." **R.**

VERSE BEFORE THE GOSPEL

R. Praise to you, O Christ, King of Eternal Glory! The seed is the word of God, Christ is the sower; all who come to him will live for ever. **R.**

GOSPEL *John 8:21–30*

Jesus said to the Pharisees: "I am going away and you will look for me, but you will die in your sin. Where I am going you cannot come." So the Jews said, "He is not going to kill himself, is he, because he said, 'Where I am going you cannot come'?" He said to them, "You belong to what is below, I belong to what is above. You belong to this world, but I do not belong to this world. That is why I told you that you will die in your sins. For if you do not believe that I AM, you will die in your sins." So they said to him, "Who are you?" Jesus said to them, "What I told you from the beginning. I have much to say about you in condemnation. But the one who sent me is true, and what I heard from him I tell the world." They did not realize that he was speaking to them of the Father. So Jesus said to them, "When you lift up the Son of Man, then you will realize that I AM, and that I do nothing on my own, but I say only what the Father taught me. The one who sent me is with me. He has not left me alone, because I always do what is pleasing to him." Because he spoke this way, many came to believe in him.

APRIL 1, 5TH WEEK OF LENT - WEDNESDAY; ST. HUGH OF GRENOBLE

FIRST READING   *Daniel 3:14–20, 91–92, 95*

King Nebuchadnezzar said: "Is it true, Shadrach, Meshach, and Abednego, that you will not serve my god, or worship the golden statue that I set up? Be ready now to fall down and worship the statue I had made, whenever you hear the sound of the trumpet, flute, lyre, harp, psaltery, bagpipe, and all the other musical instruments; otherwise, you shall be instantly cast into the white–hot furnace; and who is the God who can deliver you out of my hands?" Shadrach, Meshach, and Abednego answered King Nebuchadnezzar, "There is no need for us to defend ourselves before you in this matter. If our God, whom we serve, can save us from the white–hot furnace and from your hands, O king, may he save us! But even if he will not, know, O king, that we will not serve your god or worship the golden statue that you set up."

King Nebuchadnezzar's face became livid with utter rage against Shadrach, Meshach, and Abednego. He ordered the furnace to be heated seven times more than usual and had some of the strongest men in his army bind Shadrach, Meshach, and Abednego and cast them into the white–hot furnace.

Nebuchadnezzar rose in haste and asked his nobles, "Did we not cast three men bound into the fire?" "Assuredly, O king," they answered. "But," he replied, "I see four men unfettered and unhurt, walking in the fire, and the fourth looks like a son of God." Nebuchadnezzar exclaimed, "Blessed be the God of Shadrach, Meshach, and Abednego, who sent his angel to deliver the servants who trusted in him; they disobeyed the royal command and yielded their bodies rather than serve or worship any god except their own God."

RESPONSORIAL PSALM   *Daniel 3:52, 53, 54, 55, 56*

R. (52b) Glory and praise for ever!

"Blessed are you, O Lord, the God of our fathers, / praiseworthy and exalted above all forever; /And blessed is your holy and glorious name, / praiseworthy and exalted above all for all ages." **R.**

"Blessed are you in the temple of your holy glory, / praiseworthy and exalted above all forever. **R.**

"Blessed are you on the throne of your kingdom, / praiseworthy and exalted above all forever." **R.**

"Blessed are you who look into the depths from your throne upon the cherubim; / praiseworthy and exalted above all forever." **R.**

"Blessed are you in the firmament of heaven, / praiseworthy and glorious forever." **R.**

VERSE BEFORE THE GOSPEL   *See Luke 8:15*

R. Praise to you, O Christ, King of Eternal Glory! Blessed are they who have kept the word with a generous heart and yield a harvest through perseverance. **R.**

GOSPEL   *John 8:31–42*

Jesus said to those Jews who believed in him, "If you remain in my word, you will truly be my disciples, and you will know the truth, and the truth will set you free." They answered him, "We are descendants of Abraham and have never been enslaved to anyone. How can you say, 'You will become free'?" Jesus answered them, "Amen, amen, I say to you, everyone who commits sin is a slave of sin. A slave does not remain in a household forever, but a son always remains. So if the Son frees you, then you will truly be free. I know that you are descendants of Abraham. But you are trying to kill me, because my word has no room among you. I tell you what I have seen in the Father's presence; then do what you have heard from the Father."

They answered and said to him, "Our father is Abraham." Jesus said to them, "If you were Abraham's children, you would be doing the works of Abraham. But now you are trying to kill me, a man who has told you the truth that I heard from God; Abraham did not do this. You are doing the works of your father!" So they said to him, "We were not born of fornication. We have one Father, God." Jesus said to them, "If God were your Father, you would love me, for I came from God and am here; I did not come on my own, but he sent me."

APRIL 2, 5TH WEEK OF LENT – THURSDAY; ST. FRANCIS OF PAOLA

FIRST READING   *Genesis 17:3–9*

When Abram prostrated himself, God spoke to him: "My covenant with you is this: you are to become the father of a host of nations. No longer shall you be called Abram; your name shall be Abraham, for I am making you the father of a host of nations. I will render you exceedingly fertile; I will make nations of you; kings shall stem from you. I will maintain my covenant with you and your descendants after you throughout the ages as an everlasting pact, to be your God and the God of your descendants after you. I will give to you and to your descendants after you the land in which you are now staying, the whole land of Canaan, as a permanent possession; and I will be their God." God also said to Abraham: "On your part, you and your descendants after you must keep my covenant throughout the ages."

RESPONSORIAL PSALM   *Psalm 105:4–5, 6–7, 8–9*

R. (8a) The Lord remembers his covenant for ever.

Look to the LORD in his strength; / seek to serve him constantly. / Recall the wondrous deeds that he has wrought, / his portents, and the judgments he has uttered. **R.**

You descendants of Abraham, his servants, / sons of Jacob, his chosen ones! / He, the LORD, is our God; / throughout the earth his judgments prevail. **R.**

He remembers forever his covenant / which he made binding for a thousand generations / Which he entered into with Abraham and by his oath to Isaac. **R.**

VERSE BEFORE THE GOSPEL   *Psalm 95:8*

R. Praise to you, O Christ, King of Eternal Glory! If today you hear his voice, harden not your hearts.

GOSPEL
John 8:51–59

Jesus said to the Jews: "Amen, amen, I say to you, whoever keeps my word will never see death." So the Jews said to him, "Now we are sure that you are possessed. Abraham died, as did the prophets, yet you say, 'Whoever keeps my word will never taste death.' Are you greater than our father Abraham, who died? Or the prophets, who died? Who do you make yourself out to be?" Jesus answered, "If I glorify myself, my glory is worth nothing; but it is my Father who glorifies me, of whom you say, 'He is our God.' You do not know him, but I know him. And if I should say that I do not know him, I would be like you a liar. But I do know him and I keep his word. Abraham your father rejoiced to see my day; he saw it and was glad." So the Jews said to him, "You are not yet fifty years old and you have seen Abraham?" Jesus said to them, "Amen, amen, I say to you, before Abraham came to be, I AM." So they picked up stones to throw at him; but Jesus hid and went out of the temple area.

APRIL 3, 5TH WEEK OF LENT - FRIDAY; ST. RICHARD DE WYCHE
FIRST READING
Jeremiah 20:10–13

I hear the whisperings of many: "Terror on every side! Denounce! let us denounce him!" All those who were my friends are on the watch for any misstep of mine. APerhaps he will be trapped; then we can prevail, and take our vengeance on him." But the LORD is with me, like a mighty champion: my persecutors will stumble, they will not triumph. In their failure they will be put to utter shame, to lasting, unforgettable confusion. O LORD of hosts, you who test the just, who probe mind and heart, Let me witness the vengeance you take on them, for to you I have entrusted my cause. Sing to the LORD, praise the LORD, For he has rescued the life of the poor from the power of the wicked!

RESPONSORIAL PSALM
Psalm 18:2–3a, 3bc–4, 5–6, 7

R. (see 7) In my distress I called upon the Lord, and he heard my voice.
I love you, O LORD, my strength, / O LORD, my rock, my fortress, my deliverer. **R.**
My God, my rock of refuge, / my shield, the horn of my salvation, my stronghold! Praised be the LORD, I exclaim, / and I am safe from my enemies. **R.**
The breakers of death surged round about me, / the destroying floods overwhelmed me; / The cords of the nether world enmeshed me, / the snares of death overtook me. **R.**
In my distress I called upon the LORD / and cried out to my God; / From his temple he heard my voice, / and my cry to him reached his ears. **R.**

VERSE BEFORE THE GOSPEL
See John 6:63c, 68c

R. Praise to you, O Christ, King of Eternal Glory! Your words, Lord, are Spirit and life; you have the words of everlasting life. **R.**

GOSPEL
John 10:31–42

The Jews picked up rocks to stone Jesus. Jesus answered them, "I have shown you many good works from my Father. For which of these are you trying to stone me?" The Jews answered him, "We are not stoning you for a good work but for blasphemy. You, a man, are making yourself God." Jesus answered them, "Is it not written in your law, 'I said, You are gods'"? If it calls them gods to whom the word of God came, and Scripture cannot be set aside, can you say that the one whom the Father has consecrated and sent into the world blasphemes because I said, 'I am the Son of God'? If I do not perform my Father's works, do not believe me; but if I perform them, even if you do not believe me, believe the works, so that you may realize and understand that the Father is in me and I am in the Father." Then they tried again to arrest him; but he escaped from their power.

He went back across the Jordan to the place where John first baptized, and there he remained. Many came to him and said, "John performed no sign, but everything John said about this man was true." And many there began to believe in him.

APRIL 4, 5TH WEEK OF LENT – SATURDAY; ST. ISIDORE OF SEVILLE

FIRST READING *Ezekiel 37:21–28*

Thus says the Lord GOD: I will take the children of Israel from among the nations to which they have come, and gather them from all sides to bring them back to their land. I will make them one nation upon the land, in the mountains of Israel, and there shall be one prince for them all. Never again shall they be two nations, and never again shall they be divided into two kingdoms.

No longer shall they defile themselves with their idols, their abominations, and all their transgressions. I will deliver them from all their sins of apostasy, and cleanse them so that they may be my people and I may be their God. My servant David shall be prince over them, and there shall be one shepherd for them all; they shall live by my statutes and carefully observe my decrees. They shall live on the land that I gave to my servant Jacob, the land where their fathers lived; they shall live on it forever, they, and their children, and their children's children, with my servant David their prince forever. I will make with them a covenant of peace; it shall be an everlasting covenant with them, and I will multiply them, and put my sanctuary among them forever. My dwelling shall be with them; I will be their God, and they shall be my people. Thus the nations shall know that it is I, the LORD, who make Israel holy, when my sanctuary shall be set up among them forever.

RESPONSORIAL PSALM *Jeremiah 31:10, 11–12abcd, 13*

R. (see 10d) **The Lord will guard us, as a shepherd guards his flock.**

Hear the word of the LORD, O nations, / proclaim it on distant isles, and say: / He who scattered Israel, now gathers them together, / he guards them as a shepherd his flock. **R.**

The LORD shall ransom Jacob, / he shall redeem him from the hand of his conqueror. / Shouting, they shall mount the heights of Zion, / they shall come streaming to the LORD's blessings: / The grain, the wine, and the oil, the sheep and the oxen. **R.**

Then the virgins shall make merry and dance, / and young men and old as well. / I will turn their mourning into joy, / I will console and gladden them after their sorrows. **R.**

VERSE BEFORE THE GOSPEL *Ezekiel 18:31*

R. **Praise to you, O Christ, King of Eternal Glory!** Cast away from you all the crimes you have committed, says the Lord, and make for yourselves a new heart and a new spirit. **R.**

GOSPEL   *John 11:45–56*

Many of the Jews who had come to Mary and seen what Jesus had done began to believe in him. But some of them went to the Pharisees and told them what Jesus had done. So the chief priests and the Pharisees convened the Sanhedrin and said, "What are we going to do? This man is performing many signs. If we leave him alone, all will believe in him, and the Romans will come and take away both our land and our nation." But one of them, Caiaphas, who was high priest that year, said to them, "You know nothing, nor do you consider that it is better for you that one man should die instead of the people, so that the whole nation may not perish." He did not say this on his own, but since he was high priest for that year, he prophesied that Jesus was going to die for the nation, and not only for the nation, but also to gather into one the dispersed children of God. So from that day on they planned to kill him.

So Jesus no longer walked about in public among the Jews, but he left for the region near the desert, to a town called Ephraim, and there he remained with his disciples.

Now the Passover of the Jews was near, and many went up from the country to Jerusalem before Passover to purify themselves. They looked for Jesus and said to one another as they were in the temple area, "What do you think? That he will not come to the feast?"

APRIL 5, PALM SUNDAY OF THE LORD'S PASSION; ST. VINCENT FERRER

AT THE PROCESSION WITH PALMS

GOSPEL   *Matthew 21:1—11*

When Jesus and the disciples drew near Jerusalem and came to Bethphage on the Mount of Olives, Jesus sent two disciples, saying to them, "Go into the village opposite you, and immediately you will find an ass tethered, and a colt with her. Untie them and bring them here to me. And if anyone should say anything to you, reply, 'The master has need of them.' Then he will send them at once." This happened so that what had been spoken through the prophet might be fulfilled: *Say to daughter Zion, "Behold, your king comes to you, meek and riding on an ass, and on a colt, the foal of a beast of burden."* The disciples went and did as Jesus had ordered them. They brought the ass and the colt and laid their cloaks over them, and he sat upon them. The very large crowd spread their cloaks on the road, while others cut branches from the trees and strewed them on the road. The crowds preceding him and those following kept crying out and saying: "Hosanna to the Son of David; blessed is he who comes in the name of the Lord; hosanna in the highest." And when he entered Jerusalem the whole city was shaken and asked, "Who is this?" And the crowds replied, "This is Jesus the prophet, from Nazareth in Galilee."

AT THE MASS

FIRST READING   *Isaiah 50:4—7*

The Lord GOD has given me a well-trained tongue, that I might know how to speak to the weary a word that will rouse them. Morning after morning he opens my ear that I may hear; and I have not rebelled, have not turned back. I gave my back to those who beat me, my cheeks to those who plucked my beard; my face I did not shield from buffets and spitting.

The Lord GOD is my help, therefore I am not disgraced; I have set my face like flint, knowing that I shall not be put to shame.

RESPONSORIAL PSALM: *Psalm 22:8—9, 17—18, 19—20, 23—24 (2a)*
R. My God, my God, why have you abandoned me?
All who see me scoff at me; **/** they mock me with parted lips, **/** they wag their heads: "He relied on the LORD; **/** let him deliver him, let him rescue him, **/** if he loves him." **R.**
Indeed, many dogs surround me, **/** a pack of evildoers closes in upon me, **/** they have pierced my hands and my feet; **/** I can count all my bones. **R.**
They divide my garments among them, **/** and for my vesture they cast lots. **/** But you, O LORD, be not far from me; **/** O my help, hasten to aid me. **R.**
I will proclaim your name to my brethren; **/** in the midst of the assembly I will praise you: **/** "You who fear the LORD, praise him; **/** all you descendants of Jacob, give glory to him; **/** revere him, all you descendants of Israel!" **R.**

SECOND READING *Philippians 2:6—11*
Christ Jesus, though he was in the form of God, did not regard equality with God something to be grasped. Rather, he emptied himself, taking the form of a slave, coming in human likeness; and found human in appearance, he humbled himself, becoming obedient to the point of death, even death on a cross. Because of this, God greatly exalted him and bestowed on him the name which is above every name, that at the name of Jesus every knee should bend, of those in heaven and on earth and under the earth, and every tongue confess that Jesus Christ is Lord, to the glory of God the Father.

VERSE BEFORE THE GOSPEL *Philippians 2:8—9*
R. Praise to you, O Christ, King of Eternal Glory! Christ became obedient to the point of death, even death on a cross. Because of this, God greatly exalted him and bestowed on him the name which is above every name. **R.**

GOSPEL *Longer Form Matthew 26:14—27:66*
One of the Twelve, who was called Judas Iscariot, went to the chief priests and said, "What are you willing to give me if I hand him over to you?" They paid him thirty pieces of silver, and from that time on he looked for an opportunity to hand him over.

On the first day of the Feast of Unleavened Bread, the disciples approached Jesus and said, "Where do you want us to prepare for you to eat the Passover?" He said, "Go into the city to a certain man and tell him, 'The teacher says, "My appointed time draws near; in your house I shall celebrate the Passover with my disciples."'" The disciples then did as Jesus had ordered, and prepared the Passover.

When it was evening, he reclined at table with the Twelve. And while they were eating, he said, "Amen, I say to you, one of you will betray me." Deeply distressed at this, they began to say to him one after another, "Surely it is not I, Lord?" He said in reply, "He who has dipped his hand into the dish with me is the one who will betray me. The Son of Man indeed goes, as it is written of him, but woe to that man by whom the Son of Man is betrayed. It would be better for that man if he had never been born." Then Judas, his betrayer, said in reply, "Surely it is not I, Rabbi?" He answered, "You have said so."

While they were eating, Jesus took bread, said the blessing, broke it, and giving it to his disciples said, "Take and eat; this is my body." Then he took a cup, gave thanks, and gave it to them, saying, "Drink from it, all of you, for this is my blood of the covenant, which will be shed on behalf of many for the forgiveness of sins. I tell you, from now on I shall not drink this fruit of the vine until the day when I drink it with you new in the kingdom of my Father." Then, after singing a hymn, they went out to the Mount of Olives.

Then Jesus said to them, "This night all of you will have your faith in me shaken, for it is written: *I will strike the shepherd, and the sheep of the flock will be dispersed;* but after I have been raised up, I shall go before you to Galilee." Peter said to him in reply, "Though all may have their faith in you shaken, mine will never be." Jesus said to him, "Amen, I say to you, this very night before the cock crows, you will deny me three times." Peter said to him, "Even though I should have to die with you, I will not deny you." And all the disciples spoke likewise.

Then Jesus came with them to a place called Gethsemane, and he said to his disciples, "Sit here while I go over there and pray." He took along Peter and the two sons of Zebedee, and began to feel sorrow and distress. Then he said to them, "My soul is sorrowful even to death. Remain here and keep watch with me." He advanced a little and fell prostrate in prayer, saying, "My Father, if it is possible, let this cup pass from me; yet, not as I will, but as you will." When he returned to his disciples he found them asleep. He said to Peter, "So you could not keep watch with me for one hour? Watch and pray that you may not undergo the test. The spirit is willing, but the flesh is weak." Withdrawing a second time, he prayed again, "My Father, if it is not possible that this cup pass without my drinking it, your will be done!" Then he returned once more and found them asleep, for they could not keep their eyes open. He left them and withdrew again and prayed a third time, saying the same thing again. Then he returned to his disciples and said to them, "Are you still sleeping and taking your rest? Behold, the hour is at hand when the Son of Man is to be handed over to sinners. Get up, let us go. Look, my betrayer is at hand."

While he was still speaking, Judas, one of the Twelve, arrived, accompanied by a large crowd, with swords and clubs, who had come from the chief priests and the elders of the people. His betrayer had arranged a sign with them, saying, "The man I shall kiss is the one; arrest him." Immediately he went over to Jesus and said, "Hail, Rabbi!" and he kissed him. Jesus answered him, "Friend, do what you have come for." Then stepping forward they laid hands on Jesus and arrested him. And behold, one of those who accompanied Jesus put his hand to his sword, drew it, and struck the high priest's servant, cutting off his ear. Then Jesus said to him, "Put your sword back into its sheath, for all who take the sword will perish by the sword. Do you think that I cannot call upon my Father and he will not provide me at this moment with more than twelve legions of angels? But then how would the Scriptures be fulfilled which say that it must come to pass in this way?" At that hour Jesus said to the crowds, "Have you come out as against a robber, with swords and clubs to seize me? Day after day I sat teaching in the temple area, yet you did not arrest me. But all this has come to pass that the writings of the prophets may be fulfilled." Then all the disciples left him and fled.

Those who had arrested Jesus led him away to Caiaphas the high priest, where the scribes and the elders were assembled. Peter was following him at a distance as far as the high priest's courtyard, and going inside he sat down with the servants to see the outcome. The chief priests and the entire Sanhedrin kept trying to obtain false testimony against Jesus in order to put him to death, but they found none, though many false witnesses came forward. Finally two came forward who stated, "This man said, 'I can destroy the temple of God and within three days rebuild it.'" The high priest rose and addressed him, "Have you no answer? What are these men testifying against you?" But Jesus was silent. Then the high priest said to him, "I order you to tell us under oath before the living God whether you are the Christ, the Son of God." Jesus said to him in reply, "You have said so. But I tell you: From now on you will see the 'Son of Man seated at the right hand of the Power' and 'coming on the clouds of heaven.'" Then the high priest tore his robes and said, "He has blasphemed! What further need have we of witnesses? You have now heard the blasphemy; what is your opinion?" They said in reply, "He deserves to die!" Then they spat in his face and struck him, while some slapped him, saying, "Prophesy for us, Christ: who is it that struck you?"

Now Peter was sitting outside in the courtyard. One of the maids came over to him and said, "You too were with Jesus the Galilean." But he denied it in front of everyone, saying, "I do not know what you are talking about!" As he went out to the gate, another girl saw him and said to those who were there, "This man was with Jesus the Nazorean." Again he denied it with an oath, "I do not know the man!" A little later the bystanders came over and said to Peter, "Surely you too are one of them; even your speech gives you away." At that he began to curse and to swear, "I do not know the man." And immediately a cock crowed. Then Peter remembered the words that Jesus had spoken: "Before the cock crows you will deny me three times." He went out and began to weep bitterly.

When it was morning, all the chief priests and the elders of the people took counsel against Jesus to put him to death. They bound him, led him away, and handed him over to Pilate, the governor.

Then Judas, his betrayer, seeing that Jesus had been condemned, deeply regretted what he had done. He returned the thirty pieces of silver to the chief priests and elders, saying, "I have sinned in betraying innocent blood." They said, "What is that to us? Look to it yourself." Flinging the money into the temple, he departed and went off and hanged himself. The chief priests gathered up the money, but said, "It is not lawful to deposit this in the temple treasury, for it is the price of blood." After consultation, they used it to buy the potter's field as a burial place for foreigners. That is why that field even today is called the Field of Blood. Then was fulfilled what had been said through Jeremiah the prophet, *And they took the thirty pieces of silver, the value of a man with a price on his head, a price set by some of the Israelites, and they paid it out for the potter's field just as the Lord had commanded me.*

Now Jesus stood before the governor, and he questioned him, "Are you the king of the Jews?" Jesus said, "You say so." And when he was accused by the chief priests and elders, he made no answer. Then Pilate said to him, "Do you not hear how many things they are testifying against you?" But he did not answer him one word, so that the governor was greatly amazed.

Now on the occasion of the feast the governor was accustomed to release to the crowd one prisoner whom they wished. And at that time they had a notorious prisoner called Barabbas. So when they had assembled, Pilate said to them, "Which one do you want me to release to you, Barabbas, or Jesus called Christ?" For he knew that it was out of envy that they had handed him over. While he was still seated on the bench, his wife sent him a message, "Have nothing to do with that righteous man. I suffered much in a dream today because of him." The chief priests and the elders persuaded the crowds to ask for Barabbas but to destroy Jesus. The governor said to them in reply, "Which of the two do you want me to release to you?" They answered, "Barabbas!" Pilate said to them, "Then what shall I do with Jesus called Christ?" They all said, "Let him be crucified!" But he said, "Why? What evil has he done?" They only shouted the louder, "Let him be crucified!" When Pilate saw that he was not succeeding at all, but that a riot was breaking out instead, he took water and washed his hands in the sight of the crowd, saying, "I am innocent of this man's blood. Look to it yourselves." And the whole people said in reply, "His blood be upon us and upon our children." Then he released Barabbas to them, but after he had Jesus scourged, he handed him over to be crucified.

Then the soldiers of the governor took Jesus inside the praetorium and gathered the whole cohort around him. They stripped off his clothes and threw a scarlet military cloak about him. Weaving a crown out of thorns, they placed it on his head, and a reed in his right hand. And kneeling before him, they mocked him, saying, "Hail, King of the Jews!" They spat upon him and took the reed and kept striking him on the head. And when they had mocked him, they stripped him of the cloak, dressed him in his own clothes, and led him off to crucify him.

As they were going out, they met a Cyrenian named Simon; this man they pressed into service to carry his cross.

And when they came to a place called Golgotha —which means Place of the Skull—, they gave Jesus wine to drink mixed with gall. But when he had tasted it, he refused to drink. After they had crucified him, they divided his garments by casting lots; then they sat down and kept watch over him there. And they placed over his head the written charge against him: This is Jesus, the King of the Jews. Two revolutionaries were crucified with him, one on his right and the other on his left. Those passing by reviled him, shaking their heads and saying, "You who would destroy the temple and rebuild it in three days, save yourself, if you are the Son of God, and come down from the cross!"

Likewise the chief priests with the scribes and elders mocked him and said, "He saved others; he cannot save himself. So he is the king of Israel! Let him come down from the cross now, and we will believe in him. He trusted in God; let him deliver him now if he wants him. For he said, 'I am the Son of God.'" The revolutionaries who were crucified with him also kept abusing him in the same way.

From noon onward, darkness came over the whole land until three in the afternoon. And about three o'clock Jesus cried out in a loud voice, *"Eli, Eli, lema sabachthani?"* which means, "My God, my God, why have you forsaken me?" Some of the bystanders who heard it said, "This one is calling for Elijah." Immediately one of them ran to get a sponge; he soaked it in wine, and putting it on a reed, gave it to him to drink. But the rest said, "Wait, let us see if Elijah comes to save him." But Jesus cried out again in a loud voice, and gave up his spirit.

Here all kneel and pause for a short time.

And behold, the veil of the sanctuary was torn in two from top to bottom. The earth quaked, rocks were split, tombs were opened, and the bodies of many saints who had fallen asleep were raised. And coming forth from their tombs after his resurrection, they entered the holy city and appeared to many. The centurion and the men with him who were keeping watch over Jesus feared greatly when they saw the earthquake and all that was happening, and they said, "Truly, this was the Son of God!" There were many women there, looking on from a distance, who had followed Jesus from Galilee, ministering to him. Among them were Mary Magdalene and Mary the mother of James and Joseph, and the mother of the sons of Zebedee.

When it was evening, there came a rich man from Arimathea named Joseph, who was himself a disciple of Jesus. He went to Pilate and asked for the body of Jesus; then Pilate ordered it to be handed over. Taking the body, Joseph wrapped it in clean linen and laid it in his new tomb that he had hewn in the rock. Then he rolled a huge stone across the entrance to the tomb and departed. But Mary Magdalene and the other Mary remained sitting there, facing the tomb.

The next day, the one following the day of preparation, the chief priests and the Pharisees gathered before Pilate and said, "Sir, we remember that this impostor while still alive said, 'After three days I will be raised up.' Give orders, then, that the grave be secured until the third day, lest his disciples come and steal him and say to the people, 'He has been raised from the dead.' This last imposture would be worse than the first." Pilate said to them, "The guard is yours; go, secure it as best you can." So they went and secured the tomb by fixing a seal to the stone and setting the guard.

SHORTER FORM   *Matthew 27:11—54*

Jesus stood before the governor, Pontius Pilate, who questioned him, "Are you the king of the Jews?" Jesus said, "You say so." And when he was accused by the chief priests and elders, he made no answer. Then Pilate said to him, "Do you not hear how many things they are testifying against you?" But he did not answer him one word, so that the governor was greatly amazed.

Now on the occasion of the feast the governor was accustomed to release to the crowd one prisoner whom they wished. And at that time they had a notorious prisoner called Barabbas. So when they had assembled, Pilate said to them, "Which one do you want me to release to you, Barabbas, or Jesus called Christ?" For he knew that it was out of envy that they had handed him over. While he was still seated on the bench, his wife sent him a message, "Have nothing to do with that righteous man. I suffered much in a dream today because of him." The chief priests and the elders persuaded the crowds to ask for Barabbas but to destroy Jesus. The governor said to them in reply, "Which of the two do you want me to release to you?" They answered, "Barabbas!" Pilate said to them, "Then what shall I do with Jesus called Christ?" They all said, "Let him be crucified!" But he said, "Why? What evil has he done?" They only shouted the louder, "Let him be crucified!" When Pilate saw that he was not succeeding at all, but that a riot was breaking out instead, he took water and washed his hands in the sight of the crowd, saying, "I am innocent of this man's blood. Look to it yourselves." And the whole people said in reply, "His blood be upon us and upon our children." Then he released Barabbas to them, but after he had Jesus scourged, he handed him over to be crucified.

Then the soldiers of the governor took Jesus inside the praetorium and gathered the whole cohort around him. They stripped off his clothes and threw a scarlet military cloak about him. Weaving a crown out of thorns, they placed it on his head, and a reed in his right hand. And kneeling before him, they mocked him, saying, "Hail, King of the Jews!" They spat upon him and took the reed and kept striking him on the head. And when they had mocked him, they stripped him of the cloak, dressed him in his own clothes, and led him off to crucify him.

As they were going out, they met a Cyrenian named Simon; this man they pressed into service to carry his cross.

And when they came to a place called Golgotha —which means Place of the Skull—, they gave Jesus wine to drink mixed with gall. But when he had tasted it, he refused to drink. After they had crucified him, they divided his garments by casting lots; then they sat down and kept watch over him there. And they placed over his head the written charge against him: This is Jesus, the King of the Jews. Two revolutionaries were crucified with him, one on his right and the other on his left. Those passing by reviled him, shaking their heads and saying, "You who would destroy the temple and rebuild it in three days, save yourself, if you are the Son of God, and come down from the cross!" Likewise the chief priests with the scribes and elders mocked him and said, "He saved others; he cannot save himself. So he is the king of Israel! Let him come down from the cross now, and we will believe in him. He trusted in God; let him deliver him now if he wants him. For he said, 'I am the Son of God.'" The revolutionaries who were crucified with him also kept abusing him in the same way.

From noon onward, darkness came over the whole land until three in the afternoon. And about three o'clock Jesus cried out in a loud voice, *"Eli, Eli, lema sabachthani?"* which means, "My God, my God, why have you forsaken me?" Some of the bystanders who heard it said, "This one is calling for Elijah." Immediately one of them ran to get a sponge; he soaked it in wine, and putting it on a reed, gave it to him to drink. But the rest said, "Wait, let us see if Elijah comes to save him." But Jesus cried out again in a loud voice, and gave up his spirit.

Here all kneel and pause for a short time.

And behold, the veil of the sanctuary was torn in two from top to bottom. The earth quaked, rocks were split, tombs were opened, and the bodies of many saints who had fallen asleep were raised. And coming forth from their tombs after his resurrection, they entered the holy city and appeared to many. The centurion and the men with him who were keeping watch over Jesus feared greatly when they saw the earthquake and all that was happening, and they said, "Truly, this was the Son of God!"

APRIL 6, HOLY WEEK - MONDAY; BLESSED NOTKER

FIRST READING *Isaiah 42:1–7*

Here is my servant whom I uphold, my chosen one with whom I am pleased, Upon whom I have put my Spirit; he shall bring forth justice to the nations, Not crying out, not shouting, not making his voice heard in the street. A bruised reed he shall not break, and a smoldering wick he shall not quench, Until he establishes justice on the earth; the coastlands will wait for his teaching.

Thus says God, the LORD, who created the heavens and stretched them out, who spreads out the earth with its crops, Who gives breath to its people and spirit to those who walk on it: I, the LORD, have called you for the victory of justice, I have grasped you by the hand; I formed you, and set you as a covenant of the people, a light for the nations, To open the eyes of the blind, to bring out prisoners from confinement, and from the dungeon, those who live in darkness.

RESPONSORIAL PSALM *Psalm 27:1, 2, 3, 13–14*

R. (1a) The Lord is my light and my salvation.

The LORD is my light and my salvation; / whom should I fear? / The LORD is my life's refuge; / of whom should I be afraid? **R.**

When evildoers come at me to devour my flesh, / My foes and my enemies themselves stumble and fall. **R.**

Though an army encamp against me, / my heart will not fear; / Though war be waged upon me, / even then will I trust. **R.**

I believe that I shall see the bounty of the LORD/ in the land of the living. / Wait for the LORD with courage; / be stouthearted, and wait for the LORD. **R.**

VERSE BEFORE THE GOSPEL

R. Praise to you, O Christ, King of Eternal Glory! Hail to you, our King; you alone are compassionate with our faults. **R.**

GOSPEL *John 12:1–11*

Six days before Passover Jesus came to Bethany, where Lazarus was, whom Jesus had raised from the dead. They gave a dinner for him there, and Martha served, while Lazarus was one of those reclining at table with him. Mary took a liter of costly perfumed oil made from genuine aromatic nard and anointed the feet of Jesus and dried them with her hair; the house was filled with the fragrance of the oil. Then Judas the Iscariot, one of his disciples, and the one who would betray him, said, "Why was this oil not sold for three hundred days' wages and given to the poor?" He said this not because he cared about the poor but because he was a thief and held the money bag and used to steal the contributions. So Jesus said, "Leave her alone. Let her keep this for the day of my burial. You always have the poor with you, but you do not always have me."

The large crowd of the Jews found out that he was there and came, not only because of him, but also to see Lazarus, whom he had raised from the dead. And the chief priests plotted to kill Lazarus too, because many of the Jews were turning away and believing in Jesus because of him.

APRIL 7, HOLY WEEK - TUESDAY; ST. JOHN BAPTIST DE LA SALLE

FIRST READING   *Isaiah 49:1–6*

Hear me, O islands, listen, O distant peoples. The LORD called me from birth, from my mother's womb he gave me my name. He made of me a sharp–edged sword and concealed me in the shadow of his arm. He made me a polished arrow, in his quiver he hid me. You are my servant, he said to me, Israel, through whom I show my glory.

Though I thought I had toiled in vain, and for nothing, uselessly, spent my strength, yet my reward is with the LORD, my recompense is with my God. For now the LORD has spoken who formed me as his servant from the womb, That Jacob may be brought back to him and Israel gathered to him; And I am made glorious in the sight of the LORD, and my God is now my strength! It is too little, he says, for you to be my servant, to raise up the tribes of Jacob, and restore the survivors of Israel; I will make you a light to the nations, that my salvation may reach to the ends of the earth.

RESPONSORIAL PSALM: *Psalm 71:1–2, 3–4a, 5ab–6ab, 15 and 17*

R. (see 15ab) I will sing of your salvation.

In you, O LORD, I take refuge; / let me never be put to shame. / In your justice rescue me, and deliver me; / incline your ear to me, and save me. **R.**

Be my rock of refuge, / a stronghold to give me safety, / for you are my rock and my fortress. / O my God, rescue me from the hand of the wicked. **R.**

For you are my hope, O Lord; / my trust, O God, from my youth. / On you I depend from birth; / from my mother's womb you are my strength. **R.**

My mouth shall declare your justice, /day by day your salvation. / O God, you have taught me from my youth, / and till the present I proclaim your wondrous deeds. **R.**

VERSE BEFORE THE GOSPEL

R. Praise to you, O Christ, King of Eternal Glory! Hail to you, our King, obedient to the Father; you were led to your crucifixion like a gentle lamb to the slaughter. **R.**

GOSPEL   *John 13:21–33, 36–38*

Reclining at table with his disciples, Jesus was deeply troubled and testified, "Amen, amen, I say to you, one of you will betray me." The disciples looked at one another, at a loss as to whom he meant. One of his disciples, the one whom Jesus loved, was reclining at Jesus' side. So Simon Peter nodded to him to find out whom he meant. He leaned back against Jesus' chest and said to him, "Master, who is it?" Jesus answered, "It is the one to whom I hand the morsel after I have dipped it." So he dipped the morsel and took it and handed it to Judas, son of Simon the Iscariot. After Judas took the morsel, Satan entered him. So Jesus said to him, "What you are going to do, do quickly." Now none of those reclining at table realized why he said this to him. Some thought that since Judas kept the money bag, Jesus had told him, "Buy what we need for the feast," or to give something to the poor. So Judas took the morsel and left at once. And it was night.

When he had left, Jesus said, "Now is the Son of Man glorified, and God is glorified in him. If God is glorified in him, God will also glorify him in himself, and he will glorify him at once. My children, I will be with you only a little while longer. You will look for me, and as I told the Jews, 'Where I go you cannot come,' so now I say it to you."

Simon Peter said to him, "Master, where are you going?" Jesus answered him, "Where I am going, you cannot follow me now, though you will follow later." Peter said to him, "Master, why can I not follow you now? I will lay down my life for you." Jesus answered, "Will you lay down your life for me? Amen, amen, I say to you, the cock will not crow before you deny me three times."

APRIL 8, HOLY WEEK - WEDNESDAY; ST. JULIE BILLIART

FIRST READING   *Isaiah 50:4–9a*

The Lord GOD has given me a well–trained tongue, That I might know how to speak to the weary a word that will rouse them. Morning after morning he opens my ear that I may hear; And I have not rebelled, have not turned back. I gave my back to those who beat me, my cheeks to those who plucked my beard; My face I did not shield from buffets and spitting.

The Lord GOD is my help, therefore I am not disgraced; I have set my face like flint, knowing that I shall not be put to shame. He is near who upholds my right; if anyone wishes to oppose me, let us appear together. Who disputes my right? Let him confront me. See, the Lord GOD is my help; who will prove me wrong?

RESPONSORIAL PSALM   *Psalm 69:8–10, 21–22, 31 and 33–34*

R. (14c) Lord, in your great love, answer me.

For your sake I bear insult, / and shame covers my face. I have become an outcast to my brothers, / a stranger to my mother's sons, / because zeal for your house consumes me, / and the insults of those who blaspheme you fall upon me. **R.**

Insult has broken my heart, and I am weak, / I looked for sympathy, but there was none; / for consolers, not one could I find. / Rather they put gall in my food, / and in my thirst they gave me vinegar to drink. **R.**

I will praise the name of God in song, / and I will glorify him with thanksgiving: / "See, you lowly ones, and be glad; / you who seek God, may your hearts revive! / For the LORD hears the poor, / and his own who are in bonds he spurns not." **R.**

VERSE BEFORE THE GOSPEL

R. Praise to you, O Christ, King of Eternal Glory! Hail to you, our King; you alone are compassionate with our errors. **OR**   Hail to you, our King, obedient to the Father; you were led to your crucifixion like a gentle lamb to the slaughter. **R.**

GOSPEL

Matthew 26:14—25

One of the Twelve, who was called Judas Iscariot, went to the chief priests and said, "What are you willing to give me if I hand him over to you?" They paid him thirty pieces of silver, and from that time on he looked for an opportunity to hand him over.

On the first day of the Feast of Unleavened Bread, the disciples approached Jesus and said, "Where do you want us to prepare for you to eat the Passover?" He said, "Go into the city to a certain man and tell him, 'The teacher says, My appointed time draws near; in your house I shall celebrate the Passover with my disciples.'"" The disciples then did as Jesus had ordered, and prepared the Passover.

When it was evening, he reclined at table with the Twelve. And while they were eating, he said, "Amen, I say to you, one of you will betray me." Deeply distressed at this, they began to say to him one after another, "Surely it is not I, Lord?" He said in reply, "He who has dipped his hand into the dish with me is the one who will betray me. The Son of Man indeed goes, as it is written of him, but woe to that man by whom the Son of Man is betrayed. It would be better for that man if he had never been born." Then Judas, his betrayer, said in reply, "Surely it is not I, Rabbi?" He answered, "You have said so."

APRIL 9, HOLY THURSDAY; ST. MADELEINE SOPHIE BARAT

CHRISM MASS

FIRST READING

Isaiah 61:1—3a, 6a, 8b—9

The spirit of the Lord GOD is upon me, because the LORD has anointed me; he has sent me to bring glad tidings to the lowly, to heal the brokenhearted, to proclaim liberty to the captives and release to the prisoners, to announce a year of favor from the LORD and a day of vindication by our God, to comfort all who mourn; to place on those who mourn in Zion a diadem instead of ashes, to give them oil of gladness in place of mourning, a glorious mantle instead of a listless spirit.

You yourselves shall be named priests of the LORD, ministers of our God you shall be called.

I will give them their recompense faithfully, a lasting covenant I will make with them. Their descendants shall be renowned among the nations, and their offspring among the peoples; all who see them shall acknowledge them as a race the LORD has blessed.

RESPONSORIAL PSALM

Psalm 89:21—22, 25 and 27 (2)

R. For ever I will sing the goodness of the Lord.

"I have found David, my servant; / with my holy oil I have anointed him. / That my hand may always be with him; /and that my arm may make him strong." R.

"My faithfulness and my mercy shall be with him; / and through my name shall his horn be exalted. / He shall say of me, 'You are my father, / my God, the Rock, my savior!'" R.

SECOND READING

Revelation 1:5—8

[Grace to you and peace] from Jesus Christ who is the faithful witness, the firstborn of the dead and ruler of the kings of the earth. To him who loves us and has freed us from our sins by his Blood, who has made us into a Kingdom, priests for his God and Father, to him be glory and power forever and ever. Amen.

Behold, he is coming amid the clouds, and every eye will see him, even those who pierced him. All the peoples of the earth will lament him. Yes. Amen.

"I am the Alpha and the Omega," says the Lord God, "the one who is and who was and who is to come, the Almighty."

VERSE BEFORE THE GOSPEL
Isaiah 61:1 (cited in Luke 4:18)

R. Praise to you, O Christ, King of Eternal Glory! The Spirit of the Lord is upon me for he sent me to bring glad tidings to the poor. **R.**

GOSPEL
Luke 4:16—21

Jesus came to Nazareth, where he had grown up, and went according to his custom into the synagogue on the sabbath day. He stood up to read and was handed a scroll of the prophet Isaiah. He unrolled The scroll and found the passage where it was written:

The Spirit of the Lord is upon me, because he has anointed me to bring glad tidings to the poor. He has sent me to proclaim liberty to captives and recovery of sight to the blind, to let the oppressed go free, and to proclaim a year acceptable to the Lord.

Rolling up the scroll, he handed it back to the attendant and sat down, and the eyes of all in the synagogue looked intently at him. He said to them, "Today this Scripture passage is fulfilled in your hearing."

EVENING MASS OF THE LORD'S SUPPER

FIRST READING
Exodus 12:1—8, 11—14

The LORD said to Moses and Aaron in the land of Egypt, "This month shall stand at the head of your calendar; you shall reckon it the first month of the year. Tell the whole community of Israel: On the tenth of this month every one of your families must procure for itself a lamb, one apiece for each household. If a family is too small for a whole lamb, it shall join the nearest household in procuring one and shall share in the lamb in proportion to the number of persons who partake of it. The lamb must be a year–old male and without blemish. You may take it from either the sheep or the goats. You shall keep it until the fourteenth day of this month, and then, with the whole assembly of Israel present, it shall be slaughtered during the evening twilight. They shall take some of its blood and apply it to the two doorposts and the lintel of every house in which they partake of the lamb. That same night they shall eat its roasted flesh with unleavened bread and bitter herbs.

"This is how you are to eat it: with your loins girt, sandals on your feet and your staff in hand, you shall eat like those who are in flight. It is the Passover of the Lord. For on this same night I will go through Egypt, striking down every firstborn of the land, both man and beast, and executing judgment on all the gods of Egypt—I, the Lord! But the blood will mark the houses where you are. Seeing the blood, I will pass over you; thus, when I strike the land of Egypt, no destructive blow will come upon you.

"This day shall be a memorial feast for you, which all your generations shall celebrate with pilgrimage to the LORD, as a perpetual institution."

17—18 (see 1 Corinthians 10:16)

R. Our blessing–cup is a communion with the Blood of Christ.

How shall I make a return to the LORD / for all the good he has done for me? / The cup of salvation I will take up, / and I will call upon the name of the LORD. **R.**

Precious in the eyes of the LORD/ is the death of his faithful ones. / I am your servant, the son of your handmaid; / you have loosed my bonds. **R.**

To you will I offer sacrifice of thanksgiving, / and I will call upon the name of the LORD. / My vows to the LORD I will pay /in the presence of all his people. **R.**

SECOND READING   *1 Corinthians 11:23—26*

Brothers and sisters: I received from the Lord what I also handed on to you, that the Lord Jesus, on the night he was handed over, took bread, and, after he had given thanks, broke it and said, "This is my body that is for you. Do this in remembrance of me." In the same way also the cup, after supper, saying, "This cup is the new covenant in my blood. Do this, as often as you drink it, in remembrance of me." For as often as you eat this bread and drink the cup, you proclaim the death of the Lord until he comes.

VERSE BEFORE THE GOSPEL   *John 13:34*

R. Praise to you, O Christ, King of Eternal Glory! I give you a new commandment, says the Lord: Love one another as I have loved you. **R.**

GOSPEL   *John 13:1—15*

Before the feast of Passover, Jesus knew that his hour had come to pass from this world to the Father. He loved his own in the world and he loved them to the end. The devil had already induced Judas, son of Simon the Iscariot, to hand him over. So, during supper, fully aware that the Father had put everything into his power and that he had come from God and was returning to God, he rose from supper and took off his outer garments. He took a towel and tied it around his waist. Then he poured water into a basin and began to wash the disciples' feet and dry them with the towel around his waist. He came to Simon Peter, who said to him, "Master, are you going to wash my feet?" Jesus answered and said to him, "What I am doing, you do not understand now, but you will understand later." Peter said to him, "You will never wash my feet." Jesus answered him, "Unless I wash you, you will have no inheritance with me." Simon Peter said to him, "Master, then not only my feet, but my hands and head as well." Jesus said to him, "Whoever has bathed has no need except to have his feet washed, for he is clean all over; so you are clean, but not all." For he knew who would betray him; for this reason, he said, "Not all of you are clean."

So when he had washed their feet and put his garments back on and reclined at table again, he said to them, "Do you realize what I have done for you? You call me 'teacher' and 'master,' and rightly so, for indeed I am. If I, therefore, the master and teacher, have washed your feet, you ought to wash one another's feet. I have given you a model to follow, so that as I have done for you, you should also do."

APRIL 10, GOOD FRIDAY; BLESSED ANTOINE FRÉDÉRIC OZANAM

FIRST READING   *Isaiah 52:13—53:12*

See, my servant shall prosper, he shall be raised high and greatly exalted. Even as many were amazed at him— so marred was his look beyond human semblance and his appearance beyond that of the sons of man— so shall he startle many nations, because of him kings shall stand speechless; for those who have not been told shall see, those who have not heard shall ponder it.

Who would believe what we have heard? To whom has the arm of the LORD been revealed? He grew up like a sapling before him, like a shoot from the parched earth; there was in him no stately bearing to make us look at him, nor appearance that would attract us to him. He was spurned and avoided by people, a man of suffering, accustomed to infirmity, one of those from whom people hide their faces, spurned, and we held him in no esteem.

Yet it was our infirmities that he bore, our sufferings that he endured, while we thought of him as stricken, as one smitten by God and afflicted. But he was pierced for our offenses, crushed for our sins; upon him was the chastisement that makes us whole, by his stripes we were healed. We had all gone astray like sheep, each following his own way; but the LORD laid upon him the guilt of us all.

Though he was harshly treated, he submitted and opened not his mouth; like a lamb led to the slaughter or a sheep before the shearers, he was silent and opened not his mouth. Oppressed and condemned, he was taken away, and who would have thought any more of his destiny? When he was cut off from the land of the living, and smitten for the sin of his people, a grave was assigned him among the wicked and a burial place with evildoers, though he had done no wrong nor spoken any falsehood. But the LORD was pleased to crush him in infirmity.

If he gives his life as an offering for sin, he shall see his descendants in a long life, and the will of the LORD shall be accomplished through him.

Because of his affliction he shall see the light in fullness of days; through his suffering, my servant shall justify many, and their guilt he shall bear. Therefore I will give him his portion among the great, and he shall divide the spoils with the mighty, because he surrendered himself to death and was counted among the wicked; and he shall take away the sins of many, and win pardon for their offenses.

RESPONSORIAL PSALM: *Psalm 31:2, 6, 12—13, 15—16, 17, 25 (Luke 23:46)*
R. Father, into your hands I commend my spirit.
In you, O LORD, I take refuge; / let me never be put to shame. / In your justice rescue me. / Into your hands I commend my spirit; / you will redeem me, O LORD, O faithful God. **R.**
For all my foes I am an object of reproach, / a laughingstock to my neighbors, / and a dread to my friends; / they who see me abroad flee from me. / I am forgotten like the unremembered dead; / I am like a dish that is broken. **R.**
But my trust is in you, O LORD; / I say, "You are my God. / In your hands is my destiny; / rescue me from the clutches of my enemies and my persecutors." **R.**

Let your face shine upon your servant; / save me in your kindness. / Take courage and be stouthearted, all you who hope in the LORD. **R.**

SECOND READING

Hebrews 4:14—16; 5:7—9

Brothers and sisters: Since we have a great high priest who has passed through the heavens, Jesus, the Son of God, let us hold fast to our confession. For we do not have a high priest who is unable to sympathize with our weaknesses, but one who has similarly been tested in every way, yet without sin. So let us confidently approach the throne of grace to receive mercy and to find grace for timely help.

In the days when Christ was in the flesh, he offered prayers and supplications with loud cries and tears to the one who was able to save him from death, and he was heard because of his reverence. Son though he was, he learned obedience from what he suffered; and when he was made perfect, he became the source of eternal salvation for all who obey him.

VERSE BEFORE THE GOSPEL

Philippians 2:8—9

R. Praise to you, O Christ, King of Eternal Glory! Christ became obedient to the point of death, even death on a cross. Because of this, God greatly exalted him and bestowed on him the name which is above every other name. **R.**

GOSPEL

John 18:1—19:42

Jesus went out with his disciples across the Kidron valley to where there was a garden, into which he and his disciples entered. Judas his betrayer also knew the place, because Jesus had often met there with his disciples. So Judas got a band of soldiers and guards from the chief priests and the Pharisees and went there with lanterns, torches, and weapons. Jesus, knowing everything that was going to happen to him, went out and said to them, "Whom are you looking for?" They answered him, "Jesus the Nazorean." He said to them, "I AM." Judas his betrayer was also with them. When he said to them, "I AM," they turned away and fell to the ground. So he again asked them, "Whom are you looking for?" They said, "Jesus the Nazorean." Jesus answered, "I told you that I AM. So if you are looking for me, let these men go." This was to fulfill what he had said, "I have not lost any of those you gave me." Then Simon Peter, who had a sword, drew it, struck the high priest's slave, and cut off his right ear. The slave's name was Malchus. Jesus said to Peter, "Put your sword into its scabbard. Shall I not drink the cup that the Father gave me?"

So the band of soldiers, the tribune, and the Jewish guards seized Jesus, bound him, and brought him to Annas first. He was the father–in–law of Caiaphas, who was high priest that year. It was Caiaphas who had counseled the Jews that it was better that one man should die rather than the people.

Simon Peter and another disciple followed Jesus. Now the other disciple was known to the high priest, and he entered the courtyard of the high priest with Jesus. But Peter stood at the gate outside. So the other disciple, the acquaintance of the high priest, went out and spoke to the gatekeeper and brought Peter in. Then the maid who was the gatekeeper said to Peter, "You are not one of this man's disciples, are you?" He said, "I am not." Now the slaves and the guards were standing around a charcoal fire that they had made, because it was cold, and were warming themselves. Peter was also standing there keeping warm.

The high priest questioned Jesus about his disciples and about his doctrine. Jesus answered him, "I have spoken publicly to the world. I have always taught in a synagogue or in the temple area where all the Jews gather, and in secret I have said nothing. Why ask me? Ask those who heard me what I said to them. They know what I said." When he had said this, one of the temple guards standing there struck Jesus and said, "Is this the way you answer the high priest?" Jesus answered him, "If I have spoken wrongly, testify to the wrong; but if I have spoken rightly, why do you strike me?" Then Annas sent him bound to Caiaphas the high priest.

Now Simon Peter was standing there keeping warm. And they said to him, "You are not one of his disciples, are you?" He denied it and said, "I am not." One of the slaves of the high priest, a relative of the one whose ear Peter had cut off, said, "Didn't I see you in the garden with him?" Again Peter denied it. And immediately the cock crowed.

Then they brought Jesus from Caiaphas to the praetorium. It was morning. And they themselves did not enter the praetorium, in order not to be defiled so that they could eat the Passover. So Pilate came out to them and said, "What charge do you bring against this man?" They answered and said to him, "If he were not a criminal, we would not have handed him over to you." At this, Pilate said to them, "Take him yourselves, and judge him according to your law." The Jews answered him, "We do not have the right to execute anyone," in order that the word of Jesus might be fulfilled that he said indicating the kind of death he would die. So Pilate went back into the praetorium and summoned Jesus and said to him, "Are you the King of the Jews?" Jesus answered, "Do you say this on your own or have others told you about me?" Pilate answered, "I am not a Jew, am I? Your own nation and the chief priests handed you over to me. What have you done?" Jesus answered, "My kingdom does not belong to this world. If my kingdom did belong to this world, my attendants would be fighting to keep me from being handed over to the Jews. But as it is, my kingdom is not here." So Pilate said to him, "Then you are a king?" Jesus answered, "You say I am a king. For this I was born and for this I came into the world, to testify to the truth. Everyone who belongs to the truth listens to my voice." Pilate said to him, "What is truth?"

When he had said this, he again went out to the Jews and said to them, "I find no guilt in him. But you have a custom that I release one prisoner to you at Passover. Do you want me to release to you the King of the Jews?" They cried out again, "Not this one but Barabbas!" Now Barabbas was a revolutionary.

Then Pilate took Jesus and had him scourged. And the soldiers wove a crown out of thorns and placed it on his head, and clothed him in a purple cloak, and they came to him and said, "Hail, King of the Jews!" And they struck him repeatedly. Once more Pilate went out and said to them, "Look, I am bringing him out to you, so that you may know that I find no guilt in him." So Jesus came out, wearing the crown of thorns and the purple cloak. And he said to them, "Behold, the man!" When the chief priests and the guards saw him they cried out, "Crucify him, crucify him!" Pilate said to them, "Take him yourselves and crucify him. I find no guilt in him." The Jews answered, "We have a law, and according to that law he ought to die, because he made himself the Son of God." Now when Pilate heard this statement, he became even more afraid, and went back into the praetorium and said to Jesus, "Where are you from?" Jesus did not answer him. So Pilate said to him, "Do you not speak to me? Do you not know that I have power to release you and I have power to crucify you?" Jesus answered him, "You would have no power over me if it had not been given to you from above. For this reason the one who handed me over to you has the greater sin." Consequently, Pilate tried to release him; but the Jews cried out, "If you release him, you are not a Friend of Caesar. Everyone who makes himself a king opposes Caesar."

When Pilate heard these words he brought Jesus out and seated him on the judge's bench in the place called Stone Pavement, in Hebrew, Gabbatha. It was preparation day for Passover, and it was about noon. And he said to the Jews, "Behold, your king!" They cried out, "Take him away, take him away! Crucify him!" Pilate said to them, "Shall I crucify your king?" The chief priests answered, "We have no king but Caesar." Then he handed him over to them to be crucified.

So they took Jesus, and, carrying the cross himself, he went out to what is called the Place of the Skull, in Hebrew, Golgotha. There they crucified him, and with him two others, one on either side, with Jesus in the middle. Pilate also had an inscription written and put on the cross. It read, "Jesus the Nazorean, the King of the Jews." Now many of the Jews read this inscription, because the place where Jesus was crucified was near the city; and it was written in Hebrew, Latin, and Greek. So the chief priests of the Jews said to Pilate, "Do not write 'The King of the Jews,' but that he said, 'I am the King of the Jews'." Pilate answered, "What I have written, I have written."

When the soldiers had crucified Jesus, they took his clothes and divided them into four shares, a share for each soldier. They also took his tunic, but the tunic was seamless, woven in one piece from the top down. So they said to one another, "Let's not tear it, but cast lots for it to see whose it will be," in order that the passage of Scripture might be fulfilled that says: *They divided my garments among them, and for my vesture they cast lots.* This is what the soldiers did. Standing by the cross of Jesus were his mother and his mother's sister, Mary the wife of Clopas, and Mary of Magdala. When Jesus saw his mother and the disciple there whom he loved he said to his mother, "Woman, behold, your son." Then he said to the disciple, "Behold, your mother." And from that hour the disciple took her into his home.

After this, aware that everything was now finished, in order that the Scripture might be fulfilled, Jesus said, "I thirst." There was a vessel filled with common wine. So they put a sponge soaked in wine on a sprig of hyssop and put it up to his mouth. When Jesus had taken the wine, he said, "It is finished." And bowing his head, he handed over the spirit.

HERE   ALL   KNEEL   AND   PAUSE   A   SHORT   TIME.
Now since it was preparation day, in order that the bodies might not remain on the cross on the sabbath, for the sabbath day of that week was a solemn one, the Jews asked Pilate that their legs be broken and that they be taken down. So the soldiers came and broke the legs of the first and then of the other one who was crucified with Jesus. But when they came to Jesus and saw that he was already dead, they did not break his legs, but one soldier thrust his lance into his side, and immediately blood and water flowed out. An eyewitness has testified, and his testimony is true; he knows that he is speaking the truth, so that you also

may come to believe. For this happened so that the Scripture passage might be fulfilled: *Not a bone of it will be broken.* And again another passage says: *They will look upon him whom they have pierced.*

After this, Joseph of Arimathea, secretly a disciple of Jesus for fear of the Jews, asked Pilate if he could remove the body of Jesus. And Pilate permitted it. So he came and took his body. Nicodemus, the one who had first come to him at night, also came bringing a mixture of myrrh and aloes weighing about one hundred pounds. They took the body of Jesus and bound it with burial cloths along with the spices, according to the Jewish burial custom. Now in the place where he had been crucified there was a garden, and in the garden a new tomb, in which no one had yet been buried. So they laid Jesus there because of the Jewish preparation day; for the tomb was close by.

THE SOLEMN INTERCESSIONS

FOR HOLY CHURCH

Let us pray, dearly beloved, for the holy Church of God, that our God and Lord be pleased to give her peace, to guard her and to unite her throughout the whole world and grant that, leading our life in tranquillity and quiet, we may glorify God the Father almighty.

Prayer in silence. Then the Priest says:

Almighty ever-living God, who in Christ revealed your glory to all the nations, watch over the works of your mercy, that your Church, spread throughout all the world, may persevere with steadfast faith in confessing your name. Through Christ our Lord. **Amen.**

FOR THE POPE

Let us pray also for our most Holy Father Pope **N.**, that our God and Lord, who chose him for the Order of Bishops, may keep him safe and unharmed for the Lord's holy Church, to govern the holy People of God.

Prayer in silence. Then the Priest says:

Almighty ever-living God, by whose decree all things are founded, look with favour on our prayers and in your kindness protect the Pope chosen for us, that, under him, the Christian people, governed by you their maker, may grow in merit by reason of their faith. Through Christ our Lord. **Amen.**

FOR ALL ORDERS AND DEGREES OF THE FAITHFUL

Let us pray also for our Bishop **N.**, for all Bishops, Priests, and Deacons of the Church and for the whole of the faithful people.

Prayer in silence. Then the Priest says:

Almighty ever-living God, by whose Spirit the whole body of the Church is sanctified and governed, hear our humble prayer for your ministers, that, by the gift of your grace, all may serve you faithfully. Through Christ our Lord. **Amen.**

FOR CATECHUMENS

Let us pray also for (our) catechumens, that our God and Lord may open wide the ears of their inmost hearts and unlock the gates of his mercy, that, having received forgiveness of all their sins through the waters of rebirth, they, too, may be one with Christ Jesus our Lord.

Prayer in silence. Then the Priest says:

Almighty ever-living God, who make your Church ever fruitful with new offspring, increase the faith and understanding of (our) catechumens, that, reborn in the font of Baptism, they may be added to the number of your adopted children. Through Christ our Lord. **Amen.**

FOR THE UNITY OF CHRISTIANS

Let us pray also for all our brothers and sisters who believe in Christ, that our God and Lord may be pleased, as they live the truth, to gather them together and keep them in his one Church.

Prayer in silence. Then the Priest says:

Almighty ever-living God, who gather what is scattered and keep together what you have gathered, look kindly on the flock of your Son, that those whom one Baptism has consecrated may be joined together by integrity of faith and united in the bond of charity. Through Christ our Lord. **Amen.**

FOR THE JEWISH PEOPLE

Let us pray also for the Jewish people, to whom the Lord our God spoke first, that he may grant them to advance in love of his name and in faithfulness to his covenant.

Prayer in silence. Then the Priest says:

Almighty ever-living God, who bestowed your promises on Abraham and his descendants, graciously hear the prayers of your Church, that the people you first made your own may attain the fullness of redemption. Through Christ our Lord. **Amen.**

FOR THOSE WHO DO NOT BELIEVE IN CHRIST

Let us pray also for those who do not believe in Christ, that, enlightened by the Holy Spirit, they, too, may enter on the way of salvation.

Prayer in silence. Then the Priest says:

Almighty ever-living God, grant to those who do not confess Christ that, by walking before you with a sincere heart, they may find the truth and that we ourselves, being constant in mutual love and striving to understand more fully the mystery of your life, may be made more perfect witnesses to your love in the world. Through Christ our Lord. **Amen.**

FOR THOSE WHO DO NOT BELIEVE IN GOD

Let us pray also for those who do not acknowledge God, that, following what is right in sincerity of heart, they may find the way to God himself.

Prayer in silence. Then the Priest says:

Almighty ever-living God, who created all people to seek you always by desiring you and, by finding you, come to rest, grant, we pray, that, despite every harmful obstacle, all may recognize the signs of your fatherly love and the witness of the good works done by those who believe in you, and so in gladness confess you, the one true God and Father of our human race. Through Christ our Lord. **Amen.**

FOR THOSE IN PUBLIC OFFICE

Let us pray also for those in public office, that our God and Lord may direct their minds and hearts according to his will for the true peace and freedom of all.

Prayer in silence. Then the Priest says:

Almighty ever-living God, in whose hand lies every human heart and the rights of peoples, look with favour, we pray, on those who govern with authority over us, that throughout the whole world, the prosperity of peoples, the assurance of peace, and freedom of religion may through your gift be made secure. Through Christ our Lord. **Amen.**

FOR THOSE IN TRIBULATION

Let us pray, dearly beloved, to God the Father almighty, that he may cleanse the world of all errors, banish disease, drive out hunger, unlock prisons, loosen fetters, granting to travellers safety, to pilgrims return, health to the sick, and salvation to the dying.

Prayer in silence. Then the Priest says:

Almighty ever-living God, comfort of mourners, strength of all who toil, may the prayers of those who cry out in any tribulation come before you, that all may rejoice, because in their hour of need your mercy was at hand. **Amen.**

Prayer after Communion

Almighty ever-living God, who have restored us to life by the blessed Death and Resurrection of your Christ, preserve in us the work of your mercy, that, by partaking of this mystery, we may have a life unceasingly devoted to you. Through Christ our Lord.

Prayer over the People

May abundant blessing, O Lord, we pray, descend upon your people, who have honoured the Death of your Son in the hope of their resurrection: may pardon come, comfort be given, holy faith increase, and everlasting redemption be made secure. Through Christ our

Lord. **Amen.**

APRIL 11, HOLY SATURDAY - EASTER VIGIL; ST. STANISLAUS

The Easter Proclamation (Exsultet)

Arriving at the altar, the Priest goes to his chair, gives his candle to a minister, puts incense into the thurible and blesses the incense as at the Gospel at Mass.

If the Exsultet is to be taken by a Deacon, the Deacon goes to the Priest and saying, Your blessing, Father, *asks for and receives a blessing from the Priest, who says in a low voice:*

May the Lord be in your heart and on your lips,

that you may proclaim his paschal praise worthily and well,

in the name of the Father and of the Son, and of the Holy Spirit.

The Deacon replies:

Amen.

If the Exsultet is to be sung by a lay cantor, this dialogue is omitted, as are also the words in brackets **[...]** *below.*

LONGER FORM OF THE EASTER PROCLAMATION

Exult, let them exult, the hosts of heaven, exult, let Angel ministers of God exult, let the trumpet of salvation sound aloud our mighty King's triumph! Be glad, let earth be glad, as glory floods her, ablaze with light from her eternal King, let all corners of the earth be glad, knowing an end to gloom and darkness. Rejoice, let Mother Church also rejoice, arrayed with the lightning of his glory, let this holy building shake with joy, filled with the mighty voices of the peoples.

[Therefore, dearest friends, standing in the awesome lory of this holy light, invoke with me, I ask you, the mercy of God almighty, that he, who has been pleased to number me, though unworthy, among the Levites, may pour into me his light unshadowed, that I may sing this candle's perfect praises.]

[The Lord be with you.] [**And with your spirit.**]
Lift up your hearts. **We lift them up to the Lord.**
Let us give thanks to the Lord our God. **It is right and just.**

It is truly right and just, with ardent love of mind and heart and with devoted service of our voice, to acclaim our God invisible, the almighty Father, and Jesus Christ, our Lord, his Son, his Only Begotten.

Who for our sake paid Adam's debt to the eternal Father, and, pouring out his own dear Blood, wiped clean the record of our ancient sinfulness.

These, then, are the feasts of Passover, in which is slain the Lamb, the one true Lamb, whose Blood anoints the doorposts of believers.

This is the night, when once you led our forebears, Israel's children, from slavery in Egypt and made them pass dry-shod through the Red Sea.

This is the night that with a pillar of fire banished the darkness of sin.

This is the night that even now, throughout the world, sets Christian believers apart from worldly vices and from the gloom of sin, leading them to grace and joining them to his holy ones.

This is the night, when Christ broke the prison-bars of death and rose victorious from the underworld.

Our birth would have been no gain, had we not been redeemed. O wonder of your humble care for us! O love, O charity beyond all telling, to ransom a slave you gave away your Son!

O truly necessary sin of Adam, destroyed completely by the Death of Christ!

O happy fault that earned so great, so glorious a Redeemer!

O truly blessed night, worthy alone to know the time and hour when Christ rose from the underworld!

This is the night of which it is written: The night shall be as bright as day, dazzling is the night for me, and full of gladness.

The sanctifying power of this night dispels wickedness, washes faults away, restores innocence to the fallen, and joy to mourners, drives out hatred, fosters concord, and brings down the mighty.

On this, your night of grace, O holy Father, accept this candle, a solemn offering, the work of bees and of your servants' hands, an evening sacrifice of praise, this gift from your most holy

Church.

But now we know the praises of this pillar, which glowing fire ignites for God's honour, a fire into many flames divided, yet never dimmed by sharing of its light, for it is fed by melting wax, drawn out by mother bees to build a torch so precious.

O truly blessed night, when things of heaven are wed to those of earth, and divine to the human.

Therefore, O Lord, we pray you that this candle, hallowed to the honour of your name, may persevere undimmed, to overcome the darkness of this night. Receive it as a pleasing fragrance, and let it mingle with the lights of heaven. May this flame be found still burning by the Morning Star: the one Morning Star who never sets, Christ your Son, who, coming back from death's domain, has shed his peaceful light on humanity, and lives and reigns for ever and ever. **Amen.**

LITURGY OF THE WORD

FIRST READING   *Longer Form Genesis 1:1—2:2*

In the beginning, when God created the heavens and the earth, the earth was a formless wasteland, and darkness covered the abyss, while a mighty wind swept over the waters.

Then God said, "Let there be light," and there was light. God saw how good the light was. God then separated the light from the darkness. God called the light "day," and the darkness he called "night." Thus evening came, and morning followed—the first day.

Then God said, "Let there be a dome in the middle of the waters, to separate one body of water from the other." And so it happened: God made the dome, and it separated the water above the dome from the water below it. God called the dome "the sky." Evening came, and morning followed—the second day.

Then God said, "Let the water under the sky be gathered into a single basin, so that the dry land may appear." And so it happened: the water under the sky was gathered into its basin, and the dry land appeared. God called the dry land "the earth," and the basin of the water he called "the sea." God saw how good it was.

Then God said, "Let the earth bring forth vegetation: every kind of plant that bears seed and every kind of fruit tree on earth that bears fruit with its seed in it." And so it happened: the earth brought forth every kind of plant that bears seed and every kind of fruit tree on earth that bears fruit with its seed in it. God saw how good it was. Evening came, and morning followed—the third day.

Then God said: "Let there be lights in the dome of the sky, to separate day from night. Let them mark the fixed times, the days and the years, and serve as luminaries in the dome of the sky, to shed light upon the earth." And so it happened: God made the two great lights, the greater one to govern the day, and the lesser one to govern the night; and he made the stars. God set them in the dome of the sky, to shed light upon the earth, to govern the day and the night, and to separate the light from the darkness. God saw how good it was. Evening came, and morning followed—the fourth day.

Then God said, "Let the water teem with an abundance of living creatures, and on the earth let birds fly beneath the dome of the sky." And so it happened: God created the great sea monsters and all kinds of swimming creatures with which the water teems, and all kinds of winged birds. God saw how good it was, and God blessed them, saying, "Be fertile, multiply, and fill the water of the seas; and let the birds multiply on the earth." Evening came, and morning followed—the fifth day.

Then God said, "Let the earth bring forth all kinds of living creatures: cattle, creeping things, and wild animals of all kinds." And so it happened: God made all kinds of wild animals, all kinds of cattle, and all kinds of creeping things of the earth. God saw how good it was.

Then God said: "Let us make man in our image, after our likeness. Let them have dominion over the fish of the sea, the birds of the air, and the cattle, and over all the wild animals and all the creatures that crawl on the ground." God created man in his image; in the image of God he created him; male and female he created them. God blessed them, saying: "Be fertile and multiply; fill the earth and subdue it. Have dominion over the fish of the sea, the birds of the air, and all the living things that move on the earth." God also said: "See, I give you every seed–bearing plant all over the earth and every tree that has seed–bearing fruit on it to be your food; and to all the animals of the land, all the birds of the air, and all the living creatures that crawl on the ground, I give all the green plants for food." And so it happened. God looked at everything he had made, and he found it very good. Evening came, and morning followed—the sixth day.

Thus the heavens and the earth and all their array were completed. Since on the seventh day God was finished with the work he had been doing, he rested on the seventh day from all the work he had undertaken.

SHORTER FORM   *Genesis 1:1, 26—31a*

In the beginning, when God created the heavens and the earth, God said: "Let us make man in our image, after our likeness. Let them have dominion over the fish of the sea, the birds of the air, and the cattle, and over all the wild animals and all the creatures that crawl on the ground." God created man in his image; in the image of God he created him; male and female he created them. God blessed them, saying: "Be fertile and multiply; fill the earth and subdue it. Have dominion over the fish of the sea, the birds of the air, and all the living things that move on the earth." God also said: "See, I give you every seed–bearing plant all over the earth and every tree that has seed–bearing fruit on it to be your food; and to all the animals of the land, all the birds of the air, and all the living creatures that crawl on the ground, I give all the green plants for food." And so it happened. God looked at everything he had made, and found it very good.

RESPONSORIAL PSALM: *Psalm 104:1—2, 5—6, 10, 12, 13—14, 24, 35 (30)*
R. Lord, send out your Spirit, and renew the face of the earth.

Bless the LORD, O my soul! / O LORD, my God, you are great indeed! / You are clothed with majesty and glory, / robed in light as with a cloak. **R.**

You fixed the earth upon its foundation, / not to be moved forever; / with the ocean, as with a garment, you covered it; / above the mountains the waters stood. **R.**

You send forth springs into the watercourses that wind among the mountains. / Beside them the birds of heaven dwell; / from among the branches they send forth their song. **R.**

You water the mountains from your palace; / the earth is replete with the fruit of your works. / You raise grass for the cattle, and vegetation for man's use, / producing bread from the earth. **R.**

How manifold are your works, O LORD! / In wisdom you have wrought them all/— the earth is full of your creatures. / Bless the LORD, O my soul! **R.**

OR: *Psalm 33:4—5, 6—7, 12—13, 20 and 22 (5b)*
R. The earth is full of the goodness of the Lord.

Upright is the word of the LORD, / and all his works are trustworthy. / He loves justice and right; / of the kindness of the LORD the earth is full. **R.**

By the word of the LORD the heavens were made; / by the breath of his mouth all their host. / He gathers the waters of the sea as in a flask; / in cellars he confines the deep. **R.**

Blessed the nation whose God is the LORD, / the people he has chosen for his own inheritance. / From heaven the LORD looks down; / he sees all mankind. **R.**

Our soul waits for the LORD, / who is our help and our shield. / May your kindness, O LORD, be upon us / who have put our hope in you. **R.**

SECOND READING   *Longer Form Genesis 22:1—18*

God put Abraham to the test. He called to him, "Abraham!" "Here I am," he replied. Then God said: "Take your son Isaac, your only one, whom you love, and go to the land of Moriah. There you shall offer him up as a holocaust on a height that I will point out to you." Early the next morning Abraham saddled his donkey, took with him his son Isaac and two of his servants as well, and with the wood that he had cut for the holocaust, set out for the place of which God had told him.

On the third day Abraham got sight of the place from afar. Then he said to his servants: "Both of you stay here with the donkey, while the boy and I go on over yonder. We will worship and then come back to you." Thereupon Abraham took the wood for the holocaust and laid it on his son Isaac's shoulders, while he himself carried the fire and the knife. As the two walked on together, Isaac spoke to his father Abraham: "Father!" Isaac said. "Yes, son," he replied. Isaac continued, "Here are the fire and the wood, but where is the sheep for the holocaust?" "Son," Abraham answered, "God himself will provide the sheep for the holocaust." Then the two continued going forward.

When they came to the place of which God had told him, Abraham built an altar there and arranged the wood on it. Next he tied up his son Isaac, and put him on top of the wood on the altar. Then he reached out and took the knife to slaughter his son. But the LORD's messenger called to him from heaven, "Abraham, Abraham!" "Here I am," he answered. "Do not lay your hand on the boy," said the messenger. "Do not do the least thing to him. I know now how devoted you are to God, since you did not withhold from me your own beloved son." As Abraham looked about, he spied a ram caught by its horns in the thicket. So he went and took the ram and offered it up as a holocaust in place of his son. Abraham named the site Yahweh–yireh; hence people now say, "On the mountain the LORD will see."

Again the LORD's messenger called to Abraham from heaven and said: "I swear by myself, declares the LORD, that because you acted as you did in not withholding from me your beloved son, I will bless you abundantly and make your descendants as countless as the stars of the sky and the sands of the seashore; your descendants shall take possession of the gates of their enemies, and in your descendants all the nations of the earth shall find blessing— all this because you obeyed my command."

SHORTER FORM   *Genesis 22:1—2, 9a, 10—13, 15—18*

God put Abraham to the test. He called to him, "Abraham!" "Here I am," he replied. Then God said: "Take your son Isaac, your only one, whom you love, and go to the land of Moriah. There you shall offer him up as a holocaust on a height that I will point out to you."

When they came to the place of which God had told him, Abraham built an altar there and arranged the wood on it. Then he reached out and took the knife to slaughter his son. But the LORD's messenger called to him from heaven, "Abraham, Abraham!" "Here I am," he answered. "Do not lay your hand on the boy," said the messenger. "Do not do the least thing to him. I know now how devoted you are to God, since you did not withhold from me your own beloved son." As Abraham looked about, he spied a ram caught by its horns in the thicket. So he went and took the ram and offered it up as a holocaust in place of his son.

Again the LORD's messenger called to Abraham from heaven and said: "I swear by myself, declares the LORD, that because you acted as you did in not withholding from me your beloved son, I will bless you abundantly and make your descendants as countless as the stars of the sky and the sands of the seashore; your descendants shall take possession of the gates of their enemies, and in your descendants all the nations of the earth shall find blessing— all this because you obeyed my command."

RESPONSORIAL PSALM   *Psalm 16:5, 8, 9—10, 11 (1)*

R. You are my inheritance, O Lord.

O LORD, my allotted portion and my cup, / you it is who hold fast my lot. / I set the LORD ever before me; / with him at my right hand I shall not be disturbed. **R.**

Therefore my heart is glad and my soul rejoices, / my body, too, abides in confidence; / because you will not abandon my soul to the netherworld, / nor will you suffer your faithful one to undergo corruption. **R.**

You will show me the path to life, / fullness of joys in your presence, / the delights at your right hand forever. **R.**

THIRD READING   *Exodus 14:15—15:1*

The LORD said to Moses, "Why are you crying out to me? Tell the Israelites to go forward. And you, lift up your staff and, with hand outstretched over the sea, split the sea in two, that the Israelites may pass through it on dry land. But I will make the Egyptians so obstinate that they will go in after them. Then I will receive glory through Pharaoh and all his army, his chariots and charioteers. The Egyptians shall know that I am the LORD, when I receive glory through Pharaoh and his chariots and charioteers."

The angel of God, who had been leading Israel's camp, now moved and went around behind them. The column of cloud also, leaving the front, took up its place behind them, so that it came between the camp of the Egyptians and that of Israel. But the cloud now became dark, and thus the night passed without the rival camps coming any closer together all night long. Then Moses stretched out his hand over the sea, and the LORD swept the sea with a strong east wind throughout the night and so turned it into dry land. When the water was thus divided, the Israelites marched into the midst of the sea on dry land, with the water like a wall to their right and to their left.

The Egyptians followed in pursuit; all Pharaoh's horses and chariots and charioteers went after them right into the midst of the sea. In the night watch just before dawn the LORD cast through the column of the fiery cloud upon the Egyptian force a glance that threw it into a panic; and he so clogged their chariot wheels that they could hardly drive. With that the Egyptians sounded the retreat before Israel, because the LORD was fighting for them against the Egyptians. Then the LORD told Moses, "Stretch out your hand over the sea, that the water may flow back upon the Egyptians, upon their chariots and their charioteers." So Moses stretched out his hand over the sea, and at dawn the sea flowed back to its normal depth. The Egyptians were fleeing head on toward the sea, when the LORD hurled them into its midst. As the water flowed back, it covered the chariots and the charioteers of Pharaoh's whole army which had followed the Israelites into the sea. Not a single one of them escaped. But the Israelites had marched on dry land through the midst of the sea, with the water like a wall to their right and to their left. Thus the LORD saved Israel on that day from the power of the Egyptians. When Israel saw the Egyptians lying dead on the seashore and beheld the great power that the LORD had shown against the Egyptians, they feared the LORD and believed in him and in his servant Moses. Then Moses and the Israelites sang this song to the Lord: I will sing to the LORD, for he is gloriously triumphant; horse and chariot he has cast into the sea.

RESPONSORIAL PSALM   *Exodus 15:1—2, 3—4, 5—6, 17—18 (1b)*
R. Let us sing to the Lord; he has covered himself in glory.
I will sing to the LORD, for he is gloriously triumphant; / horse and chariot he has cast into the sea. / My strength and my courage is the LORD, / and he has been my savior. He is my God, I praise him; / the God of my father, I extol him. **R.**
The LORD is a warrior, LORD is his name! / Pharaoh's chariots and army he hurled into the sea; / the elite of his officers were submerged in the Red Sea. **R.**
The flood waters covered them, / they sank into the depths like a stone. / Your right hand, O LORD, magnificent in power, / your right hand, O LORD, has shattered the enemy. **R.**
You brought in the people you redeemed / and planted them on the mountain of your

inheritance— / the place where you made your seat, O LORD, / the sanctuary, LORD, which your hands established. / The LORD shall reign forever and ever. **R.**

FOURTH READING
Isaiah 54:5—14

The One who has become your husband is your Maker; his name is the LORD of hosts; your redeemer is the Holy One of Israel, called God of all the earth. The LORD calls you back, like a wife forsaken and grieved in spirit, a wife married in youth and then cast off, says your God. For a brief moment I abandoned you, but with great tenderness I will take you back. In an outburst of wrath, for a moment I hid my face from you; but with enduring love I take pity on you, says the LORD, your redeemer. This is for me like the days of Noah, when I swore that the waters of Noah should never again deluge the earth; so I have sworn not to be angry with you, or to rebuke you. Though the mountains leave their place and the hills be shaken, my love shall never leave you nor my covenant of peace be shaken, says the LORD, who has mercy on you. O afflicted one, storm–battered and unconsoled, I lay your pavements in carnelians, and your foundations in sapphires; I will make your battlements of rubies, your gates of carbuncles, and all your walls of precious stones. All your children shall be taught by the LORD, and great shall be the peace of your children. In justice shall you be established, far from the fear of oppression, where destruction cannot come near you.

RESPONSORIAL PSALM
Psalm 30:2, 4, 5—6, 11—12, 13 (2a)

R. I will praise you, Lord, for you have rescued me.
I will extol you, O LORD, / for you drew me clear and did not let my enemies rejoice over me. / O LORD, you brought me up from the netherworld; / you preserved me from among those going down into the pit. **R.**
Sing praise to the LORD, you his faithful ones, / and give thanks to his holy name. /For his anger lasts but a moment; / a lifetime, his good will. / At nightfall, weeping enters in, / but with the dawn, rejoicing. **R.**
Hear, O LORD, and have pity on me; / O LORD, be my helper. / You changed my mourning into dancing; / O LORD, my God, forever will I give you thanks. **R.**

FIFTH READING
Isaiah 55:1—11

Thus says the LORD: All you who are thirsty, come to the water! You who have no money, come, receive grain and eat; come, without paying and without cost, drink wine and milk! Why spend your money for what is not bread, your wages for what fails to satisfy? Heed me, and you shall eat well, you shall delight in rich fare. Come to me heedfully, listen, that you may have life. I will renew with you the everlasting covenant, the benefits assured to David. As I made him a witness to the peoples, a leader and commander of nations, so shall you summon a nation you knew not, and nations that knew you not shall run to you, because of the LORD, your God, the Holy One of Israel, who has glorified you.

Seek the LORD while he may be found, call him while he is near. Let the scoundrel forsake his way, and the wicked man his thoughts; let him turn to the LORD for mercy; to our God, who is generous in forgiving. For my thoughts are not your thoughts, nor are your ways my ways, says the LORD. As high as the heavens are above the earth, so high are my ways above your ways and my thoughts above your thoughts.

For just as from the heavens the rain and snow come down and do not return there till they have watered the earth, making it fertile and fruitful, giving seed to the one who sows and bread to the one who eats, so shall my word be that goes forth from my mouth; my word shall not return to me void, but shall do my will, achieving the end for which I sent it.

RESPONSORIAL PSALM   *Isaiah 12:2—3, 4, 5—6 (3)*

R. You will draw water joyfully from the springs of salvation.

God indeed is my savior; / I am confident and unafraid. / My strength and my courage is the LORD, / and he has been my savior. / With joy you will draw water at the fountain of salvation. **R.**

Give thanks to the LORD, acclaim his name; / among the nations make known his deeds, / proclaim how exalted is his name. **R.**

Sing praise to the LORD for his glorious achievement; / let this be known throughout all the earth. / Shout with exultation, O city of Zion, / for great in your midst is the Holy One of Israel! **R.**

SIXTH READING   *Baruch 3:9—15, 32—4:4*

Hear, O Israel, the commandments of life: listen, and know prudence! How is it, Israel, that you are in the land of your foes, grown old in a foreign land, defiled with the dead, accounted with those destined for the netherworld? You have forsaken the fountain of wisdom! Had you walked in the way of God, you would have dwelt in enduring peace. Learn where prudence is, where strength, where understanding; that you may know also where are length of days, and life, where light of the eyes, and peace. Who has found the place of wisdom, who has entered into her treasuries?

The One who knows all things knows her; he has probed her by his knowledge— the One who established the earth for all time, and filled it with four—footed beasts; he who dismisses the light, and it departs, calls it, and it obeys him trembling; before whom the stars at their posts shine and rejoice; when he calls them, they answer, "Here we are!" shining with joy for their Maker. Such is our God; no other is to be compared to him: He has traced out the whole way of understanding, and has given her to Jacob, his servant, to Israel, his beloved son.

Since then she has appeared on earth, and moved among people. She is the book of the precepts of God, the law that endures forever; all who cling to her will live, but those will die who forsake her. Turn, O Jacob, and receive her: walk by her light toward splendor. Give not your glory to another, your privileges to an alien race. Blessed are we, O Israel; for what pleases God is known to us!

RESPONSORIAL PSALM   *Psalm 19:8, 9, 10, 11 (John 6:68c)*

R. Lord, you have the words of everlasting life.

The law of the LORD is perfect, / refreshing the soul; /
the decree of the LORD is trustworthy, / giving wisdom to the simple. **R.**

The precepts of the LORD are right, / rejoicing the heart; /
the command of the LORD is clear, / enlightening the eye. **R.**
The fear of the LORD is pure, / enduring forever; /
the ordinances of the LORD are true, / all of them just. **R.**
They are more precious than gold, / than a heap of purest gold; /
sweeter also than syrup or honey from the comb. **R.**

SEVENTH READING   *Ezekiel 36:16—17a, 18—28*

The word of the LORD came to me, saying: Son of man, when the house of Israel lived in their land, they defiled it by their conduct and deeds. Therefore I poured out my fury upon them because of the blood that they poured out on the ground, and because they defiled it with idols. I scattered them among the nations, dispersing them over foreign lands; according to their conduct and deeds I judged them. But when they came among the nations wherever they came, they served to profane my holy name, because it was said of them: "These are the people of the LORD, yet they had to leave their land." So I have relented because of my holy name which the house of Israel profaned among the nations where they came. Therefore say to the house of Israel: Thus says the Lord GOD: Not for your sakes do I act, house of Israel, but for the sake of my holy name, which you profaned among the nations to which you came. I will prove the holiness of my great name, profaned among the nations, in whose midst you have profaned it. Thus the nations shall know that I am the LORD, says the Lord GOD, when in their sight I prove my holiness through you. For I will take you away from among the nations, gather you from all the foreign lands, and bring you back to your own land. I will sprinkle clean water upon you to cleanse you from all your impurities, and from all your idols I will cleanse you. I will give you a new heart and place a new spirit within you, taking from your bodies your stony hearts and giving you natural hearts. I will put my spirit within you and make you live by my statutes, careful to observe my decrees. You shall live in the land I gave your fathers; you shall be my people, and I will be your God.

RESPONSORIAL PSALM   *Psalm 42:3, 5; 43:3, 4 (42:2)*
R. Like a deer that longs for running streams, my soul longs for you, my God.
Athirst is my soul for God, the living God. When shall I go and behold the face of God? **R.**
I went with the throng and led them in procession to the house of God, amid loud cries of joy and thanksgiving, with the multitude keeping festival. **R.**
Send forth your light and your fidelity; they shall lead me on and bring me to your holy mountain, to your dwelling–place. **R.**
Then will I go in to the altar of God, the God of my gladness and joy; then will I give you thanks upon the harp, O God, my God! **R.**

OR   *Isaiah 12:2—3, 4bcd, 5—6 (3)*
R. You will draw water joyfully from the springs of salvation.

God indeed is my savior; I am confident and unafraid. My strength and my courage is the LORD, and he has been my savior. With joy you will draw water at the fountain of salvation. **R.**

Give thanks to the LORD, acclaim his name; among the nations make known his deeds, proclaim how exalted is his name. **R.**

Sing praise to the LORD for his glorious achievement; let this be known throughout all the earth. Shout with exultation, O city of Zion, for great in your midst is the Holy One of Israel! **R.**

OR   *Psalm 51:12—13, 14—15, 18—19 (12a)*
R. Create a clean heart in me, O God.

A clean heart create for me, O God, **/** and a steadfast spirit renew within me. **/** Cast me not out from your presence, **/** and your Holy Spirit take not from me. **R.**

Give me back the joy of your salvation, **/** and a willing spirit sustain in me. **/** I will teach transgressors your ways, **/** and sinners shall return to you. **R.**

For you are not pleased with sacrifices; **/** should I offer a holocaust, you would not accept it. **/** My sacrifice, O God, is a contrite spirit; **/** a heart contrite and humbled, **/** O God, you will not spurn. **R.**

EPISTLE   *Romans 6:3—11*

Brothers and sisters: Are you unaware that we who were baptized into Christ Jesus were baptized into his death? We were indeed buried with him through baptism into death, so that, just as Christ was raised from the dead by the glory of the Father, we too might live in newness of life.

For if we have grown into union with him through a death like his, we shall also be united with him in the resurrection. We know that our old self was crucified with him, so that our sinful body might be done away with, that we might no longer be in slavery to sin. For a dead person has been absolved from sin. If, then, we have died with Christ, we believe that we shall also live with him. We know that Christ, raised from the dead, dies no more; death no longer has power over him. As to his death, he died to sin once and for all; as to his life, he lives for God. Consequently, you too must think of yourselves as being dead to sin and living for God in Christ Jesus.

RESPONSORIAL PSALM   *Psalm 118:1—2, 16—17, 22—23*
R. Alleluia, alleluia, alleluia.

Give thanks to the LORD, for he is good, **/** for his mercy endures forever. **/** Let the house of Israel say, **/** "His mercy endures forever." **R.**

"The right hand of the LORD has struck with power; **/** the right hand of the LORD is exalted. **/** I shall not die, but live, **/** and declare the works of the LORD." **R.**

The stone which the builders rejected **/** has become the cornerstone. **/** By the LORD has this been done; **/** it is wonderful in our eyes. **R.**

GOSPEL   *Matthew 28:1—10*

After the sabbath, as the first day of the week was dawning, Mary Magdalene and the other Mary came to see the tomb. And behold, there was a great earthquake; for an angel of the Lord descended from heaven, approached, rolled back the stone, and sat upon it. His appearance was like lightning and his clothing was white as snow. The guards were shaken with fear of him and became like dead men. Then the angel said to the women in reply, "Do not be afraid! I know that you are seeking Jesus the crucified. He is not here, for he has been raised just as he said. Come and see the place where he lay. Then go quickly and tell his disciples, 'He has been raised from the dead, and he is going before you to Galilee; there you will see him.' Behold, I have told you." Then they went away quickly from the tomb, fearful yet overjoyed, and ran to announce this to his disciples. And behold, Jesus met them on their way and greeted them. They approached, embraced his feet, and did him homage. Then Jesus said to them, "Do not be afraid. Go tell my brothers to go to Galilee, and there they will see me."

APRIL 12, EASTER DAY - THE RESURRECTION OF THE LORD; ST. JOSEPH MOSCATI
FIRST READING   *Acts 10:34a, 37—43*

Peter proceeded to speak and said: "You know what has happened all over Judea, beginning in Galilee after the baptism that John preached, how God anointed Jesus of Nazareth with the Holy Spirit and power. He went about doing good and healing all those oppressed by the devil, for God was with him. We are witnesses of all that he did both in the country of the Jews and in Jerusalem. They put him to death by hanging him on a tree. This man God raised on the third day and granted that he be visible, not to all the people, but to us, the witnesses chosen by God in advance, who ate and drank with him after he rose from the dead. He commissioned us to preach to the people and testify that he is the one appointed by God as judge of the living and the dead. To him all the prophets bear witness, that everyone who believes in him will receive forgiveness of sins through his name."

RESPONSORIAL PSALM   *Psalm 118:1—2, 16—17, 22—23 (24)*

R. This is the day the Lord has made; let us rejoice and be glad. or R. Alleluia.

Give thanks to the LORD, for he is good, for his mercy endures forever. Let the house of Israel say, "His mercy endures forever." **R.**

"The right hand of the LORD has struck with power; the right hand of the LORD is exalted. I shall not die, but live, and declare the works of the LORD. **R.**

The stone which the builders rejected has become the cornerstone. By the LORD has this been done; it is wonderful in our eyes. **R.**

SECOND READING   *Colossians 3:1—4*

Brothers and sisters: If then you were raised with Christ, seek what is above, where Christ is seated at the right hand of God. Think of what is above, not of what is on earth. For you have died, and your life is hidden with Christ in God. When Christ your life appears, then you too will appear with him in glory.

ALTERNATIVE SECOND READING: *1 Corinthians 5:6b—8*

Brothers and sisters: Do you not know that a little yeast leavens all the dough? Clear out the old yeast, so that you may become a fresh batch of dough, inasmuch as you are unleavened. For our paschal lamb, Christ, has been sacrificed. Therefore, let us celebrate the feast, not with the old yeast, the yeast of malice and wickedness, but with the unleavened bread of sincerity and truth.

SEQUENCE

Christians, to the Paschal Victim / Offer your thankful praises! / A Lamb the sheep redeems; / Christ, who only is sinless, / Reconciles sinners to the Father.

Death and life have contended / in that combat stupendous: / The Prince of life, who died, reigns immortal. / Speak, Mary, declaring What you saw, wayfaring.

"The tomb of Christ, who is living, / the glory of Jesus' resurrection;

Bright angels attesting, / the shroud and napkin resting.

Yes, Christ my hope is arisen; / to Galilee he goes before you."

Christ indeed from death is risen, / our new life obtaining. / Have mercy, victor King, ever reigning! Amen. Alleluia.

ALLELUIA *see 1 Corinthians 5:7b—8a*

R. Alleluia, alleluia. Christ, our paschal lamb, has been sacrificed; let us then feast with joy in the Lord. **R.**

GOSPEL *John 20:1—9*

On the first day of the week, Mary of Magdala came to the tomb early in the morning, while it was still dark, and saw the stone removed from the tomb. So she ran and went to Simon Peter and to the other disciple whom Jesus loved, and told them, "They have taken the Lord from the tomb, and we don't know where they put him." So Peter and the other disciple went out and came to the tomb. They both ran, but the other disciple ran faster than Peter and arrived at the tomb first; he bent down and saw the burial cloths there, but did not go in. When Simon Peter arrived after him, he went into the tomb and saw the burial cloths there, and the cloth that had covered his head, not with the burial cloths but rolled up in a separate place. Then the other disciple also went in, the one who had arrived at the tomb first, and he saw and believed. For they did not yet understand the Scripture that he had to rise from the dead.

OR AT AN AFTERNOON OR EVENING MASS: *Luke 24:13—35*

That very day, the first day of the week, two of Jesus' disciples were going to a village seven miles from Jerusalem called Emmaus, and they were conversing about all the things that had occurred. And it happened that while they were conversing and debating, Jesus himself drew near and walked with them, but their eyes were prevented from recognizing him. He asked them, "What are you discussing as you walk along?" They stopped, looking downcast. One of them, named Cleopas, said to him in reply, "Are you the only visitor to Jerusalem who does not know of the things that have taken place there in these days?" And he replied to them, "What sort of things?" They said to him, "The things that happened to Jesus the Nazarene, who was a prophet mighty in deed and word before God and all the people, how our chief priests and rulers both handed him over to a sentence of death and crucified him. But we were hoping that he would be the one to redeem Israel; and besides all this, it is now the third day since this took place. Some women from our group, however, have astounded us: they were at the tomb early in the morning and did not find his body; they came back and reported that they had indeed seen a vision of angels who announced that he was alive. Then some of those with us went to the tomb and found things just as the women had described, but him they did not see." And he said to them, "Oh, how foolish you are! How slow of heart to believe all that the prophets spoke! Was it not necessary that the Christ should suffer these things and enter into his glory?" Then beginning with Moses and all the prophets, he interpreted to them what referred to him in all the Scriptures. As they approached the village to which they were going, he gave the impression that he was going on farther. But they urged him, "Stay with us, for it is nearly evening and the day is almost over." So he went in to stay with them. And it happened that, while he was with them at table, he took bread, said the blessing, broke it, and gave it to them. With that their eyes were opened and they recognized him, but he vanished from their sight.

Then they said to each other, "Were not our hearts burning within us while he spoke to us on the way and opened the Scriptures to us?" So they set out at once and returned to Jerusalem where they found gathered together the eleven and those with them who were saying, "The Lord has truly been raised and has appeared to Simon!" Then the two recounted what had taken place on the way and how he was made known to them in the breaking of bread.

APRIL 13, EASTER MONDAY; ST. MARTIN I

FIRST READING *Acts 2:14, 22—33*

On the day of Pentecost, Peter stood up with the Eleven, raised his voice, and proclaimed: "You who are Jews, indeed all of you staying in Jerusalem. Let this be known to you, and listen to my words.

"You who are children of Israel, hear these words. Jesus the Nazorean was a man commended to you by God with mighty deeds, wonders, and signs, which God worked through him in your midst, as you yourselves know. This man, delivered up by the set plan and foreknowledge of God, you killed, using lawless men to crucify him. But God raised him up, releasing him from the throes of death, because it was impossible for him to be held by it. For David says of him:

I saw the Lord ever before me, with him at my right hand I shall not be disturbed. Therefore my heart has been glad and my tongue has exulted; my flesh, too, will dwell in hope, because you will not abandon my soul to the netherworld, nor will you suffer your holy one to see corruption. You have made known to me the paths of life; you will fill me with joy in your presence.

My brothers, one can confidently say to you about the patriarch David that he died and was buried, and his tomb is in our midst to this day. But since he was a prophet and knew that God had sworn an oath to him that he would set one of his descendants upon his throne, he foresaw and spoke of the resurrection of the Christ, that neither was he abandoned to the netherworld nor did his flesh see corruption. God raised this Jesus; of this we are all witnesses. Exalted at the right hand of God, he poured forth the promise of the Holy Spirit that he received from the Father, as you both see and hear."

RESPONSORIAL PSALM   *Psalm 16:1—2a, 5, 7—8, 9—10, 11 (1)*
R. Keep me safe, O God; you are my hope. or R. Alleluia.
Keep me, O God, for in you I take refuge, **/** I say to the LORD, "My Lord are you." **/**
O LORD, my allotted portion and my cup, **/** you it is who hold fast my lot. **R.**
I bless the LORD who counsels me; **/** even in the night my heart exhorts me. **/**
I set the LORD ever before me; **/** with him at my right hand, **/** I shall not be disturbed. **R.**
Therefore my heart is glad and my soul rejoices, **/** my body, too, abides in confidence; **/** Because you will not abandon my soul to the nether world, **/** nor will you suffer your faithful one to undergo corruption. **R.**
You will show me the path to life, **/** fullness of joys in your presence, **/**
the delights of your right hand forever. **R.**

ALLELUIA   *Psalm 118:24*
R. Alleluia, alleluia. This is the day the Lord has made; let us be glad and rejoice in it. **R.**

GOSPEL   *Matthew 28:8—15*
Mary Magdalene and the other Mary went away quickly from the tomb, fearful yet overjoyed, and ran to announce the news to his disciples. And behold, Jesus met them on their way and greeted them. They approached, embraced his feet, and did him homage. Then Jesus said to them, "Do not be afraid. Go tell my brothers to go to Galilee, and there they will see me."

While they were going, some of the guard went into the city and told the chief priests all that had happened. The chief priests assembled with the elders and took counsel; then they gave a large sum of money to the soldiers, telling them, "You are to say, 'His disciples came by night and stole him while we were asleep.' And if this gets to the ears of the governor, we will satisfy him and keep you out of trouble." The soldiers took the money and did as they were instructed. And this story has circulated among the Jews to the present day.

APRIL 14, EASTER TUESDAY; BLESSED JAMES DUCKETT

FIRST READING *Acts 2:36—41*

On the day of Pentecost, Peter said to the Jews, "Let the whole house of Israel know for certain that God has made him both Lord and Christ, this Jesus whom you crucified."

Now when they heard this, they were cut to the heart, and they asked Peter and the other Apostles, "What are we to do, my brothers?" Peter said to them, "Repent and be baptized, every one of you, in the name of Jesus Christ, for the forgiveness of your sins; and you will receive the gift of the Holy Spirit. For the promise is made to you and to your children and to all those far off, whomever the Lord our God will call." He testified with many other arguments, and was exhorting them, "Save yourselves from this corrupt generation." Those who accepted his message were baptized, and about three thousand persons were added that day.

RESPONSORIAL PSALM *Psalm 33:4—5, 18—19, 20, 22 (5b)*

R. The earth is full of the goodness of the Lord. or R. Alleluia.

Upright is the word of the LORD, / and all his works are trustworthy. / He loves justice and right; / of the kindness of the LORD the earth is full. **R.**

See, the eyes of the LORD are upon those who fear him, / upon those who hope for his kindness, / To deliver them from death / and preserve them in spite of famine. **R.**

Our soul waits for the LORD, /who is our help and our shield. / May your kindness, O LORD, be upon us; / who have put our hope in you. **R.**

ALLELUIA *Psalm 118:24*

R. Alleluia, alleluia. This is the day the Lord has made; let us rejoice and be glad in it. **R.**

GOSPEL *John 20:11—18*

Mary Magdalene stayed outside the tomb weeping. And as she wept, she bent over into the tomb and saw two angels in white sitting there, one at the head and one at the feet where the body of Jesus had been. And they said to her, "Woman, why are you weeping?" She said to them, "They have taken my Lord, and I don't know where they laid him." When she had said this, she turned around and saw Jesus there, but did not know it was Jesus. Jesus said to her, "Woman, why are you weeping? Whom are you looking for?" She thought it was the gardener and said to him, "Sir, if you carried him away, tell me where you laid him, and I will take him." Jesus said to her, "Mary!" She turned and said to him in Hebrew, "Rabbouni," which means Teacher. Jesus said to her, "Stop holding on to me, for I have not yet ascended to the Father. But go to my brothers and tell them, 'I am going to my Father and your Father, to my God and your God.'" Mary went and announced to the disciples, "I have seen the Lord," and then reported what he had told her.

APRIL 15, EASTER WEDNESDAY; BLESSED ANNA SCHÄFFER

FIRST READING *Acts 3:1—10*

Peter and John were going up to the temple area for the three o'clock hour of prayer. And a man crippled from birth was carried and placed at the gate of the temple called "the

Beautiful Gate" every day to beg for alms from the people who entered the temple. When he saw Peter and John about to go into the temple, he asked for alms. But Peter looked intently at him, as did John, and said, "Look at us." He paid attention to them, expecting to receive something from them. Peter said, "I have neither silver nor gold, but what I do have I give you: in the name of Jesus Christ the Nazorean, rise and walk." Then Peter took him by the right hand and raised him up, and immediately his feet and ankles grew strong. He leaped up, stood, and walked around, and went into the temple with them, walking and jumping and praising God. When all the people saw him walking and praising God, they recognized him as the one who used to sit begging at the Beautiful Gate of the temple, and they were filled with amazement and astonishment at what had happened to him.

RESPONSORIAL PSALM   *Psalm 105:1—2, 3—4, 6—7, 8—9 (3b)*
R. Rejoice, O hearts that seek the Lord. or R. Alleluia.
Give thanks to the LORD, invoke his name; / make known among the nations his deeds. / Sing to him, sing his praise, / proclaim all his wondrous deeds. **R.**
Glory in his holy name; / rejoice, O hearts that seek the LORD! / Look to the LORD in his strength; / Seek to serve him constantly. **R.**
You descendants of Abraham, his servants, / sons of Jacob, his chosen ones! / He, the LORD, is our God; / throughout the earth his judgments prevail. **R.**
He remembers forever his covenant / which he made binding for a thousand generations— /Which he entered into with Abraham / and by his oath to Isaac. **R.**
ALLELUIA   *Psalm 118:24*
R. Alleluia, alleluia. This is the day the Lord has made; let us rejoice and be glad in it. **R.**

GOSPEL   *Luke 24:13—35*
That very day, the first day of the week, two of Jesus' disciples were going to a village seven miles from Jerusalem called Emmaus, and they were conversing about all the things that had occurred. And it happened that while they were conversing and debating, Jesus himself drew near and walked with them, but their eyes were prevented from recognizing him. He asked them, "What are you discussing as you walk along?" They stopped, looking downcast. One of them, named Cleopas, said to him in reply, "Are you the only visitor to Jerusalem who does not know of the things that have taken place there in these days?" And he replied to them, "What sort of things?" They said to him, "The things that happened to Jesus the Nazarene, who was a prophet mighty in deed and word before God and all the people, how our chief priests and rulers both handed him over to a sentence of death and crucified him. But we were hoping that he would be the one to redeem Israel; and besides all this, it is now the third day since this took place. Some women from our group, however, have astounded us: they were at the tomb early in the morning and did not find his Body; they came back and reported that they had indeed seen a vision of angels who announced that he was alive. Then some of those with us went to the tomb and found things just as the women had described, but him they did not see." And he said to them, "Oh, how foolish you are! How slow of heart to believe all that the prophets spoke! Was it not necessary that the Christ should suffer these things and enter into his glory?" Then beginning with Moses

and all the prophets, he interpreted to them what referred to him in all the Scriptures. As they approached the village to which they were going, he gave the impression that he was going on farther. But they urged him, "Stay with us, for it is nearly evening and the day is almost over." So he went in to stay with them. And it happened that, while he was with them at table, he took bread, said the blessing, broke it, and gave it to them. With that their eyes were opened and they recognized him, but he vanished from their sight. Then they said to each other, "Were not our hearts burning within us while he spoke to us on the way and opened the Scriptures to us?" So they set out at once and returned to Jerusalem where they found gathered together the Eleven and those with them who were saying, "The Lord has truly been raised and has appeared to Simon!" Then the two recounted what had taken place on the way and how he was made known to them in the breaking of the bread.

APRIL 16, EASTER THURSDAY; ST. BENEDICT JOSEPH LABRE

FIRST READING   *Acts 3:11—26*

As the crippled man who had been cured clung to Peter and John, all the people hurried in amazement toward them in the portico called "Solomon's Portico." When Peter saw this, he addressed the people, "You children of Israel, why are you amazed at this, and why do you look so intently at us as if we had made him walk by our own power or piety? The God of Abraham, the God of Isaac, and the God of Jacob, the God of our fathers, has glorified his servant Jesus whom you handed over and denied in Pilate's presence, when he had decided to release him. You denied the Holy and Righteous One and asked that a murderer be released to you. The author of life you put to death, but God raised him from the dead; of this we are witnesses. And by faith in his name, this man, whom you see and know, his name has made strong, and the faith that comes through it has given him this perfect health, in the presence of all of you. Now I know, brothers and sisters, that you acted out of ignorance, just as your leaders did; but God has thus brought to fulfillment what he had announced beforehand through the mouth of all the prophets, that his Christ would suffer. Repent, therefore, and be converted, that your sins may be wiped away, and that the Lord may grant you times of refreshment and send you the Christ already appointed for you, Jesus, whom heaven must receive until the times of universal restoration of which God spoke through the mouth of his holy prophets from of old.

For Moses said: *A prophet like me will the Lord, your God, raise up for you from among your own kin; to him you shall listen in all that he may say to you. Everyone who does not listen to that prophet will be cut off from the people.*

"Moreover, all the prophets who spoke, from Samuel and those afterwards, also announced these days. You are the children of the prophets and of the covenant that God made with your ancestors when he said to Abraham, *In your offspring all the families of the earth shall be blessed.* For you first, God raised up his servant and sent him to bless you by turning each of you from your evil ways."

RESPONSORIAL PSALM   *Psalm 8:2ab, 5, 6—7, 8—9 (2ab)*
R. O Lord, our God, how wonderful your name in all the earth! or R. Alleluia.

O LORD, our Lord, how glorious is your name/ over all the earth! / What is man that you should be mindful of him, / or the son of man that you should care for him? **R.**
You have made him little less than the angels, / and crowned him with glory and honor. / You have given him rule over the works of your hands, / putting all things under his feet. **R.**
All sheep and oxen, / yes, and the beasts of the field, / The birds of the air, the fishes of the sea, / and whatever swims the paths of the seas. **R.**

ALLELUIA *Psalm 118:24*

R. Alleluia, alleluia. This is the day the Lord has made; let us be glad and rejoice in it. **R.**

GOSPEL *Luke 24:35—48*

The disciples of Jesus recounted what had taken place along the way, and how they had come to recognize him in the breaking of bread.

While they were still speaking about this, he stood in their midst and said to them, "Peace be with you." But they were startled and terrified and thought that they were seeing a ghost. Then he said to them, "Why are you troubled? And why do questions arise in your hearts? Look at my hands and my feet, that it is I myself. Touch me and see, because a ghost does not have flesh and bones as you can see I have." And as he said this, he showed them his hands and his feet. While they were still incredulous for joy and were amazed, he asked them, "Have you anything here to eat?" They gave him a piece of baked fish; he took it and ate it in front of them.

He said to them, "These are my words that I spoke to you while I was still with you, that everything written about me in the law of Moses and in the prophets and psalms must be fulfilled." Then he opened their minds to understand the Scriptures. And he said to them, "Thus it is written that the Christ would suffer and rise from the dead on the third day and that repentance, for the forgiveness of sins, would be preached in his name to all the nations, beginning from Jerusalem. You are witnesses of these things."

APRIL 17, EASTER FRIDAY; ST. STEPHEN HARDING

FIRST READING *Acts 4:1—12*

After the crippled man had been cured, while Peter and John were still speaking to the people, the priests, the captain of the temple guard, and the Sadducees confronted them, disturbed that they were teaching the people and proclaiming in Jesus the resurrection of the dead. They laid hands on Peter and John and put them in custody until the next day, since it was already evening. But many of those who heard the word came to believe and the number of men grew to about five thousand.

On the next day, their leaders, elders, and scribes were assembled in Jerusalem, with Annas the high priest, Caiaphas, John, Alexander, and all who were of the high—priestly class. They brought them into their presence and questioned them, "By what power or by what name have you done this?" Then Peter, filled with the Holy Spirit, answered them, "Leaders of the people and elders: If we are being examined today about a good deed done to a cripple, namely, by what means he was saved, then all of you and all the people of Israel should know that it was in the name of Jesus Christ the Nazorean whom you crucified, whom God raised from the dead; in his name this man stands before you healed.

He is *the stone rejected by you, the builders, which has become the cornerstone.* There is no salvation through anyone else, nor is there any other name under heaven given to the human race by which we are to be saved."

RESPONSORIAL PSALM *Psalm 118:1—2, 4, 22—24, 25—27a (22)*

R. The stone rejected by the builders has become the cornerstone. or R. Alleluia.
Give thanks to the LORD, for he is good, **/** for his mercy endures forever. **/** Let the house of Israel say: **/** "His mercy endures forever." **/** Let those who fear the LORD say, **/** "His mercy endures forever." **R.**
The stone which the builders rejected **/** has become the cornerstone. **/** By the LORD has this been done; **/** it is wonderful in our eyes. **/** This is the day the LORD has made; **/** let us be glad and rejoice in it. **R.**
O LORD, grant salvation! **/** O LORD, grant prosperity! **/** Blessed is he who comes in the name of the LORD; **/** we bless you from the house of the LORD. **/** The LORD is God, and he has given us light. **R.**

ALLELUIA *Psalm 118:24*

R. Alleluia, alleluia. This is the day the Lord has made; let us be glad and rejoice in it. **R.**

GOSPEL *John 21:1—14*

Jesus revealed himself again to his disciples at the Sea of Tiberias. He revealed himself in this way. Together were Simon Peter, Thomas called Didymus, Nathanael from Cana in Galilee, Zebedee's sons, and two others of his disciples. Simon Peter said to them, "I am going fishing." They said to him, "We also will come with you." So they went out and got into the boat, but that night they caught nothing. When it was already dawn, Jesus was standing on the shore; but the disciples did not realize that it was Jesus. Jesus said to them, "Children, have you caught anything to eat?" They answered him, "No." So he said to them, "Cast the net over the right side of the boat and you will find something." So they cast it, and were not able to pull it in because of the number of fish. So the disciple whom Jesus loved said to Peter, "It is the Lord." When Simon Peter heard that it was the Lord, he tucked in his garment, for he was lightly clad, and jumped into the sea. The other disciples came in the boat, for they were not far from shore, only about a hundred yards, dragging the net with the fish. When they climbed out on shore, they saw a charcoal fire with fish on it and bread. Jesus said to them, "Bring some of the fish you just caught." So Simon Peter went over and dragged the net ashore full of one hundred fifty—three large fish. Even though there were so many, the net was not torn. Jesus said to them, "Come, have breakfast." And none of the disciples dared to ask him, "Who are you?" because they realized it was the Lord. Jesus came over and took the bread and gave it to them, and in like manner the fish. This was now the third time Jesus was revealed to his disciples after being raised from the dead.

APRIL 18, EASTER SATURDAY; BLESSED MARIE OF THE INCARNATION

FIRST READING   *Acts 4:13—21*

Observing the boldness of Peter and John and perceiving them to be uneducated, ordinary men, the leaders, elders, and scribes were amazed, and they recognized them as the companions of Jesus. Then when they saw the man who had been cured standing there with them, they could say nothing in reply. So they ordered them to leave the Sanhedrin, and conferred with one another, saying, "What are we to do with these men? Everyone living in Jerusalem knows that a remarkable sign was done through them, and we cannot deny it. But so that it may not be spread any further among the people, let us give them a stern warning never again to speak to anyone in this name."

So they called them back and ordered them not to speak or teach at all in the name of Jesus. Peter and John, however, said to them in reply, "Whether it is right in the sight of God for us to obey you rather than God, you be the judges. It is impossible for us not to speak about what we have seen and heard." After threatening them further, they released them, finding no way to punish them, on account of the people who were all praising God for what had happened.

RESPONSORIAL PSALM: *Psalm 118:1, 14—15ab, 16—18, 19—21 (21a)*
R. I will give thanks to you, for you have answered me. or R. Alleluia.
Give thanks to the LORD, for he is good, **/** for his mercy endures forever. **/** My strength and my courage is the LORD, **/** and he has been my savior. **/** The joyful shout of victory in the tents of the just. **R.**
"The right hand of the LORD is exalted; **/** the right hand of the LORD has struck with power." **/** I shall not die, but live, **/** and declare the works of the LORD. **/** Though the LORD has indeed chastised me, **/** yet he has not delivered me to death. **R.**
Open to me the gates of justice; **/** I will enter them and give thanks to the LORD. **/** This is the gate of the LORD; **/** the just shall enter it. **/** I will give thanks to you, **/** for you have answered me **/** and have been my savior. **R.**

ALLELUIA   *Psalm 118:24*
R. Alleluia, alleluia. This is the day the Lord has made; let us rejoice and be glad in it. **R.**

GOSPEL   *Mark 16:9—15*

When Jesus had risen, early on the first day of the week, he appeared first to Mary Magdalene, out of whom he had driven seven demons. She went and told his companions who were mourning and weeping. When they heard that he was alive and had been seen by her, they did not believe.

After this he appeared in another form to two of them walking along on their way to the country. They returned and told the others; but they did not believe them either.

But later, as the Eleven were at table, Jesus appeared to them and rebuked them for their unbelief and hardness of heart because they had not believed those who saw him after he had been raised. He said to them, "Go into the whole world and proclaim the Gospel to every creature."

APRIL 19, 2ND SUNDAY OF EASTER (DIVINE MERCY SUNDAY)

FIRST READING *Acts 2:42—47*

They devoted themselves to the teaching of the apostles and to the communal life, to the breaking of bread and to the prayers. Awe came upon everyone, and many wonders and signs were done through the apostles. All who believed were together and had all things in common; they would sell their property and possessions and divide them among all according to each one's need. Every day they devoted themselves to meeting together in the temple area and to breaking bread in their homes. They ate their meals with exultation and sincerity of heart, praising God and enjoying favor with all the people. And every day the Lord added to their number those who were being saved.

RESPONSORIAL PSALM *Psalm 118:2—4, 13—15, 22—24 (1)*

R. Give thanks to the Lord for he is good, his love is everlasting. or R. Alleluia.

Let the house of Israel say, / "His mercy endures forever." / Let the house of Aaron say, / "His mercy endures forever." / Let those who fear the LORD say, / "His mercy endures forever." **R.**

I was hard pressed and was falling, / but the LORD helped me. / My strength and my courage is the LORD, / and he has been my savior. / The joyful shout of victory in the tents of the just. **R.**

The stone which the builders rejected / has become the cornerstone. / By the LORD has this been done; / it is wonderful in our eyes. / This is the day the LORD has made; / let us be glad and rejoice in it. **R.**

SECOND READING *1 Peter 1:3—9*

Blessed be the God and Father of our Lord Jesus Christ, who in his great mercy gave us a new birth to a living hope through the resurrection of Jesus Christ from the dead, to an inheritance that is imperishable, undefiled, and unfading, kept in heaven for you who by the power of God are safeguarded through faith, to a salvation that is ready to be revealed in the final time. In this you rejoice, although now for a little while you may have to suffer through various trials, so that the genuineness of your faith, more precious than gold that is perishable even though tested by fire, may prove to be for praise, glory, and honor at the revelation of Jesus Christ. Although you have not seen him you love him; even though you do not see him now yet believe in him, you rejoice with an indescribable and glorious joy, as you attain the goal of your faith, the salvation of your souls.

ALLELUIA *John 20:29*

R. Alleluia, alleluia. You believe in me, Thomas, because you have seen me, says the Lord; blessed are they who have not seen me, but still believe! **R.**

GOSPEL *John 20:19—31*

On the evening of that first day of the week, when the doors were locked, where the disciples were, for fear of the Jews, Jesus came and stood in their midst and said to them, "Peace be with you." When he had said this, he showed them his hands and his side. The disciples rejoiced when they saw the Lord. Jesus said to them again, "Peace be with you. As the Father has sent me, so I send you." And when he had said this, he breathed on them and said to them, "Receive the Holy Spirit. Whose sins you forgive are forgiven them, and whose sins you retain are retained."

Thomas, called Didymus, one of the Twelve, was not with them when Jesus came. So the other disciples said to him, "We have seen the Lord." But he said to them, "Unless I see the mark of the nails in his hands and put my finger into the nailmarks and put my hand into his side, I will not believe."

Now a week later his disciples were again inside and Thomas was with them. Jesus came, although the doors were locked, and stood in their midst and said, "Peace be with you." Then he said to Thomas, "Put your finger here and see my hands, and bring your hand and put it into my side, and do not be unbelieving, but believe." Thomas answered and said to him, "My Lord and my God!" Jesus said to him, "Have you come to believe because you have seen me? Blessed are those who have not seen and have believed."

Now, Jesus did many other signs in the presence of his disciples that are not written in this book. But these are written that you may come to believe that Jesus is the Christ, the Son of God, and that through this belief you may have life in his name.

APRIL 20, 2ND WEEK OF EASTER – MONDAY; ST. AGNES OF MONTEPULCIANO
FIRST READING *Acts 4:23–31*

After their release Peter and John went back to their own people and reported what the chief priests and elders had told them. And when they heard it, they raised their voices to God with one accord and said, "Sovereign Lord, maker of heaven and earth and the sea and all that is in them, you said by the Holy Spirit through the mouth of our father David, your servant:

Why did the Gentiles rage and the peoples entertain folly? The kings of the earth took their stand and the princes gathered together against the Lord and against his anointed.

Indeed they gathered in this city against your holy servant Jesus whom you anointed, Herod and Pontius Pilate, together with the Gentiles and the peoples of Israel, to do what your hand and your will had long ago planned to take place. And now, Lord, take note of their threats, and enable your servants to speak your word with all boldness, as you stretch forth your hand to heal, and signs and wonders are done through the name of your holy servant Jesus." As they prayed, the place where they were gathered shook, and they were all filled with the Holy Spirit and continued to speak the word of God with boldness.

RESPONSORIAL PSALM *Psalm 2:1–3, 4–7a, 7b–9*
R. Blessed are all who take refuge in the Lord. or: R. Alleluia.
Why do the nations rage and the peoples utter folly? **/** The kings of the earth rise up, **/** and the princes conspire together against the LORD **/** and against his anointed: **/** "Let us break their fetters **/** and cast their bonds from us!" **R.**

He who is throned in heaven laughs; / the LORD derides them. / Then in anger he speaks to them; / he terrifies them in his wrath: / "I myself have set up my king on Zion, my holy mountain. / " I will proclaim the decree of the LORD. **R.**

The LORD said to me, / "You are my Son; / this day I have begotten you. / Ask of me and I will give you the nations for an inheritance / and the ends of the earth for your possession. / You shall rule them with an iron rod; / you shall shatter them like an earthen dish." **R.**

ALLELUIA   *Colossians 3:1*

R. Alleluia, alleluia. If then you were raised with Christ, seek what is above, where Christ is seated at the right hand of God. **R.**

GOSPEL   *John 3:1–8*

There was a Pharisee named Nicodemus, a ruler of the Jews. He came to Jesus at night and said to him, "Rabbi, we know that you are a teacher who has come from God, for no one can do these signs that you are doing unless God is with him." Jesus answered and said to him, "Amen, amen, I say to you, unless one is born from above, he cannot see the Kingdom of God." Nicodemus said to him, "How can a man once grown old be born again? Surely he cannot reenter his mother's womb and be born again, can he?" Jesus answered, "Amen, amen, I say to you, unless one is born of water and Spirit he cannot enter the Kingdom of God. What is born of flesh is flesh and what is born of spirit is spirit. Do not be amazed that I told you, 'You must be born from above.' The wind blows where it wills, and you can hear the sound it makes, but you do not know where it comes from or where it goes; so it is with everyone who is born of the Spirit."

APRIL 21, 2ND WEEK OF EASTER - TUESDAY; ST. ANSELM

FIRST READING   *Acts 4:32–37*

The community of believers was of one heart and mind, and no one claimed that any of his possessions was his own, but they had everything in common. With great power the Apostles bore witness to the resurrection of the Lord Jesus, and great favor was accorded them all. There was no needy person among them, for those who owned property or houses would sell them, bring the proceeds of the sale, and put them at the feet of the Apostles, and they were distributed to each according to need.

Thus Joseph, also named by the Apostles Barnabas (which is translated Ason of encouragement"), a Levite, a Cypriot by birth, sold a piece of property that he owned, then brought the money and put it at the feet of the Apostles.

RESPONSORIAL PSALM   *Psalm 93:1ab, 1cd–2, 5*

R. The Lord is king; he is robed in majesty. or: R. Alleluia.

The LORD is king, in splendor robed; / robed is the LORD and girt about with strength. **R.**

And he has made the world firm, / not to be moved. / Your throne stands firm from of old; / from everlasting you are, O LORD. **R.**

Your decrees are worthy of trust indeed: / holiness befits your house, / O LORD, for length of days. **R.**

ALLELUIA
John 3:14–15

R. Alleluia, alleluia. The Son of Man must be lifted up, so that everyone who believes in him may have eternal life. **R.**

GOSPEL
John 3:7b–15

Jesus said to Nicodemus: "'You must be born from above.' The wind blows where it wills, and you can hear the sound it makes, but you do not know where it comes from or where it goes; so it is with everyone who is born of the Spirit." Nicodemus answered and said to him, 'How can this happen?" Jesus answered and said to him, "You are the teacher of Israel and you do not understand this? Amen, amen, I say to you, we speak of what we know and we testify to what we have seen, but you people do not accept our testimony. If I tell you about earthly things and you do not believe, how will you believe if I tell you about heavenly things? No one has gone up to heaven except the one who has come down from heaven, the Son of Man. And just as Moses lifted up the serpent in the desert, so must the Son of Man be lifted up, so that everyone who believes in him may have eternal life."

APRIL 22, 2ND WEEK OF EASTER – WEDNESDAY; BLESSED LIDWINA

FIRST READING
Acts 5:17–26

The high priest rose up and all his companions, that is, the party of the Sadducees, and, filled with jealousy, laid hands upon the Apostles and put them in the public jail. But during the night, the angel of the Lord opened the doors of the prison, led them out, and said, "Go and take your place in the temple area, and tell the people everything about this life." When they heard this, they went to the temple early in the morning and taught. When the high priest and his companions arrived, they convened the Sanhedrin, the full senate of the children of Israel, and sent to the jail to have them brought in. But the court officers who went did not find them in the prison, so they came back and reported, "We found the jail securely locked and the guards stationed outside the doors, but when we opened them, we found no one inside." When the captain of the temple guard and the chief priests heard this report, they were at a loss about them, as to what this would come to. Then someone came in and reported to them, "The men whom you put in prison are in the temple area and are teaching the people." Then the captain and the court officers went and brought them, but without force, because they were afraid of being stoned by the people.

RESPONSORIAL PSALM
Psalm 34:2–3, 4–5, 6–7, 8–9

R. The Lord hears the cry of the poor. or: R. Alleluia.

I will bless the LORD at all times; / his praise shall be ever in my mouth. / Let my soul glory in the LORD; / the lowly will hear me and be glad. **R.**

Glorify the LORD with me, / let us together extol his name. / I sought the LORD, and he answered me / and delivered me from all my fears. **R.**

Look to him that you may be radiant with joy, / and your faces may not blush with shame. / When the poor one called out, the LORD heard, / and from all his distress he saved him. **R.**

The angel of the LORD encamps around those who fear him, / and delivers them. Taste and see how good the LORD is; / blessed the man who takes refuge in him. **R.**

ALLELUIA   *John 3:16*

R. Alleluia, alleluia. God so loved the world that he gave his only–begotten Son, so that everyone who believes in him might have eternal life. **R.**

GOSPEL   *John 3:16–21*

God so loved the world that he gave his only–begotten Son, so that everyone who believes in him might not perish but might have eternal life. For God did not send his Son into the world to condemn the world, but that the world might be saved through him. Whoever believes in him will not be condemned, but whoever does not believe has already been condemned, because he has not believed in the name of the only–begotten Son of God. And this is the verdict, that the light came into the world, but people preferred darkness to light, because their works were evil. For everyone who does wicked things hates the light and does not come toward the light, so that his works might not be exposed. But whoever lives the truth comes to the light, so that his works may be clearly seen as done in God.

APRIL 23, 2ND WEEK OF EASTER – THURSDAY; ST. ADALBERT

FIRST READING   *Acts 5:27–33*

When the court officers had brought the Apostles in and made them stand before the Sanhedrin, the high priest questioned them, "We gave you strict orders did we not, to stop teaching in that name. Yet you have filled Jerusalem with your teaching and want to bring this man's blood upon us." But Peter and the Apostles said in reply, "We must obey God rather than men. The God of our ancestors raised Jesus, though you had him killed by hanging him on a tree. God exalted him at his right hand as leader and savior to grant Israel repentance and forgiveness of sins. We are witnesses of these things, as is the Holy Spirit whom God has given to those who obey him."

When they heard this, they became infuriated and wanted to put them to death.

RESPONSORIAL PSALM   *Psalm 34:2 and 9, 17–18, 19–20*

R. The Lord hears the cry of the poor. or: R. Alleluia.

I will bless the LORD at all times; / his praise shall be ever in my mouth. / Taste and see how good the LORD is; / blessed the man who takes refuge in him. **R.**

The LORD confronts the evildoers, / to destroy remembrance of them from the earth. / When the just cry out, the LORD hears them, / and from all their distress he rescues them. **R.**

The LORD is close to the brokenhearted; / and those who are crushed in spirit he saves. / Many are the troubles of the just man, / but out of them all the LORD delivers him. **R.**

ALLELUIA   *John 20:29*

R. Alleluia, alleluia. You believe in me, Thomas, because you have seen me, says the Lord; blessed are those who have not seen, but still believe! **R.**

GOSPEL   *John 3:31–36*

The one who comes from above is above all. The one who is of the earth is earthly and speaks of earthly things. But the one who comes from heaven is above all. He testifies to what he has seen and heard, but no one accepts his testimony. Whoever does accept his testimony certifies that God is trustworthy. For the one whom God sent speaks the words of God. He does not ration his gift of the Spirit. The Father loves the Son and has given everything over to him. Whoever believes in the Son has eternal life, but whoever disobeys the Son will not see life, but the wrath of God remains upon him.

APRIL 24, 2ND WEEK OF EASTER – FRIDAY; ST. FIDELIS OF SIGMARINGEN

FIRST READING   *Acts 5:34–42*

A Pharisee in the Sanhedrin named Gamaliel, a teacher of the law, respected by all the people, stood up, ordered the Apostles to be put outside for a short time, and said to the Sanhedrin, "Fellow children of Israel, be careful what you are about to do to these men. Some time ago, Theudas appeared, claiming to be someone important, and about four hundred men joined him, but he was killed, and all those who were loyal to him were disbanded and came to nothing. After him came Judas the Galilean at the time of the census. He also drew people after him, but he too perished and all who were loyal to him were scattered. So now I tell you, have nothing to do with these men, and let them go. For if this endeavor or this activity is of human origin, it will destroy itself. But if it comes from God, you will not be able to destroy them; you may even find yourselves fighting against God." They were persuaded by him. After recalling the Apostles, they had them flogged, ordered them to stop speaking in the name of Jesus, and dismissed them. So they left the presence of the Sanhedrin, rejoicing that they had been found worthy to suffer dishonor for the sake of the name. And all day long, both at the temple and in their homes, they did not stop teaching and proclaiming the Christ, Jesus.

RESPONSORIAL PSALM   *Psalm 27:1, 4, 13–14*
R. One thing I seek: to dwell in the house of the Lord. or: R. Alleluia.
The LORD is my light and my salvation; / whom should I fear? / The LORD is my life's refuge; / of whom should I be afraid? **R.**
One thing I ask of the LORD this I seek: / To dwell in the house of the LORD / all the days of my life, / That I may gaze on the loveliness of the LORD / and contemplate his temple. **R.**
I believe that I shall see the bounty of the LORD / in the land of the living. / Wait for the LORD with courage; / be stouthearted, and wait for the LORD. **R.**
ALLELUIA   *Matthew 4:4b*
R. Alleluia, alleluia. One does not live on bread alone, but on every word that comes forth from the mouth of God. **R.**

GOSPEL   *John 6:1–15*

Jesus went across the Sea of Galilee. A large crowd followed him, because they saw the signs he was performing on the sick. Jesus went up on the mountain, and there he sat down with his disciples. The Jewish feast of Passover was near. When Jesus raised his eyes and saw that a large crowd was coming to him, he said to Philip, "Where can we buy enough food for them to eat?" He said this to test him, because he himself knew what he was going to do. Philip answered him, "Two hundred days' wages worth of food would not be enough for each of them to have a little." One of his disciples, Andrew, the brother of Simon Peter, said to him, "There is a boy here who has five barley loaves and two fish; but what good are these for so many?" Jesus said, "Have the people recline." Now there was a great deal of grass in that place. So the men reclined, about five thousand in number. Then Jesus took the loaves, gave thanks, and distributed them to those who were reclining, and also as much of the fish as they wanted. When they had had their fill, he said to his disciples, "Gather the fragments left over, so that nothing will be wasted." So they collected them, and filled twelve wicker baskets with fragments from the five barley loaves that had been more than they could eat. When the people saw the sign he had done, they said, "This is truly the Prophet, the one who is to come into the world." Since Jesus knew that they were going to come and carry him off to make him king, he withdrew again to the mountain alone.

APRIL 25, SAINT MARK, EVANGELIST – FEAST; ST. MARK THE EVANGELIST
FIRST READING *1 Peter 5:5b–14*

Beloved: Clothe yourselves with humility in your dealings with one another, for: God opposes the proud but bestows favor on the humble. So humble yourselves under the mighty hand of God, that he may exalt you in due time. Cast all your worries upon him because he cares for you.

Be sober and vigilant. Your opponent the Devil is prowling around like a roaring lion looking for someone to devour. Resist him, steadfast in faith, knowing that your brothers and sisters throughout the world undergo the same sufferings. The God of all grace who called you to his eternal glory through Christ Jesus will himself restore, confirm, strengthen, and establish you after you have suffered a little. To him be dominion forever. Amen.

I write you this briefly through Silvanus, whom I consider a faithful brother, exhorting you and testifying that this is the true grace of God. Remain firm in it. The chosen one at Babylon sends you greeting, as does Mark, my son. Greet one another with a loving kiss. Peace to all of you who are in Christ.

RESPONSORIAL PSALM *Psalm 89:2–3, 6–7, 16–17*

R. For ever I will sing the goodness of the Lord. or: R. Alleluia.

The favors of the LORD I will sing forever; / through all generations my mouth shall proclaim your faithfulness. / For you have said, / "My kindness is established forever"; / in heaven you have confirmed your faithfulness. **R.**

The heavens proclaim your wonders, O LORD, / and your faithfulness, in the assembly of the holy ones. / For who in the skies can rank with the LORD? / Who is like the LORD among the sons of God? **R.**

Blessed the people who know the joyful shout; **/** in the light of your countenance, **/** O LORD, they walk. **/** At your name they rejoice all the day, **/** and through your justice they are exalted. **R.**

ALLELUIA *1 Corinthians 1:23a–24b*

R. Alleluia, alleluia. We proclaim Christ crucified; he is the power of God and the wisdom of God. **R.**

GOSPEL *Mark 16:15–20*

Jesus appeared to the Eleven and said to them: "Go into the whole world and proclaim the Gospel to every creature. Whoever believes and is baptized will be saved; whoever does not believe will be condemned. These signs will accompany those who believe: in my name they will drive out demons, they will speak new languages. They will pick up serpents with their hands, and if they drink any deadly thing, it will not harm them. They will lay hands on the sick, and they will recover."

Then the Lord Jesus, after he spoke to them, was taken up into heaven and took his seat at the right hand of God. But they went forth and preached everywhere, while the Lord worked with them and confirmed the word through accompanying signs.

APRIL 26, 3RD SUNDAY OF EASTER; ST. ZITA

FIRST READING *Acts 2:14, 22—33*

Then Peter stood up with the Eleven, raised his voice, and proclaimed: "You who are Jews, indeed all of you staying in Jerusalem. Let this be known to you, and listen to my words. You who are Israelites, hear these words. Jesus the Nazorean was a man commended to you by God with mighty deeds, wonders, and signs, which God worked through him in your midst, as you yourselves know. This man, delivered up by the set plan and foreknowledge of God, you killed, using lawless men to crucify him. But God raised him up, releasing him from the throes of death, because it was impossible for him to be held by it. For David says of him: *I saw the Lord ever before me, with him at my right hand I shall not be disturbed. Therefore my heart has been glad and my tongue has exulted; my flesh, too, will dwell in hope, because you will not abandon my soul to the netherworld, nor will you suffer your holy one to see corruption. You have made known to me the paths of life; you will fill me with joy in your presence.*

"My brothers, one can confidently say to you about the patriarch David that he died and was buried, and his tomb is in our midst to this day. But since he was a prophet and knew that God had sworn an oath to him that he would set one of his descendants upon his throne, he foresaw and spoke of the resurrection of the Christ, that neither was he abandoned to the netherworld nor did his flesh see corruption. God raised this Jesus; of this we are all witnesses. Exalted at the right hand of God, he received the promise of the Holy Spirit from the Father and poured him forth, as you see and hear."

RESPONSORIAL PSALM *Psalm 16:1—2, 5, 7—8, 9—10, 11 (11a)*

R. Lord, you will show us the path of life. or R. Alleluia.

Keep me, O God, for in you I take refuge; / I say to the LORD, "My LORD are you." / O LORD, my allotted portion and my cup, / you it is who hold fast my lot. **R.**

I bless the LORD who counsels me; / even in the night my heart exhorts me. / I set the LORD ever before me; / with him at my right hand I shall not be disturbed. **R.**

Therefore my heart is glad and my soul rejoices, / my body, too, abides in confidence; / because you will not abandon my soul to the netherworld, / nor will you suffer your faithful one to undergo corruption. **R.**

You will show me the path to life, / abounding joy in your presence, / the delights at your right hand forever. **R.**

SECOND READING   1 Peter 1:17—21

Beloved: If you invoke as Father him who judges impartially according to each one's works, conduct yourselves with reverence during the time of your sojourning, realizing that you were ransomed from your futile conduct, handed on by your ancestors, not with perishable things like silver or gold but with the precious blood of Christ as of a spotless unblemished lamb.

He was known before the foundation of the world but revealed in the final time for you, who through him believe in God who raised him from the dead and gave him glory, so that your faith and hope are in God.

ALLELUIA   John 10:27

R. Alleluia, alleluia. Lord Jesus, open the Scriptures to us; make our hearts burn while you speak to us. **R.**

GOSPEL   Luke 24:13—35

That very day, the first day of the week, two of Jesus' disciples were going to a village seven miles from Jerusalem called Emmaus, and they were conversing about all the things that had occurred. And it happened that while they were conversing and debating, Jesus himself drew near and walked with them, but their eyes were prevented from recognizing him. He asked them, "What are you discussing as you walk along?" They stopped, looking downcast. One of them, named Cleopas, said to him in reply, "Are you the only visitor to Jerusalem who does not know of the things that have taken place there in these days?" And he replied to them, "What sort of things?" They said to him, "The things that happened to Jesus the Nazarene, who was a prophet mighty in deed and word before God and all the people, how our chief priests and rulers both handed him over to a sentence of death and crucified him. But we were hoping that he would be the one to redeem Israel; and besides all this, it is now the third day since this took place. Some women from our group, however, have astounded us: they were at the tomb early in the morning and did not find his body; they came back and reported that they had indeed seen a vision of angels who announced that he was alive. Then some of those with us went to the tomb and found things just as the women had described, but him they did not see." And he said to them, "Oh, how foolish you are! How slow of heart to believe all that the prophets spoke! Was it not necessary that the Christ should suffer these things and enter into his glory?" Then beginning with Moses and all the prophets, he interpreted to them what referred to him in all the Scriptures. As they approached the village to which they were going, he gave the impression that he was going on farther. But they urged him, "Stay with us, for it is nearly evening and the day is almost over." So he went in to stay with them. And it happened that, while he was with them at table, he took bread, said the blessing, broke it, and gave it to them. With that their eyes were opened and they recognized him, but he vanished from their sight. Then they said to each other, "Were not our hearts burning within us while he spoke to us on the way and opened the Scriptures to us?" So they set out at once and returned to Jerusalem where they found gathered together the eleven and those with them who were saying, "The Lord has truly been raised and has appeared to Simon!" Then the two recounted what had taken place on the way and how he was made known to them in the breaking of bread.

APRIL 27, 3RD WEEK OF EASTER – MONDAY; ST. GIANNA BERETTA MOLLA

FIRST READING *Acts 6:8–15*

Stephen, filled with grace and power, was working great wonders and signs among the people. Certain members of the so–called Synagogue of Freedmen, Cyreneans, and Alexandrians, and people from Cilicia and Asia, came forward and debated with Stephen, but they could not withstand the wisdom and the Spirit with which he spoke. Then they instigated some men to say, "We have heard him speaking blasphemous words against Moses and God." They stirred up the people, the elders, and the scribes, accosted him, seized him, and brought him before the Sanhedrin. They presented false witnesses who testified, "This man never stops saying things against this holy place and the law. For we have heard him claim that this Jesus the Nazorean will destroy this place and change the customs that Moses handed down to us." All those who sat in the Sanhedrin looked intently at him and saw that his face was like the face of an angel.

RESPONSORIAL PSALM *Psalm 119:23–24, 26–27, 29–30*

R. Blessed are they who follow the law of the Lord! or: R. Alleluia.

Though princes meet and talk against me, / your servant meditates on your statutes. / Yes, your decrees are my delight; / they are my counselors. **R.**

I declared my ways, and you answered me; / teach me your statutes. / Make me understand the way of your precepts, / and I will meditate on your wondrous deeds. **R.**

Remove from me the way of falsehood, / and favor me with your law. / The way of truth I have chosen; / I have set your ordinances before me. **R.**

ALLELUIA *Matthew 4:4b*

R. Alleluia, alleluia. One does not live on bread alone but on every word that comes forth from the mouth of God. **R.**

GOSPEL *John 6:22–29*

[After Jesus had fed the five thousand men, his disciples saw him walking on the sea.] The next day, the crowd that remained across the sea saw that there had been only one boat there, and that Jesus had not gone along with his disciples in the boat, but only his disciples had left. Other boats came from Tiberias near the place where they had eaten the bread when the Lord gave thanks. When the crowd saw that neither Jesus nor his disciples were there, they themselves got into boats and came to Capernaum looking for Jesus. And when they found him across the sea they said to him, "Rabbi, when did you get here?" Jesus answered them and said, "Amen, amen, I say to you, you are looking for me not because you saw signs but because you ate the loaves and were filled. Do not work for food that perishes but for the food that endures for eternal life, which the Son of Man will give you. For on him the Father, God, has set his seal." So they said to him, "What can we do to accomplish the works of God?" Jesus answered and said to them, "This is the work of God, that you believe in the one he sent."

APRIL 28, 3RD WEEK OF EASTER – TUESDAY; ST. PETER CHANEL

FIRST READING *Acts 7:51B8:1a*

Stephen said to the people, the elders, and the scribes: "You stiff-necked people, uncircumcised in heart and ears, you always oppose the Holy Spirit; you are just like your ancestors. Which of the prophets did your ancestors not persecute? They put to death those who foretold the coming of the righteous one, whose betrayers and murderers you have now become. You received the law as transmitted by angels, but you did not observe it." When they heard this, they were infuriated, and they ground their teeth at him. But Stephen, filled with the Holy Spirit, looked up intently to heaven and saw the glory of God and Jesus standing at the right hand of God, and Stephen said, "Behold, I see the heavens opened and the Son of Man standing at the right hand of God." But they cried out in a loud voice, covered their ears, and rushed upon him together. They threw him out of the city, and began to stone him. The witnesses laid down their cloaks at the feet of a young man named Saul. As they were stoning Stephen, he called out, "Lord Jesus, receive my spirit." Then he fell to his knees and cried out in a loud voice, "Lord, do not hold this sin against them"; and when he said this, he fell asleep. Now Saul was consenting to his execution.

RESPONSORIAL PSALM; *Psalm 31:3cd–4, 6 and 7b and 8a, 17 and 21ab*
R. Into your hands, O Lord, I commend my spirit. or: R. Alleluia.
Be my rock of refuge, / a stronghold to give me safety. / You are my rock and my fortress; / for your name's sake / you will lead and guide me. R.
Into your hands I commend my spirit; / you will redeem me, / O LORD, O faithful God. My trust is in the LORD; / I will rejoice and be glad of your mercy. R.
Let your face shine upon your servant; / save me in your kindness. / You hide them in the shelter of your presence / from the plottings of men. R.

ALLELUIA *John 6:35ab*
R. Alleluia, alleluia. I am the bread of life, says the Lord; whoever comes to me will never hunger. R.

GOSPEL *John 6:30–35*
The crowd said to Jesus: "What sign can you do, that we may see and believe in you? What can you do? Our ancestors ate manna in the desert, as it is written: *He gave them bread*

189

from heaven to eat." So Jesus said to them, Amen, amen, I say to you, it was not Moses who gave the bread from heaven; my Father gives you the true bread from heaven. For the bread of God is that which comes down from heaven and gives life to the world." So they said to Jesus, "Sir, give us this bread always." Jesus said to them, "I am the bread of life; whoever comes to me will never hunger, and whoever believes in me will never thirst."

APRIL 29, 3RD WEEK OF EASTER – WEDNESDAY; ST. CATHERINE OF SIENA

FIRST READING   *Acts 8:1b–8*

There broke out a severe persecution of the Church in Jerusalem, and all were scattered throughout the countryside of Judea and Samaria, except the Apostles. Devout men buried Stephen and made a loud lament over him. Saul, meanwhile, was trying to destroy the Church; entering house after house and dragging out men and women, he handed them over for imprisonment.

Now those who had been scattered went about preaching the word. Thus Philip went down to the city of Samaria and proclaimed the Christ to them. With one accord, the crowds paid attention to what was said by Philip when they heard it and saw the signs he was doing. For unclean spirits, crying out in a loud voice, came out of many possessed people, and many paralyzed and crippled people were cured. There was great joy in that city.

RESPONSORIAL PSALM   *Psalm 66:1–3a, 4–5, 6–7a*

R. Let all the earth cry out to God with joy. or: R. Alleluia.

Shout joyfully to God, all the earth, / sing praise to the glory of his name; / proclaim his glorious praise. / Say to God, / "How tremendous are your deeds!" **R.**

"Let all on earth worship and sing praise to you, / sing praise to your name!" / Come and see the works of God, / his tremendous deeds among the children of Adam. **R.**

He has changed the sea into dry land; / through the river they passed on foot; / therefore let us rejoice in him. / He rules by his might forever. **R.**

ALLELUIA   *See John 6:40*

R. Alleluia, alleluia. Everyone who believes in the Son has eternal life, and I shall raise him on the last day, says the Lord. **R.**

GOSPEL   *John 6:35–40*

Jesus said to the crowds, "I am the bread of life; whoever comes to me will never hunger, and whoever believes in me will never thirst. But I told you that although you have seen me, you do not believe. Everything that the Father gives me will come to me, and I will not reject anyone who comes to me, because I came down from heaven not to do my own will but the will of the one who sent me. And this is the will of the one who sent me, that I should not lose anything of what he gave me, but that I should raise it on the last day. For this is the will of my Father, that everyone who sees the Son and believes in him may have eternal life, and I shall raise him on the last day."

APRIL 30, 3RD WEEK OF EASTER - THURSDAY; ST. PIUS V

FIRST READING *Acts 8:26–40*

The angel of the Lord spoke to Philip, "Get up and head south on the road that goes down from Jerusalem to Gaza, the desert route." So he got up and set out. Now there was an Ethiopian eunuch, a court official of the Candace, that is, the queen of the Ethiopians, in charge of her entire treasury, who had come to Jerusalem to worship, and was returning home. Seated in his chariot, he was reading the prophet Isaiah. The Spirit said to Philip, "Go and join up with that chariot." Philip ran up and heard him reading Isaiah the prophet and said, "Do you understand what you are reading?" He replied, "How can I, unless someone instructs me?" So he invited Philip to get in and sit with him. This was the Scripture passage he was reading:

Like a sheep he was led to the slaughter, and as a lamb before its shearer is silent, so he opened not his mouth. In his humiliation justice was denied him. Who will tell of his posterity? For his life is taken from the earth.

Then the eunuch said to Philip in reply, "I beg you, about whom is the prophet saying this? About himself, or about someone else?" Then Philip opened his mouth and, beginning with this Scripture passage, he proclaimed Jesus to him. As they traveled along the road they came to some water, and the eunuch said, "Look, there is water. What is to prevent my being baptized?" Then he ordered the chariot to stop, and Philip and the eunuch both went down into the water, and he baptized him. When they came out of the water, the Spirit of the Lord snatched Philip away, and the eunuch saw him no more, but continued on his way rejoicing. Philip came to Azotus, and went about proclaiming the good news to all the towns until he reached Caesarea.

RESPONSORIAL PSALM *Psalm 66:8–9, 16–17, 20*

R. Let all the earth cry out to God with joy. or: R. Alleluia.

Bless our God, you peoples, / loudly sound his praise; / He has given life to our souls, / and has not let our feet slip. **R.**

Hear now, all you who fear God, / while I declare what he has done for me. / When I appealed to him in words, / praise was on the tip of my tongue. **R.**

Blessed be God who refused me not my prayer or his kindness! **R.**

ALLELUIA *John 6:51*

R. Alleluia, alleluia. I am the living bread that came down from heaven, says the Lord; whoever eats this bread will live forever. **R.**

GOSPEL *John 6:44–51*

Jesus said to the crowds: "No one can come to me unless the Father who sent me draw him, and I will raise him on the last day. It is written in the prophets:

They shall all be taught by God.

Everyone who listens to my Father and learns from him comes to me. Not that anyone has seen the Father except the one who is from God; he has seen the Father. Amen, amen, I say to you, whoever believes has eternal life. I am the bread of life. Your ancestors ate the manna in the desert, but they died; this is the bread that comes down from heaven so that one may eat it and not die. I am the living bread that came down from heaven; whoever eats this bread will live forever; and the bread that I will give is my Flesh for the life of the world.

7 MAY

MAY 1, SAINT JOSEPH THE WORKER
WEEK DAY READING

FIRST READING   *Acts 9:1–20*

Saul, still breathing murderous threats against the disciples of the Lord, went to the high priest and asked him for letters to the synagogues in Damascus, that, if he should find any men or women who belonged to the Way, he might bring them back to Jerusalem in chains. On his journey, as he was nearing Damascus, a light from the sky suddenly flashed around him. He fell to the ground and heard a voice saying to him, "Saul, Saul, why are you persecuting me?" He said, "Who are you, sir?" The reply came, "I am Jesus, whom you are persecuting. Now get up and go into the city and you will be told what you must do." The men who were traveling with him stood speechless, for they heard the voice but could see no one. Saul got up from the ground, but when he opened his eyes he could see nothing; so they led him by the hand and brought him to Damascus. For three days he was unable to see, and he neither ate nor drank.

There was a disciple in Damascus named Ananias, and the Lord said to him in a vision, "Ananias." He answered, "Here I am, Lord." The Lord said to him, "Get up and go to the street called Straight and ask at the house of Judas for a man from Tarsus named Saul. He is there praying, and in a vision he has seen a man named Ananias come in and lay his hands on him, that he may regain his sight." But Ananias replied, "Lord, I have heard from many sources about this man, what evil things he has done to your holy ones in Jerusalem. And here he has authority from the chief priests to imprison all who call upon your name." But the Lord said to him, "Go, for this man is a chosen instrument of mine to carry my name before Gentiles, kings, and children of Israel, and I will show him what he will have to suffer for my name." So Ananias went and entered the house; laying his hands on him, he said, "Saul, my brother, the Lord has sent me, Jesus who appeared to you on the way by which you came, that you may regain your sight and be filled with the Holy Spirit." Immediately things like scales fell from his eyes and he regained his sight. He got up and was baptized, and when he had eaten, he recovered his strength.

He stayed some days with the disciples in Damascus, and he began at once to proclaim Jesus in the synagogues, that he is the Son of God.

RESPONSORIAL PSALM   *Psalm 117:1bc, 2*
R. Go out to all the world and tell the Good News. or: R. Alleluia.
Praise the LORD, all you nations; / glorify him, all you peoples! **R.**

For steadfast is his kindness toward us, **/** and the fidelity of the LORD endures forever. **R.**

ALLELUIA   *John 6:56*

R. Alleluia, alleluia. Whoever eats my Flesh and drinks my Blood, remains in me and I in him, says the Lord. **R.**

GOSPEL   *John 6:52–59*

The Jews quarreled among themselves, saying, "How can this man give us his Flesh to eat?" Jesus said to them, "Amen, amen, I say to you, unless you eat the Flesh of the Son of Man and drink his Blood, you do not have life within you. Whoever eats my Flesh and drinks my Blood has eternal life, and I will raise him on the last day. For my Flesh is true food, and my Blood is true drink. Whoever eats my Flesh and drinks my Blood remains in me and I in him. Just as the living Father sent me and I have life because of the Father, so also the one who feeds on me will have life because of me. This is the bread that came down from heaven. Unlike your ancestors who ate and still died, whoever eats this bread will live forever." These things he said while teaching in the synagogue in Capernaum.

OR

READINGS FOR THE MEMORIAL OF ST JOSEPH THE WORKER

FIRST READING   *Genesis 1:26B2:3*

God said: "Let us make man in our image, after our likeness. Let them have dominion over the fish of the sea, the birds of the air, and the cattle, and over all the wild animals and all the creatures that crawl on the ground."

God created man in his image; in the divine image he created him; male and female he created them.

God blessed them, saying: "Be fertile and multiply; fill the earth and subdue it. Have dominion over the fish of the sea, the birds of the air, and all the living things that move on the earth." God also said: "See, I give you every seed–bearing plant all over the earth and every tree that has seed–bearing fruit on it to be your food; and to all the animals of the land, all the birds of the air, and all the living creatures that crawl on the ground, I give all the green plants for food." And so it happened. God looked at everything he had made, and he found it very good. Evening came, and morning followed—the sixth day.

Thus the heavens and the earth and all their array were completed. Since on the seventh day God was finished with the work he had been doing, God rested on the seventh day from all the work he had undertaken. So God blessed the seventh day and made it holy, because on it he rested from all the work he had done in creation.

ALTERNATIVE FIRST READING: *Colossians 3:14–15, 17, 23–24*

Brothers and sisters: Over all these things put on love, that is, the bond of perfection. And let the peace of Christ control your hearts, the peace into which you were also called in one Body. And be thankful. And whatever you do, in word or in deed, do everything in the name of the Lord Jesus, giving thanks to God the Father through him. Whatever you do, do from the heart, as for the Lord and not for men, knowing that you will receive from the Lord the due payment of the inheritance; be slaves of the Lord Christ.

RESPONSORIAL PSALM *Psalm 90:2, 3–4, 12–13, 14 and 16*

R. Lord, give success to the work of our hands. or: R. Alleluia.

Before the mountains were begotten **/** and the earth and the world were brought forth, **/** from everlasting to everlasting you are God. **R.**

You turn men back to dust, saying, **/** "Return, O children of men." **/** For a thousand years in your sight are as yesterday, **/** now that it is past, **/** or as a watch of the night. **R.**

Teach us to number our days aright, **/** that we may gain wisdom of heart. **/** Return, O LORD! How long? **/** Have pity on your servants! **R.**

Fill us at daybreak with your kindness, **/** that we may shout for joy and gladness all our days. **/** Let your work be seen by your servants **/** and your glory by their children. **R.**

ALLELUIA *Psalm 68:20*

R. Alleluia, alleluia. Blessed be the Lord day by day, God, our salvation, who bears our burdens. **R.**

GOSPEL *Matthew 13:54–58*

Jesus came to his native place and taught the people in their synagogue. They were astonished and said, "Where did this man get such wisdom and mighty deeds? Is he not the carpenter's son? Is not his mother named Mary and his brothers James, Joseph, Simon, and Judas? Are not his sisters all with us? Where did this man get all this?" And they took offense at him. But Jesus said to them, "A prophet is not without honor except in his native place and in his own house." And he did not work many mighty deeds there because of their lack of faith.

MAY 2, 3RD WEEK OF EASTER – SATURDAY; ST. ATHANASIUS

FIRST READING *Acts 9:31–42*

The Church throughout all Judea, Galilee, and Samaria was at peace. She was being built up and walked in the fear of the Lord, and with the consolation of the Holy Spirit she grew in numbers.

As Peter was passing through every region, he went down to the holy ones living in Lydda. There he found a man named Aeneas, who had been confined to bed for eight years, for he was paralyzed. Peter said to him, "Aeneas, Jesus Christ heals you. Get up and make your bed." He got up at once. And all the inhabitants of Lydda and Sharon saw him, and they turned to the Lord.

Now in Joppa there was a disciple named Tabitha (which translated is Dorcas). She was completely occupied with good deeds and almsgiving. Now during those days she fell sick and died, so after washing her, they laid her out in a room upstairs. Since Lydda was near Joppa, the disciples, hearing that Peter was there, sent two men to him with the request, "Please come to us without delay." So Peter got up and went with them. When he arrived, they took him to the room upstairs where all the widows came to him weeping and showing him the tunics and cloaks that Dorcas had made while she was with them. Peter sent them all out and knelt down and prayed. Then he turned to her body and said, "Tabitha, rise up." She opened her eyes, saw Peter, and sat up. He gave her his hand and raised her up, and when he had called the holy ones and the widows, he presented her alive. This became known all over Joppa, and many came to believe in the Lord.

RESPONSORIAL PSALM *Psalm 116:12–13, 14–15, 16–17*
R. How shall I make a return to the Lord for all the good he has done for me? or: R. Alleluia.
How shall I make a return to the LORD / for all the good he has done for me? / The cup of salvation I will take up, / and I will call upon the name of the LORD. **R.**
My vows to the LORD I will pay / in the presence of all his people. / Precious in the eyes of the LORD / is the death of his faithful ones. **R.**
O LORD, I am your servant; / I am your servant, the son of your handmaid; / you have loosed my bonds. / To you will I offer sacrifice of thanksgiving, / and I will call upon the name of the LORD. **R.**

ALLELUIA *See John 6:63c, 68c*
R. Alleluia, alleluia. Your words, Lord, are Spirit and life; you have the words of everlasting life. **R.**

GOSPEL *John 6:60–69*
Many of the disciples of Jesus who were listening said, "This saying is hard; who can accept it?" Since Jesus knew that his disciples were murmuring about this, he said to them, "Does this shock you? What if you were to see the Son of Man ascending to where he was before? It is the Spirit that gives life, while the flesh is of no avail. The words I have spoken to you are Spirit and life. But there are some of you who do not believe." Jesus knew from the beginning the ones who would not believe and the one who would betray him. And he said, "For this reason I have told you that no one can come to me unless it is granted him by my Father."

As a result of this, many of his disciples returned to their former way of life and no longer walked with him. Jesus then said to the Twelve, "Do you also want to leave?" Simon Peter answered him, "Master, to whom shall we go? You have the words of eternal life. We have come to believe and are convinced that you are the Holy One of God."

MAY 3, 4TH SUNDAY OF EASTER; ST. PHILIP & ST. JAMES
FIRST READING *Acts 2:14a, 36—41*
Then Peter stood up with the Eleven, raised his voice, and proclaimed: "Let the whole house of Israel know for certain that God has made both Lord and Christ, this Jesus whom you crucified."

Now when they heard this, they were cut to the heart, and they asked Peter and the other apostles, "What are we to do, my brothers?" Peter said to them, "Repent and be baptized, every one of you, in the name of Jesus Christ for the forgiveness of your sins; and you will receive the gift of the Holy Spirit. For the promise is made to you and to your children and to all those far off, whomever the Lord our God will call." He testified with many other arguments, and was exhorting them, "Save yourselves from this corrupt generation." Those who accepted his message were baptized, and about three thousand persons were added that day.

RESPONSORIAL PSALM *Psalm 23:1—3a, 3b—4, 5, 6 (1)*
R. The Lord is my shepherd; there is nothing I shall want. or R. Alleluia.
The LORD is my shepherd; **/** I shall not want. **/** In verdant pastures he gives me repose; **/** beside restful waters he leads me; **/** he refreshes my soul. **R.**
He guides me in right paths for his name's sake. **/** Even though I walk in the dark valley I fear no evil; **/** for you are at my side, **/** with your rod and your staff that give me courage. **R.**
You spread the table before me **/** in the sight of my foes; **/** you anoint my head with oil; **/** my cup overflows. **R.**
Only goodness and kindness follow me all the days of my life; **/** and I shall dwell in the house of the LORD **/** for years to come. **R.**

SECOND READING *1 Peter 2:20b—25*
Beloved: If you are patient when you suffer for doing what is good, this is a grace before God. For to this you have been called, because Christ also suffered for you, leaving you an example that you should follow in his footsteps. *He committed no sin, and no deceit was found in his mouth.*

When he was insulted, he returned no insult; when he suffered, he did not threaten; instead, he handed himself over to the one who judges justly. He himself bore our sins in his body upon the cross, so that, free from sin, we might live for righteousness. By his wounds you have been healed. For you had gone astray like sheep, but you have now returned to the shepherd and guardian of your souls.

ALLELUIA *John 10:14*
R. Alleluia, alleluia. I am the good shepherd, says the Lord; I know my sheep, and mine know me. **R.**

GOSPEL *John 10:1—10*
Jesus said: "Amen, amen, I say to you, whoever does not enter a sheepfold through the gate but climbs over elsewhere is a thief and a robber. But whoever enters through the gate is the shepherd of the sheep. The gatekeeper opens it for him, and the sheep hear his voice, as the shepherd calls his own sheep by name and leads them out. When he has driven out all his own, he walks ahead of them, and the sheep follow him, because they recognize his voice. But they will not follow a stranger; they will run away from him, because they do not recognize the voice of strangers." Although Jesus used this figure of speech, the Pharisees did not realize what he was trying to tell them.

So Jesus said again, "Amen, amen, I say to you, I am the gate for the sheep. All who came before me are thieves and robbers, but the sheep did not listen to them. I am the gate. Whoever enters through me will be saved, and will come in and go out and find pasture. A thief comes only to steal and slaughter and destroy; I came so that they might have life and have it more abundantly."

MAY 4, 4TH WEEK OF EASTER – MONDAY; BLESSED CEFERINO GIMÉNEZ MALLA
FIRST READING *Acts 11:1–18*

The Apostles and the brothers who were in Judea heard that the Gentiles too had accepted the word of God. So when Peter went up to Jerusalem the circumcised believers confronted him, saying, 'You entered the house of uncircumcised people and ate with them." Peter began and explained it to them step by step, saying, "I was at prayer in the city of Joppa when in a trance I had a vision, something resembling a large sheet coming down, lowered from the sky by its four corners, and it came to me. Looking intently into it, I observed and saw the four–legged animals of the earth, the wild beasts, the reptiles, and the birds of the sky. I also heard a voice say to me, 'Get up, Peter. Slaughter and eat.' But I said, 'Certainly not, sir, because nothing profane or unclean has ever entered my mouth.' But a second time a voice from heaven answered, 'What God has made clean, you are not to call profane.' This happened three times, and then everything was drawn up again into the sky. Just then three men appeared at the house where we were, who had been sent to me from Caesarea. The Spirit told me to accompany them without discriminating. These six brothers also went with me, and we entered the man's house. He related to us how he had seen the angel standing in his house, saying, 'Send someone to Joppa and summon Simon, who is called Peter, who will speak words to you by which you and all your household will be saved.' As I began to speak, the Holy Spirit fell upon them as it had upon us at the beginning, and I remembered the word of the Lord, how he had said, 'John baptized with water but you will be baptized with the Holy Spirit.' If then God gave them the same gift he gave to us when we came to believe in the Lord Jesus Christ, who was I to be able to hinder God?" When they heard this, they stopped objecting and glorified God, saying, "God has then granted life–giving repentance to the Gentiles too."

RESPONSORIAL PSALM *Psalm 42:2–3; 43:3, 4*
R. Athirst is my soul for the living God. or: R. Alleluia.
As the hind longs for the running waters, **/** so my soul longs for you, O God. **/**
Athirst is my soul for God, **/** the living God. **/** When shall I go and behold **/**
the face of God? **R.**
Send forth your light and your fidelity; **/** they shall lead me on **/**
and bring me to your holy mountain, **/** to your dwelling–place. **R.**
Then will I go in to the altar of God, **/** the God of my gladness and joy; **/**
Then will I give you thanks upon the harp, **/** O God, my God! **R.**

ALLELUIA *John 10:14*
R. Alleluia, alleluia. I am the good shepherd, says the Lord; I know my sheep, and mine know me. **R.**

GOSPEL   *John 10:11–18*

Jesus said: "I am the good shepherd. A good shepherd lays down his life for the sheep. A hired man, who is not a shepherd and whose sheep are not his own, sees a wolf coming and leaves the sheep and runs away, and the wolf catches and scatters them. This is because he works for pay and has no concern for the sheep. I am the good shepherd, and I know mine and mine know me, just as the Father knows me and I know the Father; and I will lay down my life for the sheep. I have other sheep that do not belong to this fold. These also I must lead, and they will hear my voice, and there will be one flock, one shepherd. This is why the Father loves me, because I lay down my life in order to take it up again. No one takes it from me, but I lay it down on my own. I have power to lay it down, and power to take it up again. This command I have received from my Father."

MAY 5, 4TH WEEK OF EASTER – TUESDAY; ST. MARY MAZZARELLO

FIRST READING   *Acts 11:19–26*

Those who had been scattered by the persecution that arose because of Stephen went as far as Phoenicia, Cyprus, and Antioch, preaching the word to no one but Jews. There were some Cypriots and Cyrenians among them, however, who came to Antioch and began to speak to the Greeks as well, proclaiming the Lord Jesus. The hand of the Lord was with them and a great number who believed turned to the Lord. The news about them reached the ears of the Church in Jerusalem, and they sent Barnabas to go to Antioch. When he arrived and saw the grace of God, he rejoiced and encouraged them all to remain faithful to the Lord in firmness of heart, for he was a good man, filled with the Holy Spirit and faith. And a large number of people was added to the Lord. Then he went to Tarsus to look for Saul, and when he had found him he brought him to Antioch. For a whole year they met with the Church and taught a large number of people, and it was in Antioch that the disciples were first called Christians.

RESPONSORIAL PSALM   *Psalm 87:1b–3, 4–5, 6–7*

R. All you nations, praise the Lord. or: R. Alleluia.

His foundation upon the holy mountains / the LORD loves: / The gates of Zion, more than any dwelling of Jacob. / Glorious things are said of you, / O city of God! **R.**

I tell of Egypt and Babylon / among those who know the LORD; / Of Philistia, Tyre, Ethiopia: / "This man was born there." / And of Zion they shall say: / "One and all were born in her; / And he who has established her / is the Most High LORD." **R.**

They shall note, when the peoples are enrolled: / "This man was born there." / And all shall sing, in their festive dance: / "My home is within you." **R.**

ALLELUIA   *John 10:27*

R. Alleluia, alleluia. My sheep hear my voice, says the Lord; I know them, and they follow me. **R.**

GOSPEL   *John 10:22–30*

The feast of the Dedication was taking place in Jerusalem. It was winter. And Jesus walked about in the temple area on the Portico of Solomon. So the Jews gathered around him and said to him, "How long are you going to keep us in suspense? If you are the Christ, tell us plainly." Jesus answered them, "I told you and you do not believe. The works I do in my Father's name testify to me. But you do not believe, because you are not among my sheep. My sheep hear my voice; I know them, and they follow me. I give them eternal life, and they shall never perish. No one can take them out of my hand. My Father, who has given them to me, is greater than all, and no one can take them out of the Father's hand. The Father and I are one."

MAY 6, 4TH WEEK OF EASTER - WEDNESDAY;
BLESSED FRANCOIS DE MONTMORENCY LAVAL

FIRST READING   *Acts 12:24 – 13:5a*

The word of God continued to spread and grow.

After Barnabas and Saul completed their relief mission, they returned to Jerusalem, taking with them John, who is called Mark.

Now there were in the Church at Antioch prophets and teachers: Barnabas, Symeon who was called Niger, Lucius of Cyrene, Manaen who was a close friend of Herod the tetrarch, and Saul. While they were worshiping the Lord and fasting, the Holy Spirit said, "Set apart for me Barnabas and Saul for the work to which I have called them." Then, completing their fasting and prayer, they laid hands on them and sent them off.

So they, sent forth by the Holy Spirit, went down to Seleucia and from there sailed to Cyprus. When they arrived in Salamis, they proclaimed the word of God in the Jewish synagogues.

RESPONSORIAL PSALM   *Psalm 67:2–3, 5, 6 and 8*

R. O God, let all the nations praise you! or: R. Alleluia.

May God have pity on us and bless us; / may he let his face shine upon us. / So may your way be known upon earth; / among all nations, your salvation. **R.**

May the nations be glad and exult / because you rule the peoples in equity; / the nations on the earth you guide. **R.**

May the peoples praise you, O God; / may all the peoples praise you! / May God bless us, / and may all the ends of the earth fear him! **R.**

ALLELUIA   *John 8:12*

R. Alleluia, alleluia. I am the light of the world, says the Lord; whoever follows me will have the light of life. **R.**

GOSPEL   *John 12:44–50*

Jesus cried out and said, "Whoever believes in me believes not only in me but also in the one who sent me, and whoever sees me sees the one who sent me. I came into the world as light, so that everyone who believes in me might not remain in darkness. And if anyone hears my words and does not observe them, I do not condemn him, for I did not come to condemn the world but to save the world. Whoever rejects me and does not accept my words has something to judge him: the word that I spoke, it will condemn him on the last day, because I did not speak on my own, but the Father who sent me commanded me what to say and speak. And I know that his commandment is eternal life. So what I say, I say as the Father told me."

MAY 7, 4TH WEEK OF EASTER – THURSDAY; BLESSED ROSE VENERINI

FIRST READING   *Acts 13:13–25*

From Paphos, Paul and his companions set sail and arrived at Perga in Pamphylia. But John left them and returned to Jerusalem. They continued on from Perga and reached Antioch in Pisidia. On the sabbath they entered into the synagogue and took their seats. After the reading of the law and the prophets, the synagogue officials sent word to them, "My brothers, if one of you has a word of exhortation for the people, please speak."

So Paul got up, motioned with his hand, and said, "Fellow children of Israel and you others who are God–fearing, listen. The God of this people Israel chose our ancestors and exalted the people during their sojourn in the land of Egypt. With uplifted arm he led them out, and for about forty years he put up with them in the desert. When he had destroyed seven nations in the land of Canaan, he gave them their land as an inheritance at the end of about four hundred and fifty years. After these things he provided judges up to Samuel the prophet. Then they asked for a king. God gave them Saul, son of Kish, a man from the tribe of Benjamin, for forty years. Then he removed him and raised up David as their king; of him he testified, I have found David, son of Jesse, a man after my own heart; he will carry out my every wish. From this man's descendants God, according to his promise, has brought to Israel a savior, Jesus. John heralded his coming by proclaiming a baptism of repentance to all the people of Israel; and as John was completing his course, he would say, 'What do you suppose that I am? I am not he. Behold, one is coming after me; I am not worthy to unfasten the sandals of his feet.'"

RESPONSORIAL PSALM   *Psalm 89:2–3, 21–22, 25 and 27*
R. For ever I will sing the goodness of the Lord. or: R. Alleluia.
The favors of the LORD I will sing forever; / through all generations my mouth shall proclaim your faithfulness. / For you have said, / "My kindness is established forever"; / in heaven you have confirmed your faithfulness. **R.**
"I have found David, my servant; / with my holy oil I have anointed him, / That my hand may be always with him, / and that my arm may make him strong." **R.**
"My faithfulness and my mercy shall be with him, / and through my name shall his horn be exalted. / He shall say of me, / 'You are my father, my God, / the Rock, my savior.'" **R.**
ALLELUIA   *See Revelation 1:5ab*
R. Alleluia, alleluia. Jesus Christ, you are the faithful witness, the firstborn of the dead, you have loved us and freed us from our sins by your Blood. **R.**

GOSPEL
John 13:16–20

When Jesus had washed the disciples' feet, he said to them: "Amen, amen, I say to you, no slave is greater than his master nor any messenger greater than the one who sent him. If you understand this, blessed are you if you do it. I am not speaking of all of you. I know those whom I have chosen. But so that the Scripture might be fulfilled, The one who ate my food has raised his heel against me. From now on I am telling you before it happens, so that when it happens you may believe that I AM. Amen, amen, I say to you, whoever receives the one I send receives me, and whoever receives me receives the one who sent me."

MAY 8, 4TH WEEK OF EASTER – FRIDAY; BLESSED CATHERINE OF ST. AUGUSTINE
FIRST READING
Acts 13:26–33

When Paul came to Antioch in Pisidia, he said in the synagogue: "My brothers, children of the family of Abraham, and those others among you who are God–fearing, to us this word of salvation has been sent. The inhabitants of Jerusalem and their leaders failed to recognize him, and by condemning him they fulfilled the oracles of the prophets that are read sabbath after sabbath. For even though they found no grounds for a death sentence, they asked Pilate to have him put to death, and when they had accomplished all that was written about him, they took him down from the tree and placed him in a tomb. But God raised him from the dead, and for many days he appeared to those who had come up with him from Galilee to Jerusalem. These are now his witnesses before the people. We ourselves are proclaiming this good news to you that what God promised our fathers he has brought to fulfillment for us, their children, by raising up Jesus, as it is written in the second psalm, *You are my Son; this day I have begotten you.*"

RESPONSORIAL PSALM
Psalm 2:6–7, 8–9, 10–11ab

R. You are my Son; this day I have begotten you. or: R. Alleluia.
"I myself have set up my king on Zion, **/** my holy mountain. **/** " I will proclaim the decree of the LORD: **/** The LORD said to me, "You are my Son; **/** this day I have begotten you." **R.**
"Ask of me and I will give you the nations **/** for an inheritance **/** and the ends of the earth for your possession. **/** You shall rule them with an iron rod; **/** you shall shatter them like an earthen dish." **R.**
And now, O kings, give heed; **/** take warning, you rulers of the earth. **/** Serve the LORD with fear, and rejoice before him; **/** with trembling rejoice. **R.**

ALLELUIA
John 14:6

R. Alleluia, alleluia. I am the way and the truth and the life, says the Lord; no one comes to the Father except through me. **R.**

GOSPEL
John 14:1–6

Jesus said to his disciples: "Do not let your hearts be troubled. You have faith in God; have faith also in me. In my Father's house there are many dwelling places. If there were not, would I have told you that I am going to prepare a place for you? And if I go and prepare a place for you, I will come back again and take you to myself, so that where I am you also may be. Where I am going you know the way." Thomas said to him, "Master, we do not know where you are going; how can we know the way?" Jesus said to him, "I am the way and the truth and the life. No one comes to the Father except through me."

MAY 9, 4TH WEEK OF EASTER – SATURDAY; BLESSED NICHOLAS ALBERGATI
FIRST READING
Acts 13:44–52

On the following Sabbath almost the whole city gathered to hear the word of the Lord. When the Jews saw the crowds, they were filled with jealousy and with violent abuse contradicted what Paul said. Both Paul and Barnabas spoke out boldly and said, "It was necessary that the word of God be spoken to you first, but since you reject it and condemn yourselves as unworthy of eternal life, we now turn to the Gentiles. For so the Lord has commanded us, I have made you a light to the Gentiles, that you may be an instrument of salvation to the ends of the earth."

The Gentiles were delighted when they heard this and glorified the word of the Lord. All who were destined for eternal life came to believe, and the word of the Lord continued to spread through the whole region. The Jews, however, incited the women of prominence who were worshipers and the leading men of the city, stirred up a persecution against Paul and Barnabas, and expelled them from their territory. So they shook the dust from their feet in protest against them and went to Iconium. The disciples were filled with joy and the Holy Spirit.

RESPONSORIAL PSALM
Psalm 98:1, 2–3ab, 3cd–4

R. All the ends of the earth have seen the saving power of God. or: R. Alleluia.

Sing to the LORD a new song, / for he has done wondrous deeds; / His right hand has won victory for him, / his holy arm. R.

The LORD has made his salvation known: / in the sight of the nations he has revealed his justice. / He has remembered his kindness and his faithfulness / toward the house of Israel. R.

All the ends of the earth have seen / the salvation by our God. / Sing joyfully to the LORD, / all you lands; / break into song; sing praise. R.

ALLELUIA
John 8:31b–32

R. Alleluia, alleluia. If you remain in my word, you will truly be my disciples, and you will know the truth, says the Lord. R.

GOSPEL
John 14:7–14

Jesus said to his disciples: "If you know me, then you will also know my Father. From now on you do know him and have seen him." Philip said to Jesus, "Master, show us the Father, and that will be enough for us." Jesus said to him, "Have I been with you for so long a time and you still do not know me, Philip? Whoever has seen me has seen the Father. How can you say, 'Show us the Father'? Do you not believe that I am in the Father and the Father is in me? The words that I speak to you I do not speak on my own. The Father who dwells in me is doing his works. Believe me that I am in the Father and the Father is in me, or else, believe because of the works themselves. Amen, amen, I say to you, whoever believes in me will do the works that I do, and will do greater ones than these, because I am going to the Father. And whatever you ask in my name, I will do, so that the Father may be glorified in the Son. If you ask anything of me in my name, I will do it."

MAY 10, 5TH SUNDAY OF EASTER; ST. DAMIEN JOSEPH DE VEUSTER OF MOLOKAI
FIRST READING   *Acts 6:1—7*

As the number of disciples continued to grow, the Hellenists complained against the Hebrews because their widows were being neglected in the daily distribution. So the Twelve called together the community of the disciples and said, "It is not right for us to neglect the word of God to serve at table. Brothers, select from among you seven reputable men, filled with the Spirit and wisdom, whom we shall appoint to this task, whereas we shall devote ourselves to prayer and to the ministry of the word." The proposal was acceptable to the whole community, so they chose Stephen, a man filled with faith and the Holy Spirit, also Philip, Prochorus, Nicanor, Timon, Parmenas, and Nicholas of Antioch, a convert to Judaism. They presented these men to the apostles who prayed and laid hands on them. The word of God continued to spread, and the number of the disciples in Jerusalem increased greatly; even a large group of priests were becoming obedient to the faith.

RESPONSORIAL PSALM   *Psalm 33:1—2, 4—5, 18—19 (22)*
R. Lord, let your mercy be on us, as we place our trust in you. or R. Alleluia.
Exult, you just, in the LORD; / praise from the upright is fitting. / Give thanks to the LORD on the harp; / with the ten-stringed lyre chant his praises. **R.**
Upright is the word of the LORD, / and all his works are trustworthy. / He loves justice and right; / of the kindness of the LORD / the earth is full. **R.**
See, the eyes of the LORD are upon those who fear him, / upon those who hope for his kindness, / to deliver them from death / and preserve them in spite of famine. **R.**

SECOND READING   *1 Peter 2:4—9*
Beloved: Come to him, a living stone, rejected by human beings but chosen and precious in the sight of God, and, like living stones, let yourselves be built into a spiritual house to be a holy priesthood to offer spiritual sacrifices acceptable to God through Jesus Christ. For it says in Scripture: *Behold, I am laying a stone in Zion, a cornerstone, chosen and precious, and whoever believes in it shall not be put to shame.* Therefore, its value is for you who have faith, but for those without faith: *The stone that the builders rejected has become the cornerstone, a stone that will make people stumble, and a rock that will make them fall.* They stumble by disobeying the word, as is their destiny.

You are "a chosen race, a royal priesthood, a holy nation, a people of his own, so that you may announce the praises" of him who called you out of darkness into his wonderful light.

ALLELUIA   *John 14:6*

R. Alleluia, alleluia. I am the way, the truth and the life, says the Lord; no one comes to the Father, except through me. **R.**

GOSPEL   *John 14:1—12*

Jesus said to his disciples: "Do not let your hearts be troubled. You have faith in God; have faith also in me. In my Father's house there are many dwelling places. If there were not, would I have told you that I am going to prepare a place for you? And if I go and prepare a place for you, I will come back again and take you to myself, so that where I am you also may be. Where I am going you know the way." Thomas said to him, "Master, we do not know where you are going; how can we know the way?" Jesus said to him, "I am the way and the truth and the life. No one comes to the Father except through me. If you know me, then you will also know my Father. From now on you do know him and have seen him." Philip said to him, "Master, show us the Father, and that will be enough for us." Jesus said to him, "Have I been with you for so long a time and you still do not know me, Philip? Whoever has seen me has seen the Father. How can you say, 'Show us the Father'? Do you not believe that I am in the Father and the Father is in me? The words that I speak to you I do not speak on my own. The Father who dwells in me is doing his works. Believe me that I am in the Father and the Father is in me, or else, believe because of the works themselves. Amen, amen, I say to you, whoever believes in me will do the works that I do, and will do greater ones than these, because I am going to the Father."

MAY 11, 5TH WEEK OF EASTER - MONDAY; ST. IGNATIUS OF LACONI

FIRST READING   *Acts 14:5–18*

There was an attempt in Iconium by both the Gentiles and the Jews, together with their leaders, to attack and stone Paul and Barnabas. They realized it, and fled to the Lycaonian cities of Lystra and Derbe and to the surrounding countryside, where they continued to proclaim the Good News.

At Lystra there was a crippled man, lame from birth, who had never walked. He listened to Paul speaking, who looked intently at him, saw that he had the faith to be healed, and called out in a loud voice, "Stand up straight on your feet." He jumped up and began to walk about. When the crowds saw what Paul had done, they cried out in Lycaonian, "The gods have come down to us in human form." They called Barnabas "Zeus" and Paul "Hermes," because he was the chief speaker. And the priest of Zeus, whose temple was at the entrance to the city, brought oxen and garlands to the gates, for he together with the people intended to offer sacrifice.

The Apostles Barnabas and Paul tore their garments when they heard this and rushed out into the crowd, shouting, "Men, why are you doing this? We are of the same nature as you, human beings. We proclaim to you good news that you should turn from these idols to the living God, who made heaven and earth and sea and all that is in them. In past generations he allowed all Gentiles to go their own ways; yet, in bestowing his goodness, he did not leave himself without witness, for he gave you rains from heaven and fruitful seasons, and filled you with nourishment and gladness for your hearts." Even with these words, they scarcely restrained the crowds from offering sacrifice to them.

RESPONSORIAL PSALM   *Psalm 115:1–2, 3–4, 15–16*
R. Not to us, O Lord, but to your name give the glory. or: R. Alleluia.
Not to us, O LORD, not to us **/** but to your name give glory **/** because of your mercy, **/** because of your truth. **/** Why should the pagans say, **/** "Where is their God?" **R.**
Our God is in heaven; **/** whatever he wills, he does. **/** Their idols are silver and gold, **/** the handiwork of men. **R.**
May you be blessed by the LORD, **/** who made heaven and earth. **/** Heaven is the heaven of the LORD, **/** but the earth he has given to the children of men. **R.**

ALLELUIA   *John 14:26*
R. Alleluia, alleluia. The Holy Spirit will teach you everything and remind you of all I told you. **R.**

GOSPEL   *John 14:21–26*
Jesus said to his disciples: "Whoever has my commandments and observes them is the one who loves me. Whoever loves me will be loved by my Father, and I will love him and reveal myself to him." Judas, not the Iscariot, said to him, "Master, then what happened that you will reveal yourself to us and not to the world?" Jesus answered and said to him, "Whoever loves me will keep my word, and my Father will love him, and we will come to him and make our dwelling with him. Whoever does not love me does not keep my words; yet the word you hear is not mine but that of the Father who sent me.

"I have told you this while I am with you. The Advocate, the Holy Spirit whom the Father will send in my name he will teach you everything and remind you of all that I told you."

MAY 12, 5TH WEEK OF EASTER - TUESDAY; ST. PANCRAS

FIRST READING   *Acts 14:19–28*
In those days, some Jews from Antioch and Iconium arrived and won over the crowds. They stoned Paul and dragged him out of the city, supposing that he was dead. But when the disciples gathered around him, he got up and entered the city. On the following day he left with Barnabas for Derbe.

After they had proclaimed the good news to that city and made a considerable number of disciples, they returned to Lystra and to Iconium and to Antioch. They strengthened the spirits of the disciples and exhorted them to persevere in the faith, saying, "It is necessary for us to undergo many hardships to enter the Kingdom of God." They appointed presbyters for them in each Church and, with prayer and fasting, commended them to the Lord in whom they had put their faith. Then they traveled through Pisidia and reached Pamphylia. After proclaiming the word at Perga they went down to Attalia. From there they sailed to Antioch, where they had been commended to the grace of God for the work they had now accomplished. And when they arrived, they called the

Church together and reported what God had done with them and how he had opened the door of faith to the Gentiles. Then they spent no little time with the disciples.

RESPONSORIAL PSALM   *Psalm 145:10–11, 12–13ab, 21*
R. (see 12) Your friends make known, O Lord, the glorious splendor of your kingdom. or:
R. Alleluia.
Let all your works give you thanks, O LORD, / and let your faithful ones bless you. / Let them discourse of the glory of your kingdom / and speak of your might. **R.**
Making known to men your might / and the glorious splendor of your kingdom. / Your kingdom is a kingdom for all ages, / and your dominion endures through all generations. **R.**
May my mouth speak the praise of the LORD, / and may all flesh bless his holy name forever and ever. **R.**

ALLELUIA   *See Luke 24:46, 26*
R. Alleluia, alleluia. Christ had to suffer and to rise from the dead, and so enter into his glory. **R.**

GOSPEL   *John 14:27–31a*
Jesus said to his disciples: "Peace I leave with you; my peace I give to you. Not as the world gives do I give it to you. Do not let your hearts be troubled or afraid. You heard me tell you, 'I am going away and I will come back to you.' If you loved me, you would rejoice that I am going to the Father; for the Father is greater than I. And now I have told you this before it happens, so that when it happens you may believe. I will no longer speak much with you, for the ruler of the world is coming. He has no power over me, but the world must know that I love the Father and that I do just as the Father has commanded me."

MAY 13, 5TH WEEK OF EASTER – WEDNESDAY; OUR LADY OF FATIMA
FIRST READING   *Acts 15:1–6*
Some who had come down from Judea were instructing the brothers, "Unless you are circumcised according to the Mosaic practice, you cannot be saved." Because there arose no little dissension and debate by Paul and Barnabas with them, it was decided that Paul, Barnabas, and some of the others should go up to Jerusalem to the Apostles and presbyters about this question. They were sent on their journey by the Church, and passed through Phoenicia and Samaria telling of the conversion of the Gentiles, and brought great joy to all the brethren. When they arrived in Jerusalem, they were welcomed by the Church, as well as by the Apostles and the presbyters, and they reported what God had done with them. But some from the party of the Pharisees who had become believers stood up and said, "It is necessary to circumcise them and direct them to observe the Mosaic law."

The Apostles and the presbyters met together to see about this matter.

RESPONSORIAL PSALM   *Psalm 122:1–2, 3–4ab, 4cd–5*
R. Let us go rejoicing to the house of the Lord. or: R. Alleluia.

I rejoiced because they said to me, **/** "We will go up to the house of the LORD." **/** And now we have set foot within your gates, **/** O Jerusalem. **R.**

Jerusalem, built as a city with compact unity. **/** To it the tribes go up, **/** the tribes of the LORD. **R.**

According to the decree for Israel, **/** to give thanks to the name of the LORD. **/** In it are set up judgment seats, **/** seats for the house of David. **R.**

ALLELUIA   *John 15:4a, 5b*

R. Alleluia, alleluia. Remain in me, as I remain in you, says the Lord; whoever remains in me will bear much fruit. **R.**

GOSPEL   *John 15:1–8*

Jesus said to his disciples: "I am the true vine, and my Father is the vine grower. He takes away every branch in me that does not bear fruit, and everyone that does he prunes so that it bears more fruit. You are already pruned because of the word that I spoke to you. Remain in me, as I remain in you. Just as a branch cannot bear fruit on its own unless it remains on the vine, so neither can you unless you remain in me. I am the vine, you are the branches. Whoever remains in me and I in him will bear much fruit, because without me you can do nothing. Anyone who does not remain in me will be thrown out like a branch and wither; people will gather them and throw them into a fire and they will be burned. If you remain in me and my words remain in you, ask for whatever you want and it will be done for you. By this is my Father glorified, that you bear much fruit and become my disciples."

MAY 14, SAINT MATTHIAS, APOSTLE – FEAST

FIRST READING   *Acts 1:15–17, 20–26*

Peter stood up in the midst of the brothers and sisters (there was a group of about one hundred and twenty persons in the one place). He said, "My brothers and sisters, the Scripture had to be fulfilled which the Holy Spirit spoke beforehand through the mouth of David, concerning Judas, who was the guide for those who arrested Jesus. Judas was numbered among us and was allotted a share in this ministry. For it is written in the Book of Psalms:

Let his encampment become desolate, and may no one dwell in it. and: *May another take his office.*

Therefore, it is necessary that one of the men who accompanied us the whole time the Lord Jesus came and went among us, beginning from the baptism of John until the day on which he was taken up from us, become with us a witness to his resurrection." So they proposed two, Joseph called Barsabbas, who was also known as Justus, and Matthias. Then they prayed, "You, Lord, who know the hearts of all, show which one of these two you have chosen to take the place in this apostolic ministry from which Judas turned away to go to his own place." Then they gave lots to them, and the lot fell upon Matthias, and he was counted with the Eleven Apostles.

RESPONSORIAL PSALM   *Psalm 113:1–2, 3–4, 5–6, 7–8*

R. The Lord will give him a seat with the leaders of his people. or: R. Alleluia.

Praise, you servants of the LORD, / praise the name of the LORD. / Blessed be the name of the LORD / both now and forever. **R.**

From the rising to the setting of the sun / is the name of the LORD to be praised.
High above all nations is the LORD; / above the heavens is his glory. **R.**

Who is like the LORD, our God, / who is enthroned on high / and looks upon the heavens and the earth below? **R.**

He raises up the lowly from the dust; / from the dunghill he lifts up the poor / To seat them with princes, / with the princes of his own people. **R.**

ALLELUIA   *See John 15:16*

R. Alleluia, alleluia. I chose you from the world, to go and bear fruit that will last, says the Lord. **R.**

GOSPEL   *John 15:9–17*

Jesus said to his disciples: "As the Father loves me, so I also love you. Remain in my love. If you keep my commandments, you will remain in my love, just as I have kept my Father's commandments and remain in his love.

"I have told you this so that my joy might be in you and your joy might be complete. This is my commandment: love one another as I love you. No one has greater love than this, to lay down one's life for one's friends. You are my friends if you do what I command you. I no longer call you slaves, because a slave does not know what his master is doing. I have called you friends, because I have told you everything I have heard from my Father. It was not you who chose me, but I who chose you and appointed you to go and bear fruit that will remain, so that whatever you ask the Father in my name he may give you. This I command you: love one another."

MAY 15, 5TH WEEK OF EASTER – FRIDAY; ST. ISIDORE THE FARMER

FIRST READING   *Acts 15:22–31*

The Apostles and presbyters, in agreement with the whole Church, decided to choose representatives and to send them to Antioch with Paul and Barnabas. The ones chosen were Judas, who was called Barsabbas, and Silas, leaders among the brothers. This is the letter delivered by them: "The Apostles and the presbyters, your brothers, to the brothers in Antioch, Syria, and Cilicia of Gentile origin: greetings. Since we have heard that some of our number who went out without any mandate from us have upset you with their teachings and disturbed your peace of mind, we have with one accord decided to choose representatives and to send them to you along with our beloved Barnabas and Paul, who have dedicated their lives to the name of our Lord Jesus Christ. So we are sending Judas and Silas who will also convey this same message by word of mouth: 'It is the decision of the Holy Spirit and of us not to place on you any burden beyond these necessities, namely, to abstain from meat sacrificed to idols, from blood, from meats of strangled animals, and from unlawful marriage. If you keep free of these, you will be doing what is right. Farewell.'"

And so they were sent on their journey. Upon their arrival in Antioch they called the assembly together and delivered the letter. When the people read it, they were delighted with the exhortation.

RESPONSORIAL PSALM *Psalm 57:8–9, 10 and 12*
R. I will give you thanks among the peoples, O Lord. or: R. Alleluia.
My heart is steadfast, O God; / my heart is steadfast; / I will sing and chant praise. / Awake, O my soul; / awake, lyre and harp! / I will wake the dawn. **R.**
I will give thanks to you among the peoples, / O LORD, I will chant your praise among the nations. / For your mercy towers to the heavens, / and your faithfulness to the skies. / Be exalted above the heavens, O God; / above all the earth be your glory! **R.**

ALLELUIA *John 15:15b*
R. Alleluia, alleluia. I call you my friends, says the Lord, for I have made known to you all that the Father has told me. **R.**

GOSPEL *John 15:12–17*
Jesus said to his disciples: "This is my commandment: love one another as I love you. No one has greater love than this, to lay down one's life for one's friends. You are my friends if you do what I command you. I no longer call you slaves, because a slave does not know what his master is doing. I have called you friends, because I have told you everything I have heard from my Father. It was not you who chose me, but I who chose you and appointed you to go and bear fruit that will remain, so that whatever you ask the Father in my name he may give you. This I command you: love one another."

MAY 16, 5TH WEEK OF EASTER – SATURDAY; ST. FELIX OF CANTALICE
FIRST READING *Acts 16:1–10*
Paul reached also Derbe and Lystra where there was a disciple named Timothy, the son of a Jewish woman who was a believer, but his father was a Greek. The brothers in Lystra and Iconium spoke highly of him, and Paul wanted him to come along with him. On account of the Jews of that region, Paul had him circumcised, for they all knew that his father was a Greek. As they traveled from city to city, they handed on to the people for observance the decisions reached by the Apostles and presbyters in Jerusalem. Day after day the churches grew stronger in faith and increased in number.

They traveled through the Phrygian and Galatian territory because they had been prevented by the Holy Spirit from preaching the message in the province of Asia. When they came to Mysia, they tried to go on into Bithynia, but the Spirit of Jesus did not allow them, so they crossed through Mysia and came down to Troas. During the night Paul had a vision. A Macedonian stood before him and implored him with these words, "Come over to Macedonia and help us." When he had seen the vision, we sought passage to Macedonia at once, concluding that God had called us to proclaim the Good News to them.

RESPONSORIAL PSALM *Psalm 100:1b–2, 3, 5*

R. Let all the earth cry out to God with joy. or: R. Alleluia.

Sing joyfully to the LORD, all you lands; / serve the LORD with gladness; / come before him with joyful song. **R.**

Know that the LORD is God; / he made us, his we are; / his people, the flock he tends. **R.**

The LORD is good: / his kindness endures forever, / and his faithfulness, to all generations. **R.**

ALLELUIA *Colossians 3:1*

R. Alleluia, alleluia. If then you were raised with Christ, seek what is above, where Christ is seated at the right hand of God. **R.**

GOSPEL *John 15:18–21*

Jesus said to his disciples: "If the world hates you, realize that it hated me first. If you belonged to the world, the world would love its own; but because you do not belong to the world, and I have chosen you out of the world, the world hates you. Remember the word I spoke to you, 'No slave is greater than his master.' If they persecuted me, they will also persecute you. If they kept my word, they will also keep yours. And they will do all these things to you on account of my name, because they do not know the one who sent me."

MAY 17, 6TH SUNDAY OF EASTER; ST. PASCHAL BAYLON

FIRST READING *Acts 8:5—8, 14—17*

Philip went down to the city of Samaria and proclaimed the Christ to them. With one accord, the crowds paid attention to what was said by Philip when they heard it and saw the signs he was doing. For unclean spirits, crying out in a loud voice, came out of many possessed people, and many paralyzed or crippled people were cured. There was great joy in that city.

Now when the apostles in Jerusalem heard that Samaria had accepted the word of God, they sent them Peter and John, who went down and prayed for them, that they might receive the Holy Spirit, for it had not yet fallen upon any of them; they had only been baptized in the name of the Lord Jesus. Then they laid hands on them and they received the Holy Spirit.

RESPONSORIAL PSALM *Psalm 66:1—3, 4—5, 6—7, 16, 20 (1)*

R. Let all the earth cry out to God with joy. or R. Alleluia.

Shout joyfully to God, all the earth, / sing praise to the glory of his name; / proclaim his glorious praise. / Say to God, / "How tremendous are your deeds!" **R.**

"Let all on earth worship and sing praise to you, / sing praise to your name!" / Come and see the works of God, / his tremendous deeds among the children of Adam. **R.**

He has changed the sea into dry land; / through the river they passed on foot; / therefore let us rejoice in him. / He rules by his might forever. **R.**

Hear now, all you who fear God, / while I declare what he has done for me. / Blessed be God who refused me not my prayer or his kindness! **R.**

SECOND READING   *1 Peter 3:15—18*

Beloved: Sanctify Christ as Lord in your hearts. Always be ready to give an explanation to anyone who asks you for a reason for your hope, but do it with gentleness and reverence, keeping your conscience clear, so that, when you are maligned, those who defame your good conduct in Christ may themselves be put to shame. For it is better to suffer for doing good, if that be the will of God, than for doing evil. For Christ also suffered for sins once, the righteous for the sake of the unrighteous, that he might lead you to God. Put to death in the flesh, he was brought to life in the Spirit.

ALLELUIA   *John 14:23*

R. Alleluia, alleluia. Whoever loves me will keep my word, says the Lord, and my Father will love him and we will come to him. **R.**

GOSPEL   *John 14:15—21*

Jesus said to his disciples: "If you love me, you will keep my commandments. And I will ask the Father, and he will give you another Advocate to be with you always, the Spirit of truth, whom the world cannot accept, because it neither sees nor knows him. But you know him, because he remains with you, and will be in you. I will not leave you orphans; I will come to you. In a little while the world will no longer see me, but you will see me, because I live and you will live. On that day you will realize that I am in my Father and you are in me and I in you. Whoever has my commandments and observes them is the one who loves me. And whoever loves me will be loved by my Father, and I will love him and reveal myself to him."

MAY 18, 6TH WEEK OF EASTER - MONDAY; ST. JOHN I

FIRST READING   *Acts 16:11–15*

We set sail from Troas, making a straight run for Samothrace, and on the next day to Neapolis, and from there to Philippi, a leading city in that district of Macedonia and a Roman colony. We spent some time in that city. On the Sabbath we went outside the city gate along the river where we thought there would be a place of prayer. We sat and spoke with the women who had gathered there. One of them, a woman named Lydia, a dealer in purple cloth, from the city of Thyatira, a worshiper of God, listened, and the Lord opened her heart to pay attention to what Paul was saying. After she and her household had been baptized, she offered us an invitation, "If you consider me a believer in the Lord, come and stay at my home," and she prevailed on us.

RESPONSORIAL PSALM   *Psalm 149:1b–2, 3–4, 5–6a and 9b*

R. The Lord takes delight in his people. or: R. Alleluia.

Sing to the LORD a new song of praise / in the assembly of the faithful. / Let Israel be glad in their maker, / let the children of Zion rejoice in their king. **R.**

Let them praise his name in the festive dance, / let them sing praise to him with timbrel and harp. / For the LORD loves his people, / and he adorns the lowly with victory. **R.**

Let the faithful exult in glory; / let them sing for joy upon their couches. / Let the high praises of God be in their throats. / This is the glory of all his faithful. Alleluia. **R.**

ALLELUIA   *John 15:26b, 27a*

R. Alleluia, alleluia. The Spirit of truth will testify to me, says the Lord, and you also will testify. **R.**

GOSPEL   *John 15:26B16:4a*

Jesus said to his disciples: "When the Advocate comes whom I will send you from the Father, the Spirit of truth who proceeds from the Father, he will testify to me. And you also testify, because you have been with me from the beginning.

"I have told you this so that you may not fall away. They will expel you from the synagogues; in fact, the hour is coming when everyone who kills you will think he is offering worship to God. They will do this because they have not known either the Father or me. I have told you this so that when their hour comes you may remember that I told you."

MAY 19, 6TH WEEK OF EASTER – TUESDAY; ST. CELESTINE V

FIRST READING   *Acts 16:22–34*

The crowd in Philippi joined in the attack on Paul and Silas, and the magistrates had them stripped and ordered them to be beaten with rods. After inflicting many blows on them, they threw them into prison and instructed the jailer to guard them securely. When he received these instructions, he put them in the innermost cell and secured their feet to a stake.

About midnight, while Paul and Silas were praying and singing hymns to God as the prisoners listened, there was suddenly such a severe earthquake that the foundations of the jail shook; all the doors flew open, and the chains of all were pulled loose. When the jailer woke up and saw the prison doors wide open, he drew his sword and was about to kill himself, thinking that the prisoners had escaped. But Paul shouted out in a loud voice, "Do no harm to yourself; we are all here." He asked for a light and rushed in and, trembling with fear, he fell down before Paul and Silas. Then he brought them out and said, "Sirs, what must I do to be saved?" And they said, "Believe in the Lord Jesus and you and your household will be saved." So they spoke the word of the Lord to him and to everyone in his house. He took them in at that hour of the night and bathed their wounds; then he and all his family were baptized at once. He brought them up into his house and provided a meal and with his household rejoiced at having come to faith in God.

RESPONSORIAL PSALM   *Psalm 138:1–2ab, 2cde–3, 7c–8*

R. Your right hand saves me, O Lord. or: R. Alleluia.

I will give thanks to you, O LORD, **/** with all my heart, for you have heard the words of my mouth; **/** in the presence of the angels I will sing your praise; **/** I will worship at your holy temple, **/** and give thanks to your name. **R.**

Because of your kindness and your truth, **/** you have made great above all things your name and your promise. **/** When I called, you answered me; **/** you built up strength within me. **R.**

Your right hand saves me. **/** The LORD will complete what he has done for me; **/** your kindness, O LORD, endures forever; **/** forsake not the work of your hands. **R.**

ALLELUIA　　　　　　　　　　　　　　　　　　　　*See John 16:7, 13*

R. **Alleluia, alleluia.** I will send to you the Spirit of truth, says the Lord; he will guide you to all truth. **R.**

GOSPEL　　　　　　　　　　　　　　　　　　　　　　*John 16:5–11*

Jesus said to his disciples: "Now I am going to the one who sent me, and not one of you asks me, 'Where are you going?' But because I told you this, grief has filled your hearts. But I tell you the truth, it is better for you that I go. For if I do not go, the Advocate will not come to you. But if I go, I will send him to you. And when he comes he will convict the world in regard to sin and righteousness and condemnation: sin, because they do not believe in me; righteousness, because I am going to the Father and you will no longer see me; condemnation, because the ruler of this world has been condemned."

MAY 20, 6TH WEEK OF EASTER – WEDNESDAY; ST. BERNARDINE OF SIENA

FIRST READING　　　　　　　　　　　　　　　　*Acts 17:15, 22 – 18 :1*

After Paul's escorts had taken him to Athens, they came away with instructions for Silas and Timothy to join him as soon as possible.

Then Paul stood up at the Areopagus and said: "You Athenians, I see that in every respect you are very religious. For as I walked around looking carefully at your shrines, I even discovered an altar inscribed, 'To an Unknown God.' What therefore you unknowingly worship, I proclaim to you. The God who made the world and all that is in it, the Lord of heaven and earth, does not dwell in sanctuaries made by human hands, nor is he served by human hands because he needs anything. Rather it is he who gives to everyone life and breath and everything. He made from one the whole human race to dwell on the entire surface of the earth, and he fixed the ordered seasons and the boundaries of their regions, so that people might seek God, even perhaps grope for him and find him, though indeed he is not far from any one of us. For 'In him we live and move and have our being,' as even some of your poets have said, 'For we too are his offspring.' Since therefore we are the offspring of God, we ought not to think that the divinity is like an image fashioned from gold, silver, or stone by human art and imagination. God has overlooked the times of ignorance, but now he demands that all people everywhere repent because he has established a day on which he will 'judge the world with justice' through a man he has appointed, and he has provided confirmation for all by raising him from the dead."

When they heard about resurrection of the dead, some began to scoff, but others said, "We should like to hear you on this some other time." And so Paul left them. But some did join him, and became believers. Among them were Dionysius, a member of the Court of the Areopagus, a woman named Damaris, and others with them.

After this he left Athens and went to Corinth.

RESPONSORIAL PSALM　　　　　　　　　*Psalm 148:1–2, 11–12, 13, 14*

R. **Heaven and earth are full of your glory. or: R. Alleluia.**

Praise the LORD from the heavens; / praise him in the heights. / Praise him, all you his angels; / praise him, all you his hosts. **R.**

Let the kings of the earth and all peoples, / the princes and all the judges of the earth, / Young men too, and maidens, old men and boys. **R.**

Praise the name of the LORD, / for his name alone is exalted; / His majesty is above earth and heaven. **R.**

He has lifted up the horn of his people; / Be this his praise from all his faithful ones, / from the children of Israel, / the people close to him. Alleluia. **R.**

ALLELUIA   *John 14:16*

R. Alleluia, alleluia. I will ask the Father and he will give you another Advocate to be with you always. **R.**

GOSPEL   *John 16:12–15*

Jesus said to his disciples: "I have much more to tell you, but you cannot bear it now. But when he comes, the Spirit of truth, he will guide you to all truth. He will not speak on his own, but he will speak what he hears, and will declare to you the things that are coming. He will glorify me, because he will take from what is mine and declare it to you. Everything that the Father has is mine; for this reason I told you that he will take from what is mine and declare it to you."

MAY 21, ASCENSION OF THE LORD (PARTS OF USA) OR 6TH WEEK OF EASTER - THURSDAY; ST. CHRISTOPHER MAGALLANES

If the Soleminity of Ascension is shifted to Sunday in your Diocese, please locate the readings for today below the ones for Ascesion

ASCENSION OF THE LORD

FIRST READING   *Acts 1:1—11*

In the first book, Theophilus, I dealt with all that Jesus did and taught until the day he was taken up, after giving instructions through the Holy Spirit to the apostles whom he had chosen. He presented himself alive to them by many proofs after he had suffered, appearing to them during forty days and speaking about the kingdom of God. While meeting with them, he enjoined them not to depart from Jerusalem, but to wait for "the promise of the Father about which you have heard me speak; for John baptized with water, but in a few days you will be baptized with the Holy Spirit."

When they had gathered together they asked him, "Lord, are you at this time going to restore the kingdom to Israel?" He answered them, "It is not for you to know the times or seasons that the Father has established by his own authority. But you will receive power when the Holy Spirit comes upon you, and you will be my witnesses in Jerusalem, throughout Judea and Samaria, and to the ends of the earth." When he had said this, as they were looking on, he was lifted up, and a cloud took him from their sight. While they were looking intently at the sky as he was going, suddenly two men dressed in white garments stood beside them. They said, "Men of Galilee, why are you standing there looking at the sky? This Jesus who has been taken up from you into heaven will return in the same way as you have seen him going into heaven."

RESPONSORIAL PSALM *Psalm 47:2—3, 6—7, 8—9 (6)*

R. God mounts his throne to shouts of joy: a blare of trumpets for the Lord. or R. Alleluia.

All you peoples, clap your hands, / shout to God with cries of gladness. / For the LORD, the Most High, the awesome, / is the great king over all the earth. **R.**

God mounts his throne amid shouts of joy; / the LORD, amid trumpet blasts. / Sing praise to God, sing praise; / sing praise to our king, sing praise. **R.**

For king of all the earth is God; / sing hymns of praise. / God reigns over the nations, / God sits upon his holy throne. **R.**

SECOND READING *Ephesians 1:17—23*

Brothers and sisters: May the God of our Lord Jesus Christ, the Father of glory, give you a Spirit of wisdom and revelation resulting in knowledge of him. May the eyes of your hearts be enlightened, that you may know what is the hope that belongs to his call, what are the riches of glory in his inheritance among the holy ones, and what is the surpassing greatness of his power for us who believe, in accord with the exercise of his great might, which he worked in Christ, raising him from the dead and seating him at his right hand in the heavens, far above every principality, authority, power, and dominion, and every name that is named not only in this age but also in the one to come. And he put all things beneath his feet and gave him as head over all things to the church, which is his body, the fullness of the one who fills all things in every way.

ALLELUIA *Luke 3:4, 6*

R. Alleluia, alleluia. Go and teach all nations, says the Lord; I am with you always, until the end of the world. **R.**

GOSPEL *Mathew 28:16—20*

The eleven disciples went to Galilee, to the mountain to which Jesus had ordered them. When they saw him, they worshiped, but they doubted. Then Jesus approached and said to them, "All power in heaven and on earth has been given to me. Go, therefore, and make disciples of all nations, baptizing them in the name of the Father, and of the Son, and of the Holy Spirit, teaching them to observe all that I have commanded you. And behold, I am with you always, until the end of the age."

THURSDAY MASS

FIRST READING *Acts 18:1—8*

Paul left Athens and went to Corinth. There he met a Jew named Aquila, a native of Pontus, who had recently come from Italy with his wife Priscilla because Claudius had ordered all the Jews to leave Rome. He went to visit them and, because he practiced the same trade, stayed with them and worked, for they were tentmakers by trade. Every Sabbath, he entered into discussions in the synagogue, attempting to convince both Jews and Greeks. When Silas and Timothy came down from Macedonia, Paul began to occupy himself totally with preaching the word, testifying to the Jews that the Christ was Jesus. When they opposed him and reviled him, he shook out his garments and said to them, "Your blood be on your heads! I am clear of responsibility. From now on I will go to the Gentiles." So he left there and went to a house belonging to a man named Titus Justus, a worshiper of God; his house was next to a synagogue. Crispus, the synagogue official, came to believe in the Lord along with his entire household, and many of the Corinthians who heard believed and were baptized.

RESPONSORIAL PSALM   *Psalm 98:1, 2–3ab, 3cd–4*
R. (see 2b) The Lord has revealed to the nations his saving power. or: R. Alleluia.
Sing to the LORD a new song, / for he has done wondrous deeds; / His right hand has won victory for him, / his holy arm. **R.**
The LORD has made his salvation known: / in the sight of the nations he has revealed his justice. / He has remembered his kindness and his faithfulness / toward the house of Israel. **R.**
All the ends of the earth have seen / the salvation by our God. / Sing joyfully to the LORD, all you lands; / break into song; sing praise. **R.**

ALLELUIA   *See John 14:18*
R. Alleluia, alleluia. I will not leave you orphans, says the Lord; I will come back to you, and your hearts will rejoice. **R.**

GOSPEL   *John 16:16–20*
Jesus said to his disciples: "A little while and you will no longer see me, and again a little while later and you will see me." So some of his disciples said to one another, "What does this mean that he is saying to us, 'A little while and you will not see me, and again a little while and you will see me,' and 'Because I am going to the Father'?" So they said, "What is this 'little while' of which he speaks? We do not know what he means." Jesus knew that they wanted to ask him, so he said to them, "Are you discussing with one another what I said, 'A little while and you will not see me, and again a little while and you will see me'? Amen, amen, I say to you, you will weep and mourn, while the world rejoices; you will grieve, but your grief will become joy."

MAY 22, 6TH WEEK OF EASTER – FRIDAY; ST. RITA OF CASCIA
FIRST READING   *Acts 18:9–18*
One night while Paul was in Corinth, the Lord said to him in a vision, "Do not be afraid. Go on speaking, and do not be silent, for I am with you. No one will attack and harm you, for I have many people in this city." He settled there for a year and a half and taught the word of God among them.

But when Gallio was proconsul of Achaia, the Jews rose up together against Paul and brought him to the tribunal, saying, "This man is inducing people to worship God contrary to the law." When Paul was about to reply, Gallio spoke to the Jews, "If it were a matter of some crime or malicious fraud, I should with reason hear the complaint of you Jews; but since it is a question of arguments over doctrine and titles and your own law, see to it yourselves. I do not wish to be a judge of such matters." And he drove them away from the tribunal. They all seized Sosthenes, the synagogue official, and beat him in full view of the tribunal. But none of this was of concern to Gallio.

Paul remained for quite some time, and after saying farewell to the brothers he sailed for Syria, together with Priscilla and Aquila. At Cenchreae he had shaved his head because he had taken a vow.

RESPONSORIAL PSALM   *Psalm 47:2–3, 4–5, 6–7*
R. God is king of all the earth. or: R. Alleluia.
All you peoples, clap your hands, / shout to God with cries of gladness, / For the LORD, the Most High, the awesome, / is the great king over all the earth. **R.**
He brings people under us; / nations under our feet. / He chooses for us our inheritance, / the glory of Jacob, whom he loves. **R.**
God mounts his throne amid shouts of joy; / the LORD, amid trumpet blasts. / Sing praise to God, / sing praise; / sing praise to our king, / sing praise. **R.**
ALLELUIA   *See Luke 24:46, 26*
R. Alleluia, alleluia. Christ had to suffer and to rise from the dead, and so enter into his glory. **R.**

GOSPEL   *John 16:20–23*
Jesus said to his disciples: "Amen, amen, I say to you, you will weep and mourn, while the world rejoices; you will grieve, but your grief will become joy. When a woman is in labor, she is in anguish because her hour has arrived; but when she has given birth to a child, she no longer remembers the pain because of her joy that a child has been born into the world. So you also are now in anguish. But I will see you again, and your hearts will rejoice, and no one will take your joy away from you. On that day you will not question me about anything. Amen, amen, I say to you, whatever you ask the Father in my name he will give you."

MAY 23, 6TH WEEK OF EASTER – SATURDAY; ST. JOHN BAPTIST ROSSI
FIRST READING   *Acts 18:23–28*
After staying in Antioch some time, Paul left and traveled in orderly sequence through the Galatian country and Phrygia, bringing strength to all the disciples.

A Jew named Apollos, a native of Alexandria, an eloquent speaker, arrived in Ephesus. He was an authority on the Scriptures. He had been instructed in the Way of the Lord and, with ardent spirit, spoke and taught accurately about Jesus, although he knew only the baptism of John. He began to speak boldly in the synagogue; but when Priscilla and Aquila heard him, they took him aside and explained to him the Way of God more accurately. And when he wanted to cross to Achaia, the brothers encouraged him and wrote to the disciples there to welcome him. After his arrival he gave great assistance to those who had come to believe through grace. He vigorously refuted the Jews in public, establishing from the Scriptures that the Christ is Jesus.

RESPONSORIAL PSALM *Psalm 47:2–3, 8–9, 10*

R. God is king of all the earth. or: R. Alleluia.

All you peoples, clap your hands; / shout to God with cries of gladness. / For the LORD, the Most High, the awesome, / is the great king over all the earth. **R.**

For king of all the earth is God; / sing hymns of praise. / God reigns over the nations, / God sits upon his holy throne. **R.**

The princes of the peoples are gathered together / with the people of the God of Abraham. / For God's are the guardians of the earth; / he is supreme. **R.**

ALLELUIA *John 16:28*

R. Alleluia, alleluia. I came from the Father and have come into the world; now I am leaving the world and going back to the Father. **R.**

GOSPEL *John 16:23b–28*

Jesus said to his disciples: "Amen, amen, I say to you, whatever you ask the Father in my name he will give you. Until now you have not asked anything in my name; ask and you will receive, so that your joy may be complete.

"I have told you this in figures of speech. The hour is coming when I will no longer speak to you in figures but I will tell you clearly about the Father. On that day you will ask in my name, and I do not tell you that I will ask the Father for you. For the Father himself loves you, because you have loved me and have come to believe that I came from God. I came from the Father and have come into the world. Now I am leaving the world and going back to the Father."

MAY 24, 7TH SUNDAY OF EASTER OR ASCENSION OF THE LORD (CANADA AND PARTS OF USA); BLESSED MARIE-LEONIE PARADIS

PLEASE CONSULT THE READINGS OF ASCENSION THURSDAY ABOVE IF THE CELEBRATION OF ASCENSION IS SHIFTED TO THIS SUNDAY IN YOUR LOCAL CHURCH

SEVENTH SUNDAY OF EASTER

FIRST READING *Acts 1:12—14*

After Jesus had been taken up to heaven the apostles returned to Jerusalem from the mount called Olivet, which is near Jerusalem, a sabbath day's journey away.

When they entered the city they went to the upper room where they were staying, Peter and John and James and Andrew, Philip and Thomas, Bartholomew and Matthew, James son of Alphaeus, Simon the Zealot, and Judas son of James. All these devoted themselves with one accord to prayer, together with some women, and Mary the mother of Jesus, and his brothers.

RESPONSORIAL PSALM *Psalm 27:1, 4, 7—8 (13)*

R. I believe that I shall see the good things of the Lord in the land of the living. or R. Alleluia.

The LORD is my light and my salvation; / whom should I fear? / The LORD is my life's refuge; / of whom should I be afraid? **R.**

One thing I ask of the LORD; / this I seek: to dwell in the house of the LORD all the days of my life, / that I may gaze on the loveliness of the LORD / and contemplate his temple. **R.**

Hear, O LORD, the sound of my call; / have pity on me, and answer me. / Of you my heart speaks; / you my glance seeks. **R.**

SECOND READING   *1 Peter 4:13—16*

Beloved: Rejoice to the extent that you share in the sufferings of Christ, so that when his glory is revealed you may also rejoice exultantly. If you are insulted for the name of Christ, blessed are you, for the Spirit of glory and of God rests upon you. But let no one among you be made to suffer as a murderer, a thief, an evildoer, or as an intriguer. But whoever is made to suffer as a Christian should not be ashamed but glorify God because of the name.

ALLELUIA   *see John 14:18*

R. Alleluia, alleluia. I will not leave you orphans, says the Lord. I will come back to you, and your hearts will rejoice. **R.**

GOSPEL   *John 17:1—11a*

Jesus raised his eyes to heaven and said, "Father, the hour has come. Give glory to your son, so that your son may glorify you, just as you gave him authority over all people, so that your son may give eternal life to all you gave him. Now this is eternal life, that they should know you, the only true God, and the one whom you sent, Jesus Christ. I glorified you on earth by accomplishing the work that you gave me to do. Now glorify me, Father, with you, with the glory that I had with you before the world began.

"I revealed your name to those whom you gave me out of the world. They belonged to you, and you gave them to me, and they have kept your word. Now they know that everything you gave me is from you, because the words you gave to me I have given to them, and they accepted them and truly understood that I came from you, and they have believed that you sent me. I pray for them. I do not pray for the world but for the ones you have given me, because they are yours, and everything of mine is yours and everything of yours is mine, and I have been glorified in them. And now I will no longer be in the world, but they are in the world, while I am coming to you."

MAY 25, 7TH WEEK OF EASTER – MONDAY; ST. BEDE THE VENERABLE

FIRST READING   *Acts 19:1–8*

While Apollos was in Corinth, Paul traveled through the interior of the country and down to Ephesus where he found some disciples. He said to them, "Did you receive the Holy Spirit when you became believers?" They answered him, "We have never even heard that there is a Holy Spirit." He said, "How were you baptized?" They replied, "With the baptism of John. "Paul then said, "John baptized with a baptism of repentance, telling the people to believe in the one who was to come after him, that is, in Jesus." When they heard this, they were baptized in the name of the Lord Jesus. And when Paul laid his hands on them, the Holy

Spirit came upon them, and they spoke in tongues and prophesied. Altogether there were about twelve men. He entered the synagogue, and for three months debated boldly with persuasive arguments about the Kingdom of God.

RESPONSORIAL PSALM   *Psalm 68:2–3ab, 4–5acd, 6–7ab*
R. Sing to God, O kingdoms of the earth. or: R. Alleluia.
God arises; his enemies are scattered, **/** and those who hate him flee before him. **/** As smoke is driven away, so are they driven; **/** as wax melts before the fire. **R.**
But the just rejoice and exult before God; **/** they are glad and rejoice. **/** Sing to God, chant praise to his name; **/** whose name is the LORD. **R.**
The father of orphans and the defender of widows **/** is God in his holy dwelling. **/** God gives a home to the forsaken; **/** he leads forth prisoners to prosperity. **R.**

ALLELUIA   *Colossians 3:1*
R. Alleluia, alleluia. If then you were raised with Christ, seek what is above, where Christ is seated at the right hand of God. **R.**

GOSPEL   *John 16:29–33*
The disciples said to Jesus, "Now you are talking plainly, and not in any figure of speech. Now we realize that you know everything and that you do not need to have anyone question you. Because of this we believe that you came from God." Jesus answered them, "Do you believe now? Behold, the hour is coming and has arrived when each of you will be scattered to his own home and you will leave me alone. But I am not alone, because the Father is with me. I have told you this so that you might have peace in me. In the world you will have trouble, but take courage, I have conquered the world."

MAY 26, 7TH WEEK OF EASTER – TUESDAY; ST. PHILIP NERI

FIRST READING   *Acts 20:17–27*
From Miletus Paul had the presbyters of the Church at Ephesus summoned. When they came to him, he addressed them, "You know how I lived among you the whole time from the day I first came to the province of Asia. I served the Lord with all humility and with the tears and trials that came to me because of the plots of the Jews, and I did not at all shrink from telling you what was for your benefit, or from teaching you in public or in your homes. I earnestly bore witness for both Jews and Greeks to repentance before God and to faith in our Lord Jesus. But now, compelled by the Spirit, I am going to Jerusalem. What will happen to me there I do not know, except that in one city after another the Holy Spirit has been warning me that imprisonment and hardships await me. Yet I consider life of no importance to me, if only I may finish my course and the ministry that I received from the Lord Jesus, to bear witness to the Gospel of God's grace.

"But now I know that none of you to whom I preached the kingdom during my travels will ever see my face again. And so I solemnly declare to you this day that I am not responsible for the blood of any of you, for I did not shrink from proclaiming to you the entire plan of God."

RESPONSORIAL PSALM   *Psalm 68:10–11, 20–21*
R. Sing to God, O kingdoms of the earth. or: R. Alleluia.

A bountiful rain you showered down, O God, / upon your inheritance; / you restored the land when it languished; / Your flock settled in it; / in your goodness, O God, you provided it for the needy. **R.**

Blessed day by day be the Lord, / who bears our burdens; / God, who is our salvation. / God is a saving God for us; / the LORD, my Lord, controls the passageways of death. **R.**

ALLELUIA   *John 14:16*

R. Alleluia, alleluia. I will ask the Father and he will give you another Advocate to be with you always. **R.**

GOSPEL   *John 17:1–11a*

Jesus raised his eyes to heaven and said, "Father, the hour has come. Give glory to your son, so that your son may glorify you, just as you gave him authority over all people, so that your son may give eternal life to all you gave him. Now this is eternal life, that they should know you, the only true God, and the one whom you sent, Jesus Christ. I glorified you on earth by accomplishing the work that you gave me to do. Now glorify me, Father, with you, with the glory that I had with you before the world began.

"I revealed your name to those whom you gave me out of the world. They belonged to you, and you gave them to me, and they have kept your word. Now they know that everything you gave me is from you, because the words you gave to me I have given to them, and they accepted them and truly understood that I came from you, and they have believed that you sent me. I pray for them. I do not pray for the world but for the ones you have given me, because they are yours, and everything of mine is yours and everything of yours is mine, and I have been glorified in them. And now I will no longer be in the world, but they are in the world, while I am coming to you."

MAY 27, 7TH WEEK OF EASTER – WEDNESDAY; ST. AUGUSTINE OF CANTERBURY
FIRST READING   *Acts 20:28–38*

At Miletus, Paul spoke to the presbyters of the Church of Ephesus: "Keep watch over yourselves and over the whole flock of which the Holy Spirit has appointed you overseers, in which you tend the Church of God that he acquired with his own Blood. I know that after my departure savage wolves will come among you, and they will not spare the flock. And from your own group, men will come forward perverting the truth to draw the disciples away after them. So be vigilant and remember that for three years, night and day, I unceasingly admonished each of you with tears. And now I commend you to God and to that gracious word of his that can build you up and give you the inheritance among all who are consecrated. I have never wanted anyone's silver or gold or clothing. You know well that these very hands have served my needs and my companions. In every way I have shown you that by hard work of that sort we must help the weak, and keep in mind the words of the Lord Jesus who himself said, 'It is more blessed to give than to receive.'"

When he had finished speaking he knelt down and prayed with them all. They were all weeping loudly as they threw their arms around Paul and kissed him, for they were deeply distressed that he had said that they would never see his face again. Then they escorted him to the ship.

RESPONSORIAL PSALM *Psalm 68:29–30, 33–35a, 35bc–36ab*
R. Sing to God, O kingdoms of the earth. or: R. Alleluia.
Show forth, O God, your power, / the power, O God, with which you took our part; / For your temple in Jerusalem / let the kings bring you gifts. **R.**
You kingdoms of the earth, / sing to God, chant praise to the Lord who rides on the heights of the ancient heavens. / Behold, his voice resounds, / the voice of power: Confess the power of God!" **R.**
Over Israel is his majesty; / his power is in the skies. / Awesome in his sanctuary is God, the God of Israel; / he gives power and strength to his people. **R.**
ALLELUIA *John See John 17:17b, 17a*
R. Alleluia, alleluia. Your word, O Lord, is truth; consecrate us in the truth. **R.**

GOSPEL *John 17:11b–19*
Lifting up his eyes to heaven, Jesus prayed, saying: "Holy Father, keep them in your name that you have given me, so that they may be one just as we are one. When I was with them I protected them in your name that you gave me, and I guarded them, and none of them was lost except the son of destruction, in order that the Scripture might be fulfilled. But now I am coming to you. I speak this in the world so that they may share my joy completely. I gave them your word, and the world hated them, because they do not belong to the world any more than I belong to the world. I do not ask that you take them out of the world but that you keep them from the Evil One. They do not belong to the world any more than I belong to the world. Consecrate them in the truth. Your word is truth. As you sent me into the world, so I sent them into the world. And I consecrate myself for them, so that they also may be consecrated in truth."

MAY 28, 7TH WEEK OF EASTER – THURSDAY; ST. MARIANA OF QUITO
FIRST READING *Acts 22:30; 23:6–11*
Wishing to determine the truth about why Paul was being accused by the Jews, the commander freed him and ordered the chief priests and the whole Sanhedrin to convene. Then he brought Paul down and made him stand before them.

Paul was aware that some were Sadducees and some Pharisees, so he called out before the Sanhedrin, "My brothers, I am a Pharisee, the son of Pharisees; I am on trial for hope in the resurrection of the dead." When he said this, a dispute broke out between the Pharisees and Sadducees, and the group became divided. For the Sadducees say that there is no resurrection or angels or spirits, while the Pharisees acknowledge all three. A great uproar occurred, and some scribes belonging to the Pharisee party stood up and sharply argued, "We find nothing wrong with this man. Suppose a spirit or an angel has spoken to him?" The dispute was so serious that the commander, afraid that Paul would be torn to pieces by them, ordered his troops to go down and rescue Paul from their midst and take him into the compound. The following night the Lord stood by him and said, "Take courage. For just as you have borne witness to my cause in Jerusalem, so you must also bear witness in Rome."

RESPONSORIAL PSALM *Psalm 16:1–2a and 5, 7–8, 9–10, 11*
R. Keep me safe, O God; you are my hope. or: R. Alleluia.
Keep me, O God, for in you I take refuge; / I say to the LORD, "My Lord are you." / O LORD, my allotted portion and my cup, / you it is who hold fast my lot. **R.**
I bless the LORD who counsels me; / even in the night my heart exhorts me. / I set the LORD ever before me; / with him at my right hand I shall not be disturbed. **R.**
Therefore my heart is glad and my soul rejoices, / my body, too, abides in confidence; / Because you will not abandon my soul to the nether world, / nor will you suffer your faithful one to undergo corruption. **R.**
You will show me the path to life, / fullness of joys in your presence, / the delights at your right hand forever. **R.**

ALLELUIA *John 17:21*
R. Alleluia, alleluia. May they all be one as you, Father, are in me and I in you, that the world may believe that you sent me, says the Lord. **R.**

GOSPEL *John 17:20–26*
Lifting up his eyes to heaven, Jesus prayed saying: "I pray not only for these, but also for those who will believe in me through their word, so that they may all be one, as you, Father, are in me and I in you, that they also may be in us, that the world may believe that you sent me. And I have given them the glory you gave me, so that they may be one, as we are one, I in them and you in me, that they may be brought to perfection as one, that the world may know that you sent me, and that you loved them even as you loved me. Father, they are your gift to me. I wish that where I am they also may be with me, that they may see my glory that you gave me, because you loved me before the foundation of the world. Righteous Father, the world also does not know you, but I know you, and they know that you sent me. I made known to them your name and I will make it known, that the love with which you loved me may be in them and I in them."

MAY 29, 7TH WEEK OF EASTER – FRIDAY; BLESSED EUGENE DE MAZENOD
FIRST READING *Acts 25:13b–21*
King Agrippa and Bernice arrived in Caesarea on a visit to Festus. Since they spent several days there, Festus referred Paul's case to the king, saying, "There is a man here left in custody by Felix. When I was in Jerusalem the chief priests and the elders of the Jews brought charges against him and demanded his condemnation. I answered them that it was not Roman practice to hand over an accused person before he has faced his accusers and had the opportunity to defend himself against their charge. So when they came together

here, I made no delay; the next day I took my seat on the tribunal and ordered the man to be brought in. His accusers stood around him, but did not charge him with any of the crimes I suspected. Instead they had some issues with him about their own religion and about a certain Jesus who had died but who Paul claimed was alive. Since I was at a loss how to investigate this controversy, I asked if he were willing to go to Jerusalem and there stand trial on these charges. And when Paul appealed that he be held in custody for the Emperor's decision, I ordered him held until I could send him to Caesar."

RESPONSORIAL PSALM *Psalm 103:1–2, 11–12, 19–20ab*
R. The Lord has established his throne in heaven. or: R. Alleluia.
Bless the LORD, O my soul; / and all my being, bless his holy name. / Bless the LORD, O my soul, / and forget not all his benefits. **R.**
For as the heavens are high above the earth, / so surpassing is his kindness toward those who fear him. / As far as the east is from the west, / so far has he put our transgressions from us. **R.**
The LORD has established his throne in heaven, / and his kingdom rules over all. / Bless the LORD, all you his angels, / you mighty in strength, who do his bidding. **R.**

ALLELUIA *John 14:26*
R. Alleluia, alleluia. The Holy Spirit will teach you everything and remind you of all I told you. **R.**

GOSPEL *John 21:15–19*
After Jesus had revealed himself to his disciples and eaten breakfast with them, he said to Simon Peter, "Simon, son of John, do you love me more than these?" Simon Peter answered him, "Yes, Lord, you know that I love you." Jesus said to him, "Feed my lambs." He then said to Simon Peter a second time, "Simon, son of John, do you love me?" Simon Peter answered him, "Yes, Lord, you know that I love you." He said to him, "Tend my sheep." He said to him the third time, "Simon, son of John, do you love me?" Peter was distressed that he had said to him a third time, "Do you love me?" and he said to him, "Lord, you know everything; you know that I love you." Jesus said to him, "Feed my sheep. Amen, amen, I say to you, when you were younger, you used to dress yourself and go where you wanted; but when you grow old, you will stretch out your hands, and someone else will dress you and lead you where you do not want to go." He said this signifying by what kind of death he would glorify God. And when he had said this, he said to him, "Follow me."

MAY 30, 7TH WEEK OF EASTER – SATURDAY; ST. JOAN OF ARC

FIRST READING *Acts 28:16–20, 30–31*
When he entered Rome, Paul was allowed to live by himself, with the soldier who was guarding him.

Three days later he called together the leaders of the Jews. When they had gathered he said to them, "My brothers, although I had done nothing against our people or our ancestral customs, I was handed over to the Romans as a prisoner from Jerusalem. After trying my case the Romans wanted to release me, because they found nothing against me deserving the death penalty. But when the Jews objected, I was obliged to appeal to Caesar, even though I had no accusation to make against my own nation. This is the reason, then, I have requested to see you and to speak with you, for it is on account of the hope of Israel that I wear these chains."

He remained for two full years in his lodgings. He received all who came to him, and with complete assurance and without hindrance he proclaimed the Kingdom of God and taught about the Lord Jesus Christ.

RESPONSORIAL PSALM   *Psalm 11:4, 5 and 7*
R. The just will gaze on your face, O Lord. or: R. Alleluia.
The LORD is in his holy temple; / the LORD's throne is in heaven. / His eyes behold, /
his searching glance is on mankind. **R.**
The LORD searches the just and the wicked; / the lover of violence he hates. /
For the LORD is just, he loves just deeds; / the upright shall see his face. **R.**
ALLELUIA   *John 16:7, 13*
R. Alleluia, alleluia. I will send to you the Spirit of truth, says the Lord; he will guide you to all truth. **R.**

GOSPEL   *John 21:20–25*
Peter turned and saw the disciple following whom Jesus loved, the one who had also reclined upon his chest during the supper and had said, "Master, who is the one who will betray you?" When Peter saw him, he said to Jesus, "Lord, what about him?" Jesus said to him, "What if I want him to remain until I come? What concern is it of yours? You follow me." So the word spread among the brothers that that disciple would not die. But Jesus had not told him that he would not die, just "What if I want him to remain until I come? What concern is it of yours?"

It is this disciple who testifies to these things and has written them, and we know that his testimony is true. There are also many other things that Jesus did, but if these were to be described individually, I do not think the whole world would contain the books that would be written.

SUNDAY 31 MAY, PENTECOST – VIGIL MASS
FIRST READING   *Genesis 11:1—9*
The whole world spoke the same language, using the same words. While the people were migrating in the east, they came upon a valley in the land of Shinar and settled there. They said to one another, "Come, let us mold bricks and harden them with fire." They used bricks for stone, and bitumen for mortar. Then they said, "Come, let us build ourselves a city and a tower with its top in the sky, and so make a name for ourselves; otherwise we shall be scattered all over the earth."

The LORD came down to see the city and the tower that the people had built. Then the LORD said: "If now, while they are one people, all speaking the same language, they have started to do this, nothing will later stop them from doing whatever they presume to do. Let us then go down there and confuse their language, so that one will not understand what another says." Thus the LORD scattered them from there all over the earth, and they stopped building the city. That is why it was called Babel, because there the LORD confused the speech of all the world. It was from that place that he scattered them all over the earth.

ALTERNATIVE FIRST READING *Exodus 19:3—8a, 16—20b*

Moses went up the mountain to God. Then the LORD called to him and said, "Thus shall you say to the house of Jacob; tell the Israelites: You have seen for yourselves how I treated the Egyptians and how I bore you up on eagle wings and brought you here to myself. Therefore, if you hearken to my voice and keep my covenant, you shall be my special possession, dearer to me than all other people, though all the earth is mine. You shall be to me a kingdom of priests, a holy nation. That is what you must tell the Israelites." So Moses went and summoned the elders of the people. When he set before them all that the LORD had ordered him to tell them, the people all answered together, "Everything the LORD has said, we will do."

On the morning of the third day there were peals of thunder and lightning, and a heavy cloud over the mountain, and a very loud trumpet blast, so that all the people in the camp trembled. But Moses led the people out of the camp to meet God, and they stationed themselves at the foot of the mountain. Mount Sinai was all wrapped in smoke, for the LORD came down upon it in fire. The smoke rose from it as though from a furnace, and the whole mountain trembled violently. The trumpet blast grew louder and louder, while Moses was speaking, and God answering him with thunder.

When the LORD came down to the top of Mount Sinai, he summoned Moses to the top of the mountain.

ALTERNATIVE FIRST READING: *Ezekiel 37:1—14*

The hand of the LORD came upon me, and he led me out in the spirit of the LORD and set me in the center of the plain, which was now filled with bones. He made me walk among the bones in every direction so that I saw how many they were on the surface of the plain. How dry they were! He asked me: Son of man, can these bones come to life? I answered, "Lord GOD, you alone know that." Then he said to me: Prophesy over these bones, and say to them: Dry bones, hear the word of the LORD! Thus says the Lord GOD to these bones: See! I will bring spirit into you, that you may come to life. I will put sinews upon you, make flesh grow over you, cover you with skin, and put spirit in you so that you may come to life and know that I am the LORD. I, Ezekiel, prophesied as I had been told, and even as I was prophesying I heard a noise; it was a rattling as the bones came together, bone joining bone. I saw the sinews and the flesh come upon them, and the skin cover them, but there was no spirit in them. Then the LORD said to me: Prophesy to the spirit, prophesy, son of man, and say to the spirit: Thus says the Lord GOD: From the four winds come, O spirit, and breathe into these slain that they may come to life. I prophesied as he told me, and the spirit came into them; they came alive and stood upright, a vast army. Then he said to me: Son of man, these bones are the whole house of Israel. They have been saying, "Our bones are dried up, our hope is lost, and we are cut off." Therefore, prophesy and say to them: Thus says the Lord GOD: O my people, I will open your graves and have you rise from them, and bring you back to the land of Israel. Then you shall know that I am the LORD, when I open your graves and have you rise from them, O my people! I will put my spirit in you that you may live, and I will settle you upon your land; thus you shall know that I am the LORD. I have promised, and I will do it, says the LORD.

ALTERNATIVE FIRST READING: *Joel 3:1—5*
Thus says the LORD: I will pour out my spirit upon all flesh. Your sons and daughters shall prophesy, your old men shall dream dreams, your young men shall see visions; even upon the servants and the handmaids, in those days, I will pour out my spirit. And I will work wonders in the heavens and on the earth, blood, fire, and columns of smoke; the sun will be turned to darkness, and the moon to blood, at the coming of the day of the LORD, the great and terrible day. Then everyone shall be rescued who calls on the name of the LORD; for on Mount Zion there shall be a remnant, as the LORD has said, and in Jerusalem survivors.

RESPONSORIAL PSALM: *Psalm 104:1—2, 24, 35, 27—28, 29, 30 (see 30)*
R. Lord, send out your Spirit, and renew the face of the earth. or R. Alleluia.
Bless the LORD, O my soul! / O LORD, my God, you are great indeed! / You are clothed with majesty and glory, / robed in light as with a cloak. **R.**
How manifold are your works, O LORD! / In wisdom you have wrought them all— / the earth is full of your creatures; / bless the LORD, O my soul! Alleluia. **R.**
Creatures all look to you / to give them food in due time. / When you give it to them, they gather it; / when you open your hand, they are filled with good things. **R.**
If you take away their breath, / they perish and return to their dust. / When you send forth your spirit, / they are created, / and you renew the face of the earth. **R.**

SECOND READING   *Romans 8:22—27*
Brothers and sisters: We know that all creation is groaning in labor pains even until now; and not only that, but we ourselves, who have the first fruits of the Spirit, we also groan within ourselves as we wait for adoption, the redemption of our bodies. For in hope we were saved. Now hope that sees is not hope. For who hopes for what one sees? But if we hope for what we do not see, we wait with endurance.

In the same way, the Spirit too comes to the aid of our weakness; for we do not know how to pray as we ought, but the Spirit himself intercedes with inexpressible groanings. And the one who searches hearts knows what is the intention of the Spirit, because he intercedes for the holy ones according to God's will.

ALLELUIA   *Luke 3:4, 6*
R. Alleluia, alleluia. Come, Holy Spirit, fill the hearts of the faithful and kindle in them the fire of your love. **R.**

GOSPEL   *John 7:37—39*

On the last and greatest day of the feast, Jesus stood up and exclaimed, "Let anyone who thirsts come to me and drink. As Scripture says: *Rivers of living water will flow from within him who believes in me.*"

He said this in reference to the Spirit that those who came to believe in him were to receive. There was, of course, no Spirit yet, because Jesus had not yet been glorified.

MAY 31, PENTECOST – MASS OF THE DAY

FIRST READING   *Acts 2:1—11*

When the time for Pentecost was fulfilled, they were all in one place together. And suddenly there came from the sky a noise like a strong driving wind, and it filled the entire house in which they were. Then there appeared to them tongues as of fire, which parted and came to rest on each one of them. And they were all filled with the Holy Spirit and began to speak in different tongues, as the Spirit enabled them to proclaim.

Now there were devout Jews from every nation under heaven staying in Jerusalem. At this sound, they gathered in a large crowd, but they were confused because each one heard them speaking in his own language. They were astounded, and in amazement they asked, "Are not all these people who are speaking Galileans? Then how does each of us hear them in his native language? We are Parthians, Medes, and Elamites, inhabitants of Mesopotamia, Judea and Cappadocia, Pontus and Asia, Phrygia and Pamphylia, Egypt and the districts of Libya near Cyrene, as well as travelers from Rome, both Jews and converts to Judaism, Cretans and Arabs, yet we hear them speaking in our own tongues of the mighty acts of God."

RESPONSORIAL PSALM   *Psalm 104:1, 24, 29—30, 31, 34 (see 30)*

R. Lord, send out your Spirit, and renew the face of the earth. or R. Alleluia.

Bless the LORD, O my soul! / O LORD, my God, you are great indeed! / How manifold are your works, O LORD! / the earth is full of your creatures. **R.**

If you take away their breath, / they perish and return to their dust. / When you send forth your spirit, they are created, / and you renew the face of the earth. **R.**

May the glory of the LORD endure forever; / may the LORD be glad in his works! / Pleasing to him be my theme; / I will be glad in the LORD. **R.**

SECOND READING   *1 Corinthians 12:3b—7, 12—13*

Brothers and sisters: No one can say, "Jesus is Lord," except by the Holy Spirit. There are different kinds of spiritual gifts but the same Spirit; there are different forms of service but the same Lord; there are different workings but the same God who produces all of them in everyone. To each individual the manifestation of the Spirit is given for some benefit.

As a body is one though it has many parts, and all the parts of the body, though many, are one body, so also Christ. For in one Spirit we were all baptized into one body, whether Jews or Greeks, slaves or free persons, and we were all given to drink of one Spirit.

SEQUENCE

Come, Holy Spirit, come! / And from your celestial home / Shed a ray of light divine!

Come, Father of the poor! / Come, source of all our store! / Come, within our bosoms shine.

You, of comforters the best; / You, the soul's most welcome guest; / Sweet refreshment here below;

In our labor, rest most sweet; / Grateful coolness in the heat; / Solace in the midst of woe.

O most blessed Light divine, / Shine within these hearts of yours, / And our inmost being fill!

Where you are not, we have naught, / Nothing good in deed or thought, / Nothing free from taint of ill.

Heal our wounds, our strength renew; / On our dryness pour your dew; / Wash the stains of guilt away:

Bend the stubborn heart and will; / Melt the frozen, warm the chill; / Guide the steps that go astray.

On the faithful, who adore / And confess you, evermore / In your sevenfold gift descend;

Give them virtue's sure reward; / Give them your salvation, Lord; / Give them joys that never end. Amen. Alleluia.

R. Alleluia, alleluia. Come, Holy Spirit, fill the hearts of your faithful and kindle in them the fire of your love. **R.**

GOSPEL   *John 20:19—23*

On the evening of that first day of the week, when the doors were locked, where the disciples were, for fear of the Jews, Jesus came and stood in their midst and said to them, "Peace be with you." When he had said this, he showed them his hands and his side. The disciples rejoiced when they saw the Lord. Jesus said to them again, "Peace be with you. As the Father has sent me, so I send you." And when he had said this, he breathed on them and said to them, "Receive the Holy Spirit. Whose sins you forgive are forgiven them, and whose sins you retain are retained."

JUNE 1, MONDAY OF WEEK 9;
MEMORIAL OF THE BLESSED VIRGIN MARY, MOTHER OF THE CHURCH

The readings for this memorial are proper.

FIRST READING   *Gn 3:9-15, 20*

After Adam had eaten of the tree, the LORD God called to him and asked him, "Where are you?" He answered, "I heard you in the garden; but I was afraid, because I was naked, so I hid myself." Then he asked, "Who told you that you were naked? You have eaten, then, from the tree of which I had forbidden you to eat!" The man replied, "The woman whom you put here with me—she gave me fruit from the tree, and so I ate it." The LORD God then asked the woman, "Why did you do such a thing?" The woman answered, "The serpent tricked me into it, so I ate it." Then the LORD God said to the serpent:

"Because you have done this, you shall be banned from all the animals and from all the wild creatures; On your belly shall you crawl, and dirt shall you eat all the days of your life. I will put enmity between you and the woman, and between your offspring and hers; He will strike at your head, while you strike at his heel."

The man called his wife Eve, because she became the mother of all the living.

ALTERNATIVE FIRST READING   *Acts 1:12-14*

After Jesus had been taken up to heaven, the Apostles returned to Jerusalem from the mount called Olivet, which is near Jerusalem, a sabbath day's journey away. When they entered the city they went to the upper room where they were staying, Peter and John and James and Andrew, Philip and Thomas, Bartholomew and Matthew, James son of Alphaeus, Simon the Zealot, and Judas son of James. All these devoted themselves with one accord to prayer, together with some women,

and Mary the mother of Jesus, and his brothers.

RESPONSORIAL PSALM   *Psalm 87:1-2, 3 and 5, 6-7*

R. (3) Glorious things are told of you, O city of God.

His foundation upon the holy mountains / the LORD loves: the gates of Zion, / more than any dwelling of Jacob .**R.**

Glorious things are said of you, / O city of God! / And of Zion they shall say: / "One and all were born in her; / And he who has established her / is the Most High LORD." **R.**

They shall note, when the peoples are enrolled: / "This man was born there." / And all shall sing, in their festive dance: / "My home is within you." **R.**

ALLELUIA

R. Alleluia, alleluia. O happy Virgin, you gave birth to the Lord; O blessed mother of the Church, you warm our hearts with the Spirit of your Son Jesus Christ. **R.**

GOSPEL   *Jn 19:25-34*

Standing by the cross of Jesus were his mother and his mother's sister, Mary the wife of Clopas, and Mary of Magdala. When Jesus saw his mother and the disciple there whom he loved, he said to his mother, *"Woman, behold, your son."* Then he said to the disciple, *"Behold, your mother."* And from that hour the disciple took her into his home.

After this, aware that everything was now finished, in order that the Scripture might be fulfilled, Jesus said, *"I thirst."* There was a vessel filled with common wine. So they put a sponge soaked in wine on a sprig of hyssop and put it up to his mouth. When Jesus had taken the wine, he said, *"It is finished."* And bowing his head, he handed over the spirit.

Now since it was preparation day, in order that the bodies might not remain on the cross on the sabbath, for the sabbath day of that week was a solemn one, the Jews asked Pilate that their legs be broken and they be taken down. So the soldiers came and broke the legs of the first and then of the other one who was crucified with Jesus. But when they came to Jesus and saw that he was already dead, they did not break his legs, but one soldier thrust his lance into his side, and immediately Blood and water flowed out.

JUNE 2, TUESDAY OF WEEK 9; ST. MARCELLINUS AND ST. PETER

FIRST READING   *2 Peter 3:12–15a, 17–18*

Beloved: Wait for and hasten the coming of the day of God, because of which the heavens will be dissolved in flames and the elements melted by fire. But according to his promise we await new heavens and a new earth in which righteousness dwells.

Therefore, beloved, since you await these things, be eager to be found without spot or blemish before him, at peace. And consider the patience of our Lord as salvation.

Therefore, beloved, since you are forewarned, be on your guard not to be led into the error of the unprincipled and to fall from your own stability. But grow in grace and in the knowledge of our Lord and savior Jesus Christ. To him be glory now and to the day of eternity. Amen.

RESPONSORIAL PSALM   *Psalm 90:2, 3–4, 10, 14 and 16*

R. (1) In every age, O Lord, you have been our refuge.

Before the mountains were begotten / and the earth and the world were brought forth, / from everlasting to everlasting you are God. **R.**

You turn man back to dust, saying, / "Return, O children of men." / For a thousand years in your sight are as yesterday, / now that it is past, or as a watch of the night. **R.**

Seventy is the sum of our years, / or eighty, if we are strong, / and most of them are fruitless toil, / for they pass quickly and we drift away. **R.**

Fill us at daybreak with your kindness, / that we may shout for joy and gladness all our days. / Let your work be seen by your servants / and your glory by their children. **R.**

ALLELUIA   *See Ephesians 1:17–18*

R. Alleluia, alleluia. May the Father of our Lord Jesus Christ enlighten the eyes of our hearts, that we may know what is the hope that belongs to his call. **R.**

GOSPEL   *Mark 12:13–17*

Some Pharisees and Herodians were sent to Jesus to ensnare him in his speech. They came and said to him, "Teacher, we know that you are a truthful man and that you are not concerned with anyone's opinion. You do not regard a person's status but teach the way of God in accordance with the truth. Is it lawful to pay the census tax to Caesar or not? Should we pay or should we not pay?" Knowing their hypocrisy he said to them, "Why are you testing me? Bring me a denarius to look at." They brought one to him and he said to them, "Whose image and inscription is this?" They replied to him, "Caesar's." So Jesus said to them, "Repay to Caesar what belongs to Caesar and to God what belongs to God." They were utterly amazed at him.

JUNE 3, WEDNESDAY OF WEEK 9; ST. CHARLES LWANGA & COMPANIONS

FIRST READING   *2nd Timothy 1:1–3, 6–12*

Paul, an Apostle of Christ Jesus by the will of God for the promise of life in Christ Jesus, to Timothy, my dear child: grace, mercy, and peace from God the Father and Christ Jesus our Lord.

I am grateful to God, whom I worship with a clear conscience as my ancestors did, as I remember you constantly in my prayers, night and day.

For this reason, I remind you to stir into flame the gift of God that you have through the imposition of my hands. For God did not give us a spirit of cowardice but rather of power and love and self–control. So do not be ashamed of your testimony to our Lord, nor of me, a prisoner for his sake; but bear your share of hardship for the Gospel with the strength that comes from God.

He saved us and called us to a holy life, not according to our works but according to his own design and the grace bestowed on us in Christ Jesus before time began, but now made manifest through the appearance of our savior Christ Jesus, who destroyed death and brought life and immortality to light through the Gospel, for which I was appointed preacher and Apostle and teacher. On this account I am suffering these things; but I am not ashamed, for I know him in whom I have believed and am confident that he is able to guard what has been entrusted to me until that day.

RESPONSORIAL PSALM   *Psalm 123:1b–2ab, 2cdef*

R. (1b) To you, O Lord, I lift up my eyes.

To you I lift up my eyes who are enthroned in heaven. / Behold, as the eyes of servants are on the hands of their masters. **R.**

As the eyes of a maid are on the hands of her mistress, / So are our eyes on the LORD, our God, / till he have pity on us. **R.**

ALLELUIA   *John 11:25a, 26*

R. Alleluia, alleluia. I am the resurrection and the life, says the Lord; whoever believes in me will never die. **R.**

GOSPEL   *Mark 12:18–27*

Some Sadducees, who say there is no resurrection, came to Jesus and put this question to him, saying, "Teacher, Moses wrote for us, 'If someone's brother dies, leaving a wife but no child, his brother must take the wife and raise up descendants for his brother.' Now there were seven brothers. The first married a woman and died, leaving no descendants. So the second brother married her and died, leaving no descendants, and the third likewise. And the seven left no descendants. Last of all the woman also died. At the resurrection when they arise whose wife will she be? For all seven had been married to her." Jesus said to them, "Are you not misled because you do not know the Scriptures or the power of God? When they rise from the dead, they neither marry nor are given in marriage, but they are like the angels in heaven.

As for the dead being raised, have you not read in the Book of Moses, in the passage about the bush, how God told him, *I am the God of Abraham, the God of Isaac, and the God of Jacob?* He is not God of the dead but of the living. You are greatly misled."

JUNE 4, THURSDAY OF WEEK 9; ST. FRANCIS CARACCIOLO

FIRST READING: *2nd Letter of Saint Paul to Timothy 2:8–15*

Beloved: Remember Jesus Christ, raised from the dead, a descendant of David: such is my Gospel, for which I am suffering, even to the point of chains, like a criminal. But the word of God is not chained. Therefore, I bear with everything for the sake of those who are chosen, so that they too may obtain the salvation that is in Christ Jesus, together with eternal glory. This saying is trustworthy:

If we have died with him we shall also live with him; if we persevere we shall also reign with him. But if we deny him he will deny us. If we are unfaithful he remains faithful, for he cannot deny himself.

Remind people of these things and charge them before God to stop disputing about words. This serves no useful purpose since it harms those who listen. Be eager to present yourself as acceptable to God, a workman who causes no disgrace, imparting the word of truth without deviation.

RESPONSORIAL PSALM   *Psalm 25:4–5ab, 8–9, 10 and 14*

R. (4) **Teach me your ways, O Lord.**

Your ways, O LORD, make known to me; / teach me your paths, / Guide me in your truth and teach me, / for you are God my savior. **R.**

Good and upright is the LORD; / thus he shows sinners the way. / He guides the humble to justice, / he teaches the humble his way. **R.**

All the paths of the LORD are kindness and constancy / toward those who keep his covenant and his decrees. / The friendship of the LORD is with those who fear him, / and his covenant, for their instruction. **R.**

ALLELUIA   *See 2 Timothy 1:10*

R. **Alleluia, alleluia.** Our Savior Jesus Christ has destroyed death and brought life to light through the Gospel. **R.**

GOSPEL

Mark 12:28–34

One of the scribes came to Jesus and asked him, "Which is the first of all the commandments?" Jesus replied, "The first is this:

Hear, O Israel! The Lord our God is Lord alone! You shall love the Lord your God with all your heart, with all your soul, with all your mind, and with all your strength.

The second is this: *You shall love your neighbor as yourself.*

There is no other commandment greater than these." The scribe said to him, "Well said, teacher. You are right in saying, *He is One and there is no other than he. And to love him with all your heart, with all your understanding, with all your strength, and to love your neighbor as yourself* is worth more than all burnt offerings and sacrifices."

And when Jesus saw that he answered with understanding, he said to him, "You are not far from the Kingdom of God." And no one dared to ask him any more questions.

JUNE 5, FRIDAY OF WEEK 9; ST. BONIFACE

FIRST READING: *2nd Letter of Saint Paul to Timothy 3:10–17*

You have followed my teaching, way of life, purpose, faith, patience, love, endurance, persecutions, and sufferings, such as happened to me in Antioch, Iconium, and Lystra, persecutions that I endured. Yet from all these things the Lord delivered me. In fact, all who want to live religiously in Christ Jesus will be persecuted. But wicked people and charlatans will go from bad to worse, deceivers and deceived. But you, remain faithful to what you have learned and believed, because you know from whom you learned it, and that from infancy you have known the sacred Scriptures, which are capable of giving you wisdom for salvation through faith in Christ Jesus. All Scripture is inspired by God and is useful for teaching, for refutation, for correction, and for training in righteousness, so that one who belongs to God may be competent, equipped for every good work.

RESPONSORIAL PSALM *Psalm 119:157, 160, 161, 165, 166, 168*

R. (165a) O Lord, great peace have they who love your law.

Though my persecutors and my foes are many, / I turn not away from your decrees. **R.**

Permanence is your word's chief trait; / each of your just ordinances is everlasting. **R.**

Princes persecute me without cause / but my heart stands in awe of your word. **R.**

Those who love your law have great peace, / and for them there is no stumbling block. **R.**

I wait for your salvation, O LORD, / and your commands I fulfill. **R.**

I keep your precepts and your decrees, / for all my ways are before you. **R.**

ALLELUIA *John 14:23*

R. Alleluia, alleluia. Whoever loves me will keep my word, and my Father will love him and we will come to him. **R.**

GOSPEL

Mark 12:35–37

As Jesus was teaching in the temple area he said, "How do the scribes claim that the Christ is the son of David? David himself, inspired by the Holy Spirit, said:

The Lord said to my lord, 'Sit at my right hand until I place your enemies under your feet.'

David himself calls him 'lord'; so how is he his son?" The great crowd heard this with delight.

JUNE 6, SATURDAY OF WEEK 9; ST. NORBERT

FIRST READING: *2nd Letter of Saint Paul to Timothy 4:1–8*

Beloved: I charge you in the presence of God and of Christ Jesus, who will judge the living and the dead, and by his appearing and his kingly power: proclaim the word; be persistent whether it is convenient or inconvenient; convince, reprimand, encourage through all patience and teaching. For the time will come when people will not tolerate sound doctrine but, following their own desires and insatiable curiosity, will accumulate teachers and will stop listening to the truth and will be diverted to myths. But you, be self–possessed in all circumstances; put up with hardship; perform the work of an evangelist; fulfill your ministry.

For I am already being poured out like a libation, and the time of my departure is at hand. I have competed well; I have finished the race; I have kept the faith. From now on the crown of righteousness awaits me, which the Lord, the just judge, will award to me on that day, and not only to me, but to all who have longed for his appearance.

RESPONSORIAL PSALM *Psalm 71:8–9, 14–15ab, 16–17, 22*

R. (see 15ab) **I will sing of your salvation.**

My mouth shall be filled with your praise, / with your glory day by day. / Cast me not off in my old age; / as my strength fails, forsake me not. **R.**

But I will always hope and praise you ever more and more. / My mouth shall declare your justice, / day by day your salvation. **R.**

I will treat of the mighty works of the Lord; / O GOD, I will tell of your singular justice. / O God, you have taught me from my youth, / and till the present I proclaim your wondrous deeds. **R.**

So will I give you thanks with music on the lyre, / for your faithfulness, O my God! / I will sing your praises with the harp, / O Holy One of Israel! **R.**

ALLELUIA *Matthew 5:3*

R. **Alleluia, alleluia.** Blessed are the poor in spirit; for theirs is the Kingdom of heaven. **R.**

GOSPEL *Mark 12:38–44*

In the course of his teaching Jesus said, "Beware of the scribes, who like to go around in long robes and accept greetings in the marketplaces, seats of honor in synagogues, and places of honor at banquets. They devour the houses of widows and, as a pretext, recite lengthy prayers. They will receive a very severe condemnation."

He sat down opposite the treasury and observed how the crowd put money into the treasury. Many rich people put in large sums. A poor widow also came and put in two small coins worth a few cents. Calling his disciples to himself, he said to them, "Amen, I say to you, this poor widow put in more than all the other contributors to the treasury. For they have all contributed from their surplus wealth, but she, from her poverty, has contributed all she had, her whole livelihood."

JUNE 7, SOLEMNITY OF THE MOST HOLY TRINITY; BLESSED ANNE GARCÍA

FIRST READING   *Exodus 34:4b—6, 8—9*

Early in the morning Moses went up Mount Sinai as the LORD had commanded him, taking along the two stone tablets.

Having come down in a cloud, the LORD stood with Moses there and proclaimed his name, "LORD." Thus the LORD passed before him and cried out, "The LORD, the LORD, a merciful and gracious God, slow to anger and rich in kindness and fidelity." Moses at once bowed down to the ground in worship. Then he said, "If I find favor with you, O LORD, do come along in our company. This is indeed a stiff–necked people; yet pardon our wickedness and sins, and receive us as your own."

RESPONSORIAL PSALM   *Daniel 3:52, 53, 54, 55, (52b)*

R. Glory and praise for ever!

Blessed are you, O Lord, the God of our fathers, / praiseworthy and exalted above all forever; / and blessed is your holy and glorious name, / praiseworthy and exalted above all for all ages. **R.**

Blessed are you in the temple of your holy glory, / praiseworthy and glorious above all forever. **R.**

Blessed are you on the throne of your kingdom, / praiseworthy and exalted above all forever. **R.**

Blessed are you who look into the depths from your throne upon the cherubim, / praiseworthy and exalted above all forever. **R.**

SECOND READING   *2 Corinthians 13:11—13*

Brothers and sisters, rejoice. Mend your ways, encourage one another, agree with one another, live in peace, and the God of love and peace will be with you. Greet one another with a holy kiss. All the holy ones greet you.

The grace of the Lord Jesus Christ and the love of God and the fellowship of the Holy Spirit be with all of you.

ALLELUIA   *see Revelation 1:8*

R. Alleluia, alleluia. Glory to the Father, the Son, and the Holy Spirit; to God who is, who was, and who is to come. **R.**

GOSPEL   *John 3:16—18*

God so loved the world that he gave his only Son, so that everyone who believes in him might not perish but might have eternal life. For God did not send his Son into the world to condemn the world, but that the world might be saved through him. Whoever believes in him will not be condemned, but whoever does not believe has already been condemned, because he has not believed in the name of the only Son of God.

JUNE 8, MONDAY OF WEEK 10; ST. WILLIAM OF YORK

FIRST READING *1 Kings 17:1–6*

Elijah the Tishbite, from Tishbe in Gilead, said to Ahab: "As the LORD, the God of Israel, lives, whom I serve, during these years there shall be no dew or rain except at my word." The LORD then said to Elijah: "Leave here, go east and hide in the Wadi Cherith, east of the Jordan. You shall drink of the stream, and I have commanded ravens to feed you there." So he left and did as the LORD had commanded. He went and remained by the Wadi Cherith, east of the Jordan. Ravens brought him bread and meat in the morning, and bread and meat in the evening, and he drank from the stream.

RESPONSORIAL PSALM *Psalm 121:1bc–2, 3–4, 5–6, 7–8*

R. (see 2) Our help is from the Lord, who made heaven and earth.

I lift up my eyes toward the mountains; / whence shall help come to me? / My help is from the LORD, / who made heaven and earth. **R.**

May he not suffer your foot to slip; / may he slumber not who guards you: / Indeed he neither slumbers nor sleeps, / the guardian of Israel. **R.**

The LORD is your guardian; the LORD is your shade; / he is beside you at your right hand. / The sun shall not harm you by day, / nor the moon by night. **R.**

The LORD will guard you from all evil; / he will guard your life. The LORD will guard your coming and your going, / both now and forever. **R.**

ALLELUIA *Matthew 5:12a*

R. Alleluia, alleluia. Rejoice and be glad; for your reward will be great in heaven. **R.**

GOSPEL *Matthew 5:1–12*

When Jesus saw the crowds, he went up the mountain, and after he had sat down, his disciples came to him. He began to teach them, saying:

"Blessed are the poor in spirit, for theirs is the Kingdom of heaven. Blessed are they who mourn, for they will be comforted. Blessed are the meek, for they will inherit the land. Blessed are they who hunger and thirst for righteousness, for they will be satisfied. Blessed are the merciful, for they will be shown mercy. Blessed are the clean of heart, for they will see God. Blessed are the peacemakers, for they will be called children of God. Blessed are they who are persecuted for the sake of righteousness, for theirs is the Kingdom of heaven. Blessed are you when they insult you and persecute you and utter every kind of evil against you falsely because of me. Rejoice and be glad, for your reward will be great in heaven.

JUNE 9, TUESDAY OF WEEK 10; ST. EPHREM

FIRST READING *1 Kings 17:7–16*

The brook near where Elijah was hiding ran dry, because no rain had fallen in the land. So the LORD said to Elijah: "Move on to Zarephath of Sidon and stay there. I have designated a widow there to provide for you." He left and went to Zarephath. As he arrived at the entrance of the city, a widow was gathering sticks there; he called out to her, "Please bring me a small cupful of water to drink." She left to get it, and he called out after her, "Please bring along a bit of bread." She answered, "As the LORD, your God, lives, I have nothing baked; there is only a handful of flour in my jar and a little oil in my jug. Just now I was collecting a couple of sticks, to go in and prepare something for myself and my son; when we have eaten it, we shall die." Elijah said to her, "Do not be afraid. Go and do as you propose. But first make me a little cake and bring it to me. Then you can prepare something for yourself and your son. For the LORD, the God of Israel, says, 'The jar of flour shall not go empty, nor the jug of oil run dry, until the day when the LORD sends rain upon the earth.'" She left and did as Elijah had said. She was able to eat for a year, and Elijah and her son as well; the jar of flour did not go empty, nor the jug of oil run dry, as the LORD had foretold through Elijah.

RESPONSORIAL PSALM   *Psalm 4:2–3, 4–5, 7b–8*
R. (7a) Lord, let your face shine on us.
When I call, answer me, O my just God, / you who relieve me when I am in distress; / Have pity on me, and hear my prayer! / Men of rank, how long will you be dull of heart? / Why do you love what is vain and seek after falsehood? **R.**
Know that the LORD does wonders for his faithful one; / the LORD will hear me when I call upon him. / Tremble, and sin not; / reflect, upon your beds, in silence. **R.**
O LORD, let the light of your countenance shine upon us! / You put gladness into my heart, / more than when grain and wine abound. **R.**

ALLELUIA   *Matthew 5:16*
R. Alleluia, alleluia. Let your light shine before others that they may see your good deeds and glorify your heavenly Father. **R.**

GOSPEL   *Matthew 5:13–16*
Jesus said to his disciples: "You are the salt of the earth. But if salt loses its taste, with what can it be seasoned? It is no longer good for anything but to be thrown out and trampled underfoot. You are the light of the world. A city set on a mountain cannot be hidden. Nor do they light a lamp and then put it under a bushel basket; it is set on a lampstand, where it gives light to all in the house. Just so, your light must shine before others, that they may see your good deeds and glorify your heavenly Father."
    Thus they persecuted the prophets who were before you."

JUNE 10, WEDNESDAY OF WEEK 10; BLESSED ANNA MARIA TAIGI
FIRST READING   *1 Kings 18:20–39*
Ahab sent to all the children of Israel and had the prophets assemble on Mount Carmel.
    Elijah appealed to all the people and said, "How long will you straddle the issue? If the LORD is God, follow him; if Baal, follow him." The people, however, did not answer him. So Elijah said to the people, "I am the only surviving prophet of the LORD, and there are four hundred and fifty prophets of Baal. Give us two young bulls. Let them choose one, cut it into pieces, and place it on the wood, but start no fire. I shall prepare the other and place

it on the wood, but shall start no fire. You shall call on your gods, and I will call on the LORD. The God who answers with fire is God." All the people answered, "Agreed!"

Elijah then said to the prophets of Baal, "Choose one young bull and prepare it first, for there are more of you. Call upon your gods, but do not start the fire." Taking the young bull that was turned over to them, they prepared it and called on Baal from morning to noon, saying, "Answer us, Baal!" But there was no sound, and no one answering. And they hopped around the altar they had prepared. When it was noon, Elijah taunted them: "Call louder, for he is a god and may be meditating, or may have retired, or may be on a journey. Perhaps he is asleep and must be awakened." They called out louder and slashed themselves with swords and spears, as was their custom, until blood gushed over them. Noon passed and they remained in a prophetic state until the time for offering sacrifice. But there was not a sound; no one answered, and no one was listening.

Then Elijah said to all the people, "Come here to me." When the people had done so, he repaired the altar of the LORD that had been destroyed. He took twelve stones, for the number of tribes of the sons of Jacob, to whom the LORD had said, "Your name shall be Israel." He built an altar in honor of the LORD with the stones, and made a trench around the altar large enough for two measures of grain.

When he had arranged the wood, he cut up the young bull and laid it on the wood. "Fill four jars with water," he said, "and pour it over the burnt offering and over the wood." "Do it again," he said, and they did it again. "Do it a third time," he said, and they did it a third time. The water flowed around the altar, and the trench was filled with the water.

At the time for offering sacrifice, the prophet Elijah came forward and said, "LORD, God of Abraham, Isaac, and Israel, let it be known this day that you are God in Israel and that I am your servant and have done all these things by your command. Answer me, LORD! Answer me, that this people may know that you, LORD, are God and that you have brought them back to their senses." The LORD's fire came down and consumed the burnt offering, wood, stones, and dust, and it lapped up the water in the trench. Seeing this, all the people fell prostrate and said, "The LORD is God! The LORD is God!"

RESPONSORIAL PSALM   *Psalm 16:1b–2ab, 4, 5ab and 8, 11*
R. (1b) Keep me safe, O God; you are my hope.
Keep me, O God, for in you I take refuge; / I say to the LORD, "My Lord are you." **R.**
They multiply their sorrows who court other gods. / Blood libations to them I will not pour out, / nor will I take their names upon my lips. **R.**
O LORD, my allotted portion and cup, / you it is who hold fast my lot. / I set the LORD ever before me; / with him at my right hand I shall not be disturbed. **R.**
You will show me the path to life, / fullness of joys in your presence, / the delights at your right hand forever. **R.**

ALLELUIA   *Psalm 25:4b, 5a*
R. Alleluia, alleluia. Teach me your paths, my God, and guide me in your truth. **R.**

GOSPEL *Matthew 5:17–19*

Jesus said to his disciples: "Do not think that I have come to abolish the law or the prophets. I have come not to abolish but to fulfill. Amen, I say to you, until heaven and earth pass away, not the smallest letter or the smallest part of a letter will pass from the law, until all things have taken place. Therefore, whoever breaks one of the least of these commandments and teaches others to do so will be called least in the Kingdom of heaven. But whoever obeys and teaches these commandments will be called greatest in the Kingdom of heaven."

JUNE 11, SAINT BARNABAS, APOSTLE; ST. BARNABAS

FIRST READING *Acts 11:21b–26; 13:1–3*

In those days a great number who believed turned to the Lord. The news about them reached the ears of the Church in Jerusalem, and they sent Barnabas to go to Antioch. When he arrived and saw the grace of God, he rejoiced and encouraged them all to remain faithful to the Lord in firmness of heart, for he was a good man, filled with the Holy Spirit and faith. And a large number of people was added to the Lord. Then he went to Tarsus to look for Saul, and when he had found him he brought him to Antioch. For a whole year they met with the Church and taught a large number of people, and it was in Antioch that the disciples were first called Christians.

Now there were in the Church at Antioch prophets and teachers: Barnabas, Symeon who was called Niger, Lucius of Cyrene, Manaen who was a close friend of Herod the tetrarch, and Saul. While they were worshiping the Lord and fasting, the Holy Spirit said, "Set apart for me Barnabas and Saul for the work to which I have called them." Then, completing their fasting and prayer, they laid hands on them and sent them off.

RESPONSORIAL PSALM *Psalm 98:1, 2–3ab, 3cd–4, 5–6*

R. (see 2b) The Lord has revealed to the nations his saving power.

Sing to the LORD a new song, / for he has done wondrous deeds; / His right hand has won victory for him, / his holy arm. **R.**

The LORD has made his salvation known: / in the sight of the nations he has revealed his justice. / He has remembered his kindness and his faithfulness / toward the house of Israel. **R.**

All the ends of the earth have seen / the salvation by our God. / Sing joyfully to the LORD, all you lands; / break into song; sing praise. **R.**

Sing praise to the LORD with the harp, / with the harp and melodious song. / With trumpets and the sound of the horn / sing joyfully before the King, the LORD. **R.**

ALLELUIA *Matthew 28:19a, 20b*

R. Alleluia, alleluia. Go and teach all nations, says the Lord; I am with you always, until the end of the world. **R.**

GOSPEL   *Matthew 5:20-26*

Jesus said to his disciples "You have heard that it was said to your ancestors, *'You shall not kill; and whoever kills will be liable to judgment.'* But I say to you, whoever is angry* with his brother will be liable to judgment, and whoever says to his brother, 'Raqa,' will be answerable to the Sanhedrin, and whoever says, 'You fool,' will be liable to fiery Gehenna. Therefore, if you bring your gift to the altar, and there recall that your brother has anything against you, leave your gift there at the altar, go first and be reconciled with your brother, and then come and offer your gift. Settle with your opponent quickly while on the way to court with him. Otherwise your opponent will hand you over to the judge, and the judge will hand you over to the guard, and you will be thrown into prison. Amen, I say to you, you will not be released until you have paid the last penny.

JUNE 12, FRIDAY OF WEEK 10; ST. JOHN GONZALEZ DE CASTRILLO

FIRST READING   *1 Kings 19:9a, 11–16*

At the mountain of God, Horeb, Elijah came to a cave, where he took shelter. But the word of the LORD came to him, "Go outside and stand on the mountain before the LORD; the LORD will be passing by." A strong and heavy wind was rending the mountains and crushing rocks before the LORDB but the LORD was not in the wind. After the wind there was an earthquakeB but the LORD was not in the earthquake. After the earthquake there was fireB but the LORD was not in the fire. After the fire there was a tiny whispering sound. When he heard this, Elijah hid his face in his cloak and went and stood at the entrance of the cave. A voice said to him, "Elijah, why are you here?" He replied, "I have been most zealous for the LORD, the God of hosts. But the children of Israel have forsaken your covenant, torn down your altars, and put your prophets to the sword. I alone am left, and they seek to take my life." The LORD said to him, "Go, take the road back to the desert near Damascus. When you arrive, you shall anoint Hazael as king of Aram. Then you shall anoint Jehu, son of Nimshi, as king of Israel, and Elisha, son of Shaphat of Abel–meholah, as prophet to succeed you."

RESPONSORIAL PSALM   *Psalm 27:7–8a, 8b–9abc, 13–14*

R. (8b) I long to see your face, O Lord.

Hear, O LORD, the sound of my call; / have pity on me, and answer me. / Of you my heart speaks; / you my glance seeks. **R.**

Your presence, O LORD, I seek. / Hide not your face from me; / do not in anger repel your servant. / You are my helper: cast me not off. **R.**

I believe that I shall see the bounty of the LORD/ in the land of the living. / Wait for the LORD with courage; / be stouthearted, and wait for the LORD. **R.**

ALLELUIA   *Philippians 2:15d, 16a*

R. Alleluia, alleluia. Shine like lights in the world, as you hold on to the word of life. **R.**

GOSPEL
Matthew 5:27–32

Jesus said to his disciples: "You have heard that it was said, you shall not commit adultery. But I say to you, everyone who looks at a woman with lust has already committed adultery with her in his heart. If your right eye causes you to sin, tear it out and throw it away. It is better for you to lose one of your members than to have your whole body thrown into Gehenna. And if your right hand causes you to sin, cut it off and throw it away. It is better for you to lose one of your members than to have your whole body go into Gehenna.

"It was also said, *Whoever divorces his wife must give her a bill of divorce.* But I say to you, whoever divorces his wife (unless the marriage is unlawful) causes her to commit adultery, and whoever marries a divorced woman commits adultery."

JUNE 13, SATURDAY OF WEEK 10; ST. ANTHONY OF PADUA

FIRST READING
1 Kings 19:19–21

Elijah set out, and came upon Elisha, son of Shaphat, as he was plowing with twelve yoke of oxen; he was following the twelfth. Elijah went over to him and threw his cloak over him. Elisha left the oxen, ran after Elijah, and said, "Please, let me kiss my father and mother goodbye, and I will follow you." Elijah answered, "Go back! Have I done anything to you?" Elisha left him and, taking the yoke of oxen, slaughtered them; he used the plowing equipment for fuel to boil their flesh, and gave it to his people to eat. Then he left and followed Elijah as his attendant.

RESPONSORIAL PSALM
Psalm 16:1b–2a and 5, 7–8, 9–10

R. (see 5a) You are my inheritance, O Lord.

Keep me, O God, for in you I take refuge; / I say to the LORD, "My Lord are you." / O LORD, my allotted portion and my cup, / you it is who hold fast my lot. R.

I bless the LORD who counsels me; / even in the night my heart exhorts me. / I set the LORD ever before me; / with him at my right hand I shall not be disturbed. R.

Therefore my heart is glad and my soul rejoices, / my body, too, abides in confidence; / because you will not abandon my soul to the nether world, / nor will you suffer your faithful one to undergo corruption. R.

ALLELUIA
Psalm 119:36a, 29b

R. Alleluia, alleluia. Incline my heart, O God, to your decrees; and favor me with your law. R.

GOSPEL
Matthew 5:33–37

Jesus said to his disciples: "You have heard that it was said to your ancestors, *do not take a false oath, but make good to the Lord all that you vow.* But I say to you, do not swear at all; not by heaven, for it is God's throne; nor by the earth, for it is his footstool; nor by Jerusalem, for it is the city of the great King. Do not swear by your head, for you cannot make a single hair white or black. Let your 'Yes' mean 'Yes,' and your 'No' mean 'No.' Anything more is from the Evil One."

JUNE 14, SOLEMNITY OF THE MOST HOLY BODY AND BLOOD OF CHRIST; ST. ANDREW FOURNET

FIRST READING *Deuteronomy 8:2—3, 14b—16a*

Moses said to the people: "Remember how for forty years now the LORD, your God, has directed all your journeying in the desert, so as to test you by affliction and find out whether or not it was your intention to keep his commandments. He therefore let you be afflicted with hunger, and then fed you with manna, a food unknown to you and your fathers, in order to show you that not by bread alone does one live, but by every word that comes forth from the mouth of the LORD.

"Do not forget the Lord, your God, who brought you out of the land of Egypt, that place of slavery; who guided you through the vast and terrible desert with its saraph serpents and scorpions, its parched and waterless ground; who brought forth water for you from the flinty rock and fed you in the desert with manna, a food unknown to your fathers."

RESPONSORIAL PSALM *Psalm 147:12—13, 14—15, 19—20 (12)*

R. Praise the Lord, Jerusalem. or R. Alleluia.

Glorify the LORD, O Jerusalem; / praise your God, O Zion. / For he has strengthened the bars of your gates; / he has blessed your children within you. **R.**

He has granted peace in your borders; / with the best of wheat he fills you. / He sends forth his command to the earth; / swiftly runs his word! **R.**

He has proclaimed his word to Jacob, / his statutes and his ordinances to Israel. / He has not done thus for any other nation; / his ordinances he has not made known to them. Alleluia. **R.**

SECOND READING *1 Corinthians 10:16—17*

Brothers and sisters: The cup of blessing that we bless, is it not a participation in the blood of Christ? The bread that we break, is it not a participation in the body of Christ? Because the loaf of bread is one, we, though many, are one body, for we all partake of the one loaf.

SEQUENCE – LAUDA SION

Laud, O Zion, your salvation, / Laud with hymns of exultation, / Christ, your king and shepherd true:

Bring him all the praise you know, / He is more than you bestow. / Never can you reach his due.

Special theme for glad thanksgiving / Is the quick'ning and the living / Bread today before you set:

From his hands of old partaken, / As we know, by faith unshaken, / Where the Twelve at supper met.

Full and clear ring out your chanting, / Joy nor sweetest grace be wanting, / From your heart let praises burst:

For today the feast is holden, / When the institution olden/ Of that supper was rehearsed.

Here the new law's new oblation, / By the new king's revelation, / Ends the form of ancient rite:

Now the new the old effaces, / Truth away the shadow chases, / Light dispels the gloom of night.

What he did at supper seated, / Christ ordained to be repeated, / His memorial ne'er to cease:

And his rule for guidance taking, / Bread and wine we hallow, making / Thus our sacrifice of peace.

This the truth each Christian learns, / Bread into his flesh he turns, / To his precious blood the wine:

Sight has fail'd, nor thought conceives, / But a dauntless faith believes, / Resting on a pow'r divine.

Here beneath these signs are hidden / Priceless things to sense forbidden; / Signs, not things are all we see:

Blood is poured and flesh is broken, / Yet in either wondrous token / Christ entire we know to be.

Whoso of this food partakes, / Does not rend the Lord nor breaks; / Christ is whole to all that taste:

Thousands are, as one, receivers, / One, as thousands of believers, / Eats of him who cannot waste.

Bad and good the feast are sharing, / Of what divers dooms preparing, / Endless death, or endless life.

Life to these, to those damnation, / See how like participation / Is with unlike issues rife.

When the sacrament is broken, / Doubt not, but believe 'tis spoken, / That each sever'd outward token / doth the very whole contain.

Nought the precious gift divides, / Breaking but the sign betides / Jesus still the same abides, / still unbroken does remain.

THE SHORTER FORM OF THE SEQUENCE BEGINS HERE

Lo! the angel's food is given / To the pilgrim who has striven; / see the children's bread from heaven, / which on dogs may not be spent.

Truth the ancient types fulfilling, / Isaac bound, a victim willing, / Paschal lamb, its lifeblood spilling, / manna to the fathers sent.

Very bread, good shepherd, tend us, / Jesus, of your love befriend us, / You refresh us, you defend us, / Your eternal goodness send us / In the land of life to see.

You who all things can and know, / Who on earth such food bestow, / Grant us with your saints, though lowest, / Where the heav'nly feast you show, / Fellow heirs and guests to be. Amen. Alleluia.

Alleluia   Jn 6:51
R. **Alleluia, alleluia.** I am the living bread that came down from heaven, says the Lord; whoever eats this bread will live forever. **R.**

GOSPEL   John 6:51—58
Jesus said to the Jewish crowds: "I am the living bread that came down from heaven; whoever eats this bread will live forever; and the bread that I will give is my flesh for the life of the world."

The Jews quarreled among themselves, saying, "How can this man give us his flesh to eat?" Jesus said to them, "Amen, amen, I say to you, unless you eat the flesh of the Son of Man and drink his blood, you do not have life within you. Whoever eats my flesh and drinks my blood has eternal life, and I will raise him on the last day. For my flesh is true food, and my blood is true drink. Whoever eats my flesh and drinks my blood remains in me and I in him. Just as the living Father sent me and I have life because of the Father, so also the one who feeds on me will have life because of me. This is the bread that came down from heaven. Unlike your ancestors who ate and still died, whoever eats this bread will live forever."

JUNE 15, MONDAY OF WEEK 11; ST. GERMAINE OF PIBRAC
FIRST READING   *1 Kings 21:1–16*
Naboth the Jezreelite had a vineyard in Jezreel next to the palace of Ahab, king of Samaria. Ahab said to Naboth, "Give me your vineyard to be my vegetable garden, since it is close by, next to my house. I will give you a better vineyard in exchange, or, if you prefer, I will give you its value in money." Naboth answered him, "The LORD forbid that I should give you my ancestral heritage." Ahab went home disturbed and angry at the answer Naboth the

Jezreelite had made to him: "I will not give you my ancestral heritage." Lying down on his bed, he turned away from food and would not eat.

His wife Jezebel came to him and said to him, "Why are you so angry that you will not eat?" He answered her, "Because I spoke to Naboth the Jezreelite and said to him, 'Sell me your vineyard, or, if you prefer, I will give you a vineyard in exchange.' But he refused to let me have his vineyard." His wife Jezebel said to him, "A fine ruler over Israel you are indeed! Get up. Eat and be cheerful. I will obtain the vineyard of Naboth the Jezreelite for you."

So she wrote letters in Ahab's name and, having sealed them with his seal, sent them to the elders and to the nobles who lived in the same city with Naboth. This is what she wrote in the letters: "Proclaim a fast and set Naboth at the head of the people. Next, get two scoundrels to face him and accuse him of having cursed God and king. Then take him out and stone him to death." His fellow citizensBthe elders and nobles who dwelt in his cityB did as Jezebel had ordered them in writing, through the letters she had sent them. They proclaimed a fast and placed Naboth at the head of the people. Two scoundrels came in and confronted him with the accusation, "Naboth has cursed God and king." And they led him out of the city and stoned him to death. Then they sent the information to Jezebel that Naboth had been stoned to death.

When Jezebel learned that Naboth had been stoned to death, she said to Ahab, "Go on, take possession of the vineyard of Naboth the Jezreelite that he refused to sell you, because Naboth is not alive, but dead." On hearing that Naboth was dead, Ahab started off on his way down to the vineyard of Naboth the Jezreelite, to take possession of it.

RESPONSORIAL PSALM   *Psalm 5:2–3ab, 4b–6a, 6b–7*
R. (2b) **Lord, listen to my groaning.**
Hearken to my words, O LORD, / attend to my sighing. / Heed my call for help, / my king and my God! **R.**
At dawn I bring my plea expectantly before you. / For you, O God, delight not in wickedness; / no evil man remains with you; / the arrogant may not stand in your sight. **R.**
You hate all evildoers. / You destroy all who speak falsehood; / The bloodthirsty and the deceitful / the LORD abhors. **R.**

ALLELUIA   *Psalm 119:105*
R. **Alleluia, alleluia.** A lamp to my feet is your word, a light to my path. **R.**

GOSPEL   *Matthew 5:38–42*
Jesus said to his disciples: "You have heard that it was said, *An eye for an eye and a tooth for a tooth*. But I say to you, offer no resistance to one who is evil. When someone strikes you on your right cheek, turn the other one to him as well. If anyone wants to go to law with you over your tunic, hand him your cloak as well. Should anyone press you into service for one mile, go with him for two miles. Give to the one who asks of you, and do not turn your back on one who wants to borrow."

JUNE 16, TUESDAY OF WEEK 11; ST. JOHN FRANCIS REGIS

FIRST READING   *1 Kings 21:17–29*

After the death of Naboth the LORD said to Elijah the Tishbite: "Start down to meet Ahab, king of Israel, who rules in Samaria. He will be in the vineyard of Naboth, of which he has come to take possession. This is what you shall tell him, 'The LORD says: After murdering, do you also take possession? For this, the LORD says: In the place where the dogs licked up the blood of Naboth, the dogs shall lick up your blood, too.'" Ahab said to Elijah, "Have you found me out, my enemy?" "Yes," he answered. "Because you have given yourself up to doing evil in the LORD's sight, I am bringing evil upon you: I will destroy you and will cut off every male in Ahab's line, whether slave or freeman, in Israel. I will make your house like that of Jeroboam, son of Nebat, and like that of Baasha, son of Ahijah, because of how you have provoked me by leading Israel into sin." (Against Jezebel, too, the LORD declared, "The dogs shall devour Jezebel in the district of Jezreel.") "When one of Ahab's line dies in the city, dogs will devour him; when one of them dies in the field, the birds of the sky will devour him." Indeed, no one gave himself up to the doing of evil in the sight of the LORD as did Ahab, urged on by his wife Jezebel. He became completely abominable by following idols, just as the Amorites had done, whom the LORD drove out before the children of Israel.

When Ahab heard these words, he tore his garments and put on sackcloth over his bare flesh. He fasted, slept in the sackcloth, and went about subdued. Then the LORD said to Elijah the Tishbite, "Have you seen that Ahab has humbled himself before me? Since he has humbled himself before me, I will not bring the evil in his time. I will bring the evil upon his house during the reign of his son."

RESPONSORIAL PSALM   *Psalm 51:3–4, 5–6ab, 11 and 16*

R. (see 3a) Be merciful, O Lord, for we have sinned.

Have mercy on me, O God, in your goodness; / in the greatness of your compassion wipe out my offense. / Thoroughly wash me from my guilt / and of my sin cleanse me. **R.**

For I acknowledge my offense, / and my sin is before me always: / Against you only have I sinned, / and done what is evil in your sight." **R.**

Turn away your face from my sins, / and blot out all my guilt. / Free me from blood guilt, O God, my saving God; / then my tongue shall revel in your justice. **R.**

ALLELUIA   *John 13:34*

R. Alleluia, alleluia. I give you a new commandment: love one another as I have loved you. **R.**

GOSPEL   *Matthew 5:43–48*

Jesus said to his disciples: "You have heard that it was said, *You shall love your neighbor and hate your enemy.* But I say to you, love your enemies and pray for those who persecute you, that you may be children of your heavenly Father, for he makes his sun rise on the bad and the good, and causes rain to fall on the just and the unjust. For if you love those who love you, what recompense will you have? Do not the tax collectors do the same? And if you greet your brothers only, what is unusual about that? Do not the pagans do the same? So be perfect, just as your heavenly Father is perfect."

JUNE 17, WEDNESDAY OF WEEK 11; ST. EMILY DE VIALAR

FIRST READING   *2 Kings 2:1, 6–14*

When the LORD was about to take Elijah up to heaven in a whirlwind, he and Elisha were on their way from Gilgal. Elijah said to Elisha, "Please stay here; the LORD has sent me on to the Jordan." "As the LORD lives, and as you yourself live, I will not leave you," Elisha replied. And so the two went on together. Fifty of the guild prophets followed and when the two stopped at the Jordan, they stood facing them at a distance. Elijah took his mantle, rolled it up and struck the water, which divided, and both crossed over on dry ground.

When they had crossed over, Elijah said to Elisha, "Ask for whatever I may do for you, before I am taken from you." Elisha answered, "May I receive a double portion of your spirit." "You have asked something that is not easy," Elijah replied. "Still, if you see me taken up from you, your wish will be granted; otherwise not." As they walked on conversing, a flaming chariot and flaming horses came between them, and Elijah went up to heaven in a whirlwind. When Elisha saw it happen he cried out, "My father! my father! Israel's chariots and drivers!" But when he could no longer see him, Elisha gripped his own garment and tore it in two.

Then he picked up Elijah's mantle that had fallen from him, and went back and stood at the bank of the Jordan. Wielding the mantle that had fallen from Elijah, Elisha struck the water in his turn and said, "Where is the LORD, the God of Elijah?" When Elisha struck the water it divided and he crossed over.

RESPONSORIAL PSALM   *Psalm 31:20, 21, 24*

R. (25) Let your hearts take comfort, all who hope in the Lord.

How great is the goodness, O LORD, / which you have in store for those who fear you, / and which, toward those who take refuge in you, / you show in the sight of the children of men. **R.**

You hide them in the shelter of your presence / from the plottings of men; / You screen them within your abode / from the strife of tongues. **R.**

Love the LORD, all you his faithful ones! / The LORD keeps those who are constant, / but more than requites those who act proudly. **R.**

ALLELUIA   *John 14:23*

R. Alleluia, alleluia. Whoever loves me will keep my word, and my Father will love him and we will come to him. **R.**

GOSPEL   *Matthew 6:1–6, 16–18*

Jesus said to his disciples: "Take care not to perform righteous deeds in order that people may see them; otherwise, you will have no recompense from your heavenly Father. When you give alms, do not blow a trumpet before you, as the hypocrites do in the synagogues and in the streets to win the praise of others. Amen, I say to you, they have received their reward. But when you give alms, do not let your left hand know what your right is doing, so that your almsgiving may be secret. And your Father who sees in secret will repay you.

"When you pray, do not be like the hypocrites, who love to stand and pray in the synagogues and on street corners so that others may see them. Amen, I say to you, they have received their reward. But when you pray, go to your inner room, close the door, and pray to your Father in secret. And your Father who sees in secret will repay you.

"When you fast, do not look gloomy like the hypocrites. They neglect their appearance, so that they may appear to others to be fasting. Amen, I say to you, they have received their reward. But when you fast, anoint your head and wash your face, so that you may not appear to others to be fasting, except to your Father who is hidden. And your Father who sees what is hidden will repay you."

JUNE 18, THURSDAY OF WEEK 11; ST. GREGORY BARBARIGO

FIRST READING *Sirach 48:1–14*

Like a fire there appeared the prophet Elijah whose words were as a flaming furnace. Their staff of bread he shattered, in his zeal he reduced them to straits; By the Lord's word he shut up the heavens and three times brought down fire. How awesome are you, Elijah, in your wondrous deeds! Whose glory is equal to yours? You brought a dead man back to life from the nether world, by the will of the LORD. You sent kings down to destruction, and easily broke their power into pieces. You brought down nobles, from their beds of sickness. You heard threats at Sinai, at Horeb avenging judgments. You anointed kings who should inflict vengeance, and a prophet as your successor. You were taken aloft in a whirlwind of fire, in a chariot with fiery horses. You were destined, it is written, in time to come to put an end to wrath before the day of the LORD, To turn back the hearts of fathers toward their sons, and to re–establish the tribes of Jacob. Blessed is he who shall have seen you And who falls asleep in your friendship. For we live only in our life, but after death our name will not be such. O Elijah, enveloped in the whirlwind!

Then Elisha, filled with the twofold portion of his spirit, wrought many marvels by his mere word. During his lifetime he feared no one, nor was any man able to intimidate his will. Nothing was beyond his power; beneath him flesh was brought back into life. In life he performed wonders, and after death, marvelous deeds.

RESPONSORIAL PSALM *Psalm 97:1–2, 3–4, 5–6, 7*

R. (12a) Rejoice in the Lord, you just!

The LORD is king; let the earth rejoice; / let the many isles be glad. / Clouds and darkness are round about him, / justice and judgment are the foundation of his throne. **R.**

Fire goes before him / and consumes his foes round about. / His lightnings illumine the world; / the earth sees and trembles. **R.**

The mountains melt like wax before the LORD, / before the Lord of all the earth. / The heavens proclaim his justice, / and all peoples see his glory. **R.**

All who worship graven things are put to shame, / who glory in the things of naught; / all gods are prostrate before him. **R.**

ALLELUIA   *Romans 8:15bc*

R. Alleluia, alleluia. You have received a spirit of adoption as sons through which we cry: Abba! Father! **R.**

GOSPEL   *Matthew 6:7–15*

Jesus said to his disciples: "In praying, do not babble like the pagans, who think that they will be heard because of their many words. Do not be like them. Your Father knows what you need before you ask him.

"This is how you are to pray:

'Our Father who art in heaven, hallowed be thy name, thy Kingdom come, thy will be done, on earth as it is in heaven. Give us this day our daily bread; and forgive us our trespasses, as we forgive those who trespass against us; and lead us not into temptation, but deliver us from evil.' "If you forgive others their transgressions, your heavenly Father will forgive you. But if you do not forgive others, neither will your Father forgive your transgressions".

JUNE 19, SOLEMNITY OF THE MOST SACRED HEART OF JESUS; ST. ROMUALD

FIRST READING   *Deuteronomy 7:6—11*

Moses said to the people: "You are a people sacred to the LORD, your God; he has chosen you from all the nations on the face of the earth to be a people peculiarly his own. It was not because you are the largest of all nations that the LORD set his heart on you and chose you, for you are really the smallest of all nations. It was because the LORD loved you and because of his fidelity to the oath he had sworn to your fathers, that he brought you out with his strong hand from the place of slavery, and ransomed you from the hand of Pharaoh, king of Egypt. Understand, then, that the LORD, your God, is God indeed, the faithful God who keeps his merciful covenant down to the thousandth generation toward those who love him and keep his commandments, but who repays with destruction a person who hates him; he does not dally with such a one, but makes them personally pay for it. You shall therefore carefully observe the commandments, the statutes and the decrees that I enjoin on you today."

RESPONSORIAL PSALM   *Psalm 103:1—2, 3—4, 6, 8, 10 (see 17)*

R. The Lord's kindness is everlasting to those who fear him.

Bless the LORD, O my soul; / all my being, bless his holy name. / Bless the LORD, O my soul; / and forget not all his benefits. **R.**

He pardons all your iniquities, / heals all your ills. He redeems your life from destruction, / crowns you with kindness and compassion. **R.**

Merciful and gracious is the LORD, / slow to anger and abounding in kindness. /

Not according to our sins does he deal with us, / nor does he requite us according to our crimes. **R.**

SECOND READING *1 John 4:7—16*

Beloved, let us love one another, because love is of God; everyone who loves is begotten by God and knows God. Whoever is without love does not know God, for God is love. In this way the love of God was revealed to us: God sent his only Son into the world so that we might have life through him. In this is love: not that we have loved God, but that he loved us and sent his Son as expiation for our sins. Beloved, if God so loved us, we also must love one another. No one has ever seen God. Yet, if we love one another, God remains in us, and his love is brought to perfection in us.

This is how we know that we remain in him and he in us, that he has given us of his Spirit. Moreover, we have seen and testify that the Father sent his Son as savior of the world. Whoever acknowledges that Jesus is the Son of God, God remains in him and he in God. We have come to know and to believe in the love God has for us.

God is love, and whoever remains in love remains in God and God in him.

ALLELUIA *Matthew 11:29ab*

R. Alleluia, alleluia. Take my yoke upon you, says the Lord; and learn from me, for I am meek and humble of heart. **R.**

GOSPEL *Matthew 11:25—30*

At that time Jesus exclaimed: "I give praise to you, Father, Lord of heaven and earth, for although you have hidden these things from the wise and the learned you have revealed them to little ones. Yes, Father, such has been your gracious will. All things have been handed over to me by my Father. No one knows the Son except the Father, and no one knows the Father except the Son and anyone to whom the Son wishes to reveal him.

"Come to me, all you who labor and are burdened, and I will give you rest. Take my yoke upon you and learn from me, for I am meek and humble of heart; and you will find rest for yourselves. For my yoke is easy, and my burden light."

JUNE 20, SATURDAY OF WEEK 11;
THE IMMACULATE HEART OF THE BLESSED VIRGIN MARY

FIRST READING *2 Chronicles 24:17–25*

After the death of Jehoiada, the princes of Judah came and paid homage to King Joash, and the king then listened to them. They forsook the temple of the LORD, the God of their fathers, and began to serve the sacred poles and the idols; and because of this crime of theirs, wrath came upon Judah and Jerusalem. Although prophets were sent to them to convert them to the LORD, the people would not listen to their warnings. Then the Spirit of God possessed Zechariah, son of Jehoiada the priest. He took his stand above the people and said to them: "God says, 'Why are you transgressing the LORD's commands, so that you cannot prosper? Because you have abandoned the LORD, he has abandoned you.'" But they conspired against him, and at the king's order they stoned him to death in the court of the LORD's temple. Thus King Joash was unmindful of the devotion shown him by Jehoiada, Zechariah's father, and slew his son. And as Zechariah was dying, he said, AMay the LORD see and avenge."

At the turn of the year a force of Arameans came up against Joash. They invaded Judah and Jerusalem, did away with all the princes of the people, and sent all their spoil to the king of Damascus. Though the Aramean force came with few men, the LORD surrendered a very large force into their power, because Judah had abandoned the LORD, the God of their fathers. So punishment was meted out to Joash. After the Arameans had departed from him, leaving him in grievous suffering, his servants conspired against him because of the murder of the son of Jehoiada the priest. He was buried in the City of David, but not in the tombs of the kings.

RESPONSORIAL PSALM   *Psalm 89:4–5, 29–30, 31–32, 33–34*
R. (29a) For ever I will maintain my love for my servant.
"I have made a covenant with my chosen one, / I have sworn to David my servant: / Forever will I confirm your posterity / and establish your throne for all generations." **R.**
"Forever I will maintain my kindness toward him, / and my covenant with him stands firm. / I will make his posterity endure forever / and his throne as the days of heaven." **R.**
"If his sons forsake my law and walk not according to my ordinances, / If they violate my statutes and keep not my commands." **R.**
"I will punish their crime with a rod / and their guilt with stripes. / Yet my mercy I will not take from him, / nor will I belie my faithfulness." **R.**

ALLELUIA   *2 Corinthians 8:9*
R. Alleluia, alleluia. Jesus Christ became poor although he was rich, so that by his poverty you might become rich. **R.**

GOSPEL   Luke *2:41–55*
Each year Jesus' parents went to Jerusalem for the feast of Passover, and when he was twelve years old, they went up according to festival custom. After they had completed its days, as they were returning, the boy Jesus remained behind in Jerusalem, but his parents did not know it. Thinking that he was in the caravan, they journeyed for a day and looked for him among their relatives and acquaintances, but not finding him, they returned to Jerusalem to look for him. After three days they found him in the temple, sitting in the midst of the teachers, listening to them and asking them questions, and all who heard him were astounded at his understanding and his answers. When his parents saw him, they were astonished, and his mother said to him, "Son, why have you done this to us? Your father and I have been looking for you with great anxiety." And he said to them, "Why were you looking for me? Did you not know that I must be in my Father's house?" But they did not understand what he said to them. He went down with them and came to Nazareth, and was obedient to them; and his mother kept all these things in her heart.

JUNE 21, 12TH SUNDAY IN ORDINARY TIME; ST. ALOYSIUS GONZAGA
FIRST READING   *Jeremiah 20:10—13*
Jeremiah said: "I hear the whisperings of many: 'Terror on every side! Denounce! let us denounce him!' All those who were my friends are on the watch for any misstep of mine. 'Perhaps he will be trapped; then we can prevail, and take our vengeance on him.' But the

LORD is with me, like a mighty champion: my persecutors will stumble, they will not triumph. In their failure they will be put to utter shame, to lasting, unforgettable confusion. O LORD of hosts, you who test the just, who probe mind and heart, let me witness the vengeance you take on them, for to you I have entrusted my cause. Sing to the LORD, praise the LORD, for he has rescued the life of the poor from the power of the wicked!"

RESPONSORIAL PSALM
Psalm 69:8—10, 14, 17, 33—35 (14c)

R. Lord, in your great love, answer me.
For your sake I bear insult, **/** and shame covers my face. **/** I have become an outcast to my brothers, **/** a stranger to my children, **/** because zeal for your house consumes me, **/** and the insults of those who blaspheme you fall upon me. **R.**

I pray to you, O LORD, **/** for the time of your favor, O God! **/** In your great kindness **/** answer me with your constant help. **/** Answer me, O LORD, **/** for bounteous is your kindness; **/** in your great mercy turn toward me. **R.**

"See, you lowly ones, and be glad; **/** you who seek God, may your hearts revive! **/** For the LORD hears the poor, **/** and his own who are in bonds he spurns not. **/** Let the heavens and the earth praise him, **/** the seas and whatever moves in them!" **R.**

SECOND READING
Romans 5:12—15

Brothers and sisters: Through one man sin entered the world, and through sin, death, and thus death came to all men, inasmuch as all sinned— for up to the time of the law, sin was in the world, though sin is not accounted when there is no law. But death reigned from Adam to Moses, even over those who did not sin after the pattern of the trespass of Adam, who is the type of the one who was to come.

But the gift is not like the transgression. For if by the transgression of the one the many died, how much more did the grace of God and the gracious gift of the one man Jesus Christ overflow for the many.

ALLELUIA
John 15:26b, 27a

R. Alleluia, alleluia. The Spirit of truth will testify to me, says the Lord; and you also will testify. **R.**

GOSPEL
Matthew 10:26—33

Jesus said to the Twelve: "Fear no one. Nothing is concealed that will not be revealed, nor secret that will not be known. What I say to you in the darkness, speak in the light; what you hear whispered, proclaim on the housetops. And do not be afraid of those who kill the body but cannot kill the soul; rather, be afraid of the one who can destroy both soul and body in Gehenna. Are not two sparrows sold for a small coin? Yet not one of them falls to the ground without your Father's knowledge. Even all the hairs of your head are counted. So do not be afraid; you are worth more than many sparrows. Everyone who acknowledges me before others I will acknowledge before my heavenly Father. But whoever denies me before others, I will deny before my heavenly Father."

JUNE 22, MONDAY OF WEEK 12;
ST. PAULINUS OF NOLA; ST. JOHN FISHER AND ST. THOMAS MORE

FIRST READING   *2 Kings 17:5–8, 13–15a, 18*

Shalmaneser, king of Assyria, occupied the whole land and attacked Samaria, which he besieged for three years. In the ninth year of Hoshea, king of Israel the king of Assyria took Samaria, and deported the children of Israel to Assyria, setting them in Halah, at the Habor, a river of Gozan, and the cities of the Medes.

This came about because the children of Israel sinned against the LORD, their God, who had brought them up from the land of Egypt, from under the domination of Pharaoh, king of Egypt, and because they venerated other gods. They followed the rites of the nations whom the LORD had cleared out of the way of the children of Israel and the kings of Israel whom they set up.

And though the LORD warned Israel and Judah by every prophet and seer, "Give up your evil ways and keep my commandments and statutes, in accordance with the entire law which I enjoined on your fathers and which I sent you by my servants the prophets," they did not listen, but were as stiff–necked as their fathers, who had not believed in the LORD, their God. They rejected his statutes, the covenant which he had made with their fathers, and the warnings which he had given them, till, in his great anger against Israel, the LORD put them away out of his sight. Only the tribe of Judah was left.

RESPONSORIAL PSALM   *Psalm 60:3, 4–5, 12–13*

R. (7b) Help us with your right hand, O Lord, and answer us.
O God, you have rejected us and broken our defenses; **/** you have been angry; rally us! **R.**
You have rocked the country and split it open; **/** repair the cracks in it, for it is tottering. **/**
You have made your people feel hardships; **/** you have given us stupefying wine. **R.**
Have not you, O God, rejected us, **/** so that you go not forth, O God, with our armies? Give us aid against the foe, **/** for worthless is the help of men. **R.**

ALLELUIA   *Hebrews 4:12*

R. Alleluia, alleluia. The word of God is living and effective, able to discern reflections and thoughts of the heart. **R.**

GOSPEL   *Matthew 7:1–5*

Jesus said to his disciples: "Stop judging, that you may not be judged. For as you judge, so will you be judged, and the measure with which you measure will be measured out to you. Why do you notice the splinter in your brother's eye, but do not perceive the wooden beam in your own eye? How can you say to your brother, 'Let me remove that splinter from your eye,' while the wooden beam is in your eye? You hypocrite, remove the wooden beam from your eye first; then you will see clearly to remove the splinter from your brother's eye."

JUNE 23, TUESDAY OF WEEK 12; ST. JOSEPH CAFASSO

FIRST READING   *2 Kings 19:9b–11, 14–21, 31–35a, 36*

Sennacherib, king of Assyria, sent envoys to Hezekiah with this message: "Thus shall you say to Hezekiah, king of Judah: 'Do not let your God on whom you rely deceive you by saying that Jerusalem will not be handed over to the king of Assyria. You have heard what the kings of Assyria have done to all other countries: they doomed them! Will you, then, be saved?'"

Hezekiah took the letter from the hand of the messengers and read it; then he went up to the temple of the LORD, and spreading it out before him, he prayed in the LORD's presence: "O LORD, God of Israel, enthroned upon the cherubim! You alone are God over all the kingdoms of the earth. You have made the heavens and the earth. Incline your ear, O LORD, and listen! Open your eyes, O LORD, and see! Hear the words of Sennacherib which he sent to taunt the living God. Truly, O LORD, the kings of Assyria have laid waste the nations and their lands, and cast their gods into the fire; they destroyed them because they were not gods, but the work of human hands, wood and stone. Therefore, O LORD, our God, save us from the power of this man, that all the kingdoms of the earth may know that you alone, O LORD, are God."

Then Isaiah, son of Amoz, sent this message to Hezekiah: "Thus says the LORD, the God of Israel, in answer to your prayer for help against Sennacherib, king of Assyria: I have listened! This is the word the LORD has spoken concerning him:

"'She despises you, laughs you to scorn, the virgin daughter Zion! Behind you she wags her head, daughter Jerusalem.

"'For out of Jerusalem shall come a remnant, and from Mount Zion, survivors. The zeal of the LORD of hosts shall do this.'

"Therefore, thus says the LORD concerning the king of Assyria: 'He shall not reach this city, nor shoot an arrow at it, nor come before it with a shield, nor cast up siege–works against it. He shall return by the same way he came, without entering the city, says the LORD. I will shield and save this city for my own sake, and for the sake of my servant David.'"

That night the angel of the LORD went forth and struck down one hundred and eighty–five thousand men in the Assyrian camp. So Sennacherib, the king of Assyria, broke camp, and went back home to Nineveh.

RESPONSORIAL PSALM   *Psalm 48:2–3ab, 3cd–4, 10–11*

R. (see 9d) God upholds his city for ever.

Great is the LORD and wholly to be praised / in the city of our God. / His holy mountain, fairest of heights, / is the joy of all the earth. **R.**

Mount Zion, the recesses of the North," / is the city of the great King. / God is with her castles; / renowned is he as a stronghold. **R.**

O God, we ponder your mercy within your temple. / As your name, O God, so also your praise reaches to the ends of the earth. / Of justice your right hand is full. **R.**

ALLELUIA   *John 8:12*

R. Alleluia, alleluia. I am the light of the world, says the Lord; whoever follows me will have the light of life. **R.**

GOSPEL   *Matthew 7:6, 12–14*
Jesus said to his disciples: "Do not give what is holy to dogs, or throw your pearls before swine, lest they trample them underfoot, and turn and tear you to pieces." Do to others whatever you would have them do to you. This is the Law and the Prophets.

"Enter through the narrow gate; for the gate is wide and the road broad that leads to destruction, and those who enter through it are many. How narrow the gate and constricted the road that leads to life. And those who find it are few."

JUNE 24, THE NATIVITY OF SAINT JOHN THE BAPTIST – SOLEMNITY

AT THE VIGIL MASS
FIRST READING   *Jeremiah 1:4—10*
In the days of King Josiah, the word of the LORD came to me, saying:

Before I formed you in the womb I knew you, before you were born I dedicated you, a prophet to the nations I appointed you.

"Ah, Lord GOD!" I said, "I know not how to speak; I am too young." But the LORD answered me, Say not, "I am too young." To whomever I send you, you shall go; whatever I command you, you shall speak. Have no fear before them, because I am with you to deliver you, says the LORD.

Then the LORD extended his hand and touched my mouth, saying, See, I place my words in your mouth! This day I set you over nations and over kingdoms, to root up and to tear down, to destroy and to demolish, to build and to plant.

RESPONSORIAL PSALM   *Psalm 71:1—2, 3—4a, 5—6ab, 15ab, 17 (6)*
R. Since my mother's womb, you have been my strength.
In you, O LORD, I take refuge; **/** let me never be put to shame. **/** In your justice rescue me, and deliver me; **/** incline your ear to me, and save me. **R.**
Be my rock of refuge, **/** a stronghold to give me safety, **/** for you are my rock and my fortress. **/** O my God, rescue me from the hand of the wicked. **R.**
For you are my hope, O LORD; **/** my trust, O LORD, from my youth. **/** On you I depend from birth; **/** from my mother's womb you are my strength. **R.**
My mouth shall declare your justice, **/** day by day your salvation. **/** O God, you have taught me from my youth, **/** and till the present I proclaim your wondrous deeds. **R.**

SECOND READING   *1 Peter 1:8—12*
Beloved: Although you have not seen Jesus Christ you love him; even though you do not see him now yet believe in him, you rejoice with an indescribable and glorious joy, as you attain the goal of your faith, the salvation of your souls.

Concerning this salvation, prophets who prophesied about the grace that was to be yours searched and investigated it, investigating the time and circumstances that the Spirit of Christ within them indicated when he testified in advance to the sufferings destined for Christ and the glories to follow them. It was revealed to them that they were serving not themselves but you with regard to the things that have now been announced to you by those who preached the Good News to you through the Holy Spirit sent from heaven, things into which angels longed to look.

ALLELUIA   *see John 1:7; Luke 1:17*

R. Alleluia, alleluia. He came to testify to the light, to prepare a people fit for the Lord. **R.**

GOSPEL   *Luke 1:5—17*

In the days of Herod, King of Judea, there was a priest named Zechariah of the priestly division of Abijah; his wife was from the daughters of Aaron, and her name was Elizabeth. Both were righteous in the eyes of God, observing all the commandments and ordinances of the Lord blamelessly. But they had no child, because Elizabeth was barren and both were advanced in years. Once when he was serving as priest in his division's turn before God, according to the practice of the priestly service, he was chosen by lot to enter the sanctuary of the Lord to burn incense. Then, when the whole assembly of the people was praying outside at the hour of the incense offering, the angel of the Lord appeared to him, standing at the right of the altar of incense. Zechariah was troubled by what he saw, and fear came upon him. But the angel said to him, "Do not be afraid, Zechariah, because your prayer has been heard. Your wife Elizabeth will bear you a son, and you shall name him John. And you will have joy and gladness, and many will rejoice at his birth, for he will be great in the sight of the Lord. John will drink neither wine nor strong drink. He will be filled with the Holy Spirit even from his mother's womb, and he will turn many of the children of Israel to the Lord their God. He will go before him in the spirit and power of Elijah to turn their hearts toward their children and the disobedient to the understanding of the righteous, to prepare a people fit for the Lord."

MASS DURING THE DAY

FIRST READING   *Isaiah 49:1—6*

Hear me, O coastlands, listen, O distant peoples. The LORD called me from birth, from my mother's womb he gave me my name. He made of me a sharp—edged sword and concealed me in the shadow of his arm. He made me a polished arrow, in his quiver he hid me. You are my servant, he said to me, Israel, through whom I show my glory.

Though I thought I had toiled in vain, and for nothing, uselessly, spent my strength, yet my reward is with the LORD, my recompense is with my God. For now the LORD has spoken who formed me as his servant from the womb, that Jacob may be brought back to him and Israel gathered to him; and I am made glorious in the sight of the LORD, and my God is now my strength! It is too little, he says, for you to be my servant, to raise up the tribes of Jacob, and restore the survivors of Israel; I will make you a light to the nations, that my salvation may reach to the ends of the earth.

RESPONSORIAL PSALM   *Psalm 139:1b—3, 13—14ab, 14c—15 (14)*

R. I praise you, for I am wonderfully made.

O LORD, you have probed me, you know me: / you know when I sit and when I stand; / you understand my thoughts from afar. / My journeys and my rest you scrutinize, / with all my ways you are familiar. **R.**

Truly you have formed my inmost being; / you knit me in my mother's womb. / I give you thanks that I am fearfully, wonderfully made; / wonderful are your works. **R.**

My soul also you knew full well; / nor was my frame unknown to you / When I was made in secret, / when I was fashioned in the depths of the earth. **R.**

SECOND READING   *Acts 13:22—26*

In those days, Paul said: "God raised up David as king; of him God testified, *I have found David, son of Jesse, a man after my own heart; he will carry out my every wish.* From this man's descendants God, according to his promise, has brought to Israel a savior, Jesus. John heralded his coming by proclaiming a baptism of repentance to all the people of Israel; and as John was completing his course, he would say, 'What do you suppose that I am? I am not he. Behold, one is coming after me; I am not worthy to unfasten the sandals of his feet.'

"My brothers, sons of the family of Abraham, and those others among you who are God—fearing, to us this word of salvation has been sent."

ALLELUIA   *see Luke 1:76*

R. Alleluia, alleluia. You, child, will be called prophet of the Most High, for you will go before the Lord to prepare his way. **R.**

GOSPEL   *Luke 1:57—66, 80*

When the time arrived for Elizabeth to have her child she gave birth to a son. Her neighbors and relatives heard that the Lord had shown his great mercy toward her, and they rejoiced with her. When they came on the eighth day to circumcise the child, they were going to call him Zechariah after his father, but his mother said in reply, "No. He will be called John." But they answered her, "There is no one among your relatives who has this name." So they made signs, asking his father what he wished him to be called. He asked for a tablet and wrote, "John is his name," and all were amazed. Immediately his mouth was opened, his tongue freed, and he spoke blessing God. Then fear came upon all their neighbors, and all these matters were discussed throughout the hill country of Judea. All who heard these things took them to heart, saying, "What, then, will this child be?" For surely the hand of the Lord was with him. The child grew and became strong in spirit, and he was in the desert until the day of his manifestation to Israel.

JUNE 25, THURSDAY OF WEEK 12; ST. WILLIAM OF VERCELLI

FIRST READING   *2 Kings 24:8–17*

Jehoiachin was eighteen years old when he began to reign, and he reigned three months in Jerusalem. His mother's name was Nehushta, daughter of Elnathan of Jerusalem. He did evil in the sight of the LORD, just as his forebears had done.

At that time the officials of Nebuchadnezzar, king of Babylon, attacked Jerusalem, and the city came under siege. Nebuchadnezzar, king of Babylon, himself arrived at the city while his servants were besieging it. Then Jehoiachin, king of Judah, together with his mother, his ministers, officers, and functionaries, surrendered to the king of Babylon, who, in the eighth year of his reign, took him captive. And he carried off all the treasures of the temple of the LORD and those of the palace, and broke up all the gold utensils that Solomon, king of Israel, had provided in the temple of the LORD, as the LORD had foretold. He deported all Jerusalem: all the officers and men of the army, ten thousand in number, and all the craftsmen and smiths. None were left among the people of the land except the poor. He deported Jehoiachin to Babylon, and also led captive from Jerusalem to Babylon the king's mother and wives, his functionaries, and the chief men of the land. The king of Babylon also led captive to Babylon all seven thousand men of the army, and a thousand craftsmen and smiths, all of them trained soldiers. In place of Jehoiachin, the king of Babylon appointed his uncle Mattaniah king, and changed his name to Zedekiah.

RESPONSORIAL PSALM   *Psalm 79:1b–2, 3–5, 8, 9*
R. (9) For the glory of your name, O Lord, deliver us.
O God, the nations have come into your inheritance; / they have defiled your holy temple, / they have laid Jerusalem in ruins. / They have given the corpses of your servants as food to the birds of heaven, / the flesh of your faithful ones to the beasts of the earth. **R.**
They have poured out their blood like water round about Jerusalem, / and there is no one to bury them. / We have become the reproach of our neighbors, / the scorn and derision of those around us. / O LORD, how long? / Will you be angry forever? / Will your jealousy burn like fire? **R.**
Remember not against us the iniquities of the past; / may your compassion quickly come to us, / for we are brought very low. **R.**
Help us, O God our savior, / because of the glory of your name; / Deliver us and pardon our sins for your name's sake. **R.**

ALLELUIA   *John 14:23*
R. Alleluia, alleluia. Whoever loves me will keep my word, and my Father will love him and we will come to him. **R.**

GOSPEL   *Matthew 7:21–29*
Jesus said to his disciples: "Not everyone who says to me, 'Lord, Lord,' will enter the Kingdom of heaven, but only the one who does the will of my Father in heaven. Many will say to me on that day, 'Lord, Lord, did we not prophesy in your name? Did we not drive out demons in your name? Did we not do mighty deeds in your name?' Then I will declare to them solemnly, 'I never knew you. Depart from me, you evildoers.'

"Everyone who listens to these words of mine and acts on them will be like a wise man who built his house on rock. The rain fell, the floods came, and the winds blew and buffeted the house. But it did not collapse; it had been set solidly on rock. And everyone who listens to these words of mine but does not act on them will be like a fool who built his house on sand. The rain fell, the floods came, and the winds blew and buffeted the house. And it collapsed and was completely ruined."

When Jesus finished these words, the crowds were astonished at his teaching, for he taught them as one having authority, and not as their scribes.

JUNE 26, FRIDAY OF WEEK 12; ST. JOSEMARÍA ESCRIVÁ

FIRST READING   *2 Kings 25:1–12*

In the tenth month of the ninth year of Zedekiah's reign, on the tenth day of the month, Nebuchadnezzar, king of Babylon, and his whole army advanced against Jerusalem, encamped around it, and built siege walls on every side. The siege of the city continued until the eleventh year of Zedekiah. On the ninth day of the fourth month, when famine had gripped the city, and the people had no more bread, the city walls were breached. Then the king and all the soldiers left the city by night through the gate between the two walls that was near the king's garden. Since the Chaldeans had the city surrounded, they went in the direction of the Arabah. But the Chaldean army pursued the king and overtook him in the desert near Jericho, abandoned by his whole army.

The king was therefore arrested and brought to Riblah to the king of Babylon, who pronounced sentence on him. He had Zedekiah's sons slain before his eyes. Then he blinded Zedekiah, bound him with fetters, and had him brought to Babylon.

On the seventh day of the fifth month (this was in the nineteenth year of Nebuchadnezzar, king of Babylon), Nebuzaradan, captain of the bodyguard, came to Jerusalem as the representative of the king of Babylon. He burned the house of the LORD, the palace of the king, and all the houses of Jerusalem; every large building was destroyed by fire. Then the Chaldean troops who were with the captain of the guard tore down the walls that surrounded Jerusalem.

Then Nebuzaradan, captain of the guard, led into exile the last of the people remaining in the city, and those who had deserted to the king of Babylon, and the last of the artisans. But some of the country's poor, Nebuzaradan, captain of the guard, left behind as vinedressers and farmers.

RESPONSORIAL PSALM   *Psalm 137:1–2, 3, 4–5, 6*

R. (6ab) **Let my tongue be silenced, if I ever forget you!**

By the streams of Babylon we sat and wept / when we remembered Zion. / On the aspens of that land / we hung up our harps. **R.**

Though there our captors asked of us the lyrics of our songs, / And our despoilers urged us to be joyous: / "Sing for us the songs of Zion!" **R.**

How could we sing a song of the LORD / in a foreign land? / If I forget you, Jerusalem, / may my right hand be forgotten! **R.**

May my tongue cleave to my palate / if I remember you not, / If I place not Jerusalem ahead of my joy. **R.**

ALLELUIA   *Matthew 8:17*

R. **Alleluia, alleluia.** Christ took away our infirmities and bore our diseases. **R.**

GOSPEL   *Matthew 8:1–4*

When Jesus came down from the mountain, great crowds followed him. And then a leper approached, did him homage, and said, "Lord, if you wish, you can make me clean." He stretched out his hand, touched him, and said, "I will do it. Be made clean." His leprosy was cleansed immediately. Then Jesus said to him, "See that you tell no one, but go show yourself to the priest, and offer the gift that Moses prescribed; that will be proof for them."

JUNE 27, SATURDAY OF WEEK 12; ST. CYRIL OF ALEXANDRIA

FIRST READING   *Lamentations 2:2, 10–14, 18–19*

The Lord has consumed without pity all the dwellings of Jacob; He has torn down in his anger the fortresses of daughter Judah; He has brought to the ground in dishonor her king and her princes.

On the ground in silence sit the old men of daughter Zion; They strew dust on their heads and gird themselves with sackcloth; The maidens of Jerusalem bow their heads to the ground.

Worn out from weeping are my eyes, within me all is in ferment; My gall is poured out on the ground because of the downfall of the daughter of my people, As child and infant faint away in the open spaces of the town.

In vain they ask their mothers, "Where is the grain?" As they faint away like the wounded in the streets of the city, And breathe their last in their mothers' arms.

To what can I liken or compare you, O daughter Jerusalem? What example can I show you for your comfort, virgin daughter Zion? For great as the sea is your downfall; who can heal you?

Your prophets had for you false and specious visions; They did not lay bare your guilt, to avert your fate; They beheld for you in vision false and misleading portents.

Cry out to the Lord; moan, O daughter Zion! Let your tears flow like a torrent day and night; Let there be no respite for you, no repose for your eyes.

Rise up, shrill in the night, at the beginning of every watch; Pour out your heart like water in the presence of the Lord; Lift up your hands to him for the lives of your little ones Who faint from hunger at the corner of every street.

RESPONSORIAL PSALM   *Psalm 74:1b–2, 3–5, 6–7, 20–21*

R. (19b) Lord, forget not the souls of your poor ones.

Why, O God, have you cast us off forever? / Why does your anger smolder against the sheep of your pasture? / Remember your flock which you built up of old, / the tribe you redeemed as your inheritance, / Mount Zion, where you took up your abode. **R.**

Turn your steps toward the utter ruins; / toward all the damage the enemy has done in the sanctuary. / Your foes roar triumphantly in your shrine; / they have set up their tokens of victory. / They are like men coming up with axes to a clump of trees. **R.**

With chisel and hammer they hack at all the paneling of the sanctuary. They set your sanctuary on fire; the place where your name abides they have razed and profaned. **R.**

Look to your covenant, for the hiding places in the land and the plains are full of violence. May the humble not retire in confusion; may the afflicted and the poor praise your name. **R.**

ALLELUIA *Matthew 8:17*

R. Alleluia, alleluia. Christ took away our infirmities and bore our diseases. **R.**

GOSPEL *Matthew 8:5–17*

When Jesus entered Capernaum, a centurion approached him and appealed to him, saying, "Lord, my servant is lying at home paralyzed, suffering dreadfully." He said to him, "I will come and cure him." The centurion said in reply, "Lord, I am not worthy to have you enter under my roof; only say the word and my servant will be healed. For I too am a man subject to authority, with soldiers subject to me. And I say to one, 'Go,' and he goes; and to another, 'Come here,' and he comes; and to my slave, 'Do this,' and he does it." When Jesus heard this, he was amazed and said to those following him, "Amen, I say to you, in no one in Israel have I found such faith. I say to you, many will come from the east and the west, and will recline with Abraham, Isaac, and Jacob at the banquet in the Kingdom of heaven, but the children of the Kingdom will be driven out into the outer darkness, where there will be wailing and grinding of teeth." And Jesus said to the centurion, "You may go; as you have believed, let it be done for you." And at that very hour his servant was healed.

Jesus entered the house of Peter, and saw his mother–in–law lying in bed with a fever. He touched her hand, the fever left her, and she rose and waited on him.

When it was evening, they brought him many who were possessed by demons, and he drove out the spirits by a word and cured all the sick, to fulfill what had been said by Isaiah the prophet:

He took away our infirmities and bore our diseases.

JUNE 28, 13TH SUNDAY IN ORDINARY TIME; ST. IRENAEUS

FIRST READING *2 Kings 4:8—11, 14—16a*

One day Elisha came to Shunem, where there was a woman of influence, who urged him to dine with her. Afterward, whenever he passed by, he used to stop there to dine. So she said to her husband, "I know that Elisha is a holy man of God. Since he visits us often, let us arrange a little room on the roof and furnish it for him with a bed, table, chair, and lamp, so that when he comes to us he can stay there." Sometime later Elisha arrived and stayed in the room overnight.

Later Elisha asked, "Can something be done for her?" His servant Gehazi answered, "Yes! She has no son, and her husband is getting on in years." Elisha said, "Call her." When the woman had been called and stood at the door, Elisha promised, "This time next year you will be fondling a baby son."

RESPONSORIAL PSALM *Psalm 89:2—3, 16—17, 18—19 (2a)*

R. Forever I will sing the goodness of the Lord.

The promises of the LORD I will sing forever, / through all generations my mouth shall proclaim your faithfulness. / For you have said, "My kindness is established forever"; / in heaven you have confirmed your faithfulness. **R.**

Blessed the people who know the joyful shout; / in the light of your countenance, O LORD, they walk. / At your name they rejoice all the day, / and through your justice they are exalted. **R.**

You are the splendor of their strength, / and by your favor our horn is exalted. / For to the LORD belongs our shield, / and to the Holy One of Israel, our king. **R.**

SECOND READING   *Romans 6:3—4, 8—11*

Brothers and sisters: Are you unaware that we who were baptized into Christ Jesus were baptized into his death? We were indeed buried with him through baptism into death, so that, just as Christ was raised from the dead by the glory of the Father, we too might live in newness of life.

If, then, we have died with Christ, we believe that we shall also live with him. We know that Christ, raised from the dead, dies no more; death no longer has power over him. As to his death, he died to sin once and for all; as to his life, he lives for God. Consequently, you too must think of yourselves as dead to sin and living for God in Christ Jesus.

ALLELUIA   *1 Peter 2:9*

R. Alleluia, alleluia. You are a chosen race, a royal priesthood, a holy nation; announce the praises of him who called you out of darkness into his wonderful light. **R.**

GOSPEL   *Matthew 10:37—42*

Jesus said to his apostles: "Whoever loves father or mother more than me is not worthy of me, and whoever loves son or daughter more than me is not worthy of me; and whoever does not take up his cross and follow after me is not worthy of me. Whoever finds his life will lose it, and whoever loses his life for my sake will find it.

"Whoever receives you receives me, and whoever receives me receives the one who sent me. Whoever receives a prophet because he is a prophet will receive a prophet's reward, and whoever receives a righteous man because he is a righteous man will receive a righteous man's reward. And whoever gives only a cup of cold water to one of these little ones to drink because the little one is a disciple— amen, I say to you, he will surely not lose his reward."

JUNE 29, SOLEMNITY OF SAINT PETER AND SAINT PAUL, APOSTLES

AT THE VIGIL MASS

FIRST READING   *Acts 3:1—10*

Peter and John were going up to the temple area for the three o'clock hour of prayer. And a man crippled from birth was carried and placed at the gate of the temple called "the Beautiful Gate" every day to beg for alms from the people who entered the temple. When he saw Peter and John about to go into the temple, he asked for alms. But Peter looked intently at him, as did John, and said, "Look at us." He paid attention to them, expecting to receive something from them. Peter said, "I have neither silver nor gold, but what I do have I give you: in the name of Jesus Christ the Nazorean, rise and walk." Then Peter took him by the right hand and raised him up, and immediately his feet and ankles grew strong. He leaped up, stood, and walked around, and went into the temple with them, walking and jumping and praising God. When all the people saw the man walking and praising God, they recognized him as the one who used to sit begging at the Beautiful Gate of the temple, and they were filled with amazement and astonishment at what had happened to him.

RESPONSORIAL PSALM
Psalm 19:2—3, 4—5 (5)

R. Their message goes out through all the earth.
The heavens declare the glory of God; **/** and the firmament proclaims his handiwork. **/** Day pours out the word to day; **/** and night to night imparts knowledge. **R.**
Not a word nor a discourse whose voice is not heard; **/** through all the earth their voice resounds, **/** and to the ends of the world, their message. **R.**

SECOND READING
Galatians 1:11—20

I want you to know, brothers and sisters, that the Gospel preached by me is not of human origin. For I did not receive it from a human being, nor was I taught it, but it came through a revelation of Jesus Christ.

For you heard of my former way of life in Judaism, how I persecuted the Church of God beyond measure and tried to destroy it, and progressed in Judaism beyond many of my contemporaries among my race, since I was even more a zealot for my ancestral traditions. But when God, who from my mother's womb had set me apart and called me through his grace, was pleased to reveal his Son to me, so that I might proclaim him to the Gentiles, I did not immediately consult flesh and blood, nor did I go up to Jerusalem to those who were apostles before me; rather, I went into Arabia and then returned to Damascus.

Then after three years I went up to Jerusalem to confer with Cephas and remained with him for fifteen days. But I did not see any other of the Apostles, only James the brother of the Lord. —As to what I am writing to you, behold, before God, I am not lying.

ALLELUIA
John 21:17

R. Alleluia, alleluia. Lord, you know everything; you know that I love you. **R.**

GOSPEL
John 21:15—19

Jesus had revealed himself to his disciples and, when they had finished breakfast, said to Simon Peter, "Simon, son of John, do you love me more than these?" Simon Peter answered him, "Yes, Lord, you know that I love you." Jesus said to him, "Feed my lambs." He then said to Simon Peter a second time, "Simon, son of John, do you love me?" Simon Peter answered him, "Yes, Lord, you know that I love you." He said to him, "Tend my sheep." He said to him the third time, "Simon, son of John, do you love me?" Peter was distressed that Jesus had said to him a third time, "Do you love me?" and he said to him, "Lord, you know everything; you know that I love you." Jesus said to him, "Feed my sheep. Amen, amen, I say to you, when you were younger, you used to dress yourself and go where you wanted; but when you grow old, you will stretch out your hands, and someone else will dress you and lead you where you do not want to go." He said this signifying by what kind of death he would glorify God. And when he had said this, he said to him, "Follow me."

MASS OF THE DAY

FIRST READING   *Acts 12:1—11*

In those days, King Herod laid hands upon some members of the Church to harm them. He had James, the brother of John, killed by the sword, and when he saw that this was pleasing to the Jews he proceeded to arrest Peter also. —It was the feast of Unleavened Bread.— He had him taken into custody and put in prison under the guard of four squads of four soldiers each. He intended to bring him before the people after Passover. Peter thus was being kept in prison, but prayer by the Church was fervently being made to God on his behalf.

On the very night before Herod was to bring him to trial, Peter, secured by double chains, was sleeping between two soldiers, while outside the door guards kept watch on the prison. Suddenly the angel of the Lord stood by him, and a light shone in the cell. He tapped Peter on the side and awakened him, saying, "Get up quickly." The chains fell from his wrists. The angel said to him, "Put on your belt and your sandals." He did so. Then he said to him, "Put on your cloak and follow me." So he followed him out, not realizing that what was happening through the angel was real; he thought he was seeing a vision. They passed the first guard, then the second, and came to the iron gate leading out to the city, which opened for them by itself. They emerged and made their way down an alley, and suddenly the angel left him.

RESPONSORIAL PSALM   *Psalm 34:2—3, 4—5, 6—7, 8—9 (5)*

R. The angel of the Lord will rescue those who fear him.

I will bless the LORD at all times; **/** his praise shall be ever in my mouth. **/** Let my soul glory in the LORD; **/** the lowly will hear me and be glad. **R.**

Glorify the LORD with me, **/** let us together extol his name. **/** I sought the LORD, and he answered me **/** and delivered me from all my fears. **R.**

Look to him that you may be radiant with joy, **/** and your faces may not blush with shame. **/** When the poor one called out, the LORD heard, **/** and from all his distress he saved him. **R.**

The angel of the LORD encamps **/** around those who fear him, **/** and delivers them. **/** Taste and see how good the LORD is; **/** blessed the man who takes refuge in him. **R.**

SECOND READING   *2 Timothy 4:6—8, 17—18*

I, Paul, am already being poured out like a libation, and the time of my departure is at hand. I have competed well; I have finished the race; I have kept the faith. From now on the crown of righteousness awaits me, which the Lord, the just judge, will award to me on that day, and not only to me, but to all who have longed for his appearance.

The Lord stood by me and gave me strength, so that through me the proclamation might be completed and all the Gentiles might hear it. And I was rescued from the lion's mouth. The Lord will rescue me from every evil threat and will bring me safe to his heavenly kingdom. To him be glory forever and ever. Amen.

ALLELUIA *Matthew 16:18*

R. Alleluia, alleluia. You are Peter and upon this rock I will build my Church, and the gates of the netherworld shall not prevail against it. **R.**

GOSPEL *Matthew 16:13—19*

When Jesus went into the region of Caesarea Philippi he asked his disciples, "Who do people say that the Son of Man is?" They replied, "Some say John the Baptist, others Elijah, still others Jeremiah or one of the prophets." He said to them, "But who do you say that I am?" Simon Peter said in reply, "You are the Christ, the Son of the living God." Jesus said to him in reply, "Blessed are you, Simon son of Jonah. For flesh and blood has not revealed this to you, but my heavenly Father. And so I say to you, you are Peter, and upon this rock I will build my Church, and the gates of the netherworld shall not prevail against it. I will give you the keys to the Kingdom of heaven. Whatever you bind on earth shall be bound in heaven; and whatever you loose on earth shall be loosed in heaven."

JUNE 30, TUESDAY OF WEEK 13; FIRST MARTYRS OF THE CHURCH OF ROME

FIRST READING *Amos 3:1–8; 4:11–12*

Hear this word, O children of Israel, that the LORD pronounces over you, over the whole family that I brought up from the land of Egypt:

You alone have I favored, more than all the families of the earth; therefore I will punish you for all your crimes.

Do two walk together unless they have agreed? Does a lion roar in the forest when it has no prey? Does a young lion cry out from its den unless it has seized something? Is a bird brought to earth by a snare when there is no lure for it? Does a snare spring up from the ground without catching anything? If the trumpet sounds in a city, will the people not be frightened? If evil befalls a city, has not the LORD caused it? Indeed, the Lord GOD does nothing without revealing his plan to his servants, the prophets.

The lion roars who will not be afraid! The Lord GOD speaks who will not prophesy!

I brought upon you such upheaval as when God overthrew Sodom and Gomorrah: you were like a brand plucked from the fire; Yet you returned not to me, says the LORD.

So now I will deal with you in my own way, O Israel! and since I will deal thus with you, prepare to meet your God, O Israel.

RESPONSORIAL PSALM *Psalm 5:4b–6a, 6b–7, 8*

R. (9a) Lead me in your justice, Lord.

At dawn I bring my plea expectantly before you. / For you, O God, delight not in wickedness; / no evil man remains with you; / the arrogant may not stand in your sight. **R.**
You hate all evildoers; / you destroy all who speak falsehood; / The bloodthirsty and the deceitful / the LORD abhors. **R.**

But I, because of your abundant mercy, / will enter your house; / I will worship at your holy temple / in fear of you, O LORD. **R.**

ALLELUIA *Psalm 130:5*

R. Alleluia, alleluia. I trust in the LORD; my soul trusts in his word. **R.**

GOSPEL *Matthew 8:23–27*

As Jesus got into a boat, his disciples followed him. Suddenly a violent storm came up on the sea, so that the boat was being swamped by waves; but he was asleep. They came and woke him, saying, "Lord, save us! We are perishing!" He said to them, "Why are you terrified, O you of little faith?" Then he got up, rebuked the winds and the sea, and there was great calm. The men were amazed and said, "What sort of man is this, whom even the winds and the sea obey?"

9   JULY

JULY 1, WEDNESDAY OF WEEK 13; BLESSED JUNÍPERO SERRA

FIRST READING *Amos 5:14–15, 21–24*

Seek good and not evil, that you may live; Then truly will the LORD, the God of hosts, be with you as you claim! Hate evil and love good, and let justice prevail at the gate; Then it may be that the LORD, the God of hosts, will have pity on the remnant of Joseph.

I hate, I spurn your feasts, says the LORD, I take no pleasure in your solemnities; Your cereal offerings I will not accept, nor consider your stall–fed peace offerings. Away with your noisy songs! I will not listen to the melodies of your harps. But if you would offer me burnt offerings, then let justice surge like water, and goodness like an unfailing stream.

RESPONSORIAL PSALM *Psalm 50:7, 8–9, 10–11, 12–13, 16bc–17*

R. (23b) To the upright I will show the saving power of God.

"Hear, my people, and I will speak; / Israel, I will testify against you; / God, your God, am I." **R.**

"Not for your sacrifices do I rebuke you, / for your burnt offerings are before me always. / I take from your house no bullock, / no goats out of your fold." **R.**

"For mine are all the animals of the forests, / beasts by the thousand on my mountains. / I know all the birds of the air, / and whatever stirs in the plains, belongs to me." **R.**

"If I were hungry, I should not tell you, / for mine are the world and its fullness. / Do I eat the flesh of strong bulls, / or is the blood of goats my drink?" **R.**

"Why do you recite my statutes, / and profess my covenant with your mouth, / Though you hate discipline / and cast my words behind you?" **R.**

ALLELUIA *James 1:18*

R. Alleluia, alleluia. The Father willed to give us birth by the word of truth that we may be a kind of firstfruits of his creatures. **R.**

GOSPEL

Matthew 8:28–34

When Jesus came to the territory of the Gadarenes, two demoniacs who were coming from the tombs met him. They were so savage that no one could travel by that road. They cried out, "What have you to do with us, Son of God? Have you come here to torment us before the appointed time?" Some distance away a herd of many swine was feeding. The demons pleaded with him, "If you drive us out, send us into the herd of swine." And he said to them, "Go then!" They came out and entered the swine, and the whole herd rushed down the steep bank into the sea where they drowned. The swineherds ran away, and when they came to the town they reported everything, including what had happened to the demoniacs. Thereupon the whole town came out to meet Jesus, and when they saw him they begged him to leave their district.

JULY 2, THURSDAY OF WEEK 13; ST. OLIVER PLUNKET

FIRST READING

Amos 7:10–17

Amaziah, the priest of Bethel, sent word to Jeroboam, king of Israel: "Amos has conspired against you here within Israel; the country cannot endure all his words. For this is what Amos says: Jeroboam shall die by the sword, and Israel shall surely be exiled from its land."

To Amos, Amaziah said: "Off with you, visionary, flee to the land of Judah! There earn your bread by prophesying, but never again prophesy in Bethel; for it is the king's sanctuary and a royal temple." Amos answered Amaziah, "I was no prophet, nor have I belonged to a company of prophets; I was a shepherd and a dresser of sycamores. The LORD took me from following the flock, and said to me, 'Go, prophesy to my people Israel.' Now hear the word of the LORD!"

You say: prophesy not against Israel, preach not against the house of Isaac. Now thus says the LORD: Your wife shall be made a harlot in the city, and your sons and daughters shall fall by the sword; Your land shall be divided by measuring line, and you yourself shall die in an unclean land; Israel shall be exiled far from its land.

RESPONSORIAL PSALM

Psalm 19:8, 9, 10, 11

R. (10cd) The judgments of the Lord are true, and all of them are just.

The law of the LORD is perfect, / refreshing the soul; / The decree of the LORD is trustworthy, / giving wisdom to the simple. **R.**

The precepts of the LORD are right, / rejoicing the heart; / The command of the LORD is clear, / enlightening the eye. **R.**

The fear of the LORD is pure, / enduring forever; / The ordinances of the LORD are true, / all of them just. **R.**

They are more precious than gold, / than a heap of purest gold; / Sweeter also than syrup or honey from the comb. **R.**

ALLELUIA

2 Corinthians 5:19

R. Alleluia, alleluia. God was reconciling the world to himself in Christ and entrusting to us the message of reconciliation. **R.**

GOSPEL   *Matthew 9:1–8*

After entering a boat, Jesus made the crossing, and came into his own town. And there people brought to him a paralytic lying on a stretcher. When Jesus saw their faith, he said to the paralytic, "Courage, child, your sins are forgiven." At that, some of the scribes said to themselves, "This man is blaspheming." Jesus knew what they were thinking, and said, :Why do you harbor evil thoughts? Which is easier, to say, 'Your sins are forgiven,' or to say, 'Rise and walk'? But that you may know that the Son of Man has authority on earth to forgive sins"— he then said to the paralytic, "Rise, pick up your stretcher, and go home." He rose and went home. When the crowds saw this they were struck with awe and glorified God who had given such authority to men.

JULY 3, SAINT THOMAS, APOSTLE - FEAST

FIRST READING   *Ephesians 2:19–22*

Brothers and sisters: You are no longer strangers and sojourners, but you are fellow citizens with the holy ones and members of the household of God, built upon the foundation of the Apostles and prophets, with Christ Jesus himself as the capstone. Through him the whole structure is held together and grows into a temple sacred in the Lord; in him you also are being built together into a dwelling place of God in the Spirit.

RESPONSORIAL PSALM   *Psalm 117:1bc, 2*

R. Go out to all the world and tell the Good News.

Praise the LORD, all you nations; / glorify him, all you peoples! **R.**

For steadfast is his kindness for us, / and the fidelity of the LORD endures forever. **R.**

ALLELUIA   *John 20:29*

R. Alleluia, alleluia. You believe in me, Thomas, because you have seen me, says the Lord; blessed are those who have not seen, but still believe! **R.**

GOSPEL   *John 20:24–29*

Thomas, called Didymus, one of the Twelve, was not with them when Jesus came. So the other disciples said to him, "We have seen the Lord." But Thomas said to them, "Unless I see the mark of the nails in his hands and put my finger into the nailmarks and put my hand into his side, I will not believe." Now a week later his disciples were again inside and Thomas was with them. Jesus came, although the doors were locked, and stood in their midst and said, "Peace be with you." Then he said to Thomas, "Put your finger here and see my hands, and bring your hand and put it into my side, and do not be unbelieving, but believe." Thomas answered and said to him, "My Lord and my God!" Jesus said to him, "Have you come to believe because you have seen me? Blessed are those who have not seen and have believed."

JULY 4, SATURDAY OF WEEK 13; ST. ELIZABETH OF PORTUGAL

FIRST READING *Amos 9:11–15*

Thus says the LORD: On that day I will raise up the fallen hut of David; I will wall up its breaches, raise up its ruins, and rebuild it as in the days of old, That they may conquer what is left of Edom and all the nations that shall bear my name, say I, the LORD, who will do this. Yes, days are coming, says the LORD, When the plowman shall overtake the reaper, and the vintager, him who sows the seed; The juice of grapes shall drip down the mountains, and all the hills shall run with it. I will bring about the restoration of my people Israel; they shall rebuild and inhabit their ruined cities, Plant vineyards and drink the wine, set out gardens and eat the fruits. I will plant them upon their own ground; never again shall they be plucked from the land I have given them, say I, the LORD, your God.

RESPONSORIAL PSALM *Psalm 85:9ab and 10, 11–12, 13–14*

R. (see 9b) The Lord speaks of peace to his people.

I will hear what God proclaims; / the LORD—for he proclaims peace to his people. / Near indeed is his salvation / to those who fear him, / glory dwelling in our land. **R.**

Kindness and truth shall meet; / justice and peace shall kiss. / Truth shall spring out of the earth, / and justice shall look down from heaven. **R.**

The LORD himself will give his benefits; / our land shall yield its increase. / Justice shall walk before him, / and salvation, along the way of his steps. **R.**

ALLELUIA *John 10:27*

R. Alleluia, alleluia. My sheep hear my voice, says the Lord; I know them, and they follow me. **R.**

GOSPEL *Matthew 9:14–17*

The disciples of John approached Jesus and said, "Why do we and the Pharisees fast much, but your disciples do not fast?" Jesus answered them, "Can the wedding guests mourn as long as the bridegroom is with them? The days will come when the bridegroom is taken away from them, and then they will fast. No one patches an old cloak with a piece of unshrunken cloth, for its fullness pulls away from the cloak and the tear gets worse. People do not put new wine into old wineskins. Otherwise the skins burst, the wine spills out, and the skins are ruined. Rather, they pour new wine into fresh wineskins, and both are preserved."

JULY 5, 14TH SUNDAY IN ORDINARY TIME; ST. ANTHONY MARY ZACCARIA

FIRST READING *Zechariah 9:9—10*

Thus says the LORD: Rejoice heartily, O daughter Zion, shout for joy, O daughter Jerusalem! See, your king shall come to you; a just savior is he, meek, and riding on an ass, on a colt, the foal of an ass. He shall banish the chariot from Ephraim, and the horse from Jerusalem; the warrior's bow shall be banished, and he shall proclaim peace to the nations. His dominion shall be from sea to sea, and from the River to the ends of the earth.

RESPONSORIAL PSALM   *Psalm 145:1—2, 8—9, 10—11, 13—14 (see 1)*

R. I will praise your name for ever, my king and my God. or R. Alleluia.

I will extol you, O my God and King, / and I will bless your name for ever and ever. / Every day will I bless you, / and I will praise your name for ever and ever. **R.**

The LORD is gracious and merciful, / slow to anger and of great kindness. / The LORD is good to all and compassionate toward all his works. **R.**

Let all your works give you thanks, O LORD, / and let your faithful ones bless you. / Let them discourse of the glory of your kingdom / and speak of your might. **R.**

The LORD is faithful in all his words / and holy in all his works. / The LORD lifts up all who are falling / and raises up all who are bowed down. **R.**

SECOND READING   *Romans 8:9, 11—13*

Brothers and sisters: You are not in the flesh; on the contrary, you are in the spirit, if only the Spirit of God dwells in you. Whoever does not have the Spirit of Christ does not belong to him. If the Spirit of the one who raised Jesus from the dead dwells in you, the one who raised Christ from the dead will give life to your mortal bodies also, through his Spirit that dwells in you. Consequently, brothers and sisters, we are not debtors to the flesh, to live according to the flesh. For if you live according to the flesh, you will die, but if by the Spirit you put to death the deeds of the body, you will live.

ALLELUIA   *see Matthew 11:25*

R. Alleluia, alleluia. Blessed are you, Father, Lord of heaven and earth; you have revealed to little ones the mysteries of the kingdom. **R.**

GOSPEL   *Matthew 11:25—30*

At that time Jesus exclaimed: "I give praise to you, Father, Lord of heaven and earth, for although you have hidden these things from the wise and the learned you have revealed them to little ones. Yes, Father, such has been your gracious will. All things have been handed over to me by my Father. No one knows the Son except the Father, and no one knows the Father except the Son and anyone to whom the Son wishes to reveal him.

"Come to me, all you who labor and are burdened, and I will give you rest. Take my yoke upon you and learn from me, for I am meek and humble of heart; and you will find rest for yourselves. For my yoke is easy, and my burden light."

JULY 6, MONDAY OF WEEK 14; ST. MARIA GORETTI

FIRST READING   *Hosea 2:16, 17c–18, 21–22*

Thus says the LORD: I will allure her; I will lead her into the desert and speak to her heart. She shall respond there as in the days of her youth, when she came up from the land of Egypt.

On that day, says the LORD, She shall call me "My husband," and never again "My baal."

I will espouse you to me forever: I will espouse you in right and in justice, in love and in mercy; I will espouse you in fidelity, and you shall know the LORD.

RESPONSORIAL PSALM   *Psalm 145:2–3, 4–5, 6–7, 8–9*

R. (8a) The Lord is gracious and merciful.

Every day will I bless you, / and I will praise your name forever and ever. / Great is the LORD and highly to be praised; / his greatness is unsearchable. **R.**

Generation after generation praises your works / and proclaims your might. / They speak of the splendor of your glorious majesty / and tell of your wondrous works. **R.**

They discourse of the power of your terrible deeds / and declare your greatness. / They publish the fame of your abundant goodness / and joyfully sing of your justice. **R.**

The LORD is gracious and merciful, / slow to anger and of great kindness. / The LORD is good to all and compassionate toward all his works. **R.**

ALLELUIA   *See 2 Timothy 1:10*

R. Alleluia, alleluia. Our Savior Jesus Christ has destroyed death and brought life to light through the Gospel. **R.**

GOSPEL   *Matthew 9:18–26*

While Jesus was speaking, an official came forward, knelt down before him, and said, "My daughter has just died. But come, lay your hand on her, and she will live." Jesus rose and followed him, and so did his disciples. A woman suffering hemorrhages for twelve years came up behind him and touched the tassel on his cloak. She said to herself, "If only I can touch his cloak, I shall be cured." Jesus turned around and saw her, and said, "Courage, daughter! Your faith has saved you." And from that hour the woman was cured.

When Jesus arrived at the official's house and saw the flute players and the crowd who were making a commotion, he said, "Go away! The girl is not dead but sleeping." And they ridiculed him. When the crowd was put out, he came and took her by the hand, and the little girl arose. And news of this spread throughout all that land.

JULY 7, TUESDAY OF WEEK 14;
BLESSED ROGER DICKENSON, BLESSED RALPH MILNER, AND BLESSED LAWRENCE HUMPHREY

FIRST READING   *Hosea 8:4–7, 11–13*

Thus says the LORD: They made kings in Israel, but not by my authority; they established princes, but without my approval. With their silver and gold they made idols for themselves, to their own destruction. Cast away your calf, O Samaria! My wrath is kindled against them; How long will they be unable to attain innocence in Israel? The work of an artisan, no god at all, destined for the flames, such is the calf of Samaria!

When they sow the wind, they shall reap the whirlwind; The stalk of grain that forms no ear can yield no flour; Even if it could, strangers would swallow it.

When Ephraim made many altars to expiate sin, his altars became occasions of sin. Though I write for him my many ordinances, they are considered as a stranger's. Though they offer sacrifice, immolate flesh and eat it, the LORD is not pleased with them. He shall still remember their guilt and punish their sins; they shall return to Egypt.

RESPONSORIAL PSALM   *Psalm 115:3–4, 5–6, 7ab–8, 9–10*

R. The house of Israel trusts in the Lord. or: R. Alleluia.

Our God is in heaven; / whatever he wills, he does. / Their idols are silver and gold, /
the handiwork of men. **R.**

They have mouths but speak not; / they have eyes but see not; /
They have ears but hear not; / they have noses but smell not. **R.**

They have hands but feel not; / they have feet but walk not. /
Their makers shall be like them, / everyone that trusts in them. **R.**

ALLELUIA   *John 10:14*

R. Alleluia, alleluia. I am the good shepherd, says the Lord; I know my sheep, and mine
know me. **R.**

GOSPEL   *Matthew 9:32–38*

A demoniac who could not speak was brought to Jesus, and when the demon was driven
out the mute man spoke. The crowds were amazed and said, "Nothing like this has ever
been seen in Israel." But the Pharisees said, "He drives out demons by the prince of
demons."

Jesus went around to all the towns and villages, teaching in their synagogues,
proclaiming the Gospel of the Kingdom, and curing every disease and illness. At the sight of
the crowds, his heart was moved with pity for them because they were troubled and
abandoned, like sheep without a shepherd. Then he said to his disciples, "The harvest is
abundant but the laborers are few; so ask the master of the harvest to send out laborers for
his harvest."

JULY 8, WEDNESDAY OF WEEK 14; BLESSED PIER GIORGIO FRASSATI
FIRST READING   *Hosea 10:1–3, 7–8, 12*

Israel is a luxuriant vine whose fruit matches its growth. The more abundant his fruit, the
more altars he built; The more productive his land, the more sacred pillars he set up. Their
heart is false, now they pay for their guilt; God shall break down their altars and destroy
their sacred pillars. If they would say, "We have no king"— since they do not fear the LORD,
what can the king do for them?

The king of Samaria shall disappear, like foam upon the waters. The high places of
Aven shall be destroyed, the sin of Israel; thorns and thistles shall overgrow their altars.
Then they shall cry out to the mountains, "Cover us!" and to the hills, "Fall upon us!"

"Sow for yourselves justice, reap the fruit of piety; break up for yourselves a new
field, for it is time to seek the LORD, till he come and rain down justice upon you."

RESPONSORIAL PSALM   *Psalm 105:2–3, 4–5, 6–7*

R. Seek always the face of the Lord. or: R. Alleluia.

Sing to him, sing his praise, / proclaim all his wondrous deeds. / Glory in his holy name; /
rejoice, O hearts that seek the LORD! **R.**

Look to the LORD in his strength; / seek to serve him constantly. / Recall the wondrous deeds that he has wrought, / his portents, and the judgments he has uttered. **R.**

You descendants of Abraham, his servants, / sons of Jacob, his chosen ones! / He, the LORD, is our God; / throughout the earth his judgments prevail. **R.**

ALLELUIA   *Mark 1:15*
R. Alleluia, alleluia. The Kingdom of God is at hand: repent and believe in the Gospel. **R.**

GOSPEL   *Matthew 10:1–7*
Jesus summoned his twelve disciples and gave them authority over unclean spirits to drive them out and to cure every disease and every illness. The names of the Twelve Apostles are these: first, Simon called Peter, and his brother Andrew; James, the son of Zebedee, and his brother John; Philip and Bartholomew, Thomas and Matthew the tax collector; James, the son of Alphaeus, and Thaddeus; Simon the Cananean, and Judas Iscariot who betrayed Jesus.

Jesus sent out these Twelve after instructing them thus, "Do not go into pagan territory or enter a Samaritan town. Go rather to the lost sheep of the house of Israel. As you go, make this proclamation: 'The Kingdom of heaven is at hand.'"

JULY 9, THURSDAY OF WEEK 14; ST. AUGUSTINE ZHAO RONG AND COMPANIONS
FIRST READING   *Hosea 11:1–4, 8e–9*
Thus says the LORD: When Israel was a child I loved him, out of Egypt I called my son. The more I called them, the farther they went from me, Sacrificing to the Baals and burning incense to idols. Yet it was I who taught Ephraim to walk, who took them in my arms; I drew them with human cords, with bands of love; I fostered them like one who raises an infant to his cheeks; Yet, though I stooped to feed my child, they did not know that I was their healer.

My heart is overwhelmed, my pity is stirred. I will not give vent to my blazing anger, I will not destroy Ephraim again; For I am God and not man, the Holy One present among you; I will not let the flames consume you.

RESPONSORIAL PSALM   *Psalm 80:2ac and 3b, 15–16*
R. (4b) Let us see your face, Lord, and we shall be saved.

O shepherd of Israel, hearken. / From your throne upon the cherubim, shine forth. / Rouse your power. **R.**

Once again, O LORD of hosts, / look down from heaven, and see: / Take care of this vine, and protect what your right hand has planted, / the son of man whom you yourself made strong. **R.**

ALLELUIA   *Mark 1:15*
R. Alleluia, alleluia. The Kingdom of God is at hand: repent and believe in the Gospel. **R.**

GOSPEL

Matthew 10:7–15

Jesus said to his Apostles: "As you go, make this proclamation: 'The Kingdom of heaven is at hand.' Cure the sick, raise the dead, cleanse the lepers, drive out demons. Without cost you have received; without cost you are to give. Do not take gold or silver or copper for your belts; no sack for the journey, or a second tunic, or sandals, or walking stick. The laborer deserves his keep. Whatever town or village you enter, look for a worthy person in it, and stay there until you leave. As you enter a house, wish it peace. If the house is worthy, let your peace come upon it; if not, let your peace return to you. Whoever will not receive you or listen to your words, go outside that house or town and shake the dust from your feet. Amen, I say to you, it will be more tolerable for the land of Sodom and Gomorrah on the day of judgment than for that town."

JULY 10, FRIDAY OF WEEK 14; ST. VERONICA GIULIANI

FIRST READING

Hosea 14:2–10

Thus says the LORD: Return, O Israel, to the LORD, your God; you have collapsed through your guilt. Take with you words, and return to the LORD; Say to him, "Forgive all iniquity, and receive what is good, that we may render as offerings the bullocks from our stalls. Assyria will not save us, nor shall we have horses to mount; we shall say no more, 'Our god,' to the work of our hands; for in you the orphan finds compassion." I will heal their defection, says the LORD, I will love them freely; for my wrath is turned away from them. I will be like the dew for Israel: he shall blossom like the lily; He shall strike root like the Lebanon cedar, and put forth his shoots. His splendor shall be like the olive tree and his fragrance like the Lebanon cedar. Again they shall dwell in his shade and raise grain; they shall blossom like the vine, and his fame shall be like the wine of Lebanon.

Ephraim! What more has he to do with idols? I have humbled him, but I will prosper him. "I am like a verdant cypress tree"— because of me you bear fruit!

Let him who is wise understand these things; let him who is prudent know them. Straight are the paths of the LORD, in them the just walk, but sinners stumble in them.

RESPONSORIAL PSALM

Psalm 51:3–4, 8–9, 12–13, 14 and 17

R. (17b) My mouth will declare your praise.

Have mercy on me, O God, / in your goodness; / in the greatness of your compassion wipe out my offense. / Thoroughly wash me from my guilt / and of my sin cleanse me. **R.**

Behold, you are pleased with sincerity of heart, / and in my inmost being you teach me wisdom. / Cleanse me of sin with hyssop, / that I may be purified; / wash me, and I shall be whiter than snow. **R.**

A clean heart create for me, O God, / and a steadfast spirit renew within me. / Cast me not out from your presence, / and your Holy Spirit take not from me. **R.**

Give me back the joy of your salvation, / and a willing spirit sustain in me. / O Lord, open my lips, / and my mouth shall proclaim your praise. **R.**

ALLELUIA

John 16:13a; 14:26d *14:26d*

R. Alleluia, alleluia. When the Spirit of truth comes, he will guide you to all truth and remind you of all I told you. **R.**

GOSPEL
Matthew 10:16–23

Jesus said to his Apostles: "Behold, I am sending you like sheep in the midst of wolves; so be shrewd as serpents and simple as doves. But beware of men, for they will hand you over to courts and scourge you in their synagogues, and you will be led before governors and kings for my sake as a witness before them and the pagans. When they hand you over, do not worry about how you are to speak or what you are to say. You will be given at that moment what you are to say. For it will not be you who speak but the Spirit of your Father speaking through you. Brother will hand over brother to death, and the father his child; children will rise up against parents and have them put to death. You will be hated by all because of my name, but whoever endures to the end will be saved. When they persecute you in one town, flee to another. Amen, I say to you, you will not finish the towns of Israel before the Son of Man comes."

JULY 11, SATURDAY OF WEEK 14; ST. BENEDICT

FIRST READING
Isaiah 6:1–8

In the year King Uzziah died, I saw the Lord seated on a high and lofty throne, with the train of his garment filling the temple. Seraphim were stationed above; each of them had six wings: with two they veiled their faces, with two they veiled their feet, and with two they hovered aloft.

They cried one to the other, "Holy, holy, holy is the LORD of hosts! All the earth is filled with his glory!" At the sound of that cry, the frame of the door shook and the house was filled with smoke.

Then I said, "Woe is me, I am doomed! For I am a man of unclean lips, living among a people of unclean lips; yet my eyes have seen the King, the LORD of hosts!" Then one of the seraphim flew to me, holding an ember that he had taken with tongs from the altar.

He touched my mouth with it and said, "See, now that this has touched your lips, your wickedness is removed, your sin purged."

Then I heard the voice of the Lord saying, "Whom shall I send? Who will go for us?" "Here I am," I said; "send me!"

RESPONSORIAL PSALM
Psalm 93:1ab, 1cd–2, 5

R. (1a) The Lord is king; he is robed in majesty.

The LORD is king, in splendor robed; / robed is the LORD and girt about with strength. **R.**
And he has made the world firm, / not to be moved. / Your throne stands firm from of old; / from everlasting you are, O LORD. **R.**
Your decrees are worthy of trust indeed: / holiness befits your house, / O LORD, for length of days. **R.**

ALLELUIA
1 Peter 4:14

R. Alleluia, alleluia. If you are insulted for the name of Christ, blessed are you, for the Spirit of God rests upon you. **R.**

GOSPEL

Matthew 10:24–33

Jesus said to his Apostles: "No disciple is above his teacher, no slave above his master. It is enough for the disciple that he become like his teacher, for the slave that he become like his master. If they have called the master of the house Beelzebul, how much more those of his household! "Therefore do not be afraid of them. Nothing is concealed that will not be revealed, nor secret that will not be known. What I say to you in the darkness, speak in the light; what you hear whispered, proclaim on the housetops. And do not be afraid of those who kill the body but cannot kill the soul; rather, be afraid of the one who can destroy both soul and body in Gehenna. Are not two sparrows sold for a small coin? Yet not one of them falls to the ground without your Father's knowledge. Even all the hairs of your head are counted. So do not be afraid; you are worth more than many sparrows. Everyone who acknowledges me before others I will acknowledge before my heavenly Father. But whoever denies me before others, I will deny before my heavenly Father."

JULY 12, 15TH SUNDAY IN ORDINARY TIME; ST. JOHN GAULBERT

FIRST READING

Isaiah 55:10—11

Thus says the LORD: Just as from the heavens the rain and snow come down and do not return there till they have watered the earth, making it fertile and fruitful, giving seed to the one who sows and bread to the one who eats, so shall my word be that goes forth from my mouth; my word shall not return to me void, but shall do my will, achieving the end for which I sent it.

RESPONSORIAL PSALM

Psalm 65:10, 11, 12—13, 14 (Luke 8:8)

R. The seed that falls on good ground will yield a fruitful harvest.
You have visited the land and watered it; **/** greatly have you enriched it. **/** God's watercourses are filled; **/** you have prepared the grain. **R.**
Thus have you prepared the land: **/** drenching its furrows, breaking up its clods, **/** softening it with showers, **/** blessing its yield. **R.**
You have crowned the year with your bounty, **/** and your paths overflow with a rich harvest; **/** the untilled meadows overflow with it, **/** and rejoicing clothes the hills. **R.**
The fields are garmented with flocks **/** and the valleys blanketed with grain. **/**
They shout and sing for joy. **R.**

SECOND READING

Romans 8:18—23

Brothers and sisters: I consider that the sufferings of this present time are as nothing compared with the glory to be revealed for us. For creation awaits with eager expectation the revelation of the children of God; for creation was made subject to futility, not of its own accord but because of the one who subjected it, in hope that creation itself would be set free from slavery to corruption and share in the glorious freedom of the children of

God. We know that all creation is groaning in labor pains even until now; and not only that, but we ourselves, who have the firstfruits of the Spirit, we also groan within ourselves as we wait for adoption, the redemption of our bodies.

ALLELUIA

R. Alleluia, alleluia. The seed is the word of God, Christ is the sower. All who come to him will have life forever. **R.**

GOSPEL *Longer Form Matthew 13:1—23*

On that day, Jesus went out of the house and sat down by the sea. Such large crowds gathered around him that he got into a boat and sat down, and the whole crowd stood along the shore. And he spoke to them at length in parables, saying: "A sower went out to sow. And as he sowed, some seed fell on the path, and birds came and ate it up. Some fell on rocky ground, where it had little soil. It sprang up at once because the soil was not deep, and when the sun rose it was scorched, and it withered for lack of roots. Some seed fell among thorns, and the thorns grew up and choked it. But some seed fell on rich soil, and produced fruit, a hundred or sixty or thirtyfold. Whoever has ears ought to hear."

The disciples approached him and said, "Why do you speak to them in parables?" He said to them in reply, "Because knowledge of the mysteries of the kingdom of heaven has been granted to you, but to them it has not been granted. To anyone who has, more will be given and he will grow rich; from anyone who has not, even what he has will be taken away. This is why I speak to them in parables, because *they look but do not see, and hear but do not listen or understand.* Isaiah's prophecy is fulfilled in them, which says: *You shall indeed hear but not understand, you shall indeed look but never see. Gross is the heart of this people, they will hardly hear with their ears, they have closed their eyes, lest they see with their eyes and hear with their ears and understand with their hearts and be converted, and I heal them.*

"But blessed are your eyes, because they see, and your ears, because they hear. Amen, I say to you, many prophets and righteous people longed to see what you see but did not see it, and to hear what you hear but did not hear it.

"Hear then the parable of the sower. The seed sown on the path is the one who hears the word of the kingdom without understanding it, and the evil one comes and steals away what was sown in his heart. The seed sown on rocky ground is the one who hears the word and receives it at once with joy. But he has no root and lasts only for a time. When some tribulation or persecution comes because of the word, he immediately falls away. The seed sown among thorns is the one who hears the word, but then worldly anxiety and the lure of riches choke the word and it bears no fruit. But the seed sown on rich soil is the one who hears the word and understands it, who indeed bears fruit and yields a hundred or sixty or thirtyfold."

SHORTER FORM MATTHEW 13:1 – 9

On that day, Jesus went out of the house and sat down by the sea. Such large crowds gathered around him that he got into a boat and sat down, and the whole crowd stood along the shore. And he spoke to them at length in parables, saying: "A sower went out to sow. And as he sowed, some seed fell on the path, and birds came and ate it up. Some fell on rocky ground, where it had little soil. It sprang up at once because the soil was not deep, and when the sun rose it was scorched, and it withered for lack of roots. Some seed fell among thorns, and the thorns grew up and choked it. But some seed fell on rich soil and produced fruit, a hundred or sixty or thirtyfold. Whoever has ears ought to hear."

JULY 13, MONDAY OF WEEK 15; ST. HENRY II

FIRST READING   *Isaiah 1:10–17*

Hear the word of the LORD, princes of Sodom! Listen to the instruction of our God, people of Gomorrah! What care I for the number of your sacrifices? says the LORD. I have had enough of whole–burnt rams and fat of fatlings; In the blood of calves, lambs and goats I find no pleasure.

When you come in to visit me, who asks these things of you? Trample my courts no more! Bring no more worthless offerings; your incense is loathsome to me. New moon and sabbath, calling of assemblies, octaves with wickedness: these I cannot bear. Your new moons and festivals I detest; they weigh me down, I tire of the load. When you spread out your hands, I close my eyes to you; Though you pray the more, I will not listen. Your hands are full of blood! Wash yourselves clean! Put away your misdeeds from before my eyes; cease doing evil; learn to do good. Make justice your aim: redress the wronged, hear the orphan's plea, defend the widow.

RESPONSORIAL PSALM   *Psalm 50:8–9, 16bc–17, 21 and 23*

R. (23b) To the upright I will show the saving power of God.

"Not for your sacrifices do I rebuke you, / for your burnt offerings are before me always. / I take from your house no bullock, / no goats out of your fold." **R.**

"Why do you recite my statutes, / and profess my covenant with your mouth, / Though you hate discipline / and cast my words behind you?" **R.**

"When you do these things, shall I be deaf to it? / Or do you think you that I am like yourself? / I will correct you by drawing them up before your eyes. / He that offers praise as a sacrifice glorifies me; / and to him that goes the right way I will show the salvation of God." **R.**

ALLELUIA   *Matthew 5:10*

R. Alleluia, alleluia. Blessed are they who are persecuted for the sake of righteousness, for theirs is the Kingdom of heaven. **R.**

GOSPEL   *Matthew 10:34–11:1*

Jesus said to his Apostles: "Do not think that I have come to bring peace upon the earth. I have come to bring not peace but the sword. For I have come to set a man against his father, a daughter against her mother, and a daughter–in–law against her mother–in–law; and one's enemies will be those of his household.

"Whoever loves father or mother more than me is not worthy of me, and whoever loves son or daughter more than me is not worthy of me; and whoever does not take up his cross and follow after me is not worthy of me. Whoever finds his life will lose it, and whoever loses his life for my sake will find it.

"Whoever receives you receives me, and whoever receives me receives the one who sent me. Whoever receives a prophet because he is a prophet will receive a prophet's reward, and whoever receives a righteous man because he is righteous will receive a righteous man's reward. And whoever gives only a cup of cold water to one of these little ones to drink because he is a disciple— amen, I say to you, he will surely not lose his reward."

When Jesus finished giving these commands to his Twelve disciples, he went away from that place to teach and to preach in their towns.

JULY 14, TUESDAY OF WEEK 15; BLESSED KATERI TEKAKWITHA

FIRST READING   Isaiah 7:1–9

In the days of Ahaz, king of Judah, son of Jotham, son of Uzziah, Rezin, king of Aram, and Pekah, king of Israel, son of Remaliah, went up to attack Jerusalem, but they were not able to conquer it. When word came to the house of David that Aram was encamped in Ephraim, the heart of the king and the heart of the people trembled, as the trees of the forest tremble in the wind.

Then the LORD said to Isaiah: Go out to meet Ahaz, you and your son Shear–jashub, at the end of the conduit of the upper pool, on the highway of the fuller's field, and say to him: Take care you remain tranquil and do not fear; let not your courage fail before these two stumps of smoldering brands the blazing anger of Rezin and the Arameans, and of the son Remaliah, because of the mischief that Aram, Ephraim and the son of Remaliah, plots against you, saying, "Let us go up and tear Judah asunder, make it our own by force, and appoint the son of Tabeel king there."

Thus says the LORD: This shall not stand, it shall not be! Damascus is the capital of Aram, and Rezin is the head of Damascus; Samaria is the capital of Ephraim, and Remaliah's son the head of Samaria.

But within sixty years and five, Ephraim shall be crushed, no longer a nation. Unless your faith is firm you shall not be firm!

RESPONSORIAL PSALM   *Psalm 48:2–3a, 3b–4, 5–6, 7–8*

R. (see 9d) God upholds his city for ever.

Great is the LORD and wholly to be praised / in the city of our God. / His holy mountain, fairest of heights, / is the joy of all the earth. **R.**

Mount Zion, "the recesses of the North," / is the city of the great King. / God is with her castles; / renowned is he as a stronghold. **R.**

For lo! the kings assemble, / they come on together; / They also see, / and at once are stunned, terrified, routed. **R.**

Quaking seizes them there; / anguish, like a woman's in labor, / As though a wind from the east / were shattering ships of Tarshish. **R.**

ALLELUIA   *Psalm 95:8*

R. Alleluia, alleluia. If today you hear his voice, harden not your hearts. **R.**

GOSPEL   *Matthew 11:20–24*

Jesus began to reproach the towns where most of his mighty deeds had been done, since they had not repented. "Woe to you, Chorazin! Woe to you, Bethsaida! For if the mighty deeds done in your midst had been done in Tyre and Sidon, they would long ago have repented in sackcloth and ashes. But I tell you, it will be more tolerable for Tyre and Sidon on the day of judgment than for you. And as for you, Capernaum:

Will you be exalted to heaven? You will go down to the netherworld.

For if the mighty deeds done in your midst had been done in Sodom, it would have remained until this day. But I tell you, it will be more tolerable for the land of Sodom on the day of judgment than for you."

JULY 15, WEDNESDAY OF WEEK 15; ST. BONAVENTURE

FIRST READING   *Isaiah 10:5–7, 13b–16*

Thus says the LORD: Woe to Assyria! My rod in anger, my staff in wrath. Against an impious nation I send him, and against a people under my wrath I order him to seize plunder, carry off loot, and tread them down like the mud of the streets. But this is not what he intends, nor does he have this in mind; rather, it is in his heart to destroy, to make an end of nations not a few.

For he says: "By my own power I have done it, and by my wisdom, for I am shrewd. I have moved the boundaries of peoples, their treasures I have pillaged, and, like a giant, I have put down the enthroned. My hand has seized like a nest the riches of nations; As one takes eggs left alone, so I took in all the earth; No one fluttered a wing, or opened a mouth, or chirped!"

Will the axe boast against him who hews with it? Will the saw exalt itself above him who wields it? As if a rod could sway him who lifts it, or a staff him who is not wood! Therefore the Lord, the LORD of hosts, will send among his fat ones leanness, And instead of his glory there will be kindling like the kindling of fire.

RESPONSORIAL PSALM   *Psalm 94:5–6, 7–8, 9–10, 14–15*

R. (14a) The Lord will not abandon his people.

Your people, O LORD, they trample down, **/** your inheritance they afflict. **/** Widow and stranger they slay, **/** the fatherless they murder. **R.**

And they say, "The LORD sees not; **/** the God of Jacob perceives not." **/** Understand, you senseless ones among the people; **/** and, you fools, when will you be wise? **R.**

Shall he who shaped the ear not hear? **/** Or he who formed the eye not see? **/** Shall he who instructs nations not chastise, **/** he who teaches men knowledge? **R.**

For the LORD will not cast off his people, **/** nor abandon his inheritance; **/** But judgment shall again be with justice, **/** and all the upright of heart shall follow it. **R.**

ALLELUIA   *Matthew 11:25*

R. Alleluia, alleluia. Blessed are you, Father, Lord of heaven and earth, you have revealed to little ones the mysteries of the Kingdom. **R.**

GOSPEL   *Matthew 11:25–27*

At that time Jesus exclaimed: "I give praise to you, Father, Lord of heaven and earth, for although you have hidden these things from the wise and the learned you have revealed them to the childlike. Yes, Father, such has been your gracious will. All things have been handed over to me by my Father. No one knows the Son except the Father, and no one knows the Father except the Son and anyone to whom the Son wishes to reveal him."

JULY 16, THURSDAY OF WEEK 15; OUR LADY OF MOUNT CARMEL

FIRST READING   *Isaiah 26:7–9, 12, 16–19*

The way of the just is smooth; the path of the just you make level. Yes, for your way and your judgments, O LORD, we look to you; Your name and your title are the desire of our souls. My soul yearns for you in the night, yes, my spirit within me keeps vigil for you; when your judgment dawns upon the earth, the world's inhabitants learn justice. O LORD, you mete out peace to us, for it is you who have accomplished all we have done.

O LORD, oppressed by your punishment, we cried out in anguish under your chastising. As a woman about to give birth writhes and cries out in her pains, so were we in your presence, O LORD. We conceived and writhed in pain, giving birth to wind; Salvation we have not achieved for the earth, the inhabitants of the world cannot bring it forth. But your dead shall live, their corpses shall rise; awake and sing, you who lie in the dust. For your dew is a dew of light, and the land of shades gives birth.

RESPONSORIAL PSALM   *Psalm 102:13–14ab and 15, 16–18, 19–21*

R. (20b) From heaven the Lord looks down on the earth.

You, O LORD, abide forever, / and your name through all generations. / You will arise and have mercy on Zion, / for it is time to pity her. / For her stones are dear to your servants, / and her dust moves them to pity. **R.**

The nations shall revere your name, O LORD, / and all the kings of the earth your glory, / When the LORD has rebuilt Zion / and appeared in his glory; / When he has regarded the prayer of the destitute, / and not despised their prayer. **R.**

Let this be written for the generation to come, / and let his future creatures praise the LORD: / "The LORD looked down from his holy height, / from heaven he beheld the earth, / To hear the groaning of the prisoners, / to release those doomed to die." **R.**

ALLELUIA   *Matthew 11:28*

R. Alleluia, alleluia. Come to me, all you who labor and are burdened, and I will give you rest, says the Lord. **R.**

GOSPEL   *Matthew 11:28–30*

Jesus said: "Come to me, all you who labor and are burdened, and I will give you rest. Take my yoke upon you and learn from me, for I am meek and humble of heart; and you will find rest for yourselves. For my yoke is easy, and my burden light."

JULY 17, FRIDAY OF WEEK 15; ST. LEO IV

FIRST READING   *Isaiah 38:1–6, 21–22, 7–8*

When Hezekiah was mortally ill, the prophet Isaiah, son of Amoz, came and said to him: "Thus says the LORD: Put your house in order, for you are about to die; you shall not recover." Then Hezekiah turned his face to the wall and prayed to the LORD:

"O LORD, remember how faithfully and wholeheartedly I conducted myself in your presence, doing what was pleasing to you!" And Hezekiah wept bitterly.

Then the word of the LORD came to Isaiah: "Go, tell Hezekiah: Thus says the LORD, the God of your father David: I have heard your prayer and seen your tears. I will heal you: in three days you shall go up to the LORD's temple; I will add fifteen years to your life. I will rescue you and this city from the hand of the king of Assyria; I will be a shield to this city."

Isaiah then ordered a poultice of figs to be taken and applied to the boil, that he might recover. Then Hezekiah asked, "What is the sign that I shall go up to the temple of the LORD?"

Isaiah answered: "This will be the sign for you from the LORD that he will do what he has promised: See, I will make the shadow cast by the sun on the stairway to the terrace of Ahaz go back the ten steps it has advanced." So the sun came back the ten steps it had advanced.

RESPONSORIAL PSALM   *Isaiah 38:10, 11, 12abcd, 16*

R. (see 17b) **You saved my life, O Lord; I shall not die.**
Once I said, **/** "In the noontime of life I must depart! **/** to the gates of the nether world I shall be consigned **/** for the rest of my years." **R.**
I said, "I shall see the LORD no more **/** in the land of the living. **/** No longer shall I behold my fellow men **/** among those who dwell in the world." **R.**
My dwelling, like a shepherd's tent, **/** is struck down and borne away from me; **/** You have folded up my life, **/** like a weaver who severs the last thread. **R.**
Those live whom the LORD protects; **/** yours is the life of my spirit. **/** You have given me health and life. **R.**

ALLELUIA   *John 10:27*

R. **Alleluia, alleluia.** My sheep hear my voice, says the Lord, I know them, and they follow me. **R.**

GOSPEL   *Matthew 12:1–8*

Jesus was going through a field of grain on the sabbath. His disciples were hungry and began to pick the heads of grain and eat them. When the Pharisees saw this, they said to him, "See, your disciples are doing what is unlawful to do on the sabbath." He said to the them, "Have you not read what David did when he and his companions were hungry, how he went into the house of God and ate the bread of offering, which neither he nor his companions but only the priests could lawfully eat? Or have you not read in the law that on the sabbath the priests serving in the temple violate the sabbath and are innocent? I say to you, something greater than the temple is here. If you knew what this meant, *I desire mercy, not sacrifice*, you would not have condemned these innocent men. For the Son of Man is Lord of the sabbath."

JULY 18, SATURDAY OF WEEK 15; ST. CAMILLUS DE LELLIS

FIRST READING   *Micah 2:1–5*

Woe to those who plan iniquity, and work out evil on their couches; In the morning light they accomplish it when it lies within their power. They covet fields, and seize them; houses, and they take them; they cheat an owner of his house, a man of his inheritance. Therefore thus says the LORD: behold, I am planning against this race an evil from which you shall not withdraw your necks; nor shall you walk with head high, for it will be a time of evil.

On that day a satire shall be sung over you, and there shall be a plaintive chant: "Our ruin is complete, our fields are portioned out among our captors, The fields of my people are measured out, and no one can get them back!" Thus you shall have no one to mark out boundaries by lot in the assembly of the LORD.

RESPONSORIAL PSALM   *Psalm 10:1–2, 3–4, 7–8, 14*

R. (12b) Do not forget the poor, O Lord!

Why, O LORD, do you stand aloof? / Why hide in times of distress? / Proudly the wicked harass the afflicted, / who are caught in the devices the wicked have contrived. **R.**

For the wicked man glories in his greed, / and the covetous blasphemes, /
sets the LORD at nought. / The wicked man boasts, /
"He will not avenge it"; / "There is no God," sums up his thoughts. **R.**

His mouth is full of cursing, guile and deceit; / under his tongue are mischief and iniquity. /
He lurks in ambush near the villages; / in hiding he murders the innocent; /
his eyes spy upon the unfortunate. **R.**

You do see, for you behold misery and sorrow, / taking them in your hands. /
On you the unfortunate man depends; / of the fatherless you are the helper. **R.**

ALLELUIA   *2 Corinthians 5:19*

R. Alleluia, alleluia. God was reconciling the world to himself in Christ, and entrusting to us the message of reconciliation. **R.**

GOSPEL   *Matthew 12:14–21*

The Pharisees went out and took counsel against Jesus to put him to death.

When Jesus realized this, he withdrew from that place. Many people followed him, and he cured them all, but he warned them not to make him known. This was to fulfill what had been spoken through Isaiah the prophet:

Behold, my servant whom I have chosen, my beloved in whom I delight; I shall place my Spirit upon him, and he will proclaim justice to the Gentiles. He will not contend or cry out, nor will anyone hear his voice in the streets. A bruised reed he will not break, a smoldering wick he will not quench, until he brings justice to victory. And in his name the Gentiles will hope.

JULY 19, 16TH SUNDAY IN ORDINARY TIME; BLESSED PETER TOROT

FIRST READING *Wisdom 12:13, 16—19*

There is no god besides you who have the care of all, that you need show you have not unjustly condemned. For your might is the source of justice; your mastery over all things makes you lenient to all. For you show your might when the perfection of your power is disbelieved; and in those who know you, you rebuke temerity. But though you are master of might, you judge with clemency, and with much lenience you govern us; for power, whenever you will, attends you. And you taught your people, by these deeds, that those who are just must be kind; and you gave your children good ground for hope that you would permit repentance for their sins.

RESPONSORIAL PSALM *Psalm 86:5—6, 9—10, 15—16 (5a)*

R. Lord, you are good and forgiving.

You, O LORD, are good and forgiving, / abounding in kindness to all who call upon you. / Hearken, O LORD, to my prayer / and attend to the sound of my pleading. **R.**

All the nations you have made / shall come and worship you, O LORD, / and glorify your name. /For you are great, and you do wondrous deeds; / you alone are God. **R.**

You, O LORD, are a God merciful and gracious, / slow to anger, abounding in kindness and fidelity. / Turn toward me, and have pity on me; / give your strength to your servant. **R.**

SECOND READING *Romans 8:26—27*

Brothers and sisters: The Spirit comes to the aid of our weakness; for we do not know how to pray as we ought, but the Spirit himself intercedes with inexpressible groanings. And the one who searches hearts knows what is the intention of the Spirit, because he intercedes for the holy ones according to God's will.

ALLELUIA *see Matthew 11:25*

R. Alleluia, alleluia. Blessed are you, Father, Lord of heaven and earth; you have revealed to little ones the mysteries of the kingdom. **R.**

GOSPEL *Longer Form Matthew 13:24—43*

Jesus proposed another parable to the crowds, saying: "The kingdom of heaven may be likened to a man who sowed good seed in his field. While everyone was asleep his enemy came and sowed weeds all through the wheat, and then went off. When the crop grew and bore fruit, the weeds appeared as well. The slaves of the householder came to him and said, 'Master, did you not sow good seed in your field? Where have the weeds come from?' He answered, 'An enemy has done this.' His slaves said to him, 'Do you want us to go and pull them up?' He replied, 'No, if you pull up the weeds you might uproot the wheat along with them. Let them grow together until harvest; then at harvest time I will say to the harvesters, "First collect the weeds and tie them in bundles for burning; but gather the wheat into my barn."'"

He proposed another parable to them. "The kingdom of heaven is like a mustard seed that a person took and sowed in a field. It is the smallest of all the seeds, yet when full–grown it is the largest of plants. It becomes a large bush, and the 'birds of the sky come and dwell in its branches.'"

He spoke to them another parable. "The kingdom of heaven is like yeast that a woman took and mixed with three measures of wheat flour until the whole batch was leavened."

All these things Jesus spoke to the crowds in parables. He spoke to them only in parables, to fulfill what had been said through the prophet: I will open my mouth in parables, I will announce what has lain hidden from the foundation of the world.

Then, dismissing the crowds, he went into the house. His disciples approached him and said, "Explain to us the parable of the weeds in the field." He said in reply, "He who sows good seed is the Son of Man, the field is the world, the good seed the children of the kingdom. The weeds are the children of the evil one, and the enemy who sows them is the devil. The harvest is the end of the age, and the harvesters are angels.

"Just as weeds are collected and burned up with fire, so will it be at the end of the age. The Son of Man will send his angels, and they will collect out of his kingdom all who cause others to sin and all evildoers. They will throw them into the fiery furnace, where there will be wailing and grinding of teeth. Then the righteous will shine like the sun in the kingdom of their Father. Whoever has ears ought to hear."

SHORTER FORM   *Matthew 13:24—30*
Jesus proposed another parable to the crowds, saying: "The kingdom of heaven may be likened to a man who sowed good seed in his field. While everyone was asleep his enemy came and sowed weeds all through the wheat, and then went off.

"When the crop grew and bore fruit, the weeds appeared as well. The slaves of the householder came to him and said, 'Master, did you not sow good seed in your field? Where have the weeds come from?' He answered, 'An enemy has done this.' His slaves said to him, 'Do you want us to go and pull them up?' He replied, 'No, if you pull up the weeds you might uproot the wheat along with them. Let them grow together until harvest; then at harvest time I will say to the harvesters, "First collect the weeds and tie them in bundles for burning; but gather the wheat into my barn."'"

JULY 20, MONDAY OF WEEK 16; ST. APOLLINARIUS

FIRST READING   *Micah 6:1—4, 6—8*
Hear what the LORD says: Arise, present your plea before the mountains, and let the hills hear your voice! Hear, O mountains, the plea of the LORD, pay attention, O foundations of the earth! For the LORD has a plea against his people, and he enters into trial with Israel.

O my people, what have I done to you, or how have I wearied you? Answer me! For I brought you up from the land of Egypt, from the place of slavery I released you; and I sent before you Moses, Aaron, and Miriam.

With what shall I come before the LORD, and bow before God most high? Shall I come before him with burnt offerings, with calves a year old? Will the LORD be pleased with thousands of rams, with myriad streams of oil? Shall I give my first–born for my crime, the fruit of my body for the sin of my soul? You have been told, O man, what is good, and what the LORD requires of you: Only to do the right and to love goodness, and to walk humbly with your God.

RESPONSORIAL PSALM   *Psalm 50:5–6, 8–9, 16bc–17, 21 and 23*
R. (23b) To the upright I will show the saving power of God.
"Gather my faithful ones before me, / those who have made a covenant with me by sacrifice." / And the heavens proclaim his justice; / for God himself is the judge. **R.**
"Not for your sacrifices do I rebuke you, / for your burnt offerings are before me always. / I take from your house no bullock, / no goats out of your fold." **R.**
"Why do you recite my statutes, / and profess my covenant with your mouth, / though you hate discipline / and cast my words behind you?" **R.**
"When you do these things, shall I be deaf to it? / Or do you think that I am like yourself? / I will correct you by drawing them up before your eyes. / He that offers praise as a sacrifice glorifies me; / and to him that goes the right way / I will show the salvation of God." **R.**
ALLELUIA   *Psalm 95:8*
R. Alleluia, alleluia. If today you hear his voice, harden not your hearts. **R.**

GOSPEL   *Matthew 12:38–42*
Some of the scribes and Pharisees said to Jesus, "Teacher, we wish to see a sign from you." He said to them in reply, "An evil and unfaithful generation seeks a sign, but no sign will be given it except the sign of Jonah the prophet. Just as Jonah was in the belly of the whale three days and three nights, so will the Son of Man be in the heart of the earth three days and three nights. At the judgment, the men of Nineveh will arise with this generation and condemn it, because they repented at the preaching of Jonah; and there is something greater than Jonah here. At the judgment the queen of the south will arise with this generation and condemn it, because she came from the ends of the earth to hear the wisdom of Solomon; and there is something greater than Solomon here."

JULY 21, TUESDAY OF WEEK 16; ST. LAWRENCE OF BRINDISI
FIRST READING   *Micah 7:14–15, 18–20*
Shepherd your people with your staff, the flock of your inheritance, that dwells apart in a woodland, in the midst of Carmel. Let them feed in Bashan and Gilead, as in the days of old; As in the days when you came from the land of Egypt, show us wonderful signs.

Who is there like you, the God who removes guilt and pardons sin for the remnant of his inheritance; Who does not persist in anger forever, but delights rather in clemency, And will again have compassion on us, treading underfoot our guilt? You will cast into the depths of the sea all our sins; You will show faithfulness to Jacob, and grace to Abraham, As you have sworn to our fathers from days of old.

RESPONSORIAL PSALM *Psalm 85:2–4, 5–6, 7–8*
R. (8a) Lord, show us your mercy and love.
You have favored, O LORD, your land; / you have brought back the captives of Jacob. / You have forgiven the guilt of your people; / you have covered all their sins. / You have withdrawn all your wrath; / you have revoked your burning anger. **R.**
Restore us, O God our savior, / and abandon your displeasure against us. / Will you be ever angry with us, / prolonging your anger to all generations? **R.**
Will you not instead give us life; / and shall not your people rejoice in you? / Show us, O LORD, your kindness, / and grant us your salvation. **R.**

ALLELUIA *John 14:23*
R. Alleluia, alleluia. Whoever loves me will keep my word, and my Father will love him and we will come to him. **R.**

GOSPEL *Matthew 12:46–50*
While Jesus was speaking to the crowds, his mother and his brothers appeared outside, wishing to speak with him. Someone told him, "Your mother and your brothers are standing outside, asking to speak with you." But he said in reply to the one who told him, "Who is my mother? Who are my brothers?" And stretching out his hand toward his disciples, he said, "Here are my mother and my brothers. For whoever does the will of my heavenly Father is my brother, and sister, and mother."

JULY 22, WEDNESDAY OF WEEK 16; ST. MARY MAGDALENE

FIRST READING *Song of Songs 3:1-4b*
The Bride says: On my bed at night I sought him whom my heart loves–I sought him but I did not find him. I will rise then and go about the city; in the streets and crossings I will seek Him whom my heart loves. I sought him but I did not find him. The watchmen came upon me, as they made their rounds of the city: Have you seen him whom my heart loves? I had hardly left them when I found him whom my heart loves.

ALTERNATIVE FIRST READING *2 COR 5:14-17*
Brothers and sisters: The love of Christ impels us, once we have come to the conviction that one died for all; therefore, all have died. He indeed died for all, so that those who live might no longer live for themselves but for him who for their sake died and was raised.

Consequently, from now on we regard no one according to the flesh; even if we once knew Christ according to the flesh, yet now we know him so no longer. So whoever is in Christ is a new creation: the old things have passed away; behold, new things have come.

RESPONSORIAL PSALM *PS 63:2, 3-4, 5-6, 8-9*
R. (2) My soul is thirsting for you, O Lord my God.

O God, you are my God whom I seek; / for you my flesh pines and my soul thirsts / like the earth, parched, lifeless and without water. **R.**

Thus have I gazed toward you in the sanctuary / to see your power and your glory, / For your kindness is a greater good than life; / my lips shall glorify you. **R.**

Thus will I bless you while I live; / lifting up my hands, I will call upon your name. /
As with the riches of a banquet shall my soul be satisfied, / and with exultant lips my mouth shall praise you. **R.**

You are my help, / and in the shadow of your wings I shout for joy. /
My soul clings fast to you; / your right hand upholds me. **R.**

ALLELUIA

R. Alleluia, alleluia. Tell us Mary, what did you see on the way? I saw the glory of the risen Christ, I saw his empty tomb. **R.**

Gospel   *John 20:1-2, 11-18*

On the first day of the week, Mary Magdalene came to the tomb early in the morning, while it was still dark, and saw the stone removed from the tomb. So she ran and went to Simon Peter and to the other disciple whom Jesus loved, and told them, "They have taken the Lord from the tomb, and we don't know where they put him."

Mary stayed outside the tomb weeping. And as she wept, she bent over into the tomb and saw two angels in white sitting there, one at the head and one at the feet where the Body of Jesus had been. And they said to her, "Woman, why are you weeping?" She said to them, "They have taken my Lord, and I don't know where they laid him." When she had said this, she turned around and saw Jesus there, but did not know it was Jesus. Jesus said to her, "Woman, why are you weeping? Whom are you looking for?" She thought it was the gardener and said to him, "Sir, if you carried him away, tell me where you laid him, and I will take him." Jesus said to her, "Mary!" She turned and said to him in Hebrew, "Rabbouni," which means Teacher. Jesus said to her, "Stop holding on to me, for I have not yet ascended to the Father. But go to my brothers and tell them, 'I am going to my Father and your Father, to my God and your God.'" Mary Magdalene went and announced to the disciples, "I have seen the Lord," and then reported what he told her.

JULY 23, THURSDAY OF WEEK 16; ST. BRIDGET OF SWEDEN

FIRST READING   *Jeremiah 2:1–3, 7–8, 12–13*

This word of the LORD came to me: Go, cry out this message for Jerusalem to hear!

I remember the devotion of your youth, how you loved me as a bride, following me in the desert, in a land unsown. Sacred to the LORD was Israel, the first fruits of his harvest; should any presume to partake of them, evil would befall them, says the LORD.

When I brought you into the garden land to eat its goodly fruits, You entered and defiled my land, you made my heritage loathsome. The priests asked not, "Where is the LORD?" Those who dealt with the law knew me not: the shepherds rebelled against me. The prophets prophesied by Baal, and went after useless idols.

Be amazed at this, O heavens, and shudder with sheer horror, says the LORD. Two evils have my people done: they have forsaken me, the source of living waters; they have dug themselves cisterns, broken cisterns, that hold no water.

RESPONSORIAL PSALM *Psalm 36:6–7ab, 8–9, 10–11*
R. (10a) With you is the fountain of life, O Lord.
O LORD, your mercy reaches to heaven; / your faithfulness, to the clouds. /
Your justice is like the mountains of God; / your judgments, like the mighty deep. **R.**
How precious is your mercy, O God! / The children of men take refuge in the shadow of your wings. / They have their fill of the prime gifts of your house; / from your delightful stream you give them to drink. **R.**
For with you is the fountain of life, / and in your light we see light. /
Keep up your mercy toward your friends, / your just defense of the upright of heart. **R.**

ALLELUIA *See Matthew 11:25*
R. Alleluia, alleluia. Blessed are you, Father, Lord of heaven and earth; you have revealed to little ones the mysteries of the Kingdom. **R.**

GOSPEL *Matthew 13:10–17*
The disciples approached Jesus and said, "Why do you speak to the crowd in parables?" He said to them in reply, "Because knowledge of the mysteries of the Kingdom of heaven has been granted to you, but to them it has not been granted. To anyone who has, more will be given and he will grow rich; from anyone who has not, even what he has will be taken away. This is why I speak to them in parables, because *they look but do not see and hear but do not listen or understand.* Isaiah's prophecy is fulfilled in them, which says:

You shall indeed hear but not understand, you shall indeed look but never see. Gross is the heart of this people, they will hardly hear with their ears, they have closed their eyes, lest they see with their eyes and hear with their ears and understand with their hearts and be converted and I heal them.

"But blessed are your eyes, because they see, and your ears, because they hear. Amen, I say to you, many prophets and righteous people longed to see what you see but did not see it, and to hear what you hear but did not hear it."

JULY 24, FRIDAY OF WEEK 16; ST. SHARBEL MAKHLOUF
FIRST READING *Jeremiah 3:14–17*
Return, rebellious children, says the LORD, for I am your Master; I will take you, one from a city, two from a clan, and bring you to Zion. I will appoint over you shepherds after my own heart, who will shepherd you wisely and prudently. When you multiply and become fruitful in the land, says the LORD, They will in those days no longer say, "The ark of the covenant of the LORD!" They will no longer think of it, or remember it, or miss it, or make another.

At that time they will call Jerusalem the LORD's throne; there all nations will be gathered together to honor the name of the LORD at Jerusalem, and they will walk no longer in their hardhearted wickedness.

RESPONSORIAL PSALM   *Jeremiah 31:10, 11–12abcd, 13*

R. (see 10d) The Lord will guard us as a shepherd guards his flock.

Hear the word of the LORD, O nations, / proclaim it on distant isles, and say: / He who scattered Israel, now gathers them together, / he guards them as a shepherd his flock. **R.**

The LORD shall ransom Jacob, / he shall redeem him from the hand of his conqueror. / Shouting, they shall mount the heights of Zion, / they shall come streaming to the LORD's blessings: / The grain, the wine, and the oil, / the sheep and the oxen. **R.**

Then the virgins shall make merry and dance, / and young men and old as well. / I will turn their mourning into joy, / I will console and gladden them after their sorrows. **R.**

ALLELUIA   *See Luke 8:15*

R. Alleluia, alleluia. Blessed are they who have kept the word with a generous heart and yield a harvest through perseverance. **R.**

GOSPEL   *Matthew 13:18–23*

Jesus said to his disciples: "Hear the parable of the sower. The seed sown on the path is the one who hears the word of the Kingdom without understanding it, and the Evil One comes and steals away what was sown in his heart. The seed sown on rocky ground is the one who hears the word and receives it at once with joy. But he has no root and lasts only for a time. When some tribulation or persecution comes because of the word, he immediately falls away. The seed sown among thorns is the one who hears the word, but then worldly anxiety and the lure of riches choke the word and it bears no fruit. But the seed sown on rich soil is the one who hears the word and understands it, who indeed bears fruit and yields a hundred or sixty or thirtyfold."

JULY 25, SAINT JAMES, APOSTLE - FEAST

FIRST READING   *2 Corinthians 4:7–15*

Brothers and sisters: We hold this treasure in earthen vessels, that the surpassing power may be of God and not from us. We are afflicted in every way, but not constrained; perplexed, but not driven to despair; persecuted, but not abandoned; struck down, but not destroyed; always carrying about in the body the dying of Jesus, so that the life of Jesus may also be manifested in our body. For we who live are constantly being given up to death for the sake of Jesus, so that the life of Jesus may be manifested in our mortal flesh.

So death is at work in us, but life in you. Since, then, we have the same spirit of faith, according to what is written, I believed, therefore I spoke, we too believe and therefore speak, knowing that the one who raised the Lord Jesus will raise us also with Jesus and place us with you in his presence. Everything indeed is for you, so that the grace bestowed in abundance on more and more people may cause the thanksgiving to overflow for the glory of God.

RESPONSORIAL PSALM   *Psalm 126:1bc–2ab, 2cd–3, 4–5, 6*

R.(5) Those who sow in tears shall reap rejoicing.

When the LORD brought back the captives of Zion, / we were like men dreaming. / Then our mouth was filled with laughter, / and our tongue with rejoicing. **R.**

Then they said among the nations, / "The LORD has done great things for them." / The LORD has done great things for us; / we are glad indeed. **R.**

Restore our fortunes, O LORD, / like the torrents in the southern desert. / Those that sow in tears / shall reap rejoicing. **R.**

Although they go forth weeping, / carrying the seed to be sown, / they shall come back rejoicing, / carrying their sheaves.

ALLELUIA   *See John 15:16*

R. Alleluia, alleluia. I chose you from the world, to go and bear fruit that will last, says the Lord. **R.**

GOSPEL   *Matthew 20:20–28*

The mother of the sons of Zebedee approached Jesus with her sons and did him homage, wishing to ask him for something. He said to her, "What do you wish?" She answered him, "Command that these two sons of mine sit, one at your right and the other at your left, in your Kingdom." Jesus said in reply, "You do not know what you are asking. Can you drink the chalice that I am going to drink?" They said to him, "We can." He replied, "My chalice you will indeed drink, but to sit at my right and at my left, this is not mine to give but is for those for whom it has been prepared by my Father." When the ten heard this, they became indignant at the two brothers. But Jesus summoned them and said, "You know that the rulers of the Gentiles lord it over them, and the great ones make their authority over them felt. But it shall not be so among you. Rather, whoever wishes to be great among you shall be your servant; whoever wishes to be first among you shall be your slave. Just so, the Son of Man did not come to be served but to serve and to give his life as a ransom for many."

JULY 26, 17TH SUNDAY IN ORDINARY TIME; SAINT JOACHIM AND SAINT ANNE

FIRST READING   *1 Kings 3:5, 7—12*

The LORD appeared to Solomon in a dream at night. God said, "Ask something of me and I will give it to you." Solomon answered: "O LORD, my God, you have made me, your servant, king to succeed my father David; but I am a mere youth, not knowing at all how to act. I serve you in the midst of the people whom you have chosen, a people so vast that it cannot be numbered or counted. Give your servant, therefore, an understanding heart to judge your people and to distinguish right from wrong. For who is able to govern this vast people of yours?"

The LORD was pleased that Solomon made this request. So God said to him: "Because you have asked for this— not for a long life for yourself, nor for riches, nor for the life of your enemies, but for understanding so that you may know what is right— I do as you requested. I give you a heart so wise and understanding that there has never been anyone like you up to now, and after you there will come no one to equal you."

RESPONSORIAL PSALM: *Psalm 119:57, 72, 76—77, 127—128, 129—130 (97a)*

R. Lord, I love your commands.

I have said, O LORD, / that my part is to keep your words. /
The law of your mouth is to me more precious / than thousands of gold and silver pieces. **R.**

Let your kindness comfort me / according to your promise to your servants. /
Let your compassion come to me / that I may live, for your law is my delight. **R.**

For I love your commands more than gold, / however fine. For in all your precepts I go forward; / every false way I hate. **R.**

Wonderful are your decrees; / therefore I observe them. /
The revelation of your words sheds light, / giving understanding to the simple. **R.**

SECOND READING   *Romans 8:28—30*

Brothers and sisters: We know that all things work for good for those who love God, who are called according to his purpose. For those he foreknew he also predestined to be conformed to the image of his Son, so that he might be the firstborn among many brothers and sisters. And those he predestined he also called; and those he called he also justified; and those he justified he also glorified.

ALLELUIA   *see Matthew 11:25*

R. Alleluia, alleluia. Blessed are you, Father, Lord of heaven and earth; for you have revealed to little ones the mysteries of the kingdom. **R.**

GOSPEL   *Longer Form Matthew 13:44—52*

Jesus said to his disciples: "The kingdom of heaven is like a treasure buried in a field, which a person finds and hides again, and out of joy goes and sells all that he has and buys that field. Again, the kingdom of heaven is like a merchant searching for fine pearls. When he finds a pearl of great price, he goes and sells all that he has and buys it. Again, the kingdom of heaven is like a net thrown into the sea, which collects fish of every kind. When it is full they haul it ashore and sit down to put what is good into buckets. What is bad they throw away. Thus it will be at the end of the age. The angels will go out and separate the wicked from the righteous and throw them into the fiery furnace, where there will be wailing and grinding of teeth.

"Do you understand all these things?" They answered, "Yes." And he replied, "Then every scribe who has been instructed in the kingdom of heaven is like the head of a household who brings from his storeroom both the new and the old."

SHORTER FORM   *Matthew 13:44—46*

Jesus said to his disciples: "The kingdom of heaven is like a treasure buried in a field, which a person finds and hides again, and out of joy goes and sells all that he has and buys that field. Again, the kingdom of heaven is like a merchant searching for fine pearls. When he finds a pearl of great price, he goes and sells all that he has and buys it."

JULY 27, MONDAY OF WEEK 17; BLESSED TITUS BRANDSMA

FIRST READING *Jeremiah 13:1–11*

The LORD said to me: Go buy yourself a linen loincloth; wear it on your loins, but do not put it in water. I bought the loincloth, as the LORD commanded, and put it on. A second time the word of the LORD came to me thus: Take the loincloth which you bought and are wearing, and go now to the Parath; there hide it in a cleft of the rock. Obedient to the LORD's command, I went to the Parath and buried the loincloth. After a long interval, the LORD said to me: Go now to the Parath and fetch the loincloth which I told you to hide there. Again I went to the Parath, sought out and took the loincloth from the place where I had hid it. But it was rotted, good for nothing! Then the message came to me from the LORD: Thus says the LORD: So also I will allow the pride of Judah to rot, the great pride of Jerusalem. This wicked people who refuse to obey my words, who walk in the stubbornness of their hearts, and follow strange gods to serve and adore them, shall be like this loincloth which is good for nothing. For, as close as the loincloth clings to a man's loins, so had I made the whole house of Israel and the whole house of Judah cling to me, says the LORD; to be my people, my renown, my praise, my beauty. But they did not listen.

RESPONSORIAL PSALM *Deuteronomy 32:18–19, 20, 21*

R. (see 18a) You have forgotten God who gave you birth.

You were unmindful of the Rock that begot you, / You forgot the God who gave you birth. / When the LORD saw this, / he was filled with loathing and anger / toward his sons and daughters. **R.**

"I will hide my face from them," he said, / "and see what will then become of them. / What a fickle race they are, / sons with no loyalty in them!" **R.**

"Since they have provoked me with their 'no–god' / and angered me with their vain idols, / I will provoke them with a 'no–people'; / with a foolish nation I will anger them." **R.**

ALLELUIA *James 1:18*

R. Alleluia, alleluia. The Father willed to give us birth by the word of truth that we may be a kind of firstfruits of his creatures. **R.**

GOSPEL *Matthew 13:31–35*

Jesus proposed a parable to the crowds. "The Kingdom of heaven is like a mustard seed that a person took and sowed in a field. It is the smallest of all the seeds, yet when full–grown it is the largest of plants. It becomes a large bush, and the *birds of the sky come and dwell in its branches*."

He spoke to them another parable. "The Kingdom of heaven is like yeast that a woman took and mixed with three measures of wheat flour until the whole batch was leavened."

All these things Jesus spoke to the crowds in parables. He spoke to them only in parables, to fulfill what had been said through the prophet:

I will open my mouth in parables, I will announce what has lain hidden from the foundation of the world.

JULY 28, TUESDAY OF WEEK 17; BLESSED MARY MAGDALEN MARTINENGO

FIRST READING   *Jeremiah 14:17–22*

Let my eyes stream with tears day and night, without rest, Over the great destruction which overwhelms the virgin daughter of my people, over her incurable wound. If I walk out into the field, look! those slain by the sword; If I enter the city, look! those consumed by hunger. Even the prophet and the priest forage in a land they know not.

Have you cast Judah off completely? Is Zion loathsome to you? Why have you struck us a blow that cannot be healed? We wait for peace, to no avail; for a time of healing, but terror comes instead. We recognize, O LORD, our wickedness, the guilt of our fathers; that we have sinned against you. For your name's sake spurn us not, disgrace not the throne of your glory; remember your covenant with us, and break it not. Among the nations' idols is there any that gives rain? Or can the mere heavens send showers? Is it not you alone, O LORD, our God, to whom we look? You alone have done all these things.

RESPONSORIAL PSALM   *Psalm 79:8, 9, 11 and 13*

R. (9) For the glory of your name, O Lord, deliver us.

Remember not against us the iniquities of the past; / may your compassion quickly come to us, / for we are brought very low. **R.**

Help us, O God our savior, / because of the glory of your name; /
Deliver us and pardon our sins / for your name's sake. **R.**

Let the prisoners' sighing come before you; / with your great power free those doomed to death. / Then we, your people and the sheep of your pasture, / will give thanks to you forever; / through all generations we will declare your praise. **R.**

ALLELUIA

R. Alleluia, alleluia. The seed is the word of God, Christ is the sower; all who come to him will live for ever. **R.**

GOSPEL   *Matthew 13:36–43*

Jesus dismissed the crowds and went into the house. His disciples approached him and said, "Explain to us the parable of the weeds in the field." He said in reply, "He who sows good seed is the Son of Man, the field is the world, the good seed the children of the Kingdom. The weeds are the children of the Evil One, and the enemy who sows them is the Devil. The harvest is the end of the age, and the harvesters are angels. Just as weeds are collected and burned up with fire, so will it be at the end of the age. The Son of Man will send his angels, and they will collect out of his Kingdom all who cause others to sin and all evildoers. They will throw them into the fiery furnace, where there will be wailing and grinding of teeth. Then the righteous will shine like the sun in the Kingdom of their Father. Whoever has ears ought to hear."

JULY 29, WEDNESDAY OF WEEK 17; ST. MARTHA

FIRST READING   *Jeremiah 15:10, 16–21*

Woe to me, mother, that you gave me birth! a man of strife and contention to all the land! I neither borrow nor lend, yet all curse me. When I found your words, I devoured them; they became my joy and the happiness of my heart, because I bore your name, O LORD, God of hosts. I did not sit celebrating in the circle of merrymakers; under the weight of your hand I sat alone because you filled me with indignation. Why is my pain continuous, my wound incurable, refusing to be healed? You have indeed become for me a treacherous brook, whose waters do not abide! Thus the LORD answered me: If you repent, so that I restore you, in my presence you shall stand; If you bring forth the precious without the vile, you shall be my mouthpiece. Then it shall be they who turn to you, and you shall not turn to them; And I will make you toward this people a solid wall of brass. Though they fight against you, they shall not prevail, for I am with you, to deliver and rescue you, says the LORD. I will free you from the hand of the wicked, and rescue you from the grasp of the violent.

RESPONSORIAL PSALM   *Psalm 59:2–3, 4, 10–11, 17, 18*

R. (17d) God is my refuge on the day of distress.

Rescue me from my enemies, O my God; / from my adversaries defend me. / Rescue me from evildoers; / from bloodthirsty men save me. **R.**

For behold, they lie in wait for my life; / mighty men come together against me, / Not for any offense or sin of mine, O LORD. **R.**

O my strength! for you I watch; / for you, O God, are my stronghold, / As for my God, may his mercy go before me; / may he show me the fall of my foes. **R.**

But I will sing of your strength / and revel at dawn in your mercy; / You have been my stronghold, / my refuge in the day of distress. **R.**

O my strength! your praise will I sing; / for you, O God, are my stronghold, / my merciful God! **R.**

ALLELUIA   *John 15:15b*

R. Alleluia, alleluia. I call you my friends, says the Lord, for I have made known to you all that the Father has told me. **R.**

GOSPEL   *Jn 11:19-27*

Many of the Jews had come to Martha and Mary to comfort them about their brother [Lazarus, who had died]. When Martha heard that Jesus was coming, she went to meet him; but Mary sat at home. Martha said to Jesus, "Lord, if you had been here, my brother would not have died. But even now I know that whatever you ask of God, God will give you." Jesus said to her, "Your brother will rise." Martha said to him, "I know he will rise, in the resurrection on the last day." Jesus told her, "I am the resurrection and the life; whoever believes in me, even if he dies, will live, and anyone who lives and believes in me will never die. Do you believe this?" She said to him, "Yes, Lord. I have come to believe that you are the Christ, the Son of God, the one who is coming into the world."

ALTERNATIVE GOSPEL

Lk 10:38-42

Jesus entered a village where a woman whose name was Martha welcomed him. She had a sister named Mary who sat beside the Lord at his feet listening to him speak. Martha, burdened with much serving, came to him and said, "Lord, do you not care that my sister has left me by myself to do the serving? Tell her to help me." The Lord said to her in reply, "Martha, Martha, you are anxious and worried about many things. There is need of only one thing. Mary has chosen the better part and it will not be taken from her."

JULY 30, THURSDAY OF WEEK 17; ST. PETER CHRYSOLOGUS

FIRST READING

Jeremiah 18:1–6

This word came to Jeremiah from the LORD: Rise up, be off to the potter's house; there I will give you my message. I went down to the potter's house and there he was, working at the wheel. Whenever the object of clay which he was making turned out badly in his hand, he tried again, making of the clay another object of whatever sort he pleased. Then the word of the LORD came to me: Can I not do to you, house of Israel, as this potter has done? says the LORD. Indeed, like clay in the hand of the potter, so are you in my hand, house of Israel.

RESPONSORIAL PSALM

Psalm 146:1b–2, 3–4, 5–6ab

R. Blessed is he whose help is the God of Jacob. or: R. Alleluia.

Praise the LORD, O my soul; I will praise the LORD all my life; I will sing praise to my God while I live. **R.**

Put not your trust in princes, in the sons of men, in whom there is no salvation. When his spirit departs he returns to his earth; on that day his plans perish. **R.**

Blessed he whose help is the God of Jacob, whose hope is in the LORD, his God. Who made heaven and earth, the sea and all that is in them. **R.**

ALLELUIA

See Acts 16:14b

R. Alleluia, alleluia. Open our hearts, O Lord, to listen to the words of your Son. **R.**

GOSPEL

Matthew 13:47–53

Jesus said to the disciples: "The Kingdom of heaven is like a net thrown into the sea, which collects fish of every kind. When it is full they haul it ashore and sit down to put what is good into buckets. What is bad they throw away. Thus it will be at the end of the age. The angels will go out and separate the wicked from the righteous and throw them into the fiery furnace, where there will be wailing and grinding of teeth."

"Do you understand all these things?" They answered, "Yes." And he replied, "Then every scribe who has been instructed in the Kingdom of heaven is like the head of a household who brings from his storeroom both the new and the old." When Jesus finished these parables, he went away from there.

JULY 31, FRIDAY OF WEEK 17; ST. IGNATIUS OF LOYOLA

FIRST READING *Jeremiah 26:1–9*

In the beginning of the reign of Jehoiakim, son of Josiah, king of Judah, this message came from the LORD: Thus says the LORD: Stand in the court of the house of the LORD and speak to the people of all the cities of Judah who come to worship in the house of the LORD; whatever I command you, tell them, and omit nothing. Perhaps they will listen and turn back, each from his evil way, so that I may repent of the evil I have planned to inflict upon them for their evil deeds. Say to them: Thus says the LORD: If you disobey me, not living according to the law I placed before you and not listening to the words of my servants the prophets, whom I send you constantly though you do not obey them, I will treat this house like Shiloh, and make this the city to which all the nations of the earth shall refer when cursing another.

Now the priests, the prophets, and all the people heard Jeremiah speak these words in the house of the LORD. When Jeremiah finished speaking all that the LORD bade him speak to all the people, the priests and prophets laid hold of him, crying, "You must be put to death! Why do you prophesy in the name of the LORD: 'This house shall be like Shiloh,' and 'This city shall be desolate and deserted'?" And all the people gathered about Jeremiah in the house of the LORD.

RESPONSORIAL PSALM *Psalm 69:5, 8–10, 14*

R. (14c) Lord, in your great love, answer me.

Those outnumber the hairs of my head / who hate me without cause. / Too many for my strength are they who wrongfully are my enemies. / Must I restore what I did not steal? **R.**

Since for your sake I bear insult, / and shame covers my face. / I have become an outcast to my brothers, / a stranger to my mother's sons, / because zeal for your house consumes me, / and the insults of those who blaspheme you fall upon me. **R.**

But I pray to you, O LORD, / for the time of your favor, O God! / In your great kindness answer me with your constant help. **R.**

ALLELUIA *1 Peter 1:25*

R. Alleluia, alleluia. The word of the Lord remains forever; this is the word that has been proclaimed to you. **R.**

GOSPEL *Matthew 13:54–58*

Jesus came to his native place and taught the people in their synagogue. They were astonished and said, "Where did this man get such wisdom and mighty deeds? Is he not the carpenter's son? Is not his mother named Mary and his brothers James, Joseph, Simon, and Judas? Are not his sisters all with us? Where did this man get all this?" And they took offense at him. But Jesus said to them, "A prophet is not without honor except in his native place and in his own house." And he did not work many mighty deeds there because of their lack of faith.

AUGUST 1, SATURDAY OF WEEK 17; ST. ALPHONSUS LIGUORI

FIRST READING   *Jeremiah 26:11–16, 24*

The priests and prophets said to the princes and to all the people, "This man deserves death; he has prophesied against this city, as you have heard with your own ears." Jeremiah gave this answer to the princes and all the people: "It was the LORD who sent me to prophesy against this house and city all that you have heard. Now, therefore, reform your ways and your deeds; listen to the voice of the LORD your God, so that the LORD will repent of the evil with which he threatens you. As for me, I am in your hands; do with me what you think good and right. But mark well: if you put me to death, it is innocent blood you bring on yourselves, on this city and its citizens. For in truth it was the LORD who sent me to you, to speak all these things for you to hear."

Thereupon the princes and all the people said to the priests and the prophets, "This man does not deserve death; it is in the name of the LORD, our God, that he speaks to us."

So Ahikam, son of Shaphan, protected Jeremiah, so that he was not handed over to the people to be put to death.

RESPONSORIAL PSALM   *Psalm 69:15–16, 30–31, 33–34*

R. (14c) Lord, in your great love, answer me.

Rescue me out of the mire; may I not sink! / may I be rescued from my foes, /
and from the watery depths. / Let not the flood–waters overwhelm me, /
nor the abyss swallow me up, / nor the pit close its mouth over me. **R.**

But I am afflicted and in pain; / let your saving help, O God, protect me. /
I will praise the name of God in song, / and I will glorify him with thanksgiving. **R.**

"See, you lowly ones, and be glad; / you who seek God, may your hearts revive! / For the LORD hears the poor, / and his own who are in bonds he spurns not." **R.**

ALLELUIA   *Matthew 5:10*

R. Alleluia, alleluia. Blessed are they who are persecuted for the sake of righteousness for theirs is the Kingdom of heaven. **R.**

GOSPEL   *Matthew 14:1–12*

Herod the tetrarch heard of the reputation of Jesus and said to his servants, "This man is John the Baptist. He has been raised from the dead; that is why mighty powers are at work in him."

Now Herod had arrested John, bound him, and put him in prison on account of Herodias, the wife of his brother Philip, for John had said to him, "It is not lawful for you to have her." Although he wanted to kill him, he feared the people, for they regarded him as a prophet. But at a birthday celebration for Herod, the daughter of Herodias performed a dance before the guests and delighted Herod so much that he swore to give her whatever she might ask for. Prompted by her mother, she said, "Give me here on a platter the head of John the Baptist." The king was distressed, but because of his oaths and the guests who were present, he ordered that it be given, and he had John beheaded in the prison. His head was brought in on a platter and given to the girl, who took it to her mother. His disciples came and took away the corpse and buried him; and they went and told Jesus.

AUGUST 2, 18TH SUNDAY IN ORDINARY TIME; ST. PETER JULIAN EYMARD
FIRST READING *Isaiah 55:1—3*

Thus says the LORD: All you who are thirsty, come to the water! You who have no money, come, receive grain and eat; come, without paying and without cost, drink wine and milk! Why spend your money for what is not bread; your wages for what fails to satisfy? Heed me, and you shall eat well, you shall delight in rich fare. Come to me heedfully, listen, that you may have life. I will renew with you the everlasting covenant, the benefits assured to David.

RESPONSORIAL PSALM *Psalm 145:8—9, 15—16, 17—18 (see 16)*

R. The hand of the Lord feeds us; he answers all our needs.

The LORD is gracious and merciful, **/** slow to anger and of great kindness. **/** The LORD is good to all **/** and compassionate toward all his works. **R.**

The eyes of all look hopefully to you, **/** and you give them their food in due season; **/** you open your hand and satisfy **/** the desire of every living thing. **R.**

The LORD is just in all his ways **/** and holy in all his works. **/** The LORD is near to all who call upon him, **/** to all who call upon him in truth. **R.**

SECOND READING *Romans 8:35, 37—39*

Brothers and sisters: What will separate us from the love of Christ? Will anguish, or distress, or persecution, or famine, or nakedness, or peril, or the sword? No, in all these things we conquer overwhelmingly through him who loved us. For I am convinced that neither death, nor life, nor angels, nor principalities, nor present things, nor future things, nor powers, nor height, nor depth, nor any other creature will be able to separate us from the love of God in Christ Jesus our Lord.

ALLELUIA *Matthew 4:4b*

R. Alleluia, alleluia. One does not live on bread alone, but on every word that comes forth from the mouth of God. **R.**

GOSPEL *Matthew 14:13—21*

When Jesus heard of the death of John the Baptist, he withdrew in a boat to a deserted place by himself. The crowds heard of this and followed him on foot from their towns. When he disembarked and saw the vast crowd, his heart was moved with pity for them, and he cured their sick. When it was evening, the disciples approached him and said, "This is a deserted place and it is already late; dismiss the crowds so that they can go to the villages and buy food for themselves." Jesus said to them, "There is no need for them to go away; give them some food yourselves." But they said to him, "Five loaves and two fish are all we have here." Then he said, "Bring them here to me," and he ordered the crowds to sit down on the grass. Taking the five loaves and the two fish, and looking up to heaven, he said the blessing, broke the loaves, and gave them to the disciples, who in turn gave them to the crowds. They all ate and were satisfied, and they picked up the fragments left over — twelve wicker baskets full. Those who ate were about five thousand men, not counting women and children.

AUGUST 3, MONDAY OF WEEK 18; ST. PHILIP BENIZI

FIRST READING *Jeremiah 28:1–17*

In the beginning of the reign of Zedekiah, king of Judah, in the fifth month of the fourth year, the prophet Hananiah, son of Azzur, from Gibeon, said to me in the house of the LORD in the presence of the priests and all the people: "Thus says the LORD of hosts, the God of Israel: 'I will break the yoke of the king of Babylon. Within two years I will restore to this place all the vessels of the temple of the LORD which Nebuchadnezzar, king of Babylon, took away from this place to Babylon. And I will bring back to this place Jeconiah, son of Jehoiakim, king of Judah, and all the exiles of Judah who went to Babylon,' says the LORD, 'for I will break the yoke of the king of Babylon.'"

The prophet Jeremiah answered the prophet Hananiah in the presence of the priests and all the people assembled in the house of the LORD, and said: Amen! thus may the LORD do! May he fulfill the things you have prophesied by bringing the vessels of the house of the LORD and all the exiles back from Babylon to this place! But now, listen to what I am about to state in your hearing and the hearing of all the people. From of old, the prophets who were before you and me prophesied war, woe, and pestilence against many lands and mighty kingdoms. But the prophet who prophesies peace is recognized as truly sent by the LORD only when his prophetic prediction is fulfilled.

Thereupon the prophet Hananiah took the yoke from the neck of the prophet Jeremiah and broke it, and said in the presence of all the people: "Thus says the LORD: 'Even so, within two years I will break the yoke of Nebuchadnezzar, king of Babylon, from off the neck of all the nations.'" At that, the prophet Jeremiah went away.

Some time after the prophet Hananiah had broken the yoke from off the neck of the prophet Jeremiah, The word of the Lord came to Jeremiah: Go tell Hananiah this: Thus says the LORD: By breaking a wooden yoke, you forge an iron yoke! For thus says the LORD of hosts, the God of Israel: A yoke of iron I will place on the necks of all these nations serving Nebuchadnezzar, king of Babylon, and they shall serve him; even the beasts of the field I give him.

To the prophet Hananiah the prophet Jeremiah said: Hear this, Hananiah! The LORD has not sent you, and you have raised false confidence in this people. For this, says the LORD, I will dispatch you from the face of the earth; this very year you shall die, because you have preached rebellion against the LORD. That same year, in the seventh month, Hananiah the prophet died.

RESPONSORIAL PSALM *Psalm 119:29, 43, 79, 80, 95, 102*

R. (68b) Lord, teach me your statutes.

Remove from me the way of falsehood, **/** and favor me with your law. **R.**

Take not the word of truth from my mouth, **/** for in your ordinances is my hope. **R.**

Let those turn to me who fear you **/** and acknowledge your decrees. **R.**

Let my heart be perfect in your statutes, **/** that I be not put to shame. **R.**

Sinners wait to destroy me, **/** but I pay heed to your decrees. **R.**

From your ordinances I turn not away, **/** for you have instructed me. **R.**

ALLELUIA   *Matthew 4:4*

R. Alleluia, alleluia. One does not live on bread alone, but on every word that comes forth from the mouth of God. **R. Alleluia, alleluia.**

GOSPEL   *Matthew 14:22–36*

Jesus made the disciples get into a boat and precede him to the other side of the sea, while he dismissed the crowds. After doing so, he went up on the mountain by himself to pray. When it was evening he was there alone. Meanwhile the boat, already a few miles offshore, was being tossed about by the waves, for the wind was against it. During the fourth watch of the night, he came toward them, walking on the sea. When the disciples saw him walking on the sea they were terrified. "It is a ghost," they said, and they cried out in fear. At once Jesus spoke to them, "Take courage, it is I; do not be afraid." Peter said to him in reply, "Lord, if it is you, command me to come to you on the water." He said, "Come." Peter got out of the boat and began to walk on the water toward Jesus. But when he saw how strong the wind was he became frightened; and, beginning to sink, he cried out, "Lord, save me!" Immediately Jesus stretched out his hand and caught him, and said to him, "O you of little faith, why did you doubt?" After they got into the boat, the wind died down. Those who were in the boat did him homage, saying, "Truly, you are the Son of God."

After making the crossing, they came to land at Gennesaret. When the men of that place recognized him, they sent word to all the surrounding country. People brought to him all those who were sick and begged him that they might touch only the tassel on his cloak, and as many as touched it were healed.

ALTERNATIVE READING   *Matthew 14:13–21*

When Jesus heard of the death of John the Baptist, he withdrew in a boat to a deserted place by himself. The crowds heard of this and followed him on foot from their towns. When he disembarked and saw the vast crowd, his heart was moved with pity for them, and he cured their sick. When it was evening, the disciples approached him and said, "This is a deserted place and it is already late; dismiss the crowds so that they can go to the villages and buy food for themselves." He said to them, "There is no need for them to go away; give them some food yourselves." But they said to him, "Five loaves and two fish are all we have here." Then he said, "Bring them here to me," and he ordered the crowds to sit down on the grass. Taking the five loaves and the two fish, and looking up to heaven, he said the blessing, broke the loaves, and gave them to the disciples, who in turn gave them to the crowds. They all ate and were satisfied, and they picked up the fragments left over— twelve wicker baskets full. Those who ate were about five thousand men, not counting women and children.

AUGUST 4, TUESDAY OF WEEK 18; ST. JOHN MARY VIANNEY

FIRST READING *Jeremiah 30:1–2, 12–15, 18–22*

The following message came to Jeremiah from the LORD: For thus says the LORD, the God of Israel: Write all the words I have spoken to you in a book.

For thus says the LORD: Incurable is your wound, grievous your bruise; There is none to plead your cause, no remedy for your running sore, no healing for you. All your lovers have forgotten you, they do not seek you. I struck you as an enemy would strike, punished you cruelly; why cry out over your wound? Your pain is without relief. Because of your great guilt, your numerous sins, I have done this to you.

Thus says the LORD: See! I will restore the tents of Jacob, his dwellings I will pity; City shall be rebuilt upon hill, and palace restored as it was. From them will resound songs of praise, the laughter of happy men. I will make them not few, but many; they will not be tiny, for I will glorify them. His sons shall be as of old, his assembly before me shall stand firm; I will punish all his oppressors. His leader shall be one of his own, and his rulers shall come from his kin. When I summon him, he shall approach me; how else should one take the deadly risk of approaching me? says the LORD. You shall be my people, and I will be your God.

RESPONSORIAL PSALM *Psalm 102:16–18, 19–21, 29 and 22–23*

R. (17) The Lord will build up Zion again, and appear in all his glory.

The nations shall revere your name, O LORD, / and all the kings of the earth your glory, / when the LORD has rebuilt Zion / and appeared in his glory; /
When he has regarded the prayer of the destitute, / and not despised their prayer. **R.**

Let this be written for the generation to come, / and let his future creatures praise the LORD: / "The LORD looked down from his holy height, / from heaven he beheld the earth, /
To hear the groaning of the prisoners, / to release those doomed to die." **R.**

The children of your servants shall abide, / and their posterity shall continue in your presence, / That the name of the LORD may be declared on Zion; / and his praise, in Jerusalem, / When the peoples gather together / and the kingdoms, to serve the LORD. **R.**

ALLELUIA *John 1:49b*

R. Alleluia, alleluia. Rabbi, you are the Son of God; you are the King of Israel. **R.**

GOSPEL *Matthew 14:22–36*

Jesus made the disciples get into a boat and precede him to the other side of the sea, while he dismissed the crowds. After doing so, he went up on the mountain by himself to pray. When it was evening he was there alone. Meanwhile the boat, already a few miles offshore, was being tossed about by the waves, for the wind was against it. During the fourth watch of the night, he came toward them, walking on the sea. When the disciples saw him walking on the sea they were terrified. "It is a ghost," they said, and they cried out in fear. At once Jesus spoke to them, "Take courage, it is I; do not be afraid." Peter said to him in reply, "Lord, if it is you, command me to come to you on the water." He said, "Come." Peter got out of the boat and began to walk on the water toward Jesus. But when he saw how strong the wind was he became frightened; and, beginning to sink, he cried out, "Lord, save me!" Immediately Jesus stretched out his hand and caught him, and said to him, "O you of little faith, why did you doubt?" After they got into the boat, the wind died down. Those who were in the boat did him homage, saying, "Truly, you are the Son of God."

After making the crossing, they came to land at Gennesaret. When the men of that place recognized him, they sent word to all the surrounding country. People brought to him all those who were sick and begged him that they might touch only the tassel on his cloak, and as many as touched it were healed.

ALTERNATIVE READING *MATTHEW 15:1–2, 10–14*

Some Pharisees and scribes came to Jesus from Jerusalem and said, "Why do your disciples break the tradition of the elders? They do not wash their hands when they eat a meal." He summoned the crowd and said to them, "Hear and understand. It is not what enters one's mouth that defiles the man; but what comes out of the mouth is what defiles one." Then his disciples approached and said to him, "Do you know that the Pharisees took offense when they heard what you said?" He said in reply, "Every plant that my heavenly Father has not planted will be uprooted. Let them alone; they are blind guides of the blind. If a blind man leads a blind man, both will fall into a pit."

AUGUST 5, WEDNESDAY OF WEEK 18;
DEDICATION OF THE BASILICA OF ST. MARY MAJOR

FIRST READING *Jeremiah 31:1–7*

At that time, says the LORD, I will be the God of all the tribes of Israel, and they shall be my people. Thus says the LORD: The people that escaped the sword have found favor in the desert. As Israel comes forward to be given his rest, the LORD appears to him from afar: With age–old love I have loved you; so I have kept my mercy toward you. Again I will restore you, and you shall be rebuilt, O virgin Israel; Carrying your festive tambourines, you shall go forth dancing with the merrymakers. Again you shall plant vineyards on the mountains of Samaria; those who plant them shall enjoy the fruits. Yes, a day will come when the watchmen will call out on Mount Ephraim: "Rise up, let us go to Zion, to the LORD, our God."

For thus says the LORD: Shout with joy for Jacob, exult at the head of the nations; proclaim your praise and say: The LORD has delivered his people, the remnant of Israel.

RESPONSORIAL PSALM *Jeremiah 31:10, 11–12ab, 13*

R. (see 10d) The Lord will guard us as a shepherd guards his flock.

Hear the word of the LORD, O nations, / proclaim it on distant isles, / and say: He who scattered Israel, now gathers them together, / he guards them as a shepherd his flock. **R.**

The LORD shall ransom Jacob, / he shall redeem him from the hand of his conqueror. / Shouting, they shall mount the heights of Zion, / they shall come streaming to the LORD's blessings. **R.**

Then the virgins shall make merry and dance, **/** and young men and old as well. **/** I will turn their mourning into joy. **/** I will console and gladden them after their sorrows. **R.**

ALLELUIA   *Luke 7:16*

R. Alleluia, alleluia. A great prophet has arisen in our midst and God has visited his people. **R.**

GOSPEL   *Matthew 15: 21–28*

At that time Jesus withdrew to the region of Tyre and Sidon. And behold, a Canaanite woman of that district came and called out, "Have pity on me, Lord, Son of David! My daughter is tormented by a demon." But he did not say a word in answer to her. His disciples came and asked him, "Send her away, for she keeps calling out after us." He said in reply, "I was sent only to the lost sheep of the house of Israel." But the woman came and did him homage, saying, "Lord, help me." He said in reply, "It is not right to take the food of the children and throw it to the dogs." She said, "Please, Lord, for even the dogs eat the scraps that fall from the table of their masters." Then Jesus said to her in reply, "O woman, great is your faith! Let it be done for you as you wish." And her daughter was healed from that hour.

AUGUST 6, THE TRANSFIGURATION OF THE LORD - FEAST

FIRST READING   *Daniel 7:9—10, 13—14*

As I watched: Thrones were set up and the Ancient One took his throne. His clothing was bright as snow, and the hair on his head as white as wool; his throne was flames of fire, with wheels of burning fire. A surging stream of fire flowed out from where he sat; thousands upon thousands were ministering to him, and myriads upon myriads attended him. The court was convened and the books were opened.

As the visions during the night continued, I saw:

One like a Son of man coming, on the clouds of heaven; when he reached the Ancient One and was presented before him, the one like a Son of man received dominion, glory, and kingship; all peoples, nations, and languages serve him. His dominion is an everlasting dominion that shall not be taken away, his kingship shall not be destroyed.

RESPONSORIAL PSALM   *Psalm 97:1—2, 5—6, 9 (1a, 9a)*

R. The Lord is king, the Most High over all the earth.

The LORD is king; let the earth rejoice; **/** let the many islands be glad. **/** Clouds and darkness are round about him, **/** justice and judgment are the foundation of his throne. **R.**

The mountains melt like wax before the LORD, **/** before the LORD of all the earth. **/**
The heavens proclaim his justice, **/** all peoples see his glory. **R.**

Because you, O LORD, are the Most High **/** over all the earth, **/** exalted far above all gods. **R.**

SECOND READING   *2 Peter 1:16—19*

Beloved: We did not follow cleverly devised myths when we made known to you the power and coming of our Lord Jesus Christ, but we had been eyewitnesses of his majesty. For he received honor and glory from God the Father when that unique declaration came to him from the majestic glory, "This is my Son, my beloved, with whom I am well pleased." We ourselves heard this voice come from heaven while we were with him on the holy mountain. Moreover, we possess the prophetic message that is altogether reliable. You will do well to be attentive to it, as to a lamp shining in a dark place, until day dawns and the morning star rises in your hearts.

R. Alleluia, alleluia. This is my beloved Son with whom I am well pleased; listen to him. **R.**

GOSPEL
Matthew 17:1—9

Jesus took Peter, James, and his brother, John, and led them up a high mountain by themselves. And he was transfigured before them; his face shone like the sun and his clothes became white as light. And behold, Moses and Elijah appeared to them, conversing with him. Then Peter said to Jesus in reply, "Lord, it is good that we are here. If you wish, I will make three tents here, one for you, one for Moses, and one for Elijah." While he was still speaking, behold, a bright cloud cast a shadow over them, then from the cloud came a voice that said, "This is my beloved Son, with whom I am well pleased; listen to him." When the disciples heard this, they fell prostrate and were very much afraid. But Jesus came and touched them, saying, "Rise, and do not be afraid." And when the disciples raised their eyes, they saw no one else but Jesus alone.

As they were coming down from the mountain, Jesus charged them, "Do not tell the vision to anyone until the Son of Man has been raised from the dead."

AUGUST 7, FRIDAY OF WEEK 18; ST. CAJETAN

FIRST READING
Nahum 2:1, 3; 3:1–3, 6–7

See, upon the mountains there advances the bearer of good news, announcing peace! Celebrate your feasts, O Judah, fulfill your vows! For nevermore shall you be invaded by the scoundrel; he is completely destroyed. The LORD will restore the vine of Jacob, the pride of Israel, Though ravagers have ravaged them and ruined the tendrils.

Woe to the bloody city, all lies, full of plunder, whose looting never stops! The crack of the whip, the rumbling sounds of wheels; horses a–gallop, chariots bounding, Cavalry charging, the flame of the sword, the flash of the spear, the many slain, the heaping corpses, the endless bodies to stumble upon! I will cast filth upon you, disgrace you and put you to shame; Till everyone who sees you runs from you, saying, "Nineveh is destroyed; who can pity her? Where can one find any to console her?"

RESPONSORIAL PSALM
Deuteronomy 32:35cd–36ab, 39abcd, 41

R. (39c) It is I who deal death and give life.

Close at hand is the day of their disaster, / and their doom is rushing upon them! / Surely, the LORD shall do justice for his people; / on his servants he shall have pity. **R.**

"Learn then that I, I alone, am God, / and there is no god besides me. / It is I who bring both death and life, / I who inflict wounds and heal them." **R.**

I will sharpen my flashing sword, / and my hand shall lay hold of my quiver, / "With vengeance I will repay my foes / and requite those who hate me." **R.**

ALLELUIA *Matthew 5:10*

R. Alleluia, alleluia. Blessed are they who are persecuted for the sake of righteousness; for theirs is the Kingdom of heaven. **R.**

GOSPEL *Matthew 16:24–28*

Jesus said to his disciples, "Whoever wishes to come after me must deny himself, take up his cross, and follow me. For whoever wishes to save his life will lose it, but whoever loses his life for my sake will find it. What profit would there be for one to gain the whole world and forfeit his life? Or what can one give in exchange for his life? For the Son of Man will come with his angels in his Father's glory, and then he will repay each according to his conduct. Amen, I say to you, there are some standing here who will not taste death until they see the Son of Man coming in his Kingdom."

AUGUST 8, SATURDAY OF WEEK 18; ST. DOMINIC

FIRST READING *Habakkuk 1:12—2:4*

Are you not from eternity, O LORD, my holy God, immortal? O LORD, you have marked him for judgment, O Rock, you have readied him punishment! Too pure are your eyes to look upon evil, and the sight of misery you cannot endure. Why, then, do you gaze on the faithless in silence while the wicked man devours one more just than himself? You have made man like the fish of the sea, like creeping things without a ruler. He brings them all up with his hook, he hauls them away with his net, He gathers them in his seine; and so he rejoices and exults. Therefore he sacrifices to his net, and burns incense to his seine; for thanks to them his portion is generous, and his repast sumptuous. Shall he, then, keep on brandishing his sword to slay peoples without mercy?

I will stand at my guard post, and station myself upon the rampart, and keep watch to see what he will say to me, and what answer he will give to my complaint.

Then the LORD answered me and said: Write down the vision Clearly upon the tablets, so that one can read it readily. For the vision still has its time, presses on to fulfillment, and will not disappoint; If it delays, wait for it, it will surely come, it will not be late. The rash man has no integrity; but the just man, because of his faith, shall live.

RESPONSORIAL PSALM *Psalm 9:8–9, 10–11, 12–13*

R. (11b) You forsake not those who seek you, O Lord.

The LORD sits enthroned forever; / he has set up his throne for judgment. / He judges the world with justice; / he governs the peoples with equity. **R.**

The LORD is a stronghold for the oppressed, / a stronghold in times of distress. / They trust in you who cherish your name, / for you forsake not those who seek you, O LORD. **R.**

Sing praise to the LORD enthroned in Zion; / proclaim among the nations his deeds; / For the avenger of blood has remembered; / he has not forgotten the cry of the poor. **R.**

ALLELUIA *See 2 Timothy 1:10*

R. Alleluia, alleluia. Our Savior Jesus Christ has destroyed death and brought life to light through the Gospel. **R.**

GOSPEL   *Matthew 17:14–20*

A man came up to Jesus, knelt down before him, and said, "Lord, have pity on my son, who is a lunatic and suffers severely; often he falls into fire, and often into water. I brought him to your disciples, but they could not cure him." Jesus said in reply, "O faithless and perverse generation, how long will I be with you? How long will I endure you? Bring the boy here to me." Jesus rebuked him and the demon came out of him, and from that hour the boy was cured. Then the disciples approached Jesus in private and said, "Why could we not drive it out?" He said to them, "Because of your little faith. Amen, I say to you, if you have faith the size of a mustard seed, you will say to this mountain, 'Move from here to there,' and it will move. Nothing will be impossible for you."

AUGUST 9, 19TH SUNDAY IN ORDINARY TIME; ST. EDITH STEIN

FIRST READING   *1 Kings 19:9a, 11—13a*

At the mountain of God, Horeb, Elijah came to a cave where he took shelter. Then the LORD said to him, "Go outside and stand on the mountain before the LORD; the LORD will be passing by."

A strong and heavy wind was rending the mountains and crushing rocks before the LORD— but the LORD was not in the wind. After the wind there was an earthquake — but the LORD was not in the earthquake. After the earthquake there was fire— but the LORD was not in the fire. After the fire there was a tiny whispering sound. When he heard this, Elijah hid his face in his cloak and went and stood at the entrance of the cave.

RESPONSORIAL PSALM   *Psalm 85:9, 10, 11—12, 13—14 (8)*

R. Lord, let us see your kindness, and grant us your salvation.

I will hear what God proclaims; / the LORD—for he proclaims peace. / Near indeed is his salvation to those who fear him, / glory dwelling in our land. **R.**

Kindness and truth shall meet; / justice and peace shall kiss. / Truth shall spring out of the earth, / and justice shall look down from heaven. **R.**

The LORD himself will give his benefits; / our land shall yield its increase. / Justice shall walk before him, / and prepare the way of his steps. **R.**

SECOND READING   *Romans 9:1—5*

Brothers and sisters: I speak the truth in Christ, I do not lie; my conscience joins with the Holy Spirit in bearing me witness that I have great sorrow and constant anguish in my heart. For I could wish that I myself were accursed and cut off from Christ for the sake of my own people, my kindred according to the flesh. They are Israelites; theirs the adoption, the glory, the covenants, the giving of the law, the worship, and the promises; theirs the patriarchs, and from them, according to the flesh, is the Christ, who is over all, God blessed forever. Amen.

ALLELUIA   *see Psalm 130:5*
R. Alleluia, alleluia. I wait for the Lord; my soul waits for his word. **R.**

GOSPEL   *Matthew 14:22—33*
After he had fed the people, Jesus made the disciples get into a boat and precede him to the other side, while he dismissed the crowds. After doing so, he went up on the mountain by himself to pray. When it was evening he was there alone. Meanwhile the boat, already a few miles offshore, was being tossed about by the waves, for the wind was against it. During the fourth watch of the night, he came toward them walking on the sea. When the disciples saw him walking on the sea they were terrified. "It is a ghost, " they said, and they cried out in fear. At once Jesus spoke to them, "Take courage, it is I; do not be afraid." Peter said to him in reply, "Lord, if it is you, command me to come to you on the water." He said, "Come." Peter got out of the boat and began to walk on the water toward Jesus. But when he saw how strong the wind was he became frightened; and, beginning to sink, he cried out, "Lord, save me!" Immediately Jesus stretched out his hand and caught Peter, and said to him, "O you of little faith, why did you doubt?" After they got into the boat, the wind died down. Those who were in the boat did him homage, saying, "Truly, you are the Son of God."

AUGUST 10, SAINT LAWRENCE, DEACON AND MARTYR - FEAST
FIRST READING   *2 Corinthians 9:6–10*
Brothers and sisters: Whoever sows sparingly will also reap sparingly, and whoever sows bountifully will also reap bountifully. Each must do as already determined, without sadness or compulsion, for God loves a cheerful giver. Moreover, God is able to make every grace abundant for you, so that in all things, always having all you need, you may have an abundance for every good work. As it is written:

> He scatters abroad, he gives to the poor; his righteousness endures forever.

The one who supplies seed to the sower and bread for food will supply and multiply your seed and increase the harvest of your righteousness.

RESPONSORIAL PSALM   *Psalm 112:1–2, 5–6, 7–8, 9*
R. **Blessed the man who is gracious and lends to those in need.**
Blessed the man who fears the LORD, / who greatly delights in his commands. / His posterity shall be mighty upon the earth; / the upright generation shall be blessed. **R.**
Well for the man who is gracious and lends, / who conducts his affairs with justice; / He shall never be moved; / the just one shall be in everlasting remembrance. **R.**
An evil report he shall not fear; / his heart is firm, trusting in the LORD. / His heart is steadfast; / he shall not fear till he looks down upon his foes. **R.**
Lavishly he gives to the poor, / his generosity shall endure forever; / his horn shall be exalted in glory. **R.**
ALLELUIA   *John 8:12bc*

R. Alleluia, alleluia. Whoever follows me will not walk in darkness but will have the light of life, says the Lord. **R.**

GOSPEL   *John 12:24–26*

Jesus said to his disciples: "Amen, amen, I say to you, unless a grain of wheat falls to the ground and dies, it remains just a grain of wheat; but if it dies, it produces much fruit. Whoever loves his life loses it, and whoever hates his life in this world will preserve it for eternal life. Whoever serves me must follow me, and where I am, there also will my servant be. The Father will honor whoever serves me."

AUGUST 11, TUESDAY OF WEEK 19; ST. CLARE

FIRST READING   *Ezekiel 2:8—3:4*

The Lord GOD said to me: As for you, son of man, obey me when I speak to you: be not rebellious like this house of rebellion, but open your mouth and eat what I shall give you.

It was then I saw a hand stretched out to me, in which was a written scroll which he unrolled before me. It was covered with writing front and back, and written on it was: Lamentation and wailing and woe!

He said to me: Son of man, eat what is before you; eat this scroll, then go, speak to the house of Israel. So I opened my mouth and he gave me the scroll to eat. Son of man, he then said to me, feed your belly and fill your stomach with this scroll I am giving you. I ate it, and it was as sweet as honey in my mouth. He said: Son of man, go now to the house of Israel, and speak my words to them.

RESPONSORIAL PSALM   *Psalm 119:14, 24, 72, 103, 111, 131*
R. (103a) How sweet to my taste is your promise!
In the way of your decrees I rejoice, **/** as much as in all riches. **R.**
Yes, your decrees are my delight; **/** they are my counselors. **R.**
The law of your mouth is to me **/** more precious than thousands of gold and silver pieces. **R.**
How sweet to my palate are your promises, **/** sweeter than honey to my mouth! **R.**
Your decrees are my inheritance forever; **/** the joy of my heart they are. **R.**
I gasp with open mouth, **/** in my yearning for your commands. **R.**
ALLELUIA   *Matthew 11:29ab*
R. Alleluia, alleluia. Take my yoke upon you and learn from me, for I am meek and humble of heart. **R. Alleluia, alleluia.**

GOSPEL   *Matthew 18:1–5, 10, 12–14*

The disciples approached Jesus and said, "Who is the greatest in the Kingdom of heaven?" He called a child over, placed it in their midst, and said, "Amen, I say to you, unless you turn and become like children, you will not enter the Kingdom of heaven. Whoever becomes humble like this child is the greatest in the Kingdom of heaven. And whoever receives one child such as this in my name receives me.

"See that you do not despise one of these little ones, for I say to you that their angels in heaven always look upon the face of my heavenly Father. What is your opinion? If a man has a hundred sheep and one of them goes astray, will he not leave the ninety–nine in the hills and go in search of the stray? And if he finds it, amen, I say to you, he rejoices more over it than over the ninety–nine that did not stray. In just the same way, it is not the will of your heavenly Father that one of these little ones be lost."

AUGUST 12, WEDNESDAY OF WEEK 19; ST. STANISLAUS KOSTKA

FIRST READING *Ezekiel 9:1–7; 10:18–22*

The LORD cried loud for me to hear: Come, you scourges of the city! With that I saw six men coming from the direction of the upper gate which faces the north, each with a destroying weapon in his hand. In their midst was a man dressed in linen, with a writer's case at his waist. They entered and stood beside the bronze altar. Then he called to the man dressed in linen with the writer's case at his waist, saying to him: Pass through the city, through Jerusalem, and mark a "Thau" on the foreheads of those who moan and groan over all the abominations that are practiced within it. To the others I heard the LORD say: Pass through the city after him and strike! Do not look on them with pity nor show any mercy! Old men, youths and maidens, women and children—wipe them out! But do not touch any marked with the "Thau"; begin at my sanctuary. So they began with the men, the elders, who were in front of the temple. Defile the temple, he said to them, and fill the courts with the slain; then go out and strike in the city.

Then the glory of the LORD left the threshold of the temple and rested upon the cherubim. These lifted their wings, and I saw them rise from the earth, the wheels rising along with them. They stood at the entrance of the eastern gate of the LORD's house, and the glory of the God of Israel was up above them. Then the cherubim lifted their wings, and the wheels went along with them, while up above them was the glory of the God of Israel.

RESPONSORIAL PSALM *Psalm 113:1–2, 3–4, 5–6*

R. (4b) The glory of the Lord is higher than the skies. or: R. Alleluia.

Praise, you servants of the LORD, / praise the name of the LORD. / Blessed be the name of the LORD / both now and forever. **R.**

From the rising to the setting of the sun / is the name of the LORD to be praised. / High above all nations is the LORD; / above the heavens is his glory. **R.**

Who is like the LORD, our God, / who is enthroned on high, / and looks upon the heavens and the earth below? **R.**

ALLELUIA *2 Corinthians 5:19*

R. Alleluia, alleluia. God was reconciling the world to himself in Christ, and entrusting to us the message of reconciliation. **R.**

GOSPEL *Matthew 18:15–20*

Jesus said to his disciples: "If your brother sins against you, go and tell him his fault between you and him alone. If he listens to you, you have won over your brother. If he does not listen, take one or two others along with you, so that every fact may be established on the testimony of two or three witnesses. If he refuses to listen to them, tell the Church. If he refuses to listen even to the Church, then treat him as you would a Gentile or a tax collector. Amen, I say to you, whatever you bind on earth shall be bound in heaven, and whatever you loose on earth shall be loosed in heaven. Again, amen, I say to you, if two of you agree on earth about anything for which they are to pray, it shall be granted to them by my heavenly Father. For where two or three are gathered together in my name, there am I in the midst of them."

AUGUST 13, THURSDAY OF WEEK 19; ST. PONTIAN AND ST. HIPPOLYTUS

FIRST READING   *Ezekiel 12:1–12*

The word of the LORD came to me: Son of man, you live in the midst of a rebellious house; they have eyes to see but do not see, and ears to hear but do not hear, for they are a rebellious house. Now, son of man, during the day while they are looking on, prepare your baggage as though for exile, and again while they are looking on, migrate from where you live to another place; perhaps they will see that they are a rebellious house. You shall bring out your baggage like an exile in the daytime while they are looking on; in the evening, again while they are looking on, you shall go out like one of those driven into exile; while they look on, dig a hole in the wall and pass through it; while they look on, shoulder the burden and set out in the darkness; cover your face that you may not see the land, for I have made you a sign for the house of Israel.

I did as I was told. During the day I brought out my baggage as though it were that of an exile, and at evening I dug a hole through the wall with my hand and, while they looked on, set out in the darkness, shouldering my burden.

Then, in the morning, the word of the LORD came to me: Son of man, did not the house of Israel, that rebellious house, ask you what you were doing? Tell them: Thus says the Lord GOD: This oracle concerns Jerusalem and the whole house of Israel within it. I am a sign for you: as I have done, so shall it be done to them; as captives they shall go into exile. The prince who is among them shall shoulder his burden and set out in darkness, going through a hole he has dug out in the wall, and covering his face lest he be seen by anyone.

RESPONSORIAL PSALM   *Psalm 78:56–57, 58–59, 61–62*

R. (see 7b) Do not forget the works of the Lord!

They tempted and rebelled against God the Most High, / and kept not his decrees. / They turned back and were faithless like their fathers; / they recoiled like a treacherous bow. **R.**
They angered him with their high places / and with their idols roused his jealousy. / God heard and was enraged / and utterly rejected Israel. **R.**
And he surrendered his strength into captivity, / his glory in the hands of the foe. / He abandoned his people to the sword / and was enraged against his inheritance. **R.**

ALLELUIA   *Psalm 119:135*

R. Alleluia, alleluia. Let your countenance shine upon your servant and teach me your statutes. **R.**

GOSPEL
Matthew 18:21—19:1

Peter approached Jesus and asked him, "Lord, if my brother sins against me, how often must I forgive him? As many as seven times?" Jesus answered, "I say to you, not seven times but seventy-seven times. That is why the Kingdom of heaven may be likened to a king who decided to settle accounts with his servants. When he began the accounting, a debtor was brought before him who owed him a huge amount. Since he had no way of paying it back, his master ordered him to be sold, along with his wife, his children, and all his property, in payment of the debt. At that, the servant fell down, did him homage, and said, 'Be patient with me, and I will pay you back in full.' Moved with compassion the master of that servant let him go and forgave him the loan. When that servant had left, he found one of his fellow servants who owed him a much smaller amount. He seized him and started to choke him, demanding, 'Pay back what you owe.' Falling to his knees, his fellow servant begged him, 'Be patient with me, and I will pay you back.' But he refused. Instead, he had the fellow servant put in prison until he paid back the debt. Now when his fellow servants saw what had happened, they were deeply disturbed, and went to their master and reported the whole affair. His master summoned him and said to him, 'You wicked servant! I forgave you your entire debt because you begged me to. Should you not have had pity on your fellow servant, as I had pity on you?' Then in anger his master handed him over to the torturers until he should pay back the whole debt. So will my heavenly Father do to you, unless each of you forgives his brother from his heart."

When Jesus finished these words, he left Galilee and went to the district of Judea across the Jordan.

AUGUST 14, FRIDAY OF WEEK 19; ST. MAXIMILIAN KOLBE

FIRST READING
Ezekiel 16:1–15, 60, 63

The word of the LORD came to me: Son of man, make known to Jerusalem her abominations. Thus says the Lord GOD to Jerusalem: By origin and birth you are of the land of Canaan; your father was an Amorite and your mother a Hittite. As for your birth, the day you were born your navel cord was not cut; you were neither washed with water nor anointed, nor were you rubbed with salt, nor swathed in swaddling clothes. No one looked on you with pity or compassion to do any of these things for you. Rather, you were thrown out on the ground as something loathsome, the day you were born.

Then I passed by and saw you weltering in your blood. I said to you: Live in your blood and grow like a plant in the field. You grew and developed, you came to the age of puberty; your breasts were formed, your hair had grown, but you were still stark naked. Again I passed by you and saw that you were now old enough for love. So I spread the corner of my cloak over you to cover your nakedness; I swore an oath to you and entered into a covenant with you; you became mine, says the Lord GOD. Then I bathed you with water, washed away your blood, and anointed you with oil. I clothed you with an embroidered gown, put sandals of fine leather on your feet; I gave you a fine linen sash and silk robes to wear. I adorned you with jewelry: I put bracelets on your arms, a necklace about your neck, a ring in your nose, pendants in your ears, and a glorious diadem upon your head. Thus you were adorned with gold and silver; your garments were of fine linen, silk, and embroidered cloth. Fine flour, honey, and oil were your food. You were exceedingly beautiful, with the dignity of a queen. You were renowned among the nations for your beauty, perfect as it was, because of my splendor which I had bestowed on you, says the Lord GOD.

But you were captivated by your own beauty, you used your renown to make yourself a harlot, and you lavished your harlotry on every passer–by, whose own you became.

Yet I will remember the covenant I made with you when you were a girl, and I will set up an everlasting covenant with you, that you may remember and be covered with confusion, and that you may be utterly silenced for shame when I pardon you for all you have done, says the Lord GOD.

ALTERNATIVE FIRST READING   *Ezekiel 16:59 – 63*

The word of the LORD came to me: Son of man, make known to Jerusalem her abominations. Thus says the Lord GOD to Jerusalem: By origin and birth you are of the land of Canaan; your father was an Amorite and your mother a Hittite. As for your birth, the day you were born your navel cord was not cut; you were neither washed with water nor anointed, nor were you rubbed with salt, nor swathed in swaddling clothes. No one looked on you with pity or compassion to do any of these things for you. Rather, you were thrown out on the ground as something loathsome, the day you were born.

Then I passed by and saw you weltering in your blood. I said to you: Live in your blood and grow like a plant in the field. You grew and developed, you came to the age of puberty; your breasts were formed, your hair had grown, but you were still stark naked. Again I passed by you and saw that you were now old enough for love. So I spread the corner of my cloak over you to cover your nakedness; I swore an oath to you and entered into a covenant with you; you became mine, says the Lord GOD. Then I bathed you with water, washed away your blood, and anointed you with oil. I clothed you with an embroidered gown, put sandals of fine leather on your feet; I gave you a fine linen sash and silk robes to wear. I adorned you with jewelry: I put bracelets on your arms, a necklace about your neck, a ring in your nose, pendants in your ears, and a glorious diadem upon your head. Thus you were adorned with gold and silver; your garments were of fine linen, silk, and embroidered cloth. Fine flour, honey, and oil were your food. You were exceedingly beautiful, with the dignity of a queen. You were renowned among the nations for your beauty, perfect as it was, because of my splendor which I had bestowed on you, says the Lord GOD.

But you were captivated by your own beauty, you used your renown to make yourself a harlot, and you lavished your harlotry on every passer–by, whose own you became.

Yet I will remember the covenant I made with you when you were a girl, and I will set up an everlasting covenant with you, that you may remember and be covered with confusion, and that you may be utterly silenced for shame when I pardon you for all you have done, says the Lord GOD.

Thus says the LORD: I will deal with you according to what you have done, you who despised your oath, breaking a covenant. Yet I will remember the covenant I made with you when you were a girl, and I will set up an everlasting covenant with you. Then you shall remember your conduct and be ashamed when I take your sisters, those older and younger than you, and give them to you as daughters, even though I am not bound by my covenant with you. For I will re–establish my covenant with you, that you may know that I am the LORD, that you may remember and be covered with confusion, and that you may be utterly silenced for shame when I pardon you for all you have done, says the Lord GOD.

RESPONSORIAL PSALM   *Isaiah 12:2–3, 4bcd, 5–6*

R. (1c) You have turned from your anger.

God indeed is my savior; **/** I am confident and unafraid. **/**
My strength and my courage is the LORD, **/** and he has been my savior. **/**
With joy you will draw water **/** at the fountain of salvation. **R.**

Give thanks to the LORD, acclaim his name; **/** among the nations make known his deeds, **/** proclaim how exalted is his name. **R.**

Sing praise to the LORD for his glorious achievement; **/** let this be known throughout all the earth. **/** Shout with exultation, O city of Zion, **/** for great in your midst is the Holy One of Israel! **R.**

ALLELUIA   *See 1 Thessalonians 2:13*

R. Alleluia, alleluia. Receive the word of God, not as the word of men, but, as it truly is, the word of God. **R.**

GOSPEL   *Matthew 19:3–12*

Some Pharisees approached Jesus, and tested him, saying, "Is it lawful for a man to divorce his wife for any cause whatever?" He said in reply, "Have you not read that from the beginning the Creator *made them male and female* and said, *For this reason a man shall leave his father and mother and be joined to his wife, and the two shall become one flesh?* So they are no longer two, but one flesh. Therefore, what God has joined together, man must not separate." They said to him, "Then why did Moses command that the man give the woman a bill of divorce and dismiss her?" He said to them, "Because of the hardness of your hearts Moses allowed you to divorce your wives, but from the beginning it was not so. I say to you, whoever divorces his wife (unless the marriage is unlawful) and marries another commits adultery." His disciples said to him, "If that is the case of a man with his wife, it is better not to marry." He answered, "Not all can accept this word, but only those to whom that is granted. Some are incapable of marriage because they were born so; some, because they were made so by others; some, because they have renounced marriage for the sake of the Kingdom of heaven. Whoever can accept this ought to accept it."

AUGUST 15, SOLEMNITY OF THE ASSUMPTION OF THE BLESSED VIRGIN MARY

AT THE VIGIL MASS

FIRST READING *1 Chronicles 15:3—4, 15—16; 16:1—2*

David assembled all Israel in Jerusalem to bring the ark of the LORD to the place that he had prepared for it. David also called together the sons of Aaron and the Levites.

The Levites bore the ark of God on their shoulders with poles, as Moses had ordained according to the word of the LORD.

David commanded the chiefs of the Levites to appoint their kinsmen as chanters, to play on musical instruments, harps, lyres, and cymbals, to make a loud sound of rejoicing.

They brought in the ark of God and set it within the tent which David had pitched for it. Then they offered up burnt offerings and peace offerings to God. When David had finished offering up the burnt offerings and peace offerings, he blessed the people in the name of the LORD.

RESPONSORIAL PSALM *Psalm 132:6—7, 9—10, 13—14 (8)*

R. Lord, go up to the place of your rest, you and the ark of your holiness.

Behold, we heard of it in Ephrathah; / we found it in the fields of Jaar. / Let us enter into his dwelling, / let us worship at his footstool. **R.**

May your priests be clothed with justice; / let your faithful ones shout merrily for joy. / For the sake of David your servant, / reject not the plea of your anointed. **R.**

For the Lord has chosen Zion; / he prefers her for his dwelling. / "Zion is my resting place forever; / in her will I dwell, for I prefer her." **R.**

SECOND READING *1 Corinthians 15:54b—57*

Brothers and sisters: When that which is mortal clothes itself with immortality, then the word that is written shall come about:

Death is swallowed up in victory. Where, O death, is your victory? Where, O death, is your sting?

The sting of death is sin, and the power of sin is the law. But thanks be to God who gives us the victory through our Lord Jesus Christ.

ALLELUIA *Luke 11:28*

R. Alleluia, alleluia. Blessed are they who hear the word of God and observe it. **R.**

GOSPEL *Luke 11:27—28*

While Jesus was speaking, a woman from the crowd called out and said to him, "Blessed is the womb that carried you and the breasts at which you nursed." He replied, "Rather, blessed are those who hear the word of God and observe it."

MASS OF THE DAY

FIRST READING   *Revelation 11:19a; 12:1—6a, 10ab*

God's temple in heaven was opened, and the ark of his covenant could be seen in the temple.

A great sign appeared in the sky, a woman clothed with the sun, with the moon under her feet, and on her head a crown of twelve stars. She was with child and wailed aloud in pain as she labored to give birth. Then another sign appeared in the sky; it was a huge red dragon, with seven heads and ten horns, and on its heads were seven diadems. Its tail swept away a third of the stars in the sky and hurled them down to the earth. Then the dragon stood before the woman about to give birth, to devour her child when she gave birth. She gave birth to a son, a male child, destined to rule all the nations with an iron rod. Her child was caught up to God and his throne. The woman herself fled into the desert where she had a place prepared by God.

Then I heard a loud voice in heaven say: "Now have salvation and power come, and the kingdom of our God and the authority of his Anointed One."

RESPONSORIAL PSALM   *Psalm 45:10, 11, 12, 16 (10bc)*

R. The queen stands at your right hand, arrayed in gold.

The queen takes her place at your right hand in gold of Ophir. **R.**

Hear, O daughter, and see; turn your ear, **/** forget your people and your father's house. **R.**

So shall the king desire your beauty; **/** for he is your lord. **R.**

They are borne in with gladness and joy; **/** they enter the palace of the king. **R.**

SECOND READING   *1 Corinthians 15:20—27*

Brothers and sisters: Christ has been raised from the dead, the firstfruits of those who have fallen asleep. For since death came through man, the resurrection of the dead came also through man. For just as in Adam all die, so too in Christ shall all be brought to life, but each one in proper order: Christ the firstfruits; then, at his coming, those who belong to Christ; then comes the end, when he hands over the kingdom to his God and Father, when he has destroyed every sovereignty and every authority and power. For he must reign until he has put all his enemies under his feet. The last enemy to be destroyed is death, for "he subjected everything under his feet."

ALLELUIA

R. Alleluia, alleluia. Mary is taken up to heaven; a chorus of angels exults. **R.**

GOSPEL   *Luke 1:39—56*

Mary set out and traveled to the hill country in haste to a town of Judah, where she entered the house of Zechariah and greeted Elizabeth. When Elizabeth heard Mary's greeting, the infant leaped in her womb, and Elizabeth, filled with the Holy Spirit, cried out in a loud voice and said, "Blessed are you among women, and blessed is the fruit of your womb. And how does this happen to me, that the mother of my Lord should come to me? For at the moment the sound of your greeting reached my ears, the infant in my womb leaped for joy. Blessed are you who believed that what was spoken to you by the Lord would be fulfilled."

And Mary said:

"My soul proclaims the greatness of the Lord; my spirit rejoices in God my Savior for he has looked with favor on his lowly servant. From this day all generations will call me blessed: the Almighty has done great things for me and holy is his Name. He has mercy on those who fear him in every generation. He has shown the strength of his arm, and has scattered the proud in their conceit. He has cast down the mighty from their thrones, and has lifted up the lowly. He has filled the hungry with good things, and the rich he has sent away empty. He has come to the help of his servant Israel for he has remembered his promise of mercy, the promise he made to our fathers, to Abraham and his children for ever."

Mary remained with her about three months and then returned to her home.

AUGUST 16, 20TH SUNDAY IN ORDINARY TIME; ST. STEPHEN OF HUNGARY

FIRST READING *Isaiah 56:1, 6—7*

Thus says the LORD: Observe what is right, do what is just; for my salvation is about to come, my justice, about to be revealed.

The foreigners who join themselves to the LORD, ministering to him, loving the name of the LORD, and becoming his servants— all who keep the sabbath free from profanation and hold to my covenant, them I will bring to my holy mountain and make joyful in my house of prayer; their burnt offerings and sacrifices will be acceptable on my altar, for my house shall be called a house of prayer for all peoples.

RESPONSORIAL PSALM *Psalm 67:2—3, 5, 6, 8 (4)*

R. O God, let all the nations praise you!

May God have pity on us and bless us; / may he let his face shine upon us. /
So may your way be known upon earth; / among all nations, your salvation. **R.**
May the nations be glad and exult / because you rule the peoples in equity; /
 the nations on the earth you guide. **R.**
May the peoples praise you, O God; / may all the peoples praise you! /
May God bless us, / and may all the ends of the earth fear him! **R.**

SECOND READING *Romans 11:13—15, 29—32*

Brothers and sisters: I am speaking to you Gentiles. Inasmuch as I am the apostle to the Gentiles, I glory in my ministry in order to make my race jealous and thus save some of them. For if their rejection is the reconciliation of the world, what will their acceptance be but life from the dead?

For the gifts and the call of God are irrevocable. Just as you once disobeyed God but have now received mercy because of their disobedience, so they have now disobeyed in order that, by virtue of the mercy shown to you, they too may now receive mercy. For God delivered all to disobedience, that he might have mercy upon all.

R. Alleluia, alleluia. Jesus proclaimed the Gospel of the kingdom and cured every disease among the people. **R.**

GOSPEL *Matthew 15:21—28*

At that time, Jesus withdrew to the region of Tyre and Sidon. And behold, a Canaanite woman of that district came and called out, "Have pity on me, Lord, Son of David! My daughter is tormented by a demon." But Jesus did not say a word in answer to her. Jesus' disciples came and asked him, "Send her away, for she keeps calling out after us." He said in reply, "I was sent only to the lost sheep of the house of Israel." But the woman came and did Jesus homage, saying, "Lord, help me." He said in reply, "It is not right to take the food of the children and throw it to the dogs." She said, "Please, Lord, for even the dogs eat the scraps that fall from the table of their masters." Then Jesus said to her in reply, "O woman, great is your faith! Let it be done for you as you wish." And the woman's daughter was healed from that hour.

AUGUST 17, MONDAY OF WEEK 20; BLESSED JOAN DELANOUE

FIRST READING *Ezekiel 24:15–23*

The word of the LORD came to me: Son of man, by a sudden blow I am taking away from you the delight of your eyes, but do not mourn or weep or shed any tears. Groan in silence, make no lament for the dead, bind on your turban, put your sandals on your feet, do not cover your beard, and do not eat the customary bread. That evening my wife died, and the next morning I did as I had been commanded. Then the people asked me, "Will you not tell us what all these things that you are doing mean for us?" I therefore spoke to the people that morning, saying to them: Thus the word of the LORD came to me: Say to the house of Israel: Thus says the Lord GOD: I will now desecrate my sanctuary, the stronghold of your pride, the delight of your eyes, the desire of your soul. The sons and daughters you left behind shall fall by the sword. Ezekiel shall be a sign for you: all that he did you shall do when it happens. Thus you shall know that I am the LORD. You shall do as I have done, not covering your beards nor eating the customary bread. Your turbans shall remain on your heads, your sandals on your feet. You shall not mourn or weep, but you shall rot away because of your sins and groan one to another.

RESPONSORIAL PSALM *Deuteronomy 32:18–19, 20, 21*

R. (see 18a) **You have forgotten God who gave you birth.**

You were unmindful of the Rock that begot you. **/** You forgot the God who gave you birth. **/** When the LORD saw this, he was filled with loathing **/** and anger toward his sons and daughters. **R.**

"I will hide my face from them," he said, **/** "and see what will then become of them. **/** What a fickle race they are, **/** sons with no loyalty in them!" **R.**

"Since they have provoked me with their 'no-god' **/** and angered me with their vain idols, **/** I will provoke them with a 'no-people'; **/** with a foolish nation I will anger them." **R.**

ALLELUIA   *Matthew 5:3*

R. Alleluia, alleluia. Blessed are the poor in spirit; for theirs is the Kingdom of heaven. **R.**

GOSPEL   *Matthew 19:16–22*

A young man approached Jesus and said, "Teacher, what good must I do to gain eternal life?" He answered him, "Why do you ask me about the good? There is only One who is good. If you wish to enter into life, keep the commandments." He asked him, "Which ones?" And Jesus replied, *"You shall not kill; you shall not commit adultery; you shall not steal; you shall not bear false witness; honor your father and your mother; and you shall love your neighbor as yourself.* "The young man said to him, "All of these I have observed. What do I still lack?" Jesus said to him, "If you wish to be perfect, go, sell what you have and give to the poor, and you will have treasure in heaven. Then come, follow me." When the young man heard this statement, he went away sad, for he had many possessions.

AUGUST 18, TUESDAY OF WEEK 20; ST. JANE FRANCES DE CHANTAL

FIRST READING   *Ezekiel 28:1–10*

The word of the LORD came to me: Son of man, say to the prince of Tyre: Thus says the Lord GOD:

Because you are haughty of heart, you say, "A god am I! I occupy a godly throne in the heart of the sea!"— And yet you are a man, and not a god, however you may think yourself like a god. Oh yes, you are wiser than Daniel, there is no secret that is beyond you. By your wisdom and your intelligence you have made riches for yourself; You have put gold and silver into your treasuries. By your great wisdom applied to your trading you have heaped up your riches; your heart has grown haughty from your riches— therefore thus says the Lord GOD: Because you have thought yourself to have the mind of a god, Therefore I will bring against you foreigners, the most barbarous of nations. They shall draw their swords against your beauteous wisdom, they shall run them through your splendid apparel. They shall thrust you down to the pit, there to die a bloodied corpse, in the heart of the sea. Will you then say, "I am a god!" when you face your murderers? No, you are man, not a god, handed over to those who will slay you. You shall die the death of the uncircumcised at the hands of foreigners, for I have spoken, says the Lord GOD.

RESPONSORIAL PSALM: *Deuteronomy 32:26–27ab, 27cd–28, 30, 35cd–36ab*

R. (39c) It is I who deal death and give life.

"I would have said, / 'I will make an end of them and blot out their name from men's memories,' / Had I not feared the insolence of their enemies, / feared that these foes would mistakenly boast." **R.**

"'Our own hand won the victory; / the LORD had nothing to do with it.'" / For they are a people devoid of reason, / having no understanding. **R.**

"How could one man rout a thousand, / or two men put ten thousand to flight, / Unless it was because their Rock sold them / and the LORD delivered them up?" **R.**

Close at hand is the day of their disaster, / and their doom is rushing upon them! / Surely, the LORD shall do justice for his people; / on his servants he shall have pity. **R.**

ALLELUIA   *2 Corinthians 8:9*

R. Alleluia, alleluia. Jesus Christ became poor although he was rich so that by his poverty you might become rich. **R.**

GOSPEL   *Matthew 19:23–30*

Jesus said to his disciples: "Amen, I say to you, it will be hard for one who is rich to enter the Kingdom of heaven. Again I say to you, it is easier for a camel to pass through the eye of a needle than for one who is rich to enter the Kingdom of God." When the disciples heard this, they were greatly astonished and said, "Who then can be saved?" Jesus looked at them and said, "For men this is impossible, but for God all things are possible." Then Peter said to him in reply, "We have given up everything and followed you. What will there be for us?" Jesus said to them, "Amen, I say to you that you who have followed me, in the new age, when the Son of Man is seated on his throne of glory, will yourselves sit on twelve thrones, judging the twelve tribes of Israel. And everyone who has given up houses or brothers or sisters or father or mother or children or lands for the sake of my name will receive a hundred times more, and will inherit eternal life. But many who are first will be last, and the last will be first."

AUGUST 19, WEDNESDAY OF WEEK 20; ST. JOHN EUDES

FIRST READING   *Ezekiel 34:1–11*

The word of the Lord came to me: Son of man, prophesy against the shepherds of Israel, in these words prophesy to them to the shepherds: Thus says the Lord GOD: Woe to the shepherds of Israel who have been pasturing themselves! Should not shepherds, rather, pasture sheep? You have fed off their milk, worn their wool, and slaughtered the fatlings, but the sheep you have not pastured. You did not strengthen the weak nor heal the sick nor bind up the injured. You did not bring back the strayed nor seek the lost, but you lorded it over them harshly and brutally. So they were scattered for the lack of a shepherd, and became food for all the wild beasts. My sheep were scattered and wandered over all the mountains and high hills; my sheep were scattered over the whole earth, with no one to look after them or to search for them.

Therefore, shepherds, hear the word of the LORD: As I live, says the Lord GOD, because my sheep have been given over to pillage, and because my sheep have become food for every wild beast, for lack of a shepherd; because my shepherds did not look after my sheep, but pastured themselves and did not pasture my sheep; because of this, shepherds, hear the word of the LORD: Thus says the Lord GOD: I swear I am coming against these shepherds. I will claim my sheep from them and put a stop to their shepherding my sheep so that they may no longer pasture themselves. I will save my sheep, that they may no longer be food for their mouths.

For thus says the Lord GOD: I myself will look after and tend my sheep.

RESPONSORIAL PSALM   *Psalm 23:1–3a, 3b–4, 5, 6*

R. (1) The Lord is my shepherd; there is nothing I shall want.

The LORD is my shepherd; / I shall not want. / In verdant pastures he gives me repose; / Beside restful waters he leads me; / he refreshes my soul. **R.**

He guides me in right paths / for his name's sake. / Even though I walk in the dark valley / I fear no evil; / for you are at my side with your rod / and your staff that give me courage. **R.**

You spread the table before me / in the sight of my foes; / You anoint my head with oil; / my cup overflows. **R.**

Only goodness and kindness will follow me / all the days of my life; / And I shall dwell in the house of the LORD / for years to come. **R.**

ALLELUIA   *Hebrews 4:12*

R. Alleluia, alleluia. The word of God is living and effective, able to discern the reflections and thoughts of the heart. **R.**

GOSPEL   *Matthew 20:1–16*

Jesus told his disciples this parable: "The Kingdom of heaven is like a landowner who went out at dawn to hire laborers for his vineyard. After agreeing with them for the usual daily wage, he sent them into his vineyard. Going out about nine o'clock, he saw others standing idle in the marketplace, and he said to them, 'You too go into my vineyard, and I will give you what is just.' So they went off. And he went out again around noon, and around three o'clock, and did likewise. Going out about five o'clock, he found others standing around, and said to them, 'Why do you stand here idle all day?' They answered, 'Because no one has hired us.' He said to them, 'You too go into my vineyard.' When it was evening the owner of the vineyard said to his foreman, 'Summon the laborers and give them their pay, beginning with the last and ending with the first.' When those who had started about five o'clock came, each received the usual daily wage. So when the first came, they thought that they would receive more, but each of them also got the usual wage. And on receiving it they grumbled against the landowner, saying, 'These last ones worked only one hour, and you have made them equal to us, who bore the day's burden and the heat.' He said to one of them in reply, 'My friend, I am not cheating you. Did you not agree with me for the usual daily wage? Take what is yours and go. What if I wish to give this last one the same as you? Or am I not free to do as I wish with my own money? Are you envious because I am generous?' Thus, the last will be first, and the first will be last."

AUGUST 20, THURSDAY OF WEEK 20; ST. BERNARD

FIRST READING   *Ezekiel 36:23–28*

Thus says the LORD: I will prove the holiness of my great name, profaned among the nations, in whose midst you have profaned it. Thus the nations shall know that I am the LORD, says the Lord GOD, when in their sight I prove my holiness through you. For I will take you away from among the nations, gather you from all the foreign lands, and bring you back to your own land. I will sprinkle clean water upon you to cleanse you from all your impurities, and from all your idols I will cleanse you. I will give you a new heart and place a new spirit within you, taking from your bodies your stony hearts and giving you natural hearts. I will put my spirit within you and make you live by my statutes, careful to observe my decrees. You shall live in the land I gave your ancestors; you shall be my people, and I will be your God.

RESPONSORIAL PSALM   *Psalm 51:12–13, 14–15, 18–19*
R. (Ezekiel 36:25) I will pour clean water on you and wash away all your sins.
A clean heart create for me, O God, / and a steadfast spirit renew within me. / Cast me not out from your presence, / and your Holy Spirit take not from me. **R.**
Give me back the joy of your salvation, / and a willing spirit sustain in me. / I will teach transgressors your ways, / and sinners shall return to you. **R.**
For you are not pleased with sacrifices; / should I offer a burnt offering, / you would not accept it. / My sacrifice, O God, is a contrite spirit; / a heart contrite and humbled, / O God, you will not spurn. **R.**

ALLELUIA   *Psalm 95:8*
R. Alleluia, alleluia. If today you hear his voice, harden not your hearts. **R.**

GOSPEL   *Matthew 22:1–14*
Jesus again in reply spoke to the chief priests and the elders of the people in parables saying, "The Kingdom of heaven may be likened to a king who gave a wedding feast for his son. He dispatched his servants to summon the invited guests to the feast, but they refused to come. A second time he sent other servants, saying, 'Tell those invited: "Behold, I have prepared my banquet, my calves and fattened cattle are killed, and everything is ready; come to the feast."' Some ignored the invitation and went away, one to his farm, another to his business. The rest laid hold of his servants, mistreated them, and killed them. The king was enraged and sent his troops, destroyed those murderers, and burned their city. Then the king said to his servants, 'The feast is ready, but those who were invited were not worthy to come. Go out, therefore, into the main roads and invite to the feast whomever you find.' The servants went out into the streets and gathered all they found, bad and good alike, and the hall was filled with guests. But when the king came in to meet the guests he saw a man there not dressed in a wedding garment. He said to him, 'My friend, how is it that you came in here without a wedding garment?' But he was reduced to silence. Then the king said to his attendants, 'Bind his hands and feet, and cast him into the darkness outside, where there will be wailing and grinding of teeth.' Many are invited, but few are chosen."

AUGUST 21, FRIDAY OF WEEK 20; ST. PIUS X

FIRST READING   *Ezekiel 37:1–14*
The hand of the LORD came upon me, and led me out in the Spirit of the LORD and set me in the center of the plain, which was now filled with bones. He made me walk among the bones in every direction so that I saw how many they were on the surface of the plain. How dry they were! He asked me: Son of man, can these bones come to life? I answered, "Lord

GOD, you alone know that." Then he said to me: Prophesy over these bones, and say to them: Dry bones, hear the word of the LORD! Thus says the Lord GOD to these bones: See! I will bring spirit into you, that you may come to life. I will put sinews upon you, make flesh grow over you, cover you with skin, and put spirit in you so that you may come to life and know that I am the LORD. I prophesied as I had been told, and even as I was prophesying I heard a noise; it was a rattling as the bones came together, bone joining bone. I saw the sinews and the flesh come upon them, and the skin cover them, but there was no spirit in them. Then the LORD said to me: Prophesy to the spirit, prophesy, son of man, and say to the spirit: Thus says the Lord GOD: From the four winds come, O spirit, and breathe into these slain that they may come to life. I prophesied as he told me, and the spirit came into them; they came alive and stood upright, a vast army. Then he said to me: Son of man, these bones are the whole house of Israel. They have been saying, "Our bones are dried up, our hope is lost, and we are cut off." Therefore, prophesy and say to them: Thus says the Lord GOD: O my people, I will open your graves and have you rise from them, and bring you back to the land of Israel. Then you shall know that I am the LORD, when I open your graves and have you rise from them, O my people! I will put my spirit in you that you may live, and I will settle you upon your land; thus you shall know that I am the LORD. I have promised, and I will do it, says the LORD.

RESPONSORIAL PSALM   *Psalm 107:2–3, 4–5, 6–7, 8–9*
R. (1) Give thanks to the Lord; his love is everlasting.
Let the redeemed of the LORD say, **/** those whom he has redeemed from the hand of the foe **/ a**nd gathered from the lands, **/** from the east and the west, from the north and the south. **R.**
They went astray in the desert wilderness; **/** the way to an inhabited city they did not find. **/** Hungry and thirsty, **/** their life was wasting away within them. **R.**
They cried to the LORD in their distress; **/** from their straits he rescued them. **/** And he led them by a direct way **/** to reach an inhabited city. **R.**
Let them give thanks to the LORD **/** for his mercy and his wondrous deeds to the children of men, **/** because he satisfied the longing soul **/** and filled the hungry soul with good things. **R.**
ALLELUIA   *Psalm 25:4b, 5a*
R. Alleluia, alleluia. Teach me your paths, my God, guide me in your truth. **R.**

GOSPEL   *Matthew 22:34–40*
When the Pharisees heard that Jesus had silenced the Sadducees, they gathered together, and one of them, a scholar of the law, tested him by asking, "Teacher, which commandment in the law is the greatest?" He said to him, "You shall love the Lord, your God, with all your heart, with all your soul, and with all your mind. This is the greatest and the first commandment. The second is like it: You shall love your neighbor as yourself. The whole law and the prophets depend on these two commandments."

AUGUST 22, SATURDAY OF WEEK 20; QUEENSHIP OF MARY

FIRST READING *Ezekiel 43:1–7ab*

The angel led me to the gate which faces the east, and there I saw the glory of the God of Israel coming from the east. I heard a sound like the roaring of many waters, and the earth shone with his glory. The vision was like that which I had seen when he came to destroy the city, and like that which I had seen by the river Chebar. I fell prone as the glory of the LORD entered the temple by way of the gate which faces the east, but spirit lifted me up and brought me to the inner court. And I saw that the temple was filled with the glory of the LORD. Then I heard someone speaking to me from the temple, while the man stood beside me. The voice said to me: Son of man, this is where my throne shall be, this is where I will set the soles of my feet; here I will dwell among the children of Israel forever.

RESPONSORIAL PSALM *Psalm 85:9ab and 10, 11–12, 13–14*

R. (see 10b) **The glory of the Lord will dwell in our land.**

I will hear what God proclaims; / the LORD—for he proclaims peace. / Near indeed is his salvation / to those who fear him, glory dwelling in our land. **R.**

Kindness and truth shall meet; / justice and peace shall kiss. / Truth shall spring out of the earth, / and justice shall look down from heaven. **R.**

The LORD himself will give his benefits; / our land shall yield its increase. / Justice shall walk before him, / and salvation, along the way of his steps. **R.**

ALLELUIA *Matthew 23:9b, 10b*

R. **Alleluia, alleluia.** You have but one Father in heaven; you have but one master, the Christ. **R.**

GOSPEL *Matthew 23:1–12*

Jesus spoke to the crowds and to his disciples, saying, "The scribes and the Pharisees have taken their seat on the chair of Moses. Therefore, do and observe all things whatsoever they tell you, but do not follow their example. For they preach but they do not practice. They tie up heavy burdens hard to carry and lay them on people's shoulders, but they will not lift a finger to move them. All their works are performed to be seen. They widen their phylacteries and lengthen their tassels. They love places of honor at banquets, seats of honor in synagogues, greetings in marketplaces, and the salutation 'Rabbi.' As for you, do not be called 'Rabbi.' You have but one teacher, and you are all brothers. Call no one on earth your father; you have but one Father in heaven. Do not be called 'Master'; you have but one master, the Christ. The greatest among you must be your servant. Whoever exalts himself will be humbled; but whoever humbles himself will be exalted."

AUGUST 23, 21ST SUNDAY IN ORDINARY TIME; ST. ROSE OF LIMA

FIRST READING *Isaiah 22:19—23*

Thus says the LORD to Shebna, master of the palace: "I will thrust you from your office and pull you down from your station. On that day I will summon my servant Eliakim, son of Hilkiah; I will clothe him with your robe, and gird him with your sash, and give over to him your authority. He shall be a father to the inhabitants of Jerusalem, and to the house of Judah. I will place the key of the House of David on Eliakim's shoulder; when he opens, no one shall shut, when he shuts, no one shall open. I will fix him like a peg in a sure spot, to be a place of honor for his family."

RESPONSORIAL PSALM   *Psalm 138:1—2, 2—3, 6, 8 (8bc)*
R. Lord, your love is eternal; do not forsake the work of your hands.
I will give thanks to you, O LORD, with all my heart, / for you have heard the words of my mouth; / in the presence of the angels I will sing your praise; / I will worship at your holy temple. **R.**
I will give thanks to your name, / because of your kindness and your truth: / when I called, you answered me; / you built up strength within me. **R.**
The LORD is exalted, yet the lowly he sees, / and the proud he knows from afar. / Your kindness, O LORD, endures forever; / forsake not the work of your hands. **R.**

SECOND READING   *Romans 11:33—36*
Oh, the depth of the riches and wisdom and knowledge of God! How inscrutable are his judgments and how unsearchable his ways! *For who has known the mind of the Lord or who has been his counselor? Or who has given the Lord anything that he may be repaid?* For from him and through him and for him are all things. To him be glory forever. Amen.

ALLELUIA   *Matthew 16:18*
R. Alleluia, alleluia. You are Peter and upon this rock I will build my Church, and the gates of the netherworld shall not prevail against it. **R.**

GOSPEL   *Matthew 16:13—20*
Jesus went into the region of Caesarea Philippi and he asked his disciples, "Who do people say that the Son of Man is?" They replied, "Some say John the Baptist, others Elijah, still others Jeremiah or one of the prophets." He said to them, "But who do you say that I am?" Simon Peter said in reply, "You are the Christ, the Son of the living God." Jesus said to him in reply, "Blessed are you, Simon son of Jonah. For flesh and blood has not revealed this to you, but my heavenly Father. And so I say to you, you are Peter, and upon this rock I will build my church, and the gates of the netherworld shall not prevail against it. I will give you the keys to the kingdom of heaven. Whatever you bind on earth shall be bound in heaven; and whatever you loose on earth shall be loosed in heaven." Then he strictly ordered his disciples to tell no one that he was the Christ.

AUGUST 24; SAINT BARTHOLOMEW, APOSTLE - FEAST
FIRST READING   *Revelation 21:9b—14*
The angel spoke to me, saying, "Come here. I will show you the bride, the wife of the Lamb." He took me in spirit to a great, high mountain and showed me the holy city Jerusalem coming down out of heaven from God. It gleamed with the splendor of God. Its

radiance was like that of a precious stone, like jasper, clear as crystal. It had a massive, high wall, with twelve gates where twelve angels were stationed and on which names were inscribed, the names of the twelve tribes of the children of Israel. There were three gates facing east, three north, three south, and three west. The wall of the city had twelve courses of stones as its foundation, on which were inscribed the twelve names of the twelve Apostles of the Lamb.

RESPONSORIAL PSALM   *Psalm 145:10–11, 12–13, 17–18*
R. Your friends make known, O Lord, the glorious splendor of your Kingdom.
Let all your works give you thanks, O LORD, / and let your faithful ones bless you. / Let them discourse of the glory of your Kingdom / and speak of your might. **R.**
Making known to men your might / and the glorious splendor of your Kingdom. / Your Kingdom is a Kingdom for all ages, / and your dominion endures through all generations. **R.**
The LORD is just in all his ways / and holy in all his works. /
The LORD is near to all who call upon him, / to all who call upon him in truth. **R.**
ALLELUIA   *John 1:49b*
R. Alleluia, alleluia. Rabbi, you are the Son of God; you are the King of Israel. **R.**

GOSPEL   *John 1:45–51*
Philip found Nathanael and told him, "We have found the one about whom Moses wrote in the law, and also the prophets, Jesus son of Joseph, from Nazareth." But Nathanael said to him, "Can anything good come from Nazareth?" Philip said to him, "Come and see." Jesus saw Nathanael coming toward him and said of him, "Here is a true child of Israel. There is no duplicity in him." Nathanael said to him, "How do you know me?" Jesus answered and said to him, "Before Philip called you, I saw you under the fig tree." Nathanael answered him, "Rabbi, you are the Son of God; you are the King of Israel." Jesus answered and said to him, "Do you believe because I told you that I saw you under the fig tree? You will see greater things than this." And he said to him, "Amen, amen, I say to you, you will see heaven opened and the angels of God ascending and descending on the Son of Man."

AUGUST 25, TUESDAY OF WEEK 21; ST. LOUIS OF FRANCE

FIRST READING   *2 Thessalonians 2:1–3a, 14–17*
We ask you, brothers and sisters, with regard to the coming of our Lord Jesus Christ and our assembling with him, not to be shaken out of your minds suddenly, or to be alarmed either by a "spirit," or by an oral statement, or by a letter allegedly from us to the effect that the day of the Lord is at hand. Let no one deceive you in any way.

To this end he has also called you through our Gospel to possess the glory of our Lord Jesus Christ. Therefore, brothers and sisters, stand firm and hold fast to the traditions that you were taught, either by an oral statement or by a letter of ours.

May our Lord Jesus Christ himself and God our Father, who has loved us and given us everlasting encouragement and good hope through his grace, encourage your hearts and strengthen them in every good deed and word.

RESPONSORIAL PSALM   *Psalm 96:10, 11–12, 13*

R. (13b) The Lord comes to judge the earth.

Say among the nations: The LORD is king. / He has made the world firm, not to be moved; /
he governs the peoples with equity. **R.**

Let the heavens be glad and the earth rejoice; / let the sea and what fills it resound; /
let the plains be joyful and all that is in them! / Then shall all the trees of the forest exult. **R.**

Before the LORD, for he comes; / for he comes to rule the earth. /
He shall rule the world with justice / and the peoples with his constancy. **R.**

ALLELUIA   *Hebrews 4:12*

R. Alleluia, alleluia. The word of God is living and effective, able to discern reflections and
thoughts of the heart. **R.**

GOSPEL   *Matthew 23:23–26*

Jesus said: "Woe to you, scribes and Pharisees, you hypocrites. You pay tithes of mint and
dill and cummin, and have neglected the weightier things of the law: judgment and mercy
and fidelity. But these you should have done, without neglecting the others. Blind guides,
who strain out the gnat and swallow the camel!

"Woe to you, scribes and Pharisees, you hypocrites. You cleanse the outside of cup
and dish, but inside they are full of plunder and self-indulgence. Blind Pharisee, cleanse
first the inside of the cup, so that the outside also may be clean."

AUGUST 26, WEDNESDAY OF WEEK 21; ST. ELIZABETH BICHIER

FIRST READING   *2 Thessalonians 3:6–10, 16–18*

We instruct you, brothers and sisters, in the name of our Lord Jesus Christ, to shun any
brother who walks in a disorderly way and not according to the tradition they received from
us. For you know how one must imitate us. For we did not act in a disorderly way among
you, nor did we eat food received free from anyone. On the contrary, in toil and drudgery,
night and day we worked, so as not to burden any of you. Not that we do not have the
right. Rather, we wanted to present ourselves as a model for you, so that you might imitate
us. In fact, when we were with you, we instructed you that if anyone was unwilling to work,
neither should that one eat.

May the Lord of peace himself give you peace at all times and in every way. The Lord
be with all of you.

This greeting is in my own hand, Paul's. This is the sign in every letter; this is how I
write. The grace of our Lord Jesus Christ be with all of you.

RESPONSORIAL PSALM   *Psalm 128:1–2, 4–5*

R. (1) Blessed are those who fear the Lord.

Blessed are you who fear the LORD, / who walk in his ways! / For you shall eat the fruit of
your handiwork; / blessed shall you be, and favored. **R.**

Behold, thus is the man / blessed who fears the LORD. / The LORD bless you from Zion: /
may you see the prosperity of Jerusalem / all the days of your life. **R.**

R. Alleluia, alleluia. Whoever keeps the word of Christ, the love of God is truly perfected in him. R.

GOSPEL   *Matthew 23:27–32*

Jesus said, "Woe to you, scribes and Pharisees, you hypocrites. You are like whitewashed tombs, which appear beautiful on the outside, but inside are full of dead men's bones and every kind of filth. Even so, on the outside you appear righteous, but inside you are filled with hypocrisy and evildoing.

"Woe to you, scribes and Pharisees, you hypocrites. You build the tombs of the prophets and adorn the memorials of the righteous, and you say, 'If we had lived in the days of our ancestors, we would not have joined them in shedding the prophets' blood.' Thus you bear witness against yourselves that you are the children of those who murdered the prophets; now fill up what your ancestors measured out!"

AUGUST 27, THURSDAY OF WEEK 21; ST. MONICA

FIRST READING   *1 Corinthians 1:1–9*

Paul, called to be an Apostle of Christ Jesus by the will of God, and Sosthenes our brother, to the Church of God that is in Corinth, to you who have been sanctified in Christ Jesus, called to be holy, with all those everywhere who call upon the name of our Lord Jesus Christ, their Lord and ours. Grace to you and peace from God our Father and the Lord Jesus Christ.

I give thanks to my God always on your account for the grace of God bestowed on you in Christ Jesus, that in him you were enriched in every way, with all discourse and all knowledge, as the testimony to Christ was confirmed among you, so that you are not lacking in any spiritual gift as you wait for the revelation of our Lord Jesus Christ. He will keep you firm to the end, irreproachable on the day of our Lord Jesus Christ. God is faithful, and by him you were called to fellowship with his Son, Jesus Christ our Lord.

RESPONSORIAL PSALM   *Psalm 145:2–3, 4–5, 6–7*

R. (1) I will praise your name for ever, Lord.

Every day will I bless you, / and I will praise your name forever and ever. / Great is the LORD and highly to be praised; / his greatness is unsearchable. **R.**

Generation after generation praises your works / and proclaims your might. / They speak of the splendor of your glorious majesty / and tell of your wondrous works. **R.**

They discourse of the power of your terrible deeds / and declare your greatness. / They publish the fame of your abundant goodness / and joyfully sing of your justice. **R.**

ALLELUIA   *Matthew 24:42a, 44*

R. Alleluia, alleluia. Stay awake! For you do not know when the Son of Man will come. **R.**

GOSPEL   *Matthew 24:42–51*

Jesus said to his disciples: "Stay awake! For you do not know on which day your Lord will come. Be sure of this: if the master of the house had known the hour of night when the thief was coming, he would have stayed awake and not let his house be broken into. So too, you also must be prepared, for at an hour you do not expect, the Son of Man will come.

"Who, then, is the faithful and prudent servant, whom the master has put in charge of his household to distribute to them their food at the proper time? Blessed is that servant whom his master on his arrival finds doing so. Amen, I say to you, he will put him in charge of all his property. But if that wicked servant says to himself, 'My master is long delayed,' and begins to beat his fellow servants, and eat and drink with drunkards, the servant's master will come on an unexpected day and at an unknown hour and will punish him severely and assign him a place with the hypocrites, where there will be wailing and grinding of teeth."

AUGUST 28, FRIDAY OF WEEK 21; ST. AUGUSTINE

FIRST READING   *1 Corinthians 1:17–25*

Brothers and sisters: Christ did not send me to baptize but to preach the Gospel, and not with the wisdom of human eloquence, so that the cross of Christ might not be emptied of its meaning.

The message of the cross is foolishness to those who are perishing, but to us who are being saved it is the power of God. For it is written:

I will destroy the wisdom of the wise, and the learning of the learned I will set aside.

Where is the wise one? Where is the scribe? Where is the debater of this age? Has not God made the wisdom of the world foolish? For since in the wisdom of God the world did not come to know God through wisdom, it was the will of God through the foolishness of the proclamation to save those who have faith. For Jews demand signs and Greeks look for wisdom, but we proclaim Christ crucified, a stumbling block to Jews and foolishness to Gentiles, but to those who are called, Jews and Greeks alike, Christ the power of God and the wisdom of God. For the foolishness of God is wiser than human wisdom, and the weakness of God is stronger than human strength.

RESPONSORIAL PSALM   *Psalm 33:1–2, 4–5, 10–11*

R. (5) The earth is full of the goodness of the Lord.

Exult, you just, in the LORD; / praise from the upright is fitting. / Give thanks to the LORD on the harp; / with the ten-stringed lyre chant his praises. **R.**

For upright is the word of the LORD, / and all his works are trustworthy. / He loves justice and right; / of the kindness of the LORD the earth is full. **R.**

The LORD brings to nought the plans of nations; / he foils the designs of peoples. / But the plan of the LORD stands forever; / the design of his heart, through all generations. **R.**

ALLELUIA   *Luke 21:36*

R. Alleluia, alleluia. Be vigilant at all times and pray, that you may have the strength to stand before the Son of Man. **R.**

GOSPEL   *Matthew 25:1–13*

Jesus told his disciples this parable: "The Kingdom of heaven will be like ten virgins who took their lamps and went out to meet the bridegroom. Five of them were foolish and five were wise. The foolish ones, when taking their lamps, brought no oil with them, but the wise brought flasks of oil with their lamps. Since the bridegroom was long delayed, they all became drowsy and fell asleep. At midnight, there was a cry, 'Behold, the bridegroom! Come out to meet him!' Then all those virgins got up and trimmed their lamps. The foolish ones said to the wise, 'Give us some of your oil, for our lamps are going out.' But the wise ones replied, 'No, for there may not be enough for us and you. Go instead to the merchants and buy some for yourselves.' While they went off to buy it, the bridegroom came and those who were ready went into the wedding feast with him. Then the door was locked. Afterwards the other virgins came and said, 'Lord, Lord, open the door for us!' But he said in reply, 'Amen, I say to you, I do not know you.' Therefore, stay awake, for you know neither the day nor the hour."

AUGUST 29, THE BEHEADING OF JOHN THE BAPTIST

FIRST READING   *1 Corinthians 1:26-31*

Consider your own calling, brothers. Not many of you were wise by human standards, not many were powerful, not many were of noble birth. Rather, God chose the foolish of the world to shame the wise, and God chose the weak of the world to shame the strong, and God chose the lowly and despised of the world, those who count for nothing, to reduce to nothing those who are something, so that no human being might boast before God. It is due to him that you are in Christ Jesus, who became for us wisdom from God, as well as righteousness, sanctification, and redemption, so that, as it is written, "Whoever boasts, should boast in the Lord."

RESPONSORIAL PSALM   *Psalm 71:1–2, 3–4a, 5–6ab, 15ab and 17*

R. I will sing your salvation.

In you, O LORD, I take refuge; / let me never be put to shame. / In your justice rescue me, and deliver me; / incline your ear to me, and save me. **R.**

Be my rock of refuge, / a stronghold to give me safety, / for you are my rock and my fortress. / O my God, rescue me from the hand of the wicked. **R.**

For you are my hope, O LORD; / my trust, O God, from my youth. / On you I depend from birth; / from my mother's womb you are my strength. **R.**

My mouth shall declare your justice, / day by day your salvation. / O God, you have taught me from my youth, / and till the present I proclaim your wondrous deeds. **R.**

ALLELUIA   *Matthew 5:10*

R. Alleluia, alleluia. Blessed are those who are persecuted for the sake of righteousness, for theirs is the Kingdom of heaven. **R.**

GOSPEL   *Mark 6:17–29*

Herod was the one who had John the Baptist arrested and bound in prison on account of Herodias, the wife of his brother Philip, whom he had married. John had said to Herod, "It is not lawful for you to have your brother's wife." Herodias harbored a grudge against him and wanted to kill him but was unable to do so. Herod feared John, knowing him to be a righteous and holy man, and kept him in custody. When he heard him speak he was very much perplexed, yet he liked to listen to him. She had an opportunity one day when Herod, on his birthday, gave a banquet for his courtiers, his military officers, and the leading men of Galilee. Herodias' own daughter came in and performed a dance that delighted Herod and his guests. The king said to the girl, "Ask of me whatever you wish and I will grant it to you." He even swore many things to her, "I will grant you whatever you ask of me, even to half of my kingdom." She went out and said to her mother, "What shall I ask for?" She replied, "The head of John the Baptist." The girl hurried back to the king's presence and made her request, "I want you to give me at once on a platter the head of John the Baptist." The king was deeply distressed, but because of his oaths and the guests he did not wish to break his word to her. So he promptly dispatched an executioner with orders to bring back his head. He went off and beheaded him in the prison. He brought in the head on a platter and gave it to the girl. The girl in turn gave it to her mother. When his disciples heard about it, they came and took his body and laid it in a tomb.

AUGUST 30, 22ND SUNDAY IN ORDINARY TIME; ST. FIACRE

FIRST READING   *Jeremiah 20:7—9*

You duped me, O LORD, and I let myself be duped; you were too strong for me, and you triumphed. All the day I am an object of laughter; everyone mocks me.

Whenever I speak, I must cry out, violence and outrage is my message; the word of the LORD has brought me derision and reproach all the day.

I say to myself, I will not mention him, I will speak in his name no more. But then it becomes like fire burning in my heart, imprisoned in my bones; I grow weary holding it in, I cannot endure it.

RESPONSORIAL PSALM: *Psalm 63:2, 3—4, 5—6, 8—9 (2b)*
R. My soul is thirsting for you, O Lord my God.
O God, you are my God whom I seek; / for you my flesh pines and my soul thirsts like the earth, / parched, lifeless and without water. **R.**
Thus have I gazed toward you in the sanctuary / to see your power and your glory, / for your kindness is a greater good than life; / my lips shall glorify you. **R.**
Thus will I bless you while I live; / lifting up my hands, I will call upon your name. / As with the riches of a banquet shall my soul be satisfied, / and with exultant lips my mouth shall praise you. **R.**
You are my help, / and in the shadow of your wings I shout for joy. / My soul clings fast to you; / your right hand upholds me. **R.**

SECOND READING   *Romans 12:1—2*

I urge you, brothers and sisters, by the mercies of God, to offer your bodies as a living sacrifice, holy and pleasing to God, your spiritual worship. Do not conform yourselves to this age but be transformed by the renewal of your mind, that you may discern what is the will of God, what is good and pleasing and perfect.

ALLELUIA   *see Ephesians 1:17—18*

R. Alleluia, alleluia. May the Father of our Lord Jesus Christ enlighten the eyes of our hearts, that we may know what is the hope that belongs to our call. **R.**

GOSPEL   *Matthew 16:21—27*

Jesus began to show his disciples that he must go to Jerusalem and suffer greatly from the elders, the chief priests, and the scribes, and be killed and on the third day be raised. Then Peter took Jesus aside and began to rebuke him, "God forbid, Lord! No such thing shall ever happen to you." He turned and said to Peter, "Get behind me, Satan! You are an obstacle to me. You are thinking not as God does, but as human beings do."

Then Jesus said to his disciples, "Whoever wishes to come after me must deny himself, take up his cross, and follow me. For whoever wishes to save his life will lose it, but whoever loses his life for my sake will find it. What profit would there be for one to gain the whole world and forfeit his life? Or what can one give in exchange for his life? For the Son of Man will come with his angels in his Father's glory, and then he will repay all according to his conduct."

AUGUST 31, MONDAY OF WEEK 22; ST. AIDAN OF LINDISFARNE

FIRST READING   *1 Corinthians 2:1–5*

When I came to you, brothers and sisters, proclaiming the mystery of God, I did not come with sublimity of words or of wisdom. For I resolved to know nothing while I was with you except Jesus Christ, and him crucified. I came to you in weakness and fear and much trembling, and my message and my proclamation were not with persuasive words of wisdom, but with a demonstration of spirit and power, so that your faith might rest not on human wisdom but on the power of God.

RESPONSORIAL PSALM   *Psalm 119:97, 98, 99, 100, 101, 102*

R. (97) Lord, I love your commands.

How I love your law, O LORD! / It is my meditation all the day. **R.**

Your command has made me wiser than my enemies, / for it is ever with me. **R.**

I have more understanding than all my teachers / when your decrees are my meditation. **R.**

I have more discernment than the elders, / because I observe your precepts. **R.**

From every evil way I withhold my feet, / that I may keep your words. **R.**

From your ordinances I turn not away, / for you have instructed me. **R.**

ALLELUIA   *See Luke 4:18*

R. Alleluia, alleluia. The Spirit of the Lord is upon me; he has sent me to bring glad tidings to the poor. **R.**

GOSPEL *Luke 4:16–30*

Jesus came to Nazareth, where he had grown up, and went according to his custom into the synagogue on the Sabbath day. He stood up to read and was handed a scroll of the prophet Isaiah. He unrolled the scroll and found the passage where it was written:

The Spirit of the Lord is upon me, because he has anointed me to bring glad tidings to the poor. He has sent me to proclaim liberty to captives and recovery of sight to the blind, to let the oppressed go free, and to proclaim a year acceptable to the Lord.

Rolling up the scroll, he handed it back to the attendant and sat down, and the eyes of all in the synagogue looked intently at him. He said to them, "Today this Scripture passage is fulfilled in your hearing." And all spoke highly of him and were amazed at the gracious words that came from his mouth. They also asked, "Is this not the son of Joseph?" He said to them, "Surely you will quote me this proverb, 'Physician, cure yourself,' and say, 'Do here in your native place the things that we heard were done in Capernaum.'" And he said, "Amen, I say to you, no prophet is accepted in his own native place. Indeed, I tell you, there were many widows in Israel in the days of Elijah when the sky was closed for three and a half years and a severe famine spread over the entire land. It was to none of these that Elijah was sent, but only to a widow in Zarephath in the land of Sidon. Again, there were many lepers in Israel during the time of Elisha the prophet; yet not one of them was cleansed, but only Naaman the Syrian." When the people in the synagogue heard this, they were all filled with fury. They rose up, drove him out of the town, and led him to the brow of the hill on which their town had been built, to hurl him down headlong. But he passed through the midst of them and went away.

11 SEPTEMBER

SEPTEMBER 1, TUESDAY OF WEEK 22; ST. GILES

FIRST READING *1 Corinthians 2:10b–16*

Brothers and sisters: The Spirit scrutinizes everything, even the depths of God. Among men, who knows what pertains to the man except his spirit that is within? Similarly, no one knows what pertains to God except the Spirit of God. We have not received the spirit of the world but the Spirit who is from God, so that we may understand the things freely given us by God. And we speak about them not with words taught by human wisdom, but with words taught by the Spirit, describing spiritual realities in spiritual terms.

Now the natural man does not accept what pertains to the Spirit of God, for to him it is foolishness, and he cannot understand it, because it is judged spiritually. The one who is spiritual, however, can judge everything but is not subject to judgment by anyone.

For "who has known the mind of the Lord, so as to counsel him?" But we have the mind of Christ.

RESPONSORIAL PSALM　　　　　　　　　*Psalm 145:8–9, 10–11, 12–13ab, 13cd–14*

R. (17) The Lord is just in all his ways.

The LORD is gracious and merciful, / slow to anger and of great kindness. /
The LORD is good to all / and compassionate toward all his works. **R.**

Let all your works give you thanks, O LORD, / and let your faithful ones bless you. /
Let them discourse of the glory of your Kingdom / and speak of your might. **R.**

Making known to men your might / and the glorious splendor of your Kingdom. / Your
Kingdom is a Kingdom for all ages, / and your dominion endures through all generations. **R.**

The LORD is faithful in all his words / and holy in all his works. /
The LORD lifts up all who are falling / and raises up all who are bowed down. **R.**

ALLELUIA　　　　　　　　　　　　　　　　　　　　*Luke 7:16*

R. Alleluia, alleluia. A great prophet has arisen in our midst and God has visited his
people. **R.**

GOSPEL　　　　　　　　　　　　　　　　　　　　　*Luke 4:31–37*

Jesus went down to Capernaum, a town of Galilee. He taught them on the sabbath, and
they were astonished at his teaching because he spoke with authority. In the synagogue
there was a man with the spirit of an unclean demon, and he cried out in a loud voice,
"What have you to do with us, Jesus of Nazareth? Have you come to destroy us? I know
who you are—the Holy One of God!" Jesus rebuked him and said, "Be quiet! Come out of
him!" Then the demon threw the man down in front of them and came out of him without
doing him any harm. They were all amazed and said to one another, "What is there about
his word? For with authority and power he commands the unclean spirits, and they come
out." And news of him spread everywhere in the surrounding region.

SEPTEMBER 2, WEDNESDAY OF WEEK 22;
BLESSED JOHN DULAU AND THE SEPTEMBER MARTYRS

FIRST READING　　　　　　　　　　　　　　　*1 Corinthians 3:1–9*

Brothers and sisters, I could not talk to you as spiritual people, but as fleshly people, as
infants in Christ. I fed you milk, not solid food, because you were unable to take it. Indeed,
you are still not able, even now, for you are still of the flesh. While there is jealousy and
rivalry among you, are you not of the flesh, and walking according to the manner of man?
Whenever someone says, "I belong to Paul," and another, "I belong to Apollos," are you not
merely men?

What is Apollos, after all, and what is Paul? Ministers through whom you became
believers, just as the Lord assigned each one. I planted, Apollos watered, but God caused
the growth. Therefore, neither the one who plants nor the one who waters is anything, but
only God, who causes the growth. He who plants and he who waters are one, and each will
receive wages in proportion to his labor. For we are God's co-workers; you are God's field,
God's building.

RESPONSORIAL PSALM   *Psalm 33:12–13, 14–15, 20–21*
R. (12) Blessed the people the Lord has chosen to be his own.
Blessed the nation whose God is the LORD, / the people he has chosen for his own inheritance. / From heaven the LORD looks down; / he sees all mankind. **R.**
From his fixed throne he beholds all who dwell on the earth, / He who fashioned the heart of each, / he who knows all their works. **R.**
Our soul waits for the LORD, / who is our help and our shield, / For in him our hearts rejoice; / in his holy name we trust. **R.**

ALLELUIA   *Luke 4:18*
R. Alleluia, alleluia. The Lord sent me to bring glad tidings to the poor and to proclaim liberty to captives. **R.**

GOSPEL   *Luke 4:38–44*
After Jesus left the synagogue, he entered the house of Simon. Simon's mother–in–law was afflicted with a severe fever, and they interceded with him about her. He stood over her, rebuked the fever, and it left her. She got up immediately and waited on them.

At sunset, all who had people sick with various diseases brought them to him. He laid his hands on each of them and cured them. And demons also came out from many, shouting, "You are the Son of God." But he rebuked them and did not allow them to speak because they knew that he was the Christ.

At daybreak, Jesus left and went to a deserted place. The crowds went looking for him, and when they came to him, they tried to prevent him from leaving them. But he said to them, "To the other towns also I must proclaim the good news of the Kingdom of God, because for this purpose I have been sent." And he was preaching in the synagogues of Judea.

SEPTEMBER 3, THURSDAY OF WEEK 22; ST. GREGORY THE GREAT
FIRST READING   *1 Corinthians 3:18–23*
Brothers and sisters: Let no one deceive himself. If anyone among you considers himself wise in this age, let him become a fool, so as to become wise. For the wisdom of this world is foolishness in the eyes of God, for it is written: God catches the wise in their own ruses, and again: The Lord knows the thoughts of the wise, that they are vain. So let no one boast about human beings, for everything belongs to you, Paul or Apollos or Cephas, or the world or life or death, or the present or the future: all belong to you, and you to Christ, and Christ to God.

RESPONSORIAL PSALM   *Psalm 24:1bc–2, 3–4ab, 5–6*
R. (1) To the Lord belongs the earth and all that fills it.
The LORD's are the earth and its fullness; / the world and those who dwell in it. / For he founded it upon the seas / and established it upon the rivers. **R.**
Who can ascend the mountain of the LORD? / Or who may stand in his holy place? / He whose hands are sinless, / whose heart is clean, / who desires not what is vain. **R.**

He shall receive a blessing from the LORD, / a reward from God his savior. / Such is the race that seeks for him, / that seeks the face of the God of Jacob. **R.**

ALLELUIA

Matthew 4:19

R. Alleluia, alleluia. Come after me, says the Lord, and I will make you fishers of men. **R.**

GOSPEL

Luke 5:1–11

While the crowd was pressing in on Jesus and listening to the word of God, he was standing by the Lake of Gennesaret. He saw two boats there alongside the lake; the fishermen had disembarked and were washing their nets. Getting into one of the boats, the one belonging to Simon, he asked him to put out a short distance from the shore. Then he sat down and taught the crowds from the boat. After he had finished speaking, he said to Simon, "Put out into deep water and lower your nets for a catch." Simon said in reply, "Master, we have worked hard all night and have caught nothing, but at your command I will lower the nets." When they had done this, they caught a great number of fish and their nets were tearing. They signaled to their partners in the other boat to come to help them. They came and filled both boats so that the boats were in danger of sinking. When Simon Peter saw this, he fell at the knees of Jesus and said, "Depart from me, Lord, for I am a sinful man." For astonishment at the catch of fish they had made seized him and all those with him, and likewise James and John, the sons of Zebedee, who were partners of Simon. Jesus said to Simon, "Do not be afraid; from now on you will be catching men." When they brought their boats to the shore, they left everything and followed him.

SEPTEMBER 4, FRIDAY OF WEEK 22; ST. ROSE OF VITERBO

FIRST READING

1 Corinthians 4:1–5

Brothers and sisters: thus should one regard us: as servants of Christ and stewards of the mysteries of God. Now it is of course required of stewards that they be found trustworthy. It does not concern me in the least that I be judged by you or any human tribunal; I do not even pass judgment on myself; I am not conscious of anything against me, but I do not thereby stand acquitted; the one who judges me is the Lord. Therefore, do not make any judgment before the appointed time, until the Lord comes, for he will bring to light what is hidden in darkness and will manifest the motives of our hearts, and then everyone will receive praise from God.

RESPONSORIAL PSALM

Psalm 37:3–4, 5–6, 27–28, 39–40

R. (39a) The salvation of the just comes from the Lord.

Trust in the LORD and do good, / that you may dwell in the land and be fed in security. Take delight in the LORD, / and he will grant you your heart's requests. **R.**

Commit to the LORD your way; / trust in him, and he will act. / He will make justice dawn for you like the light; / bright as the noonday shall be your vindication. **R.**

Turn from evil and do good, / that you may abide forever; /

For the LORD loves what is right, / and forsakes not his faithful ones. /

Criminals are destroyed and the posterity of the wicked is cut off. **R.**

The salvation of the just is from the LORD; **/** he is their refuge in time of distress. **/** And the LORD helps them and delivers them; **/** he delivers them from the wicked and saves them, **/** because they take refuge in him. **R.**

ALLELUIA
John 8:12

R. Alleluia, alleluia. I am the light of the world, says the Lord; whoever follows me will have the light of life. **R.**

GOSPEL
Luke 5:33–39

The scribes and Pharisees said to Jesus, "The disciples of John the Baptist fast often and offer prayers, and the disciples of the Pharisees do the same; but yours eat and drink." Jesus answered them, "Can you make the wedding guests fast while the bridegroom is with them? But the days will come, and when the bridegroom is taken away from them, then they will fast in those days." And he also told them a parable. "No one tears a piece from a new cloak to patch an old one. Otherwise, he will tear the new and the piece from it will not match the old cloak. Likewise, no one pours new wine into old wineskins. Otherwise, the new wine will burst the skins, and it will be spilled, and the skins will be ruined. Rather, new wine must be poured into fresh wineskins. And no one who has been drinking old wine desires new, for he says, 'The old is good.'"

SEPTEMBER 5, SATURDAY OF WEEK 22; ST TERESA OF CALCUTTA

FIRST READING
1 Corinthians 4:6b–15

Brothers and sisters: Learn from myself and Apollos not to go beyond what is written, so that none of you will be inflated with pride in favor of one person over against another. Who confers distinction upon you? What do you possess that you have not received? But if you have received it, why are you boasting as if you did not receive it? You are already satisfied; you have already grown rich; you have become kings without us! Indeed, I wish that you had become kings, so that we also might become kings with you.

For as I see it, God has exhibited us Apostles as the last of all, like people sentenced to death, since we have become a spectacle to the world, to angels and men alike. We are fools on Christ's account, but you are wise in Christ; we are weak, but you are strong; you are held in honor, but we in disrepute. To this very hour we go hungry and thirsty, we are poorly clad and roughly treated, we wander about homeless and we toil, working with our own hands. When ridiculed, we bless; when persecuted, we endure; when slandered, we respond gently. We have become like the world's rubbish, the scum of all, to this very moment.

I am writing you this not to shame you, but to admonish you as my beloved children. Even if you should have countless guides to Christ, yet you do not have many fathers, for I became your father in Christ Jesus through the Gospel.

RESPONSORIAL PSALM
Psalm 145:17–18, 19–20, 21

R. (18) The Lord is near to all who call upon him.

The LORD is just in all his ways / and holy in all his works. / The LORD is near to all who call upon him, / to all who call upon him in truth. **R.**

He fulfills the desire of those who fear him, / he hears their cry and saves them. / The LORD keeps all who love him, / but all the wicked he will destroy. **R.**

May my mouth speak the praise of the LORD, / and may all flesh bless his holy name forever and ever. **R.**

ALLELUIA   *John 14:6*

R. Alleluia, alleluia. I am the way and the truth and the life, says the Lord; no one comes to the Father except through me. **R.**

GOSPEL   *Luke 6:1–5*

While Jesus was going through a field of grain on a Sabbath, his disciples were picking the heads of grain, rubbing them in their hands, and eating them. Some Pharisees said, "Why are you doing what is unlawful on the Sabbath?" Jesus said to them in reply, "Have you not read what David did when he and those who were with him were hungry? How he went into the house of God, took the bread of offering, which only the priests could lawfully eat, ate of it, and shared it with his companions?" Then he said to them, "The Son of Man is lord of the Sabbath."

SEPTEMBER 6, 23RD SUNDAY IN ORDINARY TIME; BLESSED BERTRAND OF GARRIGUES

FIRST READING   *Ezekiel 33:7—9*

Thus says the LORD: You, son of man, I have appointed watchman for the house of Israel; when you hear me say anything, you shall warn them for me. If I tell the wicked, "O wicked one, you shall surely die," and you do not speak out to dissuade the wicked from his way, the wicked shall die for his guilt, but I will hold you responsible for his death. But if you warn the wicked, trying to turn him from his way, and he refuses to turn from his way, he shall die for his guilt, but you shall save yourself.

RESPONSORIAL PSALM   *Psalm 95:1—2, 6—7, 8—9 (8)*

R. If today you hear his voice, harden not your hearts.

Come, let us sing joyfully to the LORD; / let us acclaim the rock of our salvation. / Let us come into his presence with thanksgiving; / let us joyfully sing psalms to him. **R.**

Come, let us bow down in worship; / let us kneel before the LORD who made us. / For he is our God, and we are the people he shepherds, / the flock he guides. **R.**

Oh, that today you would hear his voice: / "Harden not your hearts as at Meribah, / as in the day of Massah in the desert, / where your fathers tempted me; / they tested me though they had seen my works." **R.**

SECOND READING   *Romans 13:8—10*

Brothers and sisters: Owe nothing to anyone, except to love one another; for the one who loves another has fulfilled the law. The commandments, "You shall not commit adultery;

you shall not kill; you shall not steal; you shall not covet," and whatever other commandment there may be, are summed up in this saying, namely, "You shall love your neighbor as yourself." Love does no evil to the neighbor; hence, love is the fulfillment of the law.

ALLELUIA   *2 Corinthians 5:19*

R. **Alleluia, alleluia.** God was reconciling the world to himself in Christ and entrusting to us the message of reconciliation. **R.**

GOSPEL   *Matthew 18:15—20*

Jesus said to his disciples: "If your brother sins against you, go and tell him his fault between you and him alone. If he listens to you, you have won over your brother. If he does not listen, take one or two others along with you, so that 'every fact may be established on the testimony of two or three witnesses.' If he refuses to listen to them, tell the church. If he refuses to listen even to the church, then treat him as you would a Gentile or a tax collector. Amen, I say to you, whatever you bind on earth shall be bound in heaven, and whatever you loose on earth shall be loosed in heaven. Again, amen, I say to you, if two of you agree on earth about anything for which they are to pray, it shall be granted to them by my heavenly Father. For where two or three are gathered together in my name, there am I in the midst of them."

SEPTEMBER 7, MONDAY OF WEEK 23;
BLESSED JOHN DUCKETT AND BLESSED RALPH CORBY

FIRST READING   *1 Corinthians 5:1–8*

Brothers and sisters: It is widely reported that there is immorality among you, and immorality of a kind not found even among pagans— a man living with his father's wife. And you are inflated with pride. Should you not rather have been sorrowful? The one who did this deed should be expelled from your midst. I, for my part, although absent in body but present in spirit, have already, as if present, pronounced judgment on the one who has committed this deed, in the name of our Lord Jesus: when you have gathered together and I am with you in spirit with the power of the Lord Jesus, you are to deliver this man to Satan for the destruction of his flesh, so that his spirit may be saved on the day of the Lord.

Your boasting is not appropriate. Do you not know that a little yeast leavens all the dough? Clear out the old yeast, so that you may become a fresh batch of dough, inasmuch as you are unleavened. For our Paschal Lamb, Christ, has been sacrificed. Therefore, let us celebrate the feast, not with the old yeast, the yeast of malice and wickedness, but with the unleavened bread of sincerity and truth.

RESPONSORIAL PSALM   *Psalm 5:5–6, 7, 12*

R. (9) **Lead me in your justice, Lord.**

For you, O God, delight not in wickedness; / no evil man remains with you; / the arrogant may not stand in your sight. / You hate all evildoers. **R.**

You destroy all who speak falsehood; / the bloodthirsty and the deceitful the LORD abhors. **R.**

But let all who take refuge in you be glad and exult forever. / Protect them, that you may be the joy of those who love your name. **R.**

ALLELUIA   *John 10:27*

R. Alleluia, alleluia. My sheep hear my voice, says the Lord; I know them, and they follow me. **R.**

GOSPEL   *Luke 6:6–11*

On a certain sabbath Jesus went into the synagogue and taught, and there was a man there whose right hand was withered. The scribes and the Pharisees watched him closely to see if he would cure on the sabbath so that they might discover a reason to accuse him. But he realized their intentions and said to the man with the withered hand, "Come up and stand before us." And he rose and stood there. Then Jesus said to them, "I ask you, is it lawful to do good on the sabbath rather than to do evil, to save life rather than to destroy it?" Looking around at them all, he then said to him, "Stretch out your hand." He did so and his hand was restored. But they became enraged and discussed together what they might do to Jesus.

SEPTEMBER 8, THE NATIVITY OF; THE BLESSED VIRGIN MARY - FEAST

FIRST READING   *Micah 5:1–4a*

The LORD says: You, Bethlehem–Ephrathah, too small to be among the clans of Judah, From you shall come forth for me one who is to be ruler in Israel; Whose origin is from of old, from ancient times. (Therefore the Lord will give them up, until the time when she who is to give birth has borne, And the rest of his brethren shall return to the children of Israel.) He shall stand firm and shepherd his flock by the strength of the LORD, in the majestic name of the LORD, his God; And they shall remain, for now his greatness shall reach to the ends of the earth; he shall be peace.

ALTERNATIVE READING   *Romans 8:28–30*

Brothers and sisters: We know that all things work for good for those who love God, who are called according to his purpose. For those he foreknew he also predestined to be conformed to the image of his Son, so that he might be the firstborn among many brothers. And those he predestined he also called; and those he called he also justified; and those he justified he also glorified.

RESPONSORIAL PSALM   *Psalm 13:6ab, 6c*

R. With delight I rejoice in the Lord.

Though I trusted in your mercy, let my heart rejoice in your salvation. **R.**

Let me sing of the LORD, "He has been good to me." **R.**

ALLELUIA

R. Alleluia, alleluia. Blessed are you, holy Virgin Mary, deserving of all praise; from you rose the sun of justice, Christ our God. **R.**

GOSPEL *Longer Form Matthew 1:1–16, 18–23*

The Book of the genealogy of Jesus Christ, the son of David, the son of Abraham.

Abraham became the father of Isaac, Isaac the father of Jacob, Jacob the father of Judah and his brothers. Judah became the father of Perez and Zerah, whose mother was Tamar. Perez became the father of Hezron, Hezron the father of Ram, Ram the father of Amminadab. Amminadab became the father of Nahshon, Nahshon the father of Salmon, Salmon the father of Boaz, whose mother was Rahab. Boaz became the father of Obed, whose mother was Ruth. Obed became the father of Jesse, Jesse the father of David the king.

David became the father of Solomon, whose mother had been the wife of Uriah. Solomon became the father of Rehoboam, Rehoboam the father of Abijah, Abijah the father of Asaph. Asaph became the father of Jehoshaphat, Jehoshaphat the father of Joram, Joram the father of Uzziah. Uzziah became the father of Jotham, Jotham the father of Ahaz, Ahaz the father of Hezekiah. Hezekiah became the father of Manasseh, Manasseh the father of Amos, Amos the father of Josiah. Josiah became the father of Jechoniah and his brothers at the time of the Babylonian exile.

After the Babylonian exile, Jechoniah became the father of Shealtiel, Shealtiel the father of Zerubbabel, Zerubbabel the father of Abiud. Abiud became the father of Eliakim, Eliakim the father of Azor, Azor the father of Zadok. Zadok became the father of Achim, Achim the father of Eliud, Eliud the father of Eleazar. Eleazar became the father of Matthan, Matthan the father of Jacob, Jacob the father of Joseph, the husband of Mary. Of her was born Jesus who is called the Christ.

Now this is how the birth of Jesus Christ came about. When his mother Mary was betrothed to Joseph, but before they lived together, she was found with child through the Holy Spirit. Joseph her husband, since he was a righteous man, yet unwilling to expose her to shame, decided to divorce her quietly. Such was his intention when, behold, the angel of the Lord appeared to him in a dream and said, "Joseph, son of David, do not be afraid to take Mary your wife into your home. For it is through the Holy Spirit that this child has been conceived in her. She will bear a son and you are to name him Jesus, because he will save his people from their sins." All this took place to fulfill what the Lord had said through the prophet:

Behold, the virgin shall be with child and bear a son, and they shall name him Emmanuel, which means "God is with us."

SHORTER FORM *Matthew 1:18–23*

This is how the birth of Jesus Christ came about. When his mother Mary was betrothed to Joseph, but before they lived together, she was found with child through the Holy Spirit. Joseph her husband, since he was a righteous man, yet unwilling to expose her to shame, decided to divorce her quietly. Such was his intention when, behold, the angel of the Lord appeared to him in a dream and said, "Joseph, son of David, do not be afraid to take Mary your wife into your home. For it is through the Holy Spirit that this child has been conceived in her. She will bear a son and you are to name him Jesus, because he will save his people from their sins." All this took place to fulfill what the Lord had said through the prophet:

Behold, the virgin shall be with child and bear a son, and they shall name him Emmanuel, which means "God is with us."

SEPTEMBER 9, WEDNESDAY OF WEEK 23; ST. PETER CLAVER

FIRST READING   *1 Corinthians 7:25–31*

Brothers and sisters: In regard to virgins, I have no commandment from the Lord, but I give my opinion as one who by the Lord's mercy is trustworthy. So this is what I think best because of the present distress: that it is a good thing for a person to remain as he is. Are you bound to a wife? Do not seek a separation. Are you free of a wife? Then do not look for a wife. If you marry, however, you do not sin, nor does an unmarried woman sin if she marries; but such people will experience affliction in their earthly life, and I would like to spare you that.

I tell you, brothers, the time is running out. From now on, let those having wives act as not having them, those weeping as not weeping, those rejoicing as not rejoicing, those buying as not owning, those using the world as not using it fully. For the world in its present form is passing away.

RESPONSORIAL PSALM   *Psalm 45:11–12, 14–15, 16–17*

R. (11) Listen to me, daughter; see and bend your ear.

Hear, O daughter, and see; / turn your ear, / forget your people and your father's house. / So shall the king desire your beauty; / for he is your lord, and you must worship him. **R.**

All glorious is the king's daughter as she enters; / her raiment is threaded with spun gold. / In embroidered apparel she is borne in to the king; / behind her the virgins of her train are brought to you. **R.**

They are borne in with gladness and joy; / they enter the palace of the king. / The place of your fathers your sons shall have; / you shall make them princes through all the land. **R.**

ALLELUIA   *Luke 6:23ab*

R. Alleluia, alleluia. Rejoice and leap for joy! Your reward will be great in heaven. **R.**

GOSPEL   *Luke 6:20–26*

Raising his eyes toward his disciples Jesus said:

"Blessed are you who are poor, for the Kingdom of God is yours. Blessed are you who are now hungry, for you will be satisfied. Blessed are you who are now weeping, for you will laugh. Blessed are you when people hate you, and when they exclude and insult you, and denounce your name as evil on account of the Son of Man.

Rejoice and leap for joy on that day! Behold, your reward will be great in heaven. For their ancestors treated the prophets in the same way.

But woe to you who are rich, for you have received your consolation. But woe to you who are filled now, for you will be hungry. Woe to you who laugh now, for you will grieve and weep. Woe to you when all speak well of you, for their ancestors treated the false prophets in this way."

SEPTEMBER 10, THURSDAY OF WEEK 23; ST. NICHOLAS OF TOLENTINO

FIRST READING *1 Corinthians 8:1b–7, 11–13*

Brothers and sisters: Knowledge inflates with pride, but love builds up. If anyone supposes he knows something, he does not yet know as he ought to know. But if one loves God, one is known by him.

So about the eating of meat sacrificed to idols: we know that there *is no idol in the world,* and that *there is no God but one.* Indeed, even though there are so–called gods in heaven and on earth (there are, to be sure, many "gods" and many "lords"), yet for us there is one God, the Father, from whom all things are and for whom we exist, and one Lord, Jesus Christ, through whom all things are and through whom we exist.

But not all have this knowledge. There are some who have been so used to idolatry up until now that, when they eat meat sacrificed to idols, their conscience, which is weak, is defiled.

Thus, through your knowledge, the weak person is brought to destruction, the brother for whom Christ died. When you sin in this way against your brothers and wound their consciences, weak as they are, you are sinning against Christ. Therefore, if food causes my brother to sin, I will never eat meat again, so that I may not cause my brother to sin.

RESPONSORIAL PSALM *Psalm 139:1b–3, 13–14ab, 23–24*

R. (24b) Guide me, Lord, along the everlasting way.

O LORD, you have probed me and you know me; / you know when I sit and when I stand; / you understand my thoughts from afar. / My journeys and my rest you scrutinize, / with all my ways you are familiar. **R.**

Truly you have formed my inmost being; / you knit me in my mother's womb. / I give you thanks that I am fearfully, wonderfully made; / wonderful are your works. **R.**

Probe me, O God, and know my heart; / try me, and know my thoughts; / See if my way is crooked, / and lead me in the way of old. **R.**

ALLELUIA *1 John 4:12*

R. Alleluia, alleluia. If we love one another, God remains in us, and his love is brought to perfection in us. **R.**

GOSPEL *Luke 6:27–38*

Jesus said to his disciples: "To you who hear I say, love your enemies, do good to those who hate you, bless those who curse you, pray for those who mistreat you. To the person who strikes you on one cheek, offer the other one as well, and from the person who takes your cloak, do not withhold even your tunic. Give to everyone who asks of you, and from the one who takes what is yours do not demand it back. Do to others as you would have them do to you. For if you love those who love you, what credit is that to you? Even sinners love those who love them. And if you do good to those who do good to you, what credit is that to you?

Even sinners do the same. If you lend money to those from whom you expect repayment, what credit is that to you? Even sinners lend to sinners, and get back the same amount. But rather, love your enemies and do good to them, and lend expecting nothing back; then your reward will be great and you will be children of the Most High, for he himself is kind to the ungrateful and the wicked. Be merciful, just as also your Father is merciful.

"Stop judging and you will not be judged. Stop condemning and you will not be condemned. Forgive and you will be forgiven. Give and gifts will be given to you; a good measure, packed together, shaken down, and overflowing, will be poured into your lap. For the measure with which you measure will in return be measured out to you."

SEPTEMBER 11, FRIDAY OF WEEK 23; ST. LAWRENCE JUSTINIAN

FIRST READING   *1 Corinthians 9:16–19, 22b–27*

Brothers and sisters: If I preach the Gospel, this is no reason for me to boast, for an obligation has been imposed on me, and woe to me if I do not preach it! If I do so willingly, I have a recompense, but if unwillingly, then I have been entrusted with a stewardship. What then is my recompense? That, when I preach, I offer the Gospel free of charge so as not to make full use of my right in the Gospel.

Although I am free in regard to all, I have made myself a slave to all so as to win over as many as possible. I have become all things to all, to save at least some. All this I do for the sake of the Gospel, so that I too may have a share in it.

Do you not know that the runners in the stadium all run in the race, but only one wins the prize? Run so as to win. Every athlete exercises discipline in every way. They do it to win a perishable crown, but we an imperishable one. Thus I do not run aimlessly; I do not fight as if I were shadowboxing. No, I drive my body and train it, for fear that, after having preached to others, I myself should be disqualified.

RESPONSORIAL PSALM   *Psalm 84:3, 4, 5–6, 12*

R. (2) How lovely is your dwelling place, Lord, mighty God!
My soul yearns and pines for the courts of the LORD. / My heart and my flesh cry out for the living God. **R.**
Even the sparrow finds a home, / and the swallow a nest in which she puts her young— Your altars, O LORD of hosts, / my king and my God! **R.**
Blessed they who dwell in your house! / Continually they praise you. / Blessed the men whose strength you are! / Their hearts are set upon the pilgrimage. **R.**
For a sun and a shield is the LORD God; / grace and glory he bestows; / The LORD withholds no good thing from those who walk in sincerity. **R.**

ALLELUIA   *See John 17:17b, 17a*

R. Alleluia, alleluia. Your word, O Lord, is truth; consecrate us in the truth. **R.**

GOSPEL   *Luke 6:39–42*

Jesus told his disciples a parable: "Can a blind person guide a blind person? Will not both fall into a pit? No disciple is superior to the teacher; but when fully trained, every disciple will be like his teacher. Why do you notice the splinter in your brother's eye, but do not perceive the wooden beam in your own? How can you say to your brother, 'Brother, let me remove that splinter in your eye,' when you do not even notice the wooden beam in your own eye? You hypocrite! Remove the wooden beam from your eye first; then you will see clearly to remove the splinter in your brother's eye."

SEPTEMBER 12, SATURDAY OF WEEK 23;
MOST HOLY NAME OF THE BLESSED VIRGIN MARY

FIRST READING   *1 Corinthians 10:14–22*

My beloved ones, avoid idolatry. I am speaking as to sensible people; judge for yourselves what I am saying. The cup of blessing that we bless, is it not a participation in the Blood of Christ? The bread that we break, is it not a participation in the Body of Christ? Because the loaf of bread is one, we, though many, are one Body, for we all partake of the one loaf.

Look at Israel according to the flesh; are not those who eat the sacrifices participants in the altar? So what am I saying? That meat sacrificed to idols is anything? Or that an idol is anything? No, I mean that what they sacrifice, they sacrifice to demons, not to God, and I do not want you to become participants with demons. You cannot drink the cup of the Lord and also the cup of demons. You cannot partake of the table of the Lord and of the table of demons. Or are we provoking the Lord to jealous anger? Are we stronger than him?

RESPONSORIAL PSALM   *Psalm 116:12–13, 17–18*

R. (17) To you, Lord, I will offer a sacrifice of praise.

How shall I make a return to the LORD / for all the good he has done for me? / The cup of salvation I will take up, / and I will call upon the name of the LORD. **R.**

To you will I offer sacrifice of thanksgiving, / and I will call upon the name of the LORD. / My vows to the LORD I will pay / in the presence of all his people. **R.**

ALLELUIA   *John 14:23*

R. Alleluia, alleluia. Whoever loves me will keep my word, and my Father will love him, and we will come to him. **R.**

GOSPEL   *Luke 6:43–49*

Jesus said to his disciples: "A good tree does not bear rotten fruit, nor does a rotten tree bear good fruit. For every tree is known by its own fruit. For people do not pick figs from thornbushes, nor do they gather grapes from brambles. A good person out of the store of goodness in his heart produces good, but an evil person out of a store of evil produces evil; for from the fullness of the heart the mouth speaks.

"Why do you call me, 'Lord, Lord,' but not do what I command? I will show you what someone is like who comes to me, listens to my words, and acts on them. That one is like a man building a house, who dug deeply and laid the foundation on rock; when the flood came, the river burst against that house but could not shake it because it had been well built. But the one who listens and does not act is like a person who built a house on the ground without a foundation. When the river burst against it, it collapsed at once and was completely destroyed."

SEPTEMBER 13, 24TH SUNDAY IN ORDINARY TIME; ST. JOHN CHRYSOSTOM

FIRST READING   *Sirach 27:30—28:7*

Wrath and anger are hateful things, yet the sinner hugs them tight. The vengeful will suffer the LORD's vengeance, for he remembers their sins in detail. Forgive your neighbor's injustice; then when you pray, your own sins will be forgiven. Could anyone nourish anger against another and expect healing from the LORD? Could anyone refuse mercy to another like himself, can he seek pardon for his own sins? If one who is but flesh cherishes wrath, who will forgive his sins? Remember your last days, set enmity aside; remember death and decay, and cease from sin! Think of the commandments, hate not your neighbor; remember the Most High's covenant, and overlook faults.

RESPONSORIAL PSALM   *Psalm 103:1—2, 3—4, 9—10, 11—12 (8)*

R. The Lord is kind and merciful, slow to anger, and rich in compassion.

Bless the LORD, O my soul; / and all my being, bless his holy name. / Bless the LORD, O my soul, / and forget not all his benefits. **R.**

He pardons all your iniquities, / heals all your ills, redeems your life from destruction, / he crowns you with kindness and compassion. **R.**

He will not always chide, / nor does he keep his wrath forever. / Not according to our sins does he deal with us, / nor does he requite us according to our crimes. **R.**

For as the heavens are high above the earth, / so surpassing is his kindness toward those who fear him. / As far as the east is from the west, / so far has he put our transgressions from us. **R.**

SECOND READING   *Romans 14:7—9*

Brothers and sisters: None of us lives for oneself, and no one dies for oneself. For if we live, we live for the Lord, and if we die, we die for the Lord; so then, whether we live or die, we are the Lord's. For this is why Christ died and came to life, that he might be Lord of both the dead and the living.

ALLELUIA   *John 13:34*

R. Alleluia, alleluia. I give you a new commandment, says the Lord; love one another as I have loved you. **R.**

GOSPEL   *Matthew 18:21—35*

Peter approached Jesus and asked him, "Lord, if my brother sins against me, how often must I forgive? As many as seven times?" Jesus answered, "I say to you, not seven times but seventy—seven times. That is why the kingdom of heaven may be likened to a king who decided to settle accounts with his servants. When he began the accounting, a debtor was brought before him who owed him a huge amount. Since he had no way of paying it back, his master ordered him to be sold, along with his wife, his children, and all his property, in payment of the debt. At that, the servant fell down, did him homage, and said, 'Be patient with me, and I will pay you back in full.' Moved with compassion the master of that servant let him go and forgave him the loan. When that servant had left, he found one of his fellow servants who owed him a much smaller amount. He seized him and started to choke him, demanding, 'Pay back what you owe.' Falling to his knees, his fellow servant begged him, 'Be patient with me, and I will pay you back.' But he refused. Instead, he had the fellow servant put in prison until he paid back the debt. Now when his fellow servants saw what had happened, they were deeply disturbed, and went to their master and reported the whole affair. His master summoned him and said to him, 'You wicked servant! I forgave you your entire debt because you begged me to. Should you not have had pity on your fellow servant, as I had pity on you?' Then in anger his master handed him over to the torturers until he should pay back the whole debt. So will my heavenly Father do to you, unless each of you forgives your brother from your heart."

SEPTEMBER 14; THE EXALTATION OF THE HOLY CROSS - FEAST

FIRST READING   *Numbers 21:4b—9*

With their patience worn out by the journey, the people complained against God and Moses, "Why have you brought us up from Egypt to die in this desert, where there is no food or water? We are disgusted with this wretched food!"

In punishment the LORD sent among the people saraph serpents, which bit the people so that many of them died. Then the people came to Moses and said, "We have sinned in complaining against the LORD and you. Pray the LORD to take the serpents from us." So Moses prayed for the people, and the LORD said to Moses, "Make a saraph and mount it on a pole, and if any who have been bitten look at it, they will live." Moses accordingly made a bronze serpent and mounted it on a pole, and whenever anyone who had been bitten by a serpent looked at the bronze serpent, he lived.

RESPONSORIAL PSALM: *Psalm 78:1bc—2, 34—35, 36—37, 38 (see 7b)*
R. Do not forget the works of the Lord!
Hearken, my people, to my teaching; / incline your ears to the words of my mouth. /
I will open my mouth in a parable, / I will utter mysteries from of old. **R.**
While he slew them they sought him / and inquired after God again, /
Remembering that God was their rock / and the Most High God, their redeemer. **R.**
But they flattered him with their mouths / and lied to him with their tongues, / though their hearts were not steadfast toward him, / nor were they faithful to his covenant. **R.**
But he, being merciful, forgave their sin / and destroyed them not; / Often he turned back his anger / and let none of his wrath be roused. **R.**

SECOND READING   *Philippians 2:6—11*

Brothers and sisters: Christ Jesus, though he was in the form of God, did not regard equality with God something to be grasped. Rather, he emptied himself, taking the form of a slave, coming in human likeness; and found human in appearance, he humbled himself, becoming obedient to death, even death on a cross. Because of this, God greatly exalted him and bestowed on him the name that is above every name, that at the name of Jesus every knee should bend, of those in heaven and on earth and under the earth, and every tongue confess that Jesus Christ is Lord, to the glory of God the Father.

ALLELUIA   *John 10:27*

R. Alleluia, alleluia. We adore you, O Christ, and we bless you, because by your Cross you have redeemed the world. **R.**

GOSPEL   *John 3:13—17*

Jesus said to Nicodemus: "No one has gone up to heaven except the one who has come down from heaven, the Son of Man. And just as Moses lifted up the serpent in the desert, so must the Son of Man be lifted up, so that everyone who believes in him may have eternal life."

For God so loved the world that he gave his only Son, so that everyone who believes in him might not perish but might have eternal life. For God did not send his Son into the world to condemn the world, but that the world might be saved through him.

SEPTEMBER 15, OUR LADY OF SORROWS

FIRST READING   *1 Corinthians 12:12–14, 27–31a*

Brothers and sisters: As a body is one though it has many parts, and all the parts of the body, though many, are one body, so also Christ. For in one Spirit we were all baptized into one Body, whether Jews or Greeks, slaves or free persons, and we were all given to drink of one Spirit.

Now the body is not a single part, but many.

Now you are Christ's Body, and individually parts of it. Some people God has designated in the Church to be, first, Apostles; second, prophets; third, teachers; then, mighty deeds; then gifts of healing, assistance, administration, and varieties of tongues. Are all Apostles? Are all prophets? Are all teachers? Do all work mighty deeds? Do all have gifts of healing? Do all speak in tongues? Do all interpret? Strive eagerly for the greatest spiritual gifts.

RESPONSORIAL PSALM   *Psalm 31:2 and 3b, 3cd–4, 5–6, 15–16, 20*

R. Save me, O Lord, in your kindness.

In you, O LORD, I take refuge; / let me never be put to shame. / In your justice rescue me, / make haste to deliver me! **R.**

Be my rock of refuge, / a stronghold to give me safety. / You are my rock and my fortress; / for your name's sake you will lead and guide me. **R.**

You will free me from the snare they set for me, / for you are my refuge. / Into your hands I commend my spirit; / you will redeem me, O LORD, / O faithful God. **R.**

But my trust is in you, O LORD, / I say, "You are my God." / In your hands is my destiny; / rescue me from the clutches of my enemies and my persecutors. **R.**

How great is your goodness, O LORD, / which you have in store for those who fear you, / and which, toward those who take refuge in you, / you show in the sight of the children of men. **R.**

ALLELUIA

R. Alleluia, alleluia. Blessed are you, O Virgin Mary; without dying you won the martyr's crown beneath the Cross of the Lord. **R.**

GOSPEL *John 19:25–27*

Standing by the cross of Jesus were his mother and his mother's sister, Mary the wife of Clopas, and Mary Magdalene. When Jesus saw his mother and the disciple there whom he loved he said to his mother, "Woman, behold, your son." Then he said to the disciple, "Behold, your mother." And from that hour the disciple took her into his home.

ALTERNATIVE FIRST READING *Luke 2:33–35*

Jesus' father and mother were amazed at what was said about him; and Simeon blessed them and said to Mary his mother, "Behold, this child is destined for the fall and rise of many in Israel, and to be a sign that will be contradicted and you yourself a sword will pierce so that the thoughts of many hearts may be revealed."

SEPTEMBER 16, WEDNESDAY OF WEEK 24; ST. CORNELIUS AND ST. CYPRIAN

FIRST READING *1 Corinthians 12:31–13:13*

Brothers and sisters: Strive eagerly for the greatest spiritual gifts. But I shall show you a still more excellent way.

If I speak in human and angelic tongues but do not have love, I am a resounding gong or a clashing cymbal. And if I have the gift of prophecy and comprehend all mysteries and all knowledge; if I have all faith so as to move mountains, but do not have love, I am nothing. If I give away everything I own, and if I hand my body over so that I may boast but do not have love, I gain nothing.

Love is patient, love is kind. It is not jealous, love is not pompous, it is not inflated, it is not rude, it does not seek its own interests, it is not quick–tempered, it does not brood over injury, it does not rejoice over wrongdoing but rejoices with the truth. It bears all things, believes all things, hopes all things, endures all things.

Love never fails. If there are prophecies, they will be brought to nothing; if tongues, they will cease; if knowledge, it will be brought to nothing. For we know partially and we prophesy partially, but when the perfect comes, the partial will pass away. When I was a child, I used to talk as a child, think as a child, reason as a child; when I became a man, I put aside childish things. At present we see indistinctly, as in a mirror, but then face to face. At present I know partially; then I shall know fully, as I am fully known. So faith, hope, love remain, these three; but the greatest of these is love.

RESPONSORIAL PSALM *Psalm 33:2–3, 4–5, 12 and 22*

R. (12) Blessed the people the Lord has chosen to be his own.

Give thanks to the LORD on the harp; **/** with the ten-stringed lyre chant his praises. **/** Sing to him a new song; **/** pluck the strings skillfully, with shouts of gladness. **R.**

For upright is the word of the LORD, **/** and all his works are trustworthy. **/** He loves justice and right; **/** of the kindness of the LORD the earth is full. **R.**

Blessed the nation whose God is the LORD, **/** the people he has chosen for his own inheritance. **/** May your kindness, O LORD, be upon us **/** who have put our hope in you. **R.**

ALLELUIA *See John 6:63c, 68c*

R. Alleluia, alleluia. Your words, Lord, are Spirit and life, you have the words of everlasting life. **R.**

GOSPEL *Luke 7:31–35*

Jesus said to the crowds: "to what shall I compare the people of this generation? What are they like? They are like children who sit in the marketplace and call to one another,

'We played the flute for you, but you did not dance. We sang a dirge, but you did not weep.'

For John the Baptist came neither eating food nor drinking wine, and you said, 'He is possessed by a demon.' The Son of Man came eating and drinking and you said, 'Look, he is a glutton and a drunkard, a friend of tax collectors and sinners.' But wisdom is vindicated by all her children."

SEPTEMBER 17, THURSDAY OF WEEK 24; ST. ROBERT BELLARMINE

FIRST READING *1 Corinthians 15:1–11*

I am reminding you, brothers and sisters, of the Gospel I preached to you, which you indeed received and in which you also stand. Through it you are also being saved, if you hold fast to the word I preached to you, unless you believed in vain. For I handed on to you as of first importance what I also received: that Christ died for our sins in accordance with the Scriptures; that he was buried; that he was raised on the third day in accordance with the Scriptures; that he appeared to Cephas, then to the Twelve. After that, he appeared to more than five hundred brothers at once, most of whom are still living, though some have fallen asleep. After that he appeared to James, then to all the Apostles. Last of all, as to one born abnormally, he appeared to me. For I am the least of the Apostles, not fit to be called an Apostle, because I persecuted the Church of God. But by the grace of God I am what I am, and his grace to me has not been ineffective. Indeed, I have toiled harder than all of them; not I, however, but the grace of God that is with me. Therefore, whether it be I or they, so we preach and so you believed.

RESPONSORIAL PSALM *Psalm 118:1b–2, 16ab–17, 28*

R. (1) Give thanks to the Lord, for he is good.

Give thanks to the LORD, for he is good, **/** for his mercy endures forever. **/** Let the house of Israel say, **/** "His mercy endures forever." **R.**

"The right hand of the LORD is exalted; **/** the right hand of the LORD has struck with power." **/** I shall not die, but live, **/** and declare the works of the LORD. **R.**

You are my God, and I give thanks to you; **/** O my God, I extol you. **R.**

ALLELUIA *Matthew 11:28*

R. Alleluia, alleluia. Come to me, all you who labor and are burdened, and I will give you rest, says the Lord. **R.**

GOSPEL
Luke 7:36–50

A certain Pharisee invited Jesus to dine with him, and he entered the Pharisee's house and reclined at table. Now there was a sinful woman in the city who learned that he was at table in the house of the Pharisee. Bringing an alabaster flask of ointment, she stood behind him at his feet weeping and began to bathe his feet with her tears. Then she wiped them with her hair, kissed them, and anointed them with the ointment. When the Pharisee who had invited him saw this he said to himself, "If this man were a prophet, he would know who and what sort of woman this is who is touching him, that she is a sinner." Jesus said to him in reply, "Simon, I have something to say to you." "Tell me, teacher," he said. "Two people were in debt to a certain creditor; one owed five hundred days' wages and the other owed fifty. Since they were unable to repay the debt, he forgave it for both. Which of them will love him more?" Simon said in reply, "The one, I suppose, whose larger debt was forgiven." He said to him, "You have judged rightly." Then he turned to the woman and said to Simon, "Do you see this woman? When I entered your house, you did not give me water for my feet, but she has bathed them with her tears and wiped them with her hair. You did not give me a kiss, but she has not ceased kissing my feet since the time I entered. You did not anoint my head with oil, but she anointed my feet with ointment. So I tell you, her many sins have been forgiven; hence, she has shown great love. But the one to whom little is forgiven, loves little." He said to her, "Your sins are forgiven." The others at table said to themselves, "Who is this who even forgives sins?" But he said to the woman, "Your faith has saved you; go in peace."

SEPTEMBER 18, FRIDAY OF WEEK 24; ST. JOSEPH OF CUPERTINO

FIRST READING
1 Corinthians 15:12–20

Brothers and sisters: If Christ is preached as raised from the dead, how can some among you say there is no resurrection of the dead? If there is no resurrection of the dead, then neither has Christ been raised. And if Christ has not been raised, then empty too is our preaching; empty, too, your faith. Then we are also false witnesses to God, because we testified against God that he raised Christ, whom he did not raise if in fact the dead are not raised. For if the dead are not raised, neither has Christ been raised, and if Christ has not been raised, your faith is vain; you are still in your sins. Then those who have fallen asleep in Christ have perished. If for this life only we have hoped in Christ, we are the most pitiable people of all.

But now Christ has been raised from the dead, the firstfruits of those who have fallen asleep.

RESPONSORIAL PSALM
Psalm 17:1bcd, 6–7, 8b and 15

R. (15b) Lord, when your glory appears, my joy will be full.

Hear, O LORD, a just suit; / attend to my outcry; / hearken to my prayer from lips without deceit. **R.**

I call upon you, for you will answer me, O God; / incline your ear to me; hear my word. Show your wondrous mercies, / O savior of those who flee from their foes to refuge at your right hand. **R.**

Hide me in the shadow of your wings, / but I in justice shall behold your face; / on waking, I shall be content in your presence. **R.**

ALLELUIA *See Matthew 11:25*

R. Alleluia, alleluia. Blessed are you, Father, Lord of heaven and earth; you have revealed to little ones the mysteries of the Kingdom. **R.**

GOSPEL *Luke 8:1–3*

Jesus journeyed from one town and village to another, preaching and proclaiming the good news of the Kingdom of God. Accompanying him were the Twelve and some women who had been cured of evil spirits and infirmities, Mary, called Magdalene, from whom seven demons had gone out, Joanna, the wife of Herod's steward Chuza, Susanna, and many others who provided for them out of their resources.

SEPTEMBER 19, SATURDAY OF WEEK 24; ST. JANUARIUS

FIRST READING *1 Corinthians 15:35–37, 42–49*

Brothers and sisters: Someone may say, "How are the dead raised? With what kind of body will they come back?"

You fool! What you sow is not brought to life unless it dies. And what you sow is not the body that is to be but a bare kernel of wheat, perhaps, or of some other kind.

So also is the resurrection of the dead. It is sown corruptible; it is raised incorruptible. It is sown dishonorable; it is raised glorious. It is sown weak; it is raised powerful. It is sown a natural body; it is raised a spiritual body. If there is a natural body, there is also a spiritual one.

So, too, it is written, "The first man, Adam, became a living being," the last Adam a life–giving spirit. But the spiritual was not first; rather the natural and then the spiritual. The first man was from the earth, earthly; the second man, from heaven. As was the earthly one, so also are the earthly, and as is the heavenly one, so also are the heavenly. Just as we have borne the image of the earthly one, we shall also bear the image of the heavenly one.

RESPONSORIAL PSALM *Psalm 56:10c–12, 13–14*

R. (14) I will walk in the presence of God, in the light of the living.

Now I know that God is with me. / In God, in whose promise I glory, / in God I trust without fear; / what can flesh do against me? **R.**

I am bound, O God, by vows to you; / your thank offerings I will fulfill. / For you have rescued me from death, / my feet, too, from stumbling; / that I may walk before God / in the light of the living. **R.**

ALLELUIA *See Luke 8:15*

R. Alleluia, alleluia. Blessed are they who have kept the word with a generous heart and yield a harvest through perseverance. **R.**

GOSPEL *Luke 8:4–15*

When a large crowd gathered, with people from one town after another journeying to Jesus, he spoke in a parable. "A sower went out to sow his seed. And as he sowed, some seed fell on the path and was trampled, and the birds of the sky ate it up. Some seed fell on rocky ground, and when it grew, it withered for lack of moisture. Some seed fell among thorns, and the thorns grew with it and choked it. And some seed fell on good soil, and when it grew, it produced fruit a hundredfold." After saying this, he called out, "Whoever has ears to hear ought to hear."

Then his disciples asked him what the meaning of this parable might be. He answered, "Knowledge of the mysteries of the Kingdom of God has been granted to you; but to the rest, they are made known through parables so that *they may look but not see, and hear but not understand.*

"This is the meaning of the parable. The seed is the word of God. Those on the path are the ones who have heard, but the Devil comes and takes away the word from their hearts that they may not believe and be saved. Those on rocky ground are the ones who, when they hear, receive the word with joy, but they have no root; they believe only for a time and fall away in time of temptation. As for the seed that fell among thorns, they are the ones who have heard, but as they go along, they are choked by the anxieties and riches and pleasures of life, and they fail to produce mature fruit. But as for the seed that fell on rich soil, they are the ones who, when they have heard the word, embrace it with a generous and good heart, and bear fruit through perseverance."

SEPTEMBER 20, 25TH SUNDAY IN ORDINARY TIME;
ST. ANDREW KIM DAEGEON & ST. PAUL CHO˘NG HASANG

FIRST READING *Isaiah 55:6—9*

Seek the LORD while he may be found, call him while he is near. Let the scoundrel forsake his way, and the wicked his thoughts; let him turn to the LORD for mercy; to our God, who is generous in forgiving. For my thoughts are not your thoughts, nor are your ways my ways, says the LORD. As high as the heavens are above the earth, so high are my ways above your ways and my thoughts above your thoughts.

RESPONSORIAL PSALM *Psalm 145:2—3, 8—9, 17—18 (18a)*

R. The Lord is near to all who call upon him.

Every day will I bless you, / and I will praise your name forever and ever. / Great is the LORD and highly to be praised; / his greatness is unsearchable. **R.**

The LORD is gracious and merciful, / slow to anger and of great kindness. / The LORD is good to all / and compassionate toward all his works. **R.**

The LORD is just in all his ways / and holy in all his works. / The LORD is near to all who call upon him, / to all who call upon him in truth. **R.**

SECOND READING   *Philippians 1:20c—24, 27a*

Brothers and sisters: Christ will be magnified in my body, whether by life or by death. For to me life is Christ, and death is gain. If I go on living in the flesh, that means fruitful labor for me. And I do not know which I shall choose. I am caught between the two. I long to depart this life and be with Christ, for that is far better. Yet that I remain in the flesh is more necessary for your benefit. Only, conduct yourselves in a way worthy of the gospel of Christ.

ALLELUIA   *see Acts 16:14b*

R. Alleluia, alleluia. Open our hearts, O Lord, to listen to the words of your Son. R.

GOSPEL   *Matthew 20:1—16a*

Jesus told his disciples this parable: "The kingdom of heaven is like a landowner who went out at dawn to hire laborers for his vineyard. After agreeing with them for the usual daily wage, he sent them into his vineyard. Going out about nine o'clock, the landowner saw others standing idle in the marketplace, and he said to them, 'You too go into my vineyard, and I will give you what is just.' So they went off. And he went out again around noon, and around three o'clock, and did likewise. Going out about five o'clock, the landowner found others standing around, and said to them, 'Why do you stand here idle all day?' They answered, 'Because no one has hired us.' He said to them, 'You too go into my vineyard.' "When it was evening the owner of the vineyard said to his foreman, 'Summon the laborers and give them their pay, beginning with the last and ending with the first.' When those who had started about five o'clock came, each received the usual daily wage. So when the first came, they thought that they would receive more, but each of them also got the usual wage. And on receiving it they grumbled against the landowner, saying, 'These last ones worked only one hour, and you have made them equal to us, who bore the day's burden and the heat.' He said to one of them in reply, 'My friend, I am not cheating you. Did you not agree with me for the usual daily wage? Take what is yours and go. What if I wish to give this last one the same as you? Or am I not free to do as I wish with my own money? Are you envious because I am generous?' "Thus, the last will be first, and the first will be last."

SEPTEMBER 21; ST. MATTHEW, APOSTLE & EVANGELIST - FEAST

FIRST READING   *Ephesians 4:1–7, 11–13*

Brothers and sisters: I, a prisoner for the Lord, urge you to live in a manner worthy of the call you have received, with all humility and gentleness, with patience, bearing with one another through love, striving to preserve the unity of the Spirit through the bond of peace: one Body and one Spirit, as you were also called to the one hope of your call; one Lord, one faith, one baptism; one God and Father of all, who is over all and through all and in all. But grace was given to each of us according to the measure of Christ's gift.

And he gave some as Apostles, others as prophets, others as evangelists, others as pastors and teachers, to equip the holy ones for the work of ministry, for building up the Body of Christ, until we all attain to the unity of faith and knowledge of the Son of God, to mature manhood, to the extent of the full stature of Christ.

RESPONSORIAL PSALM

Psalm 19:2–3, 4–5

R. Their message goes out through all the earth.

The heavens declare the glory of God; / and the firmament proclaims his handiwork. / Day pours out the word to day, / and night to night imparts knowledge. **R.**

Not a word nor a discourse whose voice is not heard; / Through all the earth their voice resounds, / and to the ends of the world, their message. **R.**

ALLELUIA

See Te Deum

R. Alleluia, alleluia. We praise you, O God, we acclaim you as Lord; the glorious company of Apostles praise you. **R.**

GOSPEL

Matthew 9:9–13

As Jesus passed by, he saw a man named Matthew sitting at the customs post. He said to him, "Follow me." And he got up and followed him. While he was at table in his house, many tax collectors and sinners came and sat with Jesus and his disciples. The Pharisees saw this and said to his disciples, "Why does your teacher eat with tax collectors and sinners?" He heard this and said, "Those who are well do not need a physician, but the sick do. Go and learn the meaning of the words, *I desire mercy, not sacrifice.* I did not come to call the righteous but sinners."

SEPTEMBER 22, TUESDAY OF WEEK 25; ST. THOMAS OF VILLANOVA

FIRST READING

Proverbs 21:1–6, 10–13

Like a stream is the king's heart in the hand of the LORD; wherever it pleases him, he directs it.

All the ways of a man may be right in his own eyes, but it is the LORD who proves hearts.

To do what is right and just is more acceptable to the LORD than sacrifice.

Haughty eyes and a proud heart— the tillage of the wicked is sin.

The plans of the diligent are sure of profit, but all rash haste leads certainly to poverty.

Whoever makes a fortune by a lying tongue is chasing a bubble over deadly snares.

The soul of the wicked man desires evil; his neighbor finds no pity in his eyes.

When the arrogant man is punished, the simple are the wiser; when the wise man is instructed, he gains knowledge.

The just man appraises the house of the wicked: there is one who brings down the wicked to ruin.

He who shuts his ear to the cry of the poor will himself also call and not be heard.

RESPONSORIAL PSALM

Psalm 119:1, 27, 30, 34, 35, 44

R. (35) Guide me, Lord, in the way of your commands.

Blessed are they whose way is blameless, / who walk in the law of the LORD. **R.**

Make me understand the way of your precepts, / and I will meditate on your wondrous deeds. **R.**

The way of truth I have chosen; / I have set your ordinances before me. **R.**
Give me discernment, / that I may observe your law / and keep it with all my heart. **R.**
Lead me in the path of your commands, / for in it I delight. **R.**
And I will keep your law continually, / forever and ever. **R.**

ALLELUIA *Luke 11:28*
R. Alleluia, alleluia. Blessed are those who hear the word of God and observe it. **R.**

GOSPEL *Luke 8:19–21*
The mother of Jesus and his brothers came to him but were unable to join him because of the crowd. He was told, "Your mother and your brothers are standing outside and they wish to see you." He said to them in reply, "My mother and my brothers are those who hear the word of God and act on it."

SEPTEMBER 23, WEDNESDAY OF WEEK 25; ST. PIO OF PIETRELCINA

FIRST READING *Proverbs 30:5–9*
Every word of God is tested; he is a shield to those who take refuge in him. Add nothing to his words, lest he reproves you, and you will be exposed as a deceiver.

Two things I ask of you, deny them not to me before I die: Put falsehood and lying far from me, give me neither poverty nor riches; provide me only with the food I need; lest, being full, I deny you, saying, "Who is the LORD?" Or, being in want, I steal, and profane the name of my God.

RESPONSORIAL PSALM *Psalm 119:29, 72, 89, 101, 104, 163*
R. (105) Your word, O Lord, is a lamp for my feet.
Remove from me the way of falsehood, / and favor me with your law. **R.**
The law of your mouth is to me more precious / than thousands of gold and silver pieces. **R.**
Your word, O LORD, endures forever; / it is firm as the heavens. **R.**
From every evil way I withhold my feet, / that I may keep your words. **R.**
Through your precepts I gain discernment; / therefore I hate every false way. **R.**
Falsehood I hate and abhor; / your law I love. **R.**

ALLELUIA *Mark 1:15*
R. Alleluia, alleluia. The Kingdom of God is at hand; repent and believe in the Gospel. **R.**

GOSPEL *Luke 9:1–6*
Jesus summoned the Twelve and gave them power and authority over all demons and to cure diseases, and he sent them to proclaim the Kingdom of God and to heal the sick. He said to them, "Take nothing for the journey, neither walking stick, nor sack, nor food, nor money, and let no one take a second tunic. Whatever house you enter, stay there and leave from there. And as for those who do not welcome you, when you leave that town, shake the dust from your feet in testimony against them." Then they set out and went from village to village proclaiming the good news and curing diseases everywhere.

SEPTEMBER 24, THURSDAY OF WEEK 25; ST. THECLA

FIRST READING   *Ecclesiastes 1:2–11*

Vanity of vanities, says Qoheleth, vanity of vanities! All things are vanity! What profit has man from all the labor which he toils at under the sun? One generation passes and another comes, but the world forever stays. The sun rises and the sun goes down; then it presses on to the place where it rises. Blowing now toward the south, then toward the north, the wind turns again and again, resuming its rounds. All rivers go to the sea, yet never does the sea become full. To the place where they go, the rivers keep on going. All speech is labored; there is nothing one can say. The eye is not satisfied with seeing nor is the ear satisfied with hearing.

What has been, that will be; what has been done, that will be done. Nothing is new under the sun. Even the thing of which we say, "See, this is new!" has already existed in the ages that preceded us. There is no remembrance of the men of old; nor of those to come will there be any remembrance among those who come after them.

RESPONSORIAL PSALM   *Psalm 90:3–4, 5–6, 12–13, 14 and 17bc*

R. (1) In every age, O Lord, you have been our refuge.

You turn man back to dust, saying, / "Return, O children of men." / For a thousand years in your sight are as yesterday, / now that it is past, / or as a watch of the night. **R.**

You make an end of them in their sleep; / the next morning they are like the changing grass, / which at dawn springs up anew, / but by evening wilts and fades. **R.**

Teach us to number our days aright, / that we may gain wisdom of heart. / Return, O LORD! How long? / Have pity on your servants! **R.**

Fill us at daybreak with your kindness, / that we may shout for joy and gladness all our days. / Prosper the work of our hands for us! / Prosper the work of our hands! **R.**

ALLELUIA   *John 14:6*

R. Alleluia, alleluia. I am the way and the truth and the life, says the Lord; no one comes to the Father except through me. **R.**

GOSPEL   *Luke 9:7–9*

Herod the tetrarch heard about all that was happening, and he was greatly perplexed because some were saying, "John has been raised from the dead"; others were saying, "Elijah has appeared"; still others, "One of the ancient prophets has arisen." But Herod said, "John I beheaded. Who then is this about whom I hear such things?" And he kept trying to see him.

SEPTEMBER 25, FRIDAY OF WEEK 25; ST. SERGIUS

FIRST READING   *Ecclesiastes 3:1–11*

There is an appointed time for everything, and a time for everything under the heavens.

A time to be born, and a time to die; a time to plant, and a time to uproot the plant. A time to kill, and a time to heal; a time to tear down, and a time to build. A time to weep, and a time to laugh; a time to mourn, and a time to dance. A time to scatter stones, and a time to gather them; a time to embrace, and a time to be far from embraces. A time to seek, and a time to lose; a time to keep, and a time to cast away. A time to rend, and a time to sew; a time to be silent, and a time to speak. A time to love, and a time to hate; a time of war, and a time of peace.

What advantage has the worker from his toil? I have considered the task that God has appointed for the sons of men to be busied about. He has made everything appropriate to its time, and has put the timeless into their hearts, without man's ever discovering, from beginning to end, the work which God has done.

RESPONSORIAL PSALM
Psalm 144:1b and 2abc, 3–4

R. (1) **Blessed be the Lord, my Rock!**
Blessed be the LORD, my rock, / my mercy and my fortress, / my stronghold, my deliverer, / My shield, in whom I trust. **R.**
LORD, what is man, that you notice him; / the son of man, that you take thought of him? / Man is like a breath; / his days, like a passing shadow. **R.**

ALLELUIA
Mark 10:45

R. **Alleluia, alleluia.** The Son of Man came to serve and to give his life as a ransom for many. **R.**

GOSPEL
Luke 9:18–22

Once when Jesus was praying in solitude, and the disciples were with him, he asked them, "Who do the crowds say that I am?" They said in reply, "John the Baptist; others, Elijah; still others, 'One of the ancient prophets has arisen.'" Then he said to them, "But who do you say that I am?" Peter said in reply, "The Christ of God." He rebuked them and directed them not to tell this to anyone.

He said, "The Son of Man must suffer greatly and be rejected by the elders, the chief priests, and the scribes, and be killed and on the third day be raised."

SEPTEMBER 26, SATURDAY OF WEEK 25; ST. COSMAS AND ST. DAMIAN
FIRST READING
Ecclesiastes 11:9—12:8

Rejoice, O young man, while you are young and let your heart be glad in the days of your youth. Follow the ways of your heart, the vision of your eyes; yet understand that as regards all this God will bring you to judgment. Ward off grief from your heart and put away trouble from your presence, though the dawn of youth is fleeting.

Remember your Creator in the days of your youth, before the evil days come And the years approach of which you will say, I have no pleasure in them; Before the sun is darkened, and the light, and the moon, and the stars, while the clouds return after the rain; When the guardians of the house tremble, and the strong men are bent, And the grinders are idle because they are few, and they who look through the windows grow blind; When the doors to the street are shut, and the sound of the mill is low; When one waits for the chirp of a bird, but all the daughters of song are suppressed; And one fears heights, and perils in the street; When the almond tree blooms, and the locust grows sluggish and the caper berry is without effect, Because man goes to his lasting home, and mourners go about the streets; Before the silver cord is snapped and the golden bowl is broken, And the pitcher is shattered at the spring, and the broken pulley falls into the well, And the dust returns to the earth as it once was, and the life breath returns to God who gave it.

Vanity of vanities, says Qoheleth, all things are vanity!

RESPONSORIAL PSALM   *Psalm 90:3–4, 5–6, 12–13, 14 and 17*
R. (1) In every age, O Lord, you have been our refuge.
You turn man back to dust, saying, **/** "Return, O children of men." **/** For a thousand years in your sight **/** are as yesterday, now that it is past, **/** or as a watch of the night. **R.**
You make an end of them in their sleep; **/** the next morning they are like the changing grass, **/** which at dawn springs up anew, **/** but by evening wilts and fades. **R.**
Teach us to number our days aright, **/** that we may gain wisdom of heart. **/** Return, O LORD! How long? **/** Have pity on your servants! **R.**
Fill us at daybreak with your kindness, **/** that we may shout for joy and gladness all our days. **/** And may the gracious care of the Lord our God be ours; **/** prosper the work of our hands for us! **/** Prosper the work of our hands! **R.**

ALLELUIA   *See 2 Timothy 1:10*
R. Alleluia, alleluia. Our Savior Christ Jesus destroyed death and brought life to light through the Gospel. **R.**

GOSPEL   *Luke 9:43b–45*
While they were all amazed at his every deed, Jesus said to his disciples, "Pay attention to what I am telling you. The Son of Man is to be handed over to men." But they did not understand this saying; its meaning was hidden from them so that they should not understand it, and they were afraid to ask him about this saying.

SEPTEMBER 27, 26TH SUNDAY IN ORDINARY TIME; ST. VINCENT DE PAUL
FIRST READING   *Ezekiel 18:25—28*
Thus says the LORD: You say, "The LORD's way is not fair!" Hear now, house of Israel: Is it my way that is unfair, or rather, are not your ways unfair? When someone virtuous turns away from virtue to commit iniquity, and dies, it is because of the iniquity he committed that he must die. But if he turns from the wickedness he has committed, and does what is right and just, he shall preserve his life; since he has turned away from all the sins that he has committed, he shall surely live, he shall not die.

RESPONSORIAL PSALM   *Psalm 25:4—5, 6—7, 8—9 (6a)*
R. Remember your mercies, O Lord.
Your ways, O LORD, make known to me; **/** teach me your paths, **/** guide me in your truth and teach me, **/** for you are God my savior. **R.**

Remember that your compassion, O LORD, / and your love are from of old. / The sins of my youth and my frailties remember not; / in your kindness remember me, / because of your goodness, O LORD. **R.**

Good and upright is the LORD; / thus he shows sinners the way. / He guides the humble to justice, / and teaches the humble his way. **R.**

SECOND READING   *Longer Form Philippians 2:1—11*

Brothers and sisters: If there is any encouragement in Christ, any solace in love, any participation in the Spirit, any compassion and mercy, complete my joy by being of the same mind, with the same love, united in heart, thinking one thing. Do nothing out of selfishness or out of vainglory; rather, humbly regard others as more important than yourselves, each looking out not for his own interests, but also for those of others.

Have in you the same attitude that is also in Christ Jesus, who, though he was in the form of God, did not regard equality with God something to be grasped. Rather, he emptied himself, taking the form of a slave, coming in human likeness; and found human in appearance, he humbled himself, becoming obedient to the point of death, even death on a cross. Because of this, God greatly exalted him and bestowed on him the name which is above every name, that at the name of Jesus every knee should bend, of those in heaven and on earth and under the earth, and every tongue confess that Jesus Christ is Lord, to the glory of God the Father.

SHORTER FORM   *Philippians 2:1—5*

Brothers and sisters: If there is any encouragement in Christ, any solace in love, any participation in the Spirit, any compassion and mercy, complete my joy by being of the same mind, with the same love, united in heart, thinking one thing. Do nothing out of selfishness or out of vainglory; rather, humbly regard others as more important than yourselves, each looking out not for his own interests, but also for those of others. Have in you the same attitude that is also in Christ Jesus.

ALLELUIA   *John 10:27*

R. Alleluia, alleluia. My sheep hear my voice, says the Lord; I know them, and they follow me. **R.**

GOSPEL   *Matthew 21:28—32*

Jesus said to the chief priests and elders of the people: "What is your opinion? A man had two sons. He came to the first and said, 'Son, go out and work in the vineyard today.' He said in reply, 'I will not,' but afterwards changed his mind and went. The man came to the other son and gave the same order. He said in reply, 'Yes, sir,' but did not go. Which of the two did his father's will?" They answered, "The first." Jesus said to them, "Amen, I say to you, tax collectors and prostitutes are entering the kingdom of God before you. When John came to you in the way of righteousness, you did not believe him; but tax collectors and prostitutes did. Yet even when you saw that, you did not later change your minds and believe him."

SEPTEMBER 28, MONDAY OF WEEK 26; ST. LAWRENCE RUIZ AND COMPANIONS

FIRST READING *Job 1:6–22*

One day, when the angels of God came to present themselves before the LORD, Satan also came among them. And the LORD said to Satan, "Whence do you come?" Then Satan answered the LORD and said, "From roaming the earth and patrolling it." And the LORD said to Satan, "Have you noticed my servant Job, and that there is no one on earth like him, blameless and upright, fearing God and avoiding evil?" But Satan answered the LORD and said, "Is it for nothing that Job is God–fearing? Have you not surrounded him and his family and all that he has with your protection? You have blessed the work of his hands, and his livestock are spread over the land. But now put forth your hand and touch anything that he has, and surely he will blaspheme you to your face." And the LORD said to Satan, "Behold, all that he has is in your power; only do not lay a hand upon his person." So Satan went forth from the presence of the LORD.

And so one day, while his sons and his daughters were eating and drinking wine in the house of their eldest brother, a messenger came to Job and said, "The oxen were ploughing and the asses grazing beside them, and the Sabeans carried them off in a raid. They put the herdsmen to the sword, and I alone have escaped to tell you." While he was yet speaking, another came and said, "Lightning has fallen from heaven and struck the sheep and their shepherds and consumed them; and I alone have escaped to tell you." While he was yet speaking, another messenger came and said, "The Chaldeans formed three columns, seized the camels, carried them off, and put those tending them to the sword, and I alone have escaped to tell you." While he was yet speaking, another came and said, "Your sons and daughters were eating and drinking wine in the house of their eldest brother, when suddenly a great wind came across the desert and smote the four corners of the house. It fell upon the young people and they are dead; and I alone have escaped to tell you." Then Job began to tear his cloak and cut off his hair. He cast himself prostrate upon the ground, and said,

"Naked I came forth from my mother's womb, and naked shall I go back again. The LORD gave and the LORD has taken away; blessed be the name of the LORD!"

In all this Job did not sin, nor did he say anything disrespectful of God.

RESPONSORIAL PSALM *Psalm 17:1bcd, 2–3, 6–7*

R. (6) Incline your ear to me and hear my word.

Hear, O LORD, a just suit; / attend to my outcry; / hearken to my prayer from lips without deceit. **R.**

From you let my judgment come; / your eyes behold what is right. / Though you test my heart, / searching it in the night, / though you try me with fire, / you shall find no malice in me. **R.**

I call upon you, for you will answer me, O God; / incline your ear to me; hear my word. / Show your wondrous mercies, / O savior of those who flee from their foes / to refuge at your right hand. **R.**

ALLELUIA *Mark 10:45*

R. Alleluia, alleluia. The Son of Man came to serve and to give his life as a ransom for many. **R.**

GOSPEL

Luke 9:46–50

An argument arose among the disciples about which of them was the greatest. Jesus realized the intention of their hearts and took a child and placed it by his side and said to them, "Whoever receives this child in my name receives me, and whoever receives me receives the one who sent me. For the one who is least among all of you is the one who is the greatest."

Then John said in reply, "Master, we saw someone casting out demons in your name and we tried to prevent him because he does not follow in our company." Jesus said to him, "Do not prevent him, for whoever is not against you is for you."

SEPTEMBER 29, SAINTS MICHAEL, GABRIEL AND RAPHAEL, ARCHANGELS - FEAST

FIRST READING

Daniel 7:9–10, 13–14

As I watched: Thrones were set up and the Ancient One took his throne. His clothing was bright as snow, and the hair on his head as white as wool; His throne was flames of fire, with wheels of burning fire. A surging stream of fire flowed out from where he sat; Thousands upon thousands were ministering to him, and myriads upon myriads attended him.

The court was convened, and the books were opened. As the visions during the night continued, I saw One like a son of man coming, on the clouds of heaven; When he reached the Ancient One and was presented before him, He received dominion, glory, and kingship; nations and peoples of every language serve him. His dominion is an everlasting dominion that shall not be taken away, his kingship shall not be destroyed.

ALTERNATIVE READING

Revelation 12:7–12ab

War broke out in heaven; Michael and his angels battled against the dragon. The dragon and its angels fought back, but they did not prevail and there was no longer any place for them in heaven. The huge dragon, the ancient serpent, who is called the Devil and Satan, who deceived the whole world, was thrown down to earth, and its angels were thrown down with it.

Then I heard a loud voice in heaven say: "Now have salvation and power come, and the Kingdom of our God and the authority of his Anointed.

For the accuser of our brothers is cast out, who accuses them before our God day and night. They conquered him by the Blood of the Lamb and by the word of their testimony; love for life did not deter them from death. Therefore, rejoice, you heavens, and you who dwell in them."

RESPONSORIAL PSALM

Psalm 138:1–2ab, 2cde–3, 4–5

R. In the sight of the angels I will sing your praises, Lord.

I will give thanks to you, O LORD, with all my heart, **/** for you have heard the words of my mouth; **/** in the presence of the angels I will sing your praise; **/** I will worship at your holy temple **/** and give thanks to your name. **R.**

Because of your kindness and your truth; **/** for you have made great above all things your name and your promise. **/** When I called, you answered me; **/** you built up strength within me. **R.**

All the kings of the earth shall give thanks to you, O LORD, **/** when they hear the words of your mouth; **/** And they shall sing of the ways of the LORD: **/** "Great is the glory of the LORD." **R.**

ALLELUIA *Psalm 103:21*

R. Alleluia, alleluia. Bless the LORD, all you angels, you ministers, who do his will. **R.**

GOSPEL *John 1:47–51*

Jesus saw Nathanael coming toward him and said of him, "Here is a true child of Israel. There is no duplicity in him." Nathanael said to him, "How do you know me?" Jesus answered and said to him, "Before Philip called you, I saw you under the fig tree." Nathanael answered him, "Rabbi, you are the Son of God; you are the King of Israel." Jesus answered and said to him, "Do you believe because I told you that I saw you under the fig tree? You will see greater things than this." And he said to him, "Amen, amen, I say to you, you will see heaven opened and the angels of God ascending and descending on the Son of Man."

SEPTEMBER 30, WEDNESDAY OF WEEK 26; ST. JEROME

FIRST READING *Job 9:1–12, 14–16*

Job answered his friends and said:

I know well that it is so; but how can a man be justified before God? Should one wish to contend with him, he could not answer him once in a thousand times. God is wise in heart and mighty in strength; who has withstood him and remained unscathed?

He removes the mountains before they know it; he overturns them in his anger. He shakes the earth out of its place, and the pillars beneath it tremble. He commands the sun, and it rises not; he seals up the stars.

He alone stretches out the heavens and treads upon the crests of the sea. He made the Bear and Orion, the Pleiades and the constellations of the south; He does great things past finding out, marvelous things beyond reckoning.

Should he come near me, I see him not; should he pass by, I am not aware of him; should he seize me forcibly, who can say him nay? Who can say to him, "What are you doing?"

How much less shall I give him any answer, or choose out arguments against him! Even though I were right, I could not answer him, but should rather beg for what was due me. If I appealed to him and he answered my call, I could not believe that he would hearken to my words.

RESPONSORIAL PSALM   *Psalm 88:10bc–11, 12–13, 14–15*

R. (3) Let my prayer come before you, Lord.

Daily I call upon you, O LORD; **/** to you I stretch out my hands. **/** Will you work wonders for the dead? **/** Will the shades arise to give you thanks? **R.**

Do they declare your mercy in the grave, **/** your faithfulness among those who have perished? **/** Are your wonders made known in the darkness, **/** or your justice in the land of oblivion? **R.**

But I, O LORD, cry out to you; **/** with my morning prayer I wait upon you. **/** Why, O LORD, do you reject me; **/** why hide from me your face? **R.**

ALLELUIA   *Philippians 3:8–9*

R. Alleluia, alleluia. I consider all things so much rubbish that I may gain Christ and be found in him. **R.**

GOSPEL   *Luke 9:57–62*

As Jesus and his disciples were proceeding on their journey, someone said to him, "I will follow you wherever you go." Jesus answered him, "Foxes have dens and birds of the sky have nests, but the Son of Man has nowhere to rest his head." And to another he said, "Follow me." But he replied, "Lord, let me go first and bury my father." But he answered him, "Let the dead bury their dead. But you, go and proclaim the Kingdom of God." And another said, "I will follow you, Lord, but first let me say farewell to my family at home." Jesus answered him, "No one who sets a hand to the plow and looks to what was left behind is fit for the Kingdom of God."

12   OCTOBER

OCTOBER 1, THURSDAY OF WEEK 26; ST. THÉRÈSE OF THE CHILD JESUS

FIRST READING   *Job 19:21–27*

Job said: Pity me, pity me, O you my friends, for the hand of God has struck me! Why do you hound me as though you were divine, and insatiably prey upon me?

Oh, would that my words were written down! Would that they were inscribed in a record: That with an iron chisel and with lead they were cut in the rock forever! But as for me, I know that my Vindicator lives, and that he will at last stand forth upon the dust; Whom I myself shall see: my own eyes, not another's, shall behold him, And from my flesh I shall see God; my inmost being is consumed with longing.

RESPONSORIAL PSALM   *Psalm 27:7–8a, 8b–9abc, 13–14*

R. (13) I believe that I shall see the good things of the Lord in the land of the living.

Hear, O LORD, the sound of my call; **/** have pity on me, and answer me. **/** Of you my heart speaks; **/** you my glance seeks. **R.**

Your presence, O LORD, I seek. / Hide not your face from me; / do not in anger repel your servant. / You are my helper: cast me not off. **R.**

I believe that I shall see the bounty of the LORD / in the land of the living. / Wait for the LORD with courage; / be stouthearted, and wait for the LORD. **R.**

ALLELUIA *Mark 1:15*

R. Alleluia, alleluia. The Kingdom of God is at hand; repent and believe in the Gospel. **R.**

GOSPEL *Luke 10:1–12*

Jesus appointed seventy–two other disciples whom he sent ahead of him in pairs to every town and place he intended to visit. He said to them, "The harvest is abundant but the laborers are few; so ask the master of the harvest to send out laborers for his harvest. Go on your way; behold, I am sending you like lambs among wolves. Carry no money bag, no sack, no sandals; and greet no one along the way. Into whatever house you enter, first say, 'Peace to this household.' If a peaceful person lives there, your peace will rest on him; but if not, it will return to you. Stay in the same house and eat and drink what is offered to you, for the laborer deserves his payment. Do not move about from one house to another. Whatever town you enter and they welcome you, eat what is set before you, cure the sick in it and say to them, 'The Kingdom of God is at hand for you.' Whatever town you enter and they do not receive you, go out into the streets and say, 'The dust of your town that clings to our feet, even that we shake off against you.' Yet know this: the Kingdom of God is at hand. I tell you, it will be more tolerable for Sodom on that day than for that town."

OCTOBER 2, THE GUARDIAN ANGELS

FIRST READING *Job 38:1, 12–21; 40:3–5*

The LORD addressed Job out of the storm and said:

Have you ever in your lifetime commanded the morning and shown the dawn its place For taking hold of the ends of the earth, till the wicked are shaken from its surface? The earth is changed as is clay by the seal, and dyed as though it were a garment; But from the wicked the light is withheld, and the arm of pride is shattered.

Have you entered into the sources of the sea, or walked about in the depths of the abyss? Have the gates of death been shown to you, or have you seen the gates of darkness? Have you comprehended the breadth of the earth? Tell me, if you know all: Which is the way to the dwelling place of light, and where is the abode of darkness, That you may take them to their boundaries and set them on their homeward paths? You know, because you were born before them, and the number of your years is great!

Then Job answered the LORD and said:

Behold, I am of little account; what can I answer you? I put my hand over my mouth. Though I have spoken once, I will not do so again; though twice, I will do so no more.

RESPONSORIAL PSALM *Psalm 91:1–2, 3–4ab, 4c–6, 10–11*

R. The Lord has put angels in charge of you, to guard you in all your ways.

You who dwell in the shelter of the Most High, / who abide in the shadow of the Almighty, / say to the LORD, "My refuge and my fortress, / my God, in whom I trust." **R.**

For he will rescue you from the snare of the fowler, / from the destroying pestilence. With his pinions he will cover you, / and under his wings you shall take refuge. **R.**

His faithfulness is a buckler and a shield. / You shall not fear the terror of the night / nor the arrow that flies by day; / nor the pestilence that roams in darkness, / nor the devastating plague at noon. **R.**

No evil shall befall you, / nor shall affliction come near your tent, / for to his angels he has given command about you, / that they guard you in all your ways. **R.**

ALLELUIA   *Psalm 103:21*

R. Alleluia, alleluia. Bless the LORD, all you angels, you ministers, who do his will. **R.**

GOSPEL   *Matthew 18:1–5, 10*

The disciples approached Jesus and said, "Who is the greatest in the Kingdom of heaven?" He called a child over, placed it in their midst, and said, "Amen, I say to you, unless you turn and become like children, you will not enter the Kingdom of heaven. Whoever humbles himself like this child is the greatest in the Kingdom of heaven. And whoever receives one child such as this in my name receives me.

"See that you do not despise one of these little ones, for I say to you that their angels in heaven always look upon the face of my heavenly Father."

OCTOBER 3, SATURDAY OF WEEK 26; BLESSED BARTOLO LONGO

FIRST READING   *Job 42:1–3, 5–6, 12–17*

Job answered the LORD and said: I know that you can do all things, and that no purpose of yours can be hindered. I have dealt with great things that I do not understand; things too wonderful for me, which I cannot know. I had heard of you by word of mouth, but now my eye has seen you. Therefore I disown what I have said, and repent in dust and ashes.

Thus the LORD blessed the latter days of Job more than his earlier ones. For he had fourteen thousand sheep, six thousand camels, a thousand yoke of oxen, and a thousand she–asses. And he had seven sons and three daughters, of whom he called the first Jemimah, the second Keziah, and the third Kerenhappuch. In all the land no other women were as beautiful as the daughters of Job; and their father gave them an inheritance along with their brothers. After this, Job lived a hundred and forty years; and he saw his children, his grandchildren, and even his great–grandchildren. Then Job died, old and full of years.

RESPONSORIAL PSALM   *Psalm 119:66, 71, 75, 91, 125, 130*

R. (135) Lord, let your face shine on me.

Teach me wisdom and knowledge, / for in your commands I trust. **R.**

It is good for me that I have been afflicted, / that I may learn your statutes. **R.**

I know, O LORD, that your ordinances are just, / and in your faithfulness you have afflicted me. **R.**

According to your ordinances they still stand firm: / all things serve you. **R.**

I am your servant; **/** give me discernment **/** that I may know your decrees. **R.**

The revelation of your words sheds light, **/** giving understanding to the simple. **R.**

ALLELUIA   *See Matthew 11:25*

R. Alleluia, alleluia. Blessed are you, Father, Lord of heaven and earth, you have revealed to little ones the mysteries of the Kingdom. **R.**

GOSPEL   *Luke 10:17–24*

The seventy–two disciples returned rejoicing and said to Jesus, "Lord, even the demons are subject to us because of your name." Jesus said, "I have observed Satan fall like lightning from the sky. Behold, I have given you the power 'to tread upon serpents' and scorpions and upon the full force of the enemy and nothing will harm you. Nevertheless, do not rejoice because the spirits are subject to you, but rejoice because your names are written in heaven."

At that very moment he rejoiced in the Holy Spirit and said, "I give you praise, Father, Lord of heaven and earth, for although you have hidden these things from the wise and the learned you have revealed them to the childlike. Yes, Father, such has been your gracious will. All things have been handed over to me by my Father. No one knows who the Son is except the Father, and who the Father is except the Son and anyone to whom the Son wishes to reveal him."

Turning to the disciples in private he said, "Blessed are the eyes that see what you see. For I say to you, many prophets and kings desired to see what you see, but did not see it, and to hear what you hear, but did not hear it."

OCTOBER 4, 27 TH SUNDAY IN ORDINARY TIME; ST. FRANCIS OF ASSISI

FIRST READING   *Isaiah 5:1—7*

Let me now sing of my friend, my friend's song concerning his vineyard. My friend had a vineyard on a fertile hillside; he spaded it, cleared it of stones, and planted the choicest vines; within it he built a watchtower, and hewed out a wine press. Then he looked for the crop of grapes, but what it yielded was wild grapes.

Now, inhabitants of Jerusalem and people of Judah, judge between me and my vineyard: What more was there to do for my vineyard that I had not done? Why, when I looked for the crop of grapes, did it bring forth wild grapes? Now, I will let you know what I mean to do with my vineyard: take away its hedge, give it to grazing, break through its wall, let it be trampled! Yes, I will make it a ruin: it shall not be pruned or hoed, but overgrown with thorns and briers; I will command the clouds not to send rain upon it. The vineyard of the LORD of hosts is the house of Israel, and the people of Judah are his cherished plant; he looked for judgment, but see, bloodshed! for justice, but hark, the outcry!

RESPONSORIAL PSALM: *Psalm 80:9, 12, 13—14, 15—16, 19—20 (Isaiah 5:7a)*

R. The vineyard of the Lord is the house of Israel.

A vine from Egypt you transplanted; **/** you drove away the nations and planted it. **/** It put forth its foliage to the Sea, **/** its shoots as far as the River. **R.**

Why have you broken down its walls, / so that every passer–by plucks its fruit, / the boar from the forest lays it waste, / and the beasts of the field feed upon it? **R.**

Once again, O LORD of hosts, / look down from heaven, and see; / take care of this vine, and protect what your right hand has planted, / the son of man whom you yourself made strong. **R.**

Then we will no more withdraw from you; / give us new life, and we will call upon your name. / O LORD, God of hosts, restore us; / if your face shine upon us, then we shall be saved. **R.**

SECOND READING   *Philippians 4:6—9*

Brothers and sisters: Have no anxiety at all, but in everything, by prayer and petition, with thanksgiving, make your requests known to God. Then the peace of God that surpasses all understanding will guard your hearts and minds in Christ Jesus.

Finally, brothers and sisters, whatever is true, whatever is honorable, whatever is just, whatever is pure, whatever is lovely, whatever is gracious, if there is any excellence and if there is anything worthy of praise, think about these things. Keep on doing what you have learned and received and heard and seen in me. Then the God of peace will be with you.

ALLELUIA   *see John 15:16*

R. Alleluia, alleluia. I have chosen you from the world, says the Lord, to go and bear fruit that will remain. **R.**

GOSPEL   *Matthew 21:33—43*

Jesus said to the chief priests and the elders of the people: "Hear another parable. There was a landowner who planted a vineyard, put a hedge around it, dug a wine press in it, and built a tower. Then he leased it to tenants and went on a journey. When vintage time drew near, he sent his servants to the tenants to obtain his produce. But the tenants seized the servants and one they beat, another they killed, and a third they stoned. Again he sent other servants, more numerous than the first ones, but they treated them in the same way. Finally, he sent his son to them, thinking, 'They will respect my son.' But when the tenants saw the son, they said to one another, 'This is the heir. Come, let us kill him and acquire his inheritance.' They seized him, threw him out of the vineyard, and killed him. What will the owner of the vineyard do to those tenants when he comes?" They answered him, "He will put those wretched men to a wretched death and lease his vineyard to other tenants who will give him the produce at the proper times." Jesus said to them, "Did you never read in the Scriptures: The stone that the builders rejected has become the cornerstone; by the Lord has this been done, and it is wonderful in our eyes? Therefore, I say to you, the kingdom of God will be taken away from you and given to a people that will produce its fruit."

OCTOBER 5, MONDAY OF WEEK 27; ST. MARIA FAUSTINA KOWALSKA

FIRST READING   *Galatians 1:6–12*

Brothers and sisters: I am amazed that you are so quickly forsaking the one who called you by the grace of Christ for a different gospel (not that there is another). But there are some who are disturbing you and wish to pervert the Gospel of Christ. But even if we or an angel from heaven should preach to you a gospel other than the one that we preached to you, let that one be accursed! As we have said before, and now I say again, if anyone preaches to you a gospel other than the one that you received, let that one be accursed!

Am I now currying favor with human beings or God? Or am I seeking to please people? If I were still trying to please people, I would not be a slave of Christ.

Now I want you to know, brothers and sisters, that the Gospel preached by me is not of human origin. For I did not receive it from a human being, nor was I taught it, but it came through a revelation of Jesus Christ.

RESPONSORIAL PSALM   *Psalm 111:1b–2, 7–8, 9 and 10c*

R. The Lord will remember his covenant for ever. or: R. Alleluia.

I will give thanks to the LORD with all my heart / in the company and assembly of the just. / Great are the works of the LORD, / exquisite in all their delights. **R.**

The works of his hands are faithful and just; / sure are all his precepts, / reliable forever and ever, / wrought in truth and equity. **R.**

He has sent deliverance to his people; / he has ratified his covenant forever; / holy and awesome is his name. / His praise endures forever. **R.**

ALLELUIA   *John 13:34*

R. Alleluia, alleluia. I give you a new commandment: love one another as I have loved you. **R.**

GOSPEL   *Luke 10:25–37*

There was a scholar of the law who stood up to test Jesus and said, "Teacher, what must I do to inherit eternal life?" Jesus said to him, "What is written in the law? How do you read it?" He said in reply, "You shall love the Lord, your God, with all your heart, with all your being, with all your strength, and with all your mind, and your neighbor as yourself." He replied to him, "You have answered correctly; do this and you will live."

But because he wished to justify himself, he said to Jesus, "And who is my neighbor?" Jesus replied, "A man fell victim to robbers as he went down from Jerusalem to Jericho. They stripped and beat him and went off leaving him half–dead. A priest happened to be going down that road, but when he saw him, he passed by on the opposite side. Likewise a Levite came to the place, and when he saw him, he passed by on the opposite side. But a Samaritan traveler who came upon him was moved with compassion at the sight. He approached the victim, poured oil and wine over his wounds and bandaged them. Then he lifted him up on his own animal, took him to an inn, and cared for him. The next day he took out two silver coins and gave them to the innkeeper with the instruction, 'Take care of him. If you spend more than what I have given you, I shall repay you on my way back.' Which of these three, in your opinion, was neighbor to the robbers' victim?" He answered, "The one who treated him with mercy." Jesus said to him, "Go and do likewise."

OCTOBER 6, TUESDAY OF WEEK 27; BLESSED MARIE ROSE DUROCHER

FIRST READING *Galatians 1:13–24*

Brothers and sisters: You heard of my former way of life in Judaism, how I persecuted the Church of God beyond measure and tried to destroy it, and progressed in Judaism beyond many of my contemporaries among my race, since I was even more a zealot for my ancestral traditions. But when he, who from my mother's womb had set me apart and called me through his grace, was pleased to reveal his Son to me, so that I might proclaim him to the Gentiles, I did not immediately consult flesh and blood, nor did I go up to Jerusalem to those who were Apostles before me; rather, I went into Arabia and then returned to Damascus.

Then after three years I went up to Jerusalem to confer with Cephas and remained with him for fifteen days. But I did not see any other of the Apostles, only James the brother of the Lord. (As to what I am writing to you, behold, before God, I am not lying.) Then I went into the regions of Syria and Cilicia. And I was unknown personally to the churches of Judea that are in Christ; they only kept hearing that "the one who once was persecuting us is now preaching the faith he once tried to destroy." So they glorified God because of me.

RESPONSORIAL PSALM *Psalm 139:1b–3, 13–14ab, 14c–15*

R. (24b) Guide me, Lord, along the everlasting way.

O LORD, you have probed me and you know me; / you know when I sit and when I stand; / you understand my thoughts from afar. / My journeys and my rest you scrutinize, / with all my ways you are familiar. **R.**

Truly you have formed my inmost being; / you knit me in my mother's womb. / I give you thanks that I am fearfully, wonderfully made; / wonderful are your works. **R.**

My soul also you knew full well; / nor was my frame unknown to you when I was made in secret, / when I was fashioned in the depths of the earth. **R.**

ALLELUIA *Luke 11:28*

R. Alleluia, alleluia. Blessed are those who hear the word of God and observe it. **R.**

GOSPEL *Luke 10:38–42*

Jesus entered a village where a woman whose name was Martha welcomed him. She had a sister named Mary who sat beside the Lord at his feet listening to him speak. Martha, burdened with much serving, came to him and said, "Lord, do you not care that my sister has left me by myself to do the serving? Tell her to help me." The Lord said to her in reply, "Martha, Martha, you are anxious and worried about many things. There is need of only one thing. Mary has chosen the better part and it will not be taken from her."

OCTOBER 7, WEDNESDAY OF WEEK 27; OUR LADY OF THE ROSARY

FIRST READING *Galatians 2:1–2, 7–14*

Brothers and sisters: after fourteen years I again went up to Jerusalem with Barnabas, taking Titus along also. I went up in accord with a revelation, and I presented to them the Gospel that I preach to the Gentiles— but privately to those of repute— so that I might not be running, or have run, in vain. On the contrary, when they saw that I had been entrusted with the Gospel to the uncircumcised, just as Peter to the circumcised, for the one who worked in Peter for an apostolate to the circumcised worked also in me for the Gentiles, and when they recognized the grace bestowed upon me, James and Cephas and John, who were reputed to be pillars, gave me and Barnabas their right hands in partnership, that we should go to the Gentiles and they to the circumcised. Only, we were to be mindful of the poor, which is the very thing I was eager to do.

And when Cephas came to Antioch, I opposed him to his face because he clearly was wrong. For, until some people came from James, he used to eat with the Gentiles; but when they came, he began to draw back and separated himself, because he was afraid of the circumcised. And the rest of the Jews acted hypocritically along with him, with the result that even Barnabas was carried away by their hypocrisy. But when I saw that they were not on the right road in line with the truth of the Gospel, I said to Cephas in front of all, "If you, though a Jew, are living like a Gentile and not like a Jew, how can you compel the Gentiles to live like Jews?"

RESPONSORIAL PSALM *Psalm 117:1bc, 2*

R. Go out to all the world, and tell the Good News.

Praise the LORD, all you nations, / glorify him, all you peoples! **R.**

For steadfast is his kindness toward us, / and the fidelity of the LORD endures forever. **R.**

ALLELUIA *Romans 8:15bc*

R. Alleluia, alleluia. You have received a spirit of adoption as sons through which we cry: Abba! Father! **R.**

GOSPEL *Luke 11:1–4*

Jesus was praying in a certain place, and when he had finished, one of his disciples said to him, "Lord, teach us to pray just as John taught his disciples." He said to them, "When you pray, say:

Father, hallowed be your name, your Kingdom come. Give us each day our daily bread and forgive us our sins for we ourselves forgive everyone in debt to us, and do not subject us to the final test."

OCTOBER 8, THURSDAY OF WEEK 27; ST. SIMEON

FIRST READING *Galatians 3:1–5*

O stupid Galatians! Who has bewitched you, before whose eyes Jesus Christ was publicly portrayed as crucified? I want to learn only this from you: did you receive the Spirit from works of the law, or from faith in what you heard? Are you so stupid? After beginning with the Spirit, are you now ending with the flesh? Did you experience so many things in vain? — if indeed it was in vain. Does, then, the one who supplies the Spirit to you and works mighty deeds among you do so from works of the law or from faith in what you heard?

RESPONSORIAL PSALM *Luke 1:69–70, 71–72, 73–75*
R. (68) Blessed be the Lord, the God of Israel; he has come to his people.
He has raised up for us a mighty savior, / born of the house of his servant David. **R.**
Through his holy prophets he promised of old / that he would save us from our enemies, / from the hands of all who hate us. **R.**
He promised to show mercy to our fathers / and to remember his holy covenant. **R.**
This was the oath he swore to our father Abraham: / to set us free from the hands of our enemies, / free to worship him without fear, / holy and righteous in his sight all the days of our life. **R.**

ALLELUIA *See Acts 16:14b*
R. Alleluia, alleluia. Open our hearts, O Lord, to listen to the words of your Son. **R.**

GOSPEL *Luke 11:5–13*
Jesus said to his disciples: "Suppose one of you has a friend to whom he goes at midnight and says, 'Friend, lend me three loaves of bread, for a friend of mine has arrived at my house from a journey and I have nothing to offer him,' and he says in reply from within, 'Do not bother me; the door has already been locked and my children and I are already in bed. I cannot get up to give you anything.' I tell you, if he does not get up to give him the loaves because of their friendship, he will get up to give him whatever he needs because of his persistence.

"And I tell you, ask and you will receive; seek and you will find; knock and the door will be opened to you. For everyone who asks, receives; and the one who seeks, finds; and to the one who knocks, the door will be opened. What father among you would hand his son a snake when he asks for a fish? Or hand him a scorpion when he asks for an egg? If you then, who are wicked, know how to give good gifts to your children, how much more will the Father in heaven give the Holy Spirit to those who ask him?"

OCTOBER 9, FRIDAY OF WEEK 27; ST. JOHN LEONARDI

FIRST READING *Galatians 3:7–14*
Brothers and sisters: Realize that it is those who have faith who are children of Abraham. Scripture, which saw in advance that God would justify the Gentiles by faith, foretold the good news to Abraham, saying, through you shall all the nations be blessed. Consequently, those who have faith are blessed along with Abraham who had faith. For all who depend on works of the law are under a curse; for it is written, Cursed be everyone who does not persevere in doing all the things written in the book of the law. And that no one is justified before God by the law is clear, for the one who is righteous by faith will live. But the law does not depend on faith; rather, the one who does these things will live by them. Christ ransomed us from the curse of the law by becoming a curse for us, for it is written, Cursed

be everyone who hangs on a tree, that the blessing of Abraham might be extended to the Gentiles through Christ Jesus, so that we might receive the promise of the Spirit through faith.

RESPONSORIAL PSALM *Psalm 111:1b–2, 3–4, 5–6*

R. (5) The Lord will remember his covenant for ever.

I will give thanks to the LORD with all my heart **/** in the company and assembly of the just. **/** Great are the works of the LORD, **/** exquisite in all their delights. **R.**

Majesty and glory are his work, **/** and his justice endures forever. **/** He has won renown for his wondrous deeds; **/** gracious and merciful is the LORD. **R.**

He has given food to those who fear him; **/** he will forever be mindful of his covenant. **/** He has made known to his people the power of his works, **/** giving them the inheritance of the nations. **R.**

ALLELUIA *John 12:31b–32*

R. Alleluia, alleluia. The prince of this world will now be cast out, and when I am lifted up from the earth I will draw all to myself, says the Lord. **R.**

GOSPEL *Luke 11:15–26*

When Jesus had driven out a demon, some of the crowd said: "By the power of Beelzebul, the prince of demons, he drives out demons." Others, to test him, asked him for a sign from heaven. But he knew their thoughts and said to them, "Every kingdom divided against itself will be laid waste and house will fall against house. And if Satan is divided against himself, how will his kingdom stand? For you say that it is by Beelzebul that I drive out demons. If I, then, drive out demons by Beelzebul, by whom do your own people drive them out? Therefore they will be your judges. But if it is by the finger of God that I drive out demons, then the Kingdom of God has come upon you. When a strong man fully armed guards his palace, his possessions are safe. But when one stronger than he attacks and overcomes him, he takes away the armor on which he relied and distributes the spoils. Whoever is not with me is against me, and whoever does not gather with me scatters.

"When an unclean spirit goes out of someone, it roams through arid regions searching for rest but, finding none, it says, 'I shall return to my home from which I came.' But upon returning, it finds it swept clean and put in order. Then it goes and brings back seven other spirits more wicked than itself who move in and dwell there, and the last condition of that man is worse than the first."

OCTOBER 10, SATURDAY OF WEEK 27; ST. FRANCIS BORGIA

FIRST READING *Galatians 3:22–29*

Brothers and sisters: Scripture confined all things under the power of sin, that through faith in Jesus Christ the promise might be given to those who believe.

Before faith came, we were held in custody under law, confined for the faith that was to be revealed. Consequently, the law was our disciplinarian for Christ, that we might be justified by faith. But now that faith has come, we are no longer under a disciplinarian.

For through faith you are all children of God in Christ Jesus. For all of you who were baptized into Christ have clothed yourselves with Christ. There is neither Jew nor Greek, there is neither slave nor free person, there is not male and female; for you are all one in Christ Jesus. And if you belong to Christ, then you are Abraham's descendants, heirs according to the promise.

RESPONSORIAL PSALM *Psalm 105:2–3, 4–5, 6–7*
R. The Lord remembers his covenant for ever. or: R. Alleluia.
Sing to him, sing his praise, / proclaim all his wondrous deeds. / Glory in his holy name; / rejoice, O hearts that seek the LORD! **R.**
Look to the LORD in his strength; / seek to serve him constantly. / Recall the wondrous deeds that he has wrought, / his portents, and the judgments he has uttered. **R.**
You descendants of Abraham, his servants, / sons of Jacob, his chosen ones! He, the LORD, is our God; / throughout the earth his judgments prevail. **R.**

ALLELUIA *Luke 11:28*
R. Alleluia, alleluia. Blessed are those who hear the word of God and observe it. **R.**

GOSPEL *Luke 11:27–28*
While Jesus was speaking, a woman from the crowd called out and said to him, "Blessed is the womb that carried you and the breasts at which you nursed." He replied, "Rather, blessed are those who hear the word of God and observe it."

OCTOBER 11, 28TH SUNDAY IN ORDINARY TIME; ST. KENNETH

FIRST READING *Isaiah 25:6—10a*
On this mountain the LORD of hosts will provide for all peoples a feast of rich food and choice wines, juicy, rich food and pure, choice wines. On this mountain he will destroy the veil that veils all peoples, the web that is woven over all nations; he will destroy death forever. The Lord GOD will wipe away the tears from every face; the reproach of his people he will remove from the whole earth; for the LORD has spoken. On that day it will be said: "Behold our God, to whom we looked to save us! This is the LORD for whom we looked; let us rejoice and be glad that he has saved us!" For the hand of the LORD will rest on this mountain.

RESPONSORIAL PSALM *Psalm 23:1—3a, 3b—4, 5, 6 (6cd)*
R. I shall live in the house of the Lord all the days of my life.
The LORD is my shepherd; / I shall not want. / In verdant pastures he gives me repose; / beside restful waters he leads me; / he refreshes my soul. **R.**
He guides me in right paths for his name's sake. / Even though I walk in the dark valley / I fear no evil; / for you are at my side with your rod /and your staff that give me courage. **R.**
You spread the table before me in the sight of my foes; / you anoint my head with oil; / my cup overflows. **R.**
Only goodness and kindness follow me / all the days of my life; / and I shall dwell in the house of the LORD / for years to come. **R.**

SECOND READING
Philippians 4:12—14, 19—20

Brothers and sisters: I know how to live in humble circumstances; I know also how to live with abundance. In every circumstance and in all things I have learned the secret of being well fed and of going hungry, of living in abundance and of being in need. I can do all things in him who strengthens me. Still, it was kind of you to share in my distress.

My God will fully supply whatever you need, in accord with his glorious riches in Christ Jesus. To our God and Father, glory forever and ever. Amen.

ALLELUIA
see Ephesians 1:17—18

R. Alleluia, alleluia. May the Father of Our Lord Jesus Christ enlighten the eyes of our hearts, so that we may know what is the hope that belongs to our call. R.

GOSPEL
Longer Form Matthew 22:1—14

Jesus again in reply spoke to the chief priests and elders of the people in parables, saying, "The kingdom of heaven may be likened to a king who gave a wedding feast for his son. He dispatched his servants to summon the invited guests to the feast, but they refused to come. A second time he sent other servants, saying, 'Tell those invited: "Behold, I have prepared my banquet, my calves and fattened cattle are killed, and everything is ready; come to the feast."' Some ignored the invitation and went away, one to his farm, another to his business. The rest laid hold of his servants, mistreated them, and killed them. The king was enraged and sent his troops, destroyed those murderers, and burned their city. Then he said to his servants, 'The feast is ready, but those who were invited were not worthy to come. Go out, therefore, into the main roads and invite to the feast whomever you find.' The servants went out into the streets and gathered all they found, bad and good alike, and the hall was filled with guests. But when the king came in to meet the guests, he saw a man there not dressed in a wedding garment. The king said to him, 'My friend, how is it that you came in here without a wedding garment?' But he was reduced to silence. Then the king said to his attendants, 'Bind his hands and feet, and cast him into the darkness outside, where there will be wailing and grinding of teeth.' Many are invited, but few are chosen."

SHORTER FORM
Matthew 22:1—10

Jesus again in reply spoke to the chief priests and elders of the people in parables, saying, "The kingdom of heaven may be likened to a king who gave a wedding feast for his son. He dispatched his servants to summon the invited guests to the feast, but they refused to come. A second time he sent other servants, saying, 'Tell those invited: "Behold, I have prepared my banquet, my calves and fattened cattle are killed, and everything is ready; come to the feast."' Some ignored the invitation and went away, one to his farm, another to his business. The rest laid hold of his servants, mistreated them, and killed them. The king was enraged and sent his troops, destroyed those murderers, and burned their city. Then he said to his servants, 'The feast is ready, but those who were invited were not worthy to come. Go out, therefore, into the main roads and invite to the feast whomever you find.' The servants went out into the streets and gathered all they found, bad and good alike, and the hall was filled with guests."

OCTOBER 12, MONDAY OF WEEK 28; ST. SERAPHIM OF MONTEGRANARO

FIRST READING *Galatians 4:22–24, 26–27, 31—5:1*

Brothers and sisters: It is written that Abraham had two sons, one by the slave woman and the other by the freeborn woman. The son of the slave woman was born naturally, the son of the freeborn through a promise. Now this is an allegory. These women represent two covenants. One was from Mount Sinai, bearing children for slavery; this is Hagar. But the Jerusalem above is freeborn, and she is our mother. For it is written:

Rejoice, you barren one who bore no children; break forth and shout, you who were not in labor; for more numerous are the children of the deserted one than of her who has a husband.

Therefore, brothers and sisters, we are children not of the slave woman but of the freeborn woman.

For freedom Christ set us free; so stand firm and do not submit again to the yoke of slavery.

RESPONSORIAL PSALM *Psalm 113:1b–2, 3–4, 5a and 6–7*

R. Blessed be the name of the Lord forever. or: R. Alleluia, alleluia.

Praise, you servants of the LORD, / praise the name of the LORD. / Blessed be the name of the LORD / both now and forever. **R.**

From the rising to the setting of the sun / is the name of the LORD to be praised. / High above all nations is the LORD; / above the heavens is his glory. **R.**

Who is like the LORD, our God, / who looks upon the heavens and the earth below? / He raises up the lowly from the dust; / from the dunghill he lifts up the poor. **R.**

ALLELUIA *Psalm 95:8*

R. Alleluia, alleluia. If today you hear his voice, harden not your hearts. **R.**

GOSPEL *Luke 11:29–32*

While still more people gathered in the crowd, Jesus said to them, "This generation is an evil generation; it seeks a sign, but no sign will be given it, except the sign of Jonah. Just as Jonah became a sign to the Ninevites, so will the Son of Man be to this generation. At the judgment the queen of the south will rise with the men of this generation and she will condemn them, because she came from the ends of the earth to hear the wisdom of Solomon, and there is something greater than Solomon here. At the judgment the men of Nineveh will arise with this generation and condemn it, because at the preaching of Jonah they repented, and there is something greater than Jonah here."

OCTOBER 13, TUESDAY OF WEEK 28; ST. EDWARD

FIRST READING *Galatians 5:1–6*

Brothers and sisters: For freedom Christ set us free; so stand firm and do not submit again to the yoke of slavery.

It is I, Paul, who am telling you that if you have yourselves circumcised, Christ will be of no benefit to you. Once again I declare to every man who has himself circumcised that he is bound to observe the entire law. You are separated from Christ, you who are trying to be justified by law; you have fallen from grace. For through the Spirit, by faith, we await the hope of righteousness. For in Christ Jesus, neither circumcision nor uncircumcision counts for anything, but only faith working through love.

RESPONSORIAL PSALM   *Psalm 119:41, 43, 44, 45, 47, 48*
R. Let your mercy come to me, O Lord.

Let your mercy come to me, O LORD, **/** your salvation according to your promise. **R.**
Take not the word of truth from my mouth, **/** for in your ordinances is my hope. **R.**
And I will keep your law continually, **/** forever and ever. **R.**
And I will walk at liberty, **/** because I seek your precepts. **R.**
And I will delight in your commands, which I love. **R.**
And I will lift up my hands to your commands **/** and meditate on your statutes. **R.**

ALLELUIA   *Hebrews 4:12*
R. Alleluia, alleluia. The word of God is living and effective, able to discern reflections and thoughts of the heart. **R.**

GOSPEL   *Luke 11:37–41*

After Jesus had spoken, a Pharisee invited him to dine at his home. He entered and reclined at table to eat. The Pharisee was amazed to see that he did not observe the prescribed washing before the meal. The Lord said to him, "Oh you Pharisees! Although you cleanse the outside of the cup and the dish, inside you are filled with plunder and evil. You fools! Did not the maker of the outside also make the inside? But as to what is within, give alms, and behold, everything will be clean for you."

OCTOBER 14, WEDNESDAY OF WEEK 28; ST. CALLISTUS I

FIRST READING   *Galatians 5:18–25*

Brothers and sisters: If you are guided by the Spirit, you are not under the law. Now the works of the flesh are obvious: immorality, impurity, licentiousness, idolatry, sorcery, hatreds, rivalry, jealousy, outbursts of fury, acts of selfishness, dissensions, factions, occasions of envy, drinking bouts, orgies, and the like. I warn you, as I warned you before, that those who do such things will not inherit the Kingdom of God. In contrast, the fruit of the Spirit is love, joy, peace, patience, kindness, generosity, faithfulness, gentleness, self–control. Against such there is no law. Now those who belong to Christ Jesus have crucified their flesh with its passions and desires. If we live in the Spirit, let us also follow the Spirit.

RESPONSORIAL PSALM   *Psalm 1:1–2, 3, 4 and 6*
R. (see Jn 8:12) Those who follow you, Lord, will have the light of life.

Blessed the man who follows not the counsel of the wicked **/** nor walks in the way of sinners, **/** nor sits in the company of the insolent, **/** But delights in the law of the LORD **/** and meditates on his law day and night. **R.**

He is like a tree planted near running water, / that yields its fruit in due season, / and whose leaves never fade. / Whatever he does, prospers. **R.**

Not so the wicked, not so; / they are like chaff which the wind drives away. / For the LORD watches over the way of the just, / but the way of the wicked vanishes. **R.**

ALLELUIA
John 10:27

R. Alleluia, alleluia. My sheep hear my voice, says the Lord; I know them, and they follow me. **R.**

GOSPEL
Luke 11:42–46

The Lord said: "Woe to you Pharisees! You pay tithes of mint and of rue and of every garden herb, but you pay no attention to judgment and to love for God. These you should have done, without overlooking the others. Woe to you Pharisees! You love the seat of honor in synagogues and greetings in marketplaces. Woe to you! You are like unseen graves over which people unknowingly walk."

Then one of the scholars of the law said to him in reply, "Teacher, by saying this you are insulting us too." And he said, "Woe also to you scholars of the law! You impose on people burdens hard to carry, but you yourselves do not lift one finger to touch them."

OCTOBER 15, THURSDAY OF WEEK 28; ST. TERESA OF AVILA

FIRST READING
Ephesians 1:1–10

Paul, an Apostle of Christ Jesus by the will of God, to the holy ones who are in Ephesus and faithful in Christ Jesus: grace to you and peace from God our Father and the Lord Jesus Christ.

Blessed be the God and Father of our Lord Jesus Christ, who has blessed us in Christ with every spiritual blessing in the heavens, as he chose us in him, before the foundation of the world, to be holy and without blemish before him. In love he destined us for adoption to himself through Jesus Christ, in accord with the favor of his will, for the praise of the glory of his grace that he granted us in the beloved.

In Christ we have redemption by his Blood, the forgiveness of transgressions, in accord with the riches of his grace that he lavished upon us. In all wisdom and insight, he has made known to us the mystery of his will in accord with his favor that he set forth in him as a plan for the fullness of times, to sum up all things in Christ, in heaven and on earth.

RESPONSORIAL PSALM
Psalm 98:1, 2–3ab, 3cd–4, 5–6

R. (2a) The Lord has made known his salvation.

Sing to the LORD a new song, / for he has done wondrous deeds; / His right hand has won victory for him, his holy arm. **R.**

The LORD has made his salvation known: / in the sight of the nations he has revealed his justice. / He has remembered his kindness / and his faithfulness toward the house of Israel. **R.**

All the ends of the earth have seen / the salvation by our God. / Sing joyfully to the LORD, all you lands; / break into song; sing praise. **R.**

Sing praise to the LORD with the harp, / with the harp and melodious song. / With trumpets and the sound of the horn / sing joyfully before the King, the LORD. **R.**

ALLELUIA *John 14:6*

R. Alleluia, alleluia. I am the way and the truth and the life, says the Lord; no one comes to the Father except through me. **R.**

GOSPEL *Luke 11:47–54*

The Lord said: "Woe to you who build the memorials of the prophets whom your fathers killed. Consequently, you bear witness and give consent to the deeds of your ancestors, for they killed them and you do the building. Therefore, the wisdom of God said, 'I will send to them prophets and Apostles; some of them they will kill and persecute' in order that this generation might be charged with the blood of all the prophets shed since the foundation of the world, from the blood of Abel to the blood of Zechariah who died between the altar and the temple building. Yes, I tell you, this generation will be charged with their blood! Woe to you, scholars of the law! You have taken away the key of knowledge. You yourselves did not enter and you stopped those trying to enter." When Jesus left, the scribes and Pharisees began to act with hostility toward him and to interrogate him about many things, for they were plotting to catch him at something he might say.

OCTOBER 16, FRIDAY OF WEEK 28; ST. MARGARET MARY ALACOQUE

FIRST READING *Ephesians 1:11–14*

Brothers and sisters: In Christ we were also chosen, destined in accord with the purpose of the One who accomplishes all things according to the intention of his will, so that we might exist for the praise of his glory, we who first hoped in Christ. In him you also, who have heard the word of truth, the Gospel of your salvation, and have believed in him, were sealed with the promised Holy Spirit, which is the first installment of our inheritance toward redemption as God's possession, to the praise of his glory.

RESPONSORIAL PSALM *Psalm 33:1–2, 4–5, 12–13*

R. (12) Blessed the people the Lord has chosen to be his own.

Exult, you just, in the LORD; / praise from the upright is fitting. / Give thanks to the LORD on the harp; / with the ten-stringed lyre chant his praises. **R.**

For upright is the word of the LORD, / and all his works are trustworthy. / He loves justice and right; / of the kindness of the LORD the earth is full. **R.**

Blessed the nation whose God is the LORD, / the people he has chosen for his own inheritance. / From heaven the LORD looks down; / he sees all mankind. **R.**

ALLELUIA *Psalm 33:22*

R. Alleluia, alleluia. May your kindness, O LORD, be upon us; who have put our hope in you. **R.**

GOSPEL
Luke 12:1–7

At that time: So many people were crowding together that they were trampling one another underfoot. Jesus began to speak, first to his disciples, "Beware of the leaven—that is, the hypocrisy—of the Pharisees.

"There is nothing concealed that will not be revealed, nor secret that will not be known. Therefore whatever you have said in the darkness will be heard in the light, and what you have whispered behind closed doors will be proclaimed on the housetops. I tell you, my friends, do not be afraid of those who kill the body but after that can do no more. I shall show you whom to fear. Be afraid of the one who after killing has the power to cast into Gehenna; yes, I tell you, be afraid of that one. Are not five sparrows sold for two small coins? Yet not one of them has escaped the notice of God. Even the hairs of your head have all been counted. Do not be afraid. You are worth more than many sparrows."

OCTOBER 17, SATURDAY OF WEEK 28; ST. IGNATIUS OF ANTIOCH
FIRST READING
Ephesians 1:15–23

Brothers and sisters: Hearing of your faith in the Lord Jesus and of your love for all the holy ones, I do not cease giving thanks for you, remembering you in my prayers, that the God of our Lord Jesus Christ, the Father of glory, may give you a spirit of wisdom and revelation resulting in knowledge of him. May the eyes of your hearts be enlightened, that you may know what is the hope that belongs to his call, what are the riches of glory in his inheritance among the holy ones, and what is the surpassing greatness of his power for us who believe, in accord with the exercise of his great might, which he worked in Christ, raising him from the dead and seating him at his right hand in the heavens, far above every principality, authority, power, and dominion, and every name that is named not only in this age but also in the one to come. And he put all things beneath his feet and gave him as head over all things to the Church, which is his Body, the fullness of the one who fills all things in every way.

RESPONSORIAL PSALM
Psalm 8:2–3ab, 4–5, 6–7

R. (7) You have given your Son rule over the works of your hands.

O LORD, our LORD, how glorious is your name / over all the earth! You have exalted your majesty above the heavens. / Out of the mouths of babes and sucklings / you have fashioned praise because of your foes. **R.**

When I behold your heavens, the work of your fingers, / the moon and the stars which you set in place— / What is man that you should be mindful of him, / or the son of man that you should care for him? **R.**

You have made him little less than the angels, / and crowned him with glory and honor. / You have given him rule over the works of your hands, / putting all things under his feet. **R.**

ALLELUIA
John 15:26b, 27a

R. Alleluia, alleluia. The Spirit of truth will testify to me, says the Lord, and you also will testify. **R.**

GOSPEL
Luke 12:8—12

Jesus said to his disciples: "I tell you, everyone who acknowledges me before others the Son of Man will acknowledge before the angels of God. But whoever denies me before others will be denied before the angels of God.

"Everyone who speaks a word against the Son of Man will be forgiven, but the one who blasphemes against the Holy Spirit will not be forgiven. When they take you before synagogues and before rulers and authorities, do not worry about how or what your defense will be or about what you are to say. For the Holy Spirit will teach you at that moment what you should say."

OCTOBER 18, 29TH SUNDAY IN ORDINARY TIME; SAINT LUKE
FIRST READING
Isaiah 45:1, 4—6

Thus says the LORD to his anointed, Cyrus, whose right hand I grasp, subduing nations before him, and making kings run in his service, opening doors before him and leaving the gates unbarred: For the sake of Jacob, my servant, of Israel, my chosen one, I have called you by your name, giving you a title, though you knew me not. I am the LORD and there is no other, there is no God besides me. It is I who arm you, though you know me not, so that toward the rising and the setting of the sun people may know that there is none besides me. I am the LORD, there is no other.

RESPONSORIAL PSALM
Psalm 96:1, 3, 4—5, 7—8, 9—10 (7b)

R. Give the Lord glory and honor.

Sing to the LORD a new song; / sing to the LORD, all you lands. / Tell his glory among the nations; / among all peoples, his wondrous deeds. **R.**

For great is the LORD and highly to be praised; / awesome is he, beyond all gods. / For all the gods of the nations are things of nought, / but the LORD made the heavens. **R.**

Give to the LORD, you families of nations, / give to the LORD glory and praise; / give to the LORD the glory due his name! / Bring gifts, and enter his courts. **R.**

Worship the LORD, in holy attire; / tremble before him, all the earth; / say among the nations: The LORD is king, / he governs the peoples with equity. **R.**

SECOND READING
1 Thessalonians 1:1—5b

Paul, Silvanus, and Timothy to the church of the Thessalonians in God the Father and the Lord Jesus Christ: grace to you and peace. We give thanks to God always for all of you, remembering you in our prayers, unceasingly calling to mind your work of faith and labor of love and endurance in hope of our Lord Jesus Christ, before our God and Father, knowing, brothers and sisters loved by God, how you were chosen. For our gospel did not come to you in word alone, but also in power and in the Holy Spirit and with much conviction.

ALLELUIA
Philippians 2:15d, 16a

R. Alleluia, alleluia. Shine like lights in the world as you hold on to the word of life. **R.**

GOSPEL

Matthew 22:15—21

The Pharisees went off and plotted how they might entrap Jesus in speech. They sent their disciples to him, with the Herodians, saying, "Teacher, we know that you are a truthful man and that you teach the way of God in accordance with the truth. And you are not concerned with anyone's opinion, for you do not regard a person's status. Tell us, then, what is your opinion: Is it lawful to pay the census tax to Caesar or not?" Knowing their malice, Jesus said, "Why are you testing me, you hypocrites? Show me the coin that pays the census tax." Then they handed him the Roman coin. He said to them, "Whose image is this and whose inscription?" They replied, "Caesar's." At that he said to them, "Then repay to Caesar what belongs to Caesar and to God what belongs to God."

OCTOBER 19, MONDAY OF WEEK 29 ST. ISAAC JOGUES; ST. JOHN DE BREBEUF, AND COMPANIONS

FIRST READING

Ephesians 2:1—10

Brothers and sisters: You were dead in your transgressions and sins in which you once lived following the age of this world, following the ruler of the power of the air, the spirit that is now at work in the disobedient. All of us once lived among them in the desires of our flesh, following the wishes of the flesh and the impulses, and we were by nature children of wrath, like the rest. But God, who is rich in mercy, because of the great love he had for us, even when we were dead in our transgressions, brought us to life with Christ (by grace you have been saved), raised us up with him, and seated us with him in the heavens in Christ Jesus, that in the ages to come he might show the immeasurable riches of his grace in his kindness to us in Christ Jesus. For by grace you have been saved through faith, and this is not from you; it is the gift of God; it is not from works, so no one may boast. For we are his handiwork, created in Christ Jesus for good works that God has prepared in advance, that we should live in them.

RESPONSORIAL PSALM

Psalm 100:1b—2, 3, 4ab, 4c—5

R. (3b) The Lord made us, we belong to him.

Sing joyfully to the LORD all you lands; / serve the LORD with gladness; / come before him with joyful song. **R.**

Know that the LORD is God; / he made us, his we are; his people, / the flock he tends. **R.**

Enter his gates with thanksgiving, / his courts with praise. **R.**

Give thanks to him; / bless his name, for he is good: / the LORD, whose kindness endures forever, / and his faithfulness, to all generations. **R.**

ALLELUIA

Matthew 5:3

R. Alleluia, alleluia. Blessed are the poor in spirit; for theirs is the Kingdom of heaven. **R.**

GOSPEL

Luke 12:13—21

Someone in the crowd said to Jesus, "Teacher, tell my brother to share the inheritance with me." He replied to him, "Friend, who appointed me as your judge and arbitrator?" Then he said to the crowd, "Take care to guard against all greed, for though one may be rich, one's life does not consist of possessions."

Then he told them a parable. "There was a rich man whose land produced a bountiful harvest. He asked himself, 'What shall I do, for I do not have space to store my harvest?' And he said, 'This is what I shall do: I shall tear down my barns and build larger ones. There I shall store all my grain and other goods and I shall say to myself, "Now as for you, you have so many good things stored up for many years, rest, eat, drink, be merry!"' But God said to him, 'You fool, this night your life will be demanded of you; and the things you have prepared, to whom will they belong?' Thus will it be for the one who stores up treasure for himself but is not rich in what matters to God."

OCTOBER 20, TUESDAY OF WEEK 29; BLESSED JOHN XXIII

FIRST READING   *Ephesians 2:12–22*

Brothers and sisters: You were at that time without Christ, alienated from the community of Israel and strangers to the covenants of promise, without hope and without God in the world. But now in Christ Jesus you who once were far off have become near by the Blood of Christ.

For he is our peace, he made both one and broke down the dividing wall of enmity, through his Flesh, abolishing the law with its commandments and legal claims, that he might create in himself one new person in place of the two, thus establishing peace, and might reconcile both with God, in one Body, through the cross, putting that enmity to death by it. He came and preached peace to you who were far off and peace to those who were near, for through him we both have access in one Spirit to the Father.

So then you are no longer strangers and sojourners, but you are fellow citizens with the holy ones and members of the household of God, built upon the foundation of the Apostles and prophets, with Christ Jesus himself as the capstone. Through him the whole structure is held together and grows into a temple sacred in the Lord; in him you also are being built together into a dwelling place of God in the Spirit.

RESPONSORIAL PSALM   *Psalm 85:9ab–10, 11–12, 13–14*

R. (see 9) The Lord speaks of peace to his people.

I will hear what God proclaims; / the LORD—for he proclaims peace. / Near indeed is his salvation to those who fear him, / glory dwelling in our land. **R.**

Kindness and truth shall meet; / justice and peace shall kiss. / Truth shall spring out of the earth, / and justice shall look down from heaven. **R.**

The LORD himself will give his benefits; / our land shall yield its increase. / Justice shall walk before him, / and salvation, along the way of his steps. **R.**

ALLELUIA   *Luke 21:36*

R. Alleluia, alleluia. Be vigilant at all times and pray that you may have the strength to stand before the Son of Man. **R.**

GOSPEL

GOSPEL *Luke 12:35–38*

Jesus said to his disciples: "Gird your loins and light your lamps and be like servants who await their master's return from a wedding, ready to open immediately when he comes and knocks. Blessed are those servants whom the master finds vigilant on his arrival. Amen, I say to you, he will gird himself, have them recline at table, and proceed to wait on them. And should he come in the second or third watch and find them prepared in this way, blessed are those servants."

OCTOBER 21, WEDNESDAY OF WEEK 29; ST. HILARION

FIRST READING *Ephesians 3:2–12*

Brothers and sisters: You have heard of the stewardship of God's grace that was given to me for your benefit, namely, that the mystery was made known to me by revelation, as I have written briefly earlier. When you read this you can understand my insight into the mystery of Christ, which was not made known to human beings in other generations as it has now been revealed to his holy Apostles and prophets by the Spirit, that the Gentiles are coheirs, members of the same Body, and copartners in the promise in Christ Jesus through the Gospel.

Of this I became a minister by the gift of God's grace that was granted me in accord with the exercise of his power. To me, the very least of all the holy ones, this grace was given, to preach to the Gentiles the inscrutable riches of Christ, and to bring to light for all what is the plan of the mystery hidden from ages past in God who created all things, so that the manifold wisdom of God might now be made known through the Church to the principalities and authorities in the heavens. This was according to the eternal purpose that he accomplished in Christ Jesus our Lord, in whom we have boldness of speech and confidence of access through faith in him.

RESPONSORIAL PSALM *Isaiah 12:2–3, 4bcd, 5–6*

R. (see 3) **You will draw water joyfully from the springs of salvation.**

God indeed is my savior; / I am confident and unafraid. / My strength and my courage is the LORD, / and he has been my savior. / With joy you will draw water / at the fountain of salvation. **R.**

Give thanks to the LORD, acclaim his name; / among the nations make known his deeds, / proclaim how exalted is his name. **R.**

Sing praise to the LORD for his glorious achievement; / let this be known throughout all the earth. / Shout with exultation, O city of Zion, / for great in your midst is the Holy One of Israel! **R.**

ALLELUIA *Matthew 24:42a, 44*

R. **Alleluia, alleluia.** Stay awake! For you do not know when the Son of Man will come. **R.**

GOSPEL

Luke 12:39–48

Jesus said to his disciples: "Be sure of this: if the master of the house had known the hour when the thief was coming, he would not have let his house be broken into. You also must be prepared, for at an hour you do not expect, the Son of Man will come."

Then Peter said, "Lord, is this parable meant for us or for everyone?" And the Lord replied, "Who, then, is the faithful and prudent steward whom the master will put in charge of his servants to distribute the food allowance at the proper time? Blessed is that servant whom his master on arrival finds doing so. Truly, I say to you, he will put him in charge of all his property. But if that servant says to himself, 'My master is delayed in coming,' and begins to beat the menservants and the maidservants, to eat and drink and get drunk, then that servant's master will come on an unexpected day and at an unknown hour and will punish the servant severely and assign him a place with the unfaithful. That servant who knew his master's will but did not make preparations nor act in accord with his will shall be beaten severely; and the servant who was ignorant of his master's will but acted in a way deserving of a severe beating shall be beaten only lightly. Much will be required of the person entrusted with much, and still more will be demanded of the person entrusted with more."

OCTOBER 22, THURSDAY OF WEEK 29; BLESSED TIMOTHY GIACCARDO

FIRST READING

Ephesians 3:14–21

Brothers and sisters: I kneel before the Father, from whom every family in heaven and on earth is named, that he may grant you in accord with the riches of his glory to be strengthened with power through his Spirit in the inner self, and that Christ may dwell in your hearts through faith; that you, rooted and grounded in love, may have strength to comprehend with all the holy ones what is the breadth and length and height and depth, and to know the love of Christ that surpasses knowledge, so that you may be filled with all the fullness of God.

Now to him who is able to accomplish far more than all we ask or imagine, by the power at work within us, to him be glory in the Church and in Christ Jesus to all generations, forever and ever. Amen.

RESPONSORIAL PSALM

Psalm 33:1–2, 4–5, 11–12, 18–19

R. (5b) The earth is full of the goodness of the Lord.

Exult, you just, in the LORD; / praise from the upright is fitting. / Give thanks to the LORD on the harp; / with the ten-stringed lyre chant his praises. **R.**

For upright is the word of the LORD, / and all his works are trustworthy. / He loves justice and right; / of the kindness of the LORD the earth is full. **R.**

But the plan of the LORD stands forever; / the design of his heart, through all generations. / Blessed the nation whose God is the LORD, / the people he has chosen for his own inheritance. **R.**

But see, the eyes of the LORD are upon those who fear him, / upon those who hope for his kindness, / to deliver them from death and preserve them in spite of famine. **R.**

ALLELUIA *Philippians 3:8–9*

R. Alleluia, alleluia. I consider all things so much rubbish that I may gain Christ and be found in him. **R.**

GOSPEL *Luke 12:49–53*

Jesus said to his disciples: "I have come to set the earth on fire, and how I wish it were already blazing! There is a baptism with which I must be baptized, and how great is my anguish until it is accomplished! Do you think that I have come to establish peace on the earth? No, I tell you, but rather division. From now on a household of five will be divided, three against two and two against three; a father will be divided against his son and a son against his father, a mother against her daughter and a daughter against her mother, a mother–in–law against her daughter–in–law and a daughter–in–law against her mother–in–law."

OCTOBER 23, FRIDAY OF WEEK 29; ST. JOHN OF CAPISTRANO

FIRST READING *Ephesians 4:1–6*

Brothers and sisters: I, a prisoner for the Lord, urge you to live in a manner worthy of the call you have received, with all humility and gentleness, with patience, bearing with one another through love, striving to preserve the unity of the spirit through the bond of peace; one Body and one Spirit, as you were also called to the one hope of your call; one Lord, one faith, one baptism; one God and Father of all, who is over all and through all and in all.

RESPONSORIAL PSALM *Psalm 24:1–2, 3–4ab, 5–6*

R. (see 6) Lord, this is the people that longs to see your face.

The LORD's are the earth and its fullness; / the world and those who dwell in it. / For he founded it upon the seas / and established it upon the rivers. **R.**

Who can ascend the mountain of the LORD? / or who may stand in his holy place? / He whose hands are sinless, whose heart is clean, / who desires not what is vain. **R.**

He shall receive a blessing from the LORD, / a reward from God his savior. / Such is the race that seeks for him, / that seeks the face of the God of Jacob. **R.**

ALLELUIA *See Matthew 11:25*

R. Alleluia, alleluia. Blessed are you, Father, Lord of heaven and earth; you have revealed to little ones the mysteries of the Kingdom. **R.**

GOSPEL *Luke 12:54–59*

Jesus said to the crowds, "When you see a cloud rising in the west you say immediately that it is going to rain—and so it does; and when you notice that the wind is blowing from the south you say that it is going to be hot—and so it is. You hypocrites! You know how to interpret the appearance of the earth and the sky; why do you not know how to interpret the present time?

"Why do you not judge for yourselves what is right? If you are to go with your opponent before a magistrate, make an effort to settle the matter on the way; otherwise your opponent will turn you over to the judge, and the judge hand you over to the constable, and the constable throw you into prison. I say to you, you will not be released until you have paid the last penny."

OCTOBER 24, SATURDAY OF WEEK 29; ST. ANTHONY MARY CLARET

FIRST READING *Ephesians 4:7–16*

Brothers and sisters: Grace was given to each of us according to the measure of Christ's gift. Therefore, it says:

He ascended on high and took prisoners captive; he gave gifts to men.

What does "he ascended" mean except that he also descended into the lower regions of the earth? The one who descended is also the one who ascended far above all the heavens, that he might fill all things.

And he gave some as Apostles, others as prophets, others as evangelists, others as pastors and teachers, to equip the holy ones for the work of ministry, for building up the Body of Christ, until we all attain to the unity of faith and knowledge of the Son of God, to mature manhood to the extent of the full stature of Christ, so that we may no longer be infants, tossed by waves and swept along by every wind of teaching arising from human trickery, from their cunning in the interests of deceitful scheming. Rather, living the truth in love, we should grow in every way into him who is the head, Christ, from whom the whole Body, joined and held together by every supporting ligament, with the proper functioning of each part, brings about the Body's growth and builds itself up in love.

RESPONSORIAL PSALM *Psalm 122:1–2, 3–4ab, 4cd–5*

R. (1) Let us go rejoicing to the house of the Lord.

I rejoiced because they said to me, **/** "We will go up to the house of the LORD." **/** And now we have set foot within your gates, O Jerusalem. **R.**

Jerusalem, built as a city with compact unity. **/** To it the tribes go up, **/** the tribes of the LORD. **R.**

According to the decree for Israel, **/** to give thanks to the name of the LORD. **/** In it are set up judgment seats, **/** seats for the house of David. **R.**

ALLELUIA *Ezekiel 33:11*

R. Alleluia, alleluia.

I take no pleasure in the death of the wicked man, says the Lord, but rather in his conversion that he may live. **R.**

GOSPEL *Luke 13:1–9*

Some people told Jesus about the Galileans whose blood Pilate had mingled with the blood of their sacrifices. He said to them in reply, "Do you think that because these Galileans suffered in this way they were greater sinners than all other Galileans? By no means! But I tell you, if you do not repent, you will all perish as they did! Or those eighteen people who were killed when the tower at Siloam fell on them— do you think they were more guilty than everyone else who lived in Jerusalem? By no means! But I tell you, if you do not repent, you will all perish as they did!"

And he told them this parable: "There once was a person who had a fig tree planted in his orchard, and when he came in search of fruit on it but found none, he said to the gardener, 'For three years now I have come in search of fruit on this fig tree but have found none. So cut it down. Why should it exhaust the soil?' He said to him in reply, 'Sir, leave it for this year also, and I shall cultivate the ground around it and fertilize it; it may bear fruit in the future. If not you can cut it down.'"

OCTOBER 25, 30TH SUNDAY IN ORDINARY TIME; ST. RICHARD GWYN

FIRST READING *Exodus 22:20—26*

Thus says the LORD: "You shall not molest or oppress an alien, for you were once aliens yourselves in the land of Egypt. You shall not wrong any widow or orphan. If ever you wrong them and they cry out to me, I will surely hear their cry. My wrath will flare up, and I will kill you with the sword; then your own wives will be widows, and your children orphans.

"If you lend money to one of your poor neighbors among my people, you shall not act like an extortioner toward him by demanding interest from him. If you take your neighbor's cloak as a pledge, you shall return it to him before sunset; for this cloak of his is the only covering he has for his body. What else has he to sleep in? If he cries out to me, I will hear him; for I am compassionate."

RESPONSORIAL PSALM *Psalm 18:2—3, 3—4, 47, 51 (2)*

R. I love you, Lord, my strength.
I love you, O LORD, my strength, / O LORD, my rock, my fortress, my deliverer. **R.**
My God, my rock of refuge, / my shield, the horn of my salvation, my stronghold! Praised be the LORD, I exclaim, / and I am safe from my enemies. **R.**
The LORD lives and blessed be my rock! / Extolled be God my savior. / You who gave great victories to your king / and showed kindness to your anointed. **R.**

SECOND READING *1 Thessalonians 1:5c—10*

Brothers and sisters: You know what sort of people we were among you for your sake. And you became imitators of us and of the Lord, receiving the word in great affliction, with joy from the Holy Spirit, so that you became a model for all the believers in Macedonia and in Achaia. For from you the word of the Lord has sounded forth not only in Macedonia and in Achaia, but in every place your faith in God has gone forth, so that we have no need to say anything. For they themselves openly declare about us what sort of reception we had among you, and how you turned to God from idols to serve the living and true God and to await his Son from heaven, whom he raised from the dead, Jesus, who delivers us from the coming wrath.

ALLELUIA *John 14:23*

R. Alleluia, alleluia. Whoever loves me will keep my word, says the Lord, and my Father will love him and we will come to him. **R.**

GOSPEL   *Matthew 22:34—40*

When the Pharisees heard that Jesus had silenced the Sadducees, they gathered together, and one of them, a scholar of the law, tested him by asking, "Teacher, which commandment in the law is the greatest?" He said to him, "You shall love the Lord, your God, with all your heart, with all your soul, and with all your mind. This is the greatest and the first commandment. The second is like it: You shall love your neighbor as yourself. The whole law and the prophets depend on these two commandments."

OCTOBER 26, MONDAY OF WEEK 30; THE ELEVEN MARTYRS OF ALMERIA, SPAIN
FIRST READING   *Ephesians 4:32—5:8*

Brothers and sisters: Be kind to one another, compassionate, forgiving one another as God has forgiven you in Christ.

Be imitators of God, as beloved children, and live in love, as Christ loved us and handed himself over for us as a sacrificial offering to God for a fragrant aroma. Immorality or any impurity or greed must not even be mentioned among you, as is fitting among holy ones, no obscenity or silly or suggestive talk, which is out of place, but instead, thanksgiving. Be sure of this, that no immoral or impure or greedy person, that is, an idolater, has any inheritance in the Kingdom of Christ and of God.

Let no one deceive you with empty arguments, for because of these things the wrath of God is coming upon the disobedient. So do not be associated with them. For you were once darkness, but now you are light in the Lord. Live as children of light.

RESPONSORIAL PSALM   *Psalm 1:1–2, 3, 4 and 6*
R. (see Eph. 5:1) Behave like God as his very dear children.

Blessed the man who follows not the counsel of the wicked / nor walks in the way of sinners, / nor sits in the company of the insolent, / but delights in the law of the LORD / and meditates on his law day and night. **R.**

He is like a tree planted near running water, / that yields its fruit in due season, / and whose leaves never fade. / Whatever he does, prospers. **R.**

Not so the wicked, not so; / they are like chaff which the wind drives away. / For the LORD watches over the way of the just, / but the way of the wicked vanishes. **R.**

ALLELUIA   *John 17:17b, 17a*
R. Alleluia, alleluia. Your word, O Lord, is truth; consecrate us in the truth. **R.**

GOSPEL   *Luke 13:10–17*

Jesus was teaching in a synagogue on the sabbath. And a woman was there who for eighteen years had been crippled by a spirit; she was bent over, completely incapable of standing erect. When Jesus saw her, he called to her and said, "Woman, you are set free of your infirmity." He laid his hands on her, and she at once stood up straight and glorified

God. But the leader of the synagogue, indignant that Jesus had cured on the sabbath, said to the crowd in reply, "There are six days when work should be done. Come on those days to be cured, not on the sabbath day." The Lord said to him in reply, "Hypocrites! Does not each one of you on the sabbath untie his ox or his ass from the manger and lead it out for watering? This daughter of Abraham, whom Satan has bound for eighteen years now, ought she not to have been set free on the sabbath day from this bondage?" When he said this, all his adversaries were humiliated; and the whole crowd rejoiced at all the splendid deeds done by him.

OCTOBER 27, TUESDAY OF WEEK 30; BLESSED CONTARDO FERRINI

FIRST READING *Ephesians 5:21–33*

Brothers and sisters: Be subordinate to one another out of reverence for Christ. Wives should be subordinate to their husbands as to the Lord. For the husband is head of his wife just as Christ is head of the Church, he himself the savior of the Body. As the Church is subordinate to Christ, so wives should be subordinate to their husbands in everything. Husbands, love your wives, even as Christ loved the Church and handed himself over for her to sanctify her, cleansing her by the bath of water with the word, that he might present to himself the Church in splendor, without spot or wrinkle or any such thing, that she might be holy and without blemish. So also husbands should love their wives as their own bodies. He who loves his wife loves himself. For no one hates his own flesh but rather nourishes and cherishes it, even as Christ does the Church, because we are members of his Body.

For this reason a man shall leave his father and his mother and be joined to his wife, and the two shall become one flesh.

This is a great mystery, but I speak in reference to Christ and the Church. In any case, each one of you should love his wife as himself, and the wife should respect her husband.

RESPONSORIAL PSALM *Psalm 128:1–2, 3, 4–5*

R. (1a) Blessed are those who fear the Lord.
Blessed are you who fear the LORD, / who walk in his ways! / For you shall eat the fruit of your handiwork; / blessed shall you be, and favored. **R.**
Your wife shall be like a fruitful vine / in the recesses of your home; / your children like olive plants around your table. **R.**
Behold, thus is the man blessed / who fears the LORD. The LORD bless you from Zion: / may you see the prosperity of Jerusalem / all the days of your life. **R.**

ALLELUIA *See Matthew 11:25*

R. Alleluia, alleluia. Blessed are you, Father, Lord of heaven and earth; you have revealed to little ones the mysteries of the Kingdom. **R.**

GOSPEL *Luke 13:18–21*

Jesus said, "What is the Kingdom of God like? To what can I compare it? It is like a mustard seed that a man took and planted in the garden. When it was fully grown, it became a large bush and *the birds of the sky dwelt in its branches.*"

Again he said, "To what shall I compare the Kingdom of God? It is like yeast that a woman took and mixed in with three measures of wheat flour until the whole batch of dough was leavened."

OCTOBER 28, SAINTS SIMON & JUDE, APOSTLES - FEAST

FIRST READING *Ephesians 2:19–22*

Brothers and sisters: You are no longer strangers and sojourners, but you are fellow citizens with the holy ones and members of the household of God, built upon the foundation of the Apostles and prophets, with Christ Jesus himself as the capstone. Through him the whole structure is held together and grows into a temple sacred in the Lord; in him you also are being built together into a dwelling place of God in the Spirit.

RESPONSORIAL PSALM *Psalm 19:2–3, 4–5*

R. Their message goes out through all the earth.

The heavens declare the glory of God, / and the firmament proclaims his handiwork. / Day pours out the word to day, / and night to night imparts knowledge. **R.**

Not a word nor a discourse whose voice is not heard; / Through all the earth their voice resounds, / and to the ends of the world, their message. **R.**

ALLELUIA *See Te Deum*

R. Alleluia, alleluia. We praise you, O God, we acclaim you as Lord; the glorious company of Apostles praise you. **R.**

GOSPEL *Luke 6:12-16*

Jesus went up to the mountain to pray, and he spent the night in prayer to God. When day came, he called his disciples to himself, and from them he chose Twelve, whom he also named Apostles: Simon, whom he named Peter, and his brother Andrew, James, John, Philip, Bartholomew, Matthew, Thomas, James the son of Alphaeus, Simon who was called a Zealot, and Judas the son of James, and Judas Iscariot, who became a traitor.

OCTOBER 29, THURSDAY OF WEEK 30; ST. NARCISSUS

FIRST READING *Ephesians 6:10-20*

Brothers and sisters: Draw your strength from the Lord and from his mighty power. Put on the armor of God so that you may be able to stand firm against the tactics of the Devil. For our struggle is not with flesh and blood but with the principalities, with the powers, with the world rulers of this present darkness, with the evil spirits in the heavens. Therefore, put on the armor of God, that you may be able to resist on the evil day and, having done everything, to hold your ground. So stand fast with your loins girded in truth, clothed with righteousness as a breastplate, and your feet shod in readiness for the Gospel of peace. In all circumstances, hold faith as a shield, to quench all the flaming arrows of the Evil One. And take the helmet of salvation and the sword of the Spirit, which is the word of God.

With all prayer and supplication, pray at every opportunity in the Spirit. To that end, be watchful with all perseverance and supplication for all the holy ones and also for me, that speech may be given me to open my mouth, to make known with boldness the mystery of the Gospel for which I am an ambassador in chains, so that I may have the courage to speak as I must.

RESPONSORIAL PSALM   *Psalm 144:1b, 2, 9–10*
R. (1b) Blessed be the Lord, my Rock!
Blessed be the LORD, my rock, / who trains my hands for battle, / my fingers for war. **R.**
My mercy and my fortress, / my stronghold, my deliverer, / My shield, in whom I trust, / who subdues my people under me. **R.**
O God, I will sing a new song to you; / with a ten-stringed lyre I will chant your praise, / You who give victory to kings, / and deliver David, your servant from the evil sword. **R.**
ALLELUIA   *See Luke 19:38; 2:14*
R. Alleluia, alleluia. Blessed is the king who comes in the name of the Lord. Glory to God in the highest and on earth peace to those on whom his favor rests. **R.**

GOSPEL   *Luke 13:31–35*
Some Pharisees came to Jesus and said, "Go away, leave this area because Herod wants to kill you." He replied, "Go and tell that fox, 'Behold, I cast out demons and I perform healings today and tomorrow, and on the third day I accomplish my purpose. Yet I must continue on my way today, tomorrow, and the following day, for it is impossible that a prophet should die outside of Jerusalem.'

"Jerusalem, Jerusalem, you who kill the prophets and stone those sent to you, how many times I yearned to gather your children together as a hen gathers her brood under her wings, but you were unwilling! Behold, your house will be abandoned. But I tell you, you will not see me until the time comes when you say, *Blessed is he who comes in the name of the Lord.*"

OCTOBER 30, FRIDAY OF WEEK 30; BLESSED ANGELO OF ACRI
FIRST READING   *Philippians 1:1–11*
Paul and Timothy, slaves of Christ Jesus, to all the holy ones in Christ Jesus who are in Philippi, with the bishops and deacons: grace to you and peace from God our Father and the Lord Jesus Christ.

I give thanks to my God at every remembrance of you, praying always with joy in my every prayer for all of you, because of your partnership for the Gospel from the first day until now. I am confident of this, that the one who began a good work in you will continue to complete it until the day of Christ Jesus. It is right that I should think this way about all of you, because I hold you in my heart, you who are all partners with me in grace, both in my imprisonment and in the defense and confirmation of the Gospel. For God is my witness, how I long for all of you with the affection of Christ Jesus. And this is my prayer: that your love may increase ever more and more in knowledge and every kind of perception, to discern what is of value, so that you may be pure and blameless for the day of Christ, filled with the fruit of righteousness that comes through Jesus Christ for the glory and praise of God.

RESPONSORIAL PSALM *Psalm 111:1–2, 3–4, 5–6*

R. (2) How great are the works of the Lord! or: R. Alleluia.

I will give thanks to the LORD with all my heart / in the company and assembly of the just. / Great are the works of the LORD, / exquisite in all their delights. **R.**

Majesty and glory are his work, / and his justice endures forever. / He has won renown for his wondrous deeds; / gracious and merciful is the LORD. **R.**

He has given food to those who fear him; / he will forever be mindful of his covenant. / He has made known to his people the power of his works, / giving them the inheritance of the nations. **R.**

ALLELUIA *John 10:27*

R. Alleluia, alleluia. My sheep hear my voice, says the Lord; I know them, and they follow me. **R.**

GOSPEL *Luke 14:1–6*

On a sabbath Jesus went to dine at the home of one of the leading Pharisees, and the people there were observing him carefully. In front of him there was a man suffering from dropsy. Jesus spoke to the scholars of the law and Pharisees in reply, asking, "Is it lawful to cure on the sabbath or not?" But they kept silent; so he took the man and, after he had healed him, dismissed him. Then he said to them "Who among you, if your son or ox falls into a cistern, would not immediately pull him out on the sabbath day?" But they were unable to answer his question.

OCTOBER 31, SATURDAY OF WEEK 30; ST. ALPHONSUS RODRIGUEZ

FIRST READING *Philippians 1:18b–26*

Brothers and sisters: as long as in every way, whether in pretense or in truth, Christ is being proclaimed, and in that I rejoice.

Indeed I shall continue to rejoice, for I know that this will result in deliverance for me through your prayers and support from the Spirit of Jesus Christ. My eager expectation and hope is that I shall not be put to shame in any way, but that with all boldness, now as always, Christ will be magnified in my body, whether by life or by death. For to me life is Christ, and death is gain. If I go on living in the flesh, that means fruitful labor for me. And I do not know which I shall choose. I am caught between the two. I long to depart this life and be with Christ, for that is far better. Yet that I remain in the flesh is more necessary for your benefit. And this I know with confidence, that I shall remain and continue in the service of all of you for your progress and joy in the faith, so that your boasting in Christ Jesus may abound on account of me when I come to you again.

RESPONSORIAL PSALM *Psalm 42:2, 3, 5cdef*

R. My soul is thirsting for the living God.

As the hind longs for the running waters, / so my soul longs for you, O God. **R.**

Athirst is my soul for God, / the living God. When shall I go and behold / the face of God? **R.**

I went with the throng and led them in procession **/** to the house of God. **/** Amid loud cries of joy and thanksgiving, **/** with the multitude keeping festival. **R.**

ALLELUIA *Matthew 11:29ab*

R. Alleluia, alleluia. Take my yoke upon you and learn from me, for I am meek and humble of heart. **R.**

GOSPEL *Luke 14:1, 7–11*

On a Sabbath Jesus went to dine at the home of one of the leading Pharisees, and the people there were observing him carefully.

He told a parable to those who had been invited, noticing how they were choosing the places of honor at the table. "When you are invited by someone to a wedding banquet, do not recline at table in the place of honor. A more distinguished guest than you may have been invited by him, and the host who invited both of you may approach you and say, 'Give your place to this man,' and then you would proceed with embarrassment to take the lowest place. Rather, when you are invited, go and take the lowest place so that when the host comes to you he may say, 'My friend, move up to a higher position.' Then you will enjoy the esteem of your companions at the table. For everyone who exalts himself will be humbled, but the one who humbles himself will be exalted."

13 NOVEMBER

NOVEMBER 1, ALL SAINTS - SOLEMNITY

FIRST READING *Revelation 7:2—4, 9—14*

I, John, saw another angel come up from the East, holding the seal of the living God. He cried out in a loud voice to the four angels who were given power to damage the land and the sea, "Do not damage the land or the sea or the trees until we put the seal on the foreheads of the servants of our God." I heard the number of those who had been marked with the seal, one hundred and forty–four thousand marked from every tribe of the children if Israel.

After this I had a vision of a great multitude, which no one could count, from every nation, race, people, and tongue. They stood before the throne and before the Lamb, wearing white robes and holding palm branches in their hands. They cried out in a loud voice:

"Salvation comes from our God, who is seated on the throne, and from the Lamb."

All the angels stood around the throne and around the elders and the four living creatures. They prostrated themselves before the throne, worshiped God, and exclaimed:

"Amen. Blessing and glory, wisdom and thanksgiving, honor, power, and might be to our God forever and ever. Amen."

Then one of the elders spoke up and said to me, "Who are these wearing white robes, and where did they come from?" I said to him, "My lord, you are the one who knows." He said to me, "These are the ones who have survived the time of great distress; they have washed their robes and made them white in the blood of the Lamb."

RESPONSORIAL PSALM *Psalm 24:1bc—2, 3—4ab, 5—6 (see 6)*
R. Lord, this is the people that longs to see your face.
The LORD's are the earth and its fullness; / the world and those who dwell in it. / For he founded it upon the seas / and established it upon the rivers. **R.**
Who can ascend the mountain of the LORD? or who may stand in his holy place? / One whose hands are sinless, / whose heart is clean, / who desires not what is vain. **R.**
He shall receive a blessing from the LORD, / a reward from God his savior. / Such is the race that seeks for him, / that seeks the face of the God of Jacob. **R.**

SECOND READING *1 John 3:1—3*
Beloved: See what love the Father has bestowed on us that we may be called the children of God. Yet so we are. The reason the world does not know us is that it did not know him. Beloved, we are God's children now; what we shall be has not yet been revealed. We do know that when it is revealed we shall be like him, for we shall see him as he is. Everyone who has this hope based on him makes himself pure, as he is pure.

ALLELUIA *John 10:27*
R. Alleluia, alleluia. Come to me, all you who labor and are burdened, and I will give you rest, says the Lord. **R.**

GOSPEL *Matthew 5:1—12a*
When Jesus saw the crowds, he went up the mountain, and after he had sat down, his disciples came to him. He began to teach them, saying:

"Blessed are the poor in spirit, for theirs is the Kingdom of heaven. Blessed are they who mourn, for they will be comforted. Blessed are the meek, for they will inherit the land. Blessed are they who hunger and thirst for righteousness, for they will be satisfied. Blessed are the merciful, for they will be shown mercy. Blessed are the clean of heart, for they will see God. Blessed are the peacemakers, for they will be called children of God. Blessed are they who are persecuted for the sake of righteousness, for theirs is the Kingdom of heaven. Blessed are you when they insult you and persecute you and utter every kind of evil against you falsely because of me. Rejoice and be glad, for your reward will be great in heaven."

NOVEMBER 2, ALL SOULS - SOLEMNITY

FIRST READING *Wisdom 3:1—9*
The souls of the just are in the hand of God, and no torment shall touch them. They seemed, in the view of the foolish, to be dead; and their passing away was thought an affliction and their going forth from us, utter destruction. But they are in peace. For if before men, indeed, they be punished, yet is their hope full of immortality; chastised a

little, they shall be greatly blessed, because God tried them and found them worthy of himself. As gold in the furnace, he proved them, and as sacrificial offerings he took them to himself. In the time of their visitation they shall shine, and shall dart about as sparks through stubble; they shall judge nations and rule over peoples, and the LORD shall be their King forever. Those who trust in him shall understand truth, and the faithful shall abide with him in love: because grace and mercy are with his holy ones, and his care is with his elect.

ALTERNATIVE READING   *Isaiah 25:6—9*

On this mountain the LORD of hosts will provide for all peoples. On this mountain he will destroy the veil that veils all peoples, the web that is woven over all nations; he will destroy death forever. The Lord GOD will wipe away the tears from all faces; the reproach of his people he will remove from the whole earth; for the LORD has spoken. On that day it will be said: "Behold our God, to whom we looked to save us! This is the LORD for whom we looked; Let us rejoice and be glad that he has saved us!"

RESPONSORIAL PSALM   *Psalm 23:1—3a, 3b—4, 5, 6 (1) (4ab)*

R. The Lord is my shepherd; there is nothing I shall want.

OR   R. Though I walk in the valley of darkness, I fear no evil, for you are with me.

The LORD is my shepherd; I shall not want. / In verdant pastures he gives me repose; / beside restful waters he leads me; / he refreshes my soul. **R.**

He guides me in right paths / for his name's sake. / Even though I walk in the dark valley / I fear no evil; for you are at my side/with your rod and your staff / that give me courage. **R.**

You spread the table before me / in the sight of my foes; / You anoint my head with oil; / my cup overflows. **R.**

Only goodness and kindness follow me / all the days of my life; / and I shall dwell in the house of the LORD / for years to come. **R.**

ALTERNATIVE PSALM   *Psalm 25:6, 7b, 17—18, 20—21*

R. To you, O Lord, I lift us my soul.

OR   R. No one who waits for you, O Lord, will ever be put to shame.

Remember that your compassion, O LORD; / and your love are from of old. / In your kindness remember me, / because of your goodness, O LORD. **R.**

Relieve the troubles of my heart, / and bring me out of my distress. / Put an end to my affliction and my suffering; / and take away all my sins. **R.**

Preserve my life and rescue me; / let me not be put to shame, for I take refuge in you, Let integrity and uprightness preserve me, / because I wait for you, O LORD. **R.**

SECOND READING   *Romans 5:5—11*

Brothers and sisters: Hope does not disappoint, because the love of God has been poured out into our hearts through the Holy Spirit that has been given to us. For Christ, while we were still helpless, died at the appointed time for the ungodly. Indeed, only with difficulty does one die for a just person, though perhaps for a good person one might even find courage to die. But God proves his love for us in that while we were still sinners Christ died for us. How much more then, since we are now justified by his blood, will we be saved through him from the wrath. Indeed, if, while we were enemies, we were reconciled to God through the death of his Son, how much more, once reconciled, will we be saved by his life. Not only that, but we also boast of God through our Lord Jesus Christ, through whom we have now received reconciliation.

ALTERNATIVE READING   *Romans 5:17—21*

Brothers and sisters: If, by the transgression of the one, death came to reign through that one, how much more will those who receive the abundance of grace and of the gift of justification come to reign in life through the one Jesus Christ. In conclusion, just as through one transgression condemnation came upon all, so, through one righteous act, acquittal and life came to all. For just as through the disobedience of the one man the many were made sinners, so through the obedience of the one the many will be made righteous. The law entered in so that transgression might increase but, where sin increased, grace overflowed all the more, so that, as sin reigned in death, grace also might reign through justification for eternal life through Jesus Christ our Lord.

ALTERNATIVE READING   *Romans 8:14—23*

Brothers and sisters: Those who are led by the Spirit of God are sons of God. For you did not receive a spirit of slavery to fall back into fear, but you received a Spirit of adoption, through whom we cry, "Abba, Father!" The Spirit himself bears witness with our spirit that we are children of God, and if children, then heirs, heirs of God and joint heirs with Christ, if only we suffer with him so that we may also be glorified with him. I consider that the sufferings of this present time are as nothing compared with the glory to be revealed for us. For creation awaits with eager expectation the revelation of the children of God; for creation was made subject to futility, not of its own accord but because of the one who subjected it, in hope that creation itself would be set free from slavery to corruption and share in the glorious freedom of the children of God. We know that all creation is groaning in labor pains even until now; and not only that, but we ourselves, who have the firstfruits of the Spirit, we also groan within ourselves as we wait for adoption, the redemption of our bodies.

ALTERNATIVE READING   *Romans 8:31b—35, 37—39*

Brothers and sisters: If God is for us, who can be against us? He did not spare his own Son but handed him over for us all, will he not also give us everything else along with him? Who will bring a charge against God's chosen ones? It is God who acquits us. Who will condemn? It is Christ Jesus who died, rather, was raised, who also is at the right hand of God, who indeed intercedes for us. What will separate us from the love of Christ? Will anguish, or distress or persecution, or famine, or nakedness, or peril, or the sword?

No, in all these things, we conquer overwhelmingly through him who loved us. For I am convinced that neither death, nor life, nor angels, nor principalities, nor present things, nor future things, nor powers, nor height, nor depth, nor any other creature will be able to separate us from the love of God in Christ Jesus our Lord.

ALTERNATIVE READING   *1 Corinthians 15:51—57*

Brothers and sisters: Behold, I tell you a mystery. We shall not all fall asleep, but we will all be changed, in an instant, in the blink of an eye, at the last trumpet. For the trumpet will sound, the dead will be raised incorruptible, and we shall be changed. For that which is corruptible must clothe itself with incorruptibility, and that which is mortal must clothe itself with immortality. And when this which is corruptible clothes itself with incorruptibility and this which is mortal clothes itself with immortality, then the word that is written shall come about:

Death is swallowed up in victory. Where, O death, is your victory? Where, O death, is your sting?

The sting of death is sin, and the power of sin is the law. But thanks be to God who gives us the victory through our Lord Jesus Christ.

ALTERNATIVE READING   *2 Corinthians 4:14—5:1*

Brothers and sisters: We know that the One who raised the Lord Jesus will raise us also with Jesus and place us with you in his presence. Everything indeed is for you, so that the grace bestowed in abundance on more and more people may cause the thanksgiving to overflow for the glory of God. Therefore, we are not discouraged; rather, although our outer self is wasting away, our inner self is being renewed day by day. For this momentary light affliction is producing for us an eternal weight of glory beyond all comparison, as we look not to what is seen but to what is unseen; for what is seen is transitory, but what is unseen is eternal. For we know that if our earthly dwelling, a tent, should be destroyed, we have a building from God, a dwelling not made with hands, eternal in heaven.

ALTERNATIVE READING   *2 Corinthians 5:1, 6—10*

Brothers and sisters: We know that if our earthly dwelling, a tent, should be destroyed, we have a building from God, a dwelling not made with hands, eternal in heaven.

We are always courageous, although we know that while we are at home in the body we are away from the Lord, for we walk by faith, not by sight. Yet we are courageous, and we would rather leave the body and go home to the Lord. Therefore, we aspire to please him, whether we are at home or away. For we must all appear before the judgment seat of Christ, so that each may receive recompense, according to what was done in the body, whether good or evil.

ALTERNATIVE READING   *Philippians 3:20—21*

Brothers and sisters: Our citizenship is in heaven, and from it we also await a savior, the Lord Jesus Christ. He will change our lowly body to conform with his glorified body by the power that enables him also to bring all things into subjection to himself.

ALTERNATIVE READING   *1 Thessalonians 4:13—18*

We do not want you to be unaware, brothers and sisters, about those who have fallen asleep, so that you may not grieve like the rest, who have no hope. For if we believe that Jesus died and rose, so too will God, through Jesus, bring with him those who have fallen asleep. Indeed, we tell you this, on the word of the Lord, that we who are alive, who are left until the coming of the Lord, will surely not precede those who have fallen asleep. For the Lord himself, with a word of command, with the voice of an archangel and with the trumpet of God, will come down from heaven, and the dead in Christ will rise first. Then we who are alive, who are left, will be caught up together with them in the clouds to meet the Lord in the air. Thus we shall always be with the Lord. Therefore, console one another with these words.

ALTERNATIVE READING   *1 Thessalonians 4:13—18*

Beloved: Remember Jesus Christ, raised from the dead, a descendant of David: such is my gospel, for which I am suffering, even to the point of chains, like a criminal. But the word of God is not chained. Therefore, I bear with everything for the sake of those who are chosen, so that they too may obtain the salvation that is in Christ Jesus, together with eternal glory. This saying is trustworthy: If we have died with him we shall also live with him; if we persevere we shall also reign with him. But if we deny him he will deny us. If we are unfaithful he remains faithful, for he cannot deny himself.

ALLELUIA   *Matthew 25:34* **OR:**   cf. *John 6:40*

R. Alleluia, alleluia. Come, you who are blessed by my Father; inherit the kingdom prepared for you from the foundation of the world.   **OR:**   This is the will of my Father, says the Lord, that everyone who sees the Son and believes in him may have eternal life.   **R.**

GOSPEL   *Matthew 5:1—12a*

When Jesus saw the crowds, he went up the mountain, and after he had sat down, his disciples came to him. He began to teach them, saying:

"Blessed are the poor in spirit, for theirs is the Kingdom of heaven. Blessed are they who mourn, for they will be comforted. Blessed are the meek, for they will inherit the land. Blessed are they who hunger and thirst for righteousness, for they will be satisfied. Blessed are the merciful, for they will be shown mercy. Blessed are the clean of heart, for they will see God. Blessed are the peacemakers, for they will be called children of God. Blessed are they who are persecuted for the sake of righteousness, for theirs is the Kingdom of heaven. Blessed are you when they insult you and persecute you and utter every kind of evil against you falsely because of me. Rejoice and be glad, for your reward will be great in heaven."

ALTERNATIVE GOSPEL READING   *Matthew 11:25—30*

At that time Jesus exclaimed: "I give praise to you, Father, Lord of heaven and earth, for although you have hidden these things from the wise and the learned you have revealed them to little ones. Yes, Father, such has been your gracious will. All things have been handed over to me by my Father. No one knows the Son except the Father, and no one knows the Father except the Son and anyone to whom the Son wishes to reveal him.

"Come to me, all you who labor and are burdened, and I will give you rest. Take my yoke upon you and learn from me, for I am meek and humble of heart; and you will find rest for yourselves.

For my yoke is easy, and my burden light."

NOVEMBER 3, TUESDAY OF WEEK 31; ST. MARTIN DE PORRES

FIRST READING   *Philippians 2:5–11*

Brothers and sisters: Have among yourselves the same attitude that is also yours in Christ Jesus, Who, though he was in the form of God, did not regard equality with God something to be grasped. Rather, he emptied himself, taking the form of a slave, coming in human likeness; and, found human in appearance, he humbled himself, becoming obedient to death, even death on a cross. Because of this, God greatly exalted him and bestowed on him the name that is above every name, that at the name of Jesus every knee should bend, of those in heaven and on earth and under the earth, and every tongue confess that Jesus Christ is Lord, to the glory of God the Father.

RESPONSORIAL PSALM   *Psalm 22:26b–27, 28–30ab, 30e, 31–32*

R. (26a) I will praise you, Lord, in the assembly of your people.

I will fulfill my vows before those who fear him. / The lowly shall eat their fill; / they who seek the LORD shall praise him: / "May your hearts be ever merry!" **R.**

All the ends of the earth shall remember and turn to the LORD; / All the families of the nations shall bow down before him. **R.**

For dominion is the LORD's, and he rules the nations. / To him alone shall bow down all who sleep in the earth. **R.**

To him my soul shall live; / my descendants shall serve him. / Let the coming generation be told of the LORD / that they may proclaim to a people yet to be born / the justice he has shown. **R.**

ALLELUIA   *Matthew 11:28*

R. Alleluia, alleluia. Come to me, all you who labor and are burdened, and I will give you rest, says the Lord. **R.**

GOSPEL   *Luke 14:15–24*

One of those at table with Jesus said to him, "Blessed is the one who will dine in the Kingdom of God." He replied to him, "A man gave a great dinner to which he invited many. When the time for the dinner came, he dispatched his servant to say to those invited, 'Come, everything is now ready.' But one by one, they all began to excuse themselves. The first said to him, 'I have purchased a field and must go to examine it; I ask you, consider me excused.' And another said, 'I have purchased five yoke of oxen and am on my way to evaluate them; I ask you, consider me excused.' And another said, 'I have just married a woman, and therefore I cannot come.' The servant went and reported this to his master. Then the master of the house in a rage commanded his servant, 'Go out quickly into the streets and alleys of the town and bring in here the poor and the crippled, the blind and the lame.' The servant reported, 'Sir, your orders have been carried out and still there is room.' The master then ordered the servant, 'Go out to the highways and hedgerows and make people come in that my home may be filled. For, I tell you, none of those men who were invited will taste my dinner.'"

NOVEMBER 4, WEDNESDAY OF WEEK 31; ST. CHARLES BORROMEO

FIRST READING   *Philippians 2:12–18*

My beloved, obedient as you have always been, not only when I am present but all the more now when I am absent, work out your salvation with fear and trembling. For God is the one who, for his good purpose, works in you both to desire and to work. Do everything without grumbling or questioning, that you may be blameless and innocent, children of God without blemish in the midst of a crooked and perverse generation, among whom you shine like lights in the world, as you hold on to the word of life, so that my boast for the day of Christ may be that I did not run in vain or labor in vain. But, even if I am poured out as a libation upon the sacrificial service of your faith, I rejoice and share my joy with all of you. In the same way you also should rejoice and share your joy with me.

RESPONSORIAL PSALM   *Psalm 27:1, 4, 13–14*

R. (1a) The Lord is my light and my salvation.
The LORD is my light and my salvation; / whom should I fear? / The LORD is my life's refuge; / of whom should I be afraid? **R.**
One thing I ask of the LORD; this I seek: / to dwell in the house of the LORD / all the days of my life, / That I may gaze on the loveliness of the LORD / and contemplate his temple. **R.**
I believe that I shall see the bounty of the LORD / in the land of the living. / Wait for the LORD with courage; / be stouthearted, and wait for the LORD. **R.**

ALLELUIA   *1 Peter 4:14*

R. Alleluia, alleluia. If you are insulted for the name of Christ, blessed are you, for the Spirit of God rests upon you. **R.**

GOSPEL   *Luke 14:25–33*

Great crowds were traveling with Jesus, and he turned and addressed them, "If anyone comes to me without hating his father and mother, wife and children, brothers and sisters, and even his own life, he cannot be my disciple. Whoever does not carry his own cross and come after me cannot be my disciple. Which of you wishing to construct a tower does not first sit down and calculate the cost to see if there is enough for its completion? Otherwise, after laying the foundation and finding himself unable to finish the work the onlookers should laugh at him and say, 'This one began to build but did not have the resources to finish.' Or what king marching into battle would not first sit down and decide whether with ten thousand troops he can successfully oppose another king advancing upon him with twenty thousand troops? But if not, while he is still far away, he will send a delegation to ask for peace terms. In the same way, everyone of you who does not renounce all his possessions cannot be my disciple."

NOVEMBER 5, THURSDAY OF WEEK 31; ST. BERTILLA

FIRST READING *Philippians 3:3–8a*

Brothers and sisters: We are the circumcision, we who worship through the Spirit of God, who boast in Christ Jesus and do not put our confidence in flesh, although I myself have grounds for confidence even in the flesh.

If anyone else thinks he can be confident in flesh, all the more can I. Circumcised on the eighth day, of the race of Israel, of the tribe of Benjamin, a Hebrew of Hebrew parentage, in observance of the law a Pharisee, in zeal I persecuted the Church, in righteousness based on the law I was blameless.

But whatever gains I had, these I have come to consider a loss because of Christ. More than that, I even consider everything as a loss because of the supreme good of knowing Christ Jesus my Lord.

RESPONSORIAL PSALM *Psalm 105:2–3, 4–5, 6–7*

R. Let hearts rejoice who search for the Lord. or: R. Alleluia.

Sing to him, sing his praise, / proclaim all his wondrous deeds. / Glory in his holy name; / rejoice, O hearts that seek the LORD! **R.**

Look to the LORD in his strength; / seek to serve him constantly. / Recall the wondrous deeds that he has wrought, / his portents, and the judgments he has uttered. **R.**

You descendants of Abraham, his servants, / sons of Jacob, his chosen ones! / He, the LORD, is our God; / throughout the earth his judgments prevail. **R.**

ALLELUIA *Matthew 11:28*

R. Alleluia, alleluia. Come to me, all you who labor and are burdened, and I will give you rest, says the Lord. **R.**

GOSPEL *Luke 15:1–10*

The tax collectors and sinners were all drawing near to listen to Jesus, but the Pharisees and scribes began to complain, saying, "This man welcomes sinners and eats with them." So Jesus addressed this parable to them. "What man among you having a hundred sheep and losing one of them would not leave the ninety–nine in the desert and go after the lost one until he finds it? And when he does find it, he sets it on his shoulders with great joy and, upon his arrival home, he calls together his friends and neighbors and says to them, 'Rejoice with me because I have found my lost sheep.' I tell you, in just the same way there will be more joy in heaven over one sinner who repents than over ninety–nine righteous people who have no need of repentance.

"Or what woman having ten coins and losing one would not light a lamp and sweep the house, searching carefully until she finds it? And when she does find it, she calls together her friends and neighbors and says to them, 'Rejoice with me because I have found the coin that I lost.' In just the same way, I tell you, there will be rejoicing among the angels of God over one sinner who repents."

NOVEMBER 6, FRIDAY OF WEEK 31; ST. THEOPHANE VENARD

FIRST READING   *Philippians 3:17—4:1*

Join with others in being imitators of me, brothers and sisters, and observe those who thus conduct themselves according to the model you have in us. For many, as I have often told you and now tell you even in tears, conduct themselves as enemies of the cross of Christ. Their end is destruction. Their God is their stomach; their glory is in their "shame." Their minds are occupied with earthly things. But our citizenship is in heaven, and from it we also await a savior, the Lord Jesus Christ. He will change our lowly body to conform with his glorified Body by the power that enables him also to bring all things into subjection to himself.

Therefore, my brothers and sisters, whom I love and long for, my joy and crown, in this way stand firm in the Lord, beloved.

RESPONSORIAL PSALM   *Psalm 122:1–2, 3–4ab, 4cd–5*

R. (1) Let us go rejoicing to the house of the Lord.

I rejoiced because they said to me, / "We will go up to the house of the LORD." / And now we have set foot within your gates, O Jerusalem. **R.**

Jerusalem, built as a city with compact unity. / To it the tribes go up, / the tribes of the LORD. **R.**

According to the decree for Israel, / to give thanks to the name of the LORD. / In it are set up judgment seats, / seats for the house of David. **R.**

ALLELUIA   *1 John 2:5*

R. Alleluia, alleluia. Whoever keeps the word of Christ, the love of God is truly perfected in him. **R.**

GOSPEL   *Luke 16:1–8*

Jesus said to his disciples, "A rich man had a steward who was reported to him for squandering his property. He summoned him and said, 'What is this I hear about you? Prepare a full account of your stewardship, because you can no longer be my steward.' The steward said to himself, 'What shall I do, now that my master is taking the position of steward away from me? I am not strong enough to dig and I am ashamed to beg. I know what I shall do so that, when I am removed from the stewardship, they may welcome me into their homes.' He called in his master's debtors one by one. To the first he said, 'How much do you owe my master?' He replied, 'One hundred measures of olive oil.' He said to him, 'Here is your promissory note. Sit down and quickly write one for fifty.' Then to another he said, 'And you, how much do you owe?' He replied, 'One hundred measures of wheat.' He said to him, 'Here is your promissory note; write one for eighty.' And the master commended that dishonest steward for acting prudently. For the children of this world are more prudent in dealing with their own generation than the children of light."

NOVEMBER 7, SATURDAY OF WEEK 31; BLESSED GIUSEPPE ANTONIO TOVINI

FIRST READING *Philippians 4:10–19*

Brothers and sisters: I rejoice greatly in the Lord that now at last you revived your concern for me. You were, of course, concerned about me but lacked an opportunity. Not that I say this because of need, for I have learned, in whatever situation I find myself, to be self–sufficient. I know indeed how to live in humble circumstances; I know also how to live with abundance. In every circumstance and in all things I have learned the secret of being well fed and of going hungry, of living in abundance and of being in need. I have the strength for everything through him who empowers me. Still, it was kind of you to share in my distress.

You Philippians indeed know that at the beginning of the Gospel, when I left Macedonia, not a single church shared with me in an account of giving and receiving, except you alone. For even when I was at Thessalonica you sent me something for my needs, not only once but more than once. It is not that I am eager for the gift; rather, I am eager for the profit that accrues to your account. I have received full payment and I abound. I am very well supplied because of what I received from you through Epaphroditus, "a fragrant aroma," an acceptable sacrifice, pleasing to God. My God will fully supply whatever you need, in accord with his glorious riches in Christ Jesus.

RESPONSORIAL PSALM *Psalm 112:1b–2, 5–6, 8a and 9*

R. Blessed the man who fears the Lord. or: R. Alleluia.

Blessed the man who fears the LORD, / who greatly delights in his commands. / His posterity shall be mighty upon the earth; / the upright generation shall be blessed. **R.**

Well for the man who is gracious and lends, / who conducts his affairs with justice; /He shall never be moved; / the just one shall be in everlasting remembrance. **R.**

His heart is steadfast; he shall not fear. / Lavishly he gives to the poor; / his generosity shall endure forever; / his horn shall be exalted in glory. **R.**

ALLELUIA *2 Corinthians 8:9*

R. Alleluia, alleluia. Jesus Christ became poor although he was rich, so that by his poverty you might become rich. **R.**

GOSPEL *Luke 16:9–15*

Jesus said to his disciples: "I tell you, make friends for yourselves with dishonest wealth, so that when it fails, you will be welcomed into eternal dwellings. The person who is trustworthy in very small matters is also trustworthy in great ones; and the person who is dishonest in very small matters is also dishonest in great ones. If, therefore, you are not trustworthy with dishonest wealth, who will trust you with true wealth? If you are not trustworthy with what belongs to another, who will give you what is yours? No servant can serve two masters. He will either hate one and love the other, or be devoted to one and despise the other. You cannot serve God and mammon."

The Pharisees, who loved money, heard all these things and sneered at him. And he said to them, "You justify yourselves in the sight of others, but God knows your hearts; for what is of human esteem is an abomination in the sight of God."

NOVEMBER 8, 32ND SUNDAY IN ORDINARY TIME; ST. PHILIP HOWARD

FIRST READING   *Wisdom 6:12—16*

Resplendent and unfading is wisdom, and she is readily perceived by those who love her, and found by those who seek her. She hastens to make herself known in anticipation of their desire; whoever watches for her at dawn shall not be disappointed, for he shall find her sitting by his gate.

For taking thought of wisdom is the perfection of prudence, and whoever for her sake keeps vigil shall quickly be free from care; because she makes her own rounds, seeking those worthy of her, and graciously appears to them in the ways, and meets them with all solicitude.

RESPONSORIAL PSALM   *Psalm 63:2, 3—4, 5—6, 7—8 (2b)*

R. My soul is thirsting for you, O Lord my God.

O God, you are my God whom I seek; **/** for you my flesh pines **/** and my soul thirsts like the earth, **/** parched, lifeless and without water. **R.**

Thus have I gazed toward you in the sanctuary **/** to see your power and your glory, **/** for your kindness is a greater good than life; **/** my lips shall glorify you. **R.**

Thus will I bless you while I live; **/** lifting up my hands, I will call upon your name. **/** As with the riches of a banquet shall my soul be satisfied, **/** and with exultant lips my mouth shall praise you. **R.**

I will remember you upon my couch, **/** and through the night–watches I will meditate on you: **/** you are my help, and in the shadow of your wings I shout for joy. **R.**

SECOND READING   *Longer Form 1 Thessalonians 4:13—18*

We do not want you to be unaware, brothers and sisters, about those who have fallen asleep, so that you may not grieve like the rest, who have no hope. For if we believe that Jesus died and rose, so too will God, through Jesus, bring with him those who have fallen asleep. Indeed, we tell you this, on the word of the Lord, that we who are alive, who are left until the coming of the Lord, will surely not precede those who have fallen asleep. For the Lord himself, with a word of command, with the voice of an archangel and with the trumpet of God, will come down from heaven, and the dead in Christ will rise first. Then we who are alive, who are left, will be caught up together with them in the clouds to meet the Lord in the air. Thus we shall always be with the Lord. Therefore, console one another with these words.

SHORTER FORM   *1 Thessalonians 4:13—14*

We do not want you to be unaware, brothers and sisters, about those who have fallen asleep, so that you may not grieve like the rest, who have no hope. For if we believe that Jesus died and rose, so too will God, through Jesus, bring with him those who have fallen asleep.

ALLELUIA   *Matthew 24:42a, 44*

R. Alleluia, alleluia. Stay awake and be ready! For you do not know on what day your Lord will come. **R.**

GOSPEL
Matthew 25:1—13

Jesus told his disciples this parable: "the kingdom of heaven will be like ten virgins who took their lamps and went out to meet the bridegroom. Five of them were foolish and five were wise. The foolish ones, when taking their lamps, brought no oil with them, but the wise brought flasks of oil with their lamps. Since the bridegroom was long delayed, they all became drowsy and fell asleep. At midnight, there was a cry, 'Behold, the bridegroom! Come out to meet him!' Then all those virgins got up and trimmed their lamps. The foolish ones said to the wise, 'Give us some of your oil, for our lamps are going out.' But the wise ones replied, 'No, for there may not be enough for us and you. Go instead to the merchants and buy some for yourselves.' While they went off to buy it, the bridegroom came and those who were ready went into the wedding feast with him. Then the door was locked. Afterwards the other virgins came and said, 'Lord, Lord, open the door for us!' But he said in reply, 'Amen, I say to you, I do not know you.' Therefore, stay awake, for you know neither the day nor the hour."

NOVEMBER 9, FEAST OF THE DEDICATION OF THE LATERAN BASILICA IN ROME
FIRST READING
Ezekiel 47:1—2, 8—9, 12

The angel brought me back to the entrance of the temple, and I saw water flowing out from beneath the threshold of the temple toward the east, for the façade of the temple was toward the east; the water flowed down from the southern side of the temple, south of the altar. He led me outside by the north gate, and around to the outer gate facing the east, where I saw water trickling from the southern side. He said to me, "This water flows into the eastern district down upon the Arabah, and empties into the sea, the salt waters, which it makes fresh. Wherever the river flows, every sort of living creature that can multiply shall live, and there shall be abundant fish, for wherever this water comes the sea shall be made fresh. Along both banks of the river, fruit trees of every kind shall grow; their leaves shall not fade, nor their fruit fail. Every month they shall bear fresh fruit, for they shall be watered by the flow from the sanctuary. Their fruit shall serve for food, and their leaves for medicine."

RESPONSORIAL PSALM
Psalm 46:2—3, 5—6, 8—9 (5)

R. The waters of the river gladden the city of God, the holy dwelling of the Most High!

God is our refuge and our strength, **/** an ever–present help in distress. **/** Therefore, we fear not, though the earth be shaken **/** and mountains plunge into the depths of the sea. **R.**

There is a stream whose runlets gladden the city of God, **/** the holy dwelling of the Most High. **/** God is in its midst; it shall not be disturbed; **/** God will help it at the break of dawn. **R.**

The LORD of hosts is with us; **/** our stronghold is the God of Jacob. **/** Come! behold the deeds of the LORD, **/** the astounding things he has wrought on earth. **R.**

SECOND READING   *1 Corinthians 3:9c—11, 16—17*

Brothers and sisters: You are God's building. According to the grace of God given to me, like a wise master builder I laid a foundation, and another is building upon it. But each one must be careful how he builds upon it, for no one can lay a foundation other than the one that is there, namely, Jesus Christ.

Do you not know that you are the temple of God, and that the Spirit of God dwells in you? If anyone destroys God's temple, God will destroy that person; for the temple of God, which you are, is holy.

ALLELUIA   *2 Chronicles 7:16*

R. Alleluia, alleluia. I have chosen and consecrated this house, says the Lord, that my name may be there forever. **R.**

GOSPEL   *John 2:13—22*

Since the Passover of the Jews was near, Jesus went up to Jerusalem. He found in the temple area those who sold oxen, sheep, and doves, as well as the money—changers seated there. He made a whip out of cords and drove them all out of the temple area, with the sheep and oxen, and spilled the coins of the money—changers and overturned their tables, and to those who sold doves he said, "Take these out of here, and stop making my Father's house a marketplace." His disciples recalled the words of Scripture, Zeal for your house will consume me. At this the Jews answered and said to him, "What sign can you show us for doing this?" Jesus answered and said to them, "Destroy this temple and in three days I will raise it up." The Jews said, "This temple has been under construction for forty—six years, and you will raise it up in three days?" But he was speaking about the temple of his Body. Therefore, when he was raised from the dead, his disciples remembered that he had said this, and they came to believe the Scripture and the word Jesus had spoken.

NOVEMBER 10, TUESDAY OF WEEK 32; ST. LEO THE GREAT

FIRST READING   *Titus 2:1–8, 11–14*

Beloved: You must say what is consistent with sound doctrine, namely, that older men should be temperate, dignified, self—controlled, sound in faith, love, and endurance. Similarly, older women should be reverent in their behavior, not slanderers, not addicted to drink, teaching what is good, so that they may train younger women to love their husbands and children, to be self—controlled, chaste, good homemakers, under the control of their husbands, so that the word of God may not be discredited.

Urge the younger men, similarly, to control themselves, showing yourself as a model of good deeds in every respect, with integrity in your teaching, dignity, and sound speech that cannot be criticized, so that the opponent will be put to shame without anything bad to say about us.

For the grace of God has appeared, saving all and training us to reject godless ways and worldly desires and to live temperately, justly, and devoutly in this age, as we await the blessed hope, the appearance of the glory of the great God and of our savior Jesus Christ, who gave himself for us to deliver us from all lawlessness and to cleanse for himself a people as his own, eager to do what is good.

RESPONSORIAL PSALM
Psalm 37:3–4, 18 and 23, 27 and 29

R. (39a) The salvation of the just comes from the Lord.

Trust in the LORD and do good, / that you may dwell in the land and be fed in security. / Take delight in the LORD, / and he will grant you your heart's requests. **R.**

The LORD watches over the lives of the wholehearted; / their inheritance lasts forever. / By the LORD are the steps of a man made firm, / and he approves his way. **R.**

Turn from evil and do good, / that you may abide forever; / the just shall possess the land and dwell in it forever. **R.**

ALLELUIA
John 14:23

R. Alleluia, alleluia. Whoever loves me will keep my word, and my Father will love him, and we will come to him. **R.**

GOSPEL
Luke 17:7–10

Jesus said to the Apostles: "Who among you would say to your servant who has just come in from plowing or tending sheep in the field, 'Come here immediately and take your place at table'? Would he not rather say to him, 'Prepare something for me to eat. Put on your apron and wait on me while I eat and drink. You may eat and drink when I am finished'? Is he grateful to that servant because he did what was commanded? So should it be with you. When you have done all you have been commanded, say, 'We are unprofitable servants; we have done what we were obliged to do.'"

NOVEMBER 11, WEDNESDAY OF WEEK 32; ST. MARTIN OF TOURS

FIRST READING
Titus 3:1–7

Beloved: Remind them to be under the control of magistrates and authorities, to be obedient, to be open to every good enterprise. They are to slander no one, to be peaceable, considerate, exercising all graciousness toward everyone. For we ourselves were once foolish, disobedient, deluded, slaves to various desires and pleasures, living in malice and envy, hateful ourselves and hating one another.

But when the kindness and generous love of God our savior appeared, not because of any righteous deeds we had done but because of his mercy, he saved us through the bath of rebirth and renewal by the Holy Spirit, whom he richly poured out on us through Jesus Christ our savior, so that we might be justified by his grace and become heirs in hope of eternal life.

RESPONSORIAL PSALM
Psalm 23:1b–3a, 3bc–4, 5, 6

R. (1) The Lord is my shepherd; there is nothing I shall want.

The LORD is my shepherd; I shall not want. / In verdant pastures he gives me repose; / beside restful waters he leads me; / he refreshes my soul. **R.**

He guides me in right paths / for his name's sake. / Even though I walk in the dark valley / I fear no evil; for you are at my side / with your rod and your staff / that give me courage. **R.** You spread the table before me / in the sight of my foes; / You anoint my head with oil; / my cup overflows. **R.**

Only goodness and kindness follow me / all the days of my life; / and I shall dwell in the house of the LORD / for years to come. **R.**

ALLELUIA *1 Thessalonians 5:18*
R. Alleluia, alleluia. In all circumstances, give thanks, for this is the will of God for you in Christ Jesus. **R.**

GOSPEL *Luke 17:11–19*
As Jesus continued his journey to Jerusalem, he traveled through Samaria and Galilee. As he was entering a village, ten lepers met him. They stood at a distance from him and raised their voice, saying, "Jesus, Master! Have pity on us!" And when he saw them, he said, "Go show yourselves to the priests." As they were going they were cleansed. And one of them, realizing he had been healed, returned, glorifying God in a loud voice; and he fell at the feet of Jesus and thanked him. He was a Samaritan. Jesus said in reply, "Ten were cleansed, were they not? Where are the other nine? Has none but this foreigner returned to give thanks to God?" Then he said to him, "Stand up and go; your faith has saved you."

NOVEMBER 12, THURSDAY OF WEEK 32; ST. JOSAPHAT
FIRST READING *Philemon 7–20*
Beloved: I have experienced much joy and encouragement from your love, because the hearts of the holy ones have been refreshed by you, brother. Therefore, although I have the full right in Christ to order you to do what is proper, I rather urge you out of love, being as I am, Paul, an old man, and now also a prisoner for Christ Jesus. I urge you on behalf of my child Onesimus, whose father I have become in my imprisonment, who was once useless to you but is now useful to both you and me. I am sending him, that is, my own heart, back to you. I should have liked to retain him for myself, so that he might serve me on your behalf in my imprisonment for the Gospel, but I did not want to do anything without your consent, so that the good you do might not be forced but voluntary. Perhaps this is why he was away from you for a while, that you might have him back forever, no longer as a slave but more than a slave, a brother, beloved especially to me, but even more so to you, as a man and in the Lord. So if you regard me as a partner, welcome him as you would me. And if he has done you any injustice or owes you anything, charge it to me. I, Paul, write this in my own hand: I will pay. May I not tell you that you owe me your very self? Yes, brother, may I profit from you in the Lord. Refresh my heart in Christ.

RESPONSORIAL PSALM *Psalm 146:7, 8–9a, 9bc–10*
R. Blessed is he whose help is the God of Jacob. or: R. Alleluia.
The LORD secures justice for the oppressed, / gives food to the hungry. / The LORD sets captives free. **R.**

The LORD gives sight to the blind. / The LORD raises up those who were bowed down; / the LORD loves the just. / The LORD protects strangers. **R.**

The fatherless and the widow he sustains, / but the way of the wicked he thwarts. / The LORD shall reign forever; / your God, O Zion, through all generations. Alleluia. **R.**

ALLELUIA *John 15:5*

R. Alleluia, alleluia. I am the vine, you are the branches, says the Lord: whoever remains in me and I in him will bear much fruit. **R.**

GOSPEL *Luke 17:20–25*

Asked by the Pharisees when the Kingdom of God would come, Jesus said in reply, "The coming of the Kingdom of God cannot be observed, and no one will announce, 'Look, here it is,' or, 'There it is.' For behold, the Kingdom of God is among you."

Then he said to his disciples, "The days will come when you will long to see one of the days of the Son of Man, but you will not see it. There will be those who will say to you, 'Look, there he is,' or 'Look, here he is.' Do not go off, do not run in pursuit. For just as lightning flashes and lights up the sky from one side to the other, so will the Son of Man be in his day. But first he must suffer greatly and be rejected by this generation."

NOVEMBER 13, FRIDAY OF WEEK 32; ST. FRANCES XAVIER CABRINI

FIRST READING *2 John1: 4–9*

I rejoiced greatly to find some of your children walking in the truth just as we were commanded by the Father. But now, Lady, I ask you, not as though I were writing a new commandment but the one we have had from the beginning: let us love one another. For this is love, that we walk according to his commandments; this is the commandment, as you heard from the beginning, in which you should walk.

Many deceivers have gone out into the world, those who do not acknowledge Jesus Christ as coming in the flesh; such is the deceitful one and the antichrist. Look to yourselves that you do not lose what we worked for but may receive a full recompense. Anyone who is so "progressive" as not to remain in the teaching of the Christ does not have God; whoever remains in the teaching has the Father and the Son.

RESPONSORIAL PSALM *Psalm 119:1, 2, 10, 11, 17, 18*

R. (1b) Blessed are they who follow the law of the Lord!

Blessed are they whose way is blameless, / who walk in the law of the LORD. **R.**

Blessed are they who observe his decrees, / who seek him with all their heart. **R.**

With all my heart I seek you; / let me not stray from your commands. **R.**

Within my heart I treasure your promise, / that I may not sin against you. **R.**

Be good to your servant, / that I may live and keep your words. **R.**

Open my eyes, / that I may consider the wonders of your law. **R.**

ALLELUIA *Luke 21:28*

R. Alleluia, alleluia. Stand erect and raise your heads because your redemption is at hand. **R.**

GOSPEL
Luke 17:26–37

Jesus said to his disciples: "As it was in the days of Noah, so it will be in the days of the Son of Man; they were eating and drinking, marrying and giving in marriage up to the day that Noah entered the ark, and the flood came and destroyed them all. Similarly, as it was in the days of Lot: they were eating, drinking, buying, selling, planting, building; on the day when Lot left Sodom, fire and brimstone rained from the sky to destroy them all. So it will be on the day the Son of Man is revealed. On that day, someone who is on the housetop and whose belongings are in the house must not go down to get them, and likewise one in the field must not return to what was left behind. Remember the wife of Lot. Whoever seeks to preserve his life will lose it, but whoever loses it will save it. I tell you, on that night there will be two people in one bed; one will be taken, the other left. And there will be two women grinding meal together; one will be taken, the other left." They said to him in reply, "Where, Lord?" He said to them, "Where the body is, there also the vultures will gather."

NOVEMBER 14, SATURDAY OF WEEK 32; ST. LAWRENCE O'TOOLE

FIRST READING
3 John 1: 5–8

Beloved, you are faithful in all you do for the brothers and sisters, especially for strangers; they have testified to your love before the Church. Please help them in a way worthy of God to continue their journey. For they have set out for the sake of the Name and are accepting nothing from the pagans. Therefore, we ought to support such persons, so that we may be co–workers in the truth.

RESPONSORIAL PSALM
Psalm 112:1–2, 3–4, 5–6
R. Blessed the man who fears the Lord. or: R. Alleluia.

Blessed the man who fears the LORD, who greatly delights in his commands. His posterity shall be mighty upon the earth; the upright generation shall be blessed. **R.**

Wealth and riches shall be in his house; his generosity shall endure forever. Light shines through the darkness for the upright; he is gracious and merciful and just. **R.**

Well for the man who is gracious and lends, who conducts his affairs with justice; He shall never be moved; the just one shall be in everlasting remembrance. **R.**

ALLELUIA
See 2 Thessalonians 2:14

R. Alleluia, alleluia. God has called us through the Gospel, to possess the glory of our Lord Jesus Christ. **R.**

GOSPEL
Luke 18:1–8

Jesus told his disciples a parable about the necessity for them to pray always without becoming weary. He said, "There was a judge in a certain town who neither feared God nor respected any human being. And a widow in that town used to come to him and say, 'Render a just decision for me against my adversary.' For a long time the judge was unwilling, but eventually he thought, 'While it is true that I neither fear God nor respect any human being, because this widow keeps bothering me I shall deliver a just decision for her lest she finally come and strike me.'" The Lord said, "Pay attention to what the dishonest judge says. Will not God then secure the rights of his chosen ones who call out to him day and night? Will he be slow to answer them? I tell you, he will see to it that justice is done for them speedily. But when the Son of Man comes, will he find faith on earth?"

NOVEMBER 15, 33RD SUNDAY IN ORDINARY TIME; ST. ALBERT THE GREAT

FIRST READING *Proverbs 31:10—13, 19—20, 30—31*

When one finds a worthy wife, her value is far beyond pearls. Her husband, entrusting his heart to her, has an unfailing prize. She brings him good, and not evil, all the days of her life. She obtains wool and flax and works with loving hands.

She puts her hands to the distaff, and her fingers ply the spindle. She reaches out her hands to the poor, and extends her arms to the needy. Charm is deceptive and beauty fleeting; the woman who fears the LORD is to be praised. Give her a reward for her labors, and let her works praise her at the city gates.

RESPONSORIAL PSALM *Psalm 128:1—2, 3, 4—5 (see 1a)*

R. Blessed are those who fear the Lord.

Blessed are you who fear the LORD, / who walk in his ways! / For you shall eat the fruit of your handiwork; / blessed shall you be, and favored. **R.**

Your wife shall be like a fruitful vine / in the recesses of your home; / your children like olive plants around your table. **R.**

Behold, thus is the man blessed / who fears the LORD. / The LORD bless you from Zion: / may you see the prosperity of Jerusalem / all the days of your life. **R.**

SECOND READING *1 Thessalonians 5:1—6*

Concerning times and seasons, brothers and sisters, you have no need for anything to be written to you. For you yourselves know very well that the day of the Lord will come like a thief at night. When people are saying, "Peace and security," then sudden disaster comes upon them, like labor pains upon a pregnant woman, and they will not escape.

But you, brothers and sisters, are not in darkness, for that day to overtake you like a thief. For all of you are children of the light and children of the day. We are not of the night or of darkness. Therefore, let us not sleep as the rest do, but let us stay alert and sober.

ALLELUIA *John 15:4a, 5b*

R. Alleluia, alleluia. Remain in me as I remain in you, says the Lord. Whoever remains in me bears much fruit. **R.**

GOSPEL *Longer Form Matthew 25:14—30*

Jesus told his disciples this parable: "A man going on a journey called in his servants and entrusted his possessions to them. To one he gave five talents; to another, two; to a third, one— to each according to his ability. Then he went away. Immediately the one who received five talents went and traded with them, and made another five. Likewise, the one who received two made another two. But the man who received one went off and dug a hole in the ground and buried his master's money.

"After a long time the master of those servants came back and settled accounts with them. The one who had received five talents came forward bringing the additional five. He said, 'Master, you gave me five talents. See, I have made five more.' His master said to him, 'Well done, my good and faithful servant. Since you were faithful in small matters, I will give you great responsibilities. Come, share your master's joy.' Then the one who had received two talents also came forward and said, 'Master, you gave me two talents. See, I have made two more.' His master said to him, 'Well done, my good and faithful servant. Since you were faithful in small matters, I will give you great responsibilities. Come, share your master's joy.' Then the one who had received the one talent came forward and said, 'Master, I knew you were a demanding person, harvesting where you did not plant and gathering where you did not scatter; so out of fear I went off and buried your talent in the ground. Here it is back.' His master said to him in reply, 'You wicked, lazy servant! So you knew that I harvest where I did not plant and gather where I did not scatter? Should you not then have put my money in the bank so that I could have got it back with interest on my return? Now then! Take the talent from him and give it to the one with ten. For to everyone who has, more will be given and he will grow rich; but from the one who has not, even what he has will be taken away. And throw this useless servant into the darkness outside, where there will be wailing and grinding of teeth.'"

SHORTER FORM   *Matthew 25:14—15, 19—21*
Jesus told his disciples this parable: A man going on a journey called in his servants and entrusted his possessions to them. To one he gave five talents; to another, two; to a third, one— to each according to his ability. Then he went away.

"After a long time the master of those servants came back and settled accounts with them. The one who had received five talents came forward bringing the additional five. He said, 'Master, you gave me five talents. See, I have made five more.' His master said to him, 'Well done, my good and faithful servant. Since you were faithful in small matters, I will give you great responsibilities. Come, share your master's joy.'"

NOVEMBER 16, MONDAY OF WEEK 33; ST. MARGARET OF SCOTLAND
FIRST READING   *Revelation 1:1–4; 2:1–5*
The revelation of Jesus Christ, which God gave to him, to show his servants what must happen soon. He made it known by sending his angel to his servant John, who gives witness to the word of God and to the testimony of Jesus Christ by reporting what he saw. Blessed is the one who reads aloud and blessed are those who listen to this prophetic message and heed what is written in it, for the appointed time is near.

John, to the seven churches in Asia: grace to you and peace from him who is and who was and who is to come, and from the seven spirits before his throne.

I heard the Lord saying to me: "To the angel of the Church in Ephesus, write this:

"'The one who holds the seven stars in his right hand and walks in the midst of the seven gold lampstands says this: "I know your works, your labor, and your endurance, and that you cannot tolerate the wicked; you have tested those who call themselves Apostles but are not, and discovered that they are impostors. Moreover, you have endurance and have suffered for my name, and you have not grown weary. Yet I hold this against you: you have lost the love you had at first. Realize how far you have fallen. Repent, and do the works you did at first. Otherwise, I will come to you and remove your lampstand from its place, unless you repent."'"

RESPONSORIAL PSALM *Psalm 1:1–2, 3, 4 and 6*
R. (Rev. 2:17) Those who are victorious I will feed from the tree of life.
Blessed the man who follows not the counsel of the wicked / nor walks in the way of sinners, / nor sits in the company of the insolent, / but delights in the law of the LORD / and meditates on his law day and night. **R.**
He is like a tree planted near running water, / that yields its fruit in due season, / and whose leaves never fade. / Whatever he does, prospers. **R.**
Not so the wicked, not so; / they are like chaff which the wind drives away. / For the LORD watches over the way of the just, / but the way of the wicked vanishes. **R.**

ALLELUIA *John 8:12*
R. Alleluia, alleluia. I am the light of the world, says the Lord; whoever follows me will have the light of life. **R.**

GOSPEL *Luke 18:35–43*
As Jesus approached Jericho a blind man was sitting by the roadside begging, and hearing a crowd going by, he inquired what was happening. They told him, "Jesus of Nazareth is passing by." He shouted, "Jesus, Son of David, have pity on me!" The people walking in front rebuked him, telling him to be silent, but he kept calling out all the more, "Son of David, have pity on me!" Then Jesus stopped and ordered that he be brought to him; and when he came near, Jesus asked him, "What do you want me to do for you?" He replied, "Lord, please let me see." Jesus told him, "Have sight; your faith has saved you." He immediately received his sight and followed him, giving glory to God. When they saw this, all the people gave praise to God.

NOVEMBER 17, TUESDAY OF WEEK 33; ST. ELIZABETH OF HUNGARY

FIRST READING *Revelation 3:1–6, 14–22*
I, John, heard the Lord saying to me: "To the angel of the Church in Sardis, write this: "'The one who has the seven spirits of God and the seven stars says this: "I know your works, that you have the reputation of being alive, but you are dead. Be watchful and strengthen what is left, which is going to die, for I have not found your works complete in the sight of my God. Remember then how you accepted and heard; keep it, and repent. If you are not watchful, I will come like a thief, and you will never know at what hour I will come upon you. However, you have a few people in Sardis who have not soiled their garments; they will walk with me dressed in white, because they are worthy. The victor will thus be dressed in white, and I will never erase his name from the book of life but will acknowledge his

name in the presence of my Father and of his angels. "'Whoever has ears ought to hear what the Spirit says to the churches.'"

"To the angel of the Church in Laodicea, write this: "'The Amen, the faithful and true witness, the source of God's creation, says this: "I know your works; I know that you are neither cold nor hot. I wish you were either cold or hot. So, because you are lukewarm, neither hot nor cold, I will spit you out of my mouth. For you say, 'I am rich and affluent and have no need of anything,' and yet do not realize that you are wretched, pitiable, poor, blind, and naked. I advise you to buy from me gold refined by fire so that you may be rich, and white garments to put on so that your shameful nakedness may not be exposed, and buy ointment to smear on your eyes so that you may see. Those whom I love, I reprove and chastise. Be earnest, therefore, and repent.

"'Behold, I stand at the door and knock. If anyone hears my voice and opens the door, then I will enter his house and dine with him, and he with me. I will give the victor the right to sit with me on my throne, as I myself first won the victory and sit with my Father on his throne. Whoever has ears ought to hear what the Spirit says to the churches.'"

RESPONSORIAL PSALM   *Psalm 15:2–3a, 3bc–4ab, 5*
R. (Rev. 3: 21) I will seat the victor beside me on my throne.
He who walks blamelessly and does justice; / who thinks the truth in his heart and slanders not with his tongue. **R.**
Who harms not his fellow man, / nor takes up a reproach against his neighbor; / by whom the reprobate is despised, / while he honors those who fear the LORD. **R.**
Who lends not his money at usury / and accepts no bribe against the innocent. / He who does these things shall never be disturbed. **R.**

ALLELUIA   *1 John 4:10b*
R. Alleluia, alleluia. God loved us, and sent his Son as expiation for our sins. **R.**

GOSPEL   *Luke 19:1–10*
At that time Jesus came to Jericho and intended to pass through the town. Now a man there named Zacchaeus, who was a chief tax collector and also a wealthy man, was seeking to see who Jesus was; but he could not see him because of the crowd, for he was short in stature. So he ran ahead and climbed a sycamore tree in order to see Jesus, who was about to pass that way. When he reached the place, Jesus looked up and said, "Zacchaeus, come down quickly, for today I must stay at your house." And he came down quickly and received him with joy. When they saw this, they began to grumble, saying, "He has gone to stay at the house of a sinner." But Zacchaeus stood there and said to the Lord, "Behold, half of my possessions, Lord, I shall give to the poor, and if I have extorted anything from anyone I shall repay it four times over." And Jesus said to him, "Today salvation has come to this house because this man too is a descendant of Abraham. For the Son of Man has come to seek and to save what was lost."

NOVEMBER 18, WEDNESDAY OF WEEK 33; ST. ROSE PHILIPPINE DUCHESNE

FIRST READING *Revelation 4:1–11*

I, John, had a vision of an open door to heaven, and I heard the trumpetlike voice that had spoken to me before, saying, "Come up here and I will show you what must happen afterwards." At once I was caught up in spirit. A throne was there in heaven, and on the throne sat one whose appearance sparkled like jasper and carnelian. Around the throne was a halo as brilliant as an emerald. Surrounding the throne I saw twenty–four other thrones on which twenty–four elders sat, dressed in white garments and with gold crowns on their heads. From the throne came flashes of lightning, rumblings, and peals of thunder. Seven flaming torches burned in front of the throne, which are the seven spirits of God. In front of the throne was something that resembled a sea of glass like crystal.

In the center and around the throne, there were four living creatures covered with eyes in front and in back. The first creature resembled a lion, the second was like a calf, the third had a face like that of a man, and the fourth looked like an eagle in flight. The four living creatures, each of them with six wings, were covered with eyes inside and out. Day and night they do not stop exclaiming: "Holy, holy, holy is the Lord God almighty, who was, and who is, and who is to come." Whenever the living creatures give glory and honor and thanks to the one who sits on the throne, who lives forever and ever, the twenty–four elders fall down before the one who sits on the throne and worship him, who lives forever and ever. They throw down their crowns before the throne, exclaiming:

"Worthy are you, Lord our God, to receive glory and honor and power, for you created all things; because of your will they came to be and were created."

RESPONSORIAL PSALM *Psalm 150:1b–2, 3–4, 5–6*

R. (1b) Holy, holy, holy Lord, mighty God!

Praise the LORD in his sanctuary, / praise him in the firmament of his strength. / Praise him for his mighty deeds, / praise him for his sovereign majesty. **R.**

Praise him with the blast of the trumpet, / praise him with lyre and harp, / Praise him with timbrel and dance, / praise him with strings and pipe. **R.**

Praise him with sounding cymbals, / praise him with clanging cymbals. / Let everything that has breath / praise the LORD! Alleluia. **R.**

ALLELUIA *See John 15:16*

R. Alleluia, alleluia. I chose you from the world, to go and bear fruit that will last, says the Lord. **R.**

GOSPEL *Luke 19:11–28*

While people were listening to Jesus speak, he proceeded to tell a parable because he was near Jerusalem and they thought that the Kingdom of God would appear there immediately. So he said,

"A nobleman went off to a distant country to obtain the kingship for himself and then to return. He called ten of his servants and gave them ten gold coins and told them, 'Engage in trade with these until I return.' His fellow citizens, however, despised him and sent a delegation after him to announce, 'We do not want this man to be our king.' But when he returned after obtaining the kingship, he had the servants called, to whom he had given the money, to learn what they had gained by trading. The first came forward and said, 'Sir, your gold coin has earned ten additional ones.' He replied, 'Well done, good servant! You have been faithful in this very small matter; take charge of ten cities.' Then the second came and reported, 'Your gold coin, sir, has earned five more.' And to this servant too he said, 'You, take charge of five cities.' Then the other servant came and said, 'Sir, here is your gold coin; I kept it stored away in a handkerchief, for I was afraid of you, because you are a demanding man; you take up what you did not lay down and you harvest what you did not plant.' He said to him, 'With your own words I shall condemn you, you wicked servant. You knew I was a demanding man, taking up what I did not lay down and harvesting what I did not plant; why did you not put my money in a bank? Then on my return I would have collected it with interest.' And to those standing by he said, 'Take the gold coin from him and give it to the servant who has ten.' But they said to him, 'Sir, he has ten gold coins.' He replied, 'I tell you, to everyone who has, more will be given, but from the one who has not, even what he has will be taken away. Now as for those enemies of mine who did not want me as their king, bring them here and slay them before me.'"

After he had said this, he proceeded on his journey up to Jerusalem.

NOVEMBER 19, THURSDAY OF WEEK 33; BLESSED VICTORIA RASOAMANARIVO

FIRST READING   *Revelation 5:1–10*

I, John, saw a scroll in the right hand of the one who sat on the throne. It had writing on both sides and was sealed with seven seals. Then I saw a mighty angel who proclaimed in a loud voice, "Who is worthy to open the scroll and break its seals?" But no one in heaven or on earth or under the earth was able to open the scroll or to examine it. I shed many tears because no one was found worthy to open the scroll or to examine it. One of the elders said to me, "Do not weep. The lion of the tribe of Judah, the root of David, has triumphed, enabling him to open the scroll with its seven seals."

Then I saw standing in the midst of the throne and the four living creatures and the elders a Lamb that seemed to have been slain. He had seven horns and seven eyes; these are the seven spirits of God sent out into the whole world. He came and received the scroll from the right hand of the one who sat on the throne. When he took it, the four living creatures and the twenty–four elders fell down before the Lamb. Each of the elders held a harp and gold bowls filled with incense, which are the prayers of the holy ones. They sang a new hymn:

"Worthy are you to receive the scroll and break open its seals, for you were slain and with your Blood you purchased for God those from every tribe and tongue, people and nation. You made them a kingdom and priests for our God, and they will reign on earth."

RESPONSORIAL PSALM   *Psalm 149:1b–2, 3–4, 5–6a and 9b*
R. The Lamb has made us a kingdom of priests to serve our God. or: R. Alleluia.

Sing to the LORD a new song of praise in the assembly of the faithful. Let Israel be glad in their maker, let the children of Zion rejoice in their king. **R.**

Let them praise his name in the festive dance, let them sing praise to him with timbrel and harp. For the LORD loves his people, and he adorns the lowly with victory. **R.**

Let the faithful exult in glory; let them sing for joy upon their couches; Let the high praises of God be in their throats. This is the glory of all his faithful. Alleluia. **R.**

ALLELUIA *Psalm 95:8*

R. Alleluia, alleluia. If today you hear his voice, harden not your hearts. **R.**

GOSPEL *Luke 19:41–44*

As Jesus drew near Jerusalem, he saw the city and wept over it, saying, "If this day you only knew what makes for peace— but now it is hidden from your eyes. For the days are coming upon you when your enemies will raise a palisade against you; they will encircle you and hem you in on all sides. They will smash you to the ground and your children within you, and they will not leave one stone upon another within you because you did not recognize the time of your visitation."

NOVEMBER 20, FRIDAY OF WEEK 33; ST. EDMUND

FIRST READING *Revelation 10:8–11*

I, John, heard a voice from heaven speak to me. Then the voice spoke to me and said: "Go, take the scroll that lies open in the hand of the angel who is standing on the sea and on the land." So I went up to the angel and told him to give me the small scroll. He said to me, "Take and swallow it. It will turn your stomach sour, but in your mouth it will taste as sweet as honey." I took the small scroll from the angel's hand and swallowed it. In my mouth it was like sweet honey, but when I had eaten it, my stomach turned sour. Then someone said to me, "You must prophesy again about many peoples, nations, tongues, and kings."

RESPONSORIAL PSALM *Psalm 119:14, 24, 72, 103, 111, 131*

R. (103a) How sweet to my taste is your promise!

In the way of your decrees I rejoice, / as much as in all riches. **R**

Yes, your decrees are my delight; / they are my counselors. **R.**

The law of your mouth is to me / more precious than thousands of gold and silver pieces. **R.**

How sweet to my palate are your promises, / sweeter than honey to my mouth! **R.**

Your decrees are my inheritance forever; / the joy of my heart they are. **R.**

I gasp with open mouth/ in my yearning for your commands. **R.**

ALLELUIA *John 10:27*

R. Alleluia, alleluia. My sheep hear my voice, says the Lord; I know them, and they follow me. **R.**

GOSPEL
Luke 19:45–48

Jesus entered the temple area and proceeded to drive out those who were selling things, saying to them, "It is written, *My house shall be a house of prayer, but you have made it a den of thieves.*" And every day he was teaching in the temple area. The chief priests, the scribes, and the leaders of the people, meanwhile, were seeking to put him to death, but they could find no way to accomplish their purpose because all the people were hanging on his words.

NOVEMBER 21, SATURDAY OF WEEK 33; PRESENTATION OF MARY
FIRST READING
Revelation 11:4–12

I, John, heard a voice from heaven speak to me: Here are my two witnesses: These are the two olive trees and the two lampstands that stand before the Lord of the earth. If anyone wants to harm them, fire comes out of their mouths and devours their enemies. In this way, anyone wanting to harm them is sure to be slain. They have the power to close up the sky so that no rain can fall during the time of their prophesying. They also have power to turn water into blood and to afflict the earth with any plague as often as they wish.

When they have finished their testimony, the beast that comes up from the abyss will wage war against them and conquer them and kill them. Their corpses will lie in the main street of the great city, which has the symbolic names "Sodom" and "Egypt," where indeed their Lord was crucified. Those from every people, tribe, tongue, and nation will gaze on their corpses for three and a half days, and they will not allow their corpses to be buried. The inhabitants of the earth will gloat over them and be glad and exchange gifts because these two prophets tormented the inhabitants of the earth. But after the three and a half days, a breath of life from God entered them. When they stood on their feet, great fear fell on those who saw them. Then they heard a loud voice from heaven say to them, "Come up here." So they went up to heaven in a cloud as their enemies looked on.

RESPONSORIAL PSALM
Psalm 144:1, 2, 9–10

R. (1b) Blessed be the Lord, my Rock!
Blessed be the LORD, my rock, / who trains my hands for battle, / my fingers for war. **R.**
My mercy and my fortress, my stronghold, my deliverer, / my shield, in whom I trust, who subdues my people under me. **R.**
O God, I will sing a new song to you; / with a ten-stringed lyre I will chant your praise, / You who give victory to kings, and deliver David, / your servant from the evil sword. **R.**

ALLELUIA
See 2 Timothy 1:10

R. Alleluia, alleluia. Our Savior Jesus Christ has destroyed death and brought life to light through the Gospel. **R.**

GOSPEL
Luke 20:27–40

Some Sadducees, those who deny that there is a resurrection, came forward and put this question to Jesus, saying, "Teacher, Moses wrote for us, *If someone's brother dies leaving a wife but no child, his brother must take the wife and raise up descendants for his brother.*

Now there were seven brothers; the first married a woman but died childless. Then the second and the third married her, and likewise all the seven died childless. Finally the woman also died. Now at the resurrection whose wife will that woman be? For all seven had been married to her." Jesus said to them, "The children of this age marry and remarry; but those who are deemed worthy to attain to the coming age and to the resurrection of the dead neither marry nor are given in marriage. They can no longer die, for they are like angels; and they are the children of God because they are the ones who will rise. That the dead will rise even Moses made known in the passage about the bush, when he called 'Lord' the God of Abraham, the God of Isaac, and the God of Jacob; and he is not God of the dead, but of the living, for to him all are alive." Some of the scribes said in reply, "Teacher, you have answered well." And they no longer dared to ask him anything.

NOVEMBER 22, SOLEMNITY OF CHRIST THE KING; ST. CECILIA

FIRST READING   *Ezekiel 34:11—12, 15—17*

Thus says the Lord GOD: I myself will look after and tend my sheep. As a shepherd tends his flock when he finds himself among his scattered sheep, so will I tend my sheep. I will rescue them from every place where they were scattered when it was cloudy and dark. I myself will pasture my sheep; I myself will give them rest, says the Lord GOD. The lost I will seek out, the strayed I will bring back, the injured I will bind up, the sick I will heal, but the sleek and the strong I will destroy, shepherding them rightly.

As for you, my sheep, says the Lord GOD, I will judge between one sheep and another, between rams and goats.

RESPONSORIAL PSALM   *Psalm 23:1—2, 2—3, 5—6 (1)*

The LORD is my shepherd; I shall not want. **/** In verdant pastures he gives me repose; **/** beside restful waters he leads me; **/** he refreshes my soul. **R.**
He guides me in right paths **/** for his name's sake. **/** Even though I walk in the dark valley **/** I fear no evil; for you are at my side **/** with your rod and your staff/that give me courage. **R.**
You spread the table before me **/** in the sight of my foes; **/** You anoint my head with oil; **/** my cup overflows. **R.**
Only goodness and kindness follow me **/** all the days of my life; **/** and I shall dwell in the house of the LORD **/** for years to come. **R.**

SECOND READING   *1 Corinthians 15:20—26, 28*

Brothers and sisters: Christ has been raised from the dead, the firstfruits of those who have fallen asleep. For since death came through man, the resurrection of the dead came also through man. For just as in Adam all die, so too in Christ shall all be brought to life, but each one in proper order: Christ the firstfruits; then, at his coming, those who belong to Christ; then comes the end, when he hands over the kingdom to his God and Father, when he has destroyed every sovereignty and every authority and power. For he must reign until he has put all his enemies under his feet. The last enemy to be destroyed is death. When everything is subjected to him, then the Son himself will also be subjected to the one who subjected everything to him, so that God may be all in all.

ALLELUIA *Mark 11:9, 10*

R. **Alleluia, alleluia.** Blessed is he who comes in the name of the Lord! Blessed is the kingdom of our father David that is to come! **R.**

GOSPEL *Matthew 25:31—46*

Jesus said to his disciples: "When the Son of Man comes in his glory, and all the angels with him, he will sit upon his glorious throne, and all the nations will be assembled before him. And he will separate them one from another, as a shepherd separates the sheep from the goats. He will place the sheep on his right and the goats on his left. Then the king will say to those on his right, 'Come, you who are blessed by my Father. Inherit the kingdom prepared for you from the foundation of the world. For I was hungry and you gave me food, I was thirsty and you gave me drink, a stranger and you welcomed me, naked and you clothed me, ill and you cared for me, in prison and you visited me.' Then the righteous will answer him and say, 'Lord, when did we see you hungry and feed you, or thirsty and give you drink? When did we see you a stranger and welcome you, or naked and clothe you? When did we see you ill or in prison, and visit you?' And the king will say to them in reply, 'Amen, I say to you, whatever you did for one of the least brothers of mine, you did for me.' Then he will say to those on his left, 'Depart from me, you accursed, into the eternal fire prepared for the devil and his angels. For I was hungry and you gave me no food, I was thirsty and you gave me no drink, a stranger and you gave me no welcome, naked and you gave me no clothing, ill and in prison, and you did not care for me.' Then they will answer and say, 'Lord, when did we see you hungry or thirsty or a stranger or naked or ill or in prison, and not minister to your needs?' He will answer them, 'Amen, I say to you, what you did not do for one of these least ones, you did not do for me.' And these will go off to eternal punishment, but the righteous to eternal life."

NOVEMBER 23, MONDAY OF WEEK 34; ST CLEMENT I;
OR ST COLUMBANUS; BLESSED MIGUEL AUGUSTIN PRO

FIRST READING *Revelation 14:1–3, 4b–5*

I, John, looked and there was the Lamb standing on Mount Zion, and with him a hundred and forty–four thousand who had his name and his Father's name written on their foreheads. I heard a sound from heaven like the sound of rushing water or a loud peal of thunder. The sound I heard was like that of harpists playing their harps. They were singing what seemed to be a new hymn before the throne, before the four living creatures and the elders. No one could learn this hymn except the hundred and forty–four thousand who had been ransomed from the earth. These are the ones who follow the Lamb wherever he goes. They have been ransomed as the first fruits of the human race for God and the Lamb. On their lips no deceit has been found; they are unblemished.

RESPONSORIAL PSALM *Psalm 24:1bc–2, 3–4ab, 5–6*

R. (see 6) Lord, this is the people that longs to see your face.

The LORD's are the earth and its fullness; / the world and those who dwell in it. / For he founded it upon the seas / and established it upon the rivers. **R.**

Who can ascend the mountain of the LORD? / Or who may stand in his holy place? / He whose hands are sinless, / whose heart is clean, who desires not what is vain. **R.**

He shall receive a blessing from the LORD, / a reward from God his savior. / Such is the race that seeks for him, / that seeks the face of the God of Jacob. **R.**

ALLELUIA *Matthew 24:42a, 44*

R. Alleluia, alleluia. Stay awake! For you do not know when the Son of Man will come. **R.**

GOSPEL *Luke 21:1–4*

When Jesus looked up he saw some wealthy people putting their offerings into the treasury and he noticed a poor widow putting in two small coins. He said, "I tell you truly, this poor widow put in more than all the rest; for those others have all made offerings from their surplus wealth, but she, from her poverty, has offered her whole livelihood."

NOVEMBER 24, TUESDAY OF WEEK 34; ST. ANDREW DUNG-LAC AND COMPANIONS

FIRST READING *Revelation 14:14–19*

I, John, looked and there was a white cloud, and sitting on the cloud one who looked like a son of man, with a gold crown on his head and a sharp sickle in his hand. Another angel came out of the temple, crying out in a loud voice to the one sitting on the cloud, "Use your sickle and reap the harvest, for the time to reap has come, because the earth's harvest is fully ripe." So the one who was sitting on the cloud swung his sickle over the earth, and the earth was harvested.

Then another angel came out of the temple in heaven who also had a sharp sickle. Then another angel came from the altar, who was in charge of the fire, and cried out in a loud voice to the one who had the sharp sickle, "Use your sharp sickle and cut the clusters from the earth's vines, for its grapes are ripe." So the angel swung his sickle over the earth and cut the earth's vintage. He threw it into the great wine press of God's fury.

RESPONSORIAL PSALM *Psalm 96:10, 11–12, 13*

R. (13b) The Lord comes to judge the earth.

Say among the nations: The LORD is king. / He has made the world firm, not to be moved; / he governs the peoples with equity. **R.**

Let the heavens be glad and the earth rejoice; / let the sea and what fills it resound; / let the plains be joyful and all that is in them! / Then shall all the trees of the forest exult. **R.**

Before the LORD, for he comes; / for he comes to rule the earth. / He shall rule the world with justice / and the peoples with his constancy. **R.**

ALLELUIA *Revelation 2:10c*

R. Alleluia, alleluia. Remain faithful until death, and I will give you the crown of life. **R.**

GOSPEL *Luke 21:5–11*

While some people were speaking about how the temple was adorned with costly stones and votive offerings, Jesus said, "All that you see here— the days will come when there will not be left a stone upon another stone that will not be thrown down."

Then they asked him, "Teacher, when will this happen? And what sign will there be when all these things are about to happen?" He answered, "See that you not be deceived, for many will come in my name, saying, 'I am he,' and 'The time has come.' Do not follow them! When you hear of wars and insurrections, do not be terrified; for such things must happen first, but it will not immediately be the end." Then he said to them, "Nation will rise against nation, and kingdom against kingdom. There will be powerful earthquakes, famines, and plagues from place to place; and awesome sights and mighty signs will come from the sky."

NOVEMBER 25, WEDNESDAY OF WEEK 34; ST. CATHERINE OF ALEXANDRIA

FIRST READING *Revelation 15:1–4*

I, John, saw in heaven another sign, great and awe–inspiring: seven angels with the seven last plagues, for through them God's fury is accomplished.

Then I saw something like a sea of glass mingled with fire. On the sea of glass were standing those who had won the victory over the beast and its image and the number that signified its name. They were holding God's harps, and they sang the song of Moses, the servant of God, and the song of the Lamb:

"Great and wonderful are your works, Lord God almighty. Just and true are your ways, O king of the nations. Who will not fear you, Lord, or glorify your name? For you alone are holy. All the nations will come and worship before you, for your righteous acts have been revealed."

RESPONSORIAL PSALM *Psalm 98:1, 2–3ab, 7–8, 9*

R. (Rev. 15: 3b) Great and wonderful are all your works, Lord, mighty God!

Sing to the LORD a new song, / for he has done wondrous deeds; / His right hand has won victory for him, his holy arm. **R.**

The LORD has made his salvation known: / in the sight of the nations he has revealed his justice. / He has remembered his kindness and his faithfulness / toward the house of Israel. **R.**

Let the sea and what fills it resound, / the world and those who dwell in it; / Let the rivers clap their hands, / the mountains shout with them for joy. **R.**

Before the LORD, for he comes, / for he comes to rule the earth; / He will rule the world with justice and the peoples with equity. **R.**

ALLELUIA *Revelation 2:10c*

R. Alleluia, alleluia. Remain faithful until death, and I will give you the crown of life. **R.**

GOSPEL
Luke 21:12–19

Jesus said to the crowd: "They will seize and persecute you, they will hand you over to the synagogues and to prisons, and they will have you led before kings and governors because of my name. It will lead to your giving testimony. Remember, you are not to prepare your defense beforehand, for I myself shall give you a wisdom in speaking that all your adversaries will be powerless to resist or refute. You will even be handed over by parents, brothers, relatives, and friends, and they will put some of you to death. You will be hated by all because of my name, but not a hair on your head will be destroyed. By your perseverance you will secure your lives."

NOVEMBER 26, THURSDAY OF WEEK 34; BLESSED JAMES ALBERIONE

FIRST READING
Revelation 18:1–2, 21–23; 19:1–3, 9a

I, John, saw another angel coming down from heaven, having great authority, and the earth became illumined by his splendor. He cried out in a mighty voice:

"Fallen, fallen is Babylon the great. She has become a haunt for demons. She is a cage for every unclean spirit, a cage for every unclean bird, a cage for every unclean and disgusting beast."

A mighty angel picked up a stone like a huge millstone and threw it into the sea and said:

"With such force will Babylon the great city be thrown down, and will never be found again. No melodies of harpists and musicians, flutists and trumpeters, will ever be heard in you again. No craftsmen in any trade will ever be found in you again. No sound of the millstone will ever be heard in you again. No light from a lamp will ever be seen in you again. No voices of bride and groom will ever be heard in you again. Because your merchants were the great ones of the world, all nations were led astray by your magic potion."

After this I heard what sounded like the loud voice of a great multitude in heaven, saying:

"Alleluia! Salvation, glory, and might belong to our God, for true and just are his judgments. He has condemned the great harlot who corrupted the earth with her harlotry. He has avenged on her the blood of his servants."

They said a second time:

"Alleluia! Smoke will rise from her forever and ever."

Then the angel said to me, "Write this: Blessed are those who have been called to the wedding feast of the Lamb."

RESPONSORIAL PSALM
Psalm 100:1b–2, 3, 4, 5

R. (Rev. 19: 9a) Blessed are they who are called to the wedding feast of the Lamb.

Sing joyfully to the LORD, all you lands; / serve the LORD with gladness; / come before him with joyful song. **R.**

Know that the LORD is God; / he made us, his we are; / his people, the flock he tends. **R.**

Enter his gates with thanksgiving, / his courts with praise; / Give thanks to him; bless his name. **R.**

For he is good: the LORD, whose kindness endures forever, / and his faithfulness, to all generations. **R.**

ALLELUIA *Luke 21:28*

R. Alleluia, alleluia. Stand erect and raise your heads because your redemption is at hand. **R.**

GOSPEL *Luke 21:20–28*

Jesus said to his disciples: "When you see Jerusalem surrounded by armies, know that its desolation is at hand. Then those in Judea must flee to the mountains. Let those within the city escape from it, and let those in the countryside not enter the city, for these days are the time of punishment when all the Scriptures are fulfilled. Woe to pregnant women and nursing mothers in those days, for a terrible calamity will come upon the earth and a wrathful judgment upon this people. They will fall by the edge of the sword and be taken as captives to all the Gentiles; and Jerusalem will be trampled underfoot by the Gentiles until the times of the Gentiles are fulfilled.

"There will be signs in the sun, the moon, and the stars, and on earth nations will be in dismay, perplexed by the roaring of the sea and the waves. People will die of fright in anticipation of what is coming upon the world, for the powers of the heavens will be shaken. And then they will see the Son of Man coming in a cloud with power and great glory. But when these signs begin to happen, stand erect and raise your heads because your redemption is at hand."

NOVEMBER 27, FRIDAY OF WEEK 34; ST. JOHN BERCHMANS

FIRST READING *Revelation 20:1–4, 11—21:2*

I, John, saw an angel come down from heaven, holding in his hand the key to the abyss and a heavy chain. He seized the dragon, the ancient serpent, which is the Devil or Satan, and tied it up for a thousand years and threw it into the abyss, which he locked over it and sealed, so that it could no longer lead the nations astray until the thousand years are completed. After this, it is to be released for a short time.

Then I saw thrones; those who sat on them were entrusted with judgment. I also saw the souls of those who had been beheaded for their witness to Jesus and for the word of God, and who had not worshiped the beast or its image nor had accepted its mark on their foreheads or hands. They came to life and they reigned with Christ for a thousand years.

Next I saw a large white throne and the one who was sitting on it. The earth and the sky fled from his presence and there was no place for them. I saw the dead, the great and the lowly, standing before the throne, and scrolls were opened. Then another scroll was opened, the book of life. The dead were judged according to their deeds, by what was written in the scrolls. The sea gave up its dead; then Death and Hades gave up their dead. All the dead were judged according to their deeds. Then Death and Hades were thrown into the pool of fire. (This pool of fire is the second death.) Anyone whose name was not found written in the book of life was thrown into the pool of fire.

Then I saw a new heaven and a new earth. The former heaven and the former earth had passed away, and the sea was no more. I also saw the holy city, a new Jerusalem, coming down out of heaven from God, prepared as a bride adorned for her husband.

RESPONSORIAL PSALM *Psalm 84:3, 4, 5–6a and 8a*
R. (Rev. 21:3b) Here God lives among his people.
My soul yearns and pines for the courts of the LORD. / My heart and my flesh cry out for the living God. **R.**
Even the sparrow finds a home, / and the swallow a nest in which she puts her young— / Your altars, O LORD of hosts, my king and my God! **R.**
Blessed they who dwell in your house! / continually they praise you. / Blessed the men whose strength you are! / They go from strength to strength. **R.**

ALLELUIA *Luke 21:28*
R. Alleluia, alleluia. Stand erect and raise your heads because your redemption is at hand. **R.**

GOSPEL *Luke 21:29–33*
Jesus told his disciples a parable. "Consider the fig tree and all the other trees. When their buds burst open, you see for yourselves and know that summer is now near; in the same way, when you see these things happening, know that the Kingdom of God is near. Amen, I say to you, this generation will not pass away until all these things have taken place. Heaven and earth will pass away, but my words will not pass away."

NOVEMBER 28, SATURDAY OF WEEK 34; ST. CATHERINE LABOURÉ

FIRST READING *Revelation 22:1–7*
John said: An angel showed me the river of life–giving water, sparkling like crystal, flowing from the throne of God and of the Lamb down the middle of the street, On either side of the river grew the tree of life that produces fruit twelve times a year, once each month; the leaves of the trees serve as medicine for the nations. Nothing accursed will be found anymore. The throne of God and of the Lamb will be in it, and his servants will worship him. They will look upon his face, and his name will be on their foreheads. Night will be no more, nor will they need light from lamp or sun, for the Lord God shall give them light, and they shall reign forever and ever.

And he said to me, "These words are trustworthy and true, and the Lord, the God of prophetic spirits, sent his angel to show his servants what must happen soon." "Behold, I am coming soon." Blessed is the one who keeps the prophetic message of this book.

RESPONSORIAL PSALM *Psalm 95:1–2, 3–5, 6–7ab*
R. (1 Cor 16: 22b, see Rev. 22: 20c) Marana tha! Come, Lord Jesus!

Come, let us sing joyfully to the LORD; / let us acclaim the Rock of our salvation. / Let us come into his presence with thanksgiving; / let us joyfully sing psalms to him. **R.**

For the LORD is a great God, and a great king above all gods; / In his hands are the depths of the earth, / and the tops of the mountains are his. / His is the sea, for he has made it, / and the dry land, which his hands have formed. **R.**

Come, let us bow down in worship; / let us kneel before the LORD who made us. / For he is our God, and we are the people he shepherds, / the flock he guides. **R.**

ALLELUIA *Luke 21:36*

R. Alleluia, alleluia. Be vigilant at all times and pray that you may have the strength to stand before the Son of Man. **R.**

GOSPEL *Luke 21:34–36*

Jesus said to his disciples: "Beware that your hearts do not become drowsy from carousing and drunkenness and the anxieties of daily life, and that day catch you by surprise like a trap. For that day will assault everyone who lives on the face of the earth. Be vigilant at all times and pray that you have the strength to escape the tribulations that are imminent and to stand before the Son of Man."

NOVEMBER 29, 1ST SUNDAY OF ADVENT; BLESSED FRANCIS ANTHONY OF LUCERA

FIRST READING *Isaiah 63:16b—17, 19b; 64:2—7*

You, LORD, are our father, our redeemer you are named forever. Why do you let us wander, O LORD, from your ways, and harden our hearts so that we fear you not? Return for the sake of your servants, the tribes of your heritage. Oh, that you would rend the heavens and come down, with the mountains quaking before you, while you wrought awesome deeds we could not hope for, such as they had not heard of from of old. No ear has ever heard, no eye ever seen, any God but you doing such deeds for those who wait for him. Would that you might meet us doing right, that we were mindful of you in our ways! Behold, you are angry, and we are sinful; all of us have become like unclean people, all our good deeds are like polluted rags; we have all withered like leaves, and our guilt carries us away like the wind. There is none who calls upon your name, who rouses himself to cling to you; for you have hidden your face from us and have delivered us up to our guilt. Yet, O LORD, you are our father; we are the clay and you the potter: we are all the work of your hands.

RESPONSORIAL PSALM *Psalm 80:2—3, 15—16, 18—19 (4)*

R. Lord, make us turn to you; let us see your face and we shall be saved.

O shepherd of Israel, hearken, / from your throne upon the cherubim, shine forth. / Rouse your power, and come to save us. **R.**

Once again, O LORD of hosts, / look down from heaven, and see; / take care of this vine, and protect what your right hand has planted, / the son of man whom you yourself made strong. **R.**

May your help be with the man of your right hand, **/** with the son of man whom you yourself made strong. **/** Then we will no more withdraw from you; **/** give us new life, and we will call upon your name. **R.**

SECOND READING   *1 Corinthians 1:3—9*

Brothers and sisters: Grace to you and peace from God our Father and the Lord Jesus Christ.

I give thanks to my God always on your account for the grace of God bestowed on you in Christ Jesus, that in him you were enriched in every way, with all discourse and all knowledge, as the testimony to Christ was confirmed among you, so that you are not lacking in any spiritual gift as you wait for the revelation of our Lord Jesus Christ. He will keep you firm to the end, irreproachable on the day of our Lord Jesus Christ. God is faithful, and by him you were called to fellowship with his Son, Jesus Christ our Lord.

ALLELUIA   *Psalm 85:8*

R. Alleluia, alleluia. Show us Lord, your love; and grant us your salvation. **R.**

GOSPEL   *Mark 13:33—37*

Jesus said to his disciples: "Be watchful! Be alert! You do not know when the time will come. It is like a man traveling abroad. He leaves home and places his servants in charge, each with his own work, and orders the gatekeeper to be on the watch. Watch, therefore; you do not know when the lord of the house is coming, whether in the evening, or at midnight, or at cockcrow, or in the morning. May he not come suddenly and find you sleeping. What I say to you, I say to all: 'Watch!'"

NOVEMBER 30, SAINT ANDREW, APOSTLE - FEAST

FIRST READING   *Romans 10:9–18*

Brothers and sisters: If you confess with your mouth that Jesus is Lord and believe in your heart that God raised him from the dead, you will be saved. For one believes with the heart and so is justified, and one confesses with the mouth and so is saved. The Scripture says, *No one who believes in him will be put to shame.* There is no distinction between Jew and Greek; the same Lord is Lord of all, enriching all who call upon him. *For everyone who calls on the name of the Lord will be saved.*

But how can they call on him in whom they have not believed? And how can they believe in him of whom they have not heard? And how can they hear without someone to preach? And how can people preach unless they are sent? As it is written, *How beautiful are the feet of those who bring the good news!* But not everyone has heeded the good news; for Isaiah says, *Lord, who has believed what was heard from us?* Thus faith comes from what is heard, and what is heard comes through the word of Christ. But I ask, did they not hear? Certainly they did; for *their voice has gone forth to all the earth, and their words to the ends of the world.*

RESPONSORIAL PSALM   *Psalm 19:8, 9, 10, 11*
R. The judgments of the Lord are true, and all of them are just. or: R. Your words, Lord, are Spirit and life.

The law of the LORD is perfect, refreshing the soul; **/** the decree of the LORD is trustworthy, giving wisdom to the simple. **R.**

The precepts of the LORD are right, rejoicing the heart; **/** the command of the LORD is clear, enlightening the eye. **R.**

The fear of the LORD is pure, enduring forever; **/** The ordinances of the LORD are true, all of them just. **R.**

They are more precious than gold, than a heap of purest gold; **/** Sweeter also than syrup or honey from the comb. **R.**

ALLELUIA   *Matthew 4:19*
R. Alleluia, alleluia. Come after me, says the Lord, and I will make you fishers of men. **R.**

GOSPEL   *Matthew 4:18–22*
As Jesus was walking by the Sea of Galilee, he saw two brothers, Simon who is called Peter, and his brother Andrew, casting a net into the sea; they were fishermen. He said to them, "Come after me, and I will make you fishers of men." At once they left their nets and followed him. He walked along from there and saw two other brothers, James, the son of Zebedee, and his brother John. They were in a boat, with their father Zebedee, mending their nets. He called them, and immediately they left their boat and their father and followed him.

14   DECEMBER

DECEMBER 1, 1ST WEEK OF ADVENT - TUESDAY; ST. EDMUND CAMPION
FIRST READING   *Isaiah 11:1–10*
On that day, A shoot shall sprout from the stump of Jesse, and from his roots a bud shall blossom. The Spirit of the LORD shall rest upon him: a Spirit of wisdom and of understanding, A Spirit of counsel and of strength, a Spirit of knowledge and of fear of the LORD, and his delight shall be the fear of the LORD. Not by appearance shall he judge, nor by hearsay shall he decide, but he shall judge the poor with justice, and decide aright for the land's afflicted. He shall strike the ruthless with the rod of his mouth, and with the breath of his lips he shall slay the wicked. Justice shall be the band around his waist, and faithfulness a belt upon his hips.

   Then the wolf shall be a guest of the lamb, and the leopard shall lie down with the kid; The calf and the young lion shall browse together, with a little child to guide them. The cow and the bear shall be neighbors, together their young shall rest; the lion shall eat hay like the ox. The baby shall play by the cobra's den, and the child lay his hand on the adder's lair. There shall be no harm or ruin on all my holy mountain; for the earth shall be filled with knowledge of the LORD, as water covers the sea.

On that day, The root of Jesse, set up as a signal for the nations, The Gentiles shall seek out, for his dwelling shall be glorious.

RESPONSORIAL PSALM   *Psalm 72:1–2, 7–8, 12–13, 17*

R. (see 7) Justice shall flourish in his time, and fullness of peace for ever.
O God, with your judgment endow the king, / and with your justice, the king's son; / He shall govern your people with justice / and your afflicted ones with judgment. **R.**
Justice shall flower in his days, / and profound peace, till the moon be no more. / May he rule from sea to sea, / and from the River to the ends of the earth. **R.**
He shall rescue the poor when he cries out, / and the afflicted when he has no one to help him. / He shall have pity for the lowly and the poor; / the lives of the poor he shall save. **R.**
May his name be blessed forever; / as long as the sun his name shall remain. / In him shall all the tribes of the earth be blessed; / all the nations shall proclaim his happiness. **R.**

ALLELUIA
R. Alleluia, alleluia. Behold, our Lord shall come with power; he will enlighten the eyes of his servants. **R.**

GOSPEL   *Luke 10:21–24*
Jesus rejoiced in the Holy Spirit and said, "I give you praise, Father, Lord of heaven and earth, for although you have hidden these things from the wise and the learned you have revealed them to the childlike. Yes, Father, such has been your gracious will. All things have been handed over to me by my Father. No one knows who the Son is except the Father, and who the Father is except the Son and anyone to whom the Son wishes to reveal him."

Turning to the disciples in private he said, "Blessed are the eyes that see what you see. For I say to you, many prophets and kings desired to see what you see, but did not see it, and to hear what you hear, but did not hear it."

DECEMBER 2, 1ST WEEK OF ADVENT - WEDNESDAY; ST. BIBIANA
FIRST READING   *Isaiah 25:6–10a*
On this mountain the LORD of hosts will provide for all peoples a feast of rich food and choice wines, juicy, rich food and pure, choice wines. On this mountain he will destroy the veil that veils all peoples, the web that is woven over all nations; he will destroy death forever. The Lord GOD will wipe away the tears from all faces; the reproach of his people he will remove from the whole earth; for the LORD has spoken.

On that day it will be said: "Behold our God, to whom we looked to save us! This is the LORD for whom we looked; let us rejoice and be glad that he has saved us!" For the hand of the LORD will rest on this mountain.

RESPONSORIAL PSALM   *Psalm 23:1–3a, 3b–4, 5, 6*
R. (6cd) I shall live in the house of the Lord all the days of my life.

The LORD is my shepherd; I shall not want. / In verdant pastures he gives me repose; / beside restful waters he leads me; / he refreshes my soul. **R.**

He guides me in right paths / for his name's sake. / Even though I walk in the dark valley / I fear no evil; for you are at my side / with your rod and your staff /that give me courage. **R.**

You spread the table before me / in the sight of my foes; / You anoint my head with oil; / my cup overflows. **R.**

Only goodness and kindness follow me / all the days of my life; / and I shall dwell in the house of the LORD / for years to come. **R.**

ALLELUIA

R. **Alleluia, alleluia.** Behold, the Lord comes to save his people; blessed are those prepared to meet him. **R.**

GOSPEL   *Matthew 15:29–37*

At that time: Jesus walked by the Sea of Galilee, went up on the mountain, and sat down there. Great crowds came to him, having with them the lame, the blind, the deformed, the mute, and many others. They placed them at his feet, and he cured them. The crowds were amazed when they saw the mute speaking, the deformed made whole, the lame walking, and the blind able to see, and they glorified the God of Israel.

Jesus summoned his disciples and said, "My heart is moved with pity for the crowd, for they have been with me now for three days and have nothing to eat. I do not want to send them away hungry, for fear they may collapse on the way." The disciples said to him, "Where could we ever get enough bread in this deserted place to satisfy such a crowd?" Jesus said to them, "How many loaves do you have?" "Seven," they replied, "and a few fish." He ordered the crowd to sit down on the ground. Then he took the seven loaves and the fish, gave thanks, broke the loaves, and gave them to the disciples, who in turn gave them to the crowds. They all ate and were satisfied. They picked up the fragments left over—seven baskets full.

DECEMBER 3, 1ST WEEK OF ADVENT - THURSDAY; ST. FRANCIS XAVIER

FIRST READING   *Isaiah 26:1–6*

On that day they will sing this song in the land of Judah:

"A strong city have we; he sets up walls and ramparts to protect us. Open up the gates to let in a nation that is just, one that keeps faith. A nation of firm purpose you keep in peace; in peace, for its trust in you."

Trust in the LORD forever! For the LORD is an eternal Rock. He humbles those in high places, and the lofty city he brings down; He tumbles it to the ground, levels it with the dust. It is trampled underfoot by the needy, by the footsteps of the poor.

RESPONSORIAL PSALM   *Psalm 118:1 and 8–9, 19–21, 25–27a*
R. **Blessed is he who comes in the name of the Lord. or: R. Alleluia.**

Give thanks to the LORD, for he is good, **/** for his mercy endures forever. **/** It is better to take refuge in the LORD **/** than to trust in man. It is better to take refuge in the LORD **/** than to trust in princes. **R.**

Open to me the gates of justice; **/** I will enter them and give thanks to the LORD. **/** This gate is the LORD's; the just shall enter it. **/** I will give thanks to you, for you have answered me **/** and have been my savior. **R.**

O LORD, grant salvation! **/** O LORD, grant prosperity! **/** Blessed is he who comes in the name of the LORD; **/** we bless you from the house of the LORD. **/** The LORD is God, and he has given us light. **R.**

ALLELUIA   *Isaiah 55:6*

R. Alleluia, alleluia. Seek the LORD while he may be found; call him while he is near. **R.**

GOSPEL   *Matthew 7:21, 24–27*

Jesus said to his disciples: "Not everyone who says to me, 'Lord, Lord,' will enter the Kingdom of heaven, but only the one who does the will of my Father in heaven.

"Everyone who listens to these words of mine and acts on them will be like a wise man who built his house on rock. The rain fell, the floods came, and the winds blew and buffeted the house. But it did not collapse; it had been set solidly on rock. And everyone who listens to these words of mine but does not act on them will be like a fool who built his house on sand. The rain fell, the floods came, and the winds blew and buffeted the house. And it collapsed and was completely ruined."

DECEMBER 4, 1ST WEEK OF ADVENT - FRIDAY; ST. JOHN OF DAMASCUS
FIRST READING   *Isaiah 29:17–24*

Thus says the Lord GOD: But a very little while, and Lebanon shall be changed into an orchard, and the orchard be regarded as a forest! On that day the deaf shall hear the words of a book; And out of gloom and darkness, the eyes of the blind shall see. The lowly will ever find joy in the LORD, and the poor rejoice in the Holy One of Israel. For the tyrant will be no more and the arrogant will have gone; All who are alert to do evil will be cut off, those whose mere word condemns a man, Who ensnare his defender at the gate, and leave the just man with an empty claim. Therefore thus says the LORD, the God of the house of Jacob, who redeemed Abraham: Now Jacob shall have nothing to be ashamed of, nor shall his face grow pale. When his children see the work of my hands in his midst, they shall keep my name holy; they shall reverence the Holy One of Jacob, and be in awe of the God of Israel. Those who err in spirit shall acquire understanding, and those who find fault shall receive instruction.

RESPONSORIAL PSALM   *Psalm 27:1, 4, 13–14*

R. (1a) The Lord is my light and my salvation.

The LORD is my light and my salvation; **/** whom should I fear? **/** The LORD is my life's refuge; **/** of whom should I be afraid? **R.**

One thing I ask of the LORD; this I seek: **/** To dwell in the house of the LORD all the days of my life, **/** that I may gaze on the loveliness of the LORD **/** and contemplate his temple. **R.**
I believe that I shall see the bounty of the LORD **/** in the land of the living. Wait for the LORD with courage; **/** be stouthearted, and wait for the LORD. **R.**

ALLELUIA
R. Alleluia, alleluia. Behold, our Lord shall come with power; he will enlighten the eyes of his servants. **R.**

GOSPEL   *Matthew 9:27–31*
As Jesus passed by, two blind men followed him, crying out, "Son of David, have pity on us!" When he entered the house, the blind men approached him and Jesus said to them, "Do you believe that I can do this?" "Yes, Lord," they said to him. Then he touched their eyes and said, "Let it be done for you according to your faith." And their eyes were opened. Jesus warned them sternly, "See that no one knows about this." But they went out and spread word of him through all that land.

DECEMBER 5, 1ST WEEK OF ADVENT - SATURDAY; ST. SABAS

FIRST READING   *Isaiah 30:19–21, 23–26*
Thus says the Lord GOD, the Holy One of Israel: O people of Zion, who dwell in Jerusalem, no more will you weep; He will be gracious to you when you cry out, as soon as he hears he will answer you. The Lord will give you the bread you need and the water for which you thirst. No longer will your Teacher hide himself, but with your own eyes you shall see your Teacher, While from behind, a voice shall sound in your ears: "This is the way; walk in it," when you would turn to the right or to the left.

He will give rain for the seed that you sow in the ground, and the wheat that the soil produces will be rich and abundant. On that day your flock will be given pasture and the lamb will graze in spacious meadows; the oxen and the asses that till the ground will eat silage tossed to them with shovel and pitchfork. Upon every high mountain and lofty hill there will be streams of running water. On the day of the great slaughter, when the towers fall, The light of the moon will be like that of the sun and the light of the sun will be seven times greater like the light of seven days. On the day the LORD binds up the wounds of his people, he will heal the bruises left by his blows.

RESPONSORIAL PSALM   *Psalm 147:1–2, 3–4, 5–6*
R. (see Isaiah 30:18d) Blessed are all who wait for the Lord.
Praise the LORD, for he is good; **/** sing praise to our God, for he is gracious; **/** it is fitting to praise him. **/** The LORD rebuilds Jerusalem; **/** the dispersed of Israel he gathers. **R.**
He heals the brokenhearted and binds up their wounds. **/** He tells the number of the stars; **/** he calls each by name. **R.**
Great is our LORD and mighty in power: **/** to his wisdom there is no limit. **/** The LORD sustains the lowly; **/** the wicked he casts to the ground. **R.**
ALLELUIA   *Isaiah 33:22*

R. Alleluia, alleluia. The LORD is our Judge, our Lawgiver, our King; he it is who will save us. **R.**

GOSPEL

Matthew 9:35—10:1, 5a, 6–8

Jesus went around to all the towns and villages, teaching in their synagogues, proclaiming the Gospel of the Kingdom, and curing every disease and illness. At the sight of the crowds, his heart was moved with pity for them because they were troubled and abandoned, like sheep without a shepherd. Then he said to his disciples, the harvest is abundant but the laborers are few; so ask the master of the harvest to send out laborers for his harvest."

Then he summoned his Twelve disciples and gave them authority over unclean spirits to drive them out and to cure every disease and every illness.

Jesus sent out these Twelve after instructing them thus, "Go to the lost sheep of the house of Israel. As you go, make this proclamation: 'The Kingdom of heaven is at hand.' Cure the sick, raise the dead, cleanse lepers, drive out demons. Without cost you have received; without cost you are to give."

DECEMBER 6, 2ND SUNDAY OF ADVENT; ST. NICHOLAS

FIRST READING

Isaiah 40:1—5, 9—11

Comfort, give comfort to my people, says your God. Speak tenderly to Jerusalem, and proclaim to her that her service is at an end, her guilt is expiated; indeed, she has received from the hand of the LORD double for all her sins.

A voice cries out: In the desert prepare the way of the LORD! Make straight in the wasteland a highway for our God! Every valley shall be filled in, every mountain and hill shall be made low; the rugged land shall be made a plain, the rough country, a broad valley. Then the glory of the LORD shall be revealed, and all people shall see it together; for the mouth of the LORD has spoken.

Go up onto a high mountain, Zion, herald of glad tidings; cry out at the top of your voice, Jerusalem, herald of good news! Fear not to cry out and say to the cities of Judah: Here is your God! Here comes with power the Lord GOD, who rules by his strong arm; here is his reward with him, his recompense before him. Like a shepherd he feeds his flock; in his arms he gathers the lambs, carrying them in his bosom, and leading the ewes with care.

RESPONSORIAL PSALM

Psalm 85:9—10, 11—12, 13—14 (8)

R. Lord, let us see your kindness, and grant us your salvation.

I will hear what God proclaims; / the LORD—for he proclaims peace to his people. / Near indeed is his salvation to those who fear him, / glory dwelling in our land. **R.**

Kindness and truth shall meet; / justice and peace shall kiss. / Truth shall spring out of the earth, / and justice shall look down from heaven. **R.**

The LORD himself will give his benefits; / our land shall yield its increase. / Justice shall walk before him, / and prepare the way of his steps. **R.**

SECOND READING   *2 Peter 3:8—14*

Do not ignore this one fact, beloved, that with the Lord one day is like a thousand years and a thousand years like one day. The Lord does not delay his promise, as some regard "delay," but he is patient with you, not wishing that any should perish but that all should come to repentance. But the day of the Lord will come like a thief, and then the heavens will pass away with a mighty roar and the elements will be dissolved by fire, and the earth and everything done on it will be found out.

Since everything is to be dissolved in this way, what sort of persons ought you to be, conducting yourselves in holiness and devotion, waiting for and hastening the coming of the day of God, because of which the heavens will be dissolved in flames and the elements melted by fire. But according to his promise we await new heavens and a new earth in which righteousness dwells. Therefore, beloved, since you await these things, be eager to be found without spot or blemish before him, at peace.

ALLELUIA   *Luke 3:4, 6*

R. Alleluia, alleluia. Prepare the way of the Lord, make straight his paths: all flesh shall see the salvation of God. **R.**

GOSPEL   *Mark 1:1—8*

The beginning of the gospel of Jesus Christ the Son of God. As it is written in Isaiah the prophet: *Behold, I am sending my messenger ahead of you; he will prepare your way. A voice of one crying out in the desert: "Prepare the way of the Lord, make straight his paths."*

John the Baptist appeared in the desert proclaiming a baptism of repentance for the forgiveness of sins. People of the whole Judean countryside and all the inhabitants of Jerusalem were going out to him and were being baptized by him in the Jordan River as they acknowledged their sins. John was clothed in camel's hair, with a leather belt around his waist. He fed on locusts and wild honey. And this is what he proclaimed: "One mightier than I is coming after me. I am not worthy to stoop and loosen the thongs of his sandals. I have baptized you with water; he will baptize you with the Holy Spirit."

DECEMBER 7, 2ND WEEK OF ADVENT - MONDAY; ST. AMBROSE

FIRST READING   *Isaiah 35:1—10*

The desert and the parched land will exult; the steppe will rejoice and bloom. They will bloom with abundant flowers, and rejoice with joyful song. The glory of Lebanon will be given to them, the splendor of Carmel and Sharon; They will see the glory of the LORD, the splendor of our God. Strengthen the hands that are feeble, make firm the knees that are weak, Say to those whose hearts are frightened: Be strong, fear not! Here is your God, he comes with vindication; With divine recompense he comes to save you. Then will the eyes of the blind be opened, the ears of the deaf be cleared; Then will the lame leap like a stag, then the tongue of the mute will sing.

Streams will burst forth in the desert, and rivers in the steppe. The burning sands will become pools, and the thirsty ground, springs of water; The abode where jackals lurk will be a marsh for the reed and papyrus. A highway will be there, called the holy way; No one unclean may pass over it, nor fools go astray on it. No lion will be there, nor beast of prey go up to be met upon it. It is for those with a journey to make, and on it the redeemed will walk. Those whom the LORD has ransomed will return and enter Zion singing, crowned with everlasting joy; they will meet with joy and gladness, sorrow and mourning will flee.

RESPONSORIAL PSALM
Psalm 85:9—10, 11—12, 13—14 (8)

R. (Isaiah 35:4f) Our God will come to save us!
I will hear what God proclaims; **/** the LORD—for he proclaims peace to his people. **/** Near indeed is his salvation to those who fear him, **/** glory dwelling in our land. **R.**
Kindness and truth shall meet; **/** justice and peace shall kiss. **/** Truth shall spring out of the earth, **/** and justice shall look down from heaven. **R.**
The LORD himself will give his benefits; **/** our land shall yield its increase. **/** Justice shall walk before him, **/** and prepare the way of his steps. **R.**

ALLELUIA
R. Alleluia, alleluia. Behold the king will come, the Lord of the earth, and he himself will lift the yoke of our captivity. **R.**

GOSPEL
Luke 5:17–26

One day as Jesus was teaching, Pharisees and teachers of the law, who had come from every village of Galilee and Judea and Jerusalem, were sitting there, and the power of the Lord was with him for healing. And some men brought on a stretcher a man who was paralyzed; they were trying to bring him in and set him in his presence. But not finding a way to bring him in because of the crowd, they went up on the roof and lowered him on the stretcher through the tiles into the middle in front of Jesus. When Jesus saw their faith, he said, "As for you, your sins are forgiven."

Then the scribes and Pharisees began to ask themselves, "Who is this who speaks blasphemies? Who but God alone can forgive sins?" Jesus knew their thoughts and said to them in reply, "What are you thinking in your hearts? Which is easier, to say, 'Your sins are forgiven,' or to say, 'Rise and walk'? But that you may know that the Son of Man has authority on earth to forgive sins"— he said to the one who was paralyzed, "I say to you, rise, pick up your stretcher, and go home."

He stood up immediately before them, picked up what he had been lying on, and went home, glorifying God. Then astonishment seized them all and they glorified God, and, struck with awe, they said, "We have seen incredible things today."

DECEMBER 8, SOLEMNITY OF THE IMMACULATE CONCEPTION OF THE BLESSED VIRGIN MARY

FIRST READING
Genesis 3:9—15, 20

After the man, Adam, had eaten of the tree, the LORD God called to the man and asked him, "Where are you?" He answered, "I heard you in the garden; but I was afraid, because I was naked, so I hid myself." Then he asked, "Who told you that you were naked? You have eaten, then, from the tree of which I had forbidden you to eat!" The man replied, "The woman whom you put here with me— she gave me fruit from the tree, and so I ate it." The LORD God then asked the woman, "Why did you do such a thing?" The woman answered, "The serpent tricked me into it, so I ate it."

Then the LORD God said to the serpent: "Because you have done this, you shall be banned from all the animals and from all the wild creatures; on your belly shall you crawl, and dirt shall you eat all the days of your life. I will put enmity between you and the woman, and between your offspring and hers; he will strike at your head, while you strike at his heel."

The man called his wife Eve, because she became the mother of all the living.

RESPONSORIAL PSALM *Psalm 98:1, 2—3ab, 3cd—4 (1a)*
R. Sing to the Lord a new song, for he has done marvelous deeds.
Sing to the LORD a new song, / for he has done wondrous deeds; / his right hand has won victory for him, his holy arm. **R.**
The LORD has made his salvation known: / in the sight of the nations he has revealed his justice. / He has remembered his kindness / and his faithfulness toward the house of Israel. **R.**
All the ends of the earth have seen the salvation by our God. / Sing joyfully to the LORD, all you lands; / break into song; sing praise. **R.**

SECOND READING *Ephesians 1:3—6, 11—12*
Brothers and sisters: Blessed be the God and Father of our Lord Jesus Christ, who has blessed us in Christ with every spiritual blessing in the heavens, as he chose us in him, before the foundation of the world, to be holy and without blemish before him. In love he destined us for adoption to himself through Jesus Christ, in accord with the favor of his will, for the praise of the glory of his grace that he granted us in the beloved.

In him we were also chosen, destined in accord with the purpose of the One who accomplishes all things according to the intention of his will, so that we might exist for the praise of his glory, we who first hoped in Christ.

ALLELUIA *see Luke 1:28*
R. Alleluia, alleluia. Hail, Mary, full of grace, the Lord is with you; blessed are you among women. **R.**

GOSPEL *Luke 1:26—38*
The angel Gabriel was sent from God to a town of Galilee called Nazareth, to a virgin betrothed to a man named Joseph, of the house of David, and the virgin's name was Mary. And coming to her, he said, "Hail, full of grace! The Lord is with you." But she was greatly troubled at what was said and pondered what sort of greeting this might be. Then the angel said to her, "Do not be afraid, Mary, for you have found favor with God. Behold, you will conceive in your womb and bear a son, and you shall name him Jesus. He will be great and will be called Son of the Most High, and the Lord God will give him the throne of David his father, and he will rule over the house of Jacob forever, and of his Kingdom there will be no

end." But Mary said to the angel, "How can this be, since I have no relations with a man?" And the angel said to her in reply, "The Holy Spirit will come upon you, and the power of the Most High will overshadow you. Therefore the child to be born will be called holy, the Son of God. And behold, Elizabeth, your relative, has also conceived a son in her old age, and this is the sixth month for her who was called barren; for nothing will be impossible for God." Mary said, "Behold, I am the handmaid of the Lord. May it be done to me according to your word." Then the angel departed from her.

DECEMBER 9, 2ND WEEK OF ADVENT - WEDNESDAY; ST. JUAN DIEGO

FIRST READING   *Isaiah 40:25–31*

To whom can you liken me as an equal? says the Holy One. Lift up your eyes on high and see who has created these things: He leads out their army and numbers them, calling them all by name. By his great might and the strength of his power not one of them is missing! Why, O Jacob, do you say, and declare, O Israel, "My way is hidden from the LORD, and my right is disregarded by my God"?

Do you not know or have you not heard? The LORD is the eternal God, creator of the ends of the earth. He does not faint nor grow weary, and his knowledge is beyond scrutiny. He gives strength to the fainting; for the weak he makes vigor abound. Though young men faint and grow weary, and youths stagger and fall, they that hope in the LORD will renew their strength, they will soar as with eagles' wings; they will run and not grow weary, walk and not grow faint.

RESPONSORIAL PSALM   *Psalm 103:1–2, 3–4, 8 and 10*

R. (1) O bless the Lord, my soul!

Bless the LORD, O my soul; / and all my being, bless his holy name. / Bless the LORD, O my soul, / and forget not all his benefits. **R.**

He pardons all your iniquities, / he heals all your ills. He redeems your life from destruction, / he crowns you with kindness and compassion. **R.**

Merciful and gracious is the LORD, / slow to anger and abounding in kindness. / Not according to our sins does he deal with us, / nor does he requite us according to our crimes. **R.**

ALLELUIA

R. Alleluia, alleluia. Behold, the Lord comes to save his people; blessed are those prepared to meet him. **R.**

GOSPEL   *Matthew 11:28–30*

Jesus said to the crowds: "Come to me, all you who labor and are burdened, and I will give you rest. Take my yoke upon you and learn from me, for I am meek and humble of heart; and you will find rest for yourselves. For my yoke is easy, and my burden light."

DECEMBER 10, 2ND WEEK OF ADVENT – THURSDAY; ST. JOHN ROBERTS

FIRST READING   *Isaiah 41:13–20*

I am the LORD, your God, who grasp your right hand; It is I who say to you, "Fear not, I will help you." Fear not, O worm Jacob, O maggot Israel; I will help you, says the LORD; your redeemer is the Holy One of Israel. I will make of you a threshing sledge, sharp, new, and double–edged, To thresh the mountains and crush them, to make the hills like chaff. When you winnow them, the wind shall carry them off and the storm shall scatter them. But you shall rejoice in the LORD, and glory in the Holy One of Israel.

The afflicted and the needy seek water in vain, their tongues are parched with thirst. I, the LORD, will answer them; I, the God of Israel, will not forsake them. I will open up rivers on the bare heights, and fountains in the broad valleys; I will turn the desert into a marshland, and the dry ground into springs of water. I will plant in the desert the cedar, acacia, myrtle, and olive; I will set in the wasteland the cypress, together with the plane tree and the pine, that all may see and know, observe and understand, that the hand of the LORD has done this, the Holy One of Israel has created it.

RESPONSORIAL PSALM   *Psalm 145:1 and 9, 10–11, 12–13ab*

R. (8) **The Lord is gracious and merciful; slow to anger, and of great kindness.**

I will extol you, O my God and King, / and I will bless your name forever and ever. / The LORD is good to all and compassionate toward all his works. **R.**

Let all your works give you thanks, O LORD, / and let your faithful ones bless you. / Let them discourse of the glory of your Kingdom / and speak of your might. **R.**

Let them make known to men your might / and the glorious splendor of your Kingdom. Your Kingdom is a Kingdom for all ages, / and your dominion endures through all generations. **R.**

ALLELUIA   *See Isaiah 45:8*

R. **Alleluia, alleluia.** Let the clouds rain down the Just One, and the earth bring forth a Savior. **R.**

GOSPEL   *Matthew 11:11–15*

Jesus said to the crowds: "Amen, I say to you, among those born of women there has been none greater than John the Baptist; yet the least in the Kingdom of heaven is greater than he. From the days of John the Baptist until now, the Kingdom of heaven suffers violence, and the violent are taking it by force. All the prophets and the law prophesied up to the time of John. And if you are willing to accept it, he is Elijah, the one who is to come. Whoever has ears ought to hear."

DECEMBER 11, 2ND WEEK OF ADVENT - FRIDAY; ST. DAMASUS I

FIRST READING   *Isaiah 48:17–19*

Thus says the LORD, your redeemer, the Holy One of Israel: I, the LORD, your God, teach you what is for your good, and lead you on the way you should go. If you would hearken to my commandments, your prosperity would be like a river, and your vindication like the waves of the sea; Your descendants would be like the sand, and those born of your stock like its grains, Their name never cut off or blotted out from my presence.

RESPONSORIAL PSALM *Psalm 1:1–2, 3, 4 and 6*
R. (see John 8:12) Those who follow you, Lord, will have the light of life.
Blessed the man who follows not the counsel of the wicked, / nor walks in the way of sinners, / nor sits in the company of the insolent. / But delights in the law of the LORD and meditates on his law day and night. **R.**
He is like a tree planted near running water, / that yields its fruit in due season, / and whose leaves never fade. / Whatever he does, prospers. **R.**
Not so the wicked, not so; / they are like chaff which the wind drives away. / For the LORD watches over the way of the just, / but the way of the wicked vanishes. **R.**

ALLELUIA
R. Alleluia, alleluia. The Lord will come; go out to meet him! He is the prince of peace. **R.**

GOSPEL *Matthew 11:16–19*
Jesus said to the crowds: "To what shall I compare this generation? It is like children who sit in marketplaces and call to one another, 'We played the flute for you, but you did not dance, we sang a dirge but you did not mourn.' For John came neither eating nor drinking, and they said, 'He is possessed by a demon.' The Son of Man came eating and drinking and they said, 'Look, he is a glutton and a drunkard, a friend of tax collectors and sinners.' But wisdom is vindicated by her works."

DECEMBER 12, OUR LADY OF GUADALUPE - FEAST

FIRST READING *Zechariah 2:14–17*
Sing and rejoice, O daughter Zion! See, I am coming to dwell among you, says the LORD. Many nations shall join themselves to the LORD on that day, and they shall be his people, and he will dwell among you, and you shall know that the LORD of hosts has sent me to you. The LORD will possess Judah as his portion in the holy land, and he will again choose Jerusalem. Silence, all mankind, in the presence of the LORD! For he stirs forth from his holy dwelling.

ALTERNATIVE FIRST READING *Revelation 11:19a; 12:1–6a, 10ab*
God's temple in heaven was opened, and the ark of his covenant could be seen in the temple.
A great sign appeared in the sky, a woman clothed with the sun, with the moon under her feet, and on her head a crown of twelve stars. She was with child and wailed aloud in pain as she labored to give birth. Then another sign appeared in the sky; it was a huge red dragon, with seven heads and ten horns, and on its heads were seven diadems. Its tail swept away a third of the stars in the sky and hurled them down to the earth. Then the dragon stood before the woman about to give birth, to devour her child when she gave birth. She gave birth to a son, a male child, destined to rule all the nations with an iron rod.

Her child was caught up to God and his throne. The woman herself fled into the desert where she had a place prepared by God.

Then I heard a loud voice in heaven say: "Now have salvation and power come, and the Kingdom of our God and the authority of his Anointed."

RESPONSORIAL PSALM   *Judith 13:18bcde, 19*
R. You are the highest honor of our race.
Blessed are you, daughter, by the Most High God, **/** above all the women on earth; **/** and blessed be the LORD God, **/** the creator of heaven and earth. **R.**
Your deed of hope will never be forgotten **/** by those who tell of the might of God. **R.**

ALLELUIA
R. Alleluia, alleluia. Blessed are you, holy Virgin Mary, deserving of all praise; from you rose the sun of justice, Christ our God. **R.**

GOSPEL   *Luke 1:26–38*
The angel Gabriel was sent from God to a town of Galilee called Nazareth, to a virgin betrothed to a man named Joseph, of the house of David, and the virgin's name was Mary. And coming to her, he said, "Hail, full of grace! The Lord is with you." But she was greatly troubled at what was said and pondered what sort of greeting this might be. Then the angel said to her, "Do not be afraid, Mary, for you have found favor with God. Behold, you will conceive in your womb and bear a son, and you shall name him Jesus. He will be great and will be called Son of the Most High, and the Lord God will give him the throne of David his father, and he will rule over the house of Jacob forever, and of his Kingdom there will be no end." But Mary said to the angel, "How can this be, since I have no relations with a man?" And the angel said to her in reply, "The Holy Spirit will come upon you, and the power of the Most High will overshadow you. Therefore the child to be born will be called holy, the Son of God. And behold, Elizabeth, your relative, has also conceived a son in her old age, and this is the sixth month for her who was called barren; for nothing will be impossible for God." Mary said, "Behold, I am the handmaid of the Lord. May it be done to me according to your word." Then the angel departed from her.

ALTERNATIVE GOSPEL   *Luke 1:39–47*
Mary set out and traveled to the hill country in haste to a town of Judah, where she entered the house of Zechariah and greeted Elizabeth. When Elizabeth heard Mary's greeting, the infant leaped in her womb, and Elizabeth, filled with the Holy Spirit, cried out in a loud voice and said, "Most blessed are you among women, and blessed is the fruit of your womb. And how does this happen to me, that the mother of my Lord should come to me? For at the moment the sound of your greeting reached my ears, the infant in my womb leaped for joy. Blessed are you who believed that what was spoken to you by the Lord would be fulfilled."

And Mary said: "My soul proclaims the greatness of the Lord; my spirit rejoices in God my savior."

DECEMBER 13, 3RD SUNDAY OF ADVENT; ST. LUCY

FIRST READING *Isaiah 61:1—2a, 10—11*

The spirit of the Lord GOD is upon me, because the LORD has anointed me; he has sent me to bring glad tidings to the poor, to heal the brokenhearted, to proclaim liberty to the captives and release to the prisoners, to announce a year of favor from the LORD and a day of vindication by our God.

I rejoice heartily in the LORD, in my God is the joy of my soul; for he has clothed me with a robe of salvation and wrapped me in a mantle of justice, like a bridegroom adorned with a diadem, like a bride bedecked with her jewels. As the earth brings forth its plants, and a garden makes its growth spring up, so will the Lord GOD make justice and praise spring up before all the nations.

RESPONSORIAL PSALM *Luke 1:46—48, 49—50, 53—54 (Isaiah 61:10b)*

R. My soul rejoices in my God.

My soul proclaims the greatness of the Lord; my spirit rejoices in God my Savior, for he has looked upon his lowly servant. From this day all generations will call me blessed. **R.**

The Almighty has done great things for me, and holy is his Name. He has mercy on those who fear him in every generation. **R.**

He has filled the hungry with good things, and the rich he has sent away empty. He has come to the help of his servant Israel for he has remembered his promise of mercy. **R.**

SECOND READING *1 Thessalonians 5:16—24*

Brothers and sisters: Rejoice always. Pray without ceasing. In all circumstances give thanks, for this is the will of God for you in Christ Jesus. Do not quench the Spirit. Do not despise prophetic utterances. Test everything; retain what is good. Refrain from every kind of evil.

May the God of peace make you perfectly holy and may you entirely, spirit, soul, and body, be preserved blameless for the coming of our Lord Jesus Christ. The one who calls you is faithful, and he will also accomplish it.

ALLELUIA *Isaiah 61:1 (cited in Luke 4:18)*

R. Alleluia, alleluia. The Spirit of the Lord is upon me, because he has anointed me to bring glad tidings to the poor. **R.**

GOSPEL *John 1:6—8, 19—28*

A man named John was sent from God. He came for testimony, to testify to the light, so that all might believe through him. He was not the light, but came to testify to the light.

And this is the testimony of John. When the Jews from Jerusalem sent priests and Levites to him to ask him, "Who are you?" he admitted and did not deny it, but admitted, "I am not the Christ." So they asked him, "What are you then? Are you Elijah?" And he said, "I am not." "Are you the Prophet?" He answered, "No." So they said to him, "Who are you, so we can give an answer to those who sent us? What do you have to say for yourself?" He said:

"I am the voice of one crying out in the desert, 'Make straight the way of the Lord,' as Isaiah the prophet said."

Some Pharisees were also sent. They asked him, "Why then do you baptize if you are not the Christ or Elijah or the Prophet?" John answered them, "I baptize with water; but there is one among you whom you do not recognize, the one who is coming after me, whose sandal strap I am not worthy to untie." This happened in Bethany across the Jordan, where John was baptizing.

DECEMBER 14, 3RD WEEK OF ADVENT - MONDAY; ST. JOHN OF THE CROSS

FIRST READING *Numbers 24:2–7, 15–17a*

When Balaam raised his eyes and saw Israel encamped, tribe by tribe, the spirit of God came upon him, and he gave voice to his oracle:

The utterance of Balaam, son of Beor, the utterance of a man whose eye is true, The utterance of one who hears what God says, and knows what the Most High knows, Of one who sees what the Almighty sees, enraptured, and with eyes unveiled: How goodly are your tents, O Jacob; your encampments, O Israel! They are like gardens beside a stream, like the cedars planted by the LORD. His wells shall yield free–flowing waters, he shall have the sea within reach; His king shall rise higher, and his royalty shall be exalted.

Then Balaam gave voice to his oracle: the utterance of Balaam, son of Beor, the utterance of the man whose eye is true, the utterance of one who hears what God says, and knows what the Most High knows, of one who sees what the Almighty sees, enraptured, and with eyes unveiled. I see him, though not now; I behold him, though not near: A star shall advance from Jacob, and a staff shall rise from Israel.

RESPONSORIAL PSALM *Psalm 25:4–5ab, 6 and 7bc, 8–9*

R. (4) **Teach me your ways, O Lord.**

Your ways, O LORD, make known to me; / teach me your paths, / Guide me in your truth and teach me, / for you are God my savior. **R.**

Remember that your compassion, O LORD, / and your kindness are from of old. / In your kindness remember me, / because of your goodness, O LORD. **R.**

Good and upright is the LORD; / thus he shows sinners the way. / He guides the humble to justice, / he teaches the humble his way. **R.**

ALLELUIA *Psalm 85:8*

R. **Alleluia, alleluia.** Show us, LORD, your love, and grant us your salvation. **R.**

GOSPEL *Matthew 21:23–27*

When Jesus had come into the temple area, the chief priests and the elders of the people approached him as he was teaching and said, "By what authority are you doing these things? And who gave you this authority?" Jesus said to them in reply, "I shall ask you one question, and if you answer it for me, then I shall tell you by what authority I do these things. Where was John's baptism from? Was it of heavenly or of human origin?" They discussed this among themselves and said, "If we say 'Of heavenly origin,' he will say to us,

'Then why did you not believe him?' But if we say, 'Of human origin,' we fear the crowd, for they all regard John as a prophet." So they said to Jesus in reply, "We do not know." He himself said to them, "Neither shall I tell you by what authority I do these things."

DECEMBER 15, 3RD WEEK OF ADVENT - TUESDAY; ST. MARY DI ROSA

FIRST READING   *Zephaniah 3:1–2, 9–13*

Thus says the LORD: woe to the city, rebellious and polluted, to the tyrannical city! She hears no voice, accepts no correction; In the LORD she has not trusted, to her God she has not drawn near.

For then I will change and purify the lips of the peoples, That they all may call upon the name of the LORD, to serve him with one accord; From beyond the rivers of Ethiopia and as far as the recesses of the North, they shall bring me offerings.

On that day You need not be ashamed of all your deeds, your rebellious actions against me; For then will I remove from your midst the proud braggarts, And you shall no longer exalt yourself on my holy mountain. But I will leave as a remnant in your midst a people humble and lowly, Who shall take refuge in the name of the LORD: the remnant of Israel. They shall do no wrong and speak no lies; nor shall there be found in their mouths a deceitful tongue; They shall pasture and couch their flocks with none to disturb them.

RESPONSORIAL PSALM   *Psalm 34:2–3, 6–7, 17–18, 19 and 23*

R. (7a) The Lord hears the cry of the poor.

I will bless the LORD at all times; his praise shall be ever in my mouth. Let my soul glory in the LORD; the lowly will hear me and be glad. **R.**

Look to him that you may be radiant with joy, and your faces may not blush with shame. When the poor one called out, the LORD heard, and from all his distress he saved him. **R.**

The LORD confronts the evildoers, to destroy remembrance of them from the earth. When the just cry out, the LORD hears them, and from all their distress he rescues them. **R.**

The LORD is close to the brokenhearted; and those who are crushed in spirit he saves. The LORD redeems the lives of his servants; no one incurs guilt who takes refuge in him. **R.**

R. Alleluia, alleluia. Come, O Lord, do not delay; forgive the sins of your people. **R.**

GOSPEL   *Matthew 21:28–32*

Jesus said to the chief priests and the elders of the people: "What is your opinion? A man had two sons. He came to the first and said, 'Son, go out and work in the vineyard today.' The son said in reply, 'I will not,' but afterwards he changed his mind and went. The man came to the other son and gave the same order. He said in reply, 'Yes, sir,' but did not go. Which of the two did his father's will?" They answered, "The first." Jesus said to them, "Amen, I say to you, tax collectors and prostitutes are entering the Kingdom of God before you. When John came to you in the way of righteousness, you did not believe him; but tax collectors and prostitutes did. Yet even when you saw that, you did not later change your minds and believe him."

DECEMBER 16, 3RD WEEK OF ADVENT - WEDNESDAY; ST. ADELAIDE

FIRST READING   *Isaiah 45:6c–8, 18, 21c–25*

I am the LORD, there is no other; I form the light, and create the darkness, I make well–being and create woe; I, the LORD, do all these things. Let justice descend, O heavens, like dew from above, like gentle rain let the skies drop it down. Let the earth open and salvation bud forth; let justice also spring up! I, the LORD, have created this.

For thus says the LORD, The creator of the heavens, who is God, The designer and maker of the earth who established it, Not creating it to be a waste, but designing it be lived in: I am the LORD, and there is no other.

Who announced this from the beginning and foretold it from of old? Was it not I, the LORD, besides whom there is no other God? There is no just and saving God but me.

Turn to me and be safe, all you ends of the earth, for I am God; there is no other! By myself I swear, uttering my just decree and my unalterable word: To me every knee shall bend; by me every tongue shall swear, saying, "Only in the LORD are just deeds and power. Before him in shame shall come all who vent their anger against him. In the LORD shall be the vindication and the glory of all the descendants of Israel."

RESPONSORIAL PSALM   *Psalm 85:9ab and 10, 11–12, 13–14*

R. (Isaiah 45:8) Let the clouds rain down the Just One, and the earth bring forth a Savior.
I will hear what God proclaims; the LORD—**/** for he proclaims peace to his people. **/** Near indeed is his salvation to those who fear him, **/** glory dwelling in our land. **R.**
Kindness and truth shall meet; **/** justice and peace shall kiss. **/** Truth shall spring out of the earth, **/** and justice shall look down from heaven. **R.**
The LORD himself will give his benefits; **/** our land shall yield its increase. **/** Justice shall walk before him, **/** and salvation, along the way of his steps. **R.**

ALLELUIA   *See Isaiah 40:9–10*

R. Alleluia, alleluia. Raise your voice and tell the Good News: Behold, the Lord GOD comes with power. **R.**

GOSPEL   *Luke 7:18b–23*

At that time, John summoned two of his disciples and sent them to the Lord to ask, "Are you the one who is to come, or should we look for another?" When the men came to the Lord, they said, "John the Baptist has sent us to you to ask, 'Are you the one who is to come, or should we look for another?'" At that time Jesus cured many of their diseases, sufferings, and evil spirits; he also granted sight to many who were blind. And Jesus said to them in reply, "Go and tell John what you have seen and heard: the blind regain their sight, the lame walk, lepers are cleansed, the deaf hear, the dead are raised, the poor have the good news proclaimed to them. And blessed is the one who takes no offense at me."

DECEMBER 17; ST. OLYMPIAS

FIRST READING   *Genesis 49:2, 8–10*

Jacob called his sons and said to them: "Assemble and listen, sons of Jacob, listen to Israel, your father.

"You, Judah, shall your brothers praise —your hand on the neck of your enemies; the sons of your father shall bow down to you. Judah, like a lion's whelp, you have grown up on prey, my son. He crouches like a lion recumbent, the king of beasts—who would dare rouse him? The scepter shall never depart from Judah, or the mace from between his legs, While tribute is brought to him, and he receives the people's homage."

RESPONSORIAL PSALM   *Psalm 72:1–2, 3–4ab, 7–8, 17*

R. (see 7) Justice shall flourish in his time, and fullness of peace for ever.

O God, with your judgment endow the king, / and with your justice, the king's son; / He shall govern your people with justice/ and your afflicted ones with judgment. **R.**

The mountains shall yield peace for the people, / and the hills justice. / He shall defend the afflicted among the people, / save the children of the poor. **R.**

Justice shall flower in his days, / and profound peace, till the moon be no more. / May he rule from sea to sea, / and from the River to the ends of the earth. **R.**

May his name be blessed forever; / as long as the sun his name shall remain. / In him shall all the tribes of the earth be blessed; / all the nations shall proclaim his happiness. **R.**

R. Alleluia, alleluia. O Wisdom of our God Most High, guiding creation with power and love: come to teach us the path of knowledge! **R.**

GOSPEL   *Matthew 1:1–17*

The book of the genealogy of Jesus Christ, the son of David, the son of Abraham.

Abraham became the father of Isaac, Isaac the father of Jacob, Jacob the father of Judah and his brothers. Judah became the father of Perez and Zerah, whose mother was Tamar. Perez became the father of Hezron, Hezron the father of Ram, Ram the father of Amminadab. Amminadab became the father of Nahshon, Nahshon the father of Salmon, Salmon the father of Boaz, whose mother was Rahab. Boaz became the father of Obed, whose mother was Ruth. Obed became the father of Jesse, Jesse the father of David the king.

David became the father of Solomon, whose mother had been the wife of Uriah. Solomon became the father of Rehoboam, Rehoboam the father of Abijah, Abijah the father of Asaph. Asaph became the father of Jehoshaphat, Jehoshaphat the father of Joram, Joram the father of Uzziah. Uzziah became the father of Jotham, Jotham the father of Ahaz, Ahaz the father of Hezekiah. Hezekiah became the father of Manasseh, Manasseh the father of Amos, Amos the father of Josiah. Josiah became the father of Jechoniah and his brothers at the time of the Babylonian exile.

After the Babylonian exile, Jechoniah became the father of Shealtiel, Shealtiel the father of Zerubbabel, Zerubbabel the father of Abiud. Abiud became the father of Eliakim, Eliakim the father of Azor, Azor the father of Zadok. Zadok became the father of Achim,

Achim the father of Eliud, Eliud the father of Eleazar. Eleazar became the father of Matthan, Matthan the father of Jacob, Jacob the father of Joseph, the husband of Mary. Of her was born Jesus who is called the Christ.

Thus the total number of generations from Abraham to David is fourteen generations; from David to the Babylonian exile, fourteen generations; from the Babylonian exile to the Christ, fourteen generations.

DECEMBER 18; BLESSED ANNA ROSA GATTORNO

FIRST READING   *Jeremiah 23:5–8*

Behold, the days are coming, says the LORD, when I will raise up a righteous shoot to David; As king he shall reign and govern wisely, he shall do what is just and right in the land. In his days Judah shall be saved, Israel shall dwell in security. This is the name they give him: "The LORD our justice."

Therefore, the days will come, says the LORD, when they shall no longer say, "As the LORD lives, who brought the children of Israel out of the land of Egypt"; but rather, "As the LORD lives, who brought the descendants of the house of Israel up from the land of the north"— and from all the lands to which I banished them; they shall again live on their own land.

RESPONSORIAL PSALM   *Psalm 72:1–2, 12–13, 18–19*

R. (see 7) Justice shall flourish in his time, and fullness of peace for ever.

O God, with your judgment endow the king, / and with your justice, the king's son; / He shall govern your people with justice / and your afflicted ones with judgment. **R.**

For he shall rescue the poor when he cries out, / and the afflicted when he has no one to help him. / He shall have pity for the lowly and the poor; / the lives of the poor he shall save. **R.**

Blessed be the LORD, the God of Israel, / who alone does wondrous deeds. / And blessed forever be his glorious name; / may the whole earth be filled with his glory. **R.**

R. Alleluia, alleluia. O Leader of the House of Israel, giver of the Law to Moses on Sinai: come to rescue us with your mighty power! **R.**

GOSPEL   *Matthew 1:18–25*

This is how the birth of Jesus Christ came about. When his mother Mary was betrothed to Joseph, but before they lived together, she was found with child through the Holy Spirit. Joseph her husband, since he was a righteous man, yet unwilling to expose her to shame, decided to divorce her quietly. Such was his intention when, behold, the angel of the Lord appeared to him in a dream and said, "Joseph, son of David, do not be afraid to take Mary your wife into your home. For it is through the Holy Spirit that this child has been conceived in her. She will bear a son and you are to name him Jesus, because he will save his people from their sins." All this took place to fulfill what the Lord had said through the prophet:

Behold, the virgin shall be with child and bear a son, and they shall name him Emmanuel, which means "God is with us." When Joseph awoke, he did as the angel of the Lord had commanded him and took his wife into his home. He had no relations with her until she bore a son, and he named him Jesus.

DECEMBER 19; BLESSED URBAN V

FIRST READING   *Judges 13:2–7, 24–25a*

There was a certain man from Zorah, of the clan of the Danites, whose name was Manoah. His wife was barren and had borne no children. An angel of the LORD appeared to the woman and said to her, "Though you are barren and have had no children, yet you will conceive and bear a son. Now, then, be careful to take no wine or strong drink and to eat nothing unclean. As for the son you will conceive and bear, no razor shall touch his head, for this boy is to be consecrated to God from the womb. It is he who will begin the deliverance of Israel from the power of the Philistines."

The woman went and told her husband, "A man of God came to me; he had the appearance of an angel of God, terrible indeed. I did not ask him where he came from, nor did he tell me his name. But he said to me, 'You will be with child and will bear a son. So take neither wine nor strong drink, and eat nothing unclean. For the boy shall be consecrated to God from the womb, until the day of his death.'"

The woman bore a son and named him Samson. The boy grew up and the LORD blessed him; the Spirit of the LORD stirred him.

RESPONSORIAL PSALM   *Psalm 71:3–4a, 5–6ab, 16–17*

R. (see 8) My mouth shall be filled with your praise, and I will sing your glory!

Be my rock of refuge, a stronghold to give me safety, / for you are my rock and my fortress. / O my God, rescue me from the hand of the wicked. **R.**

For you are my hope, O LORD; / my trust, O God, from my youth. / On you I depend from birth; / from my mother's womb you are my strength. **R.**

I will treat of the mighty works of the LORD; O God, / I will tell of your singular justice. / O God, you have taught me from my youth, / and till the present I proclaim your wondrous deeds. **R.**

R. Alleluia, alleluia. O Root of Jesse's stem, sign of God's love for all his people: come to save us without delay! **R.**

GOSPEL   *Luke 1:5–25*

In the days of Herod, King of Judea, there was a priest named Zechariah of the priestly division of Abijah; his wife was from the daughters of Aaron, and her name was Elizabeth. Both were righteous in the eyes of God, observing all the commandments and ordinances of the Lord blamelessly. But they had no child, because Elizabeth was barren and both were advanced in years.

Once when he was serving as priest in his division's turn before God, according to the practice of the priestly service, he was chosen by lot to enter the sanctuary of the Lord to burn incense. Then, when the whole assembly of the people was praying outside at the hour of the incense offering, the angel of the Lord appeared to him, standing at the right of the altar of incense. Zechariah was troubled by what he saw, and fear came upon him.

But the angel said to him, "Do not be afraid, Zechariah, because your prayer has been heard. Your wife Elizabeth will bear you a son, and you shall name him John. And you will have joy and gladness, and many will rejoice at his birth, for he will be great in the sight of the Lord. He will drink neither wine nor strong drink. He will be filled with the Holy Spirit even from his mother's womb, and he will turn many of the children of Israel to the Lord their God. He will go before him in the spirit and power of Elijah to turn the hearts of fathers toward children and the disobedient to the understanding of the righteous, to prepare a people fit for the Lord."

Then Zechariah said to the angel, "How shall I know this? For I am an old man, and my wife is advanced in years." And the angel said to him in reply, "I am Gabriel, who stand before God. I was sent to speak to you and to announce to you this good news. But now you will be speechless and unable to talk until the day these things take place, because you did not believe my words, which will be fulfilled at their proper time." Meanwhile the people were waiting for Zechariah and were amazed that he stayed so long in the sanctuary. But when he came out, he was unable to speak to them, and they realized that he had seen a vision in the sanctuary. He was gesturing to them but remained mute.

Then, when his days of ministry were completed, he went home. After this time his wife Elizabeth conceived, and she went into seclusion for five months, saying, "So has the Lord done for me at a time when he has seen fit to take away my disgrace before others."

DECEMBER 20, 4TH SUNDAY OF ADVENT; ST. DOMINIC OF SILOS

FIRST READING   *2 Samuel 7:1—5, 8b—12, 14a, 16*

When King David was settled in his palace, and the LORD had given him rest from his enemies on every side, he said to Nathan the prophet, "Here I am living in a house of cedar, while the ark of God dwells in a tent!" Nathan answered the king, "Go, do whatever you have in mind, for the LORD is with you." But that night the LORD spoke to Nathan and said: "Go, tell my servant David, 'Thus says the LORD: Should you build me a house to dwell in?

"'It was I who took you from the pasture and from the care of the flock to be commander of my people Israel. I have been with you wherever you went, and I have destroyed all your enemies before you. And I will make you famous like the great ones of the earth. I will fix a place for my people Israel; I will plant them so that they may dwell in their place without further disturbance. Neither shall the wicked continue to afflict them as they did of old, since the time I first appointed judges over my people Israel. I will give you rest from all your enemies. The LORD also reveals to you that he will establish a house for you. And when your time comes and you rest with your ancestors, I will raise up your heir after you, sprung from your loins, and I will make his kingdom firm. I will be a father to him, and he shall be a son to me. Your house and your kingdom shall endure forever before me; your throne shall stand firm forever.'"

RESPONSORIAL PSALM *Psalm 89:2—3, 4—5, 27, 29 (2a)*

R. Forever I will sing the goodness of the Lord.

The promises of the LORD I will sing forever; / through all generations my mouth shall proclaim your faithfulness. / For you have said, "My kindness is established forever"; / in heaven you have confirmed your faithfulness. **R.**

"I have made a covenant with my chosen one, / I have sworn to David my servant: / forever will I confirm your posterity / and establish your throne for all generations." **R.**

"He shall say of me, / 'You are my father, my God, the rock, my savior.' Forever I will maintain my kindness toward him, / and my covenant with him stands firm." **R.**

SECOND READING *Romans 16:25—27*

Brothers and sisters: To him who can strengthen you, according to my gospel and the proclamation of Jesus Christ, according to the revelation of the mystery kept secret for long ages but now manifested through the prophetic writings and, according to the command of the eternal God, made known to all nations to bring about the obedience of faith, to the only wise God, through Jesus Christ be glory forever and ever. Amen.

ALLELUIA *Luke 1:38*

R. Alleluia, alleluia. Behold, I am the handmaid of the Lord. May it be done to me according to your word. **R.**

GOSPEL *Luke 1:26—38*

The angel Gabriel was sent from God to a town of Galilee called Nazareth, to a virgin betrothed to a man named Joseph, of the house of David, and the virgin's name was Mary. And coming to her, he said, "Hail, full of grace! The Lord is with you." But she was greatly troubled at what was said and pondered what sort of greeting this might be. Then the angel said to her, "Do not be afraid, Mary, for you have found favor with God."

"Behold, you will conceive in your womb and bear a son, and you shall name him Jesus. He will be great and will be called Son of the Most High, and the Lord God will give him the throne of David his father, and he will rule over the house of Jacob forever, and of his kingdom there will be no end." But Mary said to the angel, "How can this be, since I have no relations with a man?" And the angel said to her in reply, "The Holy Spirit will come upon you, and the power of the Most High will overshadow you. Therefore the child to be born will be called holy, the Son of God. And behold, Elizabeth, your relative, has also conceived a son in her old age, and this is the sixth month for her who was called barren; for nothing will be impossible for God." Mary said, "Behold, I am the handmaid of the Lord. May it be done to me according to your word." Then the angel departed from her.

DECEMBER 21; ST. PETER CANISIUS

FIRST READING *Song of Songs 2:8—14*

Hark! my lover—here he comes springing across the mountains, leaping across the hills. My lover is like a gazelle or a young stag. Here he stands behind our wall, gazing through the windows, peering through the lattices. My lover speaks; he says to me, "Arise, my beloved, my dove, my beautiful one, and come!" For see, the winter is past, the rains are over and gone. The flowers appear on the earth, the time of pruning the vines has come, and the song of the dove is heard in our land. The fig tree puts forth its figs, and the vines, in bloom, give forth fragrance. Arise, my beloved, my beautiful one, and come!

"O my dove in the clefts of the rock, in the secret recesses of the cliff, Let me see you, let me hear your voice, For your voice is sweet, and you are lovely."

ALTERNATIVE FIRST READING   *Zephaniah 3:14–18a*

Shout for joy, O daughter Zion! Sing joyfully, O Israel! Be glad and exult with all your heart, O daughter Jerusalem! The LORD has removed the judgment against you, he has turned away your enemies; The King of Israel, the LORD, is in your midst, you have no further misfortune to fear. On that day, it shall be said to Jerusalem: Fear not, O Zion, be not discouraged! The LORD, your God, is in your midst, a mighty savior; He will rejoice over you with gladness, and renew you in his love, He will sing joyfully because of you, as one sings at festivals.

RESPONSORIAL PSALM   *Psalm 33:2–3, 11–12, 20–21*

R. (1a; 3a) Exult, you just, in the Lord! Sing to him a new song.

Give thanks to the LORD on the harp; / with the ten–stringed lyre chant his praises. / Sing to him a new song; / pluck the strings skillfully, with shouts of gladness. **R.**

But the plan of the LORD stands forever; / the design of his heart, through all generations. / Blessed the nation whose God is the LORD, / the people he has chosen for his own inheritance. **R.**

Our soul waits for the LORD, who is our help and our shield, / for in him our hearts rejoice; / in his holy name we trust. **R.**

R. Alleluia, alleluia. O Emmanuel, our King and Giver of Law: come to save us, Lord our God! **R.**

GOSPEL   *Luke 1:39–45*

Mary set out in those days and traveled to the hill country in haste to a town of Judah, where she entered the house of Zechariah and greeted Elizabeth. When Elizabeth heard Mary's greeting, the infant leaped in her womb, and Elizabeth, filled with the Holy Spirit, cried out in a loud voice and said, "Most blessed are you among women, and blessed is the fruit of your womb. And how does this happen to me, that the mother of my Lord should come to me? For at the moment the sound of your greeting reached my ears, the infant in my womb leaped for joy. Blessed are you who believed that what was spoken to you by the Lord would be fulfilled."

DECEMBER 22; ST. MARGUERITE D'YOUVILLE
FIRST READING   *1 Samuel 1:24–28*

In those days, Hannah brought Samuel with her, along with a three–year–old bull, an ephah of flour, and a skin of wine, and presented him at the temple of the LORD in Shiloh. After the boy's father had sacrificed the young bull, Hannah, his mother, approached Eli and said: "Pardon, my lord! As you live, my lord, I am the woman who stood near you here, praying to the LORD. I prayed for this child, and the LORD granted my request. Now I, in turn, give him to the LORD; as long as he lives, he shall be dedicated to the LORD." She left Samuel there.

RESPONSORIAL PSALM   *1 Samuel 2:1, 4–5, 6–7, 8abcd*
R. (see 1a) My heart exults in the Lord, my Savior.
"My heart exults in the LORD, / my horn is exalted in my God. I have swallowed up my enemies; / I rejoice in my victory." **R.**
"The bows of the mighty are broken, / while the tottering gird on strength. / The well–fed hire themselves out for bread, / while the hungry batten on spoil. / The barren wife bears seven sons, / while the mother of many languishes." **R.**
"The LORD puts to death and gives life; / he casts down to the nether world; / he raises up again. / The LORD makes poor and makes rich, / he humbles, he also exalts." **R.**
"He raises the needy from the dust; / from the dung heap he lifts up the poor, / to seat them with nobles / and make a glorious throne their heritage." **R.**
R. Alleluia, alleluia. O King of all nations and keystone of the Church: come and save man, whom you formed from the dust! **R.**

GOSPEL   *Luke 1:46–56*
Mary said: "My soul proclaims the greatness of the Lord; my spirit rejoices in God my savior. For he has looked upon his lowly servant. From this day all generations will call me blessed: the Almighty has done great things for me, and holy is his Name. He has mercy on those who fear him in every generation. He has shown the strength of his arm, and has scattered the proud in their conceit. He has cast down the mighty from their thrones and has lifted up the lowly. He has filled the hungry with good things, and the rich he has sent away empty. He has come to the help of his servant Israel for he remembered his promise of mercy, the promise he made to our fathers, to Abraham and his children for ever."
     Mary remained with Elizabeth about three months and then returned to her home.

DECEMBER 23; ST. JOHN OF KANTY

FIRST READING   *Malachi 3:1–4, 23–24*
Thus says the Lord GOD: Lo, I am sending my messenger to prepare the way before me; And suddenly there will come to the temple the LORD whom you seek, And the messenger of the covenant whom you desire. Yes, he is coming, says the LORD of hosts. But who will endure the day of his coming? And who can stand when he appears? For he is like the refiner's fire, or like the fuller's lye. He will sit refining and purifying silver, and he will purify the sons of Levi, Refining them like gold or like silver that they may offer due sacrifice to the LORD. Then the sacrifice of Judah and Jerusalem will please the LORD, as in the days of old, as in years gone by.

Lo, I will send you Elijah, the prophet, before the day of the LORD comes, the great and terrible day, To turn the hearts of the fathers to their children, and the hearts of the children to their fathers, Lest I come and strike the land with doom.

RESPONSORIAL PSALM *Psalm 25:4–5ab, 8–9, 10 and 14*
R. (see Luke 21:28) Lift up your heads and see; your redemption is near at hand.
Your ways, O LORD, make known to me; / teach me your paths, / Guide me in your truth and teach me, / for you are God my savior. **R.**
Good and upright is the LORD; / thus he shows sinners the way. / He guides the humble to justice, / he teaches the humble his way. **R.**
All the paths of the LORD are kindness / and constancy toward those who keep his covenant and his decrees. / The friendship of the LORD is with those who fear him, / and his covenant, for their instruction. **R.**
R. Alleluia, alleluia. O King of all nations and keystone of the Church: come and save man, whom you formed from the dust! **R.**

GOSPEL *Luke 1:57–66*
When the time arrived for Elizabeth to have her child she gave birth to a son. Her neighbors and relatives heard that the Lord had shown his great mercy toward her, and they rejoiced with her. When they came on the eighth day to circumcise the child, they were going to call him Zechariah after his father, but his mother said in reply, "No. He will be called John." But they answered her, "There is no one among your relatives who has this name." So they made signs, asking his father what he wished him to be called. He asked for a tablet and wrote, "John is his name," and all were amazed. Immediately his mouth was opened, his tongue freed, and he spoke blessing God. Then fear came upon all their neighbors, and all these matters were discussed throughout the hill country of Judea. All who heard these things took them to heart, saying, "What, then, will this child be? For surely the hand of the Lord was with him."

DECEMBER 24

FIRST READING *2 Samuel 7:1–5, 8b–12, 14a, 16*
When King David was settled in his palace, and the LORD had given him rest from his enemies on every side, he said to Nathan the prophet, "Here I am living in a house of cedar, while the ark of God dwells in a tent!" Nathan answered the king, "Go, do whatever you have in mind, for the LORD is with you." But that night the LORD spoke to Nathan and said: "Go, tell my servant David, 'thus says the LORD: Should you build me a house to dwell in?

"'It was I who took you from the pasture and from the care of the flock to be commander of my people Israel. I have been with you wherever you went, and I have destroyed all your enemies before you. And I will make you famous like the great ones of the earth. I will fix a place for my people Israel; I will plant them so that they may dwell in their place without further disturbance. Neither shall the wicked continue to afflict them as they did of old, since the time I first appointed judges over my people Israel. I will give you rest from all your enemies. The LORD also reveals to you that he will establish a house for you. And when your time comes and you rest with your ancestors, I will raise up your heir after you, sprung from your loins, and I will make his Kingdom firm. I will be a father to him, and he shall be a son to me. Your house and your Kingdom shall endure forever before me; your throne shall stand firm forever.'"

RESPONSORIAL PSALM
Psalm 89:2–3, 4–5, 27 and 29

R. (2) For ever I will sing the goodness of the Lord.
The favors of the LORD I will sing forever; **/** through all generations my mouth shall proclaim your faithfulness. **/** For you have said, "My kindness is established forever"; **/** in heaven you have confirmed your faithfulness. **R.**
"I have made a covenant with my chosen one, **/** I have sworn to David my servant: **/** Forever will I confirm your posterity **/** and establish your throne for all generations." **R.**
"He shall say of me, **/** 'You are my father, my God, the rock, my savior.' **/** Forever I will maintain my kindness toward him, **/** and my covenant with him stands firm." **R.**
R. Alleluia, alleluia. O Radiant Dawn, splendor of eternal light, sun of justice: come and shine on those who dwell in darkness and in the shadow of death. **R.**

GOSPEL
Luke 1:67–79

Zechariah his father, filled with the Holy Spirit, prophesied, saying: "Blessed be the Lord, the God of Israel; for he has come to his people and set them free. He has raised up for us a mighty Savior, born of the house of his servant David. Through his prophets he promised of old that he would save us from our enemies, from the hands of all who hate us. He promised to show mercy to our fathers and to remember his holy covenant. This was the oath he swore to our father Abraham: to set us free from the hand of our enemies, free to worship him without fear, holy and righteous in his sight all the days of our life. You, my child, shall be called the prophet of the Most High, for you will go before the Lord to prepare his way, to give his people knowledge of salvation by the forgiveness of their sins. In the tender compassion of our God the dawn from on high shall break upon us, to shine on those who dwell in darkness and the shadow of death, and to guide our feet into the way of peace."

DECEMBER 25
CHRISTMAS DAY – VIGIL MASS

FIRST READING
Isaiah 62:1—5

For Zion's sake I will not be silent, for Jerusalem's sake I will not be quiet, until her vindication shines forth like the dawn and her victory like a burning torch.

Nations shall behold your vindication, and all the kings your glory; you shall be called by a new name pronounced by the mouth of the LORD. You shall be a glorious crown in the hand of the LORD, a royal diadem held by your God. No more shall people call you "Forsaken," or your land "Desolate," but you shall be called "My Delight," and your land "Espoused." For the LORD delights in you and makes your land his spouse. As a young man marries a virgin, your Builder shall marry you; and as a bridegroom rejoices in his bride so shall your God rejoice in you.

RESPONSORIAL PSALM   *Psalm 89:4—5, 16—17, 27, 29 (2a)*
R. Forever I will sing the goodness of the Lord.
I have made a covenant with my chosen one, / I have sworn to David my servant: / forever will I confirm your posterity / and establish your throne for all generations. **R.**
Blessed the people who know the joyful shout; / in the light of your countenance, O LORD, they walk. / At your name they rejoice all the day, / and through your justice they are exalted. **R.**
He shall say of me, / "You are my father, my God, the rock, my savior." / Forever I will maintain my kindness toward him, / and my covenant with him stands firm. **R.**

SECOND READING   *Acts 13:16—17, 22—25*
When Paul reached Antioch in Pisidia and entered the synagogue, he stood up, motioned with his hand, and said, "Fellow Israelites and you others who are God–fearing, listen. The God of this people Israel chose our ancestors and exalted the people during their sojourn in the land of Egypt. With uplifted arm he led them out of it. Then he removed Saul and raised up David as king; of him he testified, 'I have found David, son of Jesse, a man after my own heart; he will carry out my every wish.' From this man's descendants God, according to his promise, has brought to Israel a savior, Jesus. John heralded his coming by proclaiming a baptism of repentance to all the people of Israel; and as John was completing his course, he would say, 'What do you suppose that I am? I am not he. Behold, one is coming after me; I am not worthy to unfasten the sandals of his feet.'"

ALLELUIA   *John 10:27*
R. Alleluia, alleluia. Tomorrow the wickedness of the earth will be destroyed: the Savior of the world will reign over us. **R.**

GOSPEL   *Longer Form Matthew 1:1—25*
The book of the genealogy of Jesus Christ, the son of David, the son of Abraham.

Abraham became the father of Isaac, Isaac the father of Jacob, Jacob the father of Judah and his brothers. Judah became the father of Perez and Zerah, whose mother was Tamar. Perez became the father of Hezron, Hezron the father of Ram, Ram the father of Amminadab. Amminadab became the father of Nahshon, Nahshon the father of Salmon, Salmon the father of Boaz, whose mother was Rahab. Boaz became the father of Obed, whose mother was Ruth. Obed became the father of Jesse, Jesse the father of David the king.

David became the father of Solomon, whose mother had been the wife of Uriah. Solomon became the father of Rehoboam, Rehoboam the father of Abijah, Abijah the father of Asaph. Asaph became the father of Jehoshaphat, Jehoshaphat the father of Joram, Joram the father of Uzziah. Uzziah became the father of Jotham, Jotham the father of Ahaz, Ahaz the father of Hezekiah. Hezekiah became the father of Manasseh, Manasseh the father of Amos, Amos the father of Josiah. Josiah became the father of Jechoniah and his brothers at the time of the Babylonian exile.

After the Babylonian exile, Jechoniah became the father of Shealtiel, Shealtiel the father of Zerubbabel, Zerubbabel the father of Abiud. Abiud became the father of Eliakim, Eliakim the father of Azor, Azor the father of Zadok. Zadok became the father of Achim, Achim the father of Eliud, Eliud the father of Eleazar. Eleazar became the father of Matthan, Matthan the father of Jacob, Jacob the father of Joseph, the husband of Mary. Of her was born Jesus who is called the Christ.

Thus the total number of generations from Abraham to David is fourteen generations; from David to the Babylonian exile, fourteen generations; from the Babylonian exile to the Christ, fourteen generations.

Now this is how the birth of Jesus Christ came about. When his mother Mary was betrothed to Joseph, but before they lived together, she was found with child through the Holy Spirit. Joseph her husband, since he was a righteous man, yet unwilling to expose her to shame, decided to divorce her quietly. Such was his intention when, behold, the angel of the Lord appeared to him in a dream and said, "Joseph, son of David, do not be afraid to take Mary your wife into your home. For it is through the Holy Spirit that this child has been conceived in her. She will bear a son and you are to name him Jesus, because he will save his people from their sins." All this took place to fulfill what the Lord had said through the prophet: *Behold, the virgin shall conceive and bear a son, and they shall name him Emmanuel,* which means "God is with us." When Joseph awoke, he did as the angel of the Lord had commanded him and took his wife into his home. He had no relations with her until she bore a son, and he named him Jesus.

SHORTER FORM   *Matthew 1:18—25*

This is how the birth of Jesus Christ came about. When his mother Mary was betrothed to Joseph, but before they lived together, she was found with child through the Holy Spirit. Joseph her husband, since he was a righteous man, yet unwilling to expose her to shame, decided to divorce her quietly. Such was his intention when, behold, the angel of the Lord appeared to him in a dream and said, "Joseph, son of David, do not be afraid to take Mary your wife into your home. For it is through the Holy Spirit that this child has been conceived in her. She will bear a son and you are to name him Jesus, because he will save his people from their sins." All this took place to fulfill what the Lord had said through the prophet: *Behold, the virgin shall conceive and bear a son, and they shall name him Emmanuel,* which means "God is with us." When Joseph awoke, he did as the angel of the Lord had commanded him and took his wife into his home. He had no relations with her until she bore a son, and he named him Jesus.

CHRISTMAS DAY – MIDNIGHT MASS

FIRST READING   *Isaiah 9:1—6*

The people who walked in darkness have seen a great light; upon those who dwelt in the land of gloom a light has shone. You have brought them abundant joy and great rejoicing, as they rejoice before you as at the harvest, as people make merry when dividing spoils. For the yoke that burdened them, the pole on their shoulder, and the rod of their taskmaster you have smashed, as on the day of Midian. For every boot that tramped in battle, every cloak rolled in blood, will be burned as fuel for flames. For a child is born to us, a son is given us; upon his shoulder dominion rests. They name him Wonder–Counselor, God–Hero, Father–Forever, Prince of Peace. His dominion is vast and forever peaceful, from David's throne, and over his kingdom, which he confirms and sustains by judgment and justice, both now and forever. The zeal of the LORD of hosts will do this!

RESPONSORIAL PSALM   *Psalm 96:1—2, 2—3, 11—12, 13 (Luke 2:11)*

R. Today is born our Savior, Christ the Lord.

Sing to the LORD a new song; / sing to the LORD, all you lands. / Sing to the LORD; bless his name. **R.**

Announce his salvation, day after day. / Tell his glory among the nations; / among all peoples, his wondrous deeds. **R.**

Let the heavens be glad and the earth rejoice; / let the sea and what fills it resound; / let the plains be joyful and all that is in them! / Then shall all the trees of the forest exult. **R.**

They shall exult before the LORD, for he comes; / for he comes to rule the earth. / He shall rule the world with justice / and the peoples with his constancy. **R.**

SECOND READING   *Titus 2:11—14*

Beloved: The grace of God has appeared, saving all and training us to reject godless ways and worldly desires and to live temperately, justly, and devoutly in this age, as we await the blessed hope, the appearance of the glory of our great God and savior Jesus Christ, who gave himself for us to deliver us from all lawlessness and to cleanse for himself a people as his own, eager to do what is good.

ALLELUIA   *John 10:27*

R. Alleluia, alleluia. I proclaim to you good news of great joy: today a Savior is born for us, Christ the Lord. **R.**

GOSPEL   *Luke 2:1—14*

In those days a decree went out from Caesar Augustus that the whole world should be enrolled. This was the first enrollment, when Quirinius was governor of Syria. So all went to be enrolled, each to his own town. And Joseph too went up from Galilee from the town of Nazareth to Judea, to the city of David that is called Bethlehem, because he was of the house and family of David, to be enrolled with Mary, his betrothed, who was with child. While they were there, the time came for her to have her child, and she gave birth to her firstborn son. She wrapped him in swaddling clothes and laid him in a manger, because there was no room for them in the inn.

Now there were shepherds in that region living in the fields and keeping the night watch over their flock. The angel of the Lord appeared to them and the glory of the Lord shone around them, and they were struck with great fear. The angel said to them, "Do not be afraid; for behold, I proclaim to you good news of great joy that will be for all the people. For today in the city of David a savior has been born for you who is Christ and Lord. And this will be a sign for you: you will find an infant wrapped in swaddling clothes and lying in a manger." And suddenly there was a multitude of the heavenly host with the angel, praising God and saying: "Glory to God in the highest and on earth peace to those on whom his favor rests."

CHRISTMAS DAY – MASS AT DAWN

FIRST READING *Isaiah 62:11—12*

See, the LORD proclaims to the ends of the earth: say to daughter Zion, your savior comes! Here is his reward with him, his recompense before him. They shall be called the holy people, the redeemed of the LORD, and you shall be called "Frequented," a city that is not forsaken.

RESPONSORIAL PSALM *Psalm 97:1, 6, 11—12*

R. A light will shine on us this day: the Lord is born for us.

The LORD is king; let the earth rejoice; / let the many isles be glad. / The heavens proclaim his justice, / and all peoples see his glory. **R.**

Light dawns for the just; / and gladness, for the upright of heart. / Be glad in the LORD, you just, / and give thanks to his holy name. **R.**

SECOND READING *Titus 3:4—7*

Beloved: when the kindness and generous love of God our savior appeared, not because of any righteous deeds we had done but because of his mercy, he saved us through the bath of rebirth and renewal by the Holy Spirit, whom he richly poured out on us through Jesus Christ our savior, so that we might be justified by his grace and become heirs in hope of eternal life.

ALLELUIA *Luke 2:14*

R. Alleluia, alleluia. Glory to God in the highest, and on earth peace to those on whom his favor rests. **R.**

GOSPEL *Luke 2:15—20*

When the angels went away from them to heaven, the shepherds said to one another, "Let us go, then, to Bethlehem to see this thing that has taken place, which the Lord has made known to us." So they went in haste and found Mary and Joseph, and the infant lying in the manger. When they saw this, they made known the message that had been told them about this child. All who heard it were amazed by what had been told them by the shepherds. And Mary kept all these things, reflecting on them in her heart. Then the shepherds returned, glorifying and praising God for all they had heard and seen, just as it had been told to them.

CHRISTMAS DAY – MASS OF THE DAY

FIRST READING   *Isaiah 52:7—10*

How beautiful upon the mountains are the feet of him who brings glad tidings, announcing peace, bearing good news, announcing salvation, and saying to Zion, "Your God is King!"

Hark! Your sentinels raise a cry, together they shout for joy, for they see directly, before their eyes, the LORD restoring Zion. Break out together in song, O ruins of Jerusalem! For the LORD comforts his people, he redeems Jerusalem. The LORD has bared his holy arm in the sight of all the nations; all the ends of the earth will behold the salvation of our God.

RESPONSORIAL PSALM   *Psalm 98:1, 2—3, 3—4, 5—6 (3c)*

R. All the ends of the earth have seen the saving power of God.

Sing to the LORD a new song, / for he has done wondrous deeds; / his right hand has won victory for him, his holy arm. **R.**

The LORD has made his salvation known: / in the sight of the nations he has revealed his justice. / He has remembered his kindness / and his faithfulness toward the house of Israel. **R.**

All the ends of the earth have seen the salvation by our God. / Sing joyfully to the LORD, all you lands; / break into song; sing praise. **R.**

Sing praise to the LORD with the harp, with the harp and melodious song. / With trumpets and the sound of the horn / sing joyfully before the King, the LORD. **R.**

SECOND READING   *Hebrews 1:1—6*

Brothers and sisters: in times past, God spoke in partial and various ways to our ancestors through the prophets; in these last days, he has spoken to us through the Son, whom he made heir of all things and through whom he created the universe, who is the refulgence of his glory, the very imprint of his being, and who sustains all things by his mighty word. When he had accomplished purification from sins, he took his seat at the right hand of the Majesty on high, as far superior to the angels as the name he has inherited is more excellent than theirs.

For to which of the angels did God ever say: "You are my son; this day I have begotten you"? Or again: "I will be a father to him, and he shall be a son to me"? And again, when he leads the firstborn into the world, he says: "Let all the angels of God worship him."

ALLELUIA   *John 10:27*

R. Alleluia, alleluia. A holy day has dawned upon us. Come, you nations, and adore the Lord. For today a great light has come upon the earth. **R.**

GOSPEL   *Longer Form John 1:1—18*

In the beginning was the Word, and the Word was with God, and the Word was God. He was in the beginning with God. All things came to be through him, and without him nothing came to be. What came to be through him was life, and this life was the light of the human race; the light shines in the darkness, and the darkness has not overcome it.

A man named John was sent from God. He came for testimony, to testify to the light, so that all might believe through him. He was not the light, but came to testify to the light. The true light, which enlightens everyone, was coming into the world.

He was in the world, and the world came to be through him, but the world did not know him. He came to what was his own, but his own people did not accept him.

But to those who did accept him he gave power to become children of God, to those who believe in his name, who were born not by natural generation nor by human choice nor by a man's decision but of God.

And the Word became flesh and made his dwelling among us, and we saw his glory, the glory as of the Father's only Son, full of grace and truth.

John testified to him and cried out, saying, "This was he of whom I said, 'The one who is coming after me ranks ahead of me because he existed before me.'" From his fullness we have all received, grace in place of grace, because while the law was given through Moses, grace and truth came through Jesus Christ. No one has ever seen God. The only Son, God, who is at the Father's side, has revealed him.

SHORTER FORM   *John 1:1—5, 9—14*

In the beginning was the Word, and the Word was with God, and the Word was God. He was in the beginning with God. All things came to be through him, and without him nothing came to be. What came to be through him was life, and this life was the light of the human race; the light shines in the darkness, and the darkness has not overcome it.

The true light, which enlightens everyone, was coming into the world. He was in the world, and the world came to be through him, but the world did not know him. He came to what was his own, but his own people did not accept him. But to those who did accept him he gave power to become children of God, to those who believe in his name, who were born not by natural generation nor by human choice nor by a man's decision but of God.

And the Word became flesh and made his dwelling among us, and we saw his glory, the glory as of the Father's only Son, full of grace and truth.

DECEMBER 26, SAINT STEPHEN, FIRST MARTYR - FEAST

FIRST READING   *Acts 6:8–10; 7:54–59*

Stephen, filled with grace and power, was working great wonders and signs among the people. Certain members of the so–called Synagogue of Freedmen, Cyrenians, and Alexandrians, and people from Cilicia and Asia, came forward and debated with Stephen, but they could not withstand the wisdom and the spirit with which he spoke.

When they heard this, they were infuriated, and they ground their teeth at him. But he, filled with the Holy Spirit, looked up intently to heaven and saw the glory of God and

Jesus standing at the right hand of God, and he said, "Behold, I see the heavens opened and the Son of Man standing at the right hand of God." But they cried out in a loud voice, covered their ears, and rushed upon him together. They threw him out of the city, and began to stone him. The witnesses laid down their cloaks at the feet of a young man named Saul. As they were stoning Stephen, he called out "Lord Jesus, receive my spirit."

RESPONSORIAL PSALM   *Psalm 31:3cd–4, 6 and 8ab, 16bc and 17*
R. (6) Into your hands, O Lord, I commend my spirit.
Be my rock of refuge, a stronghold to give me safety. **/** You are my rock and my fortress; **/** for your name's sake you will lead and guide me. **R.**
Into your hands I commend my spirit; **/** you will redeem me, O LORD, O faithful God. **/** I will rejoice and be glad because of your mercy. **R.**
Rescue me from the clutches of my enemies and my persecutors. **/** Let your face shine upon your servant; **/** save me in your kindness. **R.**
ALLELUIA   *Psalm 118:26a, 27a*
R. Alleluia, alleluia. Blessed is he who comes in the name of the LORD: the LORD is God and has given us light. **R.**

GOSPEL   *Matthew 10:17–22*
Jesus said to his disciples: "Beware of men, for they will hand you over to courts and scourge you in their synagogues, and you will be led before governors and kings for my sake as a witness before them and the pagans. When they hand you over, do not worry about how you are to speak or what you are to say. You will be given at that moment what you are to say. For it will not be you who speak but the Spirit of your Father speaking through you. Brother will hand over brother to death, and the father his child; children will rise up against parents and have them put to death. You will be hated by all because of my name, but whoever endures to the end will be saved."

DECEMBER 27, FEAST OF THE HOLY FAMILY; SAINT JOHN, APOSTLE
FIRST READING   *Genesis 15:1—6; 21:1—3*
The word of the Lord came to Abram in a vision, saying: "Fear not, Abram! I am your shield; I will make your reward very great." But Abram said, "O Lord GOD, what good will your gifts be, if I keep on being childless and have as my heir the steward of my house, Eliezer?" Abram continued, "See, you have given me no offspring, and so one of my servants will be my heir." Then the word of the LORD came to him: "No, that one shall not be your heir; your own issue shall be your heir." The Lord took Abram outside and said, "Look up at the sky and count the stars, if you can. Just so," he added, "shall your descendants be." Abram put his faith in the LORD, who credited it to him as an act of righteousness.

The LORD took note of Sarah as he had said he would; he did for her as he had promised. Sarah became pregnant and bore Abraham a son in his old age, at the set time that God had stated. Abraham gave the name Isaac to this son of his whom Sarah bore him.

ALTERNATIVE FIRST READING   *Sirach 3:2—6, 12—14*

God sets a father in honor over his children; a mother's authority he confirms over her sons. Whoever honors his father atones for sins, and preserves himself from them. When he prays, he is heard; he stores up riches who reveres his mother. Whoever honors his father is gladdened by children, and, when he prays, is heard. Whoever reveres his father will live a long life; he who obeys his father brings comfort to his mother.

My son, take care of your father when he is old; grieve him not as long as he lives. Even if his mind fail, be considerate of him; revile him not all the days of his life; kindness to a father will not be forgotten, firmly planted against the debt of your sins —a house raised in justice to you.

RESPONSORIAL PSALM   *Psalm 105:1—2, 3—4, 5—6, 8—9 (7a , 8a)*

R. The Lord remembers his covenant forever.

Give thanks to the LORD, invoke his name; / make known among the nations his deeds. / Sing to him, sing his praise, / proclaim all his wondrous deeds. **R.**

Glory in his holy name; / rejoice, O hearts that seek the LORD! / Look to the LORD in his strength; / constantly seek his face. **R.**

You descendants of Abraham, his servants, / sons of Jacob, his chosen ones! He, the LORD, is our God; / throughout the earth his judgments prevail. **R.**

He remembers forever his covenant / which he made binding for a thousand generations / which he entered into with Abraham and by his oath to Isaac. **R.**

SECOND READING   *Hebrews 11:8, 11—12, 17—19*

Brothers and sisters: by faith Abraham obeyed when he was called to go out to a place that he was to receive as an inheritance; he went out, not knowing where he was to go. By faith he received power to generate, even though he was past the normal age —and Sarah herself was sterile— for he thought that the one who had made the promise was trustworthy. So it was that there came forth from one man, himself as good as dead, descendants as numerous as the stars in the sky and as countless as the sands on the seashore.

By faith Abraham, when put to the test, offered up Isaac, and he who had received the promises was ready to offer his only son, of whom it was said, "Through Isaac descendants shall bear your name." He reasoned that God was able to raise even from the dead, and he received Isaac back as a symbol.

LONGER FORM   *Colossians 3:12—21*

Brothers and sisters: Put on, as God's chosen ones, holy and beloved, heartfelt compassion, kindness, humility, gentleness, and patience, bearing with one another and forgiving one another, if one has a grievance against another; as the Lord has forgiven you, so must you also do. And over all these put on love, that is, the bond of perfection. And let the peace of Christ control your hearts, the peace into which you were also called in one body. And be thankful. Let the word of Christ dwell in you richly, as in all wisdom you teach and admonish one another, singing psalms, hymns, and spiritual songs with gratitude in your hearts to

God. And whatever you do, in word or in deed, do everything in the name of the Lord Jesus, giving thanks to God the Father through him.

Wives, be subordinate to your husbands, as is proper in the Lord. Husbands, love your wives, and avoid any bitterness toward them. Children, obey your parents in everything, for this is pleasing to the Lord. Fathers, do not provoke your children, so they may not become discouraged.

SHORTER FORM   *Colossians 3:12—21*

Brothers and sisters: put on, as God's chosen ones, holy and beloved, heartfelt compassion, kindness, humility, gentleness, and patience, bearing with one another and forgiving one another, if one has a grievance against another; as the Lord has forgiven you, so must you also do. And over all these put on love, that is, the bond of perfection. And let the peace of Christ control your hearts, the peace into which you were also called in one body. And be thankful. Let the word of Christ dwell in you richly, as in all wisdom you teach and admonish one another, singing psalms, hymns, and spiritual songs with gratitude in your hearts to God. And whatever you do, in word or in deed, do everything in the name of the Lord Jesus, giving thanks to God the Father through him.

ALLELUIA   *Hebrews 1:1—2*

R. Alleluia, alleluia. In the past God spoke to our ancestors through the prophets; in these last days, he has spoken to us through the Son. R.

GOSPEL LONGER FORM   *Luke 2:22—40*

When the days were completed for their purification according to the law of Moses, they took him up to Jerusalem to present him to the Lord, just as it is written in the law of the Lord, *Every male that opens the womb shall be consecrated to the Lord,* and to offer the sacrifice of *a pair of turtledoves or two young pigeons,* in accordance with the dictate in the law of the Lord.

Now there was a man in Jerusalem whose name was Simeon. This man was righteous and devout, awaiting the consolation of Israel, and the Holy Spirit was upon him. It had been revealed to him by the Holy Spirit that he should not see death before he had seen the Christ of the Lord. He came in the Spirit into the temple; and when the parents brought in the child Jesus to perform the custom of the law in regard to him, he took him into his arms and blessed God, saying: "Now, Master, you may let your servant go in peace, according to your word, for my eyes have seen your salvation, which you prepared in sight of all the peoples, a light for revelation to the Gentiles, and glory for your people Israel." The child's father and mother were amazed at what was said about him; and Simeon blessed them and said to Mary his mother, "Behold, this child is destined for the fall and rise of many in Israel, and to be a sign that will be contradicted —and you yourself a sword will pierce— so that the thoughts of many hearts may be revealed." There was also a prophetess, Anna, the daughter of Phanuel, of the tribe of Asher. She was advanced in years, having lived seven years with her husband after her marriage, and then as a widow until she was eighty–four. She never left the temple, but worshiped night and day with fasting and prayer. And coming forward at that very time, she gave thanks to God and spoke about the child to all who were awaiting the redemption of Jerusalem.

When they had fulfilled all the prescriptions of the law of the Lord, they returned to Galilee, to their own town of Nazareth. The child grew and became strong, filled with wisdom; and the favor of God was upon him.

SHORTER FORM   *Luke 2:22, 39—40*

When the days were completed for their purification according to the law of Moses, they took him up to Jerusalem to present him to the Lord.

When they had fulfilled all the prescriptions of the law of the Lord, they returned to Galilee, to their own town of Nazareth. The child grew and became strong, filled with wisdom; and the favor of God was upon him.

DECEMBER 28, THE HOLY INNOCENTS, MARTYRS - FEAST

FIRST READING   *1 John 1:5–2:2*

Beloved: this is the message that we have heard from Jesus Christ and proclaim to you: God is light, and in him there is no darkness at all. If we say, "We have fellowship with him," while we continue to walk in darkness, we lie and do not act in truth. But if we walk in the light as he is in the light, then we have fellowship with one another, and the Blood of his Son Jesus cleanses us from all sin. If we say, "We are without sin," we deceive ourselves, and the truth is not in us. If we acknowledge our sins, he is faithful and just and will forgive our sins and cleanse us from every wrongdoing. If we say, "We have not sinned," we make him a liar, and his word is not in us.

My children, I am writing this to you so that you may not commit sin. But if anyone does sin, we have an Advocate with the Father, Jesus Christ the righteous one. He is expiation for our sins, and not for our sins only but for those of the whole world.

RESPONSORIAL PSALM   *Psalm 124:2–3, 4–5, 7cd–8*

R. (7) Our soul has been rescued like a bird from the fowler's snare.

Had not the LORD been with us / when men rose up against us, / then would they have swallowed us alive, / when their fury was inflamed against us. **R.**

Then would the waters have overwhelmed us; / the torrent would have swept over us; / over us then would have swept the raging waters. **R.**

Broken was the snare, and we were freed. / Our help is in the name of the LORD, / who made heaven and earth. **R.**

ALLELUIA   *See Te Deum*

R. Alleluia, alleluia. We praise you, O God, we acclaim you as Lord; the white–robed army of martyrs praise you. **R.**

GOSPEL   *Matthew 2:13–18*

When the magi had departed, behold, the angel of the Lord appeared to Joseph in a dream and said, "Rise, take the child and his mother, flee to Egypt, and stay there until I tell you.

Herod is going to search for the child to destroy him." Joseph rose and took the child and his mother by night and departed for Egypt. He stayed there until the death of Herod, that what the Lord had said through the prophet might be fulfilled, *Out of Egypt I called my son.*

When Herod realized that he had been deceived by the magi, he became furious. He ordered the massacre of all the boys in Bethlehem and its vicinity two years old and under, in accordance with the time he had ascertained from the magi. Then was fulfilled what had been said through Jeremiah the prophet: *A voice was heard in Ramah, sobbing and loud lamentation; Rachel weeping for her children, and she would not be consoled, since they were no more.*

DECEMBER 29, 5TH DAY IN THE OCTAVE OF CHRISTMAS; ST. THOMAS BECKET
FIRST READING *1John 2:3–11*

Beloved: the way we may be sure that we know Jesus is to keep his commandments. Whoever says, "I know him," but does not keep his commandments is a liar, and the truth is not in him. But whoever keeps his word, the love of God is truly perfected in him. This is the way we may know that we are in union with him: whoever claims to abide in him ought to walk just as he walked.

Beloved, I am writing no new commandment to you but an old commandment that you had from the beginning. The old commandment is the word that you have heard. And yet I do write a new commandment to you, which holds true in him and among you, for the darkness is passing away, and the true light is already shining. Whoever says he is in the light, yet hates his brother, is still in the darkness. Whoever loves his brother remains in the light, and there is nothing in him to cause a fall. Whoever hates his brother is in darkness; he walks in darkness and does not know where he is going because the darkness has blinded his eyes.

RESPONSORIAL PSALM *Psalm 96:1–2a, 2b–3, 5b–6*

R. (11a) Let the heavens be glad and the earth rejoice!

Sing to the LORD a new song; / sing to the LORD, all you lands. / Sing to the LORD; / bless his name. **R.**

Announce his salvation, day after day. / Tell his glory among the nations; / among all peoples, his wondrous deeds. **R.**

The LORD made the heavens. / Splendor and majesty go before him; / praise and grandeur are in his sanctuary. **R.**

ALLELUIA *Luke 2:32*

R. Alleluia, alleluia. A light of revelation to the Gentiles and glory for your people Israel. **R.**

GOSPEL *Luke 2:22–35*

When the days were completed for their purification according to the law of Moses, the parents of Jesus took him up to Jerusalem to present him to the Lord, just as it is written in the law of the Lord, *Every male that opens the womb shall be consecrated to the Lord,* and to offer the sacrifice of *a pair of turtledoves or two young pigeons,* in accordance with the dictate in the law of the Lord.

Now there was a man in Jerusalem whose name was Simeon. This man was righteous and devout, awaiting the consolation of Israel, and the Holy Spirit was upon him. It had been revealed to him by the Holy Spirit that he should not see death before he had seen the Christ of the Lord. He came in the Spirit into the temple; and when the parents brought in the child Jesus to perform the custom of the law in regard to him, he took him into his arms and blessed God, saying:

"Lord, now let your servant go in peace; your word has been fulfilled: my own eyes have seen the salvation which you prepared in the sight of every people, a light to reveal you to the nations and the glory of your people Israel."

The child's father and mother were amazed at what was said about him; and Simeon blessed them and said to Mary his mother, "Behold, this child is destined for the fall and rise of many in Israel, and to be a sign that will be contradicted (and you yourself a sword will pierce) so that the thoughts of many hearts may be revealed."

DECEMBER 30, 6TH DAY IN THE OCTAVE OF CHRISTMAS; BLESSED VICENTE VILAR DAVID

FIRST READING   *1John 2:12–17*

I am writing to you, children, because your sins have been forgiven for his name's sake.
I am writing to you, fathers, because you know him who is from the beginning.
I am writing to you, young men, because you have conquered the Evil One.
I write to you, children, because you know the Father.
I write to you, fathers, because you know him who is from the beginning.
I write to you, young men, because you are strong and the word of God remains in you, and you have conquered the Evil One.

Do not love the world or the things of the world. If anyone loves the world, the love of the Father is not in him. For all that is in the world, sensual lust, enticement for the eyes, and a pretentious life, is not from the Father but is from the world. Yet the world and its enticement are passing away. But whoever does the will of God remains forever.

RESPONSORIAL PSALM   *Psalm 96:7–8a, 8b–9, 10*

R. (11a) Let the heavens be glad and the earth rejoice!

Give to the LORD, you families of nations, / give to the LORD glory and praise; / give to the LORD the glory due his name! **R.**

Bring gifts, and enter his courts; / worship the LORD in holy attire. / Tremble before him, all the earth. **R.**

Say among the nations: / The LORD is king. / He has made the world firm, / not to be moved; / he governs the peoples with equity. **R.**

R. Alleluia, alleluia. A holy day has dawned upon us. Come, you nations, and adore the Lord. Today a great light has come upon the earth. **R.**

GOSPEL   *Luke 2:36–40*

There was a prophetess, Anna, the daughter of Phanuel, of the tribe of Asher. She was advanced in years, having lived seven years with her husband after her marriage, and then as a widow until she was eighty–four. She never left the temple, but worshiped night and day with fasting and prayer. And coming forward at that very time, she gave thanks to God and spoke about the child to all who were awaiting the redemption of Jerusalem.

When they had fulfilled all the prescriptions of the law of the Lord, they returned to Galilee, to their own town of Nazareth. The child grew and became strong, filled with wisdom; and the favor of God was upon him.

DECEMBER 31, 7TH DAY IN THE OCTAVE OF CHRISTMAS; ST. SYLVESTER I

FIRST READING   *1 John 2:18–21*

Children, it is the last hour; and just as you heard that the antichrist was coming, so now many antichrists have appeared. Thus we know this is the last hour. They went out from us, but they were not really of our number; if they had been, they would have remained with us. Their desertion shows that none of them was of our number. But you have the anointing that comes from the Holy One, and you all have knowledge. I write to you not because you do not know the truth but because you do, and because every lie is alien to the truth.

RESPONSORIAL PSALM   *Psalm 96:1–2, 11–12, 13*

R. (11a) Let the heavens be glad and the earth rejoice!

Sing to the LORD a new song; **/** sing to the LORD, all you lands. **/** Sing to the LORD; bless his name; **/** announce his salvation, day after day. **R.**

Let the heavens be glad and the earth rejoice; **/** let the sea and what fills it resound; **/** let the plains be joyful and all that is in them! **/** Then shall all the trees of the forest exult before the LORD. **R.**

The LORD comes, he comes to rule the earth. **/** He shall rule the world with justice **/** and the peoples with his constancy. **R.**

ALLELUIA   *John 1:14a, 12a*

R. Alleluia, alleluia. The Word of God became flesh and dwelt among us. To those who accepted him he gave power to become the children of God. **R.**

GOSPEL   *John 1:1–18*

In the beginning was the Word, and the Word was with God, and the Word was God. He was in the beginning with God. All things came to be through him, and without him nothing came to be. What came to be through him was life, and this life was the light of the human race; the light shines in the darkness, and the darkness has not overcome it.

A man named John was sent from God. He came for testimony, to testify to the light, so that all might believe through him. He was not the light, but came to testify to the light. The true light, which enlightens everyone, was coming into the world.

He was in the world, and the world came to be through him, but the world did not know him. He came to what was his own, but his own people did not accept him.

But to those who did accept him he gave power to become children of God, to those who believe in his name, who were born not by natural generation nor by human choice nor by a man's decision but of God.

And the Word became flesh and made his dwelling among us, and we saw his glory, the glory as of the Father's only–begotten Son, full of grace and truth.

John testified to him and cried out, saying, "This was he of whom I said, 'The one who is coming after me ranks ahead of me because he existed before me.'" From his fullness we have all received, grace in place of grace, because while the law was given through Moses, grace and truth came through Jesus Christ. No one has ever seen God. The only–begotten Son, God, who is at the Father's side, has revealed him.

ABOUT THE AUTHOR

This publication is the handiwork of the Catholic Liturgical World Team, which comprises of 15 members, some of who are laity, priests and religious persons. This team is a body specialized in publications related to the liturgy including mass reflections.

Made in the USA
Monee, IL
12 August 2020